About the Authors

Tribute to Dr. Jerry J. Bigner, Ph.D. (1944–2011)

**"There is a land of the living and a land of the dead
and the bridge is love . . ."**
(Thornton Wilder, 1897–1975)

Welcome to the ninth edition of *Parent–Child Relations: An Introduction to Parenting*. We pay tribute to the "father" of this book, Dr. Jerry J. Bigner, who nurtured and raised it from infancy to adulthood. The work was first conceived in 1972, when Dr. Bigner was in his late twenties. He meticulously tended it, much like a parent carefully watches over a child. He was working on the ninth edition at the time of his passing, in 2011.

Dr. Bigner's curriculum vitae was overwhelmingly impressive, with dozens of publications, and years of hands-on teaching and working in child-care settings as a professor of Human Development and Family Studies at Colorado State University. He had been a member of the National Council on Family Relations since 1966. He also had a noteworthy presence as the senior editor of the *Journal of GLBT Family Studies*, and was passionate about respecting human diversity in its many expressions.

In the year of the new millennium, our professional paths crossed. When we first collaborated, it was as part of a project funded by The Pew Charitable Trusts. During what was to be the last year of his life, we were in constant contact. We discussed this text several times a week, as Dr. Bigner had already decided that I was to take on a role in coparenting his life's work. Everything he planned for the ninth edition—his ideas about parenting and the directions for future editions—he co-anchored in my mind.

Dr. Bigner leaves behind a legacy—in his publications, in the influence he has had on the countless students and colleagues who have internalized aspects of his teachings, and on all the significant persons in his life, his closest and dearest. We salute him for having been a role model to family life educators, a man who was extremely generous with his professional knowledge and expertise, and a man who touched the lives of thousands of students over several decades.

Dr. Clara Gerhardt
Professor of Family Studies, Samford University

Clara Gerhardt, MBA, Ph.D., is a professor of Family Studies at Samford University. She is a clinical psychologist and a licensed marriage and family therapist, as well as a certified family life educator. Among her many publications, she documented the history of family therapy in a chapter of *Global Perspectives in Family Therapy*. She writes a regular guest column for a publication of the National Council on Family Relations. She has held positions as chair of the Department of Family Studies at Samford University and chair of a State Board of Examiners in Psychology. As an educator, she teaches parenting, life span development, and multicultural perspectives. As part of her duties as an internship supervisor, she has mentored child life and child development education students. Dr. Gerhardt has professionally presented on six continents, visited more than 60 countries, and speaks five languages fluently. Her practical training is constantly updated by being a parent and a grandparent.

NINTH EDITION

PARENT–CHILD RELATIONS
An Introduction to Parenting

JERRY J. BIGNER
Colorado State University, Professor Emeritus

CLARA GERHARDT
Samford University

PEARSON

Boston   Columbus   Indianapolis   New York   San Francisco   Upper Saddle River
Amsterdam   Cape Town   Dubai   London   Madrid   Milan   Munich   Paris   Montreal   Toronto
Delhi   Mexico City   São Paulo   Sydney   Hong Kong   Seoul   Singapore   Taipei   Tokyo

Vice President and Editorial Director:
    Jeffery W. Johnston
Senior Acquisitions Editor: Julie Peters
Editorial Assistant: Andrea Hall
Vice President, Director of Marketing: Margaret Waples
Senior Marketing Manager: Christopher Barry
Senior Managing Editor: Pamela D. Bennett
Project Manager: Kerry Rubadue
Production Manager: Laura Messerly
Senior Art Director: Jayne Conte

Cover Designer: Bruce Kenselaar
Illustrations: Claire Gerhardt Gottschalk
Cover Art: Dan Ionut Popescu/Shutterstock.com
Full-Service Project Management:
    Mansi Negi; Aptara®, Inc.
Composition: Aptara®, Inc.
Printer/Binder: Edwards Brothers Malloy
Cover Printer: Edwards Brothers Malloy
Text Font: 10/12 New Caledonia

Credits and acknowledgments for materials borrowed from other sources and reproduced, with permission, in this textbook appear on the appropriate page within the text.

Photo Credits: Duane Farnell, p. v; Caroline Summers/Samford University, p. vi; get4net/Fotolia, p. 6; pressmaster/Fotolia, p. 7; yuri4u80/Fotolia, p. 14; micromonkey/Fotolia, pp. 24, 112; sonya etchison/Fotolia, p. 33; WONG SZE FEI/Fotolia, pp. 37, 100, 103; Ryan McVay/Getty Images, Inc.-PhotoDisc, p. 39; bojorgensen/Fotolia, pp. 43, 348; GINA SMITH/Fotolia, p. 44; auremar/Fotolia, pp. 50, 133; USDA/APHIS Animal and Plant Health Inspection Service, p. 52; Monkey Business/Fotolia, pp. 70, 231, 283; elisabetta figus/Fotolia, p. 80; mangostock/Fotolia, pp. 82, 254; NatUlrich/Fotolia, p. 94; Andres Rodriguez/Fotolia, pp. 114, 236; Hogan Imaging/Fotolia, p. 121; Bryan Creely/Fotolia, p. 124; detailblick/Fotolia, p. 128; Dr. Tatum A. McArthur, p. 139; Purestock/Alamy, p. 140; Kati Molin/Fotolia, p. 142; Joanna Zielinska/Fotolia, pp. 147, 174; Svetlana Fedoseeva/Fotolia, p. 149, Dmitry Pichugin/Fotolia, p. 153; munchkinmoo/Fotolia, p. 156; mocker_bat/Fotolia, p. 163; darko64/Fotolia, p. 171; Ilike/Fotolia, p. 172; iofoto/Fotolia, p. 186; michaeljung/Fotolia, pp. 190, 339; Gail Meese/Merrill, p. 203; Yuri Arcurs/Fotolia, pp. 207, 242; Jaren Wicklund/Fotolia, p. 213; Franz Pfluegl/Fotolia, p. 223; Eric Simard/Fotolia, p. 228; kotomiti/Fotolia, p. 259; drubig-photo/Fotolia, p. 262; Image Source IS2/Fotolia, p. 270; Darren Baker/Fotolia, p. 277; SW Productions/Getty Images, p. 286; Monart Design/Fotolia, p. 289; tracyhornbrook/Fotolia, p. 292; william87/Fotolia, p. 300; Carolyn Sherer, pp. 301, 309, 313; Tatyana Gladskih/Fotolia, p. 321; EJ White/Fotolia, p. 325; Helder Almeida/Fotolia, p. 328; Woodapple/Fotolia, p. 342; archana bhartia/Fotolia, p. 344

Every effort has been made to provide accurate and current Internet information in this book. However, the Internet and information posted on it are constantly changing, so it is inevitable that some of the Internet addresses listed in this textbook will change.

Library of Congress Cataloging-in-Publication Data

Bigner, Jerry J.
    Parent-child relations: an introduction to parenting/Jerry J. Bigner, Clara Gerhardt.—9th ed.
    p. cm.
    ISBN-13: 978-0-13-285334-7
    ISBN-10: 0-13-285334-5
    1. Parenting.   2. Parent and child.   3. Child development.   4. Families.   I. Gerhardt, Clara.   II. Title.
    HQ755.8.B53 2014
    649'.1—dc23   2012036311

10 9 8 7 6 5 4 3 2

PEARSON

ISBN-10:   0-13-285334-5
ISBN-13: 978-0-13-285334-7

This text is dedicated to Dr. Jerry Bigner,
A man both giving and gifted.
May his teachings continue to nurture future family life scholars.
With appreciation and gratitude.

Preface

FEATURES OF THE TEXT

The ninth edition of *Parent–Child Relations* has been revised and updated to retain the significant pedagogical features of previous editions:

- A sharp focus on parenting. Students using this text typically study child development in a separate course.
- A strong emphasis on various theoretical models pertaining to parenting
- An emphasis on family systems theory and a systemic family development model to describe intergenerational family scenarios and life span challenges
- A focus on the ecological, social, and cultural contexts in which parent–child relations occur
- Anchoring of some parenting strategies by focusing on nurture and structure
- Expanded discussions of ethnic diversity and family structures in the United States
- *Frequently Asked Questions* allow students to see parenting concerns through the eyes of a parent or a therapist
- *Parenting Reflections* raise significant questions to promote critical thinking
- *Focus On* highlights important information

SUPPLEMENTS TO THE TEXT

Instructors will be pleased that their favorite topics may be included during lectures to supplement the text. The following online supplements are available to instructors and can be downloaded at www.pearsonhighered.com:

- **Online Instructor's Manual.** This manual provides a variety of resources that support the text, including notes from the author regarding each chapter, suggestions for supplementary lecture topics, and a listing of audiovisual materials that illustrate chapter concepts.
- **Online Test Bank.** The *Test Bank* features evaluation items, such as true–false and multiple choice.
- **Online PowerPoint® Slides.** PowerPoint presentations accompany each chapter of the text. These slides can be customized by adding comments.
- **Computerized Test Bank Software.** Known as TestGen, this computerized test bank software gives instructors electronic access to the Test Bank items, allowing them to create customized exams. TestGen is available in a dual Macintosh and PC/Windows version.
- **Course Management.** The assessment items in the Test Bank are also available in WebCT and Blackboard formats.

NEW TO THIS EDITION

- For the ninth edition, this text has undergone numerous changes and updates. Dr. Clara Gerhardt has joined the team as the coauthor.
- Many chapters were rewritten to reflect recent research and subtle changes in societal attitudes. "Culture and Diversity," "Parenting Strategies," "Transition to Parenthood," "Pregnancy and Birth," and "Family Formation and Parenting in Same-Sex Couples" have been revised in their entirety.
- The "Theoretical Perspectives" chapter was expanded and rewritten to clarify areas that students often find challenging. New visual renderings of the theoretical models were incorporated to facilitate understanding.

- The final chapter, "Best Practices in Parent–Child Relations," is a new addition to the book, and looks at the larger societal systems that cushion families. We ask the ambitious question, "What is the state of parent–child relations?" and analyze some demographics to provide us with indications of our strengths and aspirations.
- We listened to the suggestions of our reviewers, who pointed us in new directions. We asked a number of subject experts to review rewritten sections of the book and to identify leading researchers on particular topics and to highlight current trends.
- Relevant themes were added and expanded, such as parenting in military families, coparenting, sudden infant death syndrome, parental despair, shaken baby syndrome, postpartum depression, miscarriage and infant loss, the history of childhood, prenatal tests, bullying, fragile families, children's brain development and parenting, the role of family therapy in supporting parent–child relations, and commercial parenting programs, to mention a few.
- Current terminology is used. This is especially clear in the chapters on blended families, pregnancy and birth, and family formation with same-sex parents. Proposed, updated *DSM-5* terms are used. We have used gender-neutral language and randomly alternated the use of masculine and feminine pronouns such as *he* and *she*.
- The family snapshots were abbreviated and a select few were introduced with a family genogram to expose our students to this form of family notation.
- The illustrations that support theoretical models were newly rendered for clarity and reader engagement.
- The references have been checked and compared to the original sources. A serious effort was made to replace dated references with current research. This is an ongoing task which ensures that students benefit from up-to-date material.
- We have kept in mind that this is a text intended to facilitate teaching and learning. We added numerous pedagogical features and focused on reader friendliness. We updated the photos and figures, added clarity to the layout and visual engagement through bullet points, recommended reputable websites, and added charts and tables to sum up key concepts.
- The supplementary materials for this text have also undergone major restructuring to lighten the instructor's load.

ACKNOWLEDGMENTS

This ninth edition was built on the inspiring and solid foundations created by the late Dr. Jerry Bigner. My deepest gratitude extends to him, as well as to his partner, Duane Farnell, who smoothed the way to carry out Jerry's wishes for this book. My appreciation to Dr. Bigner's many collaborators, including Dr. Raymond Yang.

It takes many musicians to perform a symphony. For any creative endeavor, there is a wide net of people who inspire, support, and simply create the space so that the project can be completed. I had an entire team, not all mentioned by name, guiding and encouraging me, and importantly, believing in my ability to capture what Dr. Bigner had envisioned. For her consistent affirmation, her artistic eye, and virtually all the diagrammatic renderings in this book, I embrace Claire Gerhardt Gottschalk. My heartfelt appreciation and love I owe to Dr. Christina Gerhardt, pediatrician. She is the backup vocalist who provided the harmony for this duet. For generously sharing her photographs and her vision, my gratitude extends to award-winning photographer Carolyn Sherer.

Samford University has been the academic home which nurtured and supported me. I am deeply indebted to my colleagues and students, especially research assistants Melissa Belflower and Katrina Brown. Dr. David Finn transformed "I can't" to "I can" with cups of tea. Others created the environment in which creativity flourishes: Drs. Mary Sue Baldwin, Jeanie Box, Kristie Chandler, and David Shipley.

The thoughtful insights and comments of the reviewers are greatly appreciated: Jennifer Andres, St. Cloud State University; Ming Cui, Florida State University; Deborah J. Handy, Washington State University; and Kim Kiehl, The Ohio State University.

Many generously shared their expertise and enthusiasm, specifically Drs. Tatum McArthur, Willem Grotepass, Gisela Kreglinger, Eva Buttner, Thomas Boll, Dan Sandiver-Stech, Arlene Hayne, Bryan Johnson, Ginger Frost, Jo King, Fred van Staden, Harold Goss, Irva Hayward, Danielle Hardaman, and computer genius Paul Gerhardt. Special acknowledgment is owed to the numerous unsung experts who read sections of the manuscript and pointed me in the right direction; you know who you are and I thank you from the bottom of my heart. The editors at Pearson were my compass and anchor: Senior Acquisitions Editor Julie Peters and Editorial Assistant Andrea Hall. Kerry Rubadue, Laura Messerly, Brian Baker, Pat Onufrak, Mansi Negi, as well as the entire Pearson team responsible for editing and production, ultimately guided this book to a safe harbor.

Lastly, to my inner circle—my husband Michael and our children, their spouses and our grandchildren. They are the ones who turned me into a parent and a grandparent, the most important and rewarding learning school of all.

Brief Contents

Contents

PART I

Parent–Child Relations in Social Context

In some ways, we are all parenting experts. We have personally felt the effects of parental and coparental influences. We carry these experiences with us for life; we know about that most sacred of bonds, the one that remains with us forever. After all, we have all been parented or coparented within the diverse context of contemporary family life.

In an ideal scenario, we have been at the receiving end of our parents' and coparents' good intentions. We were the object of their hopes and dreams; we may have witnessed their challenges and sacrifices. In reality, we may have been cared for, but not all of these relationships may have amounted to loving or constructive interactions.

Not all parents can or want to parent.

Not all children take the extended opportunities.

Not all parent–child relationships have successful outcomes.

There are many shades of gray in the quality of a (co)parent–child relationship. We take it for granted that children are lovingly parented, but the reality is more complicated. Parenting can challenge us like nothing else. It can bring immense joy; disappointment and bitter tears are the flipside of that coin.

For as much as parents *parent*, the children do something in return; parents and their progeny do things to each other. It occurs against the backdrop of family histories. Parenting goes forward and backward in time; it crosses generations. We parent in the context of social, educational, and biological influences—factors that limit or enhance our effectiveness. Having some tried and true techniques and well researched literature at hand raises our intuitive knowledge to a more scholarly level. Assuming that parenting skills are innate may preclude the benefits of learning from a model of best practices.

In a parenting course, we try to describe the many visible and invisible threads that set the loom—the influences we may be aware of, as well as the somewhat imperceptible ones. By recognizing and understanding some of the patterns, learning techniques, and approaching parenting as a skill set that can be expanded, parent–child relations can become more rewarding for all participants. We can train professionals who will help parents find the most constructive and rewarding path through a forest of challenges. Biological parenthood is not a prerequisite; there are many paths toward a caring relationship of the *caretaker–care taken* configuration. We can use these skills in any responsible coparenting relationship involving children and adolescents, and in a variety of professions.

Parenting courses are anchored in countless volumes of research. In approaching parenting as a formal topic for study, we sum up the highlights and make the material accessible to those interested in this topic. We try to keep the joyful aspect of parent–child relations in mind. If these relationships seem like an occasional endurance test, learning from what has worked for others may increase our fitness level to run the parenting race gracefully and with good outcomes.

Parenting and the caring dimensions it represents has the potential for being one of life's greatest joys and ongoing gifts. As students of parent–child relations, we are particularly privileged to be close to the stage, where we can observe, encourage, and cheer on the actors partaking in one of life's true dramas, and where we can become part of the audience eavesdropping on the many dialogues that occur within the sacred space of the family.

CHAPTER 1

The Ecology of Parent–Child Relations

Learning Outcomes

■ ■ ■ ■ ■ ■ ■ ■ ■ ■ ■ ■

After completing this chapter, readers should be able to

1. Explain the current views that support formal parenting education.
2. Explain the implications of the different perspectives concerning parent–child relations.
3. Explain the social factors that contributed to the changing trends in parenthood over the past century.
4. Describe the factors that contribute to the parenthood role, and reflect on the relevance of each of these factors during the life span development of the parent.

■ ■ ■ ■ ■ ■ ■ ■ ■ ■ ■ ■

THE NEED FOR PARENTING EDUCATION

When we reflect on our own childhood experiences several questions come to mind: Why did our parents behave and react the way they did? What would we do differently if we were in their shoes? Are there lessons to be learned that will make us better parents? Are there best practices that we can follow to ensure optimal outcomes?

One of the most significant and intimate relationships among humans is that between parent and child. The parent–child bond is unique in its biological foundations and in its psychological meanings. For children, this essential relationship ensures

...l and helps shape their destinies. For adults, it ...e one of the most fulfilling human experiences ... a challenging opportunity for personal growth and ...velopment.

For many years, the need for formal parenting education was undervalued, and typically the option of training for this role was not available. Parent educators and professionals who work closely with parents agree that such skills would be a welcome addition. Our society goes to great lengths to train people for most vocational roles. A license indicating training and competence is required for a range of activities and vocations—from driving a car to the most sophisticated of professions. Other than for special circumstances such as foster parenting, no state or federal statute requires individuals to have training or preparation to become parents, or to practice parenting, even though the stakes are high and the effects are long lasting. The question concerning the feasibility of licensing parents has been asked (LaFollette, 2004). Our legal system has intervened in regulating potentially harmful activities, and promoting situations and behaviors that are "in the best interests of the child." It has played a role in adoption and parental rights issues. Even though parenting licensure would represent an attempt at raising the bar and exerting a gate-keeping role, many would see licensure as an intrusion on family privacy. Questioning a family's innate willingness to rise to the challenge of giving parenting their very best shot seems to be an intrusion into the private sphere of family life. Unless the overall emotional and physical well-being of a child is jeopardized or there is suspicion or fear that a child may be at risk, we tend to leave parenting to the parents, with varying outcomes (Tittle, 2004).

The media sometimes depicts parenthood in unrealistic ways by portraying idealistic outcomes of parent–child relations: the happily-ever-after story. It is tempting to believe that most parents and children have smooth interactions; children improve their parents' marriage; children will turn out well if they have good parents; children generally are compliant with parents' requests; and parents are solely responsible for their children's character, personality, and achievements upon attaining maturity. Learning about parenting in formal coursework, observing parents and children interact in natural settings, and hearing parents share their experiences may contribute to a more authentic understanding of parenthood.

Although most parents could profit from learning new ways to be effective in their role, there are so many opposing guidelines concerning parenting that it is hard to separate the wheat from the chaff. Researchers continue to make progress toward helping parents find more effective ways of performing their parenting roles and raising children to become competent adults.

Contemporary ideas about the nature of parent–child relations are the result of years of social evolution and many historical changes. Our concept of the relationship between a parent and a child contains numerous complex meanings. These perceptions influence an adult's decision to become a parent and also shape the subsequent parenting behavior. Our understanding of this significant family relationship has benefited from increased knowledge of the behavioral sciences. Experts continue to study parent–child interactions in the hopes of gaining a clearer understanding of how this relationship changes over time and is altered in certain social contexts. Researchers look at the dynamics of parent–child relations and try to distill the essence of competent parenting behaviors.

Disconcerting events occurring in families and in contemporary society underline the urgency of preparing parents and coparents to ensure that they are competent in their roles. It is becoming clearer that the qualities inherent in parenting relationships can benefit or harm a child's development. The prevalence of destructive behaviors in adulthood is traced to family-of-origin experiences in which poor and ineffective parenting may have played a major role (Coontz, 2006). Family experts are concerned about the effects of emotional, physical, and sexual abuse of children by their parents and close family. Poor preparation for parenthood, inadequate social support, lack of adequate skills for coping with the stresses of parenting, and resource-depleted environments all interact to put families at risk (Cheal, 2007).

The relationship between parents and children is complex and varied. Parenthood is described as a **developmental role** that changes over time, usually in response to the changing developmental needs of children. Clearly, people can learn how to be effective in raising children and may be able to improve their behavior as parents. By studying the research, theories, and approaches that have been developed and examined by practitioners, it is possible to develop a better understanding of the many facets of parenting.

• •

Parenting Reflection 1–1

At the outset and before having studied parent–child relations, what topics would you include in a course for first-time parents?

• •

Coparenting

Coparents can come in various guises and in several contexts. It refers to the people who team up or *collaborate to parent*. Think about the word *cooperate*. It contains the prefix *co*, meaning that it is an activity that we do together or jointly, where we share our resources: in short, where we collaborate. It is much more than an extended form of child care. It is a very legitimate form of parenting and can occur in many settings. It can have legal implications concerning parental rights and responsibilities.

At the heart of coparenting lies the ongoing commitment to a child's well-being in a parental manner. Coparents can be biological parents in binuclear families who take on parenting roles from two different households because of divorce or separation. Coparents can be adults who significantly support parents in the parenting role, or may take over the parenting role for an absent or incapacitated parent. In this way, grandparents, supportive family members, friends, and foster parents could act as coparents if they take on permanent and semi-permanent roles with a serious commitment to a child's upbringing. They carry the child's interests at heart and become a significant force in the child's life in a relationship that is ongoing and enduring.

The adults could have a biological link to the child, but they need not have this connection. For instance, parents and stepparents in a post-divorce situation may coparent. Same-sex couples may coparent. Unmarried parents may coparent from two different households. Foster parents could coparent occasionally with a biological parent. In summary, "[co]parenting is an enterprise undertaken by two or more adults who together take on the care and upbringing of children for whom they share responsibility" (McHale & Lindahl, 2011, p. 3).

• •

Focus Point. It is important for parents to learn how to raise children, to understand their developmental needs, and to become more effective in their roles as parents.

• •

CONCEPTS OF PARENTHOOD

In our society, the parenting role is associated with several different concepts. Originally, the idea of parenthood referred singularly to the prominent aspect of sexual reproduction. Our society, like all others, values the function of reproduction within a family setting because, traditionally, this was the only way to sustain the population.

Although advances in medical technology allow for assisted reproduction, the traditional manner of *family formation* is the most frequently occurring variation. Initial family formation is followed by years of careful supervision of the offspring.

Other ideas are also embedded in our society's concept of parenthood—namely, that parents are responsible for nurturing, teaching, and acting as guardians for their children until they reach the age of legal maturity. This extended timespan of providing care for children is unique among most species found on Earth. Human infants and children have a prolonged period of dependency on adults, partly because of the length of time it takes for maturation of the brain and the complexity of the skills that have to be attained (Stiles, 2008). The brain of a human infant, unlike that of the offspring of many other mammals, is immature at birth and continues to develop. Human infants' survival is dependent upon being protected by adults. In contrast, the offspring of many other species walk within hours of birth and are capable of running to escape danger. Human infants do not master these same motor functions until many months and years after birth. Differences in brain size and function account for many of the disparities between humans and other species.

Parents were originally considered to be a child's principal teachers. This instructional function and the responsibility given to parents by society to prepare children for adulthood is referred to as **socialization**, or learning how to conform to the conventional ways of behavior in society. In the past, parents served as educators for their children by teaching them the essential skills needed to survive in society, including reading, writing, and calculation if they were growing up within a literate society. They helped children learn the job skills necessary to provide a living upon attaining adulthood. Today these requirements are met by schools and other agents. Parents are expected to help children learn the basic rules of social functioning and to impart values to guide the behavior and decisions of their offspring.

Understanding the family relationship enhances parenting skills. Parenthood is a developmental role which changes in response to the needs of the children.

Focus Point. A number of concepts are embedded in the role of a parent. These concepts define the different meanings associated with the role.

THE ECOLOGY AND CHARACTERISTICS OF PARENTHOOD

The relationship between parents and children can be described according to several dimensions. This relationship is one of the cornerstones of human existence, largely because of its biological basis. It is an essential part of our society, and society requires the addition of new members in order to continue.

To understand the context and complexity of the unique bond between parents and their children, we examine this bond from an **ecological perspective**. Ecology is an interdisciplinary branch of biology that examines the *interrelationships* between organisms and their environment (Barry, 2007). Behavioral scientists

have placed an ecological perspective on human development and social behavior. Using this approach, the developmental changes in individuals, families, and other social groups take place within the context of interactions with changing environmental systems (Bronfenbrenner, 1979). This same perspective is used in the context of parent–child relations. To understand the parent–child relationship from an ecological angle, we must examine the context of the various environments that influence and shape behavior. We explore the basic nature of parent–child relations and identify the particular aspects that influence the roles and behaviors that parents assume.

Parenting Reflection 1–2

Try to imagine yourself as the best parent possible. What characteristics would you have? What are some things that you would try to do, and what would you try to avoid?

Following are some characteristic traits and qualities of the parent–child relationship:

1. *Parenthood is a social construct.* The parental role is a social institution based on complex values, beliefs, norms, and behaviors that focus on procreation and the need to care for the young (Bengston, Acock, Allen, Dilworth-Anderson, & Klein, 2005; Coontz, 2006). People who are not parents can also experience the parenting role—for instance, through coparenting. Coparents are significant persons within a system who collaborate and contribute to the parenting of a child (McHale & Lindahl, 2011).

The role of the parent is universally understood by diverse groups. Every society, culture, and subculture defines appropriate behavior for parents. Some cultural groups allocate a higher moral stature to parents than to nonparents. People who are not parents may be devalued by societies in which parenthood is valued.

2. *The relationship between parents and children is a subsystem of the larger social system that we call a family.* One of the most salient models for understanding family group functioning is the **family systems theory**. This approach falls within an ecological context (Becvar & Becvar, 1998). Family systems theory

describes family functioning in ways that resemble other systems found in nature, such as the solar system and ecological systems. This model explains how everyday functioning takes place in a family, how rules evolve to govern the behavior of members, how roles are assigned to regulate behavior, and how these roles relate to family goals. It explains how a family group strives to maintain stability over time and adapts rules, behaviors, roles, and goals. This model recognizes that family members experience developmental changes, resolve interpersonal conflicts, and confront crises in ways that enhance effective functioning.

Several other subsystems exist simultaneously within a larger family system, such as the committed relationship or marriage between adults and the relationships among siblings. A **subsystem** is a microcosm of the larger family system that mirrors the functioning of this group. The same principles and concepts that explain the functioning of the larger family system relate to how subsystems, including the parent–child subsystem, function.

The main priority of the parent–child relationship is to nurture children toward maturity and effective adult functioning. The family systems model describes the parent–child relationship as bidirectional. The flow of influence goes both ways. Children's behavior and development are strong factors that contribute to the quality and scope of interactions with parents. As children experience developmental changes, parents change their behavior and adapt by changing the rules, the ways they interact with children, and their goals for child rearing. Interactions between parents and children evolve in tandem with children's developmental changes. Similarly, children respond to changes in parenting behavior in ways that help them achieve the developmental tasks appropriate for their particular life span stage.

The parental role is sensitive and responsive to changes within the family system. For example, when one adult is removed from the family through divorce or death, the remaining adult's quality and style of parenting change. The parenthood role is also heavily influenced by factors arising from what is known as **family ecology**, which is the influence of the larger environment on the family system.

3. *Parenting is bidirectional.*   Our ideas and philosophies about parent–child relations are derived from diverse cultural and historical influences. Until several decades ago, the relationship between parent and child was described as a **unidirectional** model of socialization

Parenting focuses on nurturing children's growth and development to facilitate learning to become an effectively functioning adult.

(Ambert, 2001). In this model, the adult assumes the role of a teacher who is responsible for encouraging appropriate behavior patterns, values, and attitudes that prepare the child for effective participation in society upon reaching maturity. The child's role is that of being an active learner. According to the model, the flow of information is solely from parent to child. Clearly, the unidirectional model features the adult as having significant power over the child. In contrast, the subordinated child lacks social power. In the past, these were the accepted roles for parents and children, and they received strong support.

Our current ideas about parent–child relations are shaped by the insight from research that reframes this bond as being **bidirectional** (Ambert, 2001; Cui,

TABLE 1–1. Childhood and the Family in Victorian England

	Influences of Victorianism occurring from 1815–1914
Industrial Revolution: Mid 18th to mid 19th century	Childhood differed depending on the class, the generation, and the gender of the child (Frost, 2009). Breakup of the extended family. Increased urbanization as fathers, who were the breadwinners, took on factory jobs; 80 percent of the people lived in cities, often in poverty. Separation of family life from work led to the formation of the nuclear family. Less support from the extended family. Class differences were based on education, financial prospects, and family background. Children were exploited, often laboring in factories.
Early Victorian: 1830s–1840s	Queen Victoria's reign from 1837–1901. Upheaval in the economic, political, and social arenas. Depression in industry and in agriculture. Potato blight in Ireland, resulting in mass immigration to the United States. Victorians idealized the family and the middle class. Reality was different with poverty and persons in the lower classes struggling. This had a direct effect on family life and children. In 1841, about 36 percent of the population was under age 15. At worst, children were exploited, died early of infectious diseases, missed out on education, and were sometimes sexually and socially abused. At best, children were idealized for their innocence and seen as central to the family. Childhood was a very short period, and children could start working as early as age 7.
Middle Victorian: 1850–1875	Relative prosperity. Large families and low life expectancy. Children could be orphaned or have to deal with stepparents. Children born out of wedlock were stigmatized and were either absorbed by maternal families or left as foundling children to be raised in orphanages. Class differences set the stage for the different experiences of childhood. Highly religious society.
Late Victorian: 1875–1914	Rise of new technology like the telephone, chemicals, and electricity. This period culminated in World War I. Large families and high infant mortality. Also frequent loss of a parent as life expectancy was short. Children were often socialized by their siblings. Family size declined in middle-class families. Children's rights became a topic for discussion. Some social reform. Alternatives other than prisons and workhouses for troubled children. The length of childhood increased as children were schooled longer. Scotland made schooling compulsory in 1872; England had a national school system by 1870 and compulsory schooling followed by 1880. Children entered the workforce later.
General Themes: Attitudes toward children	Gradual increase in awareness of the importance of parenting. Gradual change in children's roles with the understanding and insight that childhood had its own characteristics and demands. Childhood and youth were not the first stage of adulthood, but a separate entity. Slow but steady social and legal reform occurred, fueled by political changes, and these reforms spread throughout the social classes. Child rearing entered the realm of public policy.
Discipline	Typically harsh discipline, treating children as if they were innately bad and needed correction. Corporal punishment. From about age 12, children were treated as adults. No extended transition into adulthood. No juvenile legal system; children were punished in the same manner as adults, or placed in harsh reform schools. Social reform initiated in the late 1800s.
Homeless children and orphans	Children born out of wedlock were mostly absorbed by maternal households, although some children were abandoned as a result of dire poverty. Increasing social reform movements to help these children (e.g., orphanages, schools, foundling homes). Many institutions were founded by religious groups (e.g., the Salvation Army).

TABLE 1–1. Childhood and the Family in Victorian England *(Continued)*

Abuse and neglect	Dire social conditions, including poverty, violence, and alcoholism, set the stage for child abuse (including some sexual abuse) and neglect. Prudery in middle-class families did not make them immune to the neglect and abuse of children.
Toys and play	The late Victorian period recognized the importance of play, and children had toys and playtime. Games could be seen as being educational as well as recreational. These insights represented the fragile beginnings of child centeredness. Books for children were being printed.
School	Initially, there was no compulsory schooling; children often left school during late childhood or early adolescence to learn a trade. Education was incomplete. Sunday schools were established to teach literacy, as well as religious concepts, to working children. England had a national school system by 1870, and compulsory schooling followed by 1880.
Child labor	Child labor continued throughout this era, up to World War I. In the late Victorian period, much of the child labor was part time, at least until school-leaving age, which was 14. Interrupted education precluded the hopes for a good economic future, with far-reaching effects on families.

Based on Frost, Ginger S. (2009). *Victorian childhoods*. In the series, Mitchell, Sally (Series Editor). *Victorian life and times*. Westport, Connecticut: Praeger.

Donnellan, & Conger, 2007; Parke & Buriel, 2006). This means that adults and children influence each other. Their mutual influence changes constantly, too, because of the developmental nature of the relationship over the course of a life span.

4. *Parenthood is a developmental role that can continue over the life span.* Unlike most adult social roles, parenting behavior and interactions must adapt to the developmental changes in children. Changes arising from a parent's own personal development affect the caregiving behavior. The age and developmental status of both the parent and the child affect the nature and context of the relationship at any point in time. Typically, the parent–child relationship can be a **life span** pursuit as it stretches over the entire life span of the parties involved, and the quality and characteristics of this relationship change accordingly.

• •

Focus Point. Parent–child relations were traditionally and historically described as unidirectional; that is, the adult had complete jurisdiction, power, and control over the relationship. Current mainstream thinking

describes this relationship as bidirectional, meaning that a child is acknowledged as an active participant and contributor to the relationship. Each person influences the behavior of the other. The parent–child relationship is unique to family systems and can be described in various ways.

• •

• •

Focus Point. Parenting is characterized by four important characteristics:

- Parenthood is a **social construct**. The parental role is a social institution based on complex values, beliefs, norms, and behaviors.
- The family systems theory describes parenthood as a **subsystem** of the larger social system of the family and within an ecological context.
- Both parent and child actively participate in a **bidirectional** interaction with mutual influence.
- Parenting is a **developmental** role and a **life span** pursuit: both parent and child undergo developmental changes with time and life span progressions.

• •

HISTORICAL CHANGES IN PARENT–CHILD RELATIONS

Contemporary ideas about the nature of parent–child relations are very different from those of the past. Current ideas have evolved from earlier beliefs. The nature and quality of parent–child interactions are influenced significantly by cultural values and by the historical context in which we live (Coontz, 2006).

Generally, our culture values the well-being of children and social institutions like the family, schools, and social service agencies, which focus on meeting children's needs. Our society tends to be child centered. We see childhood as a special time in the life span, a time of preparation and education for the later years. Childhood is hopefully a time for happiness and freedom from anxiety. We believe that children have special needs that are first met in their family system and later by institutions, groups, and agencies outside of the family system. Our ideas about the unique nature of childhood developed over many years of social transformation in Western culture (Coontz, 2006).

Childhood, parenthood, and the family were viewed differently during the Middle Ages, or even during the Colonial period of the United States. Most social historians agree that the love between parents and children has probably not changed over time. Changes are noted in the ways that adults define and conduct appropriate parenting behavior. Although parenting has always had a strong nurturing context, the way that adults express this nurturing has changed in culturally approved ways. Child-rearing practices have evolved throughout history to reflect the changing ideas of what children need from adults to prepare them for their own future as adults.

Infant Mortality. Where there are adults, there must have been children, and the history of humankind, as shown in Figure 1–1, is also the history of childhood. Our knowledge of children during prehistoric times, including the times of hunter–gatherers, is limited to archeological and paleontological data (Volk, 2011). We know that child mortality rates were disconcertingly high, and from archeological findings, the estimates are that around half of the children never reached adulthood. Stating this bluntly:

> In many ways, the history of childhood is perhaps best described as a history of death. Infant and child mortality rates appear to have been shockingly high for all but the most recent part of the history of childhood. (Volk, 2011, p. 475)

In Victorian times, the loss of a sibling was a likely occurrence, and it exerted an emotional toll on the entire family. The loss of a parent proved to be disruptive to the family structure and devastating to the children who were sometimes sent to live with extended family, which was not always a loving environment. The surviving parent very likely remarried, even if it was only to keep the household intact.

Walter Littler, the 14th of 18 children, describes his Victorian childhood in his memoir. Within a dozen years, eight of his siblings had passed away from infectious diseases such as measles and scarlet fever; illnesses, which a century later, would be fairly well controlled (Frost, 2009). In the Foakes family, the mother, Grace, had 14 children, of whom only five reached adulthood, while nine died in infancy or childhood.

"[The loss of a child is] an almost unimaginable loss to modern eyes. Parents faced such grief with resignation, but when siblings died, children were both frightened and saddened, a state sometimes aggravated by the Victorian custom of keeping the body in the parlor or kitchen until burial. The death of a contemporary was a shock, one that forced children to face the reality of mortality." (Frost, 2009, p. 21)

FIGURE 1–1. Family life and infant mortality in Victorian England.

Source: Frost, Ginger S. (2009). *Victorian childhoods*, chapter 1, page 21. In the series, Mitchell, Sally (Series Editor). *Victorian life and times*. Westport, Connecticut: Praeger. The following source is referenced by Frost (2009): Littler, Walter. (1997). *A Victorian childhood: Recollections and reflections*. Belbroughton, Worcestershire, England: Marion Seymour.

With the absence of a long-lasting oral or written history, the details elude us. The review of the evolution of childhood begins with the ancient cultures that influenced contemporary Western societies, and where we have greater access to more detailed historical data.

The threat of death forced parents to be both invested and disinvested in their offspring. They invested strongly in these bonds to increase the odds of survival as children represented their lineage, the hope of a next generation. At the same time, the many circumstances accompanying high child mortality demanded a certain resignation and disinvestment (Volk, 2011).

Ancient Greece and Rome

In ancient times, only two stages of the human life span were recognized: childhood and adulthood (Cunningham,

2005). Adulthood was considered to be the culmination of childhood experiences. Childhood was the time for preparing to become an adult. Achieving this status was the primary goal of an individual's developmental progress. The boundary between childhood and adulthood was distinct. Childhood commenced at birth and usually ended between the surprisingly young ages of 5 and 7 years, at which time individuals assumed adult status, along with the associated responsibilities, behaviors, and traits expected of an adult. The life span was much shorter, and many people died in their mid 30s and 40s.

The ancient cultures of Greece and Rome recognized that the experiences of childhood gave rise to the adult's character. The artistic works of these eras suggest that adulthood was considered to be of higher value and the epitome of human development (Golden, 1993). Infancy and late adulthood did not seem to receive the same degree of interest, assuming artistic attention as a valid indicator of social concern. Child sacrifices, infanticide, and slavery were common during these historical eras. On the authority of the father, infants who were deformed, weak, or of an undesired sex (usually female) could be left to the elements, drowned, or suffocated.

There was concern for children's preparation for their future roles in adulthood. Although schools taught a wide variety of subjects, parents were responsible for teaching their children basic skills and knowledge. Education was considered to benefit the well-being of the community and the state, rather than the welfare of the individual. In these cultures, a formal education was a privilege that was restricted to males. Females were expected to acquire only domestic skills related to home management and child care.

The family was recognized as the core element in both of these early civilizations. The father was the family leader, and the mother was regarded as a child's first teacher. Women and children had very few rights and were considered to be the property of an adult male. Children could be sold into slavery or even abandoned. By the 5th century, rewards were given to families who gave asylum to orphaned or deserted children. Conditions changed during the Middle Ages.

The Middle Ages to the Renaissance

The Middle Ages (400–1400) were a time in which Western societies functioned in a rural, primitive manner. Formal education was minimal and restricted to the clergy of the Roman Catholic Church. Families were structured in **extended families**, with several generations living together. Family life centered primarily on an agrarian lifestyle.

In these premodern times, children were treated with indifference to their special needs. During the Middle Ages and for some time afterward, the nature of an infant was taken for granted by adults. There was no concept that infants needed to learn to trust their caregivers. Assimilation into the adult world came early, usually between ages 5 and 7. A child's education—probably their only schooling—came from observing and imitating adult role models. Parents in the Middle Ages probably felt that children needed adult supervision and care, but this did not extend to close emotional ties. Parents did not appear to provide warmth or nurture to children, possibly because many children died in infancy and childhood from diseases that are preventable today. During this period, parenting was only one of many functions of the family, and no high priority was attached to it. Families were most concerned with the production of food, clothing, and shelter to ensure daily survival.

The prevailing attitude during the Middle Ages was that children were miniature adults. They were dressed in adult-type clothing and given responsibilities at an early age. The lives of children and adults paralleled closely. Children were exposed to adult behavior and living conditions. For example, most children of commoners in Europe were apprenticed to learn a particular skill or trade once they reached age 7.

During medieval times, infants were featured in artwork. During the early part of this era, subjects were depicted holding infants in a detached manner, with little direct eye contact between mother and child. Infant mortality rates were particularly high. The advent of medical care, and especially the availability of antibiotics, was centuries away. Because life was uncertain, adults probably did not develop a close attachment to infants and young children for fear of a disastrous, premature end to their relationship. This would change in the years that followed.

Over the next two centuries that followed the Middle Ages, that is, 1400–1600, Europe experienced a period of cultural revitalization that was marked by voyages of discovery, scientific exploration, and an explosion of artistic creativity. Adults explored their inner environments or personalities, attempting to discover their true selves. This social and cultural expansion generally did not lead to an increased understanding of children and parenting. The focus clearly was on the adult, as illustrated by the concept of the Renaissance man, that is, someone who was well rounded in almost all areas of development, including intellectual, artistic, social, and physical.

It was common practice among Italian Renaissance nobility to send their infants to live with wet nurses (i.e., peasant women who had infants of their own). The wet nurse usually cared for the nobility's infants for about 2 years, including nursing them. Apparently, the biological parents were not particularly concerned about the quality of care given to their infant during this time (Harlow & Laurence, 2010).

The artistic works produced during this period show a greater interest in children. Fra Filippo Lippi was among the first of the Renaissance artists to portray infants with accurate body proportions. In the artwork of this period, babies were usually drawn as cherubs, which was considered to be the position in the angelic hierarchy of Heaven assigned to infants and children who died. A new sentimentality about children began to emerge. This contributed to changes in attitudes about the nature and status of children in society. During the late 1500s, artists gave more attention to children in their artwork. Another indication of greater concern and attention was the creation of special clothing styles just for children. Until this time, children had been dressed in replicas of adult costumes. This change in clothing style signaled that children, at least those of the nobility, were seen as distinct and separate entities (Cunningham, 2005).

By the late 1500s, additional distinctions between the world of adults and that of children emerged. Recreational activities, stories, and types of medical care between the two groups began to differ. Advice on how to provide discipline and guidance in child rearing became more widespread (Mintz, 2006). Over the next 200 years, the rate of social change would accelerate, bringing new adjustments to the ways that people viewed parenthood and childhood.

Colonial America: 1600–1800

The cultural and religious conditions that existed at the time that America was colonized contributed to a unique view of children and the provision of care by their parents.

Children were seen as inherently depraved. Adults thought that children were basically bad or evil. It was thought that parents could overcome this by providing particular child-rearing experiences. Many parents believed that if they administered stern discipline through hard labor, children would become self-denying, pious adults upon maturity. Adults prized children for their usefulness in colonization and for being a good source of cheap labor. Their value in the colonies increased because of the high rate of infant mortality.

The premise that the nature of children was sinful stemmed primarily from the rigid Puritan religious views of the colonists (Mintz, 2006). These are illustrated in the *Day of Doom*, a catechism written by Michael Wigglesworth (1631–1705), which was learned by almost every child in Puritan New England. Puritan parents were responsible for providing rigorous moral and religious training for children, which included stern discipline. These parents believed it was their responsibility to bring children to religious salvation or conversion. This was accomplished when children were able to recognize and admit their own sinful nature and become Christians. The earlier this occurred, the better, from many parents' point of view. To help children achieve religious conversion, they were taught that they must always obey their parents unquestioningly, especially their father. They were taught to curb their natural inclination to commit sins. Aspects of childhood that are considered acceptable and developmentally appropriate today were, in Colonial times, viewed as satanic manifestations. Play was considered sinful, and children were kept occupied by memorizing scripture and religious songs. This approach to child rearing placed authority and the welfare of children squarely in the hands of parents. Based on this approach, the unidirectional model of parent–child relations became the primary model of child rearing.

During Colonial times, adults approached their parenting role in ways that we would today label as overly involved and borderline abusive. Stemming from the indifference toward children during the Renaissance, this represented a pendulum swing toward the opposite stance. There was a heavy emphasis on religious matters and the use of harsh disciplinary methods to achieve children's salvation and obedience. Despite the punitive image, parents had great affection for their children and showed concern for their welfare in ways that were thought to be appropriate at that time.

Nineteenth Century

The 19th century in the United States involved a serious internal conflict: the War Between the States. Prior to this event, several major views about parenthood and childhood emerged that had originated during the Colonial period, and which continue to influence our current ideas.

Three contradictory philosophies on how to rear children emerged during this era. These approaches prescribed appropriate parental roles for specific outcomes.

Calvinism. The strongest approach, which received the most attention, was inspired by the Calvinist religious movement. This view advocated stern, harsh use of physical punishment and strict moral instruction for children, essentially a strong, authoritarian child-rearing style. It implied a cause-and-effect between how a parent trained a child and the outcome in terms of the child's character in adulthood. This approach was thought to be based on the Biblical admonition to parents, "Train up a child in the way he should go: and when he is old, he will not depart from it" (Proverbs 22.6, p. 876). Susanna Wesley, mother of brothers John and Charles Wesley, who were attributed with founding the Methodist movement based on the principles of Methodism, wrote that her own children would cry softly in fear of punishment. From her diaries, it appears that children as young as a year old were harshly corrected. This was thought to promote quiet children and tranquil households (Cunningham, 2005). She described correction as follows: ". . . when turned a year old (and some time before) they were taught to fear the rod and cry softly, by which means they escaped abundance of correction" (Cunningham, 2005, p. 53).

The Industrial Revolution produced dramatic changes in family life and roles. During the Colonial period, the father's central role consisted of providing the economic support and moral and religious education for children and acting as the disciplinarian, as such, *authoritarianism* and fatherhood became intertwined. During and following the Industrial Revolution, fathers were increasingly employed in nonfarm jobs, which took them away from their families for long periods. To compensate, mothers assumed increasing responsibility for the character development and socialization of children. The mother became the instructor and central family figure in a child's life.

Because of this shift within parenting roles and responsibilities, a shift occurred from the harsh Calvinist approach to a greater emphasis on nurture (Cunningham, 2005). This shift is attributed to the increasing maternal involvement in all aspects of child rearing. In some very religious families, physical punishment for character molding continued.

Environmentalism. As the Calvinist approach began to wane, a second approach to child rearing emerged that was influenced by the writings of John Locke (1699). Locke was known for his *tabula rasa* theory of development. In this view, children were believed to be born with their minds and personalities empty like blank slates; the child-rearing experiences provided by parents inscribed the traits that were manifested in their adult personalities. This is a cause-and-effect view of child rearing as well, but it was a departure from the Calvinist- and highly religious-inspired approaches. It was not as harsh. It emphasized that the model of behavior presented by parents to children played an important role in children's future character development. The strength of a child's character was thought to come from exposure to a wide range of experiences while growing up.

Early Developmentalism. The third approach to child rearing that emerged during the 19th century is similar to some contemporary views. Stemming, in part, from the movement in Europe that advocated early childhood education via nursery schools and kindergartens, this approach acknowledged the developmental immaturity of children. If children did not behave appropriately, it was because they did not know any better. Parents were advised not to be overly concerned about breaking a child's will or to be fearful of indulging the child. Obedience was valued, but it could be coaxed from children in more humane ways, such as being firm, using persuasion, and giving rewards rather than physical punishment (Mann & Peabody, 1863). This view can be considered to be the first developmental approach to children because it emphasized

■ the role of meeting children's developmental needs,
■ the parents' role in shaping children's personalities,
■ the effects of neglect and harsh punishment, and
■ the effects of gentle care and nurture on development.

Since World War II, changing economic conditions and the rise of the Women's movement have left families with new ideas about gender roles involving working mothers. The current norm is a two-income family with the vast majority of women working outside the home throughout their children's childhood years.

Twentieth-Century and Current Trends

The 20th century witnessed child-rearing approaches that ranged from increasing permissiveness, encouraged by the writings of Sigmund Freud (1856–1939) and Benjamin Spock (1903–1998), to more restrictive and authoritarian approaches, advocated by John Watson (1928) and others. As scientific information increased and children were studied in a developmental context, numerous child-rearing experts offered detailed, frequently conflicting child-rearing advice (Bigner & Yang, 1996). The emphasis became more psychological. Behavior modification based on positive reinforcement or reward became increasingly popular. The use of physical punishment to shape children's behavior was discouraged.

Changes also took place in the expectations of fathers' involvement with their children. Fathers were encouraged to take an active role in preparing for and participating in the birth of their children and in bonding with children during infancy and thereafter. Men's greater involvement in family life was encouraged by the Women's Movement during the late 1960s and early 1970s. These changes produced widespread and significant social changes. The emphasis on gender equality encouraged both women and men to participate in all aspects of life: family, work, and community involvement.

Significantly, this period was also characterized by the Civil Rights Movement that forged a new awareness toward granting equal rights to all citizens, regardless of racial or ethnic origin. This movement gained momentum in the 1960s with many legislative acts at the federal, state, and local levels, shifting social attitudes about race and ethnicity. Many federal programs were initiated, with the War on Poverty program playing a significant role. One of these programs remains in effect today as Project Head Start, a proven educational approach to prepare children for public school participation. It also enhances family life, physical well-being, and parental involvement. Numerous other programs were a part of the War on Poverty and impacted the lives of many underserved, inner-city families in the United States.

The dramatic increase in the number of female parents employed outside the home had many repercussions. During World War II, large numbers of women took the place of men in the war effort to produce the goods and services needed by the military. Following the war, with the movement of many families from cities to the suburbs, women gave up some of their employment opportunities. Economic conditions, coupled with the rise of the Women's Movement, forced families to revise their ideas about gender roles involving working mothers. A two-income family has become the current norm as the vast majority of women are employed during the years when children are born and are growing up.

Teen pregnancy reached a peak following World War II. Attitudes shifted from stigmatizing adolescent parenthood to accepting it, but not necessarily condoning it. Many teen mothers relinquished parental rights when their child was born, and many children were adopted. As the numbers of teen mothers grew and families became more willing to support the young mother and her child, fewer children were made available for adoption. Teen fathers did not receive the attention and acceptance given to teen mothers. In recent years, this has changed, and public school systems allow teen parents to continue their education when they have a child.

The American public became increasingly aware of the insidious and pervasive presence of incest and sexual abuse of children by parents and family members. This was partly prompted by a number of well-known public figures and celebrities sharing information about their own victimization. The extent of family violence and addictive behaviors became better known, revealed by the dramatic increase in children in the foster care system. The number of incarcerated parents with addictive behaviors climbed dramatically. This has accounted for the increase in the number of grandparents who have custody of grandchildren and are actively raising these children.

Changes in laws and attitudes led to greater acceptance of divorce and, in turn, to the emergence of the single-parent family. Changes in American society following World War II contributed to the demise of the traditional nuclear family. Increases in the number of divorces were accompanied by a rise in the number of remarriages and blended families. By the end of the 20th century, diversity in family forms and structures became the norm rather than the exception. Today, a variety of family forms are considered functional, healthy, and effective. Poverty and homelessness continue to affect families, children, and society at large.

A number of other contemporary social issues impact parent–child relations directly or indirectly. What occurs in the larger society affects all individuals and families to some degree, and the reverse is true as well, as there is a bidirectional influence. Some of these issues are controversial and can be divisive in nature.

■ Societal issues pertaining to public education, violence, addiction, and the drawn-out economic recession, accompanied by a housing and mortgage crisis, have had far-reaching effects on childhood and family life. Record numbers of resource-strapped families are raising children in poverty, and employment prospects for young adults are especially challenging.
■ The continuing debates surrounding reproductive choices, adoption rights, general civil rights, legal and illegal immigration, and so forth continue.

The *Convention on the Rights of the Child*, drafted by the United Nations Children's Fund (UNICEF, 1959) and formally adopted in 1990, reflects a concern with the global well-being of children and is an intentional approach to create and maintain a comprehensive national agenda for children. The rights address the best interests of the child, the protection of rights, nondiscrimination, parental guidance, and survival and development to name just a few. There are 54 articles focusing on rights, as well as the implementation of measures.

FIGURE 1–2.   Rights of the child.

Source: Based on United Nations (UNICEF): Convention on the Rights of the Child www.unicef.org/crc/.

■ There was a significant turning point in American culture after September 11, 2001 (9/11). As a nation, we have been involved in wars on terrorism. Military families and especially the children in these families have been deeply affected by deployment and war-related issues.
■ The increasing presence of the World Wide Web via personal computers and handheld electronic devices, as well as the influence of the social media, have caused a ripple effect in changing communication patterns, education, and endless other areas of family life in a paradigm shift unlike anything previously experienced in history. Information overload and less real-life face time with significant others are new phenomena linked to the digital age.

Parenting Reflection 1–3

Should parents raise their children using identical methods, styles, and approaches? What effects would such uniformity in child rearing have on adult outcomes?

Focus Point.   The concepts of parenthood and childhood have undergone many changes over the last 2,000+ years. Contemporary ideas on parenting roles reflect changes in cultural values.

THE PARENTHOOD ROLE

Several factors contribute to how people see themselves as parents, and how they behave in this role (see Figure 1–3). A number of themes merge into a workable blueprint that guides the behavior of the parenting role. It is as if someone takes the pieces of a puzzle, manages to perceive how they all fit together, and puts them together into a completed object.

Some factors that contribute to an adult's concept of parenting behavior come from past experiences. New ideas are added as the person gains experience in parenting children. The contribution of a child to the delineation of parenting roles is very clear. Family ecological factors, attitudes about discipline, and an individual's past experiences all influence parenting styles.

The predisposing factors that combine to influence a parenting style and form a parenting blueprint include the following:

- *Cultural influences:* social class, education, or peer values
- *Developmental time:* period of active engagement in child rearing
- *Structure and nurture:* two dimensions that anchor parenting behavior
- *Family-of-origin influences:* modeling from the family of our own childhood
- *Child influences:* how children impact parental behavior
- *Disciplinary approach:* developmentally appropriate discipline and structure
- *Family ecological factors:* family structure and trends that affect family form
- *Attitudes and parenting styles:* beliefs that influence parental behavior

Cultural Influences

Research over the past decades assumed that cultural variations in child-rearing patterns present in the personality and behavioral differences in children. In theory, differences in social class cause corresponding differences in child rearing. The patterns found in the social class groupings are thought to be perpetuated from one generation to the next, although individual parents interpret them in different ways.

Numerous studies reported considerable variations among socioeconomic groups in the ways that children are reared and in the values that are promoted (Coontz, 2006). For example, middle-class families, in contrast to lower class families, were believed to use psychologically harsher methods to control children's behavior. Middle-class families tend to teach children to delay need gratification, while lower class families tend to promote immediate need gratification. Lower class families appear to place greater emphasis on conforming to parental values, unlike middle-class families.

Generally differences between families of different socioeconomic backgrounds have diminished. There appear to be more similarities than differences in child rearing. This has been attributed partly to the presence of the mass media, which portrays middle-class values, and the fact that more families can achieve a middle-class lifestyle through education and better paying jobs.

Children's learning styles and the ability to process information differ dramatically between disadvantaged and middle-class families (Coontz, 2006). This suggests that the potential for children's mental growth may be strongly influenced by the mothers' differences in language use and teaching styles. The middle-class values placed on education and academic achievement may result in patterns of interaction that promote children's problem-solving skills.

FIGURE 1–3. Interacting factors influencing parental role behavior.

Cultural influences

Developmental time

Structure and nurture

Family-of-origin influences

Child influences

Disciplinary approach

Family ecological factors

Attitudes and parenting styles

A parent's behavioral style is partly guided by the value system of their social class. Each group maintains essentially the same common objective in child rearing, that is, to support children's growth and development. The style of each group differs considerably. Middle-class parents tend to value social achievement, encourage children to acquire knowledge, and expect independence early in their children's lives. These differences in values translate to differences in child-rearing patterns and what the children are taught.

Synchrony of Parental Style and Child Development

Parenting style should be congruent, or synchronized, with the child's developmental level. For example, the parenting style during infancy focuses on nurture and providing tremendous amounts of physical care to meet the infant's needs. When families have children of a broad age range, parenting styles must be mixed, while still congruent with each child's developmental level. Parents must attend to the developmental needs of their children while attempting to meet their own developmental demands. For example, interactions with children may be tempered by the pressures on working parents who juggle family and work roles.

Primary Parenting Functions

Parental behavior and ways of interacting with children are usually purposeful attempts to meet their children's needs (Marsiglio, Hutchinson, & Cohan, 2000). These, in turn, relate strongly to the goals that adults wish to accomplish with regard to the socialization of their children. Two broad categories anchor parenting behavior to prepare children for their future, namely *structure* and *nurture* (Clarke & Dawson, 1998).

Structure describes those aspects of parenting behavior that aid regulation and lay the foundation for personality formation and expression. Structure teaches children personal boundaries, the limits to which they may go so that they do not infringe on others' needs and rights. Structure provides the experiences that promote a healthy sense of self-worth and a sense of safety and security so that children learn to trust in the appropriate contexts. Structure also helps children develop healthy habits in thought and behavior; learn values and ethics; and acquire valued character traits such as honesty, integrity,

and personal honor. Additionally, they develop personal responsibility for their actions. Structure provides a child with a healthy, strong sense of self-esteem that permits growth toward meeting personal potential and becoming a well-differentiated individual who is valued for distinct qualities and traits.

Nurture relates to those parenting behaviors intended to meet a child's need for unconditional love. This is necessary for healthy growth and well-being. By experiencing that he or she is lovable, a child learns to love others. The assertive care and support that are given in unconditional ways form the basis of nurture and support appropriate attachment.

Additionally, parents and caretakers should strive to provide responsive care, which includes assertive and supportive components.

Responsive care involves reacting to the child in an appropriate manner. It requires noticing, understanding, and answering to the behavioral cues and verbal requests of the child. It is expressed when adults *respond* to children's needs in loving, predictable, and trustworthy ways. It becomes part of the bidirectional communication between caretaker and child, and supports the formation of basic trust and bonding, because the child is a part of an interacting unit in which the child is acknowledged and cared for appropriately. It resembles a dialogue with bidirectional exchanges.

Two facets of responsive caregiving are **assertive** and **supportive** care. In assertive care, the caregiver initiates and extends the necessary and appropriate care to the infant or child. For instance, for new parents or caretakers, a very young infant's needs may be difficult to read, yet they initiate the appropriate assertive care, without waiting for the child to express its own needs. Supportive care is expressed when adults offer care to children but allow them the freedom to accept or reject the offer because it is offered unconditionally.

Family-of-Origin Influences

Because humans become parents largely without the assistance of instinct to guide behavior, we rely on other means to help us learn how to care for a dependent child. One of the major influences comes from observing our own parents and close caregivers. We unwittingly use them as models for how to act as a parent (Marsiglio, Hutchinson, & Cohan, 2000). The reactions, perceptions, and feelings that we have about how we were raised influence how we approach our own children. Generally, people who are satisfied with how they were raised and how they feel about themselves as adults will probably duplicate the parenting methods and attitudes of their own parents (Clarke & Dawson, 1998). Conversely, people who are dissatisfied with their parents' methods may try to do the opposite of what they experienced in their family of origin. Another response is feeling that one's parents did not provide enough love or physical affection, and this may lead one to overcompensate with one's own children.

The experiences we have in our childhood provide a blueprint for a number of interactional patterns in adulthood (Marsiglio et al., 2000). There are several sources for this blueprint:

- The goals our parents had for our growth and development
- The model of parenthood we observed from our parents' behavior
- The influence of parenting models that were handed down from one generation to the next

The parenting blueprint we assimilate may not be helpful when the time comes to assume the role ourselves. It may be outmoded, inappropriate, and unrealistic because circumstances in our family of origin may not resemble those in our current family.

Not every family system is healthy or functions in a well-adjusted manner. For example, one or both adults can be affected by addiction and related disorders, by mental or emotional disturbances, or by living conditions that hamper the ability to parent. Most attempt to hide the emotional pain that results from their inability to function healthily. When this occurs, the adults often adopt certain parenting behaviors (possibly learned from their own parental models) and assign roles to the children that mirror those in their family of origin, even if these roles are dysfunctional. This illustrates the concept of wholeness and interrelatedness in family systems theory: What affects one person in a family system affects everyone to some degree. Patterns for coping with the stress of an unhealthy family of origin tend to carry over into future generations.

Based on observations of numerous adults acting as parents, several models of parenting behavior have been developed that illustrate how an unhealthy family of origin influences a person's own patterns of parenting (Framo, Weber, & Levine, 2003). There is never a pure

assimilation of one particular model into a person's potential parenting behavior; instead, a composite of behaviors is taken from the various models.

Influence of Children on Parents

Our culture traditionally ascribes the role of learner to children. Children and adolescents are thought to need numerous learning experiences to prepare them for adulthood. They are the objects of adults' intensive socialization efforts. The relationship between parents and children focuses on the configuration of the adult as teacher and the child as learner. From this viewpoint, there is support for maintaining the unidirectional model of socialization.

Our culture also constructs the concept of children as people who are in need of adults' protection. Children obviously need assistance in learning the many skills considered necessary to ultimately function effectively as adults. Children are dependent on parents for a longer time than they were earlier in history. The relationship between parent and child has become one of the last human interactional relationships in which the use of social power by an adult is largely unquestioned. Because of the inherent teacher–student quality of this relationship, the power of adults is accentuated in interactions with children. In addition, the greater physical size and strength of adults also contributes to the greater use of their power over children. According to many psychologists and sociologists, this has caused the child to become somewhat of a victim.

Power, or rather the way in which it is used, may be the culprit. Some adults use power to control and manipulate, rather than facilitate, children's growth and development. This causes difficulty in the relationship, especially as children grow older (de Mol & Buysse, 2008).

With the advent of family systems theory, which describes interactions within family relationships as having a reciprocal effect upon participants, researchers began acknowledging the impact that children have on their parents' behavior and the effects that they have in a number of other areas, including (de Mol & Buysse, 2008):

- Parental health
- Adults' activities
- Parental employment status
- Use and availability of family financial resources
- Parents' intimate relationship
- Parents' interactions and community interactions

- Parental personality development
- Parents' values, attitudes, and belief systems
- Parents' life plans
- Adults' feelings of having control over their lives

Disciplinary Approach ✕

The approach parents take in teaching their children the values and beliefs their family hold will shape parenting styles in a variety of ways. The goals that parents hold for their children's growth and development usually arise out of altruism. What adults desire for children and how most people shape their parenting activities and behavior relate to what they believe children need to become effective adults. Ordinarily, most parents want their child to

- have a happy and fulfilling life;
- become a person who functions independently, can be employed, and have constructive relationships;
- acquire the skills and competencies that permit effective functioning as an adult in society; and
- acquire behaviors and attitudes that allow participation as a good citizen within a democratic society (Bornstein & Toole, 2010).

Parents think about the behaviors and social competencies that they feel are important for children to acquire to become effectively functioning adults. Adults believe that children need these skills, and they shape them as part of children's behavioral repertoire. **Social competence** usually refers to a group of attributes that are believed to be essential in assisting a person to make full use of personal resources to cope productively with the circumstances of life. The way that parents provide structure for children is shaped to facilitate the acquisition of these essential social skills.

The parental goals in child rearing and discipline are guided by personal and societal influences. Adults' perceptions of what children need are based on complex personal opinions that reflect the realities of life and family experiences. Parents' opinions about what children need are based on, among other things, their own past experiences, the values from their families of origin, and the philosophies of parenting they have developed as adults. These perceptions can be tempered by specific events, such as a child's physical or mental disability or when divorce changes the structure of the family.

Parenting should be adapted to the child's developmental stage. As the offspring establish goals, most parents realize that they must change how they interact with their children to facilitate new developmental goals. Parents can seek out information and assistance in learning how to adapt and change their behavior in response to developmental changes in their children (Bigner & Yang, 1996). This represents one of the major challenges of effective parenting behavior.

Family Ecological Factors ✕

The influence of various environmental systems on the functioning of the parent–child microenvironment can be observed in a variety of ways, but they can be difficult to accurately anticipate or measure. Our behavior is influenced by a number of environmental factors. Our past experience with children is one factor. Our behavior can be influenced by internal factors, such as blood sugar levels, hormone balances, sleep deprivation, and emotional states. Sociocultural factors that affect our behavior include value systems and beliefs about appropriate role behavior. Other factors are more physical, for example, where we live (e.g., in an apartment or in a single-family residence, in the city or in a rural area). Even the time of day can be an important consideration. All these factors from the past and present lead to variability in parents' behavior and affect the way interactions take place.

✕ Family ecological factors, such as the level of family income (poverty level vs. middle class), ethnic identity, or type of family structure, influence parenting styles. See Figure 1–4 to see how the family structural dynamic has changed over time. They also affect a family's ability to provide equipment and services, such as medical or dental care, clothing, and food, which, in turn, influence the quality and nature of the interactions. In this way, parents' goals for their child-rearing efforts may be tempered by a variety of family ecological factors.

Attitudes and Parenting Styles

Adult attitudes about children and child rearing are important. They are the result of socialization and past experiences and form the implicit rules, or "shoulds," that guide parental behavior. The attitudes about how one should act as a parent may be seen more clearly in disciplinary styles.

FIGURE 1–4. Households by type: 1990, 2000, and 2010.

Source: U.S. Census Bureau, *Census 2010 Summary File 1; Census 2000 Summary File 1; 1990 Census of Population; Summary Population and Housing Characteristics, United States (1990 CPH-1-1).*

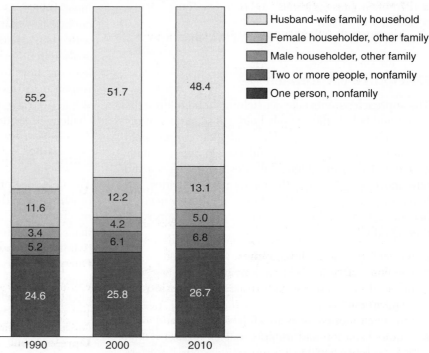

Households by type: 1990, 2000, and 2010

Husband-wife family household
Female householder, other family
Male householder, other family
Two or more people, nonfamily
One person, nonfamily

The range of attitudes about how to parent children appropriately and effectively can be viewed as a compilation of the attributes of parental control (what parents feel they should do to control children's behavior and development) and emotional warmth. They range from **authoritarian** (strict), through authoritative (balanced), to **permissive** (lenient; Baumrind, 1966). For example, an authoritarian attitude is distinctly high in parental control but also low in emotional warmth toward children. Typically, attitudes guide actual parenting behavior and can be expected to shift with the changing developmental stages of children. These attitudes have a significant influence on parenting styles, especially when children reach preschool age.

Parenting Reflection 1–4

Consider how your own disciplinary style could be influenced by various interacting factors. Would you or wouldn't you adopt the disciplinary style that you experienced in your own youth? Justify your choice.

Focus Point. Eight major categories contribute to the nature and context of an adult's potential behavior as a parent and influence the configuration of the adopted parenting style:

1. *Cultural influences:* social class, background, and associated values and beliefs
2. *Developmental time:* synchrony of parental style and a child's developmental stage
3. *Structure and nurture:* primary parenting objectives in achieving child-rearing goals
4. *Family-of-origin influences:* the model of parental behavior as experienced in family of origin
5. *Child influences:* the many ways children influence their parents' behaviors
6. *Disciplinary approach:* the approach adopted by parents in guiding their children toward goals
7. *Family ecological factors:* ethnic identity, level of family income, and type of family structure
8. *Attitudes and parenting styles:* as reflected in authoritarian, authoritative, and permissive approaches

POINTS TO CONSIDER

- Individuals in our society need training and education to be effective parents, just as for other roles in adulthood. Until recently, little preparation was provided to future parents.
- In contemporary society, there are four characteristics of the parenthood role:
  - Parenthood is a **social construct**. The parental role is a social institution based on complex values, beliefs, norms, and behaviors.
  - The family systems theory describes parenthood as a **subsystem** of the larger social system of the family and within an ecological context.
  - Both parent and child actively participate in a **bidirectional** interaction with mutual influence.
  - Parenting is a **developmental** role and a **life span** pursuit: both parent and child undergo developmental changes with time and life span progressions.
- Our current ideas about the nature of parent–child relations have evolved over time. What is considered appropriate today differs somewhat from what we practiced in the past.
- A number of factors contribute toward how behavior affects the parenthood role. Among them are our beliefs, attitudes, and values; the developmental stage of both the child and the parent; nurture and structure; family-of-origin influences, and the bidirectionality of the relationship.

USEFUL WEBSITES

Administration for Children and Families, U.S. Department of Health and Human Services
www.acf.hhs.gov

American Academy of Child and Adolescent Psychiatry
www.aacap.org

American Academy of Pediatrics
www.aap.org

Centers for Disease Control and Prevention
www.cdc.gov

National Institute of Child Health and Human Development
www.nichd.nih.gov

National Institutes of Health
www.nih.gov

CHAPTER 2

Cultural Perspectives

Learning Outcomes

After completing this chapter, readers should be able to

1. Describe the roles of socialization, cultural identity, traditions, and assimilation in effective parent–child relations.

2. Describe the principal features, forms, and structures found in contemporary American families.

3. Explain how parents and coparents can contribute in promoting multicultural competence.

4. Describe the unique characteristics and challenges of parent–child relations in ethnically diverse families in the United States.

To understand how parenthood roles function within family systems, it is essential to describe the factors that may be collectively grouped as family ecological influences. Some of these factors serve as part of the social context in which parent–child relations take place. Family ecology refers to the various social, psychological, and physical environmental systems in which parenting behaviors are contextualized. For example, the level of a family's income and resources, as well as the ethnic identity of a family, can influence parenting styles and behavior. For all practical purposes, these systems comprise cultural content as well. Culture is relative to each particular group and is characterized by some flexibility because it can change over time. Culture cannot be contained within tight boundaries; instead, it permeates into many areas of life and has fuzzy edges. There is a bidirectional influence as individuals can influence a culture and culture, in turn, can influence its group members. The cultural exchange is modified by the context within which cultural events are embedded.

We examine how culture is influential in parent–child relations and how a range of family systems are defined, structured, and characterized in contemporary American society. We explore the ecological factors of ethnicity and background from an ethnographic perspective because these influence parent–child relations.

THE ROLE OF CULTURE IN PARENT–CHILD RELATIONS

Culture

One of the most significant contexts for parent–child relations is the cultural dimension. This social construct defines what families value and believe to be important, and guides the behavior of all members subscribing to a particular cultural group. Culture is a virtual shorthand between persons sharing the same cultural context; it allows them to assume content and meaning without further clarification because as members of the same cultural perspective they have been **enculturated** in a similar manner. Culture can be likened to a computer operating system; it forms a basic layer on top of which other programs can run. Similarly, in a group of people who share cultural values, there are rituals, values, beliefs, and ways of doing things that are shared unquestioningly. This adds to the harmony within a group because there is a cohesiveness that results from these shared values, customs, and belief systems. Being part of a cultural group, members absorb the values seemingly by osmosis. In reality, culture is learned behavior that is transmitted initially in the parent–child relationship, and later by all those who assume coparenting, supportive, and other social roles in a child's life.

Culture shapes the rules or social norms that outline appropriate behavior in a variety of contexts, such as the roles that persons fulfill and the notions of acceptable and unacceptable actions. Importantly, it links them to individuals, agencies, and institutions that transmit these values and beliefs, and may impart a sense of belonging. For example, for some, these values are derived from the larger ethnic group with which they identify (Matsumoto & Juang, 2008); for others, these values come from religious beliefs and philosophies. Usually, all of the contributing agents are so intertwined that there is little point in teasing out which system contributed what in terms of culture. Matsumoto and Juang (2008, p. 7) reference Malpass (1993) when they state

that "Culture, in its truest and broadest sense, cannot simply be swallowed in a single gulp." This reflects the complexity of this multifaceted topic.

Regardless of the origin of the values, parents are charged with transmitting this cultural heritage to their children. It also plays into the scenario that children's brains are equipped with what neuroscientists call *mirror neurons*, which support children in mimicking and copying behavior, especially language, in a virtually involuntary manner (Ferrari & Coudé, 2011; Pätzold, 2010). This ability is also believed to play a supportive role in the acquisition of culture (Azar, 2005; Dobbs, 2006).

Cognitively, children learn values, attitudes, and beliefs by parental example. Negative prejudices can also be learned, which underlines the necessity of parent–child relations that focus on values and behaviors that will support and enhance **multicultural competence** in the child's later life. According to Ryder and Dere (2010), cultural competence should be regarded as a general orientation. It is also aspirational and can be fostered and strengthened with "knowledge about and comfort with the implications of cultural difference" (Ryder & Dere, 2010, pp. 11–12). These same authors use the concept **cultural humility** to describe the quality required in a professional clinical relationship.

An informal description of culture compares its effects to a global positioning device, which directs, and gently redirects, the user back to a preset destination. In cultural terms, it would mean that ongoing minor behavioral adjustments are made to meet cultural expectations. Members of a cultural group share and can reference the symbols and behaviors pertaining to that group. It becomes especially apparent in rituals for life transitions, for instance, life-span rites of passage surrounding birth, marriage, and death.

The formal definitions of culture may seem simple, but encapsulate complexity. Matsumoto and Juang (2008, p. 27) define culture as "[a] unique meaning and information system, shared by a group and transmitted across generations that allows the group to meet basic needs of survival, pursue happiness and well-being, and derive meaning from life." Shiraev and Levy (2010, p. 3) describe it in the following manner: "Culture is a set of attitudes, behaviors, and symbols shared by a large group of people and usually communicated from one generation to the next."

According to Nanda and Warms (2007, p. 86), who describe culture from an anthropological perspective,

Family events and holiday gatherings provide families with an opportunity to transmit cultural traditions to younger generations.

the following commonalities recur in definitions: It is learned behavior, it uses a symbolic "shorthand" or sets of symbols, it is integrated in a logical manner, the material is shared by members who subscribe to a particular culture, and culture adapts and changes over time.

Even though cultural constructs have a degree of permanence, there is also fluidity, allowing for change. The change can be rapid, as in some small subcultures, or relatively slow, as in intergenerational changes. Culture has blurry or indistinct boundaries in that there is no clear demarcation where the influences of culture begin or end. We live in more interconnected ways through mass media, global communication, travel, immigration, and other effects of globalization, and therefore cultures become less stable because there are so many layers of bidirectional influence.

Applied here, culture serves as the lens through which parenting behavior may be observed regarding the proper ways to raise children to maturity in accordance with cultural values and beliefs (Derbort, 2006). More specifically, each culture is likely to have its own particular ways of defining proper child rearing. From this vantage point, culture becomes a worldview possessed and practiced in unique ways by each culture or subculture.

Large societies, such as the United States, often consist of a variety of subcultures that are differentiated from the larger society according to distinct sets of behaviors,

values, and beliefs. These subcultures may be based on features held in common, such as ethnicity, nationality of origin, sexual orientation, age, gender, political affiliation, religious belief, or geographic location. It is possible that individuals may ascribe to more than one subculture based on these factors. Blending or fusing cultures may allow for both a *heritage* culture and a mainstream culture (Ryder, Alden, & Paulhus, 2000, p. 49).

In the United States, where the population has been largely derived from immigrants of many different groups over the years, multiculturalism encourages and allows various subcultures to retain their basic features while also coexisting with others as one nation. Immigrants can maintain a *heritage culture* while simultaneously assimilating to the *host culture*; leading to bi- and multicultural identities (Ryder et al., 2000). The process of acquiring a second culture, layered on top of the first or integrated with the first, is called *acculturation* (Shiraev & Levy, 2010).

Individualism and *collectivism* are two cultural conceptions of value systems (Greenfield et al., 2006). The various cultures around the world are characterized by the manner in which these two value systems are blended or balanced. Essentially, *individualism* in a culture values the person and what can be accomplished on one's own. Individual identity and self-expression are valued as well. *Collectivism* as a cultural trait emphasizes the interdependence of the individual with the larger community. Collectivism encourages people to fit in and adapt to the characteristics of the larger community. Collectivism is frequently associated with cultural groups in Asia, whereas mainstream North America is generally regarded as individualistic.

These two cultural conceptions have direct application in parent–child relations in that they influence how parents translate cultural values into interactions with their children. For example, parents in cultures characterized as *individualistic* tend to

- Encourage autonomy or independence in children.
- Promote children's self-reliance.
- Foster children's personal achievements.
- Support children's competitiveness.
- Allow children to question and explore.
- Allow children to participate in decision making.

In contrast, parents in cultures characterized as *collectivist* tend to

- Have closer emotional ties to children for longer periods in infancy and childhood.
- Emphasize the extended family network in teaching children what is valued.
- Stress obedience to all authority, especially to parents and older family members.
- Emphasize children learning and respecting social norms governing appropriate behavior.
- Emphasize the sharing of property and belongings.
- Shape children's behavior to demonstrate responsibility and obligation to others (Greenfield & Suzuki, 2001; Trumbull, Rothstein-Fisch, & Greenfield, 2000).

There are some implications concerning this interplay between collectivism and individualism. Parents who emigrate from typically collectivistic cultures may find it difficult to assimilate into individualistic cultures. The family cultural values may be at odds with the mainstream cultural values of the host country. First-generation immigrants may bear the brunt of these challenges, while second-generation immigrants (the offspring of the immigrants) may thrive as cultural "translators," understanding both the culture of the country of origin and the culture of the adopted home country (Ryder et al., 2000).

In the teaching–learning environments of educational systems, individualistic approaches emphasize dialogue, independent exploration of ideas, creativity, questioning, and active participation in the teaching–learning process (Gerhardt & Gerhardt, 2009). Traditional collectivistic environments tend to put the teacher or professor into an authoritarian position as the expert, whose opinions may be accepted unquestioningly, while placing the student into a more passive learning role. In an individualistic teaching–learning environment, original thought and action may be prized. For parents (and for teachers) in general, it is a constructive challenge to impart values promoting some cultural cohesiveness while also allowing individualistic, yet pro-social, expression.

The aspects of the cultural heritage to be maintained, versus the aspects to be silenced by the assimilation process, may contribute to adaptation to the host culture. The willingness of migrants and immigrants to find the level of assimilation best suited to integrate successfully may contribute to the family's well-being (Dere, Ryder, & Kirmayer, 2010). Typically, the assimilation and integration process occurs and strengthens from one generation to the next. Each subsequent generation becomes more assimilated into the host culture. The language of the country of origin is usually lost by the third or fourth generation post initial immigration. The United States is an example of such blending of many immigrant voices into one choir.

Behavioral scientists who study cultural influences warn us about the problems of **ethnocentrism** as we study our culture in the United States in comparison with that of others. This occurs when we use the understandings of our culture to compare, evaluate, and judge those of others. Implicit is the conclusion that our culture is superior and preferable to that of others (Matsumoto & Juang, 2012; Rogoff, 2003). For example, the use of physical punishment by parents with children has different meanings and different values from culture to culture and even from one subculture to the next. In another example, although American parents typically value children becoming autonomous at an early age, this practice is viewed as unusual in some cultures.

In studying parents and children, as well as families, we should strive to recognize that there are patterns that are likely to be shared across subcultures, as well as patterns that are unique to each, recognizing the functioning of *cultural universalism* versus *cultural relativism* in influencing our perceptions. In cultural relativism, the *cultural context* within which any cultural expression occurs is emphasized, increasing the understanding and tolerance of cultural expressions that may occur beyond the mainstream (Shiraev & Levy, 2010). Additionally, the concepts **emic** (culturally specific) and **etic** (culturally universal) are of importance. Emic (pronounced to rhyme with "scenic") refers to that which identifies us, or makes us culturally unique. Etic (pronounced to rhyme with "poetic"), on the other hand, draws together those cultural components that we share universally (Shiraev & Levy, 2010).

Socialization

The family is a universal social institution. This group has the responsibility of producing children and socializing them to become well-functioning members of the larger society in which their family is embedded. Although families have always been the basic building blocks of a society, they have also changed significantly over the past century in terms of composition, size, and functioning, as well as the characteristics that give them meaning.

Years of social evolution have produced changes in families themselves, as well as in the umbrella societies under which the families are sheltered. Family functions have altered over time as societies have changed. Of all the functions that families originally had in society, the socialization of children to prepare them for their participation in society is perhaps the principal task to which parents in contemporary families continue to subscribe.

While there are various definitions of what *socialization* comprises, we will use this term to mean "the set of interpersonal processes through which cultural meaning is passed on and changed" (Peterson, Steinmetz, & Wilson, 2005, p. 10). In a more practical vein, socialization is what parents do to teach children to conform to social rules, acquire personal values, and develop attitudes and behaviors that are typical or representative of their culture at large. Socialization occurs through the many ways that culture is transmitted to children by parents, the media, institutions, and agencies.

This process begins in earnest when children are toddlers and preschoolers, when parents and other caregivers take an active role in teaching and socializing children. The lessons are not always given in formal, verbal instruction; many are learned by children when they observe the behaviors of their parents and caregivers. Young children are excellent imitators as young brains are programmed to copy. This is a powerful way of socializing children, as well as transmitting culture, even at an early age (Azar, 2005).

Depending on the nature of a particular family system, certain standards may be promoted more than others. Despite the diversity of families today, almost all

teach certain kinds of behaviors and values to children. Embedded in the guidance about acceptable behaviors are lessons about undesirable behavior as well. All of this is based on the assumption that there are shared meanings for *acceptable/desirable* versus *unacceptable/undesirable* behaviors that are taught by all parents and other agents in society that influence individuals and families. Families can be socialization agents and function on a rigid to flexible or even permissive continuum, as reflected by their parenting styles. This depiction of socialization as a unidirectional model fails to accurately describe what truly happens in families when parents are raising children for adulthood. In reality, the process of socialization is *bidirectional* in nature because children play a role in this process. Parents change and shape the lessons of socialization based on the developmental stage and personal abilities of the child. This is also referred to as *developmental* parenting, meaning that it is appropriate for a particular child, acknowledging their individual and unique abilities while also considering their developmental age.

....

Focus Point. Parent–child relations are influenced by and take place within a cultural context. Socialization is the way that parents and other societal entities teach culture to children. Socialization is bidirectional in that children participate with their parents in this process.

....

Parenting Reflection 2–1

Try to predict how marriage, parenthood, and parent–child relations will be conceptualized in the year 2100 or even 2200. How would you rate contemporary families in their abilities to socialize children effectively for their future?

....

THE FEATURES OF CONTEMPORARY FAMILIES

Characteristics

Societal changes are reflected in families. Demographic trends indicate an increased complexity in family life and boundaries between groups that are more fluid

(Cherlin, 2010). Society and the families within it have a reciprocal relationship. What affects society affects families, and vice versa. The trends have revealed an increasing separation between what is regarded as a family and what can be described as a household. There has been an increase in childbearing among single women. Other changes are reflected in cohabiting relationships, partnership formation and dissolution, and changing marriage and divorce trends (Cherlin, 2010). Diversity is reflected by a variety of ethnic and cultural backgrounds. Immigrant families may have extended families in other countries.

Demographic data are useful for understanding contemporary American families. The conditions under which they operate influence parent–child relations. This information, much of it collected by the U.S. Census Bureau, is helpful in evaluating changes in family and population characteristics and for making predictions about the forms that American families will take. Contemporary American families exhibit trends and features that provide another ecological dimension that shapes parenthood and other family functions and relationships. Families also reflect the influences of culture and socialization in parent–child relations.

Marriage.   Generally, Americans continue to value marriage as a social institution, but a number of changes are occurring. Compared with the start of the 20th century, when the median marriage age was 25.9 years for men and 21.9 years for women, the age of first marriage has increased to 27.5 for men and 25.6 for women a century later (Carl, 2012, p. 83). Couples are marrying later and are marrying less frequently as educational responsibilities and cohabitation increase. Although the overall figures vary by geographic region, ethnicity, and race, the pattern indicates that this trend is occurring across ethnic boundaries (Carl, 2012). Important changes in marital events (marriage, divorce, and widowhood) affect family formation and the assumption of parenting roles.

The higher median ages at first marriage appear to be related to economic and social issues. The delay in assuming adult roles has to do with complex educational and career demands, obstacles in establishing an occupational path, greater gender equality, and greater economic hardship. Later marriage has contributed to delayed childbearing, smaller families, and greater marital stability (Fields, 2003; Hobbs & Stoops, 2002). It has also created new and novel approaches that affect family life: stay-at-home dads, dual-income couples, job sharing, part-time and temporary employment, semi-permanent coparenting arrangements, and moving back to the parental home (boomerang kids). These variations are frequently born out of socioeconomic challenges. Another indication of the delay in first marriage is the increasingly larger number of young, unmarried adults in the population. A sizable number of Americans are deciding whether to become parents independent of their choice about marriage.

Births.   The number of children born in the United States has been relatively stable since about 1975, following a significant decline in births from 1958 (Martin et al., 2006). The number of births increased dramatically among unmarried women within recent years, while those among adolescents have declined significantly. In recent years, Asian and Hispanic women have tended to have higher fertility rates (the number of births that a typical woman will have over her lifetime) than women in other ethnic groups. The overall population numbers continue to grow, and according to the 2010 U.S. Census, the U.S. population is about 308 million, representing an almost 10 percent increase over the census from a decade earlier. Some of this growth can be ascribed to immigration (U.S. Census Bureau, 2010f).

Only 10 percent of all American families had four children or more in 2002, a decline from 36 percent of all families in 1976 (Downs, 2003). Most commonly, parents have two children per family unit (Carl, 2012). Small family size produces other ripple effects observed in society, such as the overall age structure of the population, school enrollment, and social programming needs.

Divorce.   Divorce data are reported in many forms by different government agencies. This presents complicated and often contradictory information, made more difficult as the figures vary by ethnicity.

The rate of divorce appears to have stabilized within the last 20 or more years, although at a level that is the highest in our nation's history (Munson & Sutton, 2006). According to Carl (2012), the picture is not as bleak as commonly believed. He states, "Notably, and contrary to common belief, fewer Americans than one might assume had ever been divorced in the year 2000. While the percentage of couples divorced tends to increase based on the length of that marriage, on average, only 20 percent of people—not the 50 percent as often cited—has ever been divorced" (Carl, 2012, p. 84). He emphasizes that these figures are complex as they vary by age, cohort group, and ethnicity. For example, in the 50–59 age group, the divorce rate is very high, which approximates the often-touted one-in-two message of gloom concerning the state of American marriages. For older adults (age 70+), the figure is lower, namely around 18 percent, as it probably was influenced by harsher social disapproval of divorce and the lower earnings potential of women who tried to make it on their own. Age at first marriage and racial group membership are related to the probability of divorce. Couples facing multiple stressors may be at greater risk for divorce (Karney, 2011; McHale & Lindahl, 2011). Higher divorce rates also tend to occur in *fragile families* (families where several simultaneous stressors are present). Stressors such as poverty, unemployment, or a child with a disability can strain the resources of a family system to the breaking point. The high incidence of divorce, as well as single parenthood, has given rise to the prevalent family form in the United States, namely the single-parent family.

As divorce has become more common, it has lost much of its social stigma. For many couples, it is difficult to maintain a long-term commitment to marriage in these more liberal times. The reasons include

■ Changes in the status and roles of women in society.
■ Changes in laws that make obtaining a divorce less complicated and less stigmatizing.
■ The strong desire to achieve personal happiness (Cherlin, 2004, Cherlin, 2005).

Parenting Reflection 2–2

You are the mother of a young woman contemplating marriage. She has a concern that she wishes to discuss with you: Why do people continue to get married given the current likelihood of divorce? What would you say to her in defense of marriage?

Remarriage. Remarriage is more likely to occur among those who leave a first marriage via divorce (U.S. Census Bureau, 2010a), although since the mid-1960s there has been a general decline in the rate at which remarriages occur. The median length of a first marriage in the United States has remained at about 7 years since 1980. The median interval between divorce and remarriage is about 3 years. Fifty-four percent of divorced women tend to remarry within 5 years, 75 percent within 10 years (Bramlett & Mosher, 2002). Racial group identity also influences remarriage rates; Caucasians are more likely to remarry than are African Americans. These relationships are considered to be at high risk of divorce, often within 6 years.

For many individuals, remarriage creates blended families, increasing the likelihood of coparenting and stepparenting. Many remarried adults can expect to parent children other than their own offspring. The 2000 U.S. Census reported that about 5 percent of all children were living in stepfamilies (Kreider, 2003). In an analysis of 2010 U.S. Census data, the reciprocal influence between marriage and parenthood is clear. Parenthood has an effect on marital status. Similarly, marriage affects parenthood. This seems to be an intuitive statement, yet closer analysis of the data shows that those persons who divorced before starting a family and did not remarry, are more likely not to have children (Carl, 2012).

Family Income and Working Mothers.   Americans are reeling under the pressures of the global financial crisis. Although many adults would prefer to be working, the high unemployment rates have made this difficult. Employment of both adults in contemporary families has become the norm, if possible, but stay-at-home dads (often because they cannot find employment) and unemployment have changed the characteristics of the working population. Family income may have a more influential effect on the quality of family life and on parent–child relations than other factors that have been previously discussed. When both adults are employed, challenges in family life generally include concerns about housework, child care and child rearing, extracurricular activities during personal and leisure time, health care, and the amount of attention devoted to the marital relationship.

The median income of families in the United States provides an idea about how finances influence quality of life. The median income of all family types in the United States has risen considerably since the mid-1940s (DeNavas-Walt, Proctor, & Lee, 2006) but is dropping under current global financial pressures. The current generation will have a bleaker financial future than their parents before them. These differences in family income have a significant influence on the quality of life experienced in these families, which, in turn, plays a central role in parenting and parent–child relations. The number of working mothers rose to an unprecedented high (U.S. Census Bureau, 2010a) as fathers were losing their jobs during the economic recession.

The increase in the numbers of married women in the labor force has resulted in a concomitant increase in dual-income families. The largest segment is married mothers of children between the ages of 6 and 17. In 2001, about 68 percent of all married women worked outside the home. The number of couples who both work has remained more or less stable, namely 66 percent of the population, or 17 million (U.S. Census Bureau, 2010a). (See Figure 2–1.) Employment of both adults in an intact family produces ripple effects in other areas of family life and parenting, such as child-care arrangements, after-school care, division of labor for household chores and responsibilities, and choices pertaining to family finances.

Poverty and Homelessness.   Family well-being is threatened when homelessness occurs and a family exists at the poverty level or below. Poverty varies considerably in the United States relative to family structure, racial group, and ethnicity. Americans who make up the poorest of the poor increased and, in 2009, had reached a record high of 6.3 percent of the population. These extremely poor families have to scrape by on less than half of what is officially designated by the poverty guidelines, namely $22,350 for a family of four living in any of the 48 contiguous states in 2011 (U.S. Department of Health and Human Services, 2011). Note that these are not the same figures as the poverty thresholds referred to by the U.S. Census Bureau because poverty thresholds and poverty guidelines are slightly different versions of the federal poverty measure. The *poverty guidelines* are used in determining financial eligibility for certain federal programs (U.S. Department of Health and Human Services, 2011). Almost 18 million children, or 18 percent of all American children, live in families affected by poverty. The amount that a family of four would require to stay above the poverty threshold varies, as it is tempered by the cost of living in different regions, employment opportunities, the ages of the children, the effects of the recession, and other economic factors. The U.S. Census Bureau uses a very complex formula to determine the poverty threshold.

The higher incidence of single-parent families headed by women among minorities is a major factor in the differences in family income among racial groups. Two trends among those affected by poverty continued to be observed in recent years: (1) the feminization of poverty, as noted by the increasing number of women and children who are poor; and (2) an increase in the number of working poor, or those who may work one or more jobs earning low wages with few or no benefits. In addition to these factors, inflation has continued to erode the buying power of the American dollar, affecting those earning minimum wages the greatest.

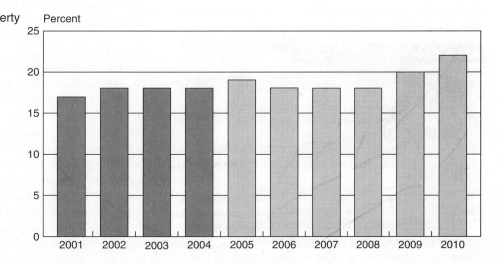

FIGURE 2–1.   U.S. Child Poverty Rate, 2001–2010 American Community Surveys.

Source: U.S. Child Poverty Rate, 2001–2010 American Community Surveys.

It is extremely difficult to estimate the number of homeless individuals currently in the United States. These are individuals who live on the streets or in public shelters. An increasingly large segment of the homeless population is women and families with children. In 2003, 42 percent of children affected by homelessness were less than 5 years of age (National Coalition for the Homeless, 2006). In rural areas, these segments of the population account for the largest numbers of those who are homeless. Other factors, such as substance abuse, mental illness, unemployment, disability, and an unstable family life, may also contribute to homelessness. Domestic violence experienced by women is a leading factor. About half of all women who were homeless were thought to be escaping from abusive relationships (American Civil Liberties Union, 2006a).

With homelessness, parenting is either terminated or inadequate because of the inability of the adult(s) to provide for themselves or for their children. The many causes of homelessness, as well as the complexity of providing solutions to end this status, represent a serious challenge to communities that are trying to reintegrate homeless children and families into the mainstream of American culture.

Many families deal with the economic pressures by moving in together. Half of young Americans ages 18 to 24 have lived with their parents, while 30 percent of those from ages 25 to 34 had moved back into the parental home (Carl, 2012).

Focus Point.   The ways that parenthood is defined, child rearing is conducted, and parent–child relations are valued vary based on how each family system experiences different ecological factors. Contemporary family life in America has certain features:

- First-time marriages occur later for both men and women.
- A great number of marriages terminate in divorce, usually after 7 years.
- There is a high probability of remarriage following divorce, leading to children growing up in blended families.
- Families tend to be smaller, often with two children.
- Family incomes have increased significantly in the years since World War II, but economic stability has been threatened by global financial recession.

- The generation currently reaching adulthood faces a more unstable economy and gloomier employment prospects than their parents did.
- Poverty and homelessness affect an increasing percentage of families in the United States each year. This situation affects minority families to a greater extent.

DIVERSITY IN CONTEMPORARY FAMILY FORMS AND STRUCTURES

The family is an important source of stability in our rapidly changing and increasingly complex society. It can be a refuge while the storms and challenges of the greater system rage. The importance of pursuing personal happiness is a basic tenet of our American society, and this noble goal is referenced in the U.S. Constitution. We have become more conscious of the diversity in our society; there is endless variety based on factors such as age, gender, race, sexual orientation, special needs, and ethnic group identity, to name a few. With increased respect for diversity and the acquisition of multicultural competence, we know that each group has its own strengths and, as Americans, we can find many threads that connect us in one common fabric. As Nobel Laureate Maya Angelou has so poignantly expressed in her poem "Human Family" (1995), "We are more alike, my friends, than we are unalike."

These social changes are reflected in family life. For example, a trend reported by the U.S. Census Bureau (2010a) is an increase in the number of nonfamily households and a decrease in the number of family households. In 1970, 70 percent of all American households were family households (at least two persons related by blood, marriage, or adoption), while today, these kinds of households are diminishing. Social conditions, such as the probability of divorce for married couples, have changed the face of the American family. Families have changed in size, structure, form, and function. Today, diversity in family form and structure is the norm. We cannot discuss every variant contained in our society and, therefore, within families because members can belong to many different groups simultaneously. To highlight every type of family where parents and children can claim membership would amount to cataloging differences, whereas we are trying to focus on unifying family trends. In this section, we will therefore focus on the predominant family types or structures that include children.

Two-Parent Families

Traditionally, families are thought to be composed of two opposite-sex, married adults and their children. For generations, this family form has been considered the ideal, normative family form in which to produce and raise children to maturity.

With gender equality on the forefront, there has been a welcome move toward **dual parenting**, with the implication that both parents will contribute whatever the parenting situation demands, regardless of traditional gender role stereotypes. In *dual-income* families, the ideal would be that all tasks are shared, from income-producing work and household-related labor, to the nurturing and raising of the offspring (Hochschild & Machung, 2003). In practice, this is not necessarily true. Dual-income families may have blurred traditional gender role divisions. Dual parenting ideally implies that both parents will contribute equally, responding to what the specific situations may demand, rather than giving a response based on traditional gender roles, even though each parent may bring different strengths to the parent–child relationship. *Androgynous* parenting is sometimes used to describe roles that are either gender neutral or that are performed by the opposite-sex parent from the one who stereotypically assumes the role. An example would be strengthening the nurturing aspect of fathers, whereas in the previous century, mothers were the primary nurturers. The blurring of gender roles in the parenting context, specifically, can enhance a greater sense of gender equality in the children. Members of Generations X and Y are more likely to be **dual centric** or **family centric**, meaning that they **emphasize work and family equally**, actively planning to allocate sufficient time to family life. These are the cohorts who were born in the 1970s and 1980s (Galinsky, 2002).

Much of the information on parent–child relations is derived from research based on individuals living in two-parent families. As such, it continues to be the predominant family form in the United States (U.S. Census Bureau, 2010c). In the general population, this family form is declining. This decline is often attributed to changes in attitudes that have made adult *cohabitation*, or living together without benefit of marriage, and divorce less stigmatized and more acceptable throughout American society (Pinsof, 2002). In addit. ward trend in two-parent families is contras. upward trend in single-parent families in ... States.

Despite the decline in this form of family, most children in the United States experience growing up with two parents (Scommegna, 2002). Many adult couples choose to cohabitate rather than marry, while raising the children of either or both partners. The literature is not clear regarding the effects or outcomes of cohabiting opposite-sex adults who are parenting children (Acs & Nelson, 2002, Federal Interagency Forum on Child and Family Statistics, 2007). It is clear that

- the number of adults who cohabit rather than marry is increasing (Fields, 2003; U.S. Census Bureau, 2010c).
- the nature of the relationship of a cohabiting couple closely resembles that of a married couple (Brown, 2000), although it has been associated with increased risk of divorce and marital distress (Stanley, Rhoades, & Markman, 2006).
- cohabitation does not necessarily lead to marriage (Heuveline & Timberlake, 2004).
- about one in nine cohabiting couples is in a same-sex partnership (Carl, 2012).

See Figure 2–2.

Single-Parent and Binuclear Families

One of the more common types of families in the United States today is composed of one adult parent and one or more children under age 18. Whether headed by a man or a woman (most often a woman), this unit is called a single-parent family. A *binuclear* family refers to children who have *access to two families*, usually as a result of parental divorce. The number of single-parent families is increasing more rapidly than any other family form today as a result of divorce, as well as the many unmarried women who are choosing to have children (Federal Interagency Forum on Child and Family Statistics, 2011b). In 2010, there were about 75 million minor children ages 0 to 17. The proportion of children under age 18 who were living with two parents decreased from 77 percent in 1980 to 66 percent in 2010, while another 3 percent lived with two biological or adoptive cohabiting parents. Older children were less likely to live with two parents. Of these children in single-parent households in 2010, 23 percent lived only

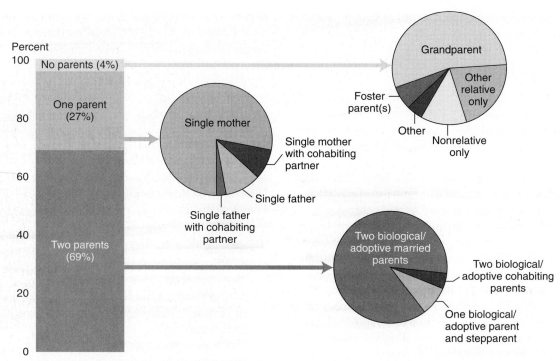

FIGURE 2–2. Percentage of children ages 0–17 living in various family arrangements, 2010.
Source: U.S. Census Bureau, Current Population Survey, Annual Social and Economic Supplements.

with their mother, 3 percent lived only with their father, and 4 percent lived with neither parent (Federal Interagency Forum on Child and Family Statistics, 2011b). Single-parent families accounted for about 26 percent of all families with children in 2010. Single-parent families are more prevalent among African Americans as a group (U.S. Census Bureau, 2007a, U.S. Census Bureau, 2007b).

A single-parent family is created through (1) divorce, desertion, or separation of the adults; (2) the death of one adult; or (3) having a child while unmarried. The most common means is through divorce. The vast majority of single-parent families are headed by women because U.S. courts typically award full physical custody of younger children to the mother, while also considering the best interests of the child.

Quality of life is a major issue for many single-parent families (Hildebrand, Phenice, Gray, & Hines, 2008). Any type of disruption in family life can produce a crisis, and divorce is one of the most stressful experiences of adulthood. It can also be traumatic for children. Although divorce has become commonplace, it is a crisis event that forces many short- and long-range adjustments.

The experience of being a single parent differs for women and men. Women generally expect to have financial difficulties, and there are significantly more children who live in poverty because they live in a single-parent family headed by a woman (Federal Interagency Forum on Child and Family Statistics, 2011b). The implications for children growing up in single-parent families, especially those headed by mothers, can be serious. While most studies report that children generally fare well while living in a single-parent family, those who live in poverty are at greater risk for problems at school, teen parenthood, unemployment, and lower wages when entering the labor force.

Life is not easy for most single-parent families. Yet many persons choose divorce over an unhappy relationship, even though a multitude of difficult adjustments are inevitable. This type of family arrangement can be more efficient and harmonious than a household marked by tensions and strife between the adults, especially if abuse is part of the scenario.

Support networks of the military and the social cohesiveness of military families contribute to their emotional resilience. The deployed parent in a military family may have to coparent from a distance.

Military Families

Military families face many unique challenges and their parenting has been aptly described as *coparenting at a distance* (Huebner, 2009). During deployment, they share some of the stressors and challenges with families who function as single-parent units, but they are also subjected to a military environment that, in some ways, is a world of its own. Military life (even without deployment) is characterized by some unique qualities that affect marital and family functioning. These are closely related to parenting and child rearing (Willerton, MacDermid Wadsworth, & Riggs, 2011). During the post-9/11 period (2001–2010), about 2 million U.S. service men and women had been deployed once (Willerton et al., 2011), while half a million plus had been deployed twice (Huebner, Mancini, Bowen, & Orthner, 2009a). By 2007, about 20,000 had been deployed five or more times (Olson, 2007). If one includes extended family, millions of Americans have experienced the deployment of a family member (Willerton et al., 2011). Considering that the period of deployment is about 15 months on average, the spouses and children in these families are under a significant strain for extended periods of time. They worry about the safety of the family member who is deployed, and they suffer from what has been called *ambiguous loss*, which is the temporary loss of a family member combined with the risks, threats, and vulnerabilities associated with injury and permanent loss of life (Huebner, Mancini, Wilcox, Grass, & Grass, 2007). To quote the Military Child Education Coalition (2011): "More than 40,000 military-dependent children have been affected by the injury, death or illness of a service member as a result of combat and deployment, a number that does not even include the young brothers, sisters and relatives of service members." Whether we concentrate on the qualities of temporary single-parent households or the characteristics of *coparenting at a distance*, these families face stressors that affect many areas of family functioning, and these stressors seem to increase with repeated deployment (Lincoln, Swift, & Shorteno-Fraser, 2008).

Significantly, many of the military children tend to be young; more than 4 in 10 military families report having children under the age of 5. Almost 2 million children are the offspring of parents in active or reservist roles in the military, and many of them have experienced a parent leaving for a war zone (Military Child Education Coalition, 2011). Between 40 and 50 percent of the soldiers are married, and of the unmarried ones, many are in serious and permanent relationships (Huebner et al., 2009a; Huebner, 2009b; Willerton et al., 2011). The sustaining and positive factors in these families are the strength and stability of the marriage relationship, combined with their social connectedness to a network of supportive and significant others, such as friends, family, and other military spouses and their families (Huebner et al., 2009a). In the work of Karney and Crown (2011), they find that, paradoxically, deployment increases the stability of many military marriages, but there are many variables that contradict generalizations because marital stability varies according to gender, race, length of deployment, and age at the time of marriage. To quote Karney and Crown: "In short, for the vast majority of the U.S. military, the longer that a service member was deployed while married, the *lower* the subsequent risk of marital dissolution. In these groups, deployment appears to enhance the stability of the marriage. The beneficial outcomes in terms of marital stability seem to increase with length of deployment" (2011, p. 37). Multiple and prolonged deployments appear to escalate difficulties (Lincoln et al., 2008). Soldiers who return with post-combat mental health problems affect the entire family, which can precipitate poor adjustment in the children of these families (Willerton et al., 2011).

Clearly, the excellent support networks of the military and the social cohesiveness of military families contribute to *emotional resilience*. In fact, Huebner et al. (2009a) state that the communities' capacity and ability to support military families is crucial in positive outcomes, as well as in providing support for the children in these challenging situations. As civilians, we should understand that there is an immense positive power contained in our expressions of care, support, and appreciation toward military families. Their well-being is also the concern of the greater community, even though the military has built excellent and exemplary support systems and provides expertise in many areas of social concern (Chawla & Solinas-Saunders, 2011).

Military personnel, as well as their families, face significant adjustment when the family member returns from deployment. There may be post-traumatic stress to deal with, the possibility of an injury is a reality, and the entire family has to readjust and rebalance to find a new equilibrium (Willerton et al., 2011). For some of the families, this adjustment cycle is repeated with redeployment and its subsequent challenges.

There are five priorities for research about military families:

- Studying marital and family relationships longitudinally.
- Studying the effects of deployment on child well-being and parent–child relationships.
- Studying the renegotiation process in military families as they readapt after deployment.
- Examining coping with the psychological and physical wounds of combat.
- Studying the impact of family members and help-seeking behavior in soldiers who are not married (Willerton et al., 2011).

It is clear from the research thus far (Willerton et al., 2011) that the support given to military families needs to incorporate the research findings to ensure efficacy. Among some of the preliminary recommendations are the use of systemic and evidence-based approaches and the power of education to inform and to teach as this will have a trickle-down effect by information and best practices being dispersed more widely. Service members, as well as their spouses, require information and training to safeguard the psychological health of their children and to optimize parent–child relations.

Blended Families

Blended families are formed when at least one of the adult partners remarries (Hildebrand et al., 2008) or when a couple cohabitates and children are involved. Because the vast majority of single-parent families are headed by women, the person usually filling the vacant adult role in the new blended family is a man. He may or may not have been divorced and may have children of his own.

Remarriage is popular, although these relationships have a higher risk of ending in divorce than first marriages (B. N. Adams, 2004; Carl, 2012). The median length of first marriages in the United States is about

7 years (Kreider, 2005). Most persons who divorce remarry within 3 years. Second marriages tend to last about the same length as first marriages. It is unusual for an individual to have been married three times or more. Blended families, by definition, involve the children of one or both remarried partners, although many remarried couples have at least one child from this new union.

Popular perception holds that blended family life is highly problematic for all involved. Researchers have found that this family form may be no better or worse than other family forms, although the challenges are unique (Hildebrand et al., 2008). These challenges include dealing with a complicated extended family network, difficulty in establishing stepparenting roles, and the unique developmental tasks associated with forming a new and cohesive family identity.

Families with Renested Adult Children

Families with renested adult children are a modern phenomenon. The renested family emerges when children who have been launched into adult lives of their own return to the home of their family of origin (Steinmetz, Clavan, & Stein, 1990). Young adult children are also referred to as *boomerang kids* (Mitchell, 2006; Mitchell & Gee, 1996). Some estimates suggest that more than 60 percent of all young adults between age 18 and 30 will, at some time, return to their family of origin to live temporarily (Piper & Balswick, 1997). It is estimated that about 56 percent of men and 43 percent of women between age 18 and 24 live with one or both parents (U.S. Census Bureau, 2010b); during extended economic downturns, these numbers tend to increase.

The phenomenon of *renested* families occurs primarily when young adult children experience some type of economic or personal crisis or transitional life event, such as job loss or divorce, and turn to their families for support. Some renested families are also formed when adult children return to their elderly parents' homes in order to care for them (Mitchell, 2006).

Very little is known about the patterns of interaction or lifestyles of renested families (Mitchell, 1998, Mitchell, 2006; Mitchell & Gee, 1996). This type of family system needs to be adaptable to respond effectively to the developmental level of a young adult. Family rules may need to be changed and new boundaries established as parents and young adult children work through interaction issues. The kind of arrangements

derived will involve new definitions of parent–child relations that depend less on the social power of the parents. Parents feel more positive about the arrangement when their boomerang kids reciprocate by contributing to the household financially and in kind, and are respectful of family rules. It is beneficial to all parties if the adult children can maintain their autonomy, even while returning to the parental home (Bold, 2001).

The *sandwich generation* refers to adults who are looking after their own parents, as well as their offspring; they are the middle generation with a generation on each side (Pierret, 2006).

Kinship Families: Custodial Grandparents and Grandchildren

"For a growing number of Americans, contemporary grandparenthood involves assuming responsibility for parenting and meeting the basic needs of one or more grandchildren" (Dolbin-MacNab, 2009, p. 207). This recent variation in family structure was first noticed in the early 1990s by researchers, public policy makers, and the media (Bryson & Casper, 1999). This family structure typically involves grandchildren who live in grandparent-maintained households, although it also includes extended family members who are caring for related children. In 1970, there were about 2.2 million of these households involving children 18 years of age and younger living with at least one grandparent. By 1997, this number increased to about 3.9 million children and constituted about 5.5 percent of all American children under age 18 (Casper & Bryson, 1998). By 2010, this number reached about 7 percent of all children in the United States, or 4.9 million children living with a grandparent. Twenty percent of these children are exclusively dependent on their grandparents. A breakdown of these figures indicates that 51 percent of the children in grandparent-maintained households are Caucasian, followed by about 24 percent African American and 19 percent Hispanic/Latino (AARP, 2010; U.S. Census Bureau, 2010b).

The family that encompasses three generations faces special challenges for all parties involved (Pierret, 2006). For the grandchildren, there may be very real reasons why their biological parents cannot raise them; they are absent and for some reason they cannot parent their offspring. The grandparents find that their lives are also transformed in unexpected ways, and that considerable financial stressors may accompany these ongoing grand-parenting responsibilities (Dolbin-MacNab, 2009). It is not surprising that a significant number of the grandparents find themselves overburdened and feel overwhelmed, especially if the children display behavioral issues, or if the grandparents have failing health. The scenario is more positive if the grandparents are healthy, coping, and have the resources to fulfill this variation of the parenting role. For some, it adds meaning to their lives in a joyful and rewarding manner (Dolbin-MacNab, 2009).

The grandmother maintains the household in the large majority of co-resident grandparent–grandchild families (Fields, 2003). Co-resident grandparent–grandchild families typically are created when parents experience some type of personal problem that prevents them from performing effectively in their caregiving role. Examples of such debilitating personal problems include incarceration, addiction and related disorders, child abuse, chronic physical or emotional illness, or even death. Economic stressors over the past few years have also added their toll. Grandparents often step in to assume custody of grandchildren under such circumstances rather than having the children placed in foster care. The motivation for assuming primary caregiving responsibilities is to provide their grandchildren with a stable environment. The children in these families (1) are likely to be age 6 and under, (2) are mostly Caucasian, (3) live in poverty, (4) lack health insurance coverage, and (5) are likely to receive some form of public assistance (Fields, 2003).

Co-resident families have difficult challenges that are not usually faced by other family structures (Edwards & Daire, 2006; Robinson & Wilkes, 2006; Ross & Aday, 2006; Smithgall & Mason, 2004). Many grandparents, while acting compassionately in the best interests of their grandchildren, find that their plans for a serene retirement must be postponed or abandoned to provide for their grandchildren. Others find it necessary to apply for public assistance upon assuming custody of grandchildren because of the increased expenses involved that tax an already-limited fixed income. The grandchildren may also arrive with multiple problems that can be traced to parental problems such as divorce, addiction and related disorders, and inconsistent parenting behavior. Additionally, grandparents in co-resident households are more likely to be poor and to experience all of the negative aspects associated with poverty. Furthermore, grandparents may not be able to cope with providing for the educational needs of grandchildren. Many have not completed high school and may not be completely aware of how to guide children's educational experiences.

Focus Point.   Diversity, in structure and form, is the principal characteristic of contemporary American families. Significant variations in the ways that families are defined and how they are composed reflect changes occurring in the larger society. The most commonly observed family types are

■ two opposite-sex adults with an intact marriage and their children.
■ single-parent adults and their children.
■ blended families composed of two opposite-sex adults who have remarried and the children of one or both.
■ renested families composed of adult parents and their adult children who have returned to the home.
■ Custodial (co-resident) grandparent–grandchild families.

It can be noted that ultimately the quality of the relationships within the diverse families are key indicators of overall well-being. Rather than making a value judgment about one particular family form or configuration over another, it is important to note how well the members of the family are functioning within their particular family group. Family wellness is affected by so many factors, from the economic to the emotional. An entire range of resources are required to ensure that the family unit avoids the pitfalls of becoming a fragile family.

A sociologist at New York University, Judith Stacey (1998a, p. 80), provides her perspective concerning the diversity of family forms:

> The most careful studies and the most careful researchers confirm what most of us know from our own lives: The quality of any family's relationships and resources readily trumps its formal structure or form. Access to economic, educational, and social resources; the quality and consistency of parental nurturance, guidance, and responsibility; and the degree of domestic harmony, conflict, and hostility affect child development and welfare far more substantially than does the particular number, gender, sexual orientation, and marital status of parents or the family structure in which children are reared.

Ethnic identity influences how family systems are organized and how they function.

ETHNIC DIVERSITY AND CONTEMPORARY FAMILIES

Cultural diversity has always been a hallmark of American society; it is the product of the immigration of various ethnic groups to the United States since pre-Colonial times. In recent years, ethnic identity has been reemphasized as Americans have become more curious about their family roots. Americans have always considered themselves to be a culturally diverse society. This diversity is reflected in the numerous ethnic and racial groups that have emigrated from other countries to make their new home in the United States (Glick, 2010).

Ethnic identity is a central family ecological factor that influences how most of these family systems are organized and how they function. It continues to play a role in each subsequent generation. Many ethnic minority families have created new lives and discovered new opportunities, but they have also struggled with the prejudice and discrimination that limits educational experiences, job opportunities, and the ability to function fully in communities. Because of these issues, family systems with minority ethnic and racial backgrounds experience problems that are not usually shared by those with a Caucasian, middle-class background.

Researchers examining family structure and functioning have tended to classify minority families according to the stereotypes promulgated within the larger society. Early researchers examining Hispanic families, for example, identified the concept of *machismo* as the prime factor shaping the dynamics of this ethnic group's family life (Staples & Mirande, 1980). Later research refuted this and other findings as not relevant to the contemporary Hispanic family (J. H. Skinner, 2001). Families are increasingly affected by mainstream cultural influences within their country of residence because the mass media is so powerful in exposing individuals to a variety of values, cultural norms, and marketing pressures.

Today, we are concerned about building bridges between all families that make up American society (Glick, 2010). Diversity, and its essential importance in our society, is not just a politically correct term; it is a critical element that has made American society what it has become today, and it predicts how the future will unfold. Ethnic diversity is a part of the sociocultural ecological system in which we live. It encompasses people's values, how their families operate as a social system, how they teach their children to function effectively, and how resources are used to promote daily functioning. While diversity is a hallmark of family systems in American society, it is important to examine these family systems from the perspective of discerning how each attempts to accomplish a common goal but in different ways: for example, how to raise children in a diverse society, in the midst of great uncertainty about the future, to become effectively functioning members of this society (Dere et al., 2010).

We will examine the challenges faced by parents and children within these cultural and racial groups that represent a cross section of families in the United States. Specifically, this section focuses on the parenting and child-rearing practices of Caucasian, African American, Hispanic, Asian American, and American Indian and Alaska Native families.

We will discuss multiracial, interethnic families, as well as newly arrived families who have immigrated to the United States. This examination uses an ethnographic perspective. Some readers will have an *emic*, or *culturally specific*, view of at least one of these groups by virtue of already being a member. By studying these groups, we are able to develop an *etic*, or *culturally universal*, perspective. In the United States, we are also connected through a common language. Many families additionally maintain the language from their culture of origin.

In studying the diverse groups within the United States, we should ideally first focus on the generalities that connect us as humans and avoid the trap of *stereotyping* specific groups. There is also the risk of *ethnocentrism*, whereby we judge people from the perspective of our own cultural heritage. The process of describing the American population in terms of five major ethnicities has been called *ethno-blocking* and is also informally referred to as "hyphenated Americans" because each groups tends to be described by hyphenating or linking these Americans to the original geographic and ethnic roots. The U.S. Census Bureau designations are based on race, rather than ethnicity or cultural background, and comprise the following: Non-Hispanic Caucasian, African American, Asian, American Indian or Alaska Native, Hispanic or Latino (Carl, 2012, pp. 40–43).

Caucasian Parents and Children

Characteristics.   Our discussion of the ethnic diversity of families in the United States begins with an examination of a few of the major features of the dominant Caucasian ethnic group. This group is also referred to as Non-Hispanic White (U.S. Census Bureau, 2010b). Persons of European extraction make up the majority of the population of the United States and have done so since the colonization process began more than 300 years ago. In 2010, slightly more than 72 percent of the population fit into this ethnic category (U.S. Census Bureau, 2010a). These individuals and their families reside in all areas of the United States, but to a lesser degree in three Southwestern states and the District of Columbia. Most are considered to be middle or working class, holding jobs that are based on educational achievement and having combined household incomes ranging from $25,000 to more than $100,000 annually.

Caucasian persons and their families have dominated American culture for a number of reasons, including their sheer size in relation to other ethnic groups and perhaps their holding positions of power, as well as social and financial stature, in communities. Many individuals and families of this group settled the Colonies that became the United States, as well as the frontier areas that gave rise to the other states that make up the nation. Another large wave of immigrants arrived between 1840 and 1930. The modern-day middle class also emerged from this group following the Great Depression of the 1930s. It is this segment of the Caucasian population whose values became a dominant force in influencing the entire culture of the United States to this day.

Parenting.   For the most part, we might assert that, until recently, the majority of what we know about parenting and parent–child relations was based on research using this group of individuals and their children as the point of reference. Until the focus on multicultural competence became more pertinent, researchers focused on the social class configuration of Caucasians as mediating considerable differences in other subcultures in terms of the ways that parenting took place and the outcomes of children exposed to these differences.

One of the fundamental findings of past research that examined social class differences was the assumption that the middle class versus the working class and the advantaged versus the disadvantaged resulted in corresponding differences in the ways that children were raised and the values that they were taught by parents (Davidson & Moore, 1992). Studies in the past indicated that middle-class parents differed from others in a number of child-rearing patterns, such as the greater use of harshness, emphasizing that children must delay the gratification of their immediate desires, the learning of a work ethic at an early age, valuing and achieving academic successes such as earning a high school diploma or a college degree, and valuing and demonstrating the value of cleanliness and neatness in one's personal life. Researchers have described differences in speech, communication styles, and interaction between middle-class and lower class parents. What realistically may have been at work were family ecological factors, such as significant differences in family income, quality of housing, availability of health care, provision of adequate nutrition, and the availability of time to devote to parenting children. The inherent message coming from these studies was ethnocentric, pointing to the relative success of middle-class parents in raising children to achieve a supposedly equally successful adulthood.

Later researchers refuted these findings, noting that social class variations have been reduced in American society because of the increased exposure of the entire population to media sources that portray middle-class values and an increase in the number of lower class individuals who have become upwardly mobile, moving into the working or middle class as a result of better-paying jobs.

Middle-class values continue to play a major role in providing a template for what is termed success and the status to which many other groups aspire. In some respects, this template comes with a price. The pressure to succeed may not always bring the happiness imagined (Drum Major Institute for Public Policy, 2006). The degree of materialism associated with middle-class success may not always grant peace of mind (Warren & Tyagi, 2004). The conspicuous consumerism of middle-class Caucasians may eventually lead to an erosion of certain moral and ethical values, although economic pressures have begun to influence this situation. Caucasian families provide one model of parent–child relations that demonstrates both cultural universalism and cultural relativism in child rearing.

•••

Focus Point.   Parent–child relations are influenced by and take place within a cultural context. Socialization is the way that parents and other societal entities teach culture to children. Socialization is bidirectional in that children participate with their parents in this process.

•••

Hispanic Parents and Children

This group is also referred to by race as Latino (U.S. Census Bureau, 2010c). Hispanic families constitute a diverse group. A commonality is the use of Spanish and the use of English as a second language (Hildebrand et al., 2008). Many families who speak a language other than English at home, which is 20 percent of the population, identify with this group (U.S. Census Bureau, 2010c). Hispanics may have the distinction of rapidly aspiring to become the largest minority group in the United States (U.S. Census Bureau, 2010c). The increases in this segment of the population are largely a result of immigration from Mexico, and other Central American countries.

Another factor accounting for the significant increases in this ethnic group is the large number of children per family, the highest among all ethnic groups in the United States. Many illegal immigrants have "anchor babies," in the hope that these children can contribute to legitimizing their residence status in the U.S. Hispanics live predominantly in southwestern states such as Texas, Arizona, New Mexico, and California, although they are represented in all the states. Most work in service occupations and in construction and earn moderately comfortable incomes. The poverty rate is about 21 percent for all Hispanic families in the United States (Fronczek, 2005). The economic downturn has increased this figure. About 59 percent of Hispanic households reported having one unemployed member, and 28 percent said that they were at risk of losing their home as a result of mortgage payment defaults (Pew Hispanic Center, 2012).

Among ethnic groups in the United States, Hispanic families have the highest number of children per family and are more likely to live in large families. Hispanics tend to be family oriented and use an extensive kinship-based support.

The role of family ecological factors has a significant influence on the nature of parent–child relations in Hispanic families (Bacallao & Smokowski, 2007). While the increasing size of this group is a significant characteristic, Hispanic families may be characterized in other ways (Hildebrand et al., 2008; McLoyd, Cauce, Takeuchi, & Wilson, 2000; Therrien & Ramirez, 2000; U.S. Census Bureau, 2010c):

■ Hispanic families are more likely to live in large families (four or more persons) as compared with non-Hispanic Caucasian families (three people or fewer).
■ There is a greater tendency for the parents and children to experience substandard levels of education. More than half of this group has not graduated from high school, and one-quarter has less than a ninth-grade education.
■ About 23 percent of Hispanic parents and their children live in poverty, compared with 8 percent of non-Latino Caucasians. Families with illegal immigration status face many additional stressors.
■ Religion plays a significant role in daily family life.
■ Hispanics may be more family oriented than Caucasians and use a more extensive kinship-based support network.

Parenting. In matters of child rearing, Hispanic parents are challenged by the traditional scripts that they learned as children that may have a poor fit with the realities of raising children in a different cultural environment. For example, differences in English and Spanish language fluency between parents and children can affect parent–child interactions, resulting in frustration and even resentment (Becerra, 1998). In a similar vein, the conditions produced by having a low income as a result of lack of educational attainment tend to promote a more authoritarian approach to child rearing known as *hierarchical parenting*. This parenting style combines emotionally warm support for children within the context of demanding exceptional respect for parents and others such as extended family members. This approach is noted for promoting a collective value system among children as opposed to the individualism promoted among Caucasians in their child-rearing approaches (McLoyd et al., 2000).

Within the context of hierarchical parenting, children learn the importance of the "three Rs" of Hispanic family values: personal relationships, respect, and responsibility (Hildebrand et al., 2008). Children also learn the role of cooperation (as opposed to competition) and other-centeredness (as opposed to self-centeredness) in their family relationships. Children are taught to make decisions based on the impact on others in their families. In this manner, they learn about family loyalty and the strength of family bonds in providing support, which in turn spills over into relationships outside of their families (Bacallao & Smokowski, 2007). The emphasis on learning these values promotes the notion of *la familia* and the high importance placed on the family group and its ability to meet the needs of all members, as well as maintaining some cultural traditions.

Educational achievement is highly valued among Hispanic families. Apart from the desire to improve their immediate and extended families' economic futures, education serves as an additional motivator fueling the desire to immigrate to the United States from other countries. Education is perceived as providing additional opportunities to the children of these families (Bacallao & Smokowski, 2007). Paradoxically, it is not unusual for educational attainment to be assigned a low priority by parents and other family members if it conflicts with a child's allegiance to the family (Hildebrand et al., 2008).

Although Hispanic children can initially be socially and educationally challenged by being bilingual, the benefits of bilingualism may surface later. Most learn Spanish as the primary language spoken at home and in the community, while learning English as a second language. For this reason, bilingual education is desirable because it recognizes these children's needs rather than making them an educational liability (Olmos, Yberra, & Monterrey, 1999). The issue of bilingual education is controversial. Hispanic parents generally favor this approach because it appears to support their children's cultural heritage, and there is the belief that bilingual classes facilitate children's learning of the English language. Current research clearly points toward the many advantages of bilingualism (Bialystok, Luk, Peets, & Yang, 2010).

Focus Point. Their strong family structure, values, and family-focused parenting styles give Hispanics a unique position among ethnic minority families in the United States. The high number of children per household contributes to making Hispanics the fastest growing ethnic group.

African American Parents and Children

Family Characteristics.   This group is also referred to by race as Black (U.S. Census Bureau, 2010c). The group constituted 12.6 percent of the total population in 2010 (U.S. Census Bureau, 2010c). In general, marriage is less likely between adults. African American women tend to have a higher fertility rate than Caucasians, and a larger proportion of families in the African American community are headed by women. As such, the poverty rate was higher for African Americans than for Caucasians, with about one-quarter of the African American community living below the poverty level. For the total population (all races), about 13.8 percent live below the poverty level (U.S. Census Bureau, 2010c).

Parenting.   The child-rearing practices of African American family systems are found to be similar to other groups in several aspects (Julian, McHenry, & McKelvey, 1994). When compared with Latino families, African Americans tend to encourage early autonomy of children, are intolerant of wasted time, appear to practice authoritative methods of discipline based on reasoning with children, and encourage egalitarian family roles (Bluestone & Tamis-LeMonda, 1999; Wiley, Warren, & Montenelli, 2002). This approach may vary with the socioeconomic status of the parents and with other factors.

One of the greatest obstacles to effective parenting among African American families relates to economic pressures (Jones, Forehand, Brody, & Armistead, 2002). Despite dire financial circumstances that can exacerbate stress in family life, effective African American parents use encouragement and shared time with children to counteract some of the negative influences of harsh economic family conditions. In spite of the obstacles and challenges facing African American families in general, stable family systems are found throughout these communities with the working class, non-poor forming the backbone of support (Billingsley, 1993).

Ethnicity is a major family ecological factor in child-rearing practices. It contributes to how children are socialized to develop a personal identity that is considered to be appropriate to their ethnic background as African Americans. Because of these and other ecological factors, such as low family incomes and the younger ages of parents compared with other families, the general child-rearing style is seen as parent centered, where children are expected to become responsible and independent at an early age (Hildebrand et al., . children in other minority groups in African American children are genera who emphasize the importance of edu a means of bettering one's quality of lif Thompson, 2003; Trosper, 2002). Whe ...can American parents consistently use authoritative methods in child rearing, their children generally perform successfully in school. The involvement of African American parents in their children's schooling is often problematic because of inconvenient meeting times with teachers, parents' own past experiences with schools that were of poor quality, and feeling intimidated by school personnel (Abdul-Adil & Farmer, 2006; Koonce & Harper, 2005). It should also be noted that religious values and church participation play a vital role in African American family life. The church has played a central role in the socialization of African American children since the days of slavery (Billingsley, 1993).

African American parents, like other minority parents, are challenged in teaching their children to have a positive ethnic group identity (Hughes, 2003). The societal movement toward multicultural competence is gaining momentum. Other aspects of parenting are unique to African Americans. For example, it is estimated that more African American parents spank their children compared with parents in other ethnic groups (Dodge, McLoyd, & Lansford, 2005; McLoyd et al., 2000). Spanking is not likely to be seen as negative, inappropriate parenting behavior among African American parents. Rather, using corporal punishment is more likely to be viewed as an appropriate positive parental behavior by both parents and children.

In addition, parenting frequently occurs within the context of single-parent family structure headed by women who may or may not have been married (Federal Interagency Forum on Child and Family Statistics, 2011b). In addition, many of the custodial co-resident grandparent–grandchild families are composed of African Americans.

Given that some of these family systems are characterized by low-income or poverty-level status, as well as living in an inner-city environment, children can be at risk of experiencing difficulties in some of the underserved schools, participating in high-risk behaviors such as drug use and gang involvement, teen pregnancy, health problems, and other difficulties. Many African American parents are successful in buffering their children from these problems by monitoring their leisure time and social contacts and through involvement with organizations such as church groups that also support constructive civic engagement. They may require younger children to tag along with older siblings, who are responsible for their care (Jarrett, 1995). As such, the family relationships are characterized as more intimate, while peer relationships are less intense than those of Caucasian teenagers.

....

Focus Point.   Research indicates many positive aspects of African American parents' parenting practices. Most problems associated with these family systems can be traced to the insidious effects of poverty; about half are single-parent families headed by a woman. Underserved schools can leave educational deficits. African American parents prepare their children by promoting and encouraging educational opportunities. African American parents possess resilience that enables them to cope with adversity.

....

Asian American Parents and Children

Family Characteristics.   Less information is available about Asian American and Pacific Islander families in comparison with other ethnic groups in the United States. Perhaps this is because these families make up a smaller percentage of the population and are located in fewer geographic areas. The majority live in the western states and in Hawaii, with substantial populations in the largest cities, such as New York City, Los Angeles, San Francisco, and San Jose (U.S. *Census Bureau*, 2010c). Like Hispanics, Asian Americans are a diverse ethnic group, including those with Chinese, Japanese, Korean, and Southeast Asian heritage. Asians with Chinese and Japanese backgrounds make up the largest and oldest established groups in the United States (Hildebrand et al., 2008). Those from Southeast Asia (including Cambodians, Vietnamese, Laotians, and Hmong) constitute the smallest groups, many having migrated as refugees.

Parenting.   Parenting styles among Asian American families appear to be more authoritarian and authoritative rather than permissive, with a greater reliance on verbal rather than physical means for disciplining children (Hildebrand et al., 2008). What appears to be a very strict parenting style to an outside observer is something entirely different to those who reside within such family systems (Gorman, 1988). These family systems typically combine nurture with control in order to shape children's behavior to conform to the family's achievement goals (Rosenthal & Feldman, 1992).

Children of Asian American parents are expected to achieve personal maturity at an early age in comparison with those of other family systems in our society (Caplan, Whitmore, & Choy, 1989). Certain behaviors are not tolerated from children, such as acting physically or verbally aggressive, especially with siblings. Older children are expected to serve as good role models of behavior for younger siblings.

Asian American parents can be intensely involved in their children's academic activities. Educational achievement is highly valued among Asian American parents (McLoyd et al., 2000). For example, more than half of Asian Americans have completed 4 years of college or more, which is an increase from the previous Census. Of all minority groups, these graduates tended to have the highest average earnings (U.S. Census Bureau, 2010c). Some researchers attribute this high level of educational achievement to the Asian American parenting style, which is commonly compared to authoritarianism (Greenfield & Suzuki, 2001). Other Asian American researchers have explained this as the *Confucian training doctrine*, which emphasizes the blending of nurture, parental involvement, and physical closeness with strict and firm control over children (McBride-Chang & Chang, 1998).

First-generation immigrants from Asia may subscribe to collectivism, whereas mainstream North America tends to be more individualistic. Researchers have investigated the cultural differences between parenting practices in China and the practices of Chinese parents living in Canada and the United States, noting that the information on fathering in these families is extremely limited. In immigrant families, fathers became more prominent in the lives of their children, as influences in the adopted country were subtly changing parenting patterns (Chuang, 2009). Chuang found that some of the parenting strategies that may have been meaningful in China were not as relevant in North American contexts. For example, promoting interdependence, obedience, and cooperation (aspects that support collectivism) was not entirely compatible with the challenges faced in more individualistic environments (Chuang, 2009).

In American Indian and Alaska Native families, children are viewed as treasured gifts and are taught to view people and things on the basis of intrinsic value.

Focus Point. Asian American families may be stereotyped as the model minority because parents heavily invest in their children and in their educational achievements. These families value strong parent–child relationships and encourage children while providing a stable family life that emphasizes closeness within a strict adherence to family rules.

American Indian and Alaska Native Parents and Children

Characteristics. The 2010 Census indicates that nearly half of American Indians and Alaska Natives report multiple races (U.S. Census Bureau, 2010c). There may be similarities with other minority groups (Glover, 2001), especially African Americans. The characteristics of American Indian or Alaska Native family systems include high fertility rates, large numbers of births to single parents, the prevalence of households headed by women, and high rates of unemployment and addiction and related disorders (Joe & Malach, 1992).

American Indian and Alaska Native families may view children differently from other groups in the United States (Hildebrand et al., 2008). Children typically are seen as treasured gifts. Parents and other extended family members are charged with discovering the unique characteristics of a child at birth to determine her or his place within the tribe. Infants are carefully observed for several months to learn about their nature. The child's name, as well as the gender role, is determined based on the characteristics that family members observe. Only then is the naming ceremony conducted, sometimes many months after birth.

Problems indigenous to life on and off of the reservation include high rates of adult alcoholism, homicide rates that are higher than those found in the rest of the U.S. population, accidents, and suicides. These problems put some of these children at a higher-than-usual risk of experiencing the loss of parents, siblings, relatives, and friends. In many tribes, the paternal uncle and male cousins, in addition to the child's father and brothers, play an important role in a child's life. Because children continually lose family members as a result of situations that are particular to their lifestyle, they are challenged to acquire coping strategies that are not usually found in children of other ethnic groups. Their response patterns frequently include disruptive, aggressive behaviors at school and at home; depression; feelings of low self-worth and self-esteem; addiction and related disorders; developmental delays; flattened emotional affect; interpersonal distancing; self-destructive behaviors, including suicidal gestures; sexual acting out; and running away from home (Hildebrand et al., 2008).

Because most American Indian and Alaska Native tribes value the personal autonomy and independence of their members, individual differences in children appear to be tolerated and accepted as part of their nature. Children are generally reared through grooming these traits as they are encouraged to learn to make personal choices and learn by the consequences of their actions. This parenting style may appear to be permissive to outsiders because parents often ignore children's behavior that is considered inappropriate.

Parenting. American Indian and Alaska Native parents might be thought to use more permissive styles of raising their children in comparison with other ethnic groups (John, 1998). Some tribes may use methods that are more punitive and controlling. Like Asian American parents, American Indian and Alaska Native parents tend to combine nurture with control in guiding children's development, especially when the children are young. Traditional styles of child rearing emphasize teaching children to maintain a sense of unity and cohesiveness with their tribal and immediate family groups and to suppress the tendency to experience conflict with others. While these practices may be useful in facilitating daily life among the people living on reservations, they may not be effective in teaching these children to function well in urban settings when they live in family units away from the reservation.

Contemporary American Indian and Alaska Native parents usually teach their children traditional values based on the practical application of personal belief systems. For example, children are taught to perceive things and people according to intrinsic rather than extrinsic traits and characteristics. Children are taught to be in touch with the rhythms of nature and to be sensitive to the needs of others. Sharing personal resources, thoughts, and knowledge is considered appropriate in smoothing interpersonal interactions.

Focus Point. American Indian and Alaska Native parents and children are challenged by sociocultural factors that are not experienced by other ethnic minorities. These relate to reconciling traditional ways and values with the necessity of adapting and acculturating to contemporary society. These parents and children may have competing allegiances to both sociocultural worlds. The family structure and functioning of tribes may be difficult for outsiders to understand and appreciate. American Indians and Alaska Natives appear to have a unique approach to child rearing and family life.

Multiracial and Interethnic Parents and Children

The number of multiracial and interethnic married couples has increased significantly; approximately 9 million individuals (or 2.9 percent of the population) described themselves as multiracial (U.S. Census Bureau, 2010c). In the not too distant past, these relationships were frowned upon and as early as 1761, colonial laws prohibited marriage between people of different races. These laws remained in effect until 1967, when the U.S. Supreme Court ruled such laws to be unconstitutional.

The reasons why these marriages have increased over the years since 1967 are varied. The general desegregation of American society presents greater opportunities for people of different racial groups to mingle socially and work together. Nowadays, increased socioeconomic opportunities encourage the socially upward mobility of ethnic minorities, which increases contact between people of all racial and ethnic groups in housing, employment, school, work, and leisure activities (McLoyd et al., 2000).

Research is limited on how multiracial children and their parents manage and learn to cope with their situation (Byrd & Garwick, 2006). Many do not experience significant adjustment challenges, but most must resolve issues related to ambiguous ethnicity and their need to define their identities (Dere et al., 2010; Gibbs, 2003). One explanation for the positive outcomes in these children can be found in the efforts of parents to provide support, encourage activities that build ethnic identity, and expose their children to effective adult role models in multi-ethnic and family contexts. A number of very successful and high-profile Americans claim multiracial backgrounds, and they have been very positive role models for the younger generation in promoting strong and respected identities. Generally, there has also been a focus on increased multicultural competence.

The number of multiracial and interethnic families is increasing. Children in multiracial–interethnic families benefit from having multiculturally competent relationships.

Immigrant Parents and Children

The United States was formed by the immigration of many different nationalities and ethnic groups over the centuries. Large numbers of persons arrived in this country to pursue their dreams of freedom, wealth, and personal happiness. Many individuals and families arrived legally and eventually assumed respected positions in their adopted communities. The amalgam of so many different ways of life, languages, family lives, parenting styles, and perspectives has given strength to the diversity of American culture.

Revisions in federal legislation in 1965 changed the criteria for lawful entry into the United States. Priority was given to those who possessed valued work skills, refugees from foreign aggression, and those who already had relatives living in the United States. Family reunification accounts for about two-thirds of legal entrants into the United States (Fix, Zimmerman, & Passel, 2001).

The number of immigrations coming into the United States has increased steadily since 1960 (Fix et al., 2001). In 2010, 20 percent of U.S. born children had one foreign-born parent, whereas 3 percent of children were foreign born themselves, with one foreign-born parent. There has been a steady increase in these figures from 15 percent in 1994, to 23 percent in 2010 (Federal Interagency Forum on Child and Family Statistics, 2011b).

Many individuals and families in the United States have become more aware of immigration issues, both legal and illegal in nature, since the terrorist attacks of September 11, 2001. Restrictions are more stringent because of security issues, and immigrant families may be scrutinized more than in the past. Much debate is currently taking place in American society as Congress attempts to revise laws dealing with immigrants who have arrived in the United States illegally.

Economic difficulties are often associated with immigrant parents and children because of language barriers and general acculturation problems (Dere et al., 2010). These challenges affect everyone in a family and hinder parent–child relations. Many parents and children are reported to be living in crowded housing units. Statistics indicate that 33 percent of the foreign-born children with foreign-born parents lived below the poverty level (Federal Interagency Forum on Child and Family Statistics, 2011b).

Immigrant parents encourage their children to achieve high levels of education and become good citizens of their new country (Detzner & Xiong, 1999). Parent–child relations in immigrant families may be strained by negative family ecological factors and by discrepancies observed in parents who may have problems with acculturation, often combined with the difficulties of learning a new language (Aroian, 2006). (See Figure 2–3.) Immigrant children may also experience problems

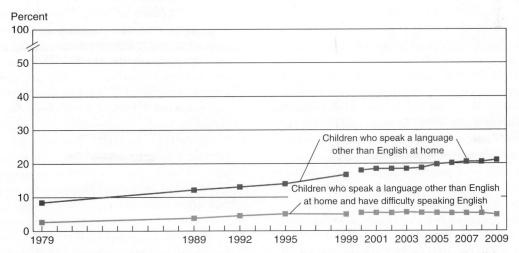

FIGURE 2–3. Percentage of children ages 5–17 who speak a language other than English at home and who have difficulty speaking English, selected years 1979–2009.

Source: U.S. Census Bureau, October (1992, 1995, and 1999) and November (1979 and 1989) Current Population Surveys, and 2000–2009 American Community Survey.

with reconciling the traditional standards and expectations of their parents with the consumer-oriented culture of contemporary American society, and it may be difficult to merge the *heritage* culture with the *host* culture (Dere et al., 2010).

••

Focus Point.   Issues confronting newly arrived immigrants involve the marginal nature of these families. Economic difficulties, problems in acquiring and using a new language, and general acculturation issues present a special challenge for immigrant parents and children.

••

POINTS TO CONSIDER

■ The most significant context in which parent–child relations take place is the cultural context. Culture defines what families value and believe to be important, which guides the behavior of all members. Culture shapes the rules or social norms that outline the appropriate behavior of people in a variety of other contexts, such as the roles they fulfill; the notions of what are acceptable and unacceptable actions; and the individuals, agencies, and institutions that transmit these values and beliefs.

■ *Individualism* and *collectivism* are two cultural conceptions of value systems. These cultural concepts have direct application in parent–child relations because they influence how parents translate cultural values into how they interact with their children.

■ In studying parents and children, as well as families, we recognize that there are patterns that are likely to be shared across subcultures; and there are also patterns that are unique. We recognize the role of *cultural universalism* versus *cultural relativism* in influencing our perceptions. *Emic* (culturally specific) and *etic* (culturally universal) dimensions address this as well.

■ Socialization is what parents do to teach children to conform to social rules, acquire personal values, and develop attitudes and behaviors that are typical or representative of their culture at large, as well as their family of origin. Socialization is the way that culture is transmitted to children by parents, the media, institutions, and agencies.

■ Socialization is bidirectional in nature because children play a role in this process. Parents change and shape the lessons of socialization on the basis of a number of factors, such as a child's age, developmental abilities, ability to use and understand language, and gender.

■ Families in contemporary American society are diverse in form and structure. Single-parent families are the fastest growing family unit today.

■ Military families have unique stressors. After 9/11, over the next decade, approximately 1.5 million service members had spent time deployed. This has significant effects on families and also the children in those families.

■ Blended families are usually formed when a biological mother remarries. These families frequently include children from the previous marriage, and remarried couples can have children of their own. Blended family maintenance requires that members rework their former family system into one that is pertinent to new participants. These families have many strengths.

■ A renested family is formed when children who have been launched into adult lives return to their home base temporarily. Relatively little is known about how these families function.

■ Custodial co-resident grandparent–grandchild families are formed when an adult child cannot function in his or her parenting role. Co-resident grandparents often need help and financial assistance to provide adequate care for their grandchildren.

■ Hispanic parents and children come from diverse groups. Children are taught family values such as developing a strong sense of belonging and loyalty, respecting other family members, and cooperation with other family members. Child rearing is characterized by hierarchical parenting, a style based on authoritarianism that combines emotional warmth and strictness. Children learn about the high value placed on family membership.

■ Many African American parents raise their children with an authoritative style. Many parents must contend with severe economic conditions but use approaches that temper this severity on family life. Educational advancement is encouraged.

■ Asian American parents and children constitute the smallest ethnic group in the United States. Asian American parents typically use a parenting style known as Confucian training doctrine.

■ American Indian and Alaska Native parents and children come from even more diverse groups. The notion of what constitutes a family usually is relative to a particular tribe. A variety of child-rearing approaches may be employed in different American Indian and Alaska Native tribes, but children generally are taught to respect authority and their elders. Because there is a division between those who live on and those who live off of reservations, American Indian and Alaska Native families are challenged by different acculturation issues than other ethnic families. Many families must cope with the insidious effects of poverty and associated problems.

■ The number of multiracial, interethnic marriages in the United States is increasing, with the accompanying larger number of multiracial and multi-ethnic children. These children generally fare well, and as a society we are valuing multicultural competence.

■ Immigrant parents and children face challenges that are unique to their situation. Many problems arise from severe economic conditions, as well as difficulties in dealing with language barriers and other acculturation issues. Quality of life is at risk, as well as the quality of parent–child relations. Parents want their children to become good citizens and responsible

individuals. Children may experience conflict between their parents pressing for adoption of the heritage culture and a contemporary society that encourages assimilation of host cultural values.

USEFUL WEBSITES

Child Welfare League of America
www.cwla.org

United Nations Children's Fund (formerly United Nations International Children's Emergency Fund [UNICEF])
www.unicef.org

United Nations Educational, Scientific and Cultural Organization (UNESCO)
www.unesco.org

United States Fund for UNICEF
www.unicefusa.org

Urban Institute
www.urban.org

CHAPTER 3

Theoretical Perspectives on Parent–Child Relations

Learning Outcomes

. . . .

After completing this chapter, readers should be able to

1. Explain how a family can be described as a social system.

2. Describe the role of attachment in parent–child relations.

3. Explain Bronfenbrenner's ecological systems theory by referring to the multiple, nested layers. Distinguish among the various layers in terms of proximity to the parent–child relationship.

4. Explain how ecological systems theory assists us in understanding individuals within the context of their family system.

5. Describe how psychosocial theory addresses parent–child relations.

6. Explain how other psychological theories address aspects of parent–child relations.

. . . .

THE FAMILY AS A SYSTEM

Families can be regarded as the building blocks of society. Families have the power to influence society, just as they themselves are being influenced. There is an interrelatedness, a give-and-take, among all of these components. If the society at large faces a recession, the families within that society will struggle. Going one layer deeper in this nested configuration, we know that individual family members are affected by what is happening within their family, and the members, in turn, have the ability to influence the climate of their family group. We are all interrelated in this complexity and the influences act in both directions; they are *bidirectional*. Anyone who has built a house of cards, stacking the cards as high as possible, knows that one false move can cause the entire structure to come tumbling down. That is because the pieces of that structure are dependent on one another; they can no longer be seen in isolation.

There is increasing alarm about the health of contemporary American families. The high incidence of family violence, divorce, child abuse, and other problems are very disruptive to family life. Basic family values are discussed, including the conscious choice to become a parent, the possibility of career changes, retirement, and other decisions. Family life is different today because of many options that were not possible in the past when choices were limited. Some people attribute the social problems in contemporary America to recent changes in family structure and functioning. Family sociologists speculate that these changes indicate the family's adaptation to societal changes.

Families have changed in size, structure, composition, and function in response to changes in the society within which they are embedded. In the past, a significant portion of family life was devoted to fulfilling cultural and socioeconomic functions. Family functioning nowadays focuses on the expression and fulfillment of family needs, especially the emotional and social needs of family members, and on training children to become effective members of society. In today's smaller families, members find that their interactions within the family group are intense and frequent. The survival and continuation of families may depend on how well each member's personal needs are met by the family group.

Survival of the family as a social institution also depends on how successfully families respond to societal changes. Parents deal with situations that are different from those encountered by families in the past. These include rapidly changing societal economic conditions, severe social pressures on children, restricted family size, the hazards of living in urban environments, and the need for both parents to work outside the home in occupations that are often highly stressful. Many families are unable to adapt in healthy ways. Family life today is described as *asynchronous*; that is, family leaders (the adults) depend on personal past experiences to guide their current behavior and to prepare children

to function as adults. The problem is that there is no guarantee that the future will be anything like the past, especially if societal changes continue to occur as rapidly as they have over the past 50 years.

The ways we define parenthood vary depending on how family ecological factors are experienced by each family system. Almost every family system adheres to the central role expectations of parenthood, including an emphasis on nurturing, teaching, and caring for children. Because of cultural and environmental variations, it is impossible to define families according to only one form, structure, or approach. At different times, theorists have added various approaches that explain child rearing and family functioning. Combined, all of these factors illuminate the relevance of family functioning against the backdrop of history.

Parents as Socialization Agents

The parent–child relationship provides an opportunity for the psychosocial development of both children and adults, especially the adults. Parents are assisted in their growth and development as adults by parenting children, while children are socialized into adulthood by parents. Although some of the theories presented do not directly address parent–child relations, it is possible to describe how the theories and their concepts may be applied to understanding the parent–child relationship. The parent–child relationship mirrors the larger family process. Using this perspective on family systems, it is possible to describe how the developmental changes being experienced by all members affect everyone within the family system.

Historically, a child was seen as an object to be socialized by the parents. This was a *unidirectional* model of socialization. The adult's behavior was the *stimulus* that caused or produced a *response* or outcome in a child. If an adult behaved well as a parent, the child would become a good person. Adults could achieve their parenting goals if they provided appropriate caregiving. Following this logic, the formula for effective parenting was based on consistently good parental performance during child rearing. Society made judgments about how child-rearing success was attained.

Behavioral and social scientists who studied parent–child relations realized that this traditional idea of parenting was too simplistic and it truly needed to address additional important aspects (Ambert, 2001). The concepts were expanded and developed; currently, three outstanding features of parent–child relations are as follows:

- *Developmental parenting:* This refers to the changes that take place as both the child and the parent experience growth and development over time, as well as the dynamic interchanges taking place.
- *Bidirectional parenting:*   The child has an impact on the parent and gives feedback in response to parental behavior. Simultaneously, the parent has an impact on the child. Communication and influence go in both directions—from the parent to the child and from the child to the parent.
- *Life span parenting:*   Parenting interactions are manifested in children's character, behavior, and competency throughout their life span development.

Although parents have a strong and vital influence on children's development, other factors also play a part. The *bidirectional* model is a more accurate depiction of parent–child relations. This model portrays the give-and-take of information and influence between parents and children; each person influences and has an impact on the behavior of the other.

Several theoretical explanations describe the bidirectional nature of the parenting process more realistically and provide a basis for understanding the influential factors and how the relationship changes over time. Child rearing is a unique statement of personal and family philosophy. These explanations show how adults shape their parenting behavior in relation to various factors.

ATTACHMENT THEORY AND PARENTING

Attachment theory is based on the work of John Bowlby (1907–1990) and Mary Ainsworth (1913–1999) and is also referred to as the *Bowlby–Ainsworth Perspective* (Posada, Longoria, Cocker, & Lu, 2011). Bowlby was a British psychologist, psychiatrist, and psychoanalyst, and Ainsworth was a Canadian developmental psychologist. Both studied at Tavistock Clinic in London where they met as colleagues. Bowlby eventually became the mental health consultant for the World Health Organization. Ainsworth is known for her contributions to play therapy with children, where she used play to explore emotions, including grief. Both Bowlby's and Ainsworth's life work centered on the effects of maternal separation on child development, now expanded to include significant and ongoing caregivers and coparenting situations.

The central tenet is that children brought up with consistent, loving parents or significant, reliable caregivers can develop a foundation of trust and attachment and can grow up to be well-adjusted adults who are capable of

This mother facilitates her child's psychosocial development by supporting or scaffolding his efforts during play.

forming trusting and loving relationships. If the stability is interrupted for any reason, such as *maternal deprivation*, problems can manifest as *separation anxiety*. Particularly during the first 2 years of an infant's life, the care should be constant and preferably provided by the dominant attachment figure. Often this is the mother, although different parenting configurations are becoming more common.

Bowlby believed that an infant's attachment was instinctive, and that both mothers and infants have a biological need for each other. This is another twist on the concept of bidirectionality in the context of parenting relations. Attachment is strengthened by *care* and *responsiveness*. John Bowlby is also remembered for the report that he wrote for the World Health Organization in 1950, entitled "Maternal Care and Mental Health," which emphasized that children's early experiences of care and parental interactions were crucial to overall healthy development and well-being, and that parental deficiencies could have far-reaching implications with detrimental outcomes. He certainly contributed insight into the caretaking relationship, specifically parenting, which we nowadays take for granted.

Attachment theory has several earlier, as well as later, underpinnings as a number of researchers and therapists each contributed insight to flesh out the overall theory. The work of the psychoanalyst Melanie Klein (1882–1960) laid some of the foundation. To place this in a historical context, Klein was born in the year that Charles Darwin died. One of her themes was that, to an infant, the mother represented completeness, and Klein talked about the good versus the bad breast, where the "good" refers to the nurturing aspect and the "bad" refers to the emotionally absent mother. She was also working with troubled children and used toys in her therapeutic sessions.

Initial attempts to study the effects of early nurturing experiences for infants began when investigators examined institutionalized infants and children in the 1940s and 1950s. At that time, infants and children who were abandoned or orphaned were placed in large group homes, where they received minimal care and attention from only a few adults. Researchers found that these children exhibited delayed development in many areas, which was attributed to inconsistent "mothering" and lack of nurture (Bowlby, 1952; Goldfarb, 1945; Ribble, 1943; Spitz, 1945). Historically, children raised in institutions were frequently suffering from malnutrition, especially protein deficiency. This could coexist with emotional and psychological difficulties such as developmental retardation, apathy, depression. The sensory deprivation would have played a role, as ongoing, predictable nurturing ar ships with caretakers. Symptoms of illness in many of these children we. attributed to the lack of appropriate interactional experiences.

Other contemporaries who explored aspects of relationships and bonding were René Spitz (1887–1974), who studied grief in children, and who linked inappropriate early care to expressions of grief. James Robertson (1911–1988), a psychoanalyst, and Bowlby collaborated in making a film in 1952 about a two-year-old, named Laura, who is going to the hospital. In the film, Laura is initially very upset about being separated from her parents. As the separation continues, she eventually calms down. The adults think that she has adjusted to the situation, but in reality she is grieving and withdrawing. This film is disturbing, and raises questions concerning the ethics of allowing this situation to progress and to be filmed. With our current research practices and ethical responsibilities of not doing harm, such observations would have to be interrupted in the interests of the child's well-being.

Several researchers contributed to the general attachment concept. William Goldfarb (1915–1995) wrote case studies near the end of World War II based on what he witnessed in orphans who suffered from the effects of parental loss and separation, as well as intense trauma. Anna Freud (1895–1982), Sigmund Freud's daughter, studied children in particular, and she formulated some of the work on defense mechanisms. She, too, observed children who had been separated from their significant and trusted caregivers during the war (World War II). Jean Piaget (1896–1980) was influential during this same period. Piaget's emphasis on cognitive development and cognitive processing was acknowledged by Bowlby as he endeavored to clarify aspects of attachment.

Harry Harlow (1905–1981) was an American psychologist who studied maternal separation, social isolation, and aspects of caregiving behavior. Behavioral scientists realized that it would be unethical and immoral to deprive a human infant of mothering experiences and chose instead to study the short- and long-term results of the lack of adequate, appropriate mothering in animals. Harlow and his associates (Harlow, 1958; Harlow, Harlow, & Hansen, 1963) examined the effects of depriving infant monkeys of significant mothering experiences. Harlow found that separating infant monkeys in their mothers following birth resulted in severe emotional trauma in the baby monkeys. The infant monkeys' lack of direct physical contact with their mothers was identified as contributing to their disturbed behavior patterns when they grew to maturity.

In this study, two groups of infant monkeys were separated from their natural mothers and placed with two artificially constructed surrogate mothers. One of the surrogates was built of bare wire mesh; the other was built of wood and covered with soft terry cloth. The infant monkeys received nourishment only from the wire-mesh surrogate, yet preferred the soft-textured surrogate. This result stressed what Harlow referred to as **contact comfort,** or an infant's need for soft, comforting, nurturing sensations provided by a caregiver.

The results of Harlow's study showed that neither group of monkeys spent more time clinging to the terry-cloth surrogate. However, infants reared with the terry-cloth surrogate were found to be more curious, more interested in exploring the environment, and better adjusted socially than those who were reared by the wire-

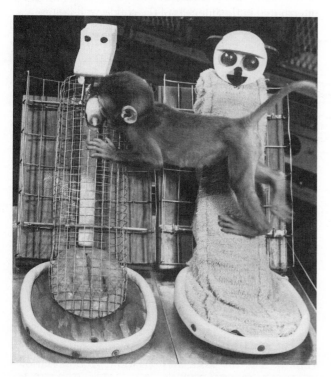

Wire-mesh and terry-cloth surrogate mothers used in Harlow's research on attachment. Photo courtesy of the University of Wisconsin Primate Laboratory and Harry F. Harlow.

mesh surrogate. Nevertheless, both groups developed in unhealthy ways into their adulthood. Neither group acquired normal monkey social skills; they were overly aggressive, preferred isolation to intimacy with other monkeys, and lacked sexual mating skills. Other behaviors included staring into space, stereotyped rocking movements, and poor social interactions with other monkeys.

Konrad Lorenz (1903–1989), a joint winner of the Nobel Prize in 1973, studied medicine and had a passion for zoology. He studied instincts in animals and is known for his work on attachment. In the context of ethology (the scientific study of animal behavior), he explored bird and mammal behavior and noted that they bonded during a critical attachment period shortly after birth. Of significance in the context of attachment is that Lorenz found that the recently hatched goslings that the researchers were feeding followed the person who wore a specific pair of rubber wading boots. Lorenz thought that the birds became permanently imprinted at an early age with significant caregivers to whom they were most frequently exposed, even if the caregivers were human. When different caretakers wore similar-looking boots, the goslings would follow the person wearing the boots.

As a result of these findings, researchers were alerted to the critical post-birth period when imprinting occurs and early bonding patterns are laid down. This knowledge is currently applied to human birthing practices, where newborn babies are placed on the mother's stomach for skin-to-skin contact as soon after birth as possible. Fathers are encouraged to be active participants during the birth and after in order to encourage bonding. Parents and their infants should have the opportunity to bond during the sensitive days and weeks following the birth.

Another situation in which we can see the effects of attachment or the lack thereof, is in international adoptions. Understanding the role of the earliest childhood experiences in orphanages prior to international adoptions has elicited further investigation, as well as recommendations for best practices. Children who are adopted fairly late during their first or second year frequently present with attachment disorders and difficulties in forming trusting relationships. These children may have spent their early months in overcrowded and understaffed orphanages. Attachment and trust issues are more recognizably expressed once they have acculturated to the new environment. Currently, pediatricians and other professionals who deal with adopted children are alert to these possible outcomes of early deprivation, and research is continuing.

According to Posada et al. (2011), the Bowlby–Ainsworth view integrates perspectives from various fields, including evolution, psychoanalytics, ethology, and cognitive psychology. It points out the range of implications that early attachment can have in later life, such as the formation of intimate relationships, the sense of self, and emotional security.

In deployed military families, we are faced with long-distance coparenting situations that are unique in terms of stressors and outcomes (Posada et al., 2011). An understanding of the implications of attachment plays a distinct role in legal decisions concerning child custody, adoption, and foster parenting.

ECOLOGICAL SYSTEMS THEORY AND PARENTING

The **ecological systems theory** proposed by Urie Bronfenbrenner (1917–2005; Bronfenbrenner, 1979, Bronfenbrenner, 1986, Bronfenbrenner, 1993) leads our attention to the role of different environments and how these affect individual and family functioning, including parent–child relations. It also represents a *sociocultural* view of development. Bronfenbrenner, a cofounder of the federal Head Start program, felt strongly that various systems in a child's life could be influential in promoting the best outcome. He focuses on the role of five distinct but related environmental settings to explain how individuals and their family systems are influenced in their development, how relationships function, and how interactions take place. A person is at the center of a set of environments that can also be described as multiple *nested* layers. From this standpoint, an individual is not a passive recipient of interactions with other people and other environments, but is actively involved in direct interactions. In fact, the interactions are *bidirectional*. Initially, the child only interacts with those closest to him or her, but these circles widen and become more complex with increasing maturity. See Figure 3–1, Environmental Settings.

The first environmental setting with which he or she interacts is that which comprises the environments provided by the family, peers, a school, or a neighborhood. This is known as the **microsystem**. The next environment is known as the **mesosystem**, which encompasses the microsystem. This system involves relations between the first and all other systems that affect the person. For

FIGURE 3–1. In Bronfenbrenner's theory, a system can be viewed in terms of interrelated, nested layers.

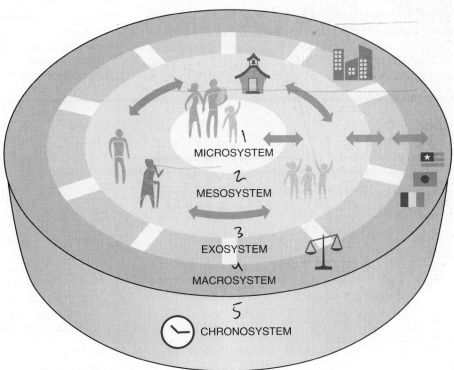

example, the family has relationships and interactions with the school that the child attends. The child's relationships at school, then, are influenced by what takes place in the family setting, and vice versa. For instance, if one or both parents have some type of addiction or related disorder, this will affect a child's interactions and relationships within the family setting and influence interactions and relationships within the child's school setting. Academic performance and social relationships and interactions with peers and teachers are influenced by what happens in the child's family life, and vice versa.

An **exosystem** also influences the individual. This setting may be visualized as encompassing the mesosystem. The individual does not have an active role in this context, but is influenced by it nevertheless. An exosystem may be government agencies, community programs, the employment settings of parents, and so on. For example, the work responsibilities or assignments of one parent may change, requiring different and extraordinary work hours. When the parent begins to work longer hours, or at night rather than during the day, the parenting experiences of the child are affected accordingly. Another example would be how the quality of the child's life is affected by funding cutbacks to community recreation programs sponsored by local governmental agencies.

A **macrosystem** is an even larger context that affects an individual. This environment involves the larger culture in which the individual lives and encompasses the exosystem and what it contains. In this context, the person is affected by the broad, generalized beliefs, behavior patterns, and value systems deemed appropriate by most members of a particular society. These influence how a person interacts with all other environmental settings. Culture would fit into this system as well.

The last environment is the **chronosystem**, which encompasses the entire network of other systems. This context involves the organization of events and changes over the life span of an individual at a particular *historical time*. For example, we know that adults are influenced in their current behaviors and interactions by events and interactions that took place during earlier stages in their lives. It is generally understood that if a person was abused as a child, the effects can last a lifetime. With therapeutic assistance, these effects can be minimized but perhaps not completely ameliorated and can continue to influence the person in various ways for years. Likewise, changes in cultural attitudes are reflected within the chronosystem and affect individuals at different historical times. Attitudes about gender roles in society are different today than 100 years ago. Androgyny, for example, is more acceptable today than a century ago. The chronosystem may also refer to the influences that an entire cohort experiences—for instance, a generation affected by the Great Depression or, in our current context, a generation that grows up with the World Wide Web and highly accessible communication technology.

It is possible to view society as an immense collection of families. As such, what goes on in families is also reflected in society, and vice versa. A family system cannot function independently from the physical, social,

Bronfenbrenner's Ecological Systems Theory
The Roles of the Layers in Parent–Child Relationships

Layer ↔	The layers have a **bidirectional** influence on one another.
Microsystem	**Micro** comes from the Greek *mikrós*, meaning "small" (think of a microscope with which very small objects can be viewed). The *microsystem* refers to the smallest or innermost system. It encompasses the very personal influences of family, neighborhood, and school. In parent–child relations, this layer would represent the relationship that is closest to the child, namely the parental relationship, as well as close family ties and the immediate environment.
Mesosystem	**Meso** comes from the Greek *meso*, meaning "in the middle." In this model, it is the middle layer sandwiched between the inner (microsystem) and the outer (exosystem) layers, and its function is to connect the structures in the child's world. For example, the teachers and the parents could be connected to each other through the *mesosystem*, yet both have an influence on the child. The mesosystem conducts (or facilitates communication) between the microsystem and the exosystem.

(Continued)

Exosystem	**Exo** comes from the Greek *exo,* meaning "outer." One could view it as the *buffer zone* between the inner circles known to the child and society at large (macrosystem), which may be anonymous to the child. The *exosystem* has an influence on the child because people and organizations from this layer interact with the parents and have an influence on the parent–child relationship. Examples from this layer are community programs, agencies, and services that may support the family.
Macrosystem	**Macro** comes from the Greek *makrós,* meaning "large." The *macrosystem* represents the largest of the nested layers. Aspects within this layer influence the child in an indirect manner. The aspects are present, and in the parent–child relationship one can feel the influence, but they may not always be apparent, as they could be somewhat abstract. Examples include cultural beliefs and values. The influence from this system can ripple right through to the parent–child relationship.
Chronosystem	**Chrono** comes from the Greek *chrónos,* meaning "time" (think of a chronometer, a very accurate timepiece). The *chronosystem* is an extra dimension. Imagine the model to be three dimensional. The chronosystem affects all of the other layers. It encompasses *time-related influences*.

This is a summary of the five distinct, but related, multiple nested layers and their roles in the parent–child relationship. Based on the work of Urie Bronfenbrenner (1979).

economical, and psychological environments of which it is a part. The ecological systems perspective outlined by Bronfenbrenner emphasizes the *dual influence* between families and societies locally and throughout the world. Essentially, what happens in one environmental aspect influences what occurs in others, as well as in families that make up a society. Likewise, what occurs in families affects the various environments in which they live. The family ecology view leads to an examination of the ways that various sociocultural environments influence family form and functioning. The presence of a reciprocal feedback loop among families that make up society and the environments that impact them produce a dynamic model that is described by the ecological systems perspective (Bubolz & Sontag, 1993). Bronfenbrenner did adapt his theory over the years, and slight variations have occurred as the theory evolved (Tudge, Mokrova, Hatfield, & Karnik, 2009).

Focus Point. Bronfenbrenner's ecological systems theory explains how individuals and families are affected by a variety of interacting environments in a bidirectional manner. An individual's family, by being part of the total environment, is also influenced by these other systems. The systems are nested within each other.

FAMILY SYSTEMS THEORY

Despite the diversity found among contemporary American families, each family operates according to certain rules that govern its performance, functioning, decision making, and conflict resolution. One of the first theoretical approaches that explains family functioning was derived from the sociological approach known as *structural functionalism.* This explanation focused on the social roles of family members and addressed the manner in which the family (as seen via the roles of its members) became integrated with other social institutions, such as schools, churches, and business and service organizations (Lamanna & Reidman, 2006).

The **general systems theory** has been applied largely in the physical sciences to explain the complex workings of naturally occurring systems such as biological ecological systems and the solar system (von Bertalanffy, 1968, von Bertalanffy, 1974). As applied to humans, families are described as operating in ways that are similar to those of other systems observed in nature. This way of looking at family functioning describes the operation of a family as a social system (Becvar & Becvar, 2008; Broderick, 1993). Systems theory is useful in explaining the complex interactions of a family and the factors that influence the processes by which a family makes decisions, sets and achieves particular goals, and establishes rules that regulate behavior. The model provided by systems theory describes how these processes govern daily interactions to maintain the stability of the family group over time. The theory also explains how a family responds to change, both developmental changes in family members and external changes that challenge its ability to function effectively as a group.

Several subsystems exist as part of a family group. For example, the relationships between parents and children, between the adult spouses, and among siblings are recognized as subsystems that reflect the patterns observed in the larger family system. The **family systems theory** is important in the context of the study of families, and specifically parent–child relations, because it also represents the dominant theoretical choice in family therapy. Almost all marriage and family therapists become very familiar with family systems theory during their training. To understand how families operate according to family systems theory, we will summarize some basic concepts.

Wholeness

A family is not simply a group of individuals who operate or behave independently from one another; rather, a family operates on the principle of **wholeness**. The family group must be considered in its entirety to understand how it works. It is not possible to do so by studying only one person from the group. In other words, a family is seen as being greater than the sum of its parts.

Interdependence

Interdependence, which is related to the principle of wholeness, means that anything that affects one person in a family also affects every other person in the family to some degree. A mobile is a good way to illustrate this concept of family systems theory. All parts

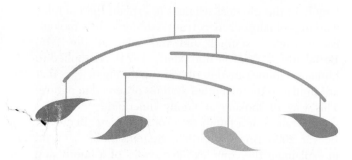

FIGURE 3–2.   A mobile can illustrate family interdependence.

of a mobile are connected, so when one part is moved abruptly, other parts are affected and respond accordingly, although to a lesser degree (Satir, 1972a, Satir, 1972b). The parts of the mobile represent different family members, and the strings connecting each piece of the mobile represent the different relationships found in a family system. Thus, the mobile illustrates the interdependence of family members. See Figure 3–2.

When one person in a family system experiences some type of change, such as becoming seriously ill, leaving the family, or receiving a job promotion, everyone in the system is affected to some degree by the change. Whether the change is good or bad, beneficial or detrimental, all members of a family system react and attempt to compensate for the imbalance caused by a change that directly affects just one member. The objective is to return to the state of balance, called *homeostasis*, which existed prior to the change that caused the imbalance.

Patterns

Within a family system, **patterns** evolve that serve to regulate the behavior of members and allow members to anticipate each other's behavior. These patterns are unique to each family system, although some patterns follow general guidelines that are common to all family systems. The patterns that are usually found in most family systems include rules, roles, and communication styles.

Rules.   A family system typically develops **rules** to govern members' behavior. Rules provide common ground for understanding which behaviors are acceptable and appropriate within each family system. In turn, the consistent application of rules helps to maintain the stability of a family system over time in general and especially in times of uncertainty or crisis. Rules govern the behavior of both adults and children in families. To be effective, rules also outline the consequences that occur when they are obeyed and when they are disobeyed.

The rules in each family system evolve, usually through the negotiations of the adults. In many instances, the rules that become established in a family system have their roots in the adults' families of origin.

Rules can be explicit or implicit. **Explicit rules** are known, stated, and outlined clearly so that all people in the family know and understand them. Because these rules are clear to all, family members can discuss them and change them if they prove to be ineffective. **Implicit rules** are unspoken and are often inferred from nonverbal behavior. Explicit rules are often stated verbally, especially when transgressions occur: "You know, the rule is that you must be home by 10 o'clock." Implicit rules are not usually discussed openly or otherwise acknowledged by family members, yet everyone is expected to know and obey them. For example, some family systems do not allow the expression of anger. In such families, everyone is expected to be pleasant and to not engage in open conflict. When conflict is imminent, family members could leave the group, be in denial about the underlying emotions, or defuse the potential conflict. It is difficult to discuss such rules and to change them when necessary because they are not readily acknowledged by family members despite their strong influence on behavior. Generally, *healthy* family systems operate with an abundance of *explicit rules* and few implicit rules, while those that are unhealthy have a greater number of implicit rules (J. I. Clarke & Dawson, 1998; Richardson, 1999).

In addition to these types of rules, most family systems develop and exercise a set of rules that are considered to be **negotiable**, as well as a set that are **nonnegotiable**. In the first instance, parents practice flexibility in the enforcement of a particular group of rules, and children may contest these rules as well. For example, a negotiable family rule might relate to coming to dinner when called. A nonnegotiable rule might require children to always inform parents of their whereabouts when away from home. Interestingly, rules that may be negotiable in some family systems are nonnegotiable in others. Each family generates these rules based initially on those that the parents experienced as children. As time passes and children grow older and become more mature, rules may change from being nonnegotiable (to protect younger children) to being negotiable to reflect children's increasing abilities to become more responsible for their own decisions.

Roles.   Roles are used in family systems to outline acceptable behavior and to regulate the system's functioning. Roles generally have associated rules that establish appropriate behavior for the person in that particular role. For example, rules may evolve that describe and outline the role of the mother. The mother's behavior is regulated by rules that reflect family members' beliefs about how a mother should act. For example, to be a good mother, she should attend all school-related functions of her children, maintain a clean and orderly home, be employed outside the home, and so on. Rules that describe the child's role might be that the child should be a willing learner; be able to perform some family tasks, but not necessarily as efficiently as an adult; and so on.

The rules provide the script to be enacted by the person filling a particular role in a family system.

Unhealthy families often develop implicit roles that are largely governed by implicit rules. Because such families often cannot or do not know how to cope with stresses effectively or in healthy ways, one family member may assume—either willingly or unknowingly—a special role in which they act out the stress on behalf of the family member under stress or for a particularly dysfunctional member (Becvar & Becvar, 2008). For example, a child may act as the family scapegoat by becoming depressed or acting out delinquently as a means of expressing stress in the parents' unhealthy relationship. In this instance, the child's role draws attention away from the parents. In a different family system, a child's implicit role may be the "best little boy." In this system, the role carries a heavy expectation of perfectionism in the child's behavior. This child acts out the script of an implicit rule that states, "We are better than other families. We are special and are expected to achieve things that others only dream of."

Communication Styles.   Communication styles relate strongly to the nature of relationships within a family system. Three basic styles are found in most families: verbal, nonverbal, and contextual (Becvar & Becvar, 2008). **Verbal communications** relate to the words used to convey information among persons in the family system. Taken at face value, verbal communication is essentially meaningless. For example, the message "It's cold outside today" simply provides descriptive information to the listener by the sender.

Nonverbal communications that accompany a verbal message include tone of voice, facial expression, body posture, and hand gestures. The purpose of the nonverbal message is to inform the receiver about what to do with the verbal message. It hints at the intent of the message and often contains an implicit command or request. For example, the message "It's cold outside today," from a mother to her daughter, may contain nonverbal elements that communicate an implicit message such as "Wear a sweater today." Hence, nonverbal communications relate to the way that a relationship is defined.

Contextual communication is allied closely with nonverbal communication, and usually the two are considered together. The context often refers to where and under what circumstances the verbal and nonverbal communications occur. If a mother says "It's cold outside today" before the daughter dresses for school,

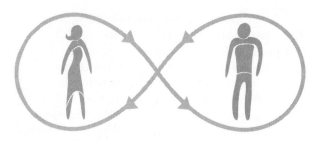

FIGURE 3–3. Reciprocal interaction.

the message has an entirely different meaning than if it occurred as the two were leaving the house.

Communication styles are unique to each family system, especially the contextual and nonverbal aspects of information exchange among members. These styles emerge as each family system evolves and develops its own meanings with regard to communications. The more frequently the family members interact and exchange information with each other and the outside world, the more flexible and receptive to change the system becomes. This flexibility occurs in ways that act to stabilize rather than disrupt healthy, effective functioning.

Reciprocal Interaction and Feedback

Systems theory does not support a cause-and-effect process of interaction among members of families or family systems. Rather, causality is seen as a **reciprocal interaction** between people and systems (Becvar & Becvar, 2008; see Figure 3–3). For example, a cause-and-effect pattern is implied in a child asserting, "I behave like a child because you treat me like a child," and the parent responding, "I treat you like a child because you behave like a child." Taken from a family systems perspective, this assertion would be reframed as "This has become a never-ending cycle: I act like a child because you treat me like a child, which makes me act in even more childish ways, which makes you continue to treat me like a child." Essentially, systems theory stresses that people in relationships or subsystems and in a family system as a whole influence one another's actions. Behavioral interactions become intertwined as one person reacts to another, setting up a chain of interactional sequences. One person's action serves as a stimulus that elicits a reaction or response from another; this reaction, in turn, acts as a stimulus that elicits a different reaction or response from the other; and the cycle continues. Behavior serves as both *stimulus* and

feedback to maintain reciprocal interaction among people in a relationship or subsystem.

Boundaries

Boundaries serve to establish limits that distinguish a family system from all others and differentiate among the persons who are members of a particular family system (Knowles, 1997; Minuchin, 1974; Wood & Talmon, 1983). These abstract, psychological dividers are based on implicit, as well as explicit, rules that also outline who participates in a particular subsystem and the role that he or she has in that subsystem.

Boundaries also assist in keeping subsystems distinct from one another because a family member can be a participant in several of these family subsystems (Orthner, Bowen, & Beare, 1990). In this regard, boundaries help prevent overlap between subsystems. For example, when conflicts occur within one subsystem, boundaries help prevent the conflict from extending into other subsystems in which family members participate. When the adults experience disagreements related to their committed relationship, boundaries help them keep the dispute from affecting the relationship with their children.

Boundaries act to regulate the degree of closeness or intimacy permissible according to a particular family system with regard to other families and among the members of that system (Goodrich, 1990). In this respect, the boundaries maintained between people and family systems assist in regulating information exchange, communication, identities, and behavior. Although boundaries can be changed and may vary by situation, families typically either have flexible boundaries, resulting in an open family system, or rigid boundaries, resulting in a closed system. Likewise, the boundaries that delineate the different subsystems within a family system can range from open to closed. For example, a healthy family system maintains closed boundaries for the expression of the adult couple's intimate relationship that does not allow for the participation of children or other family members. Family systems theory describes an *open* family as one with flexible boundaries that permit the easy flow and exchange of information and interaction with other families and individuals. When this is the case, the family system is open to input or new data from outside the system and is receptive to change. Essentially, healthy families operate as an open system. Some families operate as a *closed* system; the boundaries serve

FIGURE 3–4. Open and closed boundaries in family systems.

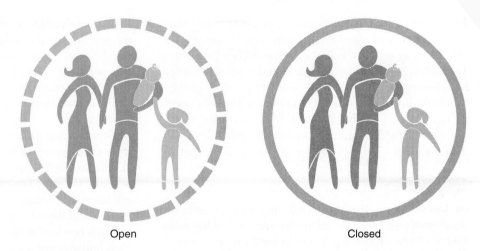

Open   Closed

to maintain the status quo of the group rather than allow external input to bring about positive changes within the system. Change is resisted rather than accepted as healthy (von Bertalanffy, 1974). When this is the case, family systems theory predicts that personal boundaries among family members in a closed system will become fused, or *enmeshed* (Minuchin, 1974). For example, children are not encouraged to differentiate themselves as individuals as part of their normal developmental process in growing toward maturity. Rather, implicit rules promote prolonged emotional attachment among family members and blurring of personal boundaries to maintain dependency among family members (Bowen, 1978). Similarly, families that are not emotionally close, and where family members are on parallel and/or different tracks that do not meet, are *disengaged*. See Figure 3–4 for illustrations of these two types of family boundaries.

In healthy family systems, boundaries are valued for helping to differentiate one person from another, even though a high level of intimacy is permitted. In such families, boundaries highlight individual differences without eliciting high degrees of anxiety among other members. Personal differences are viewed positively as another means by which the family system is enriched by behavioral, philosophical, and emotional variety among its members. In these families, the implicit rules that serve as the foundation for personal boundaries promote the balance between individuation and intimacy among family members. Some unhealthy family systems view differences in members as threatening the welfare and effective functioning of the family system. Such families demand lesser degrees of individuation and maintain less rigid personal boundaries that differentiate each member

(Richardson, 1999). These families foster an expectation of similarity among members rather than distinct differences. They support the strong belief that everyone must hold the same values, philosophies, opinions, and attitudes. Rules in these families are exceptionally strict and serve to promote the idea of sameness and maintain weak or diffuse personal boundaries among members.

Entropy

Although a family system maintains separateness from other family systems, the degree of closure is never thought to be complete (von Bertalanffy, 1968). There will always be some exchange of information among systems. **Entropy** is disorder or chaos in system functioning that results from lack of input or information from outside the system as a means of resolving a crisis or a problem. A family may react to the presence of entropy in two basic ways: (a) Positive actions involve movement of a system away from disorder and chaos by accepting and using information and energy from outside itself, such as from other family systems. (b) Negative actions occur when movement of the system enhances the level of entropy to even greater chaos or disruption. Such actions by the system may entail dedicated efforts to maintain the status quo, refusing to allow the exchange of information between the family and other environmental systems, or using denial to resist acknowledging that some problem or crisis exists.

In family systems with more open and flexible boundaries, energy and information input is accepted and used to maximize group functioning. For example, some energy in such a family system is directed toward organization and some is directed toward performing family tasks.

using information about how other ... certain problems, open systems work ... to achieve healthy solutions to their problems. In family systems that are rigidly closed, little new energy or information is allowed. This tends to promote greater family disorganization and greater expenditure of energy in random and inefficient ways. The continued maintenance of rigid boundaries enhances higher levels of entropy in such families (Becvar & Becvar, 2008).

Equifinality

All subsystems have goals that substantiate the reason for their existence. Likewise, all family systems develop goals that influence functioning and behavior. The concept of **equifinality** holds that families share common goals but reach these goals in different ways. For example, the ultimate goal of the parent–child subsystem is likely to be raising the child to become an effectively functioning adult. All parent–child relationships may have this goal as the primary endeavor. Different family systems in society accomplish this goal in diverse ways. The concept of equifinality significantly differentiates family systems theory from a unidirectional model of cause and effect.

Adaptation

A family system is challenged by both internal and external events and processes to restructure patterns to accommodate these changes. Change is a constant threat to the effective functioning of a family system because nothing is ever completely stable for families over the long term. All persons within the family system experience constant developmental changes over time. If the system is to continue to function effectively, patterns must be readjusted periodically upon discovering that they are not working properly. For example, the rules developed at the beginning of a couple's parenting career may reflect a lack of experience with children other than simple knowledge of an infant's developmental abilities. After gaining experience, the parents' rules are **adapted,** or changed, to permit a more realistic experience in nurturing an infant. By rigidly maintaining rules that clearly don't work to everyone's benefit, a family system risks becoming unhealthy by virtue of its inability to function adequately.

Homeostasis

The ultimate goal of family system functioning is to maintain stability, or *homeostasis*, over time. This is also known as *dynamic equilibrium*. There may seem to be a fundamental contradiction between a family system's needs for adaptation and its need for stability. To address this seeming contradiction, two other terms are often used to illustrate the more fundamental need for stability over time. *Morphogenesis* describes the tendency of a family system to respond to variables that cause change by experiencing growth, change, innovation, and creativity and adapting its structure and patterns accordingly (Hoffman, 1973). *Morphostasis* describes the desire of a family system to remain stable over time by attempting to retain its organization, structure, and patterns. To understand these concepts, it may be helpful to visualize them as residing at opposite ends of a continuum and to view homeostasis as an attempt to achieve dynamic equilibrium between them. Healthy family systems continually seek to maintain homeostasis between the dynamic factors of change and stability. The rules of such systems allow changes in patterns, rules, and boundaries to accommodate changing situations and conditions.

During times of stress, morphogenesis is thought to be more desirable than morphostasis in allowing a system to work out means that will ensure its continued existence and functioning. Too many and too frequent experiences in morphogenesis call for greater and more extended efforts to maintain morphostasis.

Application to Parent–Child Relations

Family systems theory has direct application to parent–child relations in several ways. It depicts this relationship as one of several that occurs as subsystems within a family. Other relationships or subsystems include the marriage or committed relationship between adults, the relationship among siblings, the relationship within the extended family (e.g., grandparent–grandchild), and the various relationships between the family and other families, agencies, and institutions with whom members interact (e.g., schools, churches, neighbors).

All subsystems within a family reflect the workings and configuration found in the larger group. For example, there are explicit rules, similar in nature to others found in the larger family systems, that are established to guide parental behavior and that of the children. These rules allow everyone to understand what is expected of each participant within his or her particular role and also allow predictability of behavior. The roles of both parents and children are outlined in this manner.

This relationship is affected by the variables just described. For example, what affects an adult will also affect children to some degree, and vice versa (i.e., interrelatedness). If a child develops a chronic illness, this condition alters the relationship with the parent(s), as well as with other family members. If the adults divorce, then we can expect children to experience effects related to this event. Likewise, we cannot completely understand the nature of parent–child relations in a family just by studying a child or an adult alone (i.e., wholeness).

Boundaries also outline what are acceptable and unacceptable behaviors within this relationship. Our culture specifically prohibits sexual activity between parents and children as it is considered totally inappropriate and unhealthy for all parties. We tend, as a culture, to separate the world of children from that of adults. In other words, we believe that children should not become involved in the affairs of their parents and other adults in their family. There is a *family hierarchy* separating the parental dyad from the children.

Adaptation and reciprocal interaction may be observed within this relationship as rules, roles, and communication styles are changed in accordance with the changing developmental abilities and stages of the children. For example, parents may have many more nonnegotiable rules in place when children are young than when they become older adolescents and young adults. Parents usually change the rules when it is discovered that they are no longer effective in achieving the desired results in children's behavior. Parents are continuously monitoring a variety of issues that are intended to maintain family homeostasis and are making adaptations when necessary.

Equifinality is observed when parents learn that there are a number of equally acceptable strategies for raising children to adulthood. Not everyone will agree on particular approaches, but there is an understanding that no absolute approach can be applied in all situations. Family theorists may be eclectic in that they apply different theories in different settings or in highlighting different aspects of the parent–child relationship.

When parents seek advice, assistance, and information from outside their family system to stabilize their situation or to help problem solve, they are actively working to avoid entropy. By showing a willingness to have an open family system in problem solving, parents demonstrate a desire to work toward constructive change as would occur in therapeutic situations. In this way, stability is promoted while chaos and disruption are avoided.

Parenting Reflection 3–1

Family therapists predominantly use variations of the systemic approaches. Explain why a systems approach lends itself to working with families. How could the principles of a systems approach be applied in other social situations (for example, work environments, committee participation, sports, church groups).

Focus Point. Family systems theory explains the complex interactions of a family group. It addresses the factors that influence the manner in which the group makes decisions, sets and achieves goals, and establishes patterns that govern members' behavior. It explains how these processes work to maintain the group's stability over time. Concepts central to this theory include wholeness, interdependence, patterns (i.e., rules, roles, and communication styles), reciprocal interaction and feedback, boundaries, entropy, equifinality, adaptation, and homeostasis (i.e., morphogenesis and morphostasis). The relationship between parents and children is one of several subsystems that make up a family system.

SYSTEMIC FAMILY DEVELOPMENT THEORY

Many years ago, pioneer sociologist Ernest Burgess (1926, p. 3) described the family as a "unity of interacting personalities." Unity in this context alludes to the concepts of *wholeness* and *interdependence* used today in family systems theory. The reference to interacting personalities denotes Burgess's observation that interaction among family members serves a vital purpose in the functioning of a family system by promoting the psychological welfare of each family member.

A family system provides an expressive function for members. This means that each member has the opportunity of being nurtured and assisted as a developing individual and is provided the means for realizing emotional needs. The idea of unity among interacting personalities implies that a family is a dynamic system that responds to changes within and outside the group's setting, especially those that impinge on its functioning. The inescapable reality in this description is echoed in the concepts of **homeostasis** and **adaptation**, concepts that also occur in family systems theory. These concepts hold that family members are dynamic, developmentally changing individuals, and hence a family system also must change its response over time.

Just as individuals follow predictable stages in their personal development, families also experience stages that follow a predictable course (O'Rand & Krecker, 1990). The progression of stages that a family follows from its establishment to its demise (Aldous, 1978; Duvall, 1988; Duvall & Miller, 1985; Mattessich & Hill, 1987) has been labeled the *family life cycle*, although it is not cyclic in the true sense of the word.

A realistic model that describes how families change in association with the passage of time is the **systemic family development theory** model (Laszloffy, 2002). The systemic model promotes the notions that families are both similar and diverse and that the concepts of wholeness and interrelatedness are strong characteristics of the complexity found in their intergenerational composition.

A Common Developmental Process in Families

All families share a common process of developmental change over time, with the details varying from family to family. The common developmental process shared by all families according to the systemic development model is the experience of *stressors* at various times

in their existence (Laszloffy, 2002). Stressors are those phenomena that force a family system to adapt, resulting in what is referred to as a *transition*. Stressors can be positive (eustress) as with happy events, such as a marriage. They can be negative (distress) when they imply loss or destruction. The transition typically produces changes in family roles and relationships.

Most transitions relieve the pressure that comes from the stressor. Sometimes a family has difficulty making a successful adaptation or transition. When this occurs, the group experiences a *snag point*, or general inflexibility (Pittman, 1987). This will likely prevent a family from using resources to cope with the stressor and the associated stress increases accordingly. The end result of the snag point is a *family crisis*, which keeps the group from progressing and making the necessary adaptations to resolve their dilemma (Joselevich, 1988).

The experience of a single stressor can usually be dealt with by making appropriate changes or using helpful resources. For example, the birth of a child is stressful in the sense that the routine in the home is altered (e.g., adult sleep patterns are disturbed by the need to feed and care for the baby) and financial resources are strained. People make changes in their roles and routines to adapt to the needs of the new baby. Stressors do not become problematic unless several occur simultaneously or within a short time. When this happens, the snag point emerges because of the accumulation of higher levels of stress from each of the events.

Focus On 3–1

Stressors in the Family

Examples of Stressors Common to Families (listed alphabetically)

- Birth of a child, adoption, infertility
- Boomerang kid moving back to the parental home
- Career, work, dual careers, income
- Chronic illness, disability, death of a family member
- Dating, marriage, separation, divorce, remarriage
- Deployment in military families
- Developmental stages of children
- Mental illness, addiction, and related disorders
- Mid-career changes, lifelong education
- New family roles (e.g., in-laws, blended families, a stepparent, grandparents)
- Relocation, moving, downsizing
- Retirement, redundancy, financial problems
- Sandwich generation, looking after elderly parents
- Simultaneous stressors occurring in all generations

As stressors continue to pile up in the family, a crisis emerges that prevents the family from adapting and making the appropriate changes. For example, suppose a family has experienced a new birth, the oldest child has begun school for the first time, and the father loses his job, all within a 2-week period. This is enough to produce a family crisis because the group is incapacitated by the cumulative stress occurring from these events and is unable to cope successfully. Taken individually and spread out over a longer period of time, the stressor events might be managed more successfully. What may help a family avoid chaos is to use effective stress management skills or to locate and use resources that will allow the group to cope effectively with the stressors. In this way, the family may prevent the crisis, or at least head off the devastating effects (Boss, 1988).

Complex and Multigenerational Family Systems

The systemic family developmental model also emphasizes the notion that families must be taken as a whole at any point in *developmental time* to understand how they function, change, and adapt. This approach comes from the concepts of wholeness and interrelatedness found in family systems theory. Unlike the stages proposed in the family life-cycle model, the systemic model assumes that it is not possible to reduce a family system to only one generation at any point in developmental time. This acknowledges the diversity of family structures.

Intergenerational Families in Developmental Time

The family systems approach clarifies that families are systems. These systems are intergenerational, and it is possible that four generations could be interacting at any given time. Each generation is on its own timeline. For that reason, each generation is also at a different point in their life span, facing the challenges of that particular stage and age group.

Typically, generations are about 20–30 years apart. By the time the fourth (or youngest) generation is born, the first (or oldest) generation is dealing with late adulthood and end-of-life themes. If we imagine each generation's life span as a track, we can stagger these tracks or life paths and see where they overlap and intersect. This would provide us with a developmental slice of the intergenerational family in terms of developmental time. Each generation is at a different point in the life span, but chronologically, we are looking at this intergenerational family system at one particular moment in the family's history. See Figure 3–5 for an illustration of intergenerational families in developmental time.

These intergenerational moments can be clearly observed at family gatherings and family transitions. If the extended family gathers for a joyous or a sad occasion, they offer each other support. It is also the time when all generations are present, allowing the observer a chance to delve into the family history and gather the anecdotes that become so precious once a generation has passed on.

Intergenerational family systems renew themselves. As the oldest generation passes on, the next generation becomes the oldest. In some ways, it is like the progression that occurs when a senior class graduates. As the oldest cohort leaves, a new group of freshmen will be entering, who will slowly mature until they, too, become graduating seniors. In families, new generations are added while older generations fall away.

A metaphor for visualizing this intergenerational family system is to view it as a layered structure.

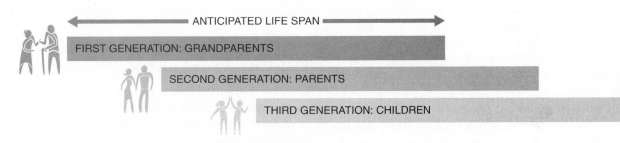

FIGURE 3–5.   Intergenerational families in developmental time.

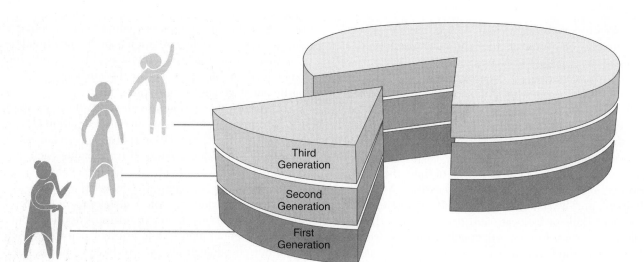

FIGURE 3–6. Intergenerational family system.

The oldest, or foundational layers, disintegrate while simultaneously new layers are added on top. This layered structure has been likened to a layered cake (Laszloffy, 2002). We view the structure as a whole, just as we must view an intergenerational family in its totality in order to understand it. The individual building blocks of the structure are like the individual family members. Individuals form a family when brought together through marriage, birth, adoption, or by choice. By losing layers of the structure (generations dying) and adding new ones (new generations being born), adjustments occur. See Figure 3–6 for a visual representation of the intergenerational family system dynamic.

To perceive what may be occurring developmentally in an intergenerational family system, we would observe the entire family group for a short time. A cross section of family life would be revealed (Laszloffy, 2002), offering a *snapshot* in time. By examining the family's place in developmental time, we can determine how the family needs to adjust to the stressors that each generation is experiencing. Those adjustments allow the family to cope in challenging times. Family members can realign their roles, patterns, and boundaries to regain homeostasis. Ideally, this would lead to a higher degree of appropriate adjustment and family cohesion.

Parenting Reflection 3–2

How can families locate resources to help them cope with stressors even before they occur? Does advance knowledge help prepare people to react appropriately? Try to illustrate this with a practical example from your own experience.

Focus Point.   Systemic family development theory allows us to understand the complexity and diversity of families. By examining a family at a particular point in its developmental time, it is possible to see that families share common stressors that challenge each generation. This model has significant practical application in working with all families.

PSYCHOSOCIAL DEVELOPMENT THEORY AND PARENTING

The two major theoretical approaches discussed thus far focused on families within larger contexts, as well as families as systems. They emphasize a strong sociological component. These approaches are valuable in understanding the extended contexts in which families function. They also form the basis of much of the therapeutic work relating to the family.

Even so, there has been a foundation of developmental research that preceded the systemically oriented theories. Major influences were exerted by leading figures such as Sigmund Freud, Alfred Adler, Jean Piaget, and Erik Erikson. They focused on various aspects, including cognitive and social development. The key characteristics of the theories of the major contributors, as well as the implications for parent–child relations, are summarized in a table near the end of the chapter.

Most modern theories focus on the development of a child during the years between birth and the end of adolescence. Many explanations consider the interaction between heredity and environmental influences in individual development. Until a few decades ago, the years of childhood and adolescence received the greatest attention. Few developmental theorists attempted to explain or interpret what took place in the various stages of adulthood (i.e., early, middle, and late adulthood). The psychosocial theory of Erik Erikson (1950, 1964, 1982; Erikson, Erikson, & Kivnick, 1986) was a notable exception. Erikson's theory features developmental change as a process that continues throughout the life span between birth and death, not just during the growth years of infancy, childhood, and adolescence.

Erikson's theory is, in part, an extension of Freud's psychoanalytical approach to explaining human personality development (Green & Piel, 2009). For the most part, classical psychoanalytical theory is not embraced by contemporary theoretical thought in explaining human development. Some of the symbolic situations Freud refers to, such as the Oedipal complex, are not easily tested by research. The Oedipal complex refers to unconscious feelings of sexual attraction toward one's own mother and is named after the fifth-century Greek mythological character Oedipus who marries his mother after unwittingly killing his father.

This brief example does not do justice to the complexity of Freud's work, which may be better understood within the context of his time as well as the rest of his theory. Freud is important in that he contributed to a paradigm shift in thinking, and the direct and indirect influences of psychoanalysis permeated not only the social sciences, but also the arts and literature. His teachings are believed to represent the beginnings of academic thought about how humans experience personality development.

Erikson's approach was regarded as more realistic, although it did not generate a vast body of supportive research. In another notable exception to Freudian thought, Erikson believed that development occurred throughout a person's life span. Each stage of the life span has its own developmental theme, which Erikson terms a *psychosocial crisis*, or a challenge to attain a healthy rather than unhealthy attitude or generalized feeling. Developmental change is enhanced or retarded by a person's experiences in confronting and handling each psychosocial crisis that occurs within each stage of the life span. The person must confront a central problem—a specific psychosocial crisis—at each life stage and is given the opportunity to develop strengths and skills leading toward a particular attitude that is healthy or unhealthy. Provided with a social and psychological environment that is conducive to developmental change, an individual faces each problem during that stage with the potential for healthy, normal accomplishment. If the person experiences overwhelming difficulty in accomplishing what is expected during one stage of the life span, the result will be difficulty in dealing with the psychosocial crises during future stages.

Developmental change does not occur within a vacuum, free from other influences. The process is structured so that a person faces the challenges and trials of life with the support of others. Developmental change occurs first within the context of a supportive family atmosphere, then within an increasingly wider social radius of friends, and later within the school environment, and so on, as life progresses. *Significant others*—those who are singularly important to a person—assist or inhibit the developmental progress at each life stage. An individual proceeds to the next stage after meeting the particular requirements of biological, social, and psychological *readiness*. This readiness to progress further along the developmental path is significantly influenced by others in the social environment. In the case of a developing child, the parents are close at hand.

The psychosocial crises during each stage of the life span present the individual with the challenge of acquiring what Erikson calls *psychosocial senses*. These are attitudes or general feelings that result from how adequately a person can meet and master the crisis at a particular stage of psychosocial development.

Erikson describes eight stages of psychosocial change over the life span and labels each in terms of healthy or unhealthy psychosocial development. It is important to note that a person's mastery of a psychosocial attitude or sense is not an all-or-nothing matter; instead, it is continually being weighed on a balance. It is possible to gain some measure of unhealthy, as well as healthy, feelings related to the psychosocial attitude associated with a particular life stage. In the balance of experiences, attitudes and feelings that promote healthy psychological development derive from attaining healthy experiences that outweigh those that are unhealthy. In early childhood, for example, children are thought to experience a psychosocial stage during which they have opportunities to acquire the ability to function independently, or what Erikson calls a sense of autonomy. Positive experiences that lead children to conclude that they can function autonomously result in a healthy sense of autonomy. Negative experiences, if occurring with sufficient consistency and intensity, lead the child to feelings of shame and doubt concerning the ability to function autonomously. The result is an unhealthy sense of shame and doubt. In Erikson's theory, at each of the eight stages, progress in development occurs when the healthy attitude in that stage is acquired, whereas future difficulty in psychosocial development will occur when the unhealthy attitude dominates.

Erikson uses a timetable to illustrate his eight stages of psychosocial development. Although the ages listed are flexible guidelines for the times at which people experience the stages, the first five occur during the growth years of infancy, childhood, and adolescence, and the remaining three occur during adulthood. See Table 3–1 for an overview view of Erikson's developmental stages.

Application to Parent–Child Relations

Erikson does not specifically indicate in his theory how it might be applied to parent–child relations, but we may infer from his writings how this may be accomplished. His theory provides a basic framework for understanding

TABLE 3–1. Erikson's Developmental Stages

Psychosocial Crisis	Ages and Persons Involved	Theme
I. Trust vs. Mistrust	Birth to 18 months Maternal person	To receive and to give, learning to trust, first relationships
II. Autonomy vs.Shame/Doubt	18 months to 3 years Paternal person	To hold on and to let go, early initiatives in self-care
III. Initiative vs. Guilt	3 to 6 years Family	To make, to imitate, exploration, expanding developmental world
IV. Industry vs. Inferiority	6 to 12 years School, neighborhood	To make things, to make together, social connectedness
V. Identity vs. Role Confusion	12 to 18 years Peer groups	To be oneself, to be with others, individuation, autonomy and peer relationships
VI. Intimacy vs. Isolation	18 to 24 years Partners in friendship, relationships, competition	To find oneself in another, relationships and intimacy
VII. Generativity vs. Self-absorption	24 to 54 years Partner	To take care of, including empathy and concern for others
VIII. Integrity vs. Despair	54 years to death Humanity	To reflect on being and not being, existential reflections

Source: Based on E. H. Erikson. (1959). Identity and the life cycle: Selected papers. *Psychological Issues 1(1).*

the psychosocial changes experienced by an individual. A family system is composed of several individuals of differing ages and developmental levels, each involved in resolving the challenges of their own particular psychosocial stage. The parents are at the stage of psychosocial development of generativity versus self-absorption. If a couple has several children, they are all likely to be at different developmental stages. For example, the oldest child may be involved in accomplishing the tasks leading toward a sense of industry versus inferiority, the middle child may be addressing the tasks involving initiative versus guilt, and the youngest may be learning to accomplish the tasks of basic trust versus mistrust.

This intertwining or congruence of developmental stages being experienced by parents and children is referred to as *reciprocal interaction* in family systems theory. In the everyday interactions taking place between parents and children, each participant in this subsystem promotes the acquisition of the healthy psychosocial sense being experienced by the other. The provision of appropriate parental care assists children in achieving the particular psychosocial attitude that they are mastering at a particular developmental point. The children, in turn, provide the parents with the opportunity to provide care. Thus, children assist their parents in mastering their sense of generativity.

In this manner, parenting behavior adapts and is modified as children grow older. By passing through the various stages of psychosocial development, children's needs change, and parenting styles are adapted to meet these new needs. Using the concepts of reciprocal interaction and adaptation, homeostasis is achieved in parent–child relations when parenting behavior is congruent with meeting the needs of children at their different stages of growth and development. For example, a child who is striving for autonomy during the latter part of infancy prompts entirely different patterns of caregiving from parents than were called for when the child was focused on developing a sense of trust. The course of parent–child relations proceeds according to these interactional sequences: The child assists or inhibits the parents in their development of a sense of generativity as the parents assist or inhibit the child in meeting the challenges of each developmental stage. Like the larger family system of which it is a part, the parent–child subsystem must adapt to changes in the individual participants to maintain stability and effective functioning.

Parenting Reflection 3–3

What are some ways at each of Erikson's developmental stages that inappropriate and ineffective caregiving by parents could impede a child's psychosocial development and encourage the acquisition of an unhealthy attitude?

Focus Point.   Erik Erikson's framework for explaining the process of psychosocial development over the life span provides another means for interpreting the relationship between parents and children. The framework focuses on developmental changes in individuals that occur in association with the passage of time. These changes occur within the context of the social environments that individuals experience throughout their life span. Parent–child relations change in response to the concept of reciprocal interaction.

PARENTING AND OTHER RELATED THEORIES

Learning Theory

Learning theory encompasses several different explanations of how individual behavior is modified or changed as a result of experiences and interactions with external factors. The explanations discussed here as they relate to parent–child relations include: (a) operant conditioning or behavior modification (B. F. Skinner, 1938), and (b) social learning theory (Bandura, 1977).

Operant conditioning, or **behavior modification**, is a powerful tool that parents can use to shape children's behavior. Briefly, behavior modification emphasizes the role of rewards or reinforcers that are associated with particular acts. If a parent wishes to teach a child a new skill or help acquire a new type of behavior, then a reward given immediately following the child's action or behavior would reinforce that behavior. Positive rewards have been repeatedly shown to be very powerful in changing a child's behavior or in teaching new skills. Positive rewards may also be social in nature, such as a hug, smile, or praise—for example, "I'm very proud of you for doing that!"

Little Albert.   A classic case study in psychology is *Little Albert*, who, in the 1920s, was exposed to classical conditioning by psychologist John B. Watson. This same case also showed the effects of the generalization of conditioned responses. Baby Albert was about nine months old, and in a sequence of conditioned responses and associations, he acquired a fear response toward a furry, white rat. He generalized this response toward a bearded Santa Claus mask. Possibly the most important long-term outcome of this experiment is the stringent ethical guidelines and rules concerning experimentation with children. In today's climate, this dubious experiment with an infant would not have been permissible, and nowadays there are several safeguards in place to ensure that ethical and responsible research standards are met, especially with minors.

Social learning theory explains how learning may occur when there is no visible reinforcer or reward. This theory is especially useful in explaining how socialization occurs or how someone learns appropriate behaviors based on family beliefs and values. According to this theory, an individual responds to a number of complex stimuli in forming associations between appropriate and inappropriate behavior. Conscious thought, rather than automatic response to a stimulus, assists in shaping behavior and actions.

This approach focuses on the importance of the role of a *model* or the effect of observation learning, also known as imitation. Many kinds of behaviors are believed to be acquired by watching the behavior of another person and then replicating the observed behavior in one's own actions.

Research shows how children learn to express such social behaviors as sharing and cooperation, as well as aggression and violence, by watching such behaviors demonstrated by a model. Models include both real people and characters seen in media presentations. Research reveals that when children see a model being rewarded for acting aggressively, for instance, they are more likely to demonstrate that same kind of behavior in their own play.

Social learning theory also explains how people acquire social values and attitudes. Social roles are learned in this manner. Children imitate behaviors that they observe in adults and in other children they perceive as models. For example, social learning partly accounts for how gender-role behaviors or scripts are acquired in childhood.

Cognitive Theory

Several theoretical approaches explain how people acquire their thought processes and problem-solving abilities, as well as organize and use information. The theories by Jean Piaget are relevant in the context of parent–child relations. His writings on this topic were based initially on observations of his own children (Piaget, 1967; Piaget & Inhelder, 1969). One of the co-authors of this book (Gerhardt) met one of Jean Piaget's personal assistants in Switzerland. The assistant, by then progressing in age, recounted how many of the experiments were conceived and then executed to determine cognitive processes in children. She also elaborated on what it was like to be part of Piaget's research team. Even at that time, it was a great honor to work in his laboratory, and his assistants were well aware of his eminence. Her description of him was that he was somewhat eccentric and was confident in taking the "path less traveled" in his research. This encouraged his coworkers to think outside the box as well. On a personal note, she remembers that he used to cycle to work, past several farms, and that he did not appreciate it if dogs chased him while he was on his bicycle. He was particularly upset when on one of his cycling trips he was bitten by a farmer's dog. In short, these human qualities resonate positively with readers who only know him through his work.

Several concepts are central to Piaget's thoughts about the development of intellect. *Cognition* and *cognitive development* are terms that refer to the way in which humans come to know and understand the world or the environments in which they live. A variety of related processes—perception, problem solving, judgment, and reasoning, for example—are involved in how people organize their mental life. Cognitive development also refers to the changes that take place as people acquire a general understanding of their environments. See Table 3–2.

Cognition is based on the acquisition of *schemes*. This refers to a consistent, reliable pattern or plan of interaction with the environment. Schemes are usually goal-oriented strategies that help a person to achieve some type of intended result from his or her behavior. For example, a rudimentary scheme is built or acquired that serves to guide a child's behavior in picking up an object that draws his or her curiosity or attention to explore by touch, sight, and even taste. This scheme acts as a script of sorts that becomes a permanent part of the child's mental abilities in learning how to manipulate objects and learn about their nature. Once the scheme is acquired when learning about one object, it can be generalized to be used in learning about all objects that a child is interested in manipulating.

Piaget believed that there are two basic types of schemes that are formed throughout infancy, childhood, and adolescence:

1. *Sensorimotor schemes,* formed in infancy and childhood, are based in motor acts and serve to help the child understand how the world operates in very rudimentary terms.
2. *Cognitive schemes* are more like ideas or patterns based on symbolism and abstract reasoning, formed from early childhood into adolescence and older years, that also permit problem solving and attainment of certain goals, for example, mathematical processes such as addition and subtraction.

Schemes evolve, once formed, from basic to more advanced and complex natures. Essentially, we are able to modify existing schemes by two processes:

1. *Assimilation* occurs when new information is incorporated into an existing scheme.

TABLE 3–2.   Piaget's Stages of Cognitive Development

Sensorimotor (Birth to 3 years)

- Establishment of sensorimotor schemes
- Assimilation and accommodation, modification of schemes
- Elementary understanding of cause-and-effect relationships
- Emergence of object permanence
- Emergence of elementary logic

Preoperational-Intuitive (3–6 years)

- Emergence of language helps to establish cognitive schemes
- Preoccupation with classification tasks
- Thinking becomes intuitive in nature
- Development of large database of knowledge and information
- Cognitive flaws include egocentrism
- Perception is based upon appearances

Concrete Operations (6–11 years)

- Understanding relationships between events and things
- Operating objects, symbols, and concepts to acquire this understanding
- Internalizing the outer environment by using mental imagery and symbolism
- Other cognitive attributes:
  - Centering
  - Mastery of conservation problems
  - Reversibility
  - Black-and-white thinking

Formal Operations (Adolescence and older)

- Increasing use of scientific reasoning
- Decrease in egocentricity
- Increasing ability to empathize
- Emergence of personal meanings
- Emergence of higher order moral reasoning

Based on Piaget, J., & Inhelder, B. (1969). *The psychology of the child*. New York: Basic Books.

2. *Accommodation* occurs when an existing scheme is altered to bring about congruence with reality. For example, an infant acquires the basic scheme for sucking on an object. After this is mastered, the baby will attempt to suck on anything that comes near his or her mouth, such as fingers, toes, and so forth. He or she may learn from interactions with parents that sucking is most appropriate with a nipple or pacifier.

Piaget proposed that individuals experience a series of four stages in infancy, childhood, and adolescence in acquiring an understanding of the world. Development proceeds from a general to a more specific understanding as children acquire greater experience with their environments. The ages at which people proceed through these stages are somewhat variable, but Piaget believed that the sequence of the stages is invariable.

Application to Parent–Child Relations

This theory is a comprehensive guide to understanding mental processes and how these are acquired and change as a person grows and develops from birth through childhood and adolescence. Central to Piaget's explanation is the role of personal experience with one's environment, both physical and social, in influencing how we think and reason. The ways in which parents interact with a child and provide a variety of physical and social experiences are an essential component of a child's development. For example, parents provide physical experiences for infants through toys and food, and in the places in the community where they take children. These shape children's understanding of their physical environment and how they can operate in this setting. Parents also provide a social environment to their infants by talking and playing with them, and teaching them rudimentary social skills in late infancy. These parental actions continue throughout childhood and adolescence. For example, when parents read to their children and encourage them to look at picture books, the children learn that information can be acquired from printed materials. What parents provide as experiences for children influences the quality of their cognitive development.

Vygotsky's Sociocultural Theory

Lev Vygotsky (1962, 1987) is a Russian psychologist who proposed a perspective of psychological development known as the **sociocultural theory**. This approach emphasizes the social aspects of cognitive development; that is, intellectual growth is stimulated by interactions with others, especially parents. Vygotsky stated that

■ Development during infancy and early childhood is specific to a particular historical time in which a person lives. Differences in development depend on when and where someone grows up.

Parents provide important life experiences for children that stimulate their cognitive, emotional and social development.

- Development takes place when a child observes an activity in group interactions and then internalizes this activity.
- Symbols such as language assist in internalizing activities.
- Culture is learned through interactions with others from the same culture.

Vygotsky proposes that children accomplish many developmental tasks within the context of what he terms the **zone of proximal development (ZPD)**. Many tasks that are too difficult for children to master alone can be accomplished successfully with the guidance and assistance of adults who are more skilled than children. The lower limit of the ZPD is what a child can accomplish in learning a task independently—without adult assistance. The upper limit of this zone is what can be accomplished when assisted by an adult. The ZPD represents an idea of a child's learning potential. It emphasizes the interpersonal context in which learning tasks occurs by implying that learning is a shared experience.

Young children are assisted by parents and other caregivers who motivate their interest in accomplishing a task that appears difficult to achieve successfully. By providing children with verbal instruction and by helping them do things themselves with guidance, parents and others assist children. The children, in turn, organize the information in their existing mental structures and transform it to accomplish increasingly difficult tasks.

Application to Parent–Child Relations

Some researchers use the term **scaffolding** to refer to any parental behavior that supports a child's efforts at more advanced skill acquisition until the child becomes competent at that behavior. We refer to such assistance as *assertive* and *supportive care*, which includes nurture and refers to the ways that parents provide appropriate and healthy support to their children. When parents instruct their preschool-age child in this manner, it may happen in the following sequence:

1. Recruiting the child's interest in performing a task or activity.
2. Simplifying the task to a number of steps that lead to a correct solution.
3. Maintaining the child's interest in the task.
4. Pointing out errors as they occur and providing guidance toward correction.
5. Controlling the child's frustration by discounting the distress caused by making mistakes.
6. Demonstrating or modeling correct solutions (Astington, 1993; Rogoff, 1990).

When seen in this manner, children learn best when parents model problem-solving skills or mentor the child in ways of reaching solutions to the problems. Vygotsky's views approximate that of social learning theory but are nested within the cultural context in which development occurs.

Vygotsky incorporates the concept of interdependence as a central part of development (Rogoff, 1990). This runs against the parenting philosophy frequently displayed in the United States. In our society, child-rearing practices tend to promote individualism as a valued trait. For example, infants are placed in separate sleeping quarters from parents and are expected to learn to comfort themselves while going to sleep. Children also conduct their own play activities with a minimal amount of adult guidance. School performance is based on competition with others, and individualism is highlighted by the heavy emphasis on personal performance in sports and athletic activities, for example. Other cultures promote collectivism rather than independence in child rearing. In Vygotsky's view, optimal development occurs within the collectivist context of relationships among individuals.

J. S. Bruner's Cognitive Learning Theory

Jerome Bruner's (1966) work on children's cognitive development reflects a rich understanding of the role of one's culture in influencing the acquisition and evolution of thinking processes. Like Piaget, Bruner believes that ideas are based on the ability to categorize according to similarities, as well as differences. Bruner proposes three modes of representation that are acquired in learning to understand one's environment: (1) enactive or action based, (2) iconic or image based, and (3) symbolic or language based. In applying these concepts, Bruner believes that new material is acquired by experiencing these three types of representation sequentially. One of Bruner's central tenets in education theory is that anything can be learned at a very early if it is properly organized. This notion is in trast to Piaget's approach.

Focus On 3–2

Comparing Theories Related to Parent–Child Relations

Theory	Proponent(s)	Major Concepts/Ideas Related to Parent–Child Relations
Psychoanalytic	Sigmund Freud (1886–1939)	■ A child's personality develops in five distinct stages from infancy through adolescence. ■ Experiences early in life significantly shape later development. ■ Parents must be careful not to do anything that will fixate (stagnate) a child's development at any stage. ■ Parental strictness/restrictiveness inhibits children's healthy personality development. ■ Adult/child neuroses are caused by psychological trauma. ■ Parents must do and say the right thing at the right time to influence healthy development. **Early childhood experiences, especially the traumatic ones, can play a role throughout the life span.**
	Alfred Adler (1870–1937)	■ Social interest plays an important part in behavior. Behavior is motivated to maintain one's social interest. ■ Everyone strives for perfection/superiority in their behavior and interactions. ■ A child's personality is highly influenced by their birth order; parents treat children differently according to their birth order. ■ Boys are held in higher esteem than girls (masculine protest). ■ Behavior is drawn toward meeting goals, purposes, and ideals; we are drawn toward the future rather than motivated by our past. ■ Our current focus on three parenting styles is partly attributed to Adler's work. He opened the first child guidance clinic in Vienna in 1921 and was a pioneer in developing parent education programs. **Overindulgence, as well as neglect, of children (disengaged parenting) can cause problems in adulthood, especially in relationships.**
Psychosocial	Erik Erikson (1902–1994)	■ Personality development occurs over the life span in eight distinct stages; individual must master a crisis or challenge in order to move from one stage to the next. ■ Parents can assist or hinder healthy development of children during the first four stages of their development. ■ Children assist parents in mastering their major developmental task of adulthood by providing a means for caregiving to be expressed in healthy ways. ■ Parents adapt their parenting behaviors as children grow older; they assist children in mastering each developmental crisis confronted at each stage, from infancy through early adulthood. ■ Stability or homeostasis is maintained with this balancing of interactions between parents and children. **Healthy development at each stage lays the foundation for the subsequent stage. A good childhood is the foundation for appropriate adult development.**

Behaviorism	Ivan Pavlov (1849–1936)	■ Described classical conditioning; first scientific method of learning demonstrated in animals. ■ Behavior can be established and shaped by structured learning experiences; learning occurs strictly by association. **Associations, especially negative ones, can shape behavior in both animals and children.**
	John B. Watson (1878–1959)	■ Attempted to extend Pavlov's findings to human infants and children; "Little Albert" experiment (later ruled unethical). ■ Careful structuring of parental behavior produces certain predictable outcomes in child behavior. ■ Children's behavior can be carefully altered through conditioning experiences. **Strong focus on the nurture component of the nature/nurture debate.**
Operant Conditioning	B. F. Skinner (1904–1990)	■ Children learn by parent's use of rewards and punishments. ■ Positive reinforcement (reward) is the most powerful tool for parents to use in raising children to behave appropriately. ■ Parents use operant conditioning when a child makes an association between an act and a consequence for that act. ■ Rewards can be used excessively; parents should use a mixed reinforcement schedule to extend the life and effectiveness of positive reinforcers. ■ Children can habituate to parental overuse of rewards. ■ To be effective, a positive reinforcer should immediately follow the desired act of a child. **The principles of conditioning can be found in certain disciplinary approaches in the form of reward and punishment.**
Social Learning	Albert Bandura (b. 1925)	■ Direct reinforcement doesn't account for all types of learning. ■ Children also learn by watching others' behavior (observational learning). ■ Internal mental processes, such as pride, enjoyment, and happiness, help learning to occur. ■ Children can learn new information without any other behavioral changes. ■ In order to learn, children must pay attention; something that is new or interesting gains their full attention. ■ Children must retain information in order to perform a specific act. ■ For learning to be successful, children must be motivated to learn. ■ Encouragement also promotes a child's learning experience. ■ A child's belief that he or she will succeed in learning, solving a particular problem, or mastering a situation influences the behavior directed toward the task. **There is an emphasis on self-efficacy and self-esteem, which, if nurtured in children, will contribute toward success in adulthood.**

(Continued)

Focus On 3–2 **(Continued)**

Cognition	Lev Vygotsky (1896–1934)	■ Social interaction is the basis of a child's learning to make meaning of and understand the world.

■ Social interaction is the basis of a child's learning to make meaning of and understand the world.

■ Social learning precedes and promotes children's development; a child's culture shapes his or her cognitive development or way of thinking about and understanding the world.

■ Children are curious and are actively involved in their own learning processes.

■ A skillful tutor (e.g., a child's parent) acts as a More Knowledgeable Other (MKO) who models appropriate behaviors and provides instructions for understanding the world; peers, others, and objects can also be MKOs.

■ The Zone of Proximal Development (ZPD) outlines what a child can accomplish on his or her own and what can be accomplished with the help and instruction provided by an MKO. Understanding this zone allows an MKO to know when and where to intervene in a child's learning process to promote skill development and higher mental functioning. It is a similar to learning to ride a bike while being supported by training wheels.

■ Language is a child's tool for powering mental development.

Children learn while being scaffolded (supported) by significant adults.

Jean Piaget (1896–1980)

■ Innate mechanisms and processes allow children to learn how to organize their understanding of the world and how it functions, leading to the ability to use logic and form hypotheses.

■ Mental development is organized into five distinct, but related, stages—from infancy to late adolescence.

■ Experiences with the world form the basis of understanding; children spend much of their time developing a database of meanings by which to understand the world.

■ Language is the tool that accelerates mental development and enhances the ability to use thought and images to form mental representations of the world .

■ Symbolic thought emerges in childhood as children learn how the world operates; this limited understanding is later transformed into a more fluid way of understanding how the world operates in late childhood and adolescence.

■ Scientific thinking emerges in late childhood and adolescence based on the child's experiences in understanding how the world operates.

■ Parental guidance and help are important in providing a wide variety of experiences that help children learn how to organize their thoughts and promote advanced learning and understanding.

Piaget emphasizes cognitive development (i.e., mental and thinking abilities), which parallels the physical development of the child.

Jerome Bruner
(b. 1915)

- Children must learn how to represent their environment(s) in various ways in order to learn how to think and to think creatively.
- Interactions with others, especially parents, as well as with cultural technologies, are important for promoting mental development.
- Children (and adults) learn to represent their environment in three distinct, but related, ways.
- Children of any age are capable of learning anything as long as it is properly organized.
- Parents can help promote a child's mental development by providing stimulating language experiences. **Bruner further elaborated on the concept of scaffolding (used by Vygotsky). Interactions need to be framed within a social context. The role of culture is recognized.**

Vygotsky, Piaget, and Bruner all emphasized that learning happens within a social context. This has far-reaching educational implications.

Parenthood as a Developmental Role: Developmental Interaction

We have presented and discussed a number of different, but related, ideas about the nature of the parenting role, the variety of factors that are thought to influence parental behaviors, and how these relate to child outcomes. It is important to reemphasize that individuals experience changes in how they conduct themselves in their role as a parent. These changes are developmental in nature and occur in association with the passage of time. Like other patterns observed in family systems, the parenting role must evolve in relation to the needs of the children and the parent(s). Most people enter this role with ideas about what it is like to be a parent, and what might be expected from children. Parents need to change and evolve their parenting skills and abilities, often in response to the developmental changes that children experience. Several writers, including Ellen Galinsky (1987), have developed the topic in greater detail.

Parenthood is traditionally considered to be a developmental task of adulthood. Although this is not necessarily an essential component of adult development, many people experience a sense of generativity by becoming a parent. Galinsky describes six stages

in the evolution of one's parenthood role that were observed in individuals as they grow and change in response to the developmental changes being experienced by their children. We refer to this process as **developmental interaction** (sometimes called developmental parenting), which is the motivating factor that produces such mutual developmental changes in parents and children.

Drawing from the theoretical work of Levinson (1978) and Erikson (1950) on adult development, Galinsky outlines the following six stages of parenthood:

1. *Image-making Stage.* During this period, a potential parent uses imagery to rehearse what it must be like to be a parent. This is a time for individuals to develop their vision of what kind of parent they wish to be. It is a time for preparation for parenthood that is particularly stimulated by the initiation of a pregnancy. Pregnancy brings many changes, especially for a woman. Her body changes, her image of her body changes, and she experiences the unique feeling of a new life developing within her body. This image-making stage is a time for individuals to examine their relationship with their own parents, a relationship that often serves as a guide for how they themselves may act as a parent. It is a time

for evaluating how changes might occur in the relationship between partners. Ultimately, this stage is also a time for preparing for the child's birth and confronting fears, especially those of the unknown if this is the first pregnancy.

2. *The Nurturing Stage.* The major focus of this stage of emerging parenthood is establishing an attachment to the new infant. For new parents, this involves reconciling the reality of what the child is actually like with how they may have imagined him or her to be. This stage necessitates redefining a couple's relationship and their relationships with their parents, in-laws, friends, and coworkers. Paradoxically, by getting to know the baby, each parent has the opportunity to get to know him- or herself even better than before. The experience of nurturing a baby reflects back to the parent the kind of person that she or he is.

3. *The Authority Stage.* This period is characterized by the realization that parenthood involves a strong element of adult authority. This is partially stimulated by the changes taking place in children that allow them to master an increasingly wider range of skills that challenge parental interactions. The changing nature of children at this time calls for greater reliance on the parent as a person of authority who decides much of what is right or wrong, appropriate or inappropriate, regarding children's behavior. Essentially, this is the time when adults must accept the responsibility for guiding the life, behavior, and development of the child. The authority stage involves the emergence of rules as a means for governance and the clear establishment of personal boundaries between parents and children.

4. *The Interpretative Stage.* At this time, adults assume the responsibility of acting as interpreters of the world for their children. This means that they begin to impart their interpretation of their own particular world view or family values to their children. Parents answer children's innumerable questions, help them to acquire skills for making personal decisions about their behavior, and pass on family values. This stage ends with the child's entrance into adolescence.

5. *The Interdependent Stage.* This period includes parenting adolescent children and demands that adults reexamine the issue of parental authority and how this is to be played out. The new child who emerges during adolescence is one who increasingly demands to be independent from parental control and authority. The reality of development for both adults and children is that although parents must recognize this desire for independence, it is not reasonable to permit adolescent children to have complete control over their decisions and behavior. The challenge of this stage of parenthood is for parents and adolescents to adapt and redefine their relationship to allow negotiation and discussion of rules, appropriate behavior, limits, and so forth.

6. *The Departing Stage.* At this time, parents reexamine all of their experiences in raising children. Parents begin to let go of their children and relinquish authority over them. They recognize that their parenting career is coming to a close and that the tasks of parenthood are almost completed. To be truly mastered, the relationship between adult children and parents must be redefined to encompass the new adult status of the children. This means that the relationship takes on an adult-to-adult quality in which the authority of the parent is no longer paramount.

Parenting Reflection 3–4

How has information from the behavioral sciences contributed to the understanding of parent–child relations?

Focus Point. Theoretical approaches may be useful in understanding the social context of parent–child relations. Learning theory components (e.g., behavior modification and social learning) explain how parents teach children by using rewards to reinforce the behaviors that they desire in children and by serving as models of behavior. Cognitive theory stresses the importance of the experiences that parents provide for children, which are both physical and social in nature, as a means of shaping their mental life. Vygotsky's views expand on social learning to explain how parents teach skills to their children.

POINTS TO CONSIDER

- Several different, but related, theories can be applied to understand and study parent–child relations. Each provides insight into a particular aspect of this relationship. Some describe how the relationship changes over time; others describe how the relationship functions.
- Attachment theory is attributed to the work of Bowlby, who emphasized the importance of the early mother and infant relationship in terms of trust, nurturance, and responsiveness. He believed that this mutual focus on each other is instinctual. Several other important researchers, such as Klein, Ainsworth, Lorenz, and Harlow, added to our understanding of attachment and bonding. The theory is important in our understanding of early child-care situations. It has implications for international adoptions where some children spent their infancy in orphanages. It is also of importance in the legal setting, with implications for custody, adoption, and foster parenting.
- Ecological systems theory proposed by Bronfenbrenner, offers a way to understand family functioning against the backdrop of increasingly larger social systems. Bronfenbrenner suggests that five distinct environmental settings influence persons in their developmental progress. These are the micro-, meso-, exo-, macro- and chronosystems. The relationships function in interaction with various environments and the people in those environments. The environments are nested within each other. This theory is also referred to as an ecological theory of development.
- Systems theory has been applied to the study of families. Family systems theory is useful in explaining the processes by which a family group makes decisions, sets and achieves particular goals, and establishes methods for governing the behavior of its members. This theory is helpful in describing how these processes work to maintain the stability of a family group over time and how the family reacts to changes that affect individual members and the group. According to this theory, several subsystems can be found within the larger family system— for instance, parental systems and systems comprising the children. These are usually based on relationships between two or more members, such as the adult spouses, parents and children, or brothers and sisters. Each subsystem has its own patterns that mirror those of the larger family system.

- Family systems theory uses several concepts to explain family functioning: wholeness, interdependence, patterns (i.e., rules, roles, and communication styles), reciprocal interaction and feedback, boundaries, entropy, equifinality, adaptation, and homeostasis. This approach is especially popular in the context of marriage and family therapy.
- Systemic family development theory is an extension of family systems theory that is useful in understanding how a family group changes in response to stressors that occur as part of the normal developmental processes of individuals. This realistic model of family life recognizes that families are complex and are composed of several interrelated generations. By taking a snapshot or slice of developmental time being experienced by a family, it is possible to examine the stressors that affect each generation in a family and study how a family responds to and copes with these stressors. By making adaptations in patterns, families are able to make the necessary changes to reestablish the stability in their functioning.
- Erikson proposes a theory of eight stages that describe the psychosocial development of individuals over the life span. The stages start with trust versus mistrust in infancy, with resolution of the psychosocial crisis at each stage, and culminate with integrity versus despair in middle to late adulthood. This theory stresses
  - The continuity of developmental changes over a person's entire life span.
  - The resolution of a central crisis or challenge in each stage.
  - The mastery or acquisition of a healthy or unhealthy psychosocial attitude at the completion of each stage.
  - The assistance and support from significant others who assist or impede an individual's developmental progress.
- Erikson's theory may be applied to parent–child relations by examining the congruence between the psychosocial stages of parents and children. The concepts of reciprocal interaction and adaptation explain the changes in parenting behavior in response to the changing developmental needs of children. In turn, children help parents achieve their particular psychosocial attitude as they are the recipients of the caregiving behavior.

■ Other theories can be applied to parent–child relations. Learning theory stresses how behavior is modified through rewards and by observing the behavior of others. Cognitive theory, as described by Piaget, focuses on the cognitive development of the child and the role of physical and social experiences provided by parents in shaping how children come to understand their world. Vygotsky's observations emphasize how parents structure learning experiences in teaching children to master skills.

■ Parenthood is a developmental role experienced in six distinct stages as proposed by Galinsky. These stages start with the image-making stage and proceed through the nurturing, authority, interpretive, and interdependent stages, culminating in the departing stage. The changes in the parental role are stimulated by the developmental changes in the child as the child grows older.

USEFUL WEBSITES

Bronfenbrenner Center for Translational Research, Cornell University
www.bctr.cornell.edu

Erikson Institute, Graduate School in Child Development
www.erikson.edu

Jean Piaget Society, Society for the Study of Knowledge and Development
www.piaget.org

CHAPTER 4

Parenting Styles and Strategies

Learning Outcomes

■ ■ ■ ■ ■ ■ ■ ■ ■ ■ ■ ■

After completing this chapter, readers should be able to:

1. Explain the qualities that characterize a competent parent by reflecting on the teaching aspect of parenting.

2. Explain the definition of discipline and what contributes to making parents effective disciplinarians.

3. Explain why structure and nurture are the cornerstones of effective discipline.

4. Describe the common elements of the basic methods of discipline and how these programs can be applied.

5. Describe some of the behavioral problems that are considered a normal aspect of children's development. Distinguish between developmentally appropriate and developmentally inappropriate behavior problems.

■ ■ ■ ■ ■ ■ ■ ■ ■ ■ ■ ■

THE NECESSITY OF PARENT EDUCATION

Even though our culture is child friendly and many social, educational, and legal settings support the well-being of children, relatively little preparation or assistance is provided in training people to act competently in parental roles. Parental behavior may be guided partly by trial-and-error learning and self-education. It is often based on parental role family of origin, and a vague idea of developmental milestones and whether progress is being made. Professionals and those who work closely with parents believe there is considerable need for such training (C. Smith et al., 2002). Most people could benefit from learning new ways to be effective in their parenting role, and researchers continue to make progress in helping parents find more effective ways of child rearing.

Ineffective parenting reveals itself when children and teenagers present with behavioral problems. Professionals who promote parenting education believe that people can learn methods to improve their parenting abilities. Education is a means of preventing or minimizing problems in child rearing; as in wellness and health maintenance, prevention is better than cure. Specific methods and techniques of child rearing have emerged as a result of social changes, as well as from information derived from behavioral science research.

· ·

Parenting Reflection 4–1

Parenting occurs in the many contexts in which children grow and develop. Reflect on the needs that unify us as parents—what we universally share in our parenting efforts, regardless of ethnicity or origin.

· ·

PARENTS AS TEACHERS

From ancient times to the present, societies have recognized that parents are their children's first and most important teachers. Long before public school systems were established in the United States, parents held the responsibility for training and teaching their children the essential skills and knowledge to become effectively functioning adults. While formal educational functions have been assumed by other agents, society has never relinquished the socialization responsibilities of parents in equipping children with basic skills and knowledge.

Comparing past and present times, we can easily conclude that the complexity of the 21st century challenges parents as teachers. The dilemma is distinguishing between what children need and do not need in order to develop into healthy adults. It is practically impossible to know what kind of occupation children will hold in the future. Additionally, the vast advances in science and technology make it difficult for parents (or anyone else) to predict the nature of the world in a few decades from now. Parents have always taught their children the skills and knowledge that they believe children will need to function effectively as adults. With societal changes, other institutions have assumed many of the family's primary functions so that children's socialization is the main concern of parenting today.

In addition to loving and nurturing children, parents should provide structure and developmentally appropriate guidance.

People in developed countries require years of education and training to become competent in an occupation or a profession. With a few exceptions, this formal training is typically not required for parenting. (Francis-Connolly, 2003). Society delegates the responsibility for socializing children to parents, but does little to prepare them to meet that responsibility. Preparing the next generation to cope emotionally and to have social and interpersonal skills is usually a matter of trial and error. It is understandable that parents feel overwhelmed. Parents have to model values that will have meaning and usefulness to their children when they are grown, regardless of the changes in society. These may include

- Integrity that will guide appropriate civic, law-abiding behavior.
- The ability to attain goals and objectives, including an education.
- Interpersonal and coping skills.
- Respecting the needs of others, as well as one's own.

The childhood experiences of today's parents differ from those that their children will encounter in the future. Additionally, the isolated nuclear family system has few outside supports to assist in its child-rearing efforts. According to respected voices in the field of parenting (Bronfenbrenner, 1985; Kagan, 1976), children generally need

- To feel valued by parents and a few significant adults, such as a teacher or a relative.
- To develop their own personal attitudes, values, and opinions in order to become autonomous.
- To develop and master skills and abilities that are valued by society.
- To love and to be able to accept love from others.

Parental competency requires knowledge of a variety of approaches for guiding children toward adulthood. Parental love and nurture of children is important for their healthy growth and development. Being a competent and effective parent requires additional skills. There are a number of strategies and parenting styles that focus on fostering the emotional needs and character development of both parents and children. Some strategies are therapeutic, some attempt to resolve conflicts between parents and children and teach interpersonal skills, and some propose a humane approach to parent–child interactions. Rather than offering a recipe for child rearing, these strategies and parenting styles provide parents with skills for raising children to become competent adults.

....

Focus Point. There are many strategies that parents can use to become competent teachers and to socialize children effectively. It is helpful to learn a variety of these strategies in order to be an effective parent.

....

DEALING WITH DISCIPLINE

The term **discipline** contains the root of the Latin verb *discere*, meaning "to learn." It is found in Middle English and is used in the context of instruction. A derivative of the term is *disciple*, which means "pupil" or "student." Nowadays, many people equate discipline to a rigorous regimen of control or training. This often translates to the use of punishment in response to children's misbehavior, although discipline in the context of child rearing should have the more positive meaning of instructional *guidance*. For discipline to be effective, parents need to view it in light of the term's original meaning.

- Discipline is teaching children to behave in socially approved ways.
- Discipline guides children to internalize rules, values, and beliefs.
- Discipline helps to control impulses, allowing appropriate behavioral choices.
- Discipline guides social skills, facilitating work, family life, and other social interactions.
- Parental disciplinary actions should be positive, reasonable, and temperate.
- Methods and strategies for discipline should be developmentally appropriate.
- Effective discipline requires an understanding of the child.
- Consistency, as well as flexibility, plays a role in effective discipline.
- Discipline provides structure by developing rules within a family system.
- Rules are found in both healthy and unhealthy family systems.

Knowing the guidelines regarding acceptable and unacceptable behaviors and their consequences in well-functioning families is helpful. In healthy family systems, there are negotiable rules. Children in healthy families learn that the rules are for their protection and freedom. They know that they can talk with their parents about making occasional exceptions to the rules. Each family system must develop its own rules, policies, and values rearing and socialization. These evolve and depend on many factors, such as personalities, family of origin, values, financial and social status, and the number and birth order of the children. Some common guidelines for parents are as follows:

1. *Understand the concept of equifinality as it applies to a program of discipline.*   The concept of equifinality from family systems theory implies that families attain similar goals in different and varied ways. Different methods for socializing children may result in adults who hold similar values and attitudes and may behave in a similar manner. A variety of techniques and practices can help accomplish socialization. There is no single disciplinary program that will meet all parenting goals.

2. *Do not use abusive corporal punishment.*   Spanking and other abusive corporal punishments do not appear to be effective in achieving desired behaviors (Kazdin & Benjet, 2003). Such physical violence incorrectly models aggressive behavior as a means for resolving conflict and can lead to violent behavior in children (Kyriacou, 2002; Sandberg, Feldhousen, & Busby, 2012). The connection between harsh physical punishment in childhood and violence in adult dating has also been observed (Swinford, DeMaris, Cernkovich, & Giordano, 2000). Many adults were spanked by their parents in an attempt to control childhood misbehavior. Researchers increasingly note that it is the consistency with which punishment and other punitive measures are used rather than the act itself that helps children learn to control their actions (Kazdin & Benjet, 2003). Spanking and other forms of physical punishment usually occur within the context of expressions of parental anger, which can result in overly aggressive actions that harm the child.

Considering the danger and the negative effect on a child's self-esteem, alternatives such as positive reinforcement, time-out, and other less damaging methods are viewed as more appropriate disciplinary measures (Saadeh, Rizzo, & Roberts, 2002). These do require an expanded skill set on the part of the parents.

When the reasoning approach is combined with noncorporal, nonabusive punishment (e.g., time-out, withdrawal of privileges), then disciplinary programs become more effective and toddlers learn to comply with parental wishes. Developmentally appropriate reasoning is the key.

3. *Try to understand children's feelings and motivations.*   Many parents consider the misbehavior of

a child to be a personal attack with malicious intent. This is rarely the case. The child's misbehavior may be a learned response or action that is logical at a particular time. Parents who attempt to develop an understanding of their children in a loving, noncritical way will feel less hostile when their offspring misbehave. As a result, parents will be more rational in developing corrective action that teaches children to think before they act. Such an approach will also facilitate the parent's position as the child's ally in solving a particular problem. On the other hand, the parent who sees misbehavior as a personal and malicious attack will likely respond with anger and frustration, which will only intensify the problem.

A parent can gain an understanding of a child's feelings and motivations for unacceptable behavior. The

Parents who have been subjected to physical punishment or abuse as children are more likely to use spanking as a means of resolving conflict.

parent can listen carefully to a child's verbal and non-verbal communications and reflect the feelings being expressed by the child. This exercise will help the child verbalize feelings and help the parent understand the emotional aspects that underlie the child's actions. This attitude is based on compassion and empathy. Parents, who are angry and critical of a child because of misbehavior often dictate their own solution to a problem, which discounts the child. The goal of good parental discipline is to foster an understanding of the child.

Parenting Reflection 4–2

Does anyone have the right to intervene when parents use physical punishment as a disciplinary technique with their child, especially in public? What would you say to a parent who is a stranger, regarding what he or she is doing?

Focus On 4–1

The Link Between Spanking and Aggressive Behavior

Consider these issues and findings from research studies on the effects of spanking children. Draw your own conclusions as to the advisability of using spanking as a means of discipline.

- Adults who spank children are likely to have been spanked by their parents as a primary means of controlling their misbehavior.

  There is a very strong association between experiencing harsh, abusive, physical punishment in childhood and being a perpetrator of violence in intimate relationships in adulthood (Douglas, 2006; Sandberg et al., 2012; Swinford et al., 2000).

- Spanking as a means of discipline appears to be strongly ingrained in certain ethnic and cultural groups (Dodge et al., 2005; Hall, 2005; Hawkins et al., 2010; McLoyd, Kaplan, Hardaway, & Wood, 2007; Taylor et al., 2011).

- Spanking appears to be a prevalent means of child maltreatment, frequently used as a last resort in gaining children's compliance to adult wishes.

  Most spankings occur when adults are angry with children (Bensley et al., 2004; Del Vecchio & O'Leary, 2008).

- Parents who are considered abusive by mental health professionals and by the courts consider spanking to be an acceptable means of discipline (Stafford, 2004).

- Spanking is frequently used instead of positive reinforcement of desirable behavior (Flora, 2004).

- Parents spank younger children (infants through preschool age) more than older children (school age through adolescent; Magnuson & Waldfogel, 2005; Socolar, Savage & Evans, 2007; Walsh, 2002).

- Children who are spanked exhibit more aggressive behaviors than children who are not spanked. Spanking is associated with children's negative feelings of self-esteem and personal worth (Aucoin et al., 2006).

- Males are more likely than females to approve of spanking children even though mothers are more likely to spank children than fathers are, especially if they are young (Ateah & Durrant, 2005). Parents spank boys more frequently than girls (Gámez-Guadix et al., 2010).

- Spanking may produce a child's conformity to parental wishes in an immediate situation, but its long-term effects may include increased probability of deviance, including delinquency in adolescence and violent crime in adulthood (Barry, 2007).

- Parents who are members of fundamentalist Protestant religious groups prefer the use of spanking (corporal punishment) to alternate methods of discipline (Grogan-Kaylor & Otis, 2007).

- Individuals who are considered to be bullies have been subjected to physical punishment/abuse as children and have incorrectly learned that the use of physical force is an "acceptable" means of resolving conflicts with others (Dussich & Maekoya, 2007); note that this is not mainstream-recommended behavior.

- The use of corporal punishment (including spanking) is controversial. A number of countries prohibit this practice by law (M. Bailey, 2003; Baumrind, Larzelere, & Cowan, 2002; Kazdin & Benjet, 2003; Kelly, 2011).

A parent might also attempt to help the child identify and rectify the cause of the misbehavior. This approach is similar to that used by a mechanic fixing a malfunctioning engine. Ordinarily, mechanics do not shout out in anger, condemn, or strike an engine because it has malfunctioned. They simply discover the cause of the malfunction and make the repairs. A parent can approach a malfunctioning child in a similar manner, first by attempting to identify what caused the problem behavior and then by helping the child make the necessary adjustments to his or her behavior.

4. *Facilitate opportunities for children to learn to think, reason, and make choices regarding their actions.* A child who is granted the right to make personal decisions and to experience the consequences, both positive and negative, of those decisions will learn to be responsible for his or her actions. Here the parent's role is to help generate alternatives without supplying all of the answers, options, or solutions all of the time. The adult must determine which decisions a child can make and at what age, and must always keep the safety and well-being of the child in mind. The parent who continually makes all of the child's decisions and accepts responsibility for all of the child's actions fosters dependency rather than autonomy in the child. By making their own decisions and living with the results, children learn to differentiate themselves from others and to establish personal boundaries.

5. *Learn to value the individual differences of children as interesting and positive tools for personal growth rather than requiring that everyone in the family system be the same.* Some family systems value sameness or rigid conformity in all members rather than seeing the benefits of individual differences in values, opinions, ideas, or means of self-expression. The parenting and disciplining of children in such family systems are approached with a cookie-cutter mentality: Children are required to think and act like their parents and hold identical values and beliefs. The demand for sameness can kill a child's spirit and self-perception as an autonomous, unique human being who has the ability to reason and think and the right to be who he or she is.

Faced with the demand for sameness among family members, a child may react in one of several ways:

■ The child may comply with the demand for sameness by denying his or her true self. The child will avoid conflict and seek peace at any price.

■ The child may rebel and seek self-definition by not acting as the parents wish, often in ways that are contrary to his or her own wishes.
■ The child may project blame onto others rather than admit his or her own part in conflicts. A power struggle with parents typically results.
■ When the demand for sameness becomes overwhelming, the child may disengage emotionally from the parents.

6. *Maintain a clear understanding that discipline should be based on helping children develop an internal structure that is based on healthy self-esteem rather than fear, guilt, or shame.* Structure refers to the internalized controls that people acquire through socialization experiences that guide their behavior. Parents provide socialization experiences to their children through care, instruction, and rules that result in children's self-disciplined actions. This differs drastically from the experiences of children who are raised by parents who use criticism, sarcasm, nagging, discounting, shame, and guilt to provide children with internal controls for their behavior. When parents attempt to shape and motivate children's development by instilling fear and shame about misbehavior, children suffer a loss of self-esteem. Such children internalize what psychologists refer to as a *critical parent* aspect of their personality to motivate and regulate their behavior. As adults, such individuals respond to committing an error or transgression with guilt and shame. These emotions tend to block effective problem solving because the person's thinking skills become frozen and ineffective when attempting to reach a rational solution.

Rules help children learn structure. When applied appropriately, rules provide children with a sense of protection and foster a sense of trust and security. Parents must teach children rules that are rational and that serve to outline the boundaries of acceptable behavior for children. If rules derive from parents' critical, judgmental, and unloving positions promoted by authoritarian attitudes, the resulting discipline and structure provided for children will tend to be rigid and inflexible. Such rules and the ways that parents enforce them become similar to the *poisonous pedagogy* of authoritarianism that causes children to acquire negative rather than positive structure.

Some parents provide implicit rules and inconsistent experiences, resulting in very permissive parenting,

---

Focus On 4–2

Identifying Positive and Negative Structure by Parenting Style

There are six possible ways that parents provide or fail to provide structure for their children. These can be arranged on a continuum according to the degree of strictness. For example, the **Rigidity** parenting style is characterized by having the highest degree of strictness, whereas the **Abandonment** parenting style has no rules. Although these two styles lie at opposite ends of the continuum, they are similar in their effects upon children. The two central parenting styles, namely, **Nonnegotiable Rules** and **Negotiable Rules**, are the patterns that support children's development of healthy structure and are the most helpful to both children and parents. The pairs of parenting styles at the two opposite ends of the continuum—**Rigidity** and **Criticism** on the left and **Permissiveness** and **Abandonment** on the right—do not provide children with healthy structure and are considered to have negative effects (Figure 4–1).

Based on Clarke, J. I., & Dawson, C. (1998). *Growing Up Again: Parenting Ourselves, Parenting Our Children* (2nd ed.). Minneapolis, MN: Hazelden. Note: These authors produced the parenting program Self-Esteem: A Family Affair® (SEFA) (1978).

---

or abandonment of children's needs for adequate structure. Some rules will be negotiable while others, by necessity, will not. Negotiable rules will lead to healthy feelings of self-esteem in children. On the other hand, rigidity, inflexibility, having mostly nonnegotiable rules, and abandoning children's needs will damage children's self-esteem. When enforcing rules, it is wise for parents to decide how and when to use their authority, when to be lenient, and when to penalize children for misbehavior. Rules constitute a significant aspect of the patterns that govern the functioning of the family system and the parent–child microenvironment. Without some form of rules, the family system cannot function effectively for the benefit of its members. It is essential that rules for children's welfare and development be formed rationally rather than emotionally.

7. *Discipline is most effective when provided to children within a nurturing atmosphere.* By nurturing their children, parents show them that they are loved unconditionally and are lovable (J. I. Clarke & Dawson, 1998).

Nurture relates to all of the ways in which we demonstrate love, not only for others but also for ourselves. Nurturing involves touching, noticing, and caring in healthy ways. Nurture that is shown toward children takes two basic forms, and each of those forms has many variations. **Assertive care** is expressed when a parent determines what a child's needs are and responds to those needs in a loving way that generates a sense of trust in the child. Assertive care involves noticing and listening to the child and understanding the cues and

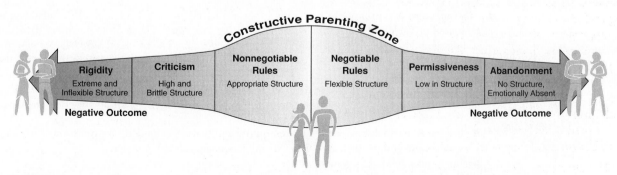

FIGURE 4–1. Continuum of structure in parenting styles. The central shaded area represents the zone of constructive parenting behavior.

requests that the child offers. **Supportive care** is provided as children grow older and can make decisions for themselves about what kinds of attention and care they need from their parents. In providing supportive care, parents offer care at appropriate times, and children are free to accept or decline that care.

Both forms of care are derived from love that is unconditional. This means that love is given freely, without expectations, limits, or measure. The parent's message to the child is "I love you because you are who you are."

In reality, both assertive and supportive care can be given by parents in ways that are both positive and negative. When such care is offered positively and consistently, children's growth and development as individuals are facilitated in healthy ways. When care is offered negatively or inconsistently, love is conditional rather than unconditional and is manifested as conditional care, indulgence, or abuse and neglect (J. I. Clarke & Dawson, 1998). This form of care and these behaviors on the part of parents indicate harshness in dealing with children, which results in negative and harmful effects that are manifested as unhealthy self-esteem. Parents' treatment of children when applying discipline teaches children about themselves and leads them to make conclusions about their self-worth.

Both assertive and responsive care can be dimensions of **responsive** care, in which both parent and child interact in an ongoing bidirectional manner and the parent is sensitive to the needs of the child.

● ●

Parenting Reflection 4–3

What is the difference between child abuse and disciplining children? At what point does discipline become abusive?

● ●

● ●

Focus Point. Many people believe that discipline is synonymous with punishment. Discipline refers to teaching children appropriate behaviors through positive means. Parents need to determine acceptable methods for disciplining children and to develop rules and boundaries that provide children with structure and teach them to internalize self-discipline.

● ●

Parenting FAQ 4–1

As parents of a young child, we would like to take a formal parenting course to guide us. Any suggestions on how to choose the most appropriate parenting program?

In reviewing parenting programs, an estimate was that over 15,000 different parenting programs are available worldwide. That figure includes programs in many languages. Narrowing it down to programs in English still leaves an overwhelming number of choices. The following decision tree may help to narrow down the possibilities:

■ The outcomes of a number of parenting programs have been assessed, and a brief selection is tabulated in Table 4–1 as *Evidence-based Parenting Programs.* These programs meet stringent standards and have been tested in various population groups. The research results have been statistically analyzed and published. There are about 250 programs that meet these requirements, and the list is growing.

■ Determine the age of the child or the needs of the target group. Programs can be quite specific in addressing specific content areas and age groups. Among the various programs are the following:
  ■ Programs presented by trained group leaders.
  ■ Programs in which formal training is required and that are intended for professionals working with certain groups, such as youths with addiction and related disorders.
  ■ Programs intended for parents within the family context.

(Continued)

- Programs requiring group sessions with other parents. These programs can be highly beneficial in forming a support group and in understanding what other parents are experiencing.
- Programs that can be studied individually, through DVDs and printed material.
- Programs based on different theoretical underpinnings. This can be a challenging choice, and guidance from a trained professional may be helpful in making the final decision.
- Non-evidence-based parenting programs vary tremendously in quality. Some advice you may get can be outright harmful. For that reason, it is important to choose wisely. Look at the context of the program, check online reviews from reputable sources, and become an informed user.
- Seek guidance from people who, through their training and background, are knowledgeable and well informed—for instance, Certified Family Life Educators (CFLEs), Licensed Social Workers (LSWs), Licensed Professional Counselors (LPCs), educators, and licensed psychologists.

Focus On 4–3

Mental Health Resources

Including Parenting Programs

National Registry of Evidence-based Programs and Practices (NREPP)

www.nrepp.samhsa.gov

The U.S. Department of Health and Human Services maintains an objective and detailed registry of resources related to *mental health promotion* in the broadest sense. Many of these interventions focus on *parenting* and *child-related themes*. Prevention of addiction and related disorders features strongly in the formula for supporting mental health. The NREPP acts as a liaison between persons seeking programs to implement and the program developers. For many organizations and professionals in the helping professions, this is a valued and trusted resource.

This registry is not exhaustive; instead, it is constantly growing, with more than 250 interventions, and many more programs in the pipeline for review (NREPP, 2012). A search for programs focusing on *parenting* listed around 40 results, and more programs may be suitable, depending on the age of the child, parental concerns and the context in which the program is administered.

To be included in the registry, programs need to reflect evidence-based practices, as supported by the quality of the program's research and its readiness for dissemination. Interventions and programs are reviewed by panels of experts and have to meet stringent criteria in the following areas:

- For quality of research (QOR),
  - Reliability of measures
  - Validity of measures
  - Intervention fidelity
  - Missing data and attrition
  - Potentially confounding variables
  - Appropriateness of analysis
- For readiness for dissemination (RFD),
  - Availability of implementation materials
  - Availability of training and support resources
  - Availability of quality assurance procedures

Source: U.S. Department of Health and Human Services, Substance Abuse and Mental Health Services Administration (SAMHSA). (2012). *National Registry of Evidence-based Programs and Practices* (NREPP). www.samhsa.gov

PARENTING STRATEGIES

Many child-rearing approaches have emerged over the past 75 years, each advocating a particular approach to discipline. These strategies are representative of modern applied behavioral science. None guarantees consistent results in children's behavior or in parents' interactions with children.

Strategies are developed by considering a variety of approaches that will hopefully accomplish something desirable. Parents develop strategies for child rearing as well, hoping that they will accomplish both short- and long-term goals. In the short term, parents may set limits on children's behavior for the safety and well-being of children and in order to help them behave in socially approved ways in public. In the long term, parents may develop rules that teach children the fundamentals of human interaction, as well as the consequences of particular behaviors.

Systematic reviews of parenting programs identify a number of theoretical frameworks, and the following broad classifications are based on this extensive research (Bunting, 2004):

- *Behavioral Parenting Programs* are based on social learning principles that use positive reinforcement, negotiation, and finding alternatives to punishment.
- *Cognitive Behavioral Parenting Programs* use the principles of behavioral parenting, but add cognitive elements to help parents restructure and reframe their thinking about their children and parenting their children.
- *Relationship-Based Parenting Programs* focus on listening and communication skills. Many basic principles used in counseling are applied to parent–child communications.
- *Multimodal Parenting Programs* combine the elements of various programs and are eclectic in nature.

Rational emotive therapy parenting programs also exist, although these are in the minority. They aim to reduce emotional stress and reinforce rational beliefs (Bunting, 2004).

Based on the National Society for the Prevention of Cruelty to Children in the United Kingdom (www.nspcc.org.uk). The website presents a number of available parenting programs. Included are reviews by the Cochrane Collaboration, among the largest organizations in the world that are engaged in producing systematic reviews (Bunting, 2004). Of all the parenting programs reviewed, 75 percent were carried out in the United States, 17 percent in Canada.

Different reviews have used different categorizations, and there is a lot of overlap between the programs. In general, most parenting programs seem to focus on the *behavioral* component, although combining approaches is also popular (*multimodal* approach), especially a combination of the behavioral and the relationship dimensions. See Table 4–1 for more information.

| Focus On 4–4 | **Identifying Positive and Negative Nurture** |

Positive nurture represents love for a child which reflects parenting behaviors that act in the best interests of the child. These actions lead children to experience positive nurture in the form of unconditional love, which facilitates joy and hope. These attributes in turn promote self-confidence and positive self-esteem.

Negative nurture: When parents abuse children physically, mentally, and/or emotionally; provide conditional care; act indulgently; and neglect children physically, mentally, and/or emotionally, the nurture provided is negative. Such treatment leads children to experience despair, joylessness, depression, and loneliness, all of which are damaging to self-esteem and self-worth.

Sometimes this negative parenting behavior is referred to as "poisonous pedagogy" or "toxic parenting."

Based on Clarke, J. L., & Dawson, D. (1998). *Growing Up Again: Parenting Ourselves, Parenting Our Children* (2nd ed.). Minneapolis, MN: Hazelden.

Behavioral Parenting Programs

Behavior Modification. Using behavior modification techniques (Bloch, 2003), parents teach children acceptable behavior by reinforcing desirable behavior and weakening undesirable behavior. According to this view, all behavior is a learned response. Just as children are taught to read, they are taught to behave appropriately in a variety of situations. A parent intentionally or unintentionally encourages and shapes certain behaviors in a child by responding to how the child acts. A child learns to adopt a given behavior pattern if it accomplishes a desired goal (Van Houten & Hall, 2001).

TABLE 4–1. Evidence-based Parenting Programs

Useful Resources	Evidence-based Parenting Programs
National Registry of Evidence-based Programs and Practices (NREPP) U.S. Department of Health and Human Services	The U.S. Department of Health and Human Services maintains an objective and detailed registry of *Parenting* programs, which have met certain standards of evidence-based practice. Program details such as cost, resources, implementation practices and potential target audiences, are also available at this site. www.nrepp.samhsa.gov **Selection of Some Evidence-based Parenting Programs Listed in NREPP**
Active Parenting Now	Based on Adlerian parenting theory. Ages 2–12. Video based. Defined by mutual respect and democratic family functioning.
Combined Parent-Child Cognitive Behavioral Therapy (CPC-CBT)	Empowering families who are at risk for physical abuse. A structured treatment program. Children ages 3–17 and their parents.
Incredible Years	A highly rated, award winning, *exemplary* program. Comprehensive, multifaceted and developmentally based for children ages 2–12, their parents and teachers. Implemented worldwide, the program translated into numerous languages. Developed by Carolyn Webster-Stratton, PhD.
Nurturing Parenting Programs (NPP)	Family Based Programs. Focus: prevention and treatment of child abuse and neglect. Target groups include high risk families. Developed by Stephen Bavolek, PhD.
Parenting Through Change (PTC)	Theory-based intervention to promote healthy child adjustment. Based on Parent Management Training–Oregon Model (PMTO). Learning effective parenting practices. Target groups include post-divorce parents and single mothers.
Parenting Wisely	Interactive computer-based training programs for parents of children ages 3–18 years. Theoretical underpinnings: Cognitive behavioral, social learning and family systems theory. Developed by Donald A. Gordon, PhD.
Parents as Teachers (PAT)	Early childhood family support and parent education home visiting model. Can enroll during pregnancy through to kindergarten.
Strengthening Families Program (SFP)	A highly rated exemplary program. Life skills courses over 14 weeks, with skill development for both parents and children. Implemented worldwide, program translated into numerous languages. Developed by Virginia Molgaard, PhD & Richard Spoth, PhD.
Triple P – Positive Parenting Program	Multilevel system of parenting and family support strategies. Birth to age 12, with extensions for teenagers, aged 13–16.

TABLE 4–2. Selection of Research Centers Focusing on Child Development

Useful Resources	Description
Center on the Developing Child National Scientific Council on the Developing Child Harvard University	Founded in 2006. Healthy child development is viewed as the foundation of economic prosperity, strong communities, and a just society. Science is applied to promote innovations in policy and practice, with child well-being as the overarching theme. It is funded by numerous foundations and individual donors. Committed to research, education, and public engagement. http://developingchild.harvard.edu
Center on Social and Emotional Foundations for Early Learning (CSEFEL)® Vanderbilt University	Directed at early care, health and education providers, as well as parents. It focuses on birth to age 5 and disseminates research and evidence-based practices to early childhood programs across the United States. User friendly materials. Funded by *Head Start* and *Child Care Bureau.* Under auspices of Administration on Children, Youth and Families, US Department of Health and Human Services. Spanish materials available. Developed the Pyramid Plus® Model together with TACSEI. http://csefel.vanderbilt.edu
National Registry of Evidence-based Programs and Practices (NREPP) U.S. Department of Health and Human Services	The U.S. Department of Health and Human Services maintains an objective and detailed registry of resources related to mental health promotion in the broadest sense. Many of these interventions focus on *parenting* and *child* related programs. To be included in the registry, programs need to reflect evidence-based practices as supported by research and readiness for dissemination. Subsidiary of Substance Abuse and Mental Health Services Administration (SAMHSA) of the U.S. government. www.nrepp.samhsa.gov
Technical Assistance Center on Social Emotional Intervention for Young Children (TACSEI)	Provides free products and resources to help decision makers and caretakers, as well as parents, in their work. Material can be downloaded free from their website. It is based on best practices and evidence-based research. Made possible by U.S. Department of Education, Special Education Programs. Developed the Pyramid Plus® Model together with CSEFEL. http://www.tacsei.org http://challengingbehavior.org
Center for Early Childhood Mental Health Consultation Georgetown University	Created through a grant from the offices of *HeadStart*. Center develops materials and makes them available to targeted audiences, including parents. http://www.ecmhc.org
Centers for Disease Control and Prevention (CDC)	Focus Child Development: Contains many resources ranging from information for parents and educators to research reports, data and statistics. www.cdc.gov
Jumpstart	Jumpstart is a national supplemental program that accesses the community as well as adult–child relationships, to build language and literacy skills. A subsidiary makes new books accessible in underserved settings. Recipient of numerous awards and recognitions including "Best in America" seal from Independent Charities of America. www.jstart.org

TABLE 4–3.   Selection of Commercially Available Parenting Programs

Parenting Programs	Description
Boot Camp for New Dads® (1990)	This program is validated by research and best practices and focuses on *father involvement* in pregnancy, birth, and parenting. As such it fills a vital role in strengthening the fatherhood movement and thus the family. It relies on father-to-father support. It is operated by the New Fathers Foundation, Inc. Spanish version available.
Parent Effectiveness Training® (PET) Thomas Gordon (1975)	A relationship based program, with a strong influence of the work of Carl Rogers (Humanism). Emphasizes skills such as active listening, empathy, negotiation, and a generally democratic parenting style. The program has expanded into related fields such as work contexts.
Self-Esteem: A Family Affair® (SEFA) Jean Illsley Clarke (1978)	A cognitive approach, emphasizing three parts of the personality. Uses affirmations, clear thinking, problem solving and improved self-esteem in both children and their parents. Spanish version available.
Active Parenting® Michael Popkin (1983)	Theoretically multimodal or eclectic: A commercial blend of the ideas of Carl Rogers (Humanism), Alfred Adler (Democratic Parenting), Richard Dreikurs, and Thomas Gordon (PET). Renames the three parenting styles of authoritarian, permissive, and authoritative. Applies active listening, "I"-messages, family meetings, logical consequences, and responsibility.
Systematic Training for Effective Parenting® (STEP) Don Dinkmeyer & Gary McKay (1976)	Theoretically multimodal or eclectic: Influences of Carl Rogers (Humanism), Alfred Adler (Democratic Parenting), and Thomas Gordon. Strong relationship elements. Concepts: democratic parenting, encouragement, active (reflective) listening, I-messages, family meetings. Includes parent homework. Spanish version available.
Behavioral Parent Training® (BPT) Developed by many people, based on B. F. Skinner's work	In essence a behavioral parenting program. Based on the work of Skinner: operant conditioning, rewards and punishments to shape behavior. Course examines how behavior is learned, how to target behavior, how to use reinforcement, tokens and time-out.
The Incredible Years® Carolyn Webster-Stratton (1980)	In essence a behavioral parenting program. Includes aspects of modeling (Albert Bandura). Sometimes referred to as the Webster-Stratton program.
Triple P: Positive Parenting Program® Matthew Sanders et al.: (1977) Sanders, Cann & Markie-Dadds	Theoretically multimodal or eclectic: focuses on prevention. Authors affiliated with the University of Queensland, Australia. Includes social learning models, family behavior therapy, developmental research on parenting and child competence, risk and protective factors, social information processing models. Strengthens parents and incorporates interventions and evidence-based practices. Spanish version available.
Love and Logic® Foster Cline & Jim Fay (1980)	This program has been expanded to fit in educational classroom settings (Schools). Autocratic as well as democratic control. Parents/teachers require "healthy control." Set limits; give choices, responsibility, consequences, child participation. Many interventional tips for specific situations. Reduces stress and anger in parenting and teaching interactions.
Other parenting programs reviewed by Carter & Kahn (1996) in the comprehensive report funded by the Pew Charitable Trusts	HIPPY: Home Instruction Program for Preschool Youngsters MELD: Formerly Minnesota Early Learning Design PAT: Parents as Teachers ECFE: Early Childhood Family Education High/Scope Foundation Avance: Spanish for Advance, Serves Latino Populations

(Continued)

TABLE 4–3.　(*Continued*)

Parenting Programs	Description
Pew Charitable Trusts: Report by Carter & Kahn (1996)	For a detailed summary of some major federal Initiatives as well as the most notable parenting and educational programs of the previous decades, refer to an extensive report funded by the Pew Charitable Trusts. Much additional development has occurred since the publication of the report, but it remains a very comprehensive summary and of historical value (Reference below).

Summary of some well-known commercial parenting programs. Mentioning a commercial program in the text does not represent an endorsement by the authors or the publishers. The sequence of presentation is random and is based on the following sources:

Bredehoft, D. J. (1995). Contemporary Parent Education Programs. In Bredehoft, D. J., & Cassidy, D. *Family life education curriculum guidelines* (2nd ed.). Minneapolis: National Council on Family Relations (NCFR), www.ncfr.org

Bredehoft, D. J., & Walcheski, M. J. (Eds.). (2007). *Family Life Education: Integrating Theory and Practice* (2nd ed.). Minneapolis: National Council on Family Relations (NCFR), www.ncfr.org

Bunting, L. (2004). Parenting Programs: The Best Available Evidence. *Childcare in Practice*. 10(4):327–343. London: National Society for the Prevention of Cruelty to Children (NSPCC), www.nspcc.org.uk

Carter, N., & Kahn, L. (1996). *See How We Grow: A Report on the Status of Parenting Education in the US.* Philadelphia: Pew Charitable Trusts.

Basic Concepts.　The basic tenets of behavior modification are as follows:

- All behavior is learned.
- Behavior is a function of its consequences.
- A given behavior is encouraged and taught when it is immediately rewarded or reinforced.
- Reinforcement may be either positive or negative in nature.
- Learning may be generalized from one situation or setting to another.

Approaches based on behavior modification emphasize an awareness of environmental events and context to fully understand the nature of the stimuli that control behavior. These approaches stress that in the same manner that behavior is learned, it can also be unlearned, changed, or modified. Individuals adjust their behavior according to its consequences. Essentially, people behave in ways that result in positive consequences and avoid behaving in ways that result in negative consequences. In addition, one has to consider the complexity of both learning and unlearning/modifying behavior.

Reinforcement.　Reinforcement maintains that a reward (which serves as the *reinforcement*) must immediately follow a particular behavior to increase the likelihood of that behavior reoccurring in the future. All reinforcers are considered to be stimuli and are either positive or negative. A *positive reward* (positive reinforcer) increases the likelihood that a particular behavior will occur again. An example of positive reinforcement might be praising a child for using good table manners. It is important that the positive reinforcement (praise, in this instance) *immediately follows* the occurrence of the desired behavior. The behavior then becomes associated with its reinforcement.

Negative reinforcement occurs when an unpleasant stimulus is removed, increasing the likelihood of the behavior reoccurring. An unpleasant stimulus associated with a certain type of behavior becomes reinforcing when its withdrawal is a positive or pleasurable experience. For example, *time-out* could be experienced as a negative situation; when it is over, the reward is the withdrawal of this intervention, which is a positive feeling. *Time-out* is an intervention whereby the child is removed from the social environment and has to sit or stand in a specific spot for a short period of time (depending on the age of the child). Often a minute is sufficient. This interrupts the misbehavior.

Parenting Reflection 4–4

If positive reinforcement is so effective in producing desirable behavior in children, why do so many parents continue to resort to physical punishment as a means of discipline?

Extinction.   Behavior modification includes the concept of extinction of behaviors that are undesirable or unpleasant. This concept is illustrated by a teacher who ignores the whining of students. The undesirable behavior is not reinforced when the teacher deliberately does not pay attention to it. Likewise, the undesirable behaviors of children that are not reinforced by attention from parents will eventually cease. This is a difficult process for many parents. The number of times a behavior must be ignored is often high, and it may take a long time for the child to eliminate the undesirable behavior from his or her repertoire.

Reinforcement Schedule.   The frequency with which reinforcers are used is important. Researchers have found that continuous reinforcement of behaviors is not desirable. Intermittent reinforcement is more effective. Two dimensions should be considered:

■ The desired behavior may be reinforced according to the number of occurrences. For example, a child may receive reinforcement only after pronouncing five words correctly.
■ The amount of time between behaviors may determine when reinforcement is given. For example, the child may receive reinforcement every other minute while talking, or there may be a variable amount of time between reinforcements, such as once after 1 minute, again after 3 minutes, and again after 10 minutes.

The use of reinforcement to teach children desirable behavior is one of the most powerful tools available to adults. Because behavior can be bidirectional, children affect the behavior of adults. Through reciprocal feedback, children teach behavior patterns to their parents by applying their own brand of reinforcers. When an adult nags loudly, for example, a child usually tunes out the adult's unpleasant behavior by not listening, thus reinforcing the nagging behavior. Similarly, a child who seeks the attention of parents learns to act in a manner that reinforces parental attention.

Social Learning Theory

The social learning theory is based on the work of Albert Bandura (b. 1925). This theory is especially useful in the context of education and human development, and it explains how socialization occurs and how someone learns appropriate behaviors by modeling. Bandura acknowledged many of the concepts from traditional learning theory, but he added a social element. Three important concepts in this theory are as follows:

■ *Observational learning:*   People (and children, in the context of parenting) can learn from social observation.
■ *Intrinsic reinforcement:*   Internal mental states are part of this learning process.
■ *The modeling process:*   Several factors can play a role in this process, such as the participants, attention, retention, reproduction, and motivation. Learning something does not necessarily imply that it will result in a change in behavior.

According to this theory, an individual responds to a number of complex stimuli in forming associations between appropriate and inappropriate behavior. Conscious thoughts, rather than an automatic response to a stimulus, assist in shaping behaviors and actions.

This approach focuses on the importance and role of a *model*, or learning through *imitation*. Many behaviors are acquired by observing the behavior of others and then replicating them. Research shows that children learn to express social behaviors such as sharing and cooperation, as well as aggression and violence, by seeing a model demonstrate such behaviors. Models include actual people and characters in media presentations. Research indicates that when children see a model being rewarded for acting aggressively, they are more likely to demonstrate the same kind of behavior in their own play. Social learning theory also explains how people acquire social values and attitudes. Social roles are learned and children imitate the behaviors that they observe in adults and in other children who serve as role models.

Parenting Reflection 4–5

When parents model undesirable behavior, for instance, prejudice and discrimination, they are teaching their children these values, attitudes, and behaviors by example. Explain how appropriate parental modeling could contribute to multicultural competence.

Developmentally appropriate interventions are effective in teaching children pro-social behavior.

....

Focus Point.   Behavior modification is a highly reliable method for eliciting desired behaviors from children through the effective, conscientious application of positive reinforcement. Behaviors can be shaped by using reinforcement and paying close attention to the time when the reinforcement is given. Social learning theory emphasizes the influence of modeling and observation for learning a variety of social behaviors and roles.

....

Relationship-Based Parenting Programs

A number of programs and approaches can be grouped within this broad category. Some very well-known programs, including Adlerian-based programs, Parent Effectiveness Training (based on the work of Gordon), and some positive parenting programs (Bunting, 2004)

The democratic approach is based on the following assumptions:

- Behavior is purposeful and has a cause; it does not happen by chance.
- It is necessary to understand behavior within its social context.
- The goals of misbehavior explain the unacceptable actions of children.
- The child's interpretation of the experienced event is important.
- Belonging to social groups is a basic need, regardless of age.
- People, including children, develop a life plan (script) that guides their behavioral decisions, even though these decisions may be based on faulty assumptions and logic.

FIGURE 4–2.   The democratic approach to parenting. Based on Dinkmeyer, 1979; Dinkmeyer & Dreikurs, 2000; Dinkmeyer & McKay, 1981; Dreikurs, 1950.

rely heavily on improving the communication and the relationship between the parent and the child.

The **democratic approach** to child training is based on the work of Alfred Adler (1870–1937) and is incorporated into **Adlerian** psychology (Figure 4–2). In the context of the history of parenting, this is very important, because Adler was one of the pioneers who focused on the unique needs of children. He is credited with opening the first parent–child guidance clinic in Vienna, and he made a significant contribution to mental health and the prevention of mental disorders. Adler thought that good parent–child relations were a key factor in achieving mental health and parental education was emphasized. He ultimately emigrated from Austria to the United States in the early 1930s and took up a professorship at the Long Island College of Medicine.

Rudolf Dreikurs (1897–1972) and his colleagues present a strategy for parenting and discipline, based on Adler's work, that emphasizes democratic approaches such as encouragement, setting appropriate limits, practicing mutual respect for family members, and collective decision making (Dreikurs, 1950). The starting point for developing an effective, loving relationship with a child is for the adult to learn about the impact of the *family system* in shaping the child's emerging patterns of behavior. The family system is seen as the child's model for all social interactions with others (Dreikurs, 1950).

A parental educational curriculum that teaches this strategy is called Systematic Training for Effective Parenting (STEP). Some research reports that the democratic approach appears to show more consistently significant outcomes as a means for attaining parenting goals (Dembo, Switzer, & Lauritzen, 1985; Krebs, 1986; Ring, 2001). Other work does not support this claim (P. W. Robinson, Robinson, & Dunn, 2003).

The *life plan* or *script* is the consistent pattern of decision making by which people make choices regarding their behavior. It is initially encouraged and developed within the family system. The life plan is based on decisions about how to act, which relate to goals and actions. A child discovers that this plan is effective in solving certain interaction problems within the family system, especially within the sibling and parent–child subsystems. As a child grows older, he or she develops a personal logic to justify the actions that make up the life plan. Different life plans emerge under each of the different parenting conditions: abuse, neglect, conditional love, indulgence, assertive care, and supportive care. If a parent consistently responds to a child's behavior in an indulgent manner, the child may adopt a life plan that involves being manipulative, self-indulgent, and self-centered. When children are taught in ways that cause them to reach faulty conclusions about themselves, or they draw these conclusions on their own, they develop life scripts that contain behavioral choices that support these faulty conclusions. See Figure 4–3 for more details.

Democratic child training recognizes the impact of a child's sibling subsystem in influencing behavior. Dreikurs, following Adler's premise, believes that birth order and position among siblings in the family system act to shape the child's life plan. Within a given family, there are differences in the siblings and their life plans as the participants vie for parental attention, sibling alliances, and varying parental expectations. For instance, being the oldest child generally brings heavy responsibilities and high expectations from the parents. The middle child may learn power-oriented or attention-getting types of behavior in order to be noticed. The youngest child may learn attention-seeking patterns by displaying inadequacy.

Logical Versus Natural Consequences. A key element of this strategy, featured strongly in the STEP program, is teaching children the logical consequences of their behavior as opposed to using rewards or

Four basic goals of misbehavior are identified in this approach:

1. *Attention seeking.* The child exhibits negative behaviors that attract attention, such as showing off or crying. Although it seems counterintuitive to an adult, the child will misbehave or act out in order to receive attention. To the child, negative attention is better than no attention at all. An alternative for the parent may be to give attention for positive behavior when the child is not making a bid for it. Ignore misbehavior when possible.
2. *Social power.* The child controls others by only doing what he or she wants to do and by refusing to cooperate. An alternative for the parent may be to withdraw from the conflict. The parent can help the child learn how to use power constructively by appealing for the child's help and enlisting cooperation. Fighting or giving in only increases the child's desire for power.
3. *Revenge.* The child retaliates when he or she feels hurt or unloved by misbehaving. An alternative for the parent may be to avoid hurting the child's feelings, avoiding punishment and thus retaliation. The parent should strive to build a trusting relationship and convince the child that she or he is loved.
4. *Displaying inadequacy.* Failure in all endeavors becomes expected and is used by the child to avoid participation in interactions with others. An alternative for the parent may be to stop all criticism; encourage any positive attempt, no matter how small; and focus on the child's assets. Above all, the parent should neither pity the child nor give up.

FIGURE 4–3. The rules of misbehavior according to systematic training for effective parenting (STEP).

Based on the work of Dinkmeyer, D., & McKay, G. D. (1981). *Parents' Handbook: Systematic Training for Effective Parenting*. Pines, MN: American Guidance Services.

punishment. The child assumes personal responsibility for his or her actions (Ring, 2001), reducing the need for authoritarian behavior by the parents. For example, if you touch a hot stove, you get burned. Natural consequences are sometimes either too dangerous to be allowed or too remote in time to be effective for teaching children about the results of their actions. In such cases, the parent must substitute a logical consequence—a consequence that is a rational result of a given action. For example, if a child arrives home after the evening meal has been served, the logical consequence of the child's tardiness (which should have been established and agreed to by all family members in advance) is that the child must prepare a meal or eat cold food. When administered consistently, the child concludes that to avoid the unpleasant consequence, he or she must be more punctual.

This technique places the responsibility for the choice of behavior, as well as its consequences, on the child, not the parent. A child learns to think, make plans, weigh the consequences of decisions, and accept responsibility for those decisions. A consequence must be experienced fully and consistently by a child before it can be an effective learning tool. Parents must resist the temptation to intervene and prevent the child from experiencing the consequence.

Encouragement Instead of Reward or Punishment. A major tenet of this strategy is that stimulation from within is more effective in producing desirable behavior than is pressure from without. With this strategy, encouragement replaces reward, and a logical consequence replaces punishment. Encouragement and reward are different in both timing and effect. Encouragement is given before an act takes place; a reward is given afterward. Encouragement is given when an attempt is made, regardless of any difficulty or failure experienced. A reward is given only when the child succeeds.

The Family Council. The democratic basis of this strategy is reflected in the use of the family council, or meeting, as a means for reaching agreements, communicating effectively, and helping children develop a sense of participation in the family. It is suggested that these meetings occur on a regular basis, and that children be allowed an equal voice and vote in reaching family decisions. Such decisions may be related to establishing logical consequences for disobeying family rules, determining the use of family resources, and resolving disputes among members of the family.

• •

Focus Point. The democratic approach to discipline strives to help children learn to become self-disciplined by experiencing the logical consequences of their behavior. Children's misbehaviors are seen to relate to the particular goal that they wish to achieve through their behavior, which, in turn, is related to their particular life script. Encouragement is an important tool that is preferred over reward or punishment. Family councils are recommended as a means to enable children to participate in family decision making.

• •

Relationship-Based Principles to Increase Parental Effectiveness

A number of parenting programs incorporate basic counseling techniques that can be applied in many communication situations across disciplines, for example, with children, in marriages, and at work. One of the earlier programs that seems to have withstood the test of time (Wood & Davidson, 2003) is *Parent Effectiveness Training* (Gordon, 1975/2000), which represents a humanistic strategy for promoting a healthy relationship between parents and children. These approaches also teach parents how to be more effective in their caregiving and disciplinary activities.

The counseling-based strategies focus primarily on the communication skills developed by the parent and a method for resolving the conflicts that occur between the parent and the child. As with other humanistic methods, such as those promoted by Haim Ginott (1922–1973; Ginott, 1965), these strategies teach the parent when to act as a counselor to children regarding their behavior. These approaches are firmly grounded in proven counseling techniques and are applied to parenting skills. Although these techniques are effective when performed appropriately, their overuse may lead a child to tune out the parents, rendering their efforts ineffective. Children of parents who have received this training exhibit greater self-reliance with regard to problem solving and a higher degree of self-esteem.

In essence, the following proven counseling principles are applied to achieve a more effective manner of communicating and interacting with children:

1. *Active listening.* The parent engages in active listening, a common therapeutic technique used in counseling. Instead of rescuing the child by offering solutions and suggestions for solving the problem for the child, the parent listens to the child and sifts through the child's statements to determine the feelings being covertly communicated. The parent then sums up the perceived problem. The goal is for the parent to empathize with the child, providing a nurturing response, and objectively reflect back to the child

Parenting FAQ 4–2

Should a parent use threats to gain a child's cooperation with parental wishes?

Threats are used when a parent feels exasperated, tired, and powerless. Sometimes they are used because a parent does not know of any other way in which to gain a child's cooperation. Threats often act to stimulate a child's noncompliance with parental wishes, promoting an "I dare you" stance between a parent and the child. Such interactions can become power struggles between the parent and the child, which are not healthy for the relationship. Instead of helping a child learn how to achieve win–win solutions to problems, threats force a no-win outcome on the child. Threats can be an exhibition of power. Using forceful threats can lead a child to fear the parent, which does not support an open, respectful communication style. Additionally, threats can damage the self-esteem of some children. If threats are overused and applied incorrectly, they will be discounted by the child.

A major problem with using threats is that they often involve hollow consequences or ones that are difficult to enforce. Imagine the reaction of a 5-year-old to hearing a mother's threat: "If you don't stop doing that, I'll throw you out of the window!" The preschooler may not fully grasp all the implications, namely, that the threat is dangerous and irresponsible to enforce, nor may the child understand that the parent will not carry out the threat. The threat may instill fear and mistrust in the child.

Threats are also undesirable if one parent plays off the other—for instance, if the parent who is present evokes the powers of the absent parent to strengthen his or her own authority. The absent parent is pulled into a battle that he or she did not choose to fight, and this could push unsolicited responsibility on the absent parent.

Using positive alternatives, such as choices rather than threats, may help to gain a child's cooperation with regard to rules that have clearly identifiable consequences. Give the child time to mentally and physically complete a task. Making children aware of time constraints can foster time management skills so that children can plan their activities to fit into schedules. Remember the courtesy of saying "please" and "thank you." These, too, should be modeled to show respect and appreciation. Here is an example of a threat and an appropriate alternative:

Threat: "This is the last time I'm telling you to stop what you're doing and come to dinner, or else you'll go hungry tonight!"

Alternative: "We'll be having dinner in about 10 minutes. Please finish up what you are doing, stop playing, and put away your toys so you'll be ready for dinner. Thanks for doing this!"

Based on Faber, A. (1995). *How to Talk So Kids Can Learn: At Home and in School.* New York: Rawson Associates.

the parent's perception of the problem. The child is allowed to search for his or her own solution.

Parenting Reflection 4–6

When is it developmentally appropriate to use effective communication techniques, and would these ever become ineffective with a child?

2. *"I" Messages.* Parents can express their feelings to children about troublesome behavior in *nondamaging* ways. On those occasions when a child's behavior is a problem to a parent, the child may not know that he or she is causing a problem, or the child may be testing a parent's limits. At times, children just can't seem to resist the temptation to misbehave, even though they know that they will get into trouble for doing so. In such situations, the parent "owns" the problem. The child's behavior is problematic because it is troublesome to the

parent. A trusted technique used in many applications of good communication is to reframe messages so that they are "I" messages. In other words, the child is not attacked by the parent; instead, the parent describes the effect of the behavior on him or herself.

Without having learned to do otherwise, most adults, when discussing someone's offensive behavior, begin with *you*: "You're acting stupid." "You are doing that all wrong." or "You are driving me crazy with all that noise." Such "you" messages often occur in cases where the adult is angry about the other person's behavior. A more effective presentation, especially when an adult wants a child to listen to what he or she is saying, takes into consideration the following:

a. Begin the message with the word "I."
b. Next, add how the parent feels ("I get angry . . .").
c. Then label the problem ("I get angry when I see you hit your sister").

"I" messages differ from "you" messages in that they enable a parent to effectively communicate a message to a child without damaging the child's self-esteem. "You" messages can contain content that would hurt the child's self-esteem, such as "You are acting stupid" or "You are doing that all wrong."

"I" messages are used to get a child to listen to what an adult has to say, to communicate facts to the child, and to help the child modify the unacceptable behavior. When parents learn to use this format, children also acquire the skill and begin to express their feelings to parents in nondamaging ways. "I" messages place the responsibility for changing the child's behavior on the child rather than on the parent, and they are less likely to promote resistance and rebellion in children. The communication has to be adjusted to meet the developmental level and characteristics of the child concerned.

3. *Negotiation skills and conflict resolution.* In essence, this process is based on a bidirectional interaction, where both parties bring something to the table and a mutually agreeable resolution is sought. All too often, individuals in families believe that in resolving conflicts there must be someone who wins and someone who loses. This belief tends to promote adversarial situations in which the parent and the child are pitted against one another in a power struggle, each attempting to win by gaining his or her own way. In employing

a no-lose strategy, the parent and the child strive to reach a win–win solution based on a compromise that is satisfactory to both. Neither the parent nor the child wins or loses when resolving the conflict; they come to an understanding that mutual needs must be satisfied to some degree in order for both persons to be happy with the solution. A logical sequence for working through a problem may contribute to a better outcome. This applies to work and partnership situations as well, and it also is an element of good negotiation skills. Keys to good conflict resolution practices include the following:

■ Identify the conflict and share the responsibility for conflict resolution.
■ Generate possible solutions, which at the same time develop the child's cognitive skills.
■ Evaluate the solutions, thereby increasing communication between the parent and the child.
■ Decide on the best solution for both parties, thus avoiding destructive emotional effects.
■ Work out ways to implement the solution without the parent exerting power over the child.
■ Evaluate how well the solution worked, considering the benefits of encouraging autonomous behavior from the child.

In *bidirectional* parenting, it is helpful to recognize the influence of children's behavior on parents and to teach children to recognize the rights and needs of parents. Respectful parenting allows both parents and children to interact on a more equal basis instead of relying on power-assertive methods that damage children's self-esteem.

Nonnegotiable situations: Importantly: When children's safety is endangered or there are time pressures, it is the adult's responsibility to behave in the best interests of the child, keeping safety in mind.

In practice that means that the responsible adult makes an appropriate decision and the situation is nonnegotiable.

The rules are (1) *safety first*, and (2) do that which is *in the best interests of the child*.

....

Focus Point. Bidirectional communication between parents and children allow both parties to actively participate. There are times when adults can be helpful to

**Parenting
FAQ 4–3**
My partner and I often disagree about how to discipline our children. We usually get into arguments about who's right and which rules our children have to follow: hers or mine. Sometimes the kids will play us off against one another. How can we resolve this?

There are always going to be differences between parenting partners. These usually happen because we are raised by different families of origin having different rules and different values. Many people believe that both parenting partners *must* agree on everything—every rule and every consequence for obeying or disobeying the rules. It may be essential to reach an agreement about how to prioritize those rules, which ones are more important than others and which are negotiable and which are not. Rather than reaching a consensus by trial and error, it is best to do so through explicit discussion and agreement. This will help everyone realize that there are some things that both parenting partners do not budge on, whereas some rule are important to one parent but are not an issue for the other parent. Such arrangements usually are not harmful to children.

children by simply listening to their problems, using active listening techniques. When a child's behavior is offensive or problematic, parents need to communicate this to the child in nondamaging ways by using "I" messages. When there is mutual respect during conflict resolution, parents and children learn to develop satisfactory compromises.

• •

Ineffective Disciplinary Methods

A review of the research literature on parental disciplinary practices suggests that there are at least four methods that do not work well in providing structure for children and gaining their compliance (Chamberlain & Patterson, 1995):

■ Discipline or parental behavior that is inconsistent
■ Irritable, explosive practices
■ Inflexible, rigid discipline
■ Low parental supervision and minimal involvement

Inconsistency in parental behavior and discipline serves primarily to confuse children about how they are expected to behave. Children receive mixed signals when a parent enforces a rule with its attendant consequences, but at another time relents and does not enforce the rule or its consequences. When parents fail to agree on certain policies or rules about children's

behavior, children may also interpret this response as parental inconsistency.

Some parents appear to have only one type of reaction to children's transgressions, for example, loud emotional outbursts such as yelling, screaming, or exhibiting violent physical acts of aggression. The intensity of the parental reaction and the degree of punitiveness usually escalates in relation to the frequency that the child misbehaves.

When parents employ inflexible, rigid discipline, they appear to rely on one type of punitive strategy regardless of the nature of a child's transgression. No matter what a child does that is unacceptable, the parent reacts the same way. What is lacking is a *hierarchy* in an organization of parental reactions that links the seriousness of the offense to the nature of the parental reaction. Typically, when parents rely on this inflexible approach, they do not employ verbal reasoning with a child when transgressions occur. Rather, the parent reacts in the same manner with little assistance given to the child on how to learn from the mistake.

When parents provide poor supervision combined with minimal involvement, children feel like they have been abandoned and neglected emotionally. Left to their own devices under such circumstances, children are at risk for experiencing a wide range of behavioral problems, poor school performance, and failure to develop effective interpersonal skills.

Parental responses to child behavior that are positive in nature, such as hugs and smiles, can shape future behavior by strengthening the child's self-esteem.

PARENTING STYLES AND MODELS

Parenting styles refer to those collections of child-rearing behaviors that tend to be global in nature. They refer to an umbrella of parental behaviors. Parenting styles characterize an overall approach to parenting, while parents can display a variety of behaviors that change and are modified by a number of real-life circumstances. Parenting styles also reflect a philosophy of parenting that characterizes what parents emphasize in shaping children's developmental behaviors. Parenting styles encapsulate those attitudes and beliefs that form the implicit rules that guide a person's behavior as a parent. These have a significant influence on behavioral choices in interacting with and guiding the child toward adulthood.

Behavioral and social scientists recognize a group of basic categories in parenting styles. Initial work revealed three basic styles: authoritarian, authoritative, and permissive (Baumrind, 1966). It is thought that parents initially adopt one particular style that strongly influences the manner in which they interact with children, but that this position shifts according to particular situations, for example, in public or private settings and in response to children's needs as they change developmentally. Parenting styles are adaptable within family systems as parents attempt to maintain homeostasis within this relationship. For example, when a child is preschool age, authoritarian-style parenting provides assertive care, and promotes appropriate standards for children to control impulses. The parenting style shifts toward the authoritative style when children reach school age and supportive care is mixed with assertive care. Later, as children reach adolescence, parenting styles relax and become more permissive as teens take increasing responsibility for their own decisions and actions. *Developmentally appropriate* parenting is called for to accommodate developmental changes in children.

Parenting styles may vary according to ethnic group or social class. For example, middle-class parents might be more authoritative, while blue collar parents may operate within a more authoritarian approach.

Authoritarian Styles

Authoritarian styles are firmly grounded in traditional methods of child rearing. Authoritarian parenting relies predominately on controlling children's behavior and places value on obtaining children's immediate and long-range obedience to their wishes (Baumrind, 1966). Typically, this parenting style involves controlling children's behavior in every respect. Obedience is obtained in numerous ways, but physical punishment and other forceful means are often used to gain the child's cooperation. A typical response to a child's questioning of rules (and an authoritarian parent has many, many nonnegotiable rules) may be, "Because I said so." Usually this parenting approach evaluates, judges, and shapes the behavior of a child according to an established and often absolute standard to which the child is expected to conform. The parent's word is law for the child, who is taught to believe that the parent's actions are always in his or her best interests. Children raised according to such standards are not encouraged to think for themselves or to think critically, but to look to their parents for approval and solutions to problems.

Authoritarian styles are not considered to be especially conducive to promoting children's emotional health (A. Miller, 1990, 2002, 2006) because parents intimidate children rather than promote healthy feelings of self-worth. Authoritarian parents heavily incorporate negative criticisms to provide what they consider appropriate child guidance into adulthood. Alice Miller (1990) refers to authoritarian parenting as *poisonous pedagogy* because this style appears to promote parenting behavior that is, in effect, emotionally abusive and damaging to a child's self-esteem. Miller believes that the net result of this parenting style robs children of their spirit, promotes the development of self-doubt, and inhibits normal emotional development in later life.

Some authoritarian-based parenting programs are commercially available. A particularly hazardous approach guides parents toward rigid scheduling of infants, with the advice to let babies cry while they learn to fall into a schedule. This approach has been associated with *failure to thrive* (FTT) in babies, as well as involuntary early weaning of infants. Another authoritarian approach is applied to preschoolers and sanctions spanking. This can be particularly risky advice to parents who themselves are recovering from abuse in their families of origin.

Dealing with out-of-control and high-risk teenagers in special educational "boot camp" settings should not be confused with parenting programs for normally developing children. These are therapeutic interventions for select high-risk populations, who frequently already have a history of family court involvement.

Clearly, authoritarian-based programs address the parental need for control, whereas the research repeatedly emphasizes bidirectionality in parent–child relations and *responsiveness* to infant and child needs in order to lay the foundations for further healthy and well-adjusted development.

Permissive Styles

Permissive parenting avoids excessive control, does not enforce obedience to externally defined standards, and basically allows children to regulate their own activities (Baumrind, 1966). Parents who use this style believe that they should respond to their children as individuals and encourage them to be autonomous. This style typically incorporates reasoning and manipulation rather than overt demonstrations of power to gain children's cooperation. Parenting behaviors are expressed in ways that communicate these beliefs. For example, a permissive parent is not interested in being viewed by a child as an authority figure or as an ideal person to be imitated; rather, this parent wishes to be seen as a resource that the child can use for learning about the world.

People who practice permissive parenting styles allow greater latitude in children's behavior. Policies or limits to behavior are determined in consultation with children in an attempt to allow them to voice their own opinions. Children are expected to learn from their mistakes and to use the consequences of their actions as a guide for how to act in the future. However, Baumrind found that the least self-reliant, curious, and self-controlled children were being parented under this style. The anti-establishment movement in the mid-1960s favored this type of child-rearing approach, but the pendulum has swung in the opposite direction with later generations of "helicopter" parents, who hover over their children (Figure 4–4).

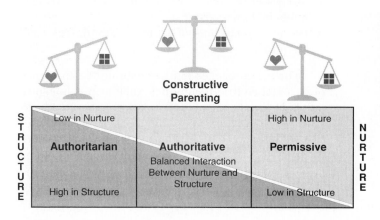

FIGURE 4–4. The degree of structure and nurture displayed in three parenting styles. From left to right the figures represent:

Authoritarian: High in structure, low in nurture.

Authoritative: Balanced interaction between structure and nurture; optimal parenting style.

Permissive: High on nurture, low on structure.

Styles

...les combine the best features of both
...an and permissive orientations. Authori-
... ...mphasize the development of autonomy
in childre... ...ut within reasonable limits. When providing structure, authoritative parents may resort to tac-
tics such as reasoning, overt demonstrations of power
through mild punishment, or psychological reinforcement (Figure 4–5). The structure is expressed in a
verbal give and take, where the reasoning behind the
policies that the parent establishes is shared with the
child, and the child's opinion is heard in the appropriate
context (Baumrind, 1966). Children of parents using
this approach tend to be self-reliant, self-controlled,
content, and curious about learning and exploring their
environment.

Later research (Baumrind, 1991, 1994, 1996)
found that this parenting style is particularly effective
when children become adolescents because it coin-
cides with the appropriate autonomy that young adults
seek. This parenting style encourages a child's success
in school, development of a healthy sense of personal
autonomy, and positive work attitudes (Steinberg,
Elmen, & Mounts, 1989). Breaking down this parenting style into certain behaviors by parents, Gray and
Steinberg (1999) report that three particular types of
parenting behaviors make this style effective with adolescents:

- *Acceptance and involvement* in the ways that parents
  respond to their children's needs and individual differences
- *Strictness and supervision* in parental monitoring
  and supervision of their children's behavior in order
  to bring conformity to family rules
- *Granting autonomy* to encourage the teen's expression of individuality and permitting participation in
  family decision making

Other Classifications

Another way to classify parenting styles uses the dimensions of *warmth/responsiveness* and *control/demand*
(Maccoby & Martin, 1983). When the basic parenting
styles are viewed through these lenses, authoritative
styles are seen to be high in warmth and high in control, authoritarian styles are seen to be low in warmth
and high in control, and indulgent or permissive styles
are seen to be high in warmth and low in control. A
fourth parenting style identified using this typology,
termed *neglectful*, is seen to be low in warmth and low
in control.

Based on these observations, Baumrind (1991, 1994,
1996) states that authoritative parental approaches appear to promote healthy, socially responsible outcomes
for children that include

- Acceptance rather than rejection and firm, but not
  rigid, policies.
- Emphasis on critical thinking skills, individuality, and
  self-initiative.
- Models of the behaviors and attitudes that parents
  want children to adopt.
- Parental explanations of the reasons for the rules and
  the policies.

These approaches omit examining the influence
of parental control techniques, such as psychological
and behavioral control, as a means for shaping desirable children's behaviors and behavioral outcomes
(Bean, Barber, & Crane, 2006). It is not clear whether
these types of categorizations are effective in helping
parents understand the effects of parental models and
strategies on child outcomes (Grolnick & Pomerantz,
2009).

Authoritarian

"Mom, can I go outside and play with Sophia?"
"No."
"Why not?"
"Because I said so; don't ask again."

Permissive

"Mom, can I go outside and play with Sophia?"
"Whatever; you can go outside and play with Sophia,
then we'll be late for the movie. Do as you like."

Authoritative

"Mom, can I go outside and play with Sophia?"
"I don't think that's such a good idea right now because
we're running late and we are trying to make it to the
movies in time. Remember, we had decided to go to
the movies together? There will be another time for
you to play with her later, okay?"

FIGURE 4–5. Parenting styles.

Parenting FAQ 4-4

My friends are using time-outs as a way to discipline their children. Are there any guidelines for using time-outs?

The best interventions occur when the parent is calm. Do not discipline in anger. A *time-out* is an effective way to interrupt negative and disruptive behavior. It is time away from play or from disruptive behavior. Here are some helpful guidelines:

- Time-out periods should not be too long; often a minute or two is sufficient for younger children.
- It is helpful to have a designated spot for time-outs, such as a specific mat, stool, or step on the stairs.
- Do not send a child to their room for a time-out because they may develop a negative association with their own room.
- Stay in the vicinity to supervise the child and to ensure his or her safety, but do not interact verbally with the child.
- When parents and children are calm, it may be a good opportunity to explain why the time-out occurred, and why the particular behavior was unacceptable. Do this *after* the time-out, when the child has calmed down.
- Once a time-out is over, do not continue to remind the child about it or, even worse, shame the child about the behavior. A time-out should be a period that ends with a brief explanation and the child's apology. The intention is that the child learns from the situation.
- Do not overuse a time-out as an intervention because it may become ineffective if it is the only form of discipline that the parent uses. Regard a time-out as one approach among many and use it only when the situation calls for it.

Families who celebrate together develop a sense of unity, which promotes family cohesion.

...lels

...all families are healthy nor do they ...ith positive outcomes. The reality is ...s can be abusive to children. The blueprints for... positive and negative parenting styles are acquired by way of observing and modeling the behavior of one's parents in the family of origin. Social learning theory states that many social behaviors are acquired through observation while growing up. These models can have long-lasting, long-term effects that are manifested in a child's adult years and may even have an afterlife in how the next generation is parented. Several parenting models, along with their common traits, are described below.

Demanding parents often conduct child rearing using an authoritarian style. These parents require children to believe that they must live their lives according to the adult's standards and ideas about what is acceptable and appropriate. Guilt and manipulation are used. Children are treated consistently as if they are totally helpless and must be dependent on their parents, regardless of their abilities or age. Children react to such treatment over a long period of time by developing a high need for parental approval, as well as exhibiting learned helplessness or practicing deception.

Critical parents interact with children by criticizing and being judgmental. This tactic can be used as a means to achieve control over children. Such behavior can motivate both the parents and the children to maintain a high degree of family secrecy. Substantial personal boundaries minimize intimacy, and rigid rules regulate behavior. Both the adults and the children suffer from low levels of personal esteem because of the pervasive air of failure that permeates their relationship. Children have overdeveloped feelings of guilt and sensitivity when errors are made.

Overfunctioning parents send consistent messages to children about their ineptitude that sustain the parents' overprotective behavior. These parents feel overly responsible for a child's actions and manage almost every aspect of a child's life. Some family therapists feel that overfunctioning parental behavior arises out of a deep fear of being abandoned.

Disengaged parents are emotionally uninvolved. These individuals appear to be too busy or self-absorbed to function adequately as parents. They might not have learned to love or be loved as children, and as parents they are unable to express these emotions. Depression in parents can make it very difficult for them to engage in social contexts. Chronic illness, disability, and mental illness can intrude on a good parent–child relationship and represent an obstacle in establishing and maintaining appropriate parenting behavior.

Ineffective parents are incapable of meeting the needs of children and accepting the responsibilities of parenting. Many reasons may underlie this parenting model, such as addiction and related disorders or chronic illness. Children assume roles that are far beyond their abilities—for example, when an older child assumes the full-time care of younger children.

Abusive parents harm children emotionally, physically, and even sexually. These parents were often abused by their own parents and are prone to repeating such actions. The emotional scars left on children take much effort and time to heal when they become adults (Sandberg et al., 2012).

It is possible to alter one's parenting style by consciously becoming aware of one's actions and how these actions impact a child's growth and development. Working with a competent family therapist is one way of making constructive changes.

● ●

Parenting Reflection 4–7

Reflect on the parenting style/model exhibited by your own parents. Based on what you observed and what you remember, can you predict what model/style you will adopt when you become a parent?

● ●

● ●

Focus Point. Three basic parenting approaches include authoritarian, permissive, and authoritative. Each influences child outcomes differently. *Authoritative* parenting appears to be especially effective in child rearing. Other models of parenting behavior may be unhealthy and are acquired through observation and modeling of one's own parents. More constructive parenting behaviors can be learned as one breaks the destructive patterns from the family of origin.

● ●

NORMAL BEHAVIORAL PROBLEMS OF CHILDREN

Frequently, there are conflicts between parents and children over socialization tasks, relationship concerns, and gaining compliance from children. Many situations that are termed normal behavioral problems are actually a problem for the adult and not the child. Similarly, many problems are simply a normal part of development as children strive to accomplish specific tasks but experience difficulty in mastering them. These may relate to the age of a child: What is normal behavior at one stage may be problematic at another and may indicate some type of developmental or emotional disturbance. Parents need to be aware of the difference between normal behavioral problems and problems that are indicative of a serious disorder that calls for professional attention.

POINTS TO CONSIDER

■ Parents serve as children's first teachers about life, including how to interact with others and the imparting of important values and attitudes. A competent parent actively acquires knowledge about children's growth and development and gains experience in using a variety of methods and strategies that facilitate healthy parent–child interactions.

■ One of the greatest parental concerns is providing adequate and appropriate discipline. Discipline is used to help children acquire socially appropriate behavior according to the patterns supported by their family system. Effective discipline should be positive, moderate, developmentally appropriate, and acknowledge the particular child's needs.

■ Discipline is often mistakenly seen as the punishment used to control children's misbehavior. Spanking and other forms of physical punishment are not recommended as part of any disciplinary program. Effective discipline aims to provide children with structure (self-discipline) and nurture (love).

■ Discipline is facilitated when caregivers (a) attempt to identify and understand a child's feelings and motivations; (b) discuss and adopt a consistent plan of disciplinary methods; (c) attempt to accomplish effective communication with children by listening to their opinions and feelings; (d) allow children to learn to make decisions, as well as mistakes, and to take responsibility for their actions; and (e) base discipline on the use of rules, some negotiable and some non-negotiable, as well as assertive and supportive care.

■ A variety of methods or strategies are available to contemporary parents for use in establishing disciplinary programs for children.

■ The disciplinary strategies discussed are derived from modern behavioral science and range from reward and reinforcement to ways to facilitate effective communication between parents and children. These strategies include behavior modification and programs that incorporate basic principles from counseling, such as active listening, respectful negotiation, and developmentally appropriate communication styles.

■ Four characteristics describe these disciplinary strategies: (a) Each seeks to reduce parental power over the child's behavior and fosters reacting in positive ways that do not damage children's self-esteem. (b) Children are taught to learn self-discipline in controlling their actions. (c) Caregivers are provided with proven, effective means of communication that help reduce conflict and facilitate healthy interpersonal interactions. (d) Each seeks to help parents gain a better understanding of children's growth and development.

■ Behavior modification involves the use of positive rewards and the reinforcement of desired behaviors from the child. Caregivers use these methods to teach children how to behave appropriately. Reinforcers must immediately follow a desired act in order to be effective. Caregivers may teach a complex task to children in sequential stages using reinforcement as children master progressively more difficult behaviors. In addition, caregivers must be aware of the ability of children to reinforce certain parental behaviors because the relationship is bidirectional.

■ A central tenet of the democratic approach to parenting presumes that (a) there are reasons for children's actions; (b) parents must attempt to understand children's behavior by determining and analyzing the child's reasoning for his or her behavior; (c) everyone has a basic need to belong to a social group; and (d) people develop a life plan that guides decisions to behave in certain ways, and that a life plan may be founded on faulty assumptions. A child's birth order in a family has a strong influence on the kind of life plan that the child develops. Parents are encouraged to teach children that there are logical consequences, either positive or negative, to behaviors, and family rules and policies should be supported. Children's behavior is positively shaped rather than resorting to the use of overt rewards. Regular family meetings establish policies and rules that are used to resolve conflicts, as well as the consequences for obeying or disobeying the rules. Children and parents should have an equal voice during such meetings.

■ Principles from counseling enhance communication skills and conflict resolution between parents and children. Effective communication (a) allows the parent to act as a counselor when a child has a problem, (b) allows an intervention when a child's behavior is causing a problem, and (c) recommends compromise in order to resolve conflicts between parents and children. An example of this type of approach is Parent Effectiveness Training.

■ There are three basic parenting styles: authoritarian, permissive, and authoritative. These styles are modified by the dimensions of warmth and control.

■ Some models of parenting behavior, ranging from neglectful to toxic, are acquired by observing the model provided by one's own parents in the family of origin.

■ Parenting education can teach parents constructive skills, supporting them in breaking destructive cycles and offering the next generation an improved parenting experience.

USEFUL WEBSITES

American Academy of Pediatrics
www.healthychildren.org

Australian Institute of Family Studies: Parenting Styles and Strategies
www.aifs.gov.au/cfca/bibliographies/parentingstyles.php

Children's Defense Fund
www.childrensdefense.org

Family and Parenting Institute, United Kingdom
www.familyandparenting.org

Institute for Education Sciences: What Works Clearinghouse.
www.ies.ed.gov/ncee/wwc/

National Institute of Child Health and Human Development
www.nichd.nih.gov

What Works: Effective Prevention Programs for Children, Youth and Families: University of Wisconsin-Madison
http://whatworks.uwex.edu/Pages/2evidenceregistries.html

PART II

The Work of Parenting

The work of parenting encompasses the active socialization of children into adulthood and usually spans about 25 years, or a third of the average adult life span. Parenting clearly becomes one of the very strong themes in most adult lives. On-the-job training, especially while rearing the firstborn child, seems to be the norm.

One of the distinctive characteristics of the process of parenting children is that parental developmental needs are evolving in tandem with the changing developmental needs of the child. There are numerous subtle shifts, refinements, and adaptations over a lifetime of parenting. For example, as a child matures and grows, parents must change from being physical helpers to psychological helpers and assist the child in coping with cultural, as well as family, expectations.

Other expressions of caregiving also change as parents adapt their ways of providing structure and nurture to accommodate the needs of growing children. When children are young, physical expressions of nurture dominate parenting styles. Increasingly, the emphasis shifts to also include experiences that teach structure. As children grow older, these physical expressions of nurture are replaced by verbal methods such as providing encouragement and reassurance, and listening to their problems. Parents change their methods for controlling a child's behavior in response to the life span development of the child. Psychological and verbal guidance methods play a greater role when children enter their preschool, school-age, and adolescent years.

We will review the process of becoming a parent in all its richness and variety. It is a commitment that will continue over a lifetime.

His own parents, He that had father'd him, and she that had conceiv'd him in her womb, and birth'd him, They gave this child more of themselves than that; They gave him afterward every day—they became part of him.

Walt Whitman (1819–1892), American Poet, From Leaves of Grass

---

CHAPTER 5

The Transition to Parenthood

Learning Outcomes

After completing this chapter, readers should be able to

1. Explain how some of the justifications for parenthood have shifted over the centuries and how the decision to become a parent has become more complex.

2. Explain the impact of first-time parenthood on a couple's committed relationship.

3. Describe some of the typical adjustments and reactions to pregnancy.

4. Describe some of the challenges, legal as well as social, in fostering or adopting children.

5. Explain why new parents could benefit from support and describe the types of support systems generally available to them.

DO I WANT TO BE A PARENT?

Historically, it was taken for granted that married couples would have children if they were biologically able to do so. With medical advances, circumstances have changed. Family formation can be planned, even timed, and assisted reproductive technology can help certain couples move toward their dreams of parenthood. People have greater freedom of choice, but this, too, has been accompanied by some unique challenges. In many cases, couples emotionally plan to have children long before conception and birth. Couples typically discuss how many children they want and prepare for the entry of children into their family system.

Complex issues are considered in making this decision. Nowadays, economic considerations play a central role (Lino, 2011). Children are no longer considered to be an economic asset as they were in the past. To a contemporary American family, children can be an economic liability; for this reason, many people delay childbearing until they have established a sound financial base in order to cover the many expenses involved. Others delay having children until further educational or lifestyle goals have been achieved. In addition, a variety of social pressures, as well as emotional factors, contribute to the decision to become a parent. Potential parents must examine the role that children play in fulfilling their different needs, values, and functions within a particular family system.

● ●

Parenting Reflection 5–1

Explain why our society's views have gradually changed toward someone who does not desire to be a parent. What factors may motivate someone to remain childless? Would you consider parenthood a prerequisite to being emotionally and socially fulfilled, or is it unrelated? Justify your position.

● ●

Economic Factors

People consider the economic costs of having children very carefully, possibly because they often have a choice in whether or not to become a parent. Economic factors relate to a couple's desired lifestyle, as well as educational outcomes, and can contribute to delayed parenthood. Although the costs of childbearing and child rearing vary widely, it has been estimated that for a middle-class working family in the United States, about one fourth of the total lifetime income is devoted to meeting the costs of raising a child from birth through age 18 (Lino, 2011). Another way to look at the financial outlay is the estimated total costs required for child rearing. For a child born in 2010, this may require an estimated $225,000 until the child reaches age 18. This translates to about a thousand dollars per month. In a breakdown of family expenses, expenses related to

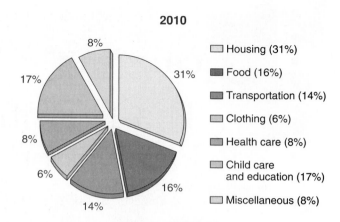

2010

- ☐ Housing (31%)
- ■ Food (16%)
- ■ Transportation (14%)
- ☐ Clothing (6%)
- ■ Health care (8%)
- ☐ Child care and education (17%)
- ☐ Miscellaneous (8%)

Total = $226,920

FIGURE 5–1. Expenditures on a child from birth through age 17, total expenses and budgetary component shares, 2010[1].

[1]U.S. average for a child in middle-income, husband-wife families.

raising a child rank about third, after the family home and health care. A more specific estimate of the large-ticket items are home (31%), health care (22%), child-related expenses (17%), food (16%), and transportation (14%; Lino, 2011). Thus, family expenditures to provide housing, to meet the needs of children, for transportation, and for food consume the majority of a family's income (see Figure 5–1). These costs account for about half of the total outlay necessary for raising children to maturity (Lino, 2011).

Another cost of child rearing, which is not often considered by those contemplating parenthood, is the potential loss of family income while one parent is not gainfully employed outside the home, although that is counterbalanced by the stay-at-home parent providing care that might otherwise prove to be costly. Increasingly, and especially during the economic recession, fathers have taken on child-rearing responsibilities while mothers have been able to find gainful employment in economically competitive and challenging times. Some parents choose not to reenter the workforce until the youngest child enters kindergarten. The ability to raise children with full-time parental supervision is regarded as such a valuable privilege that some parents choose this option, even if it is accompanied by financial and career sacrifices (see Figure 5–2).

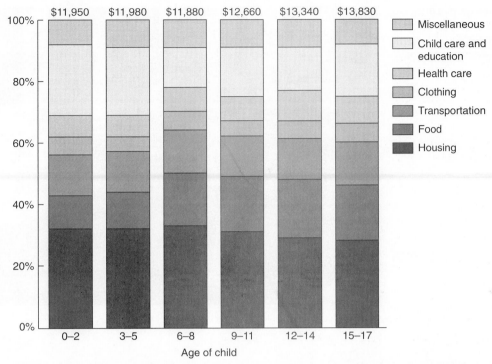

FIGURE 5–2. Total expenses and expenditure shares on a child (as a percentage of total child-rearing expenditures), by age of child,[1] 2010.

[1]U.S. average for the younger child in middle-income, husband-wife families with two children. Child care and education expenses only for families with expense.

Structural Factors

Several structural factors that relate to and influence economic considerations enter into the decision to become a parent. The marital and employment status of the parents are an important consideration (Federal Interagency Forum on Child and Family Statistics, 2010). Single mothers tend to have significantly lower household incomes than married women. This directly influences the quality of life that a woman can expect when raising a child as a single mother versus as a married mother. The factors that play a role in this outcome are that a younger single mother might interrupt her education for parenthood, and this closes the door to obtaining higher wages from jobs that require a longer educational path. Additionally, a single mother has to carry the burden of an entire household, whereas in a partnership or marriage, this responsibility would be shared.

Child care is a top priority when both parents return to the workforce. Finding a source of reliable,

economical child care, especially for an infant, calls for careful consideration. Many families in the United States rely on relatives or in-home (family) care of children when parents are both employed outside the home. Others rely on agencies, nonprofit organizations, co-ops, and proprietary services for substitute child care. Use of these services is often seen as less desirable than parental care, although research strongly suggests that children are not harmed by nonparental care during the early years of their lives, as long as it is good-quality care and there is continuity of the significant caregivers (Griffin, 2011).

The socioeconomic status and ethnic group of a family also influences the decision to pursue parenthood. These factors are associated with the values and functions that adults ascribe to having children and the number of children that a couple desires.

A group's *fertility rate*—the number of biological children that a woman has—reflects these factors as well. Hispanics are currently the fastest growing minority in

Planning for child care is an important parenting decision. Parents rely on high quality child care and consistent caregivers.

the United States, partly because they have larger families than other ethnic groups (Humes, Jones, & Ramirez, 2011). Additionally, more women are completing college educations, entering the workforce, and postponing marriage into the later years of early adulthood. These trends tend to promote fewer births and are also related to more prevalent use of birth control, differences in the rate and type of employment, and a tendency to limit family size to maintain a certain lifestyle (Hamilton, Martin, & Ventura, 2010).

Because of our culture's strong *pronatalist* (pro-birth) bias, adults who are married are socially coerced to become parents. Perhaps the greatest pressure comes from a couple's parents, who express their desire to become grandparents. Simultaneously, there is also a veiled message to couples to limit the number of children that they have because of concerns regarding overpopulation and general economic pressures.

Psychosocial Factors

Complex psychosocial factors contribute to the decision to become parents (Clark, Richard-Davis, Hayes, Murphy, & Theall, 2009). The reasons for having children have shifted from the need for a strong familial workforce in the past to reasons of a psychological and

social nature today. The many factors that affect the decision about whether to become a parent are shown in Figure 5–3.

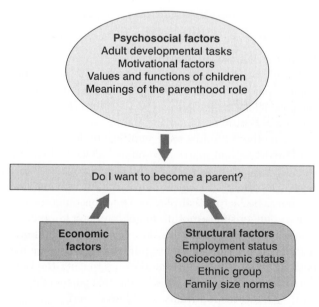

FIGURE 5–3. Complex interrelated factors influence decisions concerning parenthood.

Parenting FAQ 5–1

I've been married for several years and have a very good relationship with my spouse. There are no children and we probably won't have any in the future. There are times when I'm uncertain that this is what I want. What should I consider with regard to my decision about having kids?

This is something that should be a joint discussion between you and your partner; and you need to find common ground concerning your decision. Each family may have unique circumstances that contribute to decisions regarding parenthood; for instance, blended families may face slightly different challenges from those of first-time marriages. Whether one has children from a previous marriage may play a role. Some issues to consider include the following:

- Are you conforming to group pressure because all of your friends have kids?
- Are you prepared financially, emotionally, and socially to experience the changes associated with having a child?
- How does a newborn fit into your and your spouse's life plans?
- What do you think you'll do if you second guess your decision to have become a parent?
- A child doesn't necessarily improve a marriage relationship; instead, it may introduce new challenges.
- A child is not a remedy for improving an ailing marriage. Seek counseling first.
- Do you like children? Do you enjoy playing with them? Have you spent time with children and know how they change everything else about your life?
- How might you feel if you have a child who has special needs?
- How might you feel about your decision to become a parent a decade or two from now?
- Your children are not a mirror of yourself nor can you live your dreams through your children. Each child is unique.
- Can you accept your child as an individual who is distinctly different from you or your spouse?
- Are you aware that you are not responsible for your adult children's successes or failures?

Parenting Reflection 5–2

What are some advantages and disadvantages of having children nowadays? What are some ways that society's expectations of parents can be made more realistic?

Reasons for Becoming a Parent. Many personal reasons enter into a person's decision about whether to become a parent, and most people genuinely appear to want children. These reasons may have their basis in the beliefs of one's family of origin, social class, or ethnic group. Motivations for becoming a parent may be present long before an individual has children and are seen as antecedents of the varying attitudes that people have toward this adult role. When children are born, adults' underlying reasons for becoming parents may be played out in a child-rearing script that they follow without questioning it. In many ways, the reasons for wanting to be a parent may be closely associated with the experience that a person expects to have when interacting with a child. Although these reasons are highly personal and unique to each individual, there is a strong psychosocial theme that reflects pleasure in child rearing, feelings of love and affection, and attitudes of generativity.

There is a *fatalistic* component to the desire to become a parent. Some people may be strongly motivated to become a parent because they believe that procreation is the primary reason for their existence. These beliefs may be supported by religious doctrines.

A different aspect of a fatalistic reason to have children is to ensure the continuation of one's family name and genetic line. In some cultures and family systems, males continue to be highly valued because family names are perpetuated through them, or there

There are a variety of reasons for wanting to become a parent. Children represent many things to parents, and the parenthood role holds a variety of meanings.

may be special significance attached to male heirs. In some countries, this gender-biased thinking has led to a surplus of male offspring and now there is a shortage of available women to marry.

The primary motivation for having children and becoming a parent can be *altruistic* in nature. Such reasons include an unselfish desire to express affection and concern for children. The desire to express one's

---

Focus On 5–1 **Some Reasons for Having Children**

There are more reasons for having children than we can possibly count because there are so many different motivations that people have for wanting to assume the role of a parent. On the flip side, there must be many reasons for someone to rationalize not becoming a parent.

Here are some reasons for becoming a parent that were obtained from Internet blogs:

■ The experience of delivering a new life into the world is singularly exhilarating. If you fear pain, there's this lovely thing called an epidural.
■ A couple becomes a family; the whole becomes greater than its parts.
■ Children are some of the most charming little people I know: full of wonder, curiosity, and innate kindness. Properly nurtured, they become equally charming adults.
■ I am not ideal . . . why should I expect my children to be? Kids teach us the joy of unconditional love and acceptance.
■ Relive childhood and all of its innocent wonder and mirth.
■ To have a happier marriage or committed relationship.
■ Free entertainment: Kids are hilarious!
■ Having someone to help you when you're old.
■ The pains of labor are worth it.

Based on Karen Edmisten (2007). "40 Reasons to Have Kids." Retrieved from http://karenedmisten.blogspot.com/2007/10/40-reasons-to-have-kids.html; and Kim C. (2010). "100+ Reasons to Have Children." Retrieved from http://inashoe.com/2010/07/reasons-children

sense of generativity may be satisfied through parenting experiences.

Parenthood provides an outlet for the fulfillment of one's psychological need to be needed, according to Erikson's concept of generativity. This aspect can also be considered a *narcissistic* motivation to become a parent. Narcissism in this context refers to the expectation that having children will reflect on the goodness of a person and serve as a concrete, visible statement of maturity and adequacy as a sexually active adult. It is also related to the need to conform to one's peers. Another narcissistic aspect is the idea that children will provide their parents with emotional security and love. There is no guarantee that children will reciprocate a parent's love; in some ways, love has to be earned.

Other reasons for becoming a parent are *instrumental* in nature; that is, the children become instruments for the wishes of the parents. For example, many parents wish for children to achieve specific goals because they believe that children are obligated to please their parents and meet the desires and goals of the parents. Their expectation is that children will reach levels of achievement that they were not able to achieve, such as getting a college education, learning a particular skill, or being successful in a certain career. In essence, parenting is then seen as a second chance at life. Some parents may unconsciously believe that they can relive their own childhood through their children. Similarly, some parents are motivated by the hope that their children will not repeat their mistakes. Many young men appear to want children, but they are concerned about being an ideal father, for example, providing adequately for a family (R. Thompson & Lee, 2011).

Another instrumental reason for becoming a parent is to secure an intimate relationship. Some people mistakenly believe that having children will rescue a troubled marriage. In reality, the presence of children does not appear to help or hinder marital satisfaction. Unfortunately, the increased strain on adults caused by managing multiple roles is likely to contribute to difficulties in a marriage. Studies that compare marriages with and without children find that marital satisfaction is greatest or is enhanced among couples who do not have children (Schulz, Cowan, & Cowan, 2006). Clearly this is a complex situation, and contrary to these findings, some parents—especially older first-time parents and parents with good support systems—report predominantly positive outcomes from having children.

Having a child can also be a way to please one's own parents. It is not unusual for older parents to pressure, either subtly or directly, their adult children to become parents. The desire to be a grandparent may be the paramount explanation. Middle-aged parents wish to conform to their peers who are grandparents. Adult children may give in to this coercion to reduce the guilt that arises from disappointing one's own parents.

● ●

Parenting Reflection 5–3

Is it possible to fail to successfully adapt to parenthood? What happens when someone has a surprise pregnancy, is opposed to abortion, or does not wish to give a child up for adoption? How do they face the many challenges of involuntary parenthood?

● ●

Parenthood and Committed Relationships

The committed relationship of a couple acts as a foundation for their family system. Forming such a relationship requires time, effort, and commitment to resolving conflicts, developing patterns, and achieving a level of healthy functioning. The focus of the first years following the commitment of marriage is devoted to achieving these ends.

Our culture supports romantic notions about parenthood and child rearing that may deceive adults about what these roles require. Folklore or common sense implies that parenthood improves a couple's marital relationship and that a truly successful marriage is one in which happiness predominates all of the time. Many childhood fairy tales end with the words ". . . and they lived happily ever after." We grow up with the unrealistic expectation that somehow marriage is the panacea for all of life's challenges.

Reality introduces the couple to their parenting roles. Like other everyday routines, becoming a parent requires restructuring and reorganizing of a couple's committed relationship. A new baby, especially a firstborn, elicits both positive and challenging reactions. Researchers who study the effects of parenthood on marital satisfaction have consistently reported that rather than improving a couple's relationship, the presence of children is associated with decreasing marital satisfaction (Carlson, Pilkauskas, McLanahan, & Brooks-Gunn, 2011). The quality of marital satisfaction begins to decline following the birth of the first child (Lawrence, Nylen, & Cobb, 2007). It continues to do so as the child grows, culminating in its lowest point when the child reaches middle childhood, and then improves as the children goes through adolescence and on into early adulthood.

Role Strain.   At first, research seems to indicate that children are detrimental to a couple's marital happiness. This is *not* the direct reason. The children are part of a configuration that leads to increasing *role strain* during the initial years of child rearing, and it is this feeling of being pulled in all directions that causes the decline in marital satisfaction. Role strain occurs when adults attempt to succeed at several competing social roles. In most family systems, this means that both adults attempt to cope with the multiple roles of worker, parent, and marriage partner. When individuals try to perform all of these roles at a very high level of proficiency, the effect is that performance in all roles suffers to some degree.

Because most individuals understand that children's needs often take priority over personal needs, their roles as marriage partners take less precedence in terms of expending energy and resources (see Figure 5–4). Essentially, while coparenting arrangements become part of a couple's committed relationship, these are likely to be maintained at the expense of other aspects of the couple's relationship (Fagan & Palkovitz, 2011). New parents may experience a decline in sexual relations or in social activities during their transition to parenthood because infant care demands a greater proportion of their energy, time, and resources.

This information strongly suggests that it is important for couples to develop a strong committed relationship prior to having children because the marital relationship typically receives less attention while they are actively involved in child rearing. Most couples have some idea that their lives will change when they become parents and that their marital relationship will be challenged to some degree. Other couples are surprised that the introduction of children tends to reorganize the marriage into a traditional gender-role orientation. Women frequently assume traditional mothering and housekeeping roles, while men gravitate more toward their careers and their role as a provider. This tends to occur even among couples who are gender neutral about roles within the home and family. However, there is a generation of men who are involved and dedicated fathers, and take pride in this role.

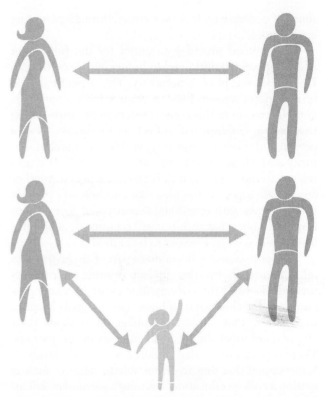

FIGURE 5–4.   The addition of a child into the family unit adds to the complexity of the system.

Becoming a parent for the first time involves certain costs, as well as benefits, regarding a couple's committed relationship (Woo & Raley, 2005). One of the costs is with regard to cohabitation versus marriage in the transition to parenthood. Apparently, cohabitating women experience greater declines in social and psychological well-being upon becoming a first-time mother. Cohabitating couples who believe that they have a future together are likely to continue a pregnancy (Sassler, Miller, & Favinger, 2009). If couples realize that problems can be anticipated in their committed relationship following the birth of a child, especially a firstborn, then they are likely to have an increased awareness of the need to maintain their relationship (Hofferth & Goldscheider, 2010). Cohabiting women may also see a pregnancy as an added strain on the relationship.

The arrival of a child is unlikely to destroy a couple's relationship, but it is not likely to salvage one that is troubled. Although both partners may expect decreases in opportunities for shared leisure activities, many partners find other ways to experience their intimate relationship.

Parenting Reflection 5–4

How can couples prepare and successfully cope with the anticipated decline in marital satisfaction if they know in advance that this is a likely outcome of having children?

Focus Point.   New parents experience a period of adjustment regarding their new roles following the birth of their first child. Although early researchers viewed this as a crisis event in the family's life span, a more contemporary view is one of transition. The transition to parenthood is influenced by several factors, such as the timing of the birth of the first child and the gender of the adult. One of the major adjustments is the shift in priorities within the marital relationship toward the parental roles. Satisfaction with marriage often declines because of the stress that adults experience in managing their new roles.

ALTERNATIVE AVENUES TO PARENTHOOD

Assisted Reproductive Technology

Approximately 12 to 15 percent of couples desiring offspring require medical intervention to fulfill their desires for parenthood (National Center for Chronic Disease Prevention and Health Promotion & American Society for Reproductive Medicine, 2009). The field of assisted reproductive technology (ART) is developing rapidly. The accompanying legal and ethical issues demand attention as well. In a social context, ART has become so well accepted that couples are no longer secretive about it. The media has also given this theme ample attention in popular films, bringing it out in the open as a viable and accepted alternative. The reasons for infertility are often medically related. In some instances, the reasons for seeking medical intervention can be social in nature, as when a single woman seeks to become a mother.

Medical technology has advanced to levels that were unimaginable in the past, allowing persons to have children under some of the most incapacitating reproductive

situations. These services first became available in the early 1980s and have become increasingly sophisticated. The success rates of the various methods vary because so many factors play a role, such as the cause of infertility, the age of the mother, and the particular treatment methods used to attempt to achieve a pregnancy. The treatments may cost thousands of dollars and often are not covered by insurance plans. Many people are willing to endure significant hardships in order to achieve biological parenthood. Other individuals who have fertility problems adopt children or become foster parents as a means of achieving parenthood.

There are a number of techniques available to a couple who desires to become biological parents. Medical teams specializing in ART can guide the couple toward making the best decisions. Some of the better known approaches include the following:

- Fertility drugs
- Artificial insemination by donor
- In Vitro Fertilization/Embryo Transfer (IVF-ET)
- IVF combined with intracytoplasmic sperm injection (ICSI)
- Ovum transfer
- Gestational surrogacy (surrogate mother)

Challenges Related to ART.   A number of ethical, legal, and psychosocial issues are involved in ART, some of these are related to the cultural values associated with parenting (see Figure 5–5). Difficult decisions must be made regarding embryo selection and preservation. When a surrogate parent is involved, the legal issues multiply. Payment for donor eggs or for carrying a pregnancy to term involves moral issues as well. How often should the sperm of a particular donor be used? If the same donor fathers too many children, is there a chance that his offspring may possibly date and marry later in life? Some sperm donors have wanted to get to know the children conceived. Is this fair to the children? Should children who are conceived using this technology be told of their origins? How accessible should the information concerning biological donors be to the child conceived through ART?

Some concerns exist about the quality of parenting among those who have used ART. The role of biological parenthood in influencing the strength of psychological attachment between children and parents has been studied. One study suggests that this factor is not as important

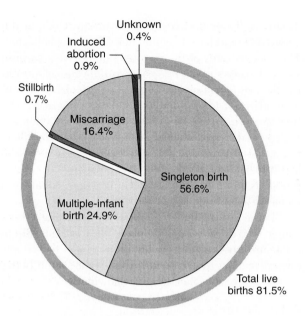

FIGURE 5–5. Outcomes of pregnancies resulting from ART cycles using fresh nondonor eggs or embryos,*† 2009.

*Maternal deaths prior to birth are not displayed due to small number (n = 7).
†Total does not equal 100% due to rounding.

as it might appear because the quality of parenting was judged to be better among those using these techniques for conception when compared with parents who conceived children naturally (Golombok, Murray, Brinsden, & Abdalla, 2003). In fact, adoptive and medically assisted parents scored similarly in this regard. In some cases, the lengths to which couples with fertility difficulties are willing to go to attain parenthood act as significant motivators to perform well in their parenting roles (V. Mitchell & Green, 2008). This can also add greatly to the stress of parenting, particularly if a parent feels that he or she is performing less than optimally with regard to the parenting task. Children conceived via ART are reported to be no different from children conceived naturally (Bos & van Balen, 2010; Bos, van Balen, & van den Boom, 2007).

Couples who use ART may encounter many setbacks because success is not guaranteed. The experience is emotionally demanding, physically exhausting, and financially draining. The process is psychologically invasive in that the areas of private life become the object of medical concern. Clinic staff and professionals dealing with these situations understand these added stressors, and the patients receive various forms of emotional support and counseling before, during, and after the procedure. There is also a certain amount of grieving if the technique fails and the couple has to relinquish their dreams of biological parenthood.

Surrogate Mothers. Sometimes if a woman has fertility difficulties, a couple can contract with a fertile woman to conceive a child by artificial insemination with the partner's sperm (i.e., the sperm of the infertile woman's partner). The surrogate mother is paid a fee, plus the cost of prenatal care and delivery. According to the contract, the surrogate mother agrees to relinquish all parental rights to the father and his partner when the baby is born. Surrogate parenthood is not adoption, because the father is a legal parent. Another issue that is likely to arise following the child's birth is the child's right to information about the surrogate mother's medical history.

Another variation is the *gestational mother*, who carries a fertilized ovum to term. Although she hosts the pregnancy, the chromosomal material of the embryo is that of the biological donors and, in this case, the gestational mother does not have a genetic link to the embryo.

Parenthood can create greater closeness with grandparents and heightened self-esteem for the couple (Bergman, Rubio, Green, & Padron, 2010). Research on the long-term implications for the children who were created through various assisted reproductive techniques continues. The legal and ethical study of assisted reproduction has been a rapidly evolving area of specialization.

Parenting Reflection 5–5

Is it likely that in the future all pregnancies will be managed by in vitro methods? What would be some circumstances that could lead to such an occurrence?

Focus Point. ART is available for helping many individuals who are experiencing infertility. These methods are very costly emotionally, physically, and financially. It is a rapidly developing area of medical research and intervention. Some couples go through a grieving process when ART fails to culminate in a live birth. Ideally, it can help couples realize their dreams of parenthood.

Adoption

Adoption is a way of caring for children whose biological parents are unable to do so (Ostrea, 2003). The decision to adopt often takes place after a number of unsuccessful fertility treatments (Bausch, 2006). Some families with biological children adopt because they perceive adoption as their altruistic calling. In some blended families, a child may be adopted by the stepparent, giving this parent legal parental rights. This is referred to as second-parent adoption.

Adoption involves the legal, social, and psychological processes of including a younger person into a family system and coming to accept this person as one's relative (L. L. Schwartz, 2000; see Figure 5–6). When adoption laws were originally written in the United States, custom placed a significant emphasis on the importance of blood ties among family members. This was particularly important because of the way that family property was inherited. In more recent times, laws in this country have been revised to make adoption easier and more accessible. It is possible for parents with diverse backgrounds to adopt children from equally diverse circumstances (DeBlander & DeBlander, 2004;

A. E. Goldberg, Kinkler, & Hines, 2011; Varon, 2003; Wells, 2011).

Several factors are associated with the decision to adopt a child (Berkowitz, 2011; Bitler & Zavodny, 2002; Child Welfare Information Gateway, 2011):

- Domestic adoption has slowed in recent years and has been supplemented by international adoption.
- More single mothers retain custody of their children, reducing the population of potential adoptees.
- Adopting a child is primarily a function of childlessness, infertility, age, and altruistic reasons.
- Adopted children are frequently economically more advantaged than children raised by never-married, single-parent mothers.
- There is a greater preference for adopting newborn infants. Although a number of older children and children in foster care seek adoptive parents, it may be more difficult to place them.
- As far as international or intercountry adoptions are concerned, the highest number of adoptees came from China, followed by Ethiopia and Russia. More girls than boys were available for adoption, especially if they were born in China. Most of these children were adopted within the first year of life, although a significant number were adopted during their second year. (Source: U.S. Department of State, Intercountry adoption, 2011, at http://adoption.state.gov/about_us/statistics.php)
- Through prior years to 2009, 60,000 children had been adopted from Russia alone. This gives an indication of the numbers of children settling into families as a result of international adoptions.

The process by which most adoptions take place can be lengthy, expensive, and frustrating. Not every application for adoption is approved by a particular agency, and not all result in a completed adoption. Typically, potential adoptive parents can expect several hurdles as they attempt to achieve parenthood:

- Contacting an agency that will facilitate the adoption of eligible children.
- Screening of the potential parents. Undergoing a home study to determine and support eligibility of the parents.
- Searching for an appropriate child for adoption.
- Seeking a court decree declaring the adoption to be legal and final.

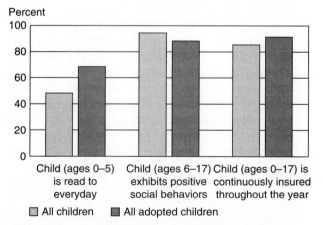

Percent

FIGURE 5–6. Percentage of children with selected well-being measures by adoptive status.

Source: Department of Health and Human Services, Office of the Assistant Secretary for Planning and Evaluation, Administration for Children and Families and National Center for Health Statistics (NCHS), State and Local Area Integrated Telephone Survey (SLAITS), National Survey of Adoptive Parents; and Maternal and Child Health Bureau and NCHS, SLAITS, National Survey of Children's Health.

Types of Adoptions.   A variety of options are available to potential parents and to those placing children for adoption. No local, state, or federal registries maintain a central database for matching potential parents with adoptive children. This is partially due to differences from state to state and from nation to nation regarding the laws governing adoption. The presence of laws that govern adoption, the age and developmental status of an available child, and the potential compatibility between the parents and an available child play a role in the type of adoption that a couple might pursue.

Public Adoption.   Public adoption typically takes place through an agency licensed for placing children for adoption (U.S. Department of Health and Human Services, 2004). These agencies may be nonprofit and sponsored by charities or religious organizations. Potential parents locate the agencies through word of mouth; Web searches; or referrals from lawyers, social workers, or medical sources. The agencies typically offer counseling and education for potential parents regarding the adoption process and what to expect following adoption. There can be a waiting period of up to 5 years as the potential parents are screened and a search is made for an appropriate child. Potential parents can expect to pay an application fee (often quite high), the legal fees involved in formalizing the adoption, the medical costs incurred by the birth mother, and travel costs to collect the child.

Private Adoption.   Private adoptions do not involve an agency; instead, a third party, often an attorney, arranges the adoption between the potential parents and the birth mother (Varon, 2003). These adoptions offer greater control to the potential parents, but may be significantly more expensive than public adoption. It is not unusual for this to be a more risky adoption in that the birth mother has greater latitude in changing her mind, even after the potential parents have paid her medical expenses and signed a contract.

Closed, Open, or Semi-Open Adoption.   Whether public or private, an adoption may be closed, open, or semi-open. Until about two decades ago, all adoptions were *closed* in that the identities of both the adoptive and biological parents were unknown to each party and no communication between these families took place. It was thought that this was the best way to handle identity and attachment issues for both the adoptive parents and the adopted children. An increasing number of adoptions are now *open*. It is possible to determine the identity of the biological parents. Adoptees and their adoptive parents have access to information records. A *semi-open* adoption permits access to information for all parties, but no contact may take place.

Open adoption arrangements are controversial (Sobol, Daly, & Kelloway, 2000). Biological parents may wish for anonymity regardless of the desires of the biological child. Adoptees often cite a need to know the medical history of the biological parents and the family for a variety of reasons. Because many states have laws allowing an adoptee access to the records of their adoption, reunions with birth parents, most frequently the mother, are occurring (Pavao, 2004). These have unpredictable outcomes that may range from very positive to very negative.

Transracial Adoption.   The problems encountered by adoptive families are sometimes heightened when the race of the child is different from that of the adoptive parents and other family members. Several issues have been identified as critical adjustment challenges for multiracial adoptive families (Kennedy, 2004):

- When adoptive parents see themselves as rescuing a child from a potentially disadvantaged life, they tend to cast the child into the role of the victim and expect the child to be grateful for their generosity.
- Some extended family members may have to adjust to a child who is of a different racial background, and this will challenge them in their ability to grow toward greater multicultural competence.
- The insidious influence of racial stereotyping may affect adoptive families; for example, an Asian child may be expected to excel in academics or an African American child in athletics.
- Despite these challenges, research has repeatedly demonstrated that transracially adopted children are not harmed by their experiences, although there are reports of identity issues. In fact, children may benefit from such placements (Swize, 2002). The high visibility of interracial adoptions by celebrities have aided increased tolerance. The frequency of international adoptions has also enhanced tolerance and acceptance.

The issues involved in transracial foster care and adoption are especially accentuated among African American and American Indian and Alaska Native children (Ishizawa,

Kenny, Kubo, & Stevens, 2006). These groups of children are overrepresented in the foster care population when compared to the representation of children in the general population. (Perez, O'Neil, & Gesiriech, 2004). The Multi-Ethnic Placement Act of 1994 and the Adoption and Safe Families Act of 1997 prohibit the delay or denial of placement of children on the basis of disparities between the race, color, or national origin of foster and adoptive parents and that of the child (Barth, Webster, & Lee, 2002).

● ●

Parenting Reflection 5–6

You are the parent of a transracial adopted child. You've been asked to address a group of potential adoptive parents who are likely to pursue this option for creating a family. What advice would you give these adults about what to expect, what to avoid, and ways to react to others who might fail to display multicultural competence?

● ●

International Adoption. Some potential parents tire of the lengthy waiting period often involved in domestic adoption and turn to agencies that assist in placing international children (Robi & Shaw, 2006). The numbers of these adoptions have increased in recent years. Americans have adopted from all over the world, with the majority coming from Asian countries (Office of Immigration Statistics, 2007). The majority of these children were infants at the time of adoption, lessening the cultural adaptation challenges encountered with older adopted children. The Child Citizenship Act of 2001 confers U.S. citizenship to foreign-born children when the adoption is finalized.

International adoptions are noted for their high risk and many difficulties (Bowie, 2004; Gunnar & van Dulmen, 2007; Layne, 2004; M.-K. Murphy & Knoll, 2003). The health histories received may be inaccurate or falsified, increasing the risk of adopting a child with unanticipated medical needs. Prospective parents must pay significant fees, such as all agency and in-country expenses, medical checkups, documents, visa and travel expenses, meals, and lodging. They may not be able to choose a desired child. In addition, the difficulties in gathering a health history for the child and government restrictions may make for a daunting obstacle course. (Humphries & Parks, 2006). American families, including adoptive families, are increasingly multicultural (Chasmoff, Schwartz, Pratt, & Neuberger, 2006). Ultimately, the success of an international adoption may depend on several interacting factors (McGuinness & Pallansch, 2000).

International adoptions have increased. Transracially adopted children may benefit from such placements.

There have also been unsuccessful international adoptions, where the adopting parents wanted to return the child, as if it were an object, after finding out that the challenges were insurmountable. Some cases of aggressive children who attacked their adoptive families have been documented. Contributing factors are early and severe neglect, parental deprivation, and **reactive attachment disorders**. Some of the antecedents to these situations include the following:

■ The adoptive parents may get insufficient or inaccurate information about the adoptee, and the medical histories are incomplete. With limited background information on the biological parents, it is difficult to ascertain whether the child was at risk prenatally, for instance, whether the child was exposed to alcohol or drugs by the mother.

■ According to ethical adoption practices, children should be clearly identified as having special needs or medical concerns so that adoptive parents know how to offer the relevant support and are informed of the unique challenges.

■ If a monetary exchange is involved, which it usually is, it becomes difficult to draw the line between necessary expenses and a possible profit motive on the part of international agencies in the countries of birth of the adoptees. It is unethical to ever attach a dollar amount to the life of a child.

■ Problems with lengthy stays in overcrowded orphanages, extreme neglect, sensory deprivation, and the absence of constant caregivers have been linked to changes in brain development presenting as reactive attachment disorders and developmental delays (Belsky & de Haas, 2011; Sue Gerhardt, 2004).

■ Interventions and psychological techniques aimed at addressing the outcomes of early parental deprivation and concomitant attachment disorders are being researched (Belsky & de Haas, 2011).

Foster Care

Some parents are separated from their children and may be denied visitation or even parental rights because of their abusive and neglectful behavior. Accompanying a dramatic increase in the number of families who experience poverty and related challenges is an equally distressing increase in the number of children who experience out-of-home placements. When a community or state agency has determined that children are not safe in their parents' home or that it is not in their best interest to be exposed to an unhealthy parent–child environment, children can be legally removed from their parents.

The most common placement is into **foster care** or **family foster care**. In this setting, children are cared for by trained and licensed adults who provide substitute parental care. Some of these homes are intended for children with special needs. Foster care could also be provided by a child's relatives. This arrangement is referred to as *kinship care*. In each of these settings, the foster parents are compensated for the services that they provide, although expenses typically exceed the amount that is provided by the supervising agency.

Demographic Data on Foster Care in the United States. The federal government collects information related to foster care and publishes this information annually (Children's Bureau, 2010).

■ The number of children in foster care in 2009 was 423,773, a decline of about 20 percent from 2000. The average age was 9.6 years. The largest numbers were infants less than a year old and adolescents up to 17 years old.

■ The average length of stay in foster care for all children was 2 years 7 months.

■ About 70 percent of all children in foster care were African American or Caucasian. African American children are overrepresented in the foster care population in comparison with the general population.

■ The majority of children in foster care are boys.

■ Most children in foster care wish to be reunited with their parents or to be adopted. These goals are most often attained when foster care is terminated.

■ Those children who were waiting to be adopted spent about 3 years in the system. The majority of these children were between 12 and 16 years of age.

■ The parents of approximately 17 percent of all children in foster care had their parental rights terminated.

Parental abuse and neglect are the most common reasons for placement into foster care. As many as 80 percent of all families involved with child protective services are affected by addictions and related disorders (Children's Defense Fund, 2010).

Parenting Reflection 5–7

Suppose you are a caseworker for child protective services. How would you explain what was happening to a child being placed into foster care because her parents had been charged with running a methamphetamine operation in the family home?

Foster Parents.   Foster parents may be married or single. They come from all social backgrounds and may or may not be fully employed outside of the home (Dickerson, Allen, & Pollack, 2011). Every state has its own criteria for accepting individuals as foster parents. Some criteria for foster parents include

- Being a minimum of 21 years of age.
- Being of good character, being motivated, and providing positive references.
- Having no criminal record or history of child abuse or neglect.
- Having a regular source of income.
- Successfully completing foster care training.
- Being certified in first aid through the Red Cross.
- Passing a home inspection.

Adults who become foster parents are often motivated by their own childhood experiences in foster care or by an altruistic desire to meet the needs of children who come from difficult family circumstances. Many of the children arrive with emotional and behavioral problems and may have been placed repeatedly since being removed from their parents' care.

Foster parents are uniquely challenged by dealing with a variety of issues that are not typically experienced by other adults who care for children (National Foster Parent Association, 2011):

- Supervising a child who has been abused, rejected, or unloved, and has trust issues.
- Being paid little for demanding work.
- Dealing with agencies; social workers; and even angry, defensive biological parents.
- Having little community support or respect for being a foster parent.
- Experiencing a high rate of burnout.

Parenting Reflection 5–8

You are in charge of developing a training program for potential foster parents. Classes will be given weekly for about 3 months. What major topics would you include in the training? What outside speakers would you invite to address the trainees?

Focus Point.   When children are removed from their parents' care, they are placed into foster care or family foster care. This frequently occurs due to parental abuse or neglect, and it is intended to be a temporary solution. Data collected by the federal government indicates that the length of stay in the foster care system is far from temporary for most children. In addition, certain demographic variables are characteristic of children in foster care.

A foster parent is usually not related to the child being cared for, although some children are cared for by relatives. Foster parents resemble other adults in most communities and must meet criteria established by state social agencies in order to be licensed. In addition, they must complete approved training to be foster parents. These parents face challenges that are unique to their situation of caring for unwanted or neglected children.

FACILITATING THE TRANSITION TO PARENTHOOD

Several kinds of support can assist individuals and couples in their transition to parenthood. *Support groups* offer information and education about parenthood (Doherty, Erickson, & LaRossa, 2006). These groups assist individuals and couples in several ways:

- Men are included and welcomed, giving the message that they are essential participants in the parenting process.
- People gain reassurance that others share similar fears, misgivings, and stress regarding becoming or being parents.
- Expectations about parenthood and child rearing can be examined in a safe environment.

First-time parenthood is a transitional point in adulthood and in a couple's committed relationship.

■ Couples can network and create social supports that can take the place of family support that may not be available. It can also help couples strengthen their relationship during the challenging time when they are transitioning to parenthood (Schulz, Cowan, & Cowan, 2006).

Parenting classes may be particularly helpful to new parents, especially during the first few weeks and months following a child's birth (Kelley, Schwerin, Farrar, & Lane, 2007). These classes may be structured according to topics (e.g., infant nutrition, physical care) and may meet for several weeks. The Boot Camp for New Dads® is run by the New Fathers Foundation, Inc. It addresses the unique needs of fathers and strengthens their role in family formation. The all-day session is offered on a weekend, and new fathers are asked to bring their children to the session with them. They are assigned to an experienced father who has previously graduated and whose children are older. This exposes new fathers to a mentor with whom they can relate. The fathers gain insight into what it means to be a new father, what infants are like, what kind of care infants need, and what to expect from themselves and their partners.

Such educational experiences help new parents learn about resources, equipment, and methods for child care. In addition, new mothers who might be at risk of experiencing *postpartum depression* have been assisted in reducing their level of anxiety and parenting difficulties via a program that provides a workbook and weekly support by telephone (Milgrom, Schrembri, Ericksen, Ross, & Gemmill, 2011). New parents who conceived and experienced a successful pregnancy that was facilitated by any of the ART methods also benefit from making a successful transition into their new roles when they have the positive social support of their nuclear and extended families, as well as friends (Gamiero, Moura-Ramos, Canavarro, & Soares, 2011).

The transition to new parenthood can be facilitated when couples successfully negotiate coparenting roles and changes in the division of labor in household tasks, and then renegotiate these issues when conflicts arise (Cowan, Cowan, & Pruett, 2007). Families continue to provide support for new parents, but usually for a limited period following the child's birth. Grandparents are often called upon to provide assistance with older children, help with household chores, provide information about child care, and be generally supportive. If long distances separate extended families, some families consider moving closer to grandparents and to their family of origin to have additional support after the birth of a child.

Another aspect of support for new parents is family leave time from employment. The *Family and Medical Leave Act of 1993*, a federal law, requires qualified employers to grant up to 12 weeks of unpaid leave and continued benefits during any 12-month period to employees for the birth and care of a newborn child. Jobs are also protected during this period and are reinstated upon completion of the leave. Parental leave that is shorter than 12 weeks frequently results in poorer adjustment to work, relationships, and parenting responsibilities by both new mothers and fathers.

Finally, the transition to parenthood becomes very concrete during childbirth. One of the most important preparations that an individual or a couple can make in anticipating childbirth is to participate in childbirth education classes. These are frequently offered as part of one's health insurance coverage by participating physicians, churches, and nonprofit community groups.

POINTS TO CONSIDER

- The decision to become a parent is often based on a conscious decision-making process by adults. It can be influenced by complex issues, such as
  - *Economic considerations* related to the costs of childbearing and child rearing.
  - *Structural factors*, including employment status, values and beliefs, and the desired family size.
  - *Psychosocial influences*. For example, parenthood may be seen as an expected developmental task of adulthood.
  - *Personal reasons*, for example, the values and functions that children may serve for adults.
- Medical technologies are available for assisting individuals and couples who face fertility issues. These expensive technologies include artificial insemination, in vitro fertilization, ovum transfer, and surrogate motherhood. Ethical and legal issues are relevant. This is a fast-developing area of medical research and intervention.
- Adoption involves challenges for both adults and children. Adopted children usually have a greater chance for an improved life situation.
- There are a number of reasons people choose to become adoptive parents, such as completing their family through the addition of children, experiencing parenthood, and for altruistic reasons.

- Prospective parents may choose to pursue different options for adoption, each with its own advantages and disadvantages.
- Adults are encouraged to openly discuss the circumstances surrounding a child's adoption.
- Children are separated from parents and parental rights are terminated temporarily or permanently when children are abused or live in an unsafe home environment. When this occurs, they are usually placed in the foster care system to be cared for by a nonrelative.
- Children in the foster care system wish to find a permanent place within loving families. If their family of origin fails them, they wish to remain with their foster families or to be adopted. Ideally, and to justify the placement, the stability in the foster family should be greater than that in the family of origin.
- Adults who become foster parents must meet criteria established by the state in which they reside and become certified by attending a training course. Adults assume this foster parenting role for a variety of reasons, often because they feel called or for altruistic reasons.
- Foster parenting is a challenge because children have often been abused, are suspicious of adults, and have emotional or behavioral problems. Some of the children have special needs and may present with problems because the mother abused alcohol or drugs during her pregnancy and did not follow up on prenatal care.
- Parents who lose custody of their children may have addiction and related disorders, suffer psychiatric problems, face extreme poverty, and possess a criminal record. They are not capable of fulfilling the parenting role responsibly and successfully, nor can they provide a stable and nurturing home environment.
- Foster parents must deal with different agencies and officials. The pay that they receive for providing housing and food for a child is quite low as most payments are intended to cover the basic costs of caring for a foster child, not as an incentive to profit from the unfortunate situation. A high degree of burnout is observed among many foster parents.
- New parents may need assistance as they become adjusted to their new role. Sources of assistance include support groups for new mothers, new fathers, or both; parenting classes; and assistance from family members.

USEFUL WEBSITES

American Academy of Pediatrics
www.aap.org

Forum on Child and Family Statistics, America's Children: Key National Indicators of Well-Being, 2011
http://childstats.gov

National Institute of Child Health and Human Development
www.nichd.nih.gov

The Pew Charitable Trusts Section: Our Work: Focus Children and Youth
www.pewtrusts.org/our_work_category. aspx?id=328798

U.S. Department of Health and Human Services, Administration for Children and Families
www.acf.hhs.gov/

CHAPTER 6

Pregnancy and Childbirth

Learning Outcomes

▪ ▪ ▪ ▪ ▪ ▪ ▪ ▪ ▪ ▪ ▪ ▪

After completing this chapter, readers should be able to

1. Explain why the critical factors influencing the course of a pregnancy include several dimensions such as social, biological, and psychological factors.

2. Explain why prenatal care includes planning for the pregnancy before conception and describe aspects to be considered in this planning process.

3. Describe the current trends in childbirth management and why they have significantly reduced birth trauma, as well as infant and mother mortality.

4. Explain some of the contributing factors as to why some mothers do not access medical support during prenatal and perinatal care.

5. Explain the emotional considerations accompanying pregnancy and childbirth.

6. Describe the effects of public awareness regarding postpartum depression and sudden infant death syndrome (SIDS) and how these issues are currently addressed.

▪ ▪ ▪ ▪ ▪ ▪ ▪ ▪ ▪ ▪ ▪ ▪

The birth of a first child transforms individuals into parents. Assuming this new family role in addition to other roles is both challenging and rewarding. People gradually evolve into their parenthood roles as they assume increasing responsibility in raising and caring for children. This transition is usually initiated when a couple learns that they are pregnant.

The birth of a baby is a significant event in the lives of parents and for the family system that it enters. The baby's arrival is anticipated with an array of feelings, ranging from great excitement to high anxiety. This may be particularly so when a couple is

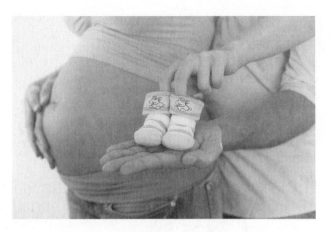

The birth of a baby is a significant event in the lives of parents and for the family system it joins.

having their first child, whose conception was desired and carefully planned.

Many Americans carefully plan and time the conception of their children. The high cost of bearing and rearing children is one important reason that this occurs. Pregnancy provides the first opportunity for the parents-to-be to offer nurturing care to their unborn child. Pregnancy and childbirth are important aspects of parenting.

CONSIDERATIONS DURING PREGNANCY

The period in the uterus before birth is one of the most crucial stages in an individual's life span. During the average 280-day period, biological foundations are established that will influence much of the person's developmental potential over his or her lifetime. Ensuring a good beginning for a child is imperative during this phase of human development.

In earlier times, development before birth was a mystery. Historically, much of what occurs during this period was hidden from direct observation, so the beginnings of life were largely misunderstood and were explained through superstition and speculation. Folklore about pregnancy encouraged the belief that almost everything a pregnant woman experienced would ultimately affect the developing child. Physical defects in a baby were believed to be caused by maternal experiences. For example, birthmarks were thought to result from the mother spilling wine or eating too many

strawberries during pregnancy. A facial cleft deformity, previously referred to by the now defunct term *harelip*, was thought to result from the mother having seen a hare or rabbit. Similarly, it was believed that if a pregnant woman read a lot of classical literature, the child would have strong literary tendencies. These examples illustrate the belief that random events could permanently influence the unborn child, which put misplaced guilt upon the mother if something went wrong during pregnancy.

Such folklore has been discarded as scientists have gained information about how life begins, how the genetic code is transmitted, and how genes are expressed. The influences of the maternal environment, both internal and external, become crucial variables in fetal development. Dramatic advances have been made with regard to knowledge about caring for babies pre- and post-birth, especially for premature neonates and those with low birth weight.

Characteristics of Prenatal Development

The time before the birth of an individual is significant and unique in many ways. Many experts consider this time during the life span to be the most important because of its crucial effects on the later stages. It can be characterized briefly in the following three ways:

1. *It is the shortest stage of the life span.* The average length of pregnancy is 280 days (about 40 weeks), although this period does vary somewhat for every pregnancy. Remarkably, during this relatively short time, the individual develops from a one-celled organism at conception to having more than 200 billion cells at birth.

2. *It is the period of most rapid growth and development during the human life span.* The first trimester (90 days) of pregnancy is the *embryonic stage*, or the formative phase of an individual's growth and development. During this stage, the fertilized egg differentiates into specialized cells that make up the systems of the body. By the end of this embryonic stage, the body has a distinctly recognizable human form and contains all of the organs that are essential for functioning after birth. The second and third trimesters are the *fetal period* of the pregnancy. During this time, the body experiences refinement and the most rapid increase in weight and length. At the beginning of this period, the fetus weighs approximately 1 ounce and is about 1½ inches long. At

birth, the infant weights about 7½ pounds and is about 21 inches long.

3. *It is a highly critical period during human development.* The embryo is vulnerable to many factors that can enhance or hinder its development. Environmental and genetic factors can have permanent effects, adversely or positively, on the embryo. These factors can result in congenital birth defects, miscarriage, prematurity, low birth weight, and tendencies toward certain behavioral traits. The prenatal conditions can also set the stage for adult wellness, or the lack thereof. The biological father's health is relevant in determining the quality of sperm, which, in turn, contributes to the outcome of the pregnancy. It is also the genetic material contributed by the father that will determine the sex of the infant.

Focus Point. The period of prenatal development is one of the most crucial stages in the life cycle. During this short period of rapid growth, many factors can affect the individual's future development.

CRITICAL FACTORS BEFORE AND DURING PREGNANCY

The Responsibility of Parenthood: Preparation for Conception

Responsibly managed parenthood is a major challenge for which parents need all of the information, support, and medical care they can get in order to contribute to an optimal outcome. Ideally, a visit to a gynecologist or health care provider at least 3 months *prior to conception* promotes planning for a successful pregnancy and addresses current medical issues (American Pregnancy Association, 2012a). Prospective parents may also be urged to attend a "Well Baby" clinic prior to conception so that they can receive guidance concerning best practices and preparation for a pregnancy. Prospective parents should access some of the excellent material regarding parenthood that is available in print and on websites.

Under medical supervision, prospective mothers should be weaned off of medications that may be harmful to a developing child and prospective fathers can optimize their health in order to produce healthier sperm. Destructive behaviors, such as smoking, using illicit drugs, misusing prescription drugs, and imbibing alcohol, are detrimental to a healthy pregnancy. Prospective parents who have addictions and related disorders should undergo rehabilitation *before* considering pregnancy, because a child could suffer severely from parental abuse engendered by poor lifestyle choices. For example, infants born to women who are addicted to crack cocaine (cocaine in a smokable form) are also addicted and must receive special medical care following birth. These infants are colloquially referred to as "crack babies." Any recreational drug use amounts to parental irresponsibility that can lead to many problems in later parent–child relations. Such problems are frequently linked to other ones in *high-risk* families.

An expectant mother's health can be adversely affected by her emotional state. High levels of anxiety and depression before and during pregnancy may signal other stressors in the mother's life that require expert medical and, possibly, psychiatric attention.

Genetic counseling. Potential parents can be given information, some of it based on statistical analyses, to assist them in making decisions regarding beginning a pregnancy. In **genetic counseling**, a genetic counselor investigates the potential parents' medical backgrounds by obtaining their family history. A chromosomal analysis of the parents can be carried out to identify genetic abnormalities. If a pregnancy is already in progress, various types of prenatal diagnostic tools are available to determine the status of the baby's health.

Intensive research to learn more about hereditary influences on birth defects has led to the development of remarkable new diagnostic tools and methods. Prospective parents, as well as parents who have had a child with a birth defect, benefit from the information provided by genetic counselors.

Parenting Reflection 6–1

Is it a good idea to require couples, as part of the process for obtaining a marriage license, to submit blood samples to screen for potential problems with regard to pregnancy and genetic abnormalities?

Focus Point. During pregnancy, the baby is exposed to a number of environmental influences that can have both short- and long-term effects on its development. Environmental influences that can be harmful to an unborn child should be avoided over the course of a pregnancy. Appropriate parenting before a child's birth involves being mindful of these factors and how they can affect the unborn child's development over the life span.

The Ages of the Parents

Both parents contribute genetic material to their off-spring, so mothers as well as fathers have been implicated in the etiology of neurodevelopmental and other disorders. The age of the mother and factors such as maternal smoking and caffeine consumption contribute to the probability of having a baby with low birth weight (Harms, Johnson, & Murry, 2004). Babies who weigh 5½ pounds or less at birth are considered to be of moderately low birth weight; very low birth weight includes those below about 3.3 pounds (Federal Interagency Forum on Child and Family Statistics, 2011b). Low birth weight is often associated not only with higher rates of infant mortality, but also with neurodevelopmental disorders (Newburn-Cook et al., 2002). For these reasons, low birth weight has implications for the health and well-being of the infant, not only at birth, but also later in life. For example, learning difficulties and cognitive problems among school-age children are associated with low birth weight (F. R. Lawrence & Blair, 2003).

Women under age 20 and over 40 have a higher probability of delivering babies of low birth weight, especially if they are African American. The infant mortality rates for African American women are also higher than the national average (Federal Interagency Forum on Child and Family Statistics, 2011). Women can experience high-risk pregnancies that are related to social factors such as poverty, poor prenatal care, and lack of social support. The age of the mother is an additional risk factor. Older women experience higher rates of miscarriage and are more likely to give birth to children who have some type of genetic disorder. For example, the incidence of Down syndrome, a genetic disorder that presents with a number of medical conditions and associated developmental delays, increases significantly among women who bear children after 40 years of age (Vontver, 2003).

The age of the father also appears to be significant. Mutations in paternal genetic material increase exponentially with paternal aging. Some of the findings presented in this section are based on the work of Kári Stefánsson and his colleagues in Iceland, who compared the whole-genome sequences of 78 trios of a mother, father, and child (Callaway, 2012; Sun, Helgason, Masson, et al., 2012). Many of these mutations are harmless, but there is strong evidence that some mutations contribute to neurodevelopmental disorders (Callaway, 2012).

Adolescent girls who become pregnant deliver babies with problems that are more likely due to attitudinal and behavioral factors rather than physical problems. For example, lack of information concerning pregnancy, improper nutrition, and lack of adequate prenatal care and supervision contribute to the high incidence of birth complications among teenage mothers (see Figure 6–1). There has been a recent drop in birth rates among adolescents to about 20 per 1,000. This was accompanied by a drop in preterm deliveries, as well as infant mortality, to about 6 per 1,000 births. This downward trend is reassuring, bringing the United States in line with other developed nations (Federal Interagency Forum on Child and Family Statistics, 2011b).

Other factors contributing to the rates of low birth weight in the United States include the increasing numbers of multiple births resulting from fertility treatments; about 15 percent of live births are multiples. The general trend in delaying childbirth to later years in adulthood has an influence as well. The low birth rate trend has been increasing over the past two decades (Federal Interagency Forum on Child and Family Statistics, 2011b).

Nevertheless, because of both physical and social factors, and especially because of good prenatal care and good delivery practices with excellent medical support, most women experience healthy pregnancies.

Nutrition During Pregnancy

The nutrition and health of a pregnant woman are important related factors that influence the quality of development of the growing child (C. Anderson, 2003). These factors have a strong impact on the well-being of both the fetus and the mother, and they can influence the course of subsequent pregnancies (Evans & Aaronson, 2005).

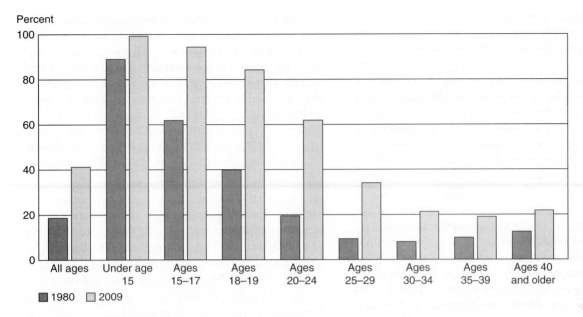

FIGURE 6–1.   Percentage of all births to unmarried women by age of mother, 1980 and 2009.
Note: Data for 2009 are preliminary.
Source: National Center for Health Statistics, *National Vital Statistics System.*

Intrauterine growth, as well as the mother's nutrition and health during pregnancy, directly influence the unborn child, and the influences can extend through the life span of the as-yet unborn (Cosmi, Fanelli, Visentin, Trevisanuto, & Zanardo, 2011). Placental insufficiency can contribute to compromised prenatal development. Disturbed intrauterine growth and premature delivery can set the stage for the development of health-related problems presenting later in the life span.

An important aspect of nutrition during pregnancy is the association between adequate weight gain by the mother and an increase in the infant's birth weight. Equally significant is preventing excessive weight gain because this can be accompanied by its own set of risk factors. Current guidelines indicate that for a mother with a body mass index (BMI) in the normal range (that is, a BMI between 18.5 and 24.9), the desired weight gain is about 25–35 pounds. It is higher for multiples and lower for women with a weight in the overweight to obese range. This weight gain is attributed to several factors other than the infant's weight, which will be about 7–8 pounds. It includes increases in blood volume (3–4 lb), larger uterus (2 lb), larger breasts (1–3 lb), placenta (1½ lb), amniotic fluid (2 lb), fat stores (7–8 lb), and

increased fluid volume (3–4 lb; Mayo Clinic, 2011a, p. 43). Steady weight gain is characteristic of the second and third trimesters.

An important part of good prenatal care is expert dietary and nutritional advice, which should include foods, medications and substances that the expectant mother may take, and those that she should avoid, which decreases the chances of a negative birth outcome. Some nutrients may play a critical role in influencing the quality and nature of a baby's development before birth. For example, an adequate amount of folic acid (a type of B vitamin) in a pregnant woman's diet appears to counteract the risk of spinal cord defects (e.g., spina bifida) in a developing baby. Folic acid is available in prenatal supplements and is available naturally in fresh fruits and vegetables. It is recommended that women of reproductive age take prenatal vitamins and folic acid when preparing for a pregnancy.

Fetal Origins of Adult Disease.   Research indicates that the prenatal period of a person's life appears to be one of the crucial periods in determining the later spectrum of health and disease (Cosmi et al., 2011). One theory associated with this premise is sometimes referred to as the *Barker hypothesis*, attributed to David J. P. Barker, a British physician and epidemiologist who first published the theory in 1992 (see www.thebarker-theory.org).

Barker and his coresearchers refer to factors that contribute to *developmental plasticity*. This means that *a given genotype can be expressed in different ways in response to environmental factors* (Bateson et al., 2004). In other words, a given developmental situation, such as intrauterine development, can develop in many directions, ranging from optimal to threatening for the development of the fetus. Various factors will interact to contribute to the outcome, and in this manner the fetus has developmental plasticity, or the ability to mold the situation.

Barker and his colleagues studied the relationships between prenatal (in utero) conditions influenced by intrauterine growth and maternal nutrition and some of the following conditions and diseases: coronary heart disease, high blood pressure, stroke, type 2 diabetes and obesity, osteoporosis, aging, and breast and ovarian cancer.

Mothers in both developed and developing countries can unwittingly influence later health outcomes for their unborn children by being poorly nourished and/or chronically malnourished (Barker, Eriksson, Forsén, & Osmond, 2002). Many chronic disorders that present themselves in adult life can be linked to prenatal conditions (Barker, 2004). Mothers who live in poverty and are malnourished and underweight can present with intrauterine conditions that result in low birth weight and prematurity, both of which can have long-ranging health effects. One of these effects is the development of a "thrifty metabolism," meaning that the fetus protects itself against malnutrition by using calories in a conservative way. When the baby is later exposed to overnutrition, as is common in our society, that baby is more at risk for obesity and all the complications of obesity, including type 2 diabetes and coronary heart disease. Further research has shown that mothers with a high body mass index at the beginning of their pregnancies, as well as those gaining an excessive amount of weight during pregnancy (for example, overweight and obese mothers), could also unwittingly be setting up their offspring for later obesity and possible type 2 diabetes, because insulin sensitivity and insulin production rates may be established in the womb (Eriksson, Forsén, Tuomilehto, Osmond, & Barker, 2003).

This hypothesis about developmental plasticity emphasizes the crucial importance of good prenatal nutrition, general prenatal care that promotes intrauterine growth, and factors associated with preventing premature births (Cosmi et al., 2011). This very sensitive period of an infant's life, namely the **prenatal** (before the time of birth) and the **perinatal** (around the time of birth) periods, can determine many facets of his or her future well-being, as well as disease development. This is one of the many reasons why, ideally, mothers should receive early prenatal care and babies should be monitored and delivered in hospital environments with specialized care, where this *optimal outcome* is more likely.

Focus Point. Short- and long-term outcomes are directly related to intrauterine conditions before birth, making the period before birth one of the key developmental stages of the life span. This critical period forms the foundation on which the later stages will be built. As mentioned earlier, various factors interact to contribute to developmental plasticity in the fetus.

Exercise

Pregnant women can prepare their bodies for pregnancy and childbirth by participating in moderate levels of physical exercise. Examples of these activities include swimming, walking, and prenatal exercises focused specifically on an expectant mother's needs and limitations. Sports with a higher risk of impact and injury should be avoided. Care needs to be taken that dehydration does not occur because that could be harmful to both the mother and the unborn child (Mayo Clinic, 2011b).

Regular exercise provides many health benefits to an expectant mother, such as improving respiration, circulation, and muscle tone. Regular exercise is also associated with an elevated mood; it boosts energy levels and reduces the risk of gestational diabetes and pregnancy-related high blood pressure. It can contribute to moderating the effects of potential postpartum depression. The mother-to-be should discuss her exercise needs and limitations with the medical team providing her prenatal care.

A note of caution is warranted as certain medical conditions may require additional medical attention. Expectant mothers need to follow the guidelines provided by their physicians very carefully. Some examples of these medical conditions are poorly controlled diabetes, high blood pressure, pregnancy-induced hypertension or

Once a woman becomes pregnant, medical supervision is key to having a healthy, full-term baby. Couples should work together to ensure optimal outcomes. Alcohol, nicotine, and caffeine intake can be harmful to the developing baby. All medications require medical approval.

preeclampsia, hypo- and hyperthyroidism, heart disease, and placenta previa, which may cause excessive bleeding. Mothers of multiples should be cautious regarding exercise and follow the guidelines from their health providers (Mayo Clinic, 2011a, p. 44). Typically, mothers of multiples are carefully monitored for the risks inherent in the birth of multiples.

Preparation for Birth

Birth preparation classes are helpful to most couples, especially for those expecting their first child because a prospective father will learn how to support the mother during childbirth. These classes will also focus on breathing exercises that assist the mother during labor and delivery. A couple will typically be advised to think about a "birthing plan" that encompasses where the mother will deliver the baby and such issues as pain management during labor and the delivery. It is helpful for prospective parents to take an *infant and child cardio-pulmonary resuscitation* (CPR) class during this time, and many hospitals with birthing centers will offer these as part of the preparations. Ideally, parents should choose a pediatrician at this time so that all support systems are in place before the birth. Parents are encouraged to take advantage of opportunities provided by the hospital or birthing center to visit the facility in order to familiarize themselves with the environment and the procedures. Good preparation, both mental and physical, will help parents to avoid panic and incorrect decisions when time is of the essence. It also creates an emotionally supportive environment when parents know in advance what to expect.

Prenatal Medical Supervision

Part of good prenatal parenting is providing the mother with medical supervision. A mother who has at least five or more prenatal visits with a health-care professional beginning in the first trimester increases the chances of having a healthy, full-term baby (Gabbe, Niebyl, & Simpson, 2003).

Physicians generally urge their pregnant patients not to take *any* type of drug—prescription, nonprescription, or recreational—without medical advice (Bailey, Cook, Hodge, & McGrady, 2011). Although a developing baby is well protected within the uterus, many substances pass across the placenta to the baby via the mother's blood. Certain drugs and chemical agents can cause malformations and other problems. The developing embryo is most sensitive to interference from these agents during the first trimester because it is during this embryonic period—the first 90 days of gestation—when organ systems are being formed. The effects of drug use or exposure during pregnancy can be manifested following a child's birth as well.

Mercury is present in many species of fish, and pregnant women are warned to be cautious about consuming fish, which often contains high concentrations of mercury (American Pregnancy Association, 2012a).

High levels of mercury in food can affect brain development and the nervous system.

A number of drugs and other chemical agents are known to have **teratogenic** effects; that is, they cause the abnormal development of an embryo. Among the most common ones are certain psychotropic medications, drugs used to treat acne, certain medications for psoriasis, thalidomide, and certain anticancer drugs (Mayo Clinic, 2011a). It is advisable to read the package inserts for medications, which list warnings, and to receive counseling from a pharmacist or health-care provider.

A woman should never self-medicate while pregnant, or even if she suspects that she may be pregnant. Even over-the-counter medications can be harmful. It is important to review every substance that one considers taking with the medical team that is providing the prenatal care. Some health conditions, such as diabetes, may require ongoing medication during pregnancy, and these situations need to be monitored by a medical team. Other substances must be avoided during pregnancy, including alcohol, nicotine, and caffeine.

Alcohol. Alcohol consumption during pregnancy is associated with birth defects in babies (Lumeng, Cabral, & Gannon, 2007). As one parental guideline states: *If you drink, so does your baby* (Mayo Clinic, 2011a, p. 48). It is estimated that about 0.2 to 1.5 births per 1,000 in the United States involve some type of defect related to **fetal alcohol syndrome (FAS;** Centers for Disease Control and Prevention, 2004). This is comparable to the number of infants born with Down syndrome or spina bifida. FAS-related defects include learning disabilities and hyperactivity, which affect school performance; indeed, these defects are serious and can last a lifetime (Coggins, Timler, & Olswang, 2007; Sokol, Delaney-Black, & Nordstrom, 2003).

Even what a mother may consider to be moderate drinking, that is, one alcoholic drink daily, is likely to cause harm to a developing baby. Because the risks to the baby are so high, physicians urge women to abstain from alcohol completely from the time that they begin thinking about becoming pregnant to the time when they wean their child from breast feeding (American Academy of Pediatrics Committee on Substance Abuse, 2001; Bailey et al., 2011).

Parenting Reflection 6–2

Should a mother who has an addiction or a related disorder be allowed to have custody of a new baby? Would the decision to allow custody have conditions such as the mother participating in a treatment program? Do medical personnel have an obligation to report such mothers to child protective services?

Tobacco (Nicotine). When an expectant mother smokes, or passively inhales the smoke of others, nicotine and many other toxic chemical agents found in cigarettes have adverse effects on the developing fetus. The risks include premature birth, low birth weight, stillbirth, and sudden infant death syndrome (SIDS; Bailey et al., 2011; Mayo Clinic, 2011a). The long-range effects in children of mothers who smoke during their prenatal development include poorer school performance, hyperactivity, perceptual-motor difficulties, and learning disabilities (Gabbe et al., 2003; Marlow, Wolke, Bracewell, & Samara, 2005).

Caffeine. Because caffeine is present in many soft drinks and is also found in chocolate, tea, coffee, and in especially high dosages in certain energy drinks and espresso, prospective mothers may not realize the extent of their caffeine intake. Weaning oneself off of caffeine is difficult because withdrawal initially causes headaches. Nevertheless, pregnant women need to restrict their intake to less than 200 milligrams of caffeine per day, which is approximately one cup of coffee (Mayo Clinic, 2011a).

Focus Point. The use of illicit drugs, as well as the misuse of prescription and over-the-counter drugs, by a pregnant woman has many deleterious effects on a developing fetus, affecting especially brain and neural development. These effects are likely to continue to manifest themselves in a number of ways, including developmental delays in the child.

Infectious Diseases

Several types of infectious diseases can be transmitted from mother to child, both before birth through the placental membrane and during birth from contact with the mother's vaginal tract. The severity of these infections depends on when the disease is contracted by the mother during the course of her pregnancy. Of special concern is rubella (German measles); fortunately, most women in the United States were vaccinated against this disease during adolescence and, ideally, well before a pregnancy. There is a strict medical protocol concerning vaccinations that can and vaccinations that cannot be administered during a pregnancy (www.mayoclinic.com/health/vaccines-during-pregnancy).

Other diseases are known to damage the baby's central nervous system during the fetal stage of development. For example, the *cytomegalovirus* (a herpes virus) and the disease *toxoplasmosis* can contribute to brain damage, learning disabilities, sensory problems, and even death (March of Dimes Foundation, 2011). Toxoplasmosis is linked to a parasite that can be found in cat litter boxes, among other places. Pregnant women should avoid the potentially risky activity of cleaning out litter boxes.

Sexually transmitted diseases, such as syphilis and gonorrhea, and the human immunodeficiency virus (HIV), which causes acquired immune deficiency syndrome (AIDS), can also be transmitted by a pregnant or lactating (nursing) woman to her developing fetus or baby (Williams, Norris, & Bedor, 2003). Chlamydia and the human papilloma virus (HPV) are other common sexually transmitted diseases. There is a vaccine available to prevent certain strains of the HPV virus.

Paternal Risk Factors in Prenatal Development. Mothers are not solely responsible for conditions that place a developing baby at risk. While the evidence points mainly to the maternal environment with regard to the developing fetus, the behavior of the father has an effect as well. For example, abnormal sperm development can be attributed to a man's exposure to lead, recreational drugs such as marijuana and cocaine, cigarettes, alcohol, radiation, and environmental chemicals such as pesticides (Brott & Ash, 2010; Westheimer & Lopater, 2004). In addition, current research has shown that the number of mutations in the genetic material of fathers increases with aging (Sun, Helgason, Masson, et al., 2012).

Parenting Reflection 6–3

What can government agencies do to help disadvantaged mothers-to-be to have healthier pregnancies?

Focus Point. The quality of an individual's development before birth may be influenced positively or negatively by a number of factors. Such factors include the age of the mother; the quality of her diet; the quality of the medical care received during pregnancy; the mother's exposure to certain drugs, chemicals, or disease agents; and uncontrolled diabetes. Certain risk factors are also related to the father.

CURRENT TRENDS IN PRENATAL CARE

The field of maternal–fetal medicine, also known as **perinatology** has emerged in recent years to address the management of high-risk pregnancies and to detect and treat conditions in developing individuals during the prenatal stage while they are still in the uterus (Sinclair, 2003).

Adequate prenatal supervision may be an important factor in reducing the incidence of low birth weight and prematurity in infants (Lawrence & Blair, 2003), a condition that has long-range implications for parents as well as children. The quality of prenatal care that a woman receives varies according to her social, ethnic, and demographic backgrounds (Federal Interagency Forum on Child and Family Statistics, 2011). A woman's educational level is an important factor that affects whether she seeks prenatal care. A pregnant woman who has not completed high school is more likely to begin care late in her pregnancy or receive no care at all.

Pregnancy and Infant Loss

Miscarriage and spontaneous abortion are terms used for a pregnancy that spontaneously ends within the first 20 weeks of gestation, although most end within the first trimester (American Pregnancy Association, 2012b). The rate of pregnancy loss is about 10–15 percent of all recognized pregnancies. The reasons are varied and can be linked to maternal health, hormone levels, issues with implantation, and chromosomal abnormalities within the developing embryo, to name a few. The risk of miscarriage increases with the mother's age. Physical trauma (such as being involved in an auto accident) can also be a factor. Depending on the reasons for the loss of the fetus, and the individual circumstances surrounding family formation, the distress associated with a miscarriage can range from mild to severe. For some parents who went through lengthy treatment for infertility, the loss of a pregnancy, perhaps one of many, can be devastating. They will experience repeated cycles of grieving as their hopes for biological parenthood seem to have been shattered. Several factors can aggravate the couple's distress (Shreffler, Greil & McQuillan, 2011):

■ A history of infertility and ART interventions
■ Whether it was a planned pregnancy, and whether there have been live births
■ Whether the loss is recent and whether there is a medical explanation
■ The desire to be a parent

Infant loss. Carrying a baby virtually to term and then facing a stillborn delivery is extremely traumatic (Shreffler et al., 2011). There are several situations for which parents require ongoing emotional support in addition to medical intervention: infertility, preterm birth, miscarriage, stillbirth, early infant death, and SIDS. Women who have experienced any of these losses can be devastated, and it can present as guilt, anxiety, depression, and grief (Shreffler et al., 2011). It is important to acknowledge the presence and the importance of the lost infant in the lives of the parents. Parents are encouraged to name the child and to go through culturally appropriate mourning and burial rites. Parents also need to see the baby, even if it was stillborn, because this can facilitate a farewell and ensue closure.

Professionals who deal with grief and loss are available in most hospitals and can guide the family toward the appropriate support systems. Professional counselors can help the family overcome emotional difficulties. For grieving families, volunteer associations offer support groups for miscarriage and infant loss. The national *Share* organization is one such network that guides participants toward help and support (www.nationalshare.org).

Prenatal screening and diagnostic tests. Prenatal screening and diagnostic tests are listed chronologically in Table 6–1 as they can occur during pregnancy. The medical team supporting the parents will decide which tests are appropriate at what time. Not all tests may be indicated for each pregnancy, and this list is not exhaustive. Even though the table has been laid out in trimesters, there are no absolutes; tests can overlap trimesters, and some tests can be repeated.

TABLE 6–1. Prenatal Screening and Diagnostic Tests

FIRST TRIMESTER SCREENING	Tests are usually performed near the end of the first trimester (first 3 months of pregnancy) and the beginning of the second trimester. An optimal period is between the 11th and 14th weeks of pregnancy. Usually, first trimester screenings are not invasive and are not known to cause miscarriage or other complications.
Ultrasound tests	This common medical imaging test uses sound waves to visualize the fetus. There are several types of ultrasound tests. The process of using ultrasound to obtain more information concerning the pregnancy is called prenatal ultrasound. The sonogram that is produced is usually the first time that the parents "meet" their unborn child.
• Standard ultrasound	This two-dimensional imaging technique takes about 20 minutes to perform and provides information concerning the size, location, and development of the fetus, and the position of the placenta.
• Nuchal translucency test, or nuchal fold scan	Women in the United States are encouraged to have this test, which is typically the first official ultrasound screening provided during the first trimester. The nuchal (neck) region is scanned during weeks 11–13. This is the earliest point at which the mother can know whether her child is at risk for a chromosomal abnormality. The quadruple, or quad, screening test is offered as a follow-up later during the pregnancy. The results of these two tests are analyzed to determine whether chromosomal abnormalities are suspected and further testing is warranted.

(Continued)

TABLE 6–1. *(Continued)*

• Advanced ultrasound	Also called a targeted ultrasound, this test takes about 30 minutes to perform. More sophisticated equipment is used to explore an area in greater detail. This test may be indicated in high-risk pregnancies as a first screening, before further tests are indicated.
• Transvaginal ultrasound	Often used during the first trimester, this test can provide a clearer image of the fetus than trans-abdominal ultrasound can. It can also be used to screen the condition of the cervix. This test is also used to examine the pelvic area of women who are not pregnant.
• Three-dimensional ultrasound: Surface rendering and volume capture	There are two types of 3D ultrasound. One provides an image of the fetus that is similar to standard ultrasound and is called a *surface rendering*. The other is called *volume capture*, which interfaces with a computer program that translates the information into sophisticated images, which are similar to the results obtained through computerized tomography (CT) and magnetic resonance imaging (MRI).
• Doppler ultrasound	This sophisticated and detailed ultrasound technique utilizes the Doppler effect to measure movement or flow in the body.
• Fetal echocardiography	This ultrasound technique provides more information on the heart of the fetus, including its anatomy and functioning.
Blood tests	Blood tests used during the first trimester to assess for increased risk of chromosomal anomalies include hCG and PAPP-A. These two blood tests are used in conjunction with the results of the nuchal translucency ultrasound test to evaluate risk.
SECOND TRIMESTER SCREENING	These tests are usually performed during the fourth through sixth months of pregnancy.
Ultrasound tests	These tests take place throughout the pregnancy, especially during the 18th through the 20th weeks. During this time, structural information can be obtained regarding the development of the fetus.
Blood tests	The quad screen measures the levels of four substances in the blood of a pregnant woman. These four tests require only one procedure. Quad screens evaluate the risk of spina bifida, anencephaly, Down syndrome (Trisomy 21), and Edwards syndrome (Trisomy 18). These screens are typically done between the 15th and 18th weeks of pregnancy, but can be done up to the 22nd week of pregnancy. The results of the quad screen are compared with the first trimester screening results to get a final risk assessment.

The following tests further investigate the possibility of chromosomal/genetic anomalies. Risks of these procedures include fetal death and permanent disability.

Amniocentesis	This test is typically used to follow up on a quad screen if there were abnormal results. Ultrasound guides the physician in safely withdrawing amniotic fluid from the sac surrounding the fetus. This test is typically done between the 15th and 20th weeks of pregnancy. There are two types of amniocentesis: genetic and maturity amniocentesis. The latter may be performed in the last trimester.
• Genetic amniocentesis	A culture is grown in a laboratory from cells in the amniotic fluid, and genes can be checked for the occurrence of Down syndrome and spina bifida. Highly specialized tests can be added for known or suspected risks, depending on the results of genetic counseling.

(Continued)

TABLE 6–1. *(Continued)*

Chorionic villus sampling (CVS)	This test can detect a number of genetic abnormalities. It carries a higher risk of miscarriage than amniocentesis and for that reason it is only done if specifically indicated.
Percutaneous umbilical blood sampling (PUBS)	Typically performed after the 18th week of pregnancy, this test may be indicated when the other tests were unable to provide adequate information. It is seldom the first choice because it carries risks, such as fetal death. The test can provide information which enables chromosomal analysis, and may be used to diagnose certain blood disorders and Rh (Rhesus) incompatibility between the mother and the fetus.
THIRD-TRIMESTER SCREENING	These tests are usually performed during the last 3 months of the pregnancy.
Ultrasound tests	These tests take place throughout pregnancy, in all trimesters, and form part of standard prenatal care, although they are not performed at each prenatal visit.
Fetal nonstress test	This noninvasive, nonstress test monitors the baby over 20–30 minutes, recording movement, heart rate, and heart rate in response to movement.
Maturity amniocentesis	Amniotic fluid is analyzed to determine the maturity of the lungs of the unborn child to determine whether they will be able to function normally at birth.
Biophysical profile testing	An ultrasound test is combined with a fetal nonstress test to assess heart rate, breathing movements, body movement, muscle tone, and amniotic fluid level. The test is typically done between the 26th and 32nd weeks of pregnancy.
Doppler ultrasound	Used for babies who may be at risk for blood- and blood flow-related conditions, this technique can detect movement and is sensitive enough to measure the blood flow within the baby, as well as between the placenta and the baby.
Three-dimensional ultrasound	This technology is similar to CT and MRI scans, and is used to enhance diagnosis. Although it provides a fairly clear image of the baby, it is typically only used when there are medical indications. The parents' curiosity concerning the appearance of their unborn child is usually not regarded as a valid reason.

Based on information published by the Mayo Clinic (2011a, pp. 305–319) and the American Pregnancy Association (2012a), www.americanpregnancy.org

---

Focus Point. Maternal–fetal medicine, also known as perinatology, is the management of high-risk pregnancies. Genetic counseling, new methods for diagnosing fetal health conditions, and equipment for monitoring prenatal development are advancements that contribute to the care and well-being of fetuses.

ADJUSTING TO PREGNANCY

Expectant Parents' Reactions to Pregnancy

When a couple learns that they are pregnant, especially with their first child, they can expect several reactions.

A pregnancy affects the couple in several ways, although the experience is unique to each parent and each couple.

An expectant mother undergoes a variety of physical, emotional, and social changes. These include adjusting to a changing body image as the pregnancy progresses, challenges to physical and psychological well-being, feelings about what it is like to be pregnant (especially for the first time), dealing with fears of the unknown, and shifting moods that may be related to fluctuations in hormone levels. Emotional reactions in pregnancy are important as well, because high levels of anxiety in mothers have been associated with increased fetal activity, which may contribute partially to lower birth weights in these infants. High-activity levels continue to be observed in these babies following birth (Monk et al., 2000).

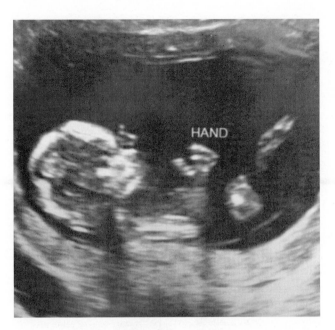

A sonogram of a fetus can assist in determining important information such as fetal age, sex, and in ruling out possible abnormalities.

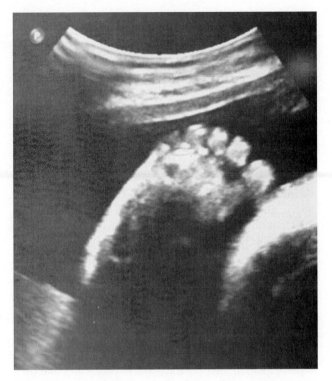

This is an ultrasound image of a normal intrauterine pregnancy (IUP) at 25 weeks. During the anatomy scan which is performed during the second trimester, the extremities are evaluated.

For the most part, women and their partners react favorably and with great anticipation to the news that a pregnancy has been confirmed. This appears to be especially the case when the pregnancy is the first one and when it is desired. Many women look forward to their child's birth with great anticipation; the alleged glow of a woman's pregnancy often refers to the state of happiness and pleasure that is experienced in the process of bringing new life into the world.

Like parenthood, pregnancy has different connotations and meanings for different individuals. For some, pregnancy validates one's sexuality. For many individuals, the initiation of a pregnancy revives memories of childhood and brings anticipation of the parenthood role.

Not everyone who learns of the beginning of a pregnancy reacts with joy, pleasure, or anticipation. Less positive reactions are attributed to other sources: frustration with the economic issues that plague families, especially among young starter families; lack of social support from families of origin and other networks; feelings of uncertainty about whether one wishes to continue a relationship with a partner; the discovery of possible developmental defects prior to birth; and feelings that the

pregnancy is generally poorly timed for one's current circumstances. These negative attitudes may contribute to the decision to terminate a pregnancy and also have a bearing on the manner in which labor and delivery are experienced should the pregnancy be brought to term (McCoyd, 2010).

It is important to note that a woman's optimistic or negative expectations about parenthood prior to a child's birth influence the quality of her experiences as a parent following the birth (Harwood, McLean, & Durkin, 2007). One study found that couples report higher levels of relationship functioning once they have adjusted to an unplanned pregnancy (Bouchard, Boudreau, & Hébert, 2006). This may be due to stressors which necessitate that a couple works harder to resolve conflict.

When a pregnancy is confirmed, a couple must focus on new issues that they have not yet considered in their relationship. For example, they reflect on what it will be like to have a child and to be a parent, what kind of parents they will be, in what kinds of activities they will participate, and what kind of person the child will become. Expectations of parenthood include how each partner will contribute to this effort, which has important bearings on what happens after a child is born (McHale & Rotman, 2007). One of the benefits of the 9 months of pregnancy is that it allows such mental preparations to take place before one actually has to perform as a parent. Expectant parents have time to begin thinking of themselves as a family rather than as a couple. By attending childbirth education classes, reading books and articles about child rearing and child development, and arranging and participating in prenatal medical care, couples begin their preparations for this change in their family system. They equip a nursery, have baby showers, and shop for the things they will need in caring for an infant. This change is significant, and it will prompt related adjustments in the family system as the couple moves from being a twosome, to being a couple in the process of producing children.

Expectant Fathers. Expectant fathers are encouraged to participate in the prenatal process. Many feel that they should be actively involved during the pregnancy and find it rewarding to do so. Additionally, it adds to the bond between the couple. Research shows that expectant fathers' involvement in the pregnancy of the wife or partner acts as an important source of support (Jungmarker, Lindgren, & Hildingsson, 2010). By involving expectant fathers in childbirth education classes, they become better prepared for the actual birthing experience. This involvement prior to a child's birth promotes a greater interest in the child's growth and development and helps the father develop a healthy understanding about what is involved in good parenting (Genosini & Tallandini, 2009). Expectant fathers have particular needs that should be addressed by the professionals assisting in the process (Fletcher, Vimpani, Russell, & Sibbritt, 2008). For example, expectant fathers would like to know how to cope with the stresses of the partner's pregnancy and how to care for a new baby. Professionals need to provide resources that will assist new fathers in assuming their role and its associated responsibilities. Boot Camp for New Dads® is a program that addresses some of these needs. Prospective and novice fathers are mentored by veteran fathers with the aim of achieving competence. The program is offered in various locations nationally and empowers fathers by supporting them as they learn best practices in parenting infants.

Focus Point. The prospect of becoming parents brings about changes for both partners. Women who anticipate motherhood positively adjust better to pregnancy, labor, and delivery. Pregnancy signals impending changes in personal and marital identities for a couple. It prepares them to adjust to the next stage in their family life. Expectant fathers play an important role and they may need assistance in successfully transitioning into their new role in the family.

Involving these expectant fathers in childbirth education classes prepares the couple for the actual birth experience. It promotes a positive attitude toward good fathering practices.

The Timing of the First Birth.   Researchers generally report that the timing of the first birth in a person's life and marriage is determined by rather complex social factors (Chakraborty, 2002). There is a trend in the United States toward delaying first marriage and childbearing (U.S. Census Bureau, 2011). In the past, couples typically had children within 2 years of their first marriage. Many couples delay having their first child for a variety of reasons, including unfavorable economic conditions and the pressures of obtaining an education and career goals (Cohn, Passel, Wang, & Livingstone, 2011). Delayed marriage is associated with having fewer children.

The age of the parents upon the birth of their first child is associated with repercussions in other areas of their lives. A particular dilemma is when parenthood is developmentally off-time when compared to the norm for one's peers. Teenage pregnancy is an example where having the first child at a younger age hampers the ability to pursue educational goals (Christoffersen & Lausten, 2009). Similarly, the older parent may face challenges in juggling professional and parenthood roles. While older parents are parenting infants, their peers who had their children earlier in life are parenting adolescents.

THE BIRTHING EXPERIENCE

The birth of a baby is a momentous event for a family. It is a particularly memorable occasion for couples who are experiencing it for the first time. During the mid-20th century, Western culture approached birth as a medical event rather than as a family affair (Molter, 2003). This has changed, and current birthing practices support the family and encourage the involvement of the father. Medical teams are aware of the emotional and social aspects surrounding the birth of a child, and these needs are respected and incorporated into modern birthing practices. The interior architecture of modern hospitals caters to the family's comfort and well-being, and labor rooms and the rooms where the parents subsequently stay are designed to promote family cohesiveness in order to facilitate bonding with the new infant. If the newborn is healthy, then he or she will stay in the room with the parents (a practice known as *rooming-in*). A lactation specialist will guide the mother to facilitate nursing. There may be a sleeper couch in the room so that the father can stay at the hospital to support the mother in this new and challenging adventure while both parents get to know their newborn.

Cesarean Deliveries.   A **cesarean section** (also known as a C-section) is a surgical procedure named after Julius Caesar, the ancient Roman emperor who, according to legend, was born in this manner. The procedure is performed by making an incision through the woman's abdominal wall and into the uterus. The fetus and placenta are removed through this opening. In some situations, it is not possible or desirable for a woman to experience a vaginal delivery. In such cases, a cesarean section is performed to protect the health and well-being of both the infant and the mother. In the United States, the incidence of C-sections is fairly high and can amount to a third of all deliveries (Centers for Disease Control and Prevention, 2011). At the same time, the entire birthing process is safer than ever before, and maternal and infant mortality have dropped significantly. There has also been a dramatic reduction in birth trauma. These are very desirable outcomes for ensuring an optimal start for the newborn.

Childbirth Coach.   A childbirth coach or a labor support companion (sometimes referred to as a *doula*) cares for the mother while she is in labor and sometimes for a period following the delivery (M. T. Stein, Kennell, & Fulcher, 2004). For centuries, they have been present in numerous cultures. Doulas are not medically trained, nor are they midwives. For that reason, they *do not* deliver babies and they do not have a clinical role. They act in an emotionally supportive role as a labor coach and companion for the mother. These individuals provide useful social, emotional, and some physical support for new mothers and have a positive impact on the mother's experiences during the days following the birth. They can also coach the father on how to be supportive. They provide continuity when some of the medical attendants may change. Women who have the support of a childbirth coach are reported to cope more effectively with the responsibilities of being a new mother (Campbell, Lake, Falk, & Backstrand, 2006). Information is available from DONA International (www.dona.org).

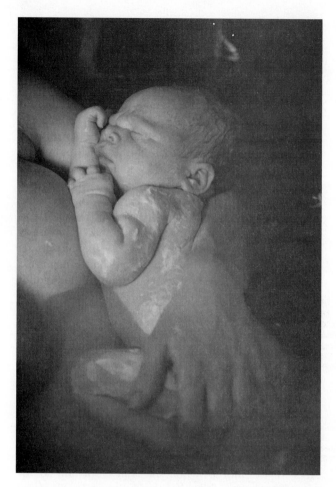

The first few minutes following birth are very important to the parent–child relationship. Ensuring that each parent has skin-to-skin contact, eye contact, and the opportunity to show physical affection toward the newborn can facilitate emotional bonding.

The Effects of the Birthing Experience on Adults

The type of birthing experience can be linked to a variety of outcomes for the couple. Childbirth is recognized as being both a psychological and a physical event that has implications beyond the immediate (Ratcliffe, 2007). Reactions to childbirth range from ecstasy and intense spirituality to singularly negative (Kendall-Tackett, 2001). One of the most significant aspects of this event is the importance and role of the birthing experience in promoting bonding, or attachment, between

the parents and the child. Some research suggests that the first few minutes following birth are crucial and constitute a critical period for the parent–child relationship (Sears & Sears, 2001). *Skin-to-skin contact* between each parent and the newborn, as well as the expression of physical affection and eye contact, are believed to facilitate emotional bonding. Family-centered childbirth methods enhance the process. A birth experience that promotes bonding between the parents and the infant contributes toward preventing later parenting difficulties. Even when prolonged separation is necessary, as with a premature birth that requires neonatal intensive care, health-care professionals may guide the parents regarding how to be actively involved in the infant's care, thus facilitating the bonding process. If the premature infant can take in liquids orally, the lactating mother is encouraged to express milk by using a lactation pump and to store the milk, which can be fed to the infant by the mother or the nursing staff. Breast milk imparts the benefits of some of the mother's immunity to the infant.

Immediate access to the newborn by the mother and father is accomplished when the infant stays in the same room as the mother (rooming-in). This increases the confidence of the parents in performing competent child care under supervised conditions. This may also lead to fewer incidences of future *parenting inadequacy*. If the care of an infant is otherwise optimal, there appears to be no long-term deficits in the mother–child relationship when these early contacts do not occur (Salonen et al., 2009).

Adults experience birth-related stress in different ways (Martin & Fleming, 2011). The level of stress experienced may be higher among first-time parents. This is related to *role transition* and other changes that first-time parents experience. For parents who are having their second or third child, there continues to be some stress associated with childbirth. This may be related to the memories of past experiences. These stimulate a more realistic appraisal of the impact that a newborn has on family life, routines, and resources. In addition, a mother's emotional satisfaction with the birth experience is related to the frequency and intrusiveness of obstetrical interventions; although, ideally, informed mothers know that the interventions safeguard the infant and the mother and contribute to a good birth outcome.

Fathers can experience varying emotions. On the positive side, most fathers are deeply touched by the miracle of birth, especially if they are with the mother during the delivery. This is a special time for bonding. The realities of increased responsibility may add stress, and some negative emotions may also be experienced related to feelings of lack of social and emotional support, feeling overwhelmed, changing family dynamics, the demands of infant care, and sleepless nights.

Some women experience an emotional letdown following birth as an expected outcome of the delivery process, and this can be hormone related. An estimated 15 percent of women suffer from significant depression, perinatal mood and anxiety disorders, and related conditions. These can occur regardless of age, income, race, or ethnicity (Postpartum Support International, 2012). These reactions occur much more frequently than the general public realizes.

Postpartum depression. Some women experience *postpartum depression.* This is a serious condition that requires medical intervention; the mother needs intense and ongoing support until she is healthier. Sometimes a mother is unable to report how she feels, or tries to keep up appearances. For that reason, family members and friends need to be alert; if they suspect depression, they need to call in medical help immediately. Ignoring this condition can have very serious repercussions for both the mother and the infant because the mother is sometimes unable to recognize her infant's needs, leading to *failure to thrive* in the child. Suicide and infant homicide have also been reported, underlining the seriousness of this condition.

Postpartum depression is a type of clinical depression that includes feelings of not wanting to provide care for the infant, severe mood swings, continual fatigue, lack of joy in life, and/or withdrawal from relationships (Mays & Lechman, 2007). It is treatable, often with antidepressants in combination with psychotherapy. This condition has implications for the quality of the relationship between the affected mother and the infant. Of particular concern is the interference that can occur in the attachment process between the mother and the child. Postpartum depression seems to have a clear organic basis, but there are contributing psychological factors as well. Our society holds out the blissful mother as the norm, and almost all women are given the message that motherhood is rewarding and wonderful. If mothers are not able to cope, they may feel as if they have somehow failed in their role as a woman and as a mother, imparting unnecessary guilt onto an already fragile mother. It is helpful to acknowledge that parental

strain and despair are among the feelings that parents experience, and that sleep deprivation and lack of social support are likely contributors to the strain.

Fathers can also experience postpartum depression, although their depression may be reactive in nature (Paulson & Bazemore, 2010). About 10 percent of the fathers in a study experienced an episode of depression following the birth of an infant. The episode typically occurred between 3 and 6 months postpartum. Fathers can also feel overwhelmed, which may result in a depressive episode.

The symptoms of these depression-related illnesses can vary, so it is advisable to get medical advice. Situations that add extra stress to the pregnancy can contribute, although several factors have to interact to precipitate the condition. Researchers have shown that mothers who were exposed to stress and even violence during pregnancy may be more prone to depression after the birth, and their infants show higher than normal levels of stress hormones in their blood. In other words, prenatal exposure to maternal stress can have lifelong effects on the offspring (Radtke et al., 2011).

Some of the factors that increase the risk of postpartum depression include the following:

- The birth of multiples
- Treatment for infertility
- An infant in a neonatal intensive care unit
- Complications during pregnancy
- Breast feeding challenges
- Medical conditions
- Poor social support system
- Abusive relationship

Postpartum psychosis. *Postpartum psychosis* is a serious psychiatric condition. Mothers who experience this condition may lose contact with reality. They may have delusions, such as believing that their child is satanic. Hallucinations can also occur. Some mothers with this condition have killed their children during psychotic episodes.

• •

Parenting Reflection 6–4

What advice would you offer new parents about what to expect in the coming months as it affects their marriage, work, home routines, and social life?

• •

Parenting FAQ 6–1

My wife wants me present when it's time for her to give birth to our child. This is our first child and I want to be supportive. What are the benefits?

Being a part of the birthing experience is a good way to show your support at a time when your partner really needs you. Today, almost all couples make childbirth a team effort. The benefits of your presence and involvement are many and long term. Being involved in the birthing experience helps you bond with your child. Your presence makes childbirth a family experience and it is an important step in your role as a father. Fathers should prepare for childbirth so that they can anticipate events and be supportive.

Focus Point. Adults can expect several outcomes in association with childbirth. The type of delivery may influence the adults' reaction, affecting the quality of emotional bonding that occurs between the parents and the newborn. The active involvement of the newborn's father during the birthing experience may facilitate his involvement in future child-rearing experiences. Rooming-in may facilitate the emotional bonding of the parents and the child, as well as bolster the confidence of the parents in their ability to provide competent care for their infant.

Focus Point. Childbirth is a family event that allows the parents and the newborn to bond emotionally. In a developed country like the United States, giving birth in a hospital, with medical support, optimizes a good outcome for both the mother and the child. In addition, and most importantly, it minimizes the risks should unforeseen complications occur. Complications cannot always be anticipated, and the ability to react quickly and appropriately is crucial in preventing infant and maternal mortality, as well as preventing permanent negative outcomes from complications. Parents who choose home births, declining the support of obstetricians, pediatricians, and a supportive medical team, run the risk of lifelong remorse if complications occur that should have been managed in a medical setting.

CULTURAL SNAPSHOTS

If circumstances are optimal, the birth of a child is a joyous occasion in all cultures. People from different ethnicities celebrate this occasion differently. In the United States, the gender of the child is often "color coded" with pink or blue, although in an increasingly gender equal environment, this practice is not followed in all circles. We can all share in the joy of this new life, even if we do not know the family personally.

In Mexico, a pregnant woman may attach two safety pins in the form of a cross to her underwear to protect the unborn child. This is believed to be especially important during a lunar eclipse due to the Aztec belief that a bite had been taken out of the moon and it was feared that that a bite could be taken out of the baby's mouth. Folklore advises women not to cut their hair during pregnancy, and some think it may have to do with diminishing strength. In some Latin American cultures, food prohibitions are taken very seriously. Mothers are discouraged from eating strawberries in order to prevent the baby from being born with a red blemish (e.g., a hemangioma). In Mexico and Central America, *la cuarentena* refers to the 40 days after the child's birth when a mother is expected to rest and adjust to motherhood while another member of the family takes care of household tasks and any other children. There are also home remedies for postpartum depression.

POINTS TO CONSIDER

- Development before birth has some unique characteristics in that it is
  - The shortest stage of the human life span.
  - The stage during which growth occurs most rapidly.
  - A highly critical period of human development because of the extreme vulnerability of the embryo to a variety of factors.

- Some factors that can positively or adversely influence the developmental progress of a fetus include the following:
  - Environmental factors
  - The age of the mother
  - Maternal nutrition and exercise
  - Exposure to medications, illicit drugs, and chemical agents
  - Exposure to infectious disease agents via the mother
  - The mother's prenatal medical care
- There are a variety of procedures available for prenatal diagnostic screening, such as sonography (ultrasound), blood tests (e.g., the quad screen test), amniocentesis, chorionic villus sampling (CVS), and percutaneous umbilical blood sampling (PUBS). These are summarized in Table 6–1.
- Most expectant parents welcome a pregnancy, especially if it has been planned and desired. The birth experience can be either a highly significant event in one's life or a highly stressful, negative experience.
- Active involvement and participation of both the mother and her partner in preparing for childbirth is important in making the transition toward parenthood. Active caretaking of the newborn by the parents facilitates and enhances bonding and good attachment between the infant and the parents.
- The birth of a couple's first child prompts the transition of the family system into the childbearing stage. The adjustments that adults make initially focus on the realignment of patterns established early in the relationship.
- The challenges that some couples experience upon the birth of their first child relate to inadequate preparation for parenthood and the abruptness with which these changes take place. Several factors mediate these adjustments:
  - The timing of the birth in the adult's personal developmental path
  - The level of personal self-esteem
  - The employment status of the mother
  - The quality of the patterns established in the family system prior to the birth of the first child
  - The degree of commitment to being a parent
  - The health of the mother and the child
  - The expectations, either positive or negative, regarding what it will be like to be a parent
- The economic, social, and psychological costs of childbearing are considered when individuals decide whether to become parents. Parenthood affects a couple's committed relationship in that satisfaction usually declines during those years that a family is involved in child rearing. This is believed to be a result of the role strain experienced by the adults rather than the presence of children within the family system.
- Postpartum depression requires early recognition and medical support because it can put both the mother and her infant at risk as it prevents good bonding; mothers who suffer from this condition cannot take adequate care of their infants. Often an informed partner or family and friends may recognize this condition before a mother admits to herself that she needs help. Fortunately, effective interventions are available.

USEFUL WEBSITES

Academic Pediatric Association
http://ambpeds.org

American Academy of Pediatrics
www.aap.org

The American Congress of Obstetricians and Gynecologists
www.acog.org

American Pregnancy Association
www.americanpregnancy.org

Mayo Clinic
www.mayoclinic.com

Postpartum Support International
www.postpartum.net

CHAPTER 7

Parenting Infants and Toddlers

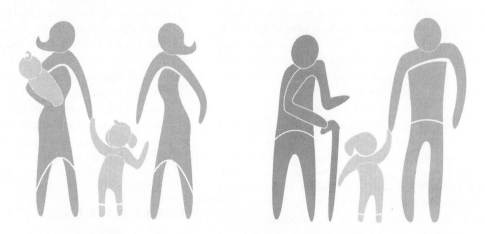

Learning Outcomes

After completing this chapter, readers should be able to

1. Describe the principal developmental landmarks of infancy and how they guide the parents in meeting infant needs appropriately.

2. Explain the differences and similarities between parenting and parent–infant relations.

3. Explain why the parenthood role is a constantly evolving role.

4. Explain why community supports are important to parents of infants and toddlers, especially while dealing with stressors.

Infancy is the period of the life span that extends between the birth and the first year following the birth. Recent research findings about the nature of infant development depict an infant as showing highly competent behaviors and being actively involved in learning to master interactions with the environment (Shelov, 2010). Most people are aware that infants require much attention, supervision, and care to grow and develop properly. Theorists and researchers also acknowledge infancy as a landmark stage in the human life span.

For most of the developmental periods between infancy and early childhood, parents provide caregiving that addresses physical as well as emotional needs.

● ●

Parenting Reflection 7–1

What are some sources of contemporary ideas about the nature of infants? Are these depictions realistic?

● ●

DEVELOPMENTAL LANDMARKS OF INFANCY

As with other stages of the life span, infancy has its own unique developmental tasks and landmarks that lay the foundation for current and future developmental progress. Several complex developmental changes and events are uniquely linked to this time of life. Many developmental events that occur in infancy are the product of maturational changes, such as changes in size, weight, and body proportions; changes in physiological structures and functions; and the development of particular physical skills, including walking and speaking. Other significant developmental events are more psychological in nature and are more sensitive to environmental influences. These are important as they contribute to the parent–child relationship and are configured in particular ways that are unique to the individual and the family system.

Healthy adjustment in infancy focuses on accomplishing the challenges of the developmental tasks and landmarks that are appropriate to this time of life. Traditionally, these lead from complete dependence and helplessness at birth to the ability to function somewhat independently of adults in some contexts. For this development to take place, infants need to acquire a trusting attitude about their caregivers and their environment and establish initial personal boundaries that permit self-individuation. They need caretakers who are *responsive* to the infant's needs.

Knowledge of developmental events that occur at each stage of a child's life span is important to parents and other caregivers. All humans are born with a capacity for certain events that have been programmed to occur and for other events that are subject to environmental influences. Infants are active participants in influencing their social environment and the responses of those who provide their care. As a result, parents and caregivers need to be aware of certain cues that a baby will provide to assist caregivers regarding behavior. These cues are often part of the developmental process, and to recognize them, caregivers need to observe a baby's behavior and know what occurs appropriately at different times.

PARENTING INFANTS AND TODDLERS

Meeting the Needs of Infants and Toddlers

Most adults are cognizant of the extreme degree of dependency of an infant on its parents or caregivers. Dependence on adults is necessary for survival and for enhancing a child's developmental progress; in turn, adults need to be *responsive*. In humans, the nature and degree of dependency in infancy and childhood differs from that observed among the young of other species. Anthropologists have attributed this to the larger brain of humans that allows for higher order mental processes that are not found in other species (Morris & Masnick, 2008). It takes much more developmental time for a human's brain to be wired in establishing the myriad neural circuits that allow mature functioning. For example, the brain at birth weighs only 25 percent of its total adult weight, but by age 3, the brain has attained about 90 percent of its adult weight. There is more to attaining maturity than achieving an adult brain weight. Socialization and education continue for many years beyond age 3. For most of the developmental period between infancy and early

Focus On 7–1   **Major Developmental Landmarks in Infancy**

The Newborn (Birth to 2 weeks)

■ Establishing respiration within normal limits.
■ Establishing circulation to the lungs and away from the umbilical cord.
■ Establishing body temperature regulation.
■ Establishing feeding and elimination processes.
■ Exercising neonatal reflexes.
■ Adjusting to light and sound.

The Infant (3 weeks to 12 months)

■ Acquiring self-regulated skills of locomotion (walking), manipulation (hand skills), and self-feeding with solid food.
■ Beginning to establish a sleep pattern and maintaining a sleep–wake cycle.
■ Exploring sound production in preparation for speech.
■ Establishing initial sensorimotor schemes and mastering object permanence.
■ Establishing an emotional attachment to parents and primary caregivers.
■ Experiencing basic emotional states that are related to infancy (e.g., social smiling and crying) as a means of communication.
■ Establishing an attitude of basic trust versus mistrust.

The Toddler (Second and third years of life)

■ Refining self-regulated skills.
■ Establishing early speech patterns.
■ Refining and modifying basic sensorimotor schemes and establishing elementary logic and reasoning.
■ Learning to control the elimination of body wastes.
■ Establishing an attitude of autonomy versus shame and doubt (Erikson, 1950).
■ Establishing self-differentiation and exploring personal boundaries.
■ Developing an initial conscience.

childhood, parents provide caregiving that is largely physical and emotionally nurturing. As children grow older, physical caregiving diminishes somewhat while psychological caregiving increases.

Feeding and Breast-feeding. To promote the health of both infants and their mothers, the Centers for Disease Control and Prevention (Centers for Disease Control and Prevention, 2012a) recommend breast-feeding. There has been a steady rise in exclusively breast-fed infants, especially at 3–6 months. This implies that mothers are nursing longer and both the mothers and the infants receive the health benefits. The statistics for the United States are encouraging and indicate that about 75 percent of children have been breast-fed at some time, meaning that some nursing occurred, supplemented with formula. At least

a third of all mothers have managed to exclusively breast-feed until the baby was 3 months old; in several states, this figure was as high as 50 percent, meeting one of the goals of Healthy People 2020 (Centers for Disease Control and Prevention, 2012b). There are distinct cultural variations, with 80 percent of Hispanic/Latina mothers initiating breast-feeding.

One of the initial decisions in providing infant care is to commit to breast-feeding for at least 4–6 months so that the mother's antibodies (proteins that fight infection) can be transmitted to the infant through her breast milk. This, in itself, is a priceless gift that helps the infant to develop increased immunity against disease. Almost all fathers are supportive and encourage breast-feeding for their newborns because they have been educated regarding the many benefits to both the mother and the infant. Hospital lactation specialists, specifically

Breastfeeding provides numerous benefits to mother and infant. Breastfeeding allows the mother's antibodies to be transmitted to the infant through her breast milk. Nursing is a healthy bonding opportunity.

certified International Board of Lactation consultants, can guide the mother in establishing good lactation patterns and coping with nursing. The lactation specialist will also counsel mothers concerning pumping breast milk for feeding when she is not available to nurse and supplementation with formula, if needed. Ideally, the mother will produce as much milk as the infant requires. It is optimal to exclusively breast-feed for 6 months (American Academy of Pediatrics, 2012), followed by the addition of complementary age-appropriate foods.

The benefits of nursing extend well beyond the actual infant feeding process. Infants who have been breast-fed are less likely to become obese and develop diabetes in later life (Centers for Disease Control and Prevention, 2012a). Mothers who have nursed lower their risk for breast cancer, diabetes, and heart disease (Stuebe & Schwarz, 2010). Additionally, the mothers who nurse lose the weight gained during pregnancy faster. The time spent nursing is an excellent bonding opportunity for the infant and the mother. Some family-friendly workplaces and child-care centers will provide a lactation room for female employees. Child-care regulations have been adjusted nationally to support nursing mothers, and it is regarded as a *best practice*. Research supports breast-feeding because the health-related benefits far outweigh any perceived inconvenience (American Academy of Pediatrics, 2012).

On the other hand, under certain medical conditions, a mother *should not* nurse because infectious agents can be transmitted via the breast milk (e.g., hepatitis, untreated tuberculosis, and HIV). In addition, certain medications and other substances can be excreted in the milk of lactating mothers. Also, lactating mothers should abstain from nicotine and alcohol and greatly limit their caffeine intake. With regard to medications, mothers should take the same precautions during lactation as they did during pregnancy. Medical guidance is indicated (American Medical Association, 2012). For the same reasons, and to ensure safety, unscreened human milk should not be fed to another mother's child; preferably, an infant should receive the milk from its own biological mother.

Under some special circumstances, such as extreme prematurity and when babies are fragile, breast milk can be purchased if it is not available from the mother. This breast milk and the donor mother will have been screened and the milk pasteurized. Some hospitals maintain milk banks that adhere to strict guidelines of the Human Milk Banking Association of North America. Nursing mothers who are able to do so can donate their surplus human milk to milk bank depots.

The sucking reflex is one of the earliest reflexes to appear during prenatal development and is exceptionally well developed at birth in full-term newborns. This necessary reflex, which is easily elicited by almost any stimulation to the lips, cheeks, or mouth area, ensures that an infant can obtain nourishment before teeth emerge for chewing. The infant also has a rooting reflex, seeking out the mother's breast in order to nurse.

Most normal infants require feeding every 2 to 4 hours during the first few months after birth. After adding solid foods to a baby's diet, usually after about the sixth month (American Academy of Pediatrics, 2012), the number of feedings is reduced and continues to decline as the infant grows older. Mothers can continue to supplement feedings with breast milk.

Toddlers can generally feed themselves after they have developed the motor skills and coordination necessary to hold a cup and drink from it and to bring food to their mouths and chew. These events are a result of maturational processes and cultural expectations or experiences. Developmental norms have been established that show the times at which these events can be expected to occur.

● ●

Parenting Reflection 7–2

Explain some of the many far-reaching positive outcomes of breast-feeding for both mother and infant. How can fathers be supportive in meeting the needs of a new baby?

● ●

Introducing Solid Foods.   Infants are introduced to age-appropriate solid foods when they indicate a readiness to begin taking solid foods. Such indications include the ability to hold the head steady and to transfer food from the front of the tongue to the back and to swallow. Infant specialists recommend that solid foods are preferably introduced at about 6 months. If introduced too early, the solid foods can interfere with the intake of human milk (American Academy of Pediatrics, 2012).

A major concern in the infant's diet is providing adequate amounts of protein, iron, and vitamin D to meet the infant's requirements for growth. Lack of adequate sources of these nutrients can lead to malnutrition and eventually to permanent damage, especially to the brain and central nervous system (Spock & Needleman, 2011). It is necessary to follow the advice of a pediatrician.

As the toddler matures, he or she will learn a more mature style of eating that parallels the physical growth. The child will also learn the many complex social, cultural, sociological, and physiological aspects that are part of eating.

Health and Medical Care.   If a woman experienced relatively good health during her pregnancy, then it is likely that the baby will also enter the world in a healthy state. Certain physical conditions that appear to be of concern are relatively normal for infants:

■ Spitting up or vomiting is common; the infant should be adequately burped after each feeding to prevent bloating and cramps.

■ Sneezing and hiccupping, especially during the first few months following birth, are common.

■ The appearance of the stool varies by age and diet of the infant. The stools of breast-fed babies typically are mustard- yellow, runny, and seedy or curdled in texture. Rashes are common, especially in the diaper area.

■ Other skin conditions may be observed, such as cradle cap (seborrhea), heat rash, and if breast-fed, occasional skin rashes and slight breast budding or swelling, caused by hormones in the lactating mother's breast milk.

■ Obstructed tear ducts sometimes occur, and in the majority of cases there is spontaneous remission within the first year.

It is important to follow up with well-baby medical care that will allow health-care professionals to examine the baby regularly and to judge whether any conditions require medical intervention and treatment. Many physical disorders can be detected early. Immunizations during infancy provide protection from communicable diseases such as measles, diphtheria, mumps, and polio. A schedule of planned vaccinations is recommended. While most families have medical insurance to cover this care, families living in poverty will be able to get all vaccinations and care at no cost at public clinics.

Sleep–Wake Cycle.   A popular belief about infants is that they sleep a great deal of the time, at least 16 hours a day. This may be so during the early months, but individual sleeping patterns are subject to wide variations (Spock & Needleman, 2011). Informative

---

Focus On 7–2   Early Warning Signs and Infant Care

It is important to know that an infant does not have the same resilience as an adult. It is better to be overcautious and to get medical advice as soon as problems manifest, because the consequences can be irreversible if there is no speedy intervention. For instance, diarrhea can cause dehydration very quickly and can be life threatening. Be informed so that, as a parent, you recognize early warning signs that warrant professional intervention. Regard the medical pediatric team as your support system in raising infants optimally.

material, based on best practices, is available to guide parents concerning their child's sleep (American Academy of Pediatrics, 2012). Sleep during the first few months after birth is interrupted only long enough for the baby to feed. This round-the-clock pattern of alternating periods of sleep with feeding extends to longer intervals of wakefulness after the third month. During the remainder of the time until the baby approaches age 2, sleep decreases to 10 to 14 hours daily. Most toddlers need a morning and afternoon nap through the preschool years, which is definitely welcomed by parents who need a little time off from child care. See Figure 7–1 for tips on safe sleeping for infants.

SAFE SLEEPING

- *Back-to-Sleep*: Infants should sleep on their backs in a supine position.
- A firm crib mattress, covered by a tight-fitting sheet, should be used in a safety-approved crib.
- There should be no bedding; loose and soft bedding and soft toys in the crib can contribute to suffocation.
- Swaddling infants older than 2 months for sleep is not recommended because it increases the risk of sudden infant death syndrome (SIDS).
- One-piece clothing for sleeping is recommended, depending on the temperature.
- Infant should not overheat; be aware of the room temperature.
- Infants should not nap or sleep in a car safety seat or a bouncy seat, instead of a crib. If an infant falls asleep in a car safety seat while traveling, remove the child immediately upon arrival and place the infant in a supine position in a crib. Monitor the child while traveling.
- Avoid baby necklaces, bibs, or anything around the baby's neck that could cause strangulation.
- There should be only one child per crib—no crib sharing.
- Infants should not sleep in adult beds, nor should they bed share with an adult.
- Pacifiers may be used, but consult the safety protocols.
- Infants should be observed by sight and sound at all times.

FIGURE 7–1. Safe sleeping for infants.

Based on the recommendations of the National Resource Center for Health and Safety in Child Care and Early Education (2012), www.nrckids.org.

Providing Structure and Nurture for Infants.   The psychosocial focus of an infant is on learning to trust the integrity of caregivers and the environment in providing and meeting the infant's needs. The child relies on the *responsiveness* of the caretaker. At some level of consciousness, infants are likely to make decisions about themselves, others, and things in their world that relate to trust (J. I. Clarke & Dawson, 1998). Interactions with people, the environment, and things in the environment lead the infant to conclusions and expectations about how his or her needs will be met. Understandably, most of the parenting behaviors that are observed in providing care for infants between birth and 6 months of age are nurturing, whereas those that are observed in providing care between 18 months and 3 years include increasing elements of structure.

Parents of toddlers are especially concerned about initiating efforts to control their child's behavior and to elicit compliance with their demands. One study provides insightful information on how parenting style influences child compliance (Kuczynski & Kochanska, 1995). The researchers observed a group of 70 mothers and their toddlers in a realistic setting. Three types of maternal demands were observed:

1. *Caretaking demands* were related to providing physical care and supervision (e.g., "Wash your hands." "Watch out for the stairs.").
2. *Demands for appropriate behavior* involved teaching and reinforcing the rules for acceptable behavior (e.g., "Don't do that!").
3. *Demands for competent action* helped the child or others (e.g., "Please share your toy."). Younger toddlers received more of the first type of guidance from mothers, while older toddlers received more of the third type.

The parenting style agreed with the type of demand that a mother used with her toddler. Those using an authoritarian style peppered their demands with prohibitions for the toddler's behavior, while those using an authoritative style couched their demands in terms that promoted competencies within a rationale of guidance. The researchers found that mothers using an authoritative style were more likely to gain compliance from their toddler than mothers using an authoritarian style. When the children and their mothers were again observed by the researchers after the children had reached 5 years of age, fewer behavior problems

Parenting FAQ 7–1

We have a toddler who just doesn't want to stay in her bed once she's put down at night. She'll get up five or six times before going to sleep. It's exhausting for us to go through this every night. Any suggestions?

Children at this age often experience separation anxiety in relation to bedtime. Some children perform this kind of routine to gain parental attention. If your child is being cared for by someone else during the day, it might be helpful to sit with her with the understanding that it will only be for a short time, during which she is to go to sleep. You are helping your child to develop a bedtime routine that is healthy for all concerned. Consistently, but firmly, lead her back to bed each time that she reappears after being put down to sleep. Developing a bedtime routine of reading calm, peaceful stories helps children settle down; a pleasant bath is also helpful for many children.

were observed among the children of the authoritative-style mothers.

Promoting Brain Development. Parents play an important role in promoting an infant's brain development. This influence begins with the environment provided by the mother during pregnancy and continues following the birth of the child with the provision of adequate nutrition, health care, stimulation, nurture, and interaction.

An infant's brain experiences rapid growth during the first 2 years following birth. At birth, the brain is functionally operational, but lacks the ability to perform critical thinking skills and to use language. The neonatal reflexes that are present at birth, such as sucking and grasping, are formed at the subcortical level. This part of the brain contains those mechanisms that regulate heart rate, respiration, sleeping patterns, and so forth. These reflexes are important in that they serve as the first avenues for allowing the infant to interact with its environment. These reflexes lay the foundation for all mental functioning during this stage and in the stages that follow.

At birth, there are immense numbers of neurons in the brain that are unconnected. The infant's brain is basically in an unsculpted state at birth regarding these neural connections that allow for the development of many physical, motor, and cognitive skills (Stiles, 2008). Meeting an infant's nutritional needs and providing appropriate sensory stimulation is critical for these brain changes to take place.

Parents play a particularly important role in providing stimulating experiences and interactions that

RESPONSIVE AND RESPONSIBLE PARENTING

- Give loving and consistent care that meets and anticipates the infant's needs.
- Provide a safe environment.
- Respond to cues regarding hunger and the need to sleep.
- Provide appropriate stimulation.
- Talk and sing to the baby.
- Hold the infant lovingly.
- Be a responsible, loving, and trustworthy caretaker.
- Seek information on child-care best practices.
- Adjust the parenting style to meet the child's developmental needs.

FIGURE 7–2. Parenting behaviors for infants.

promote brain development (see Figure 7–2). The quality of parental caretaking, especially in how nurture is expressed to an infant, plays a critical role (Kim & Swain, 2006). When a parent holds an infant in a nurturing manner (with a loving touch) while it is being fed, looks into its eyes (visual stimulation), and talks soothingly (auditory stimulation), then several sensory modalities are being stimulated simultaneously. Later, as the baby grows older, the brain appears to be constantly fine-tuning the neural connections, as well as continuing to develop new ones. This is dependent, in part, upon parents and family members continuing to provide nurture and interactions that help infants learn to be curious and to want to explore, touch, taste, and thoroughly experience their world through their senses. Social and physical stimulation are important and necessary components of providing appropriate infant care.

Attachment in infancy is a strong emotional tie to the primary caregiver and can influence relationship formation in later developmental stages.

Later, cultural aspects are transmitted via language, observation of family and community members, and by socialization experiences provided by the parents. The young brains are equipped with *mirror neurons*, which support this imitative behavior (Ferrari & Coudé, 2011; Pätzold, 2010).

Facilitating Attachment. **Attachment** is an attraction to someone that is based on psychological bonding. It is also described as a strong affectional tie between an infant and his or her primary caregivers (Ainsworth, 1973). This process affects both the parents and the infant. It is one of the few developmental phenomena that appear to be found universally in all humans and in all cultural settings. It is essential for an infant's survival and well-being. When an infant fails to attach properly to caregivers, the consequences are damaging to his or her emotional, physical, social, and psychological well-being.

Attachment is constructed through the interactions of an infant with the primary caregivers. An infant who is experiencing normal developmental progress behaves in ways that signal a desire to be near caregivers, and the behaviors usually serve to attract the caregivers' attention. Infant behaviors that stimulate attachment to caregivers include crying, smiling, clutching, and touching. Such infant behaviors elicit *responses* from the caregivers that facilitate the attachment process, for example, smiling at, gently handling, stroking, feeding, and talking to the infant.

Attachment between the infant and the caregiver is believed to occur in four phases (Bowlby, 1982):

Focus On 7–3

Parenting and Children's Brain Development

- For optimal development, infants and children need ongoing, consistent, responsive, loving and constructive parenting and care (Sue Gerhardt, 2004).
- A current theme in child development and in parenting concerns the effects of extreme childhood adversity and brain development, as well as subsequent developmental implications.
- Cutting-edge research questions the relationship between parenting and later emotional, cognitive, and social outcomes.
- Most of the studies examining the link between parenting and brain structure have focused on high-risk groups, such as children in settings with severe institutional deprivation and neglect as well as maltreated children (Sue Gerhardt, 2004; Pollak, 2008).
- Certain areas of the brain appear to be adversely affected by deprivation and trauma during sensitive periods in infancy and childhood (Sue Gerhardt, 2004; Marshall, 2011).
- It is presumed that, because not all sections of the brain develop simultaneously or at the same rate, the outcomes of early experiences, including the effects of parenting behavior, can differ, depending on when these influences occur (Nagel, 2012; Vanderwert, Marshall, Nelson, Zeanah, & Fox, 2010).
- Research seems to support the hypothesis that children, and thereby their developing brains, differ in their responses to varying parenting behaviors (Belsky & de Haan, 2011).
- Research outcomes also suggest that there is a link between emotional and social trauma in early childhood and the development and function of brain structures (Belsky & de Haan, 2011).

(Continued)

Focus On 7–3   (*Continued*)

- Delayed maturation and reduced functional connectivity of the frontal cortex, as well as the involvement of other areas of the brain, may contribute to scholastic and emotional difficulties in children with a history of deprivation, abuse, and neglect. The neurodevelopmental effects appear to continue post institutionalization (Nagel, 2012; Pollak, Nelson, Schlaak, Roeber, et al., 2010).
- It is important to establish whether subsequent optimal parenting, as well as therapeutic interventions, can ameliorate the effects of earlier trauma and deprivation.
- Further research is necessary, especially examining the outcome of parenting under relatively normal circumstances with subjects who have not endured extreme adversity (Belskey & de Haan, 2011).

Based on Belskey, Jay, & de Haan, Michelle (2011). Annual research review: parenting and children's brain development: the end of the beginning. *Journal of Child Psychology and Psychiatry* 52:4 (2011), pp. 409–428. Oxford, UK: Blackwell Publishing.

Gerhardt, Sue (2004).*Why love matters: how affection shapes a baby's brain*. NY: Brunner-Routledge.

Nagel, M. C. (2012). *In the beginning: the brain, early development and learning.* Sydney: Australian Council for Educational Research.

1. *Undiscriminating social responsiveness* is observed at about 2 to 3 months of age. This stage is characterized by an infant's orientation toward all humans as seen in the baby's visual tracking, visual exploration, listening and becoming quiet when being addressed by someone, and becoming relaxed when held. Opportunities to examine the faces of caregivers appear to facilitate this phase of attachment.
2. *Discriminating social responsiveness* is observed at about 4 to 5 months of age. This phase is characterized by an infant's recognition of familiar persons, by smiling in response, and by restless behavior when the person leaves its field of vision. Also indicative of this stage is anxiety when encountering unfamiliar people.
3. *Active proximity seeking*—that is, seeking physical proximity and contact with familiar people—occurs at about 7 months of age. At this stage, an infant clings to, crawls toward, and actively seeks to touch and have contact with a familiar person.
4. *Goal-corrected partnership* occurs at about age 3 and completes the attachment process. The child has now learned to predict the behavior of the caregivers and to adjust his or her own behavior to maintain some degree of physical closeness to them.

Attachment is important in establishing an infant's sense of basic trust in people and the environment, and in helping the infant feel secure in exploring the environment (Ainsworth, 1977). Children who successfully

attach to caregivers learn to express curiosity in their world, which helps promote mental and social growth throughout their life span. Children who have successfully attached during infancy appear to have a greater capacity to deal with novel situations, cope with failure, exert greater perseverance in problem solving, participate in loving relationships with others, and maintain healthy self-esteem.

Social referencing appears to be related to attachment. This behavior is observed when infants look to their parents' faces as a means of obtaining informational cues (Baldwin & Moses, 1996). Facial cues guide infants' decisions about how to act and how to react to situations. Apparently, cues and emotional information from the parents program many reactions that become automatic and habitual responses to similar situations that arise later in life.

Attachment is not a one-sided affair that only affects the infant. While this is critical for a baby's survival and well-being, parents also must experience a positive, secure attachment to an infant in order to fully provide for its care. The elementary basis of this interactional pattern that helps both infants and parents to bond was explored first through studies of what occurs in infant development when the infant is deprived of adequate parental stimulation and interaction.

A controversial issue about contemporary family life relates to attachment during infancy. In about 65 percent of all married couples in the United States, both adults are employed outside the home (U.S. Bureau of Labor Statistics, 2010). Most single parents are employed as well. The daily separations that result raise concerns about the ability of infants to form attachments with caregivers and the quality of those attachments. Some studies find significant differences in the attachments between the infants of employed mothers and the infants of unemployed mothers, while others do not. The question concerns whether there should be less out-of-home child care or whether the child care be different (Maccoby & Lewis, 2003). *The essence of the issue relates to the quality and consistency of the child care. This also applies to in-home care, which will vary according to the quality of the care provided by the caretaker.*

The important element of nurturing behavior from caregivers is sensory stimulation that communicates love and nurture to an infant. Touching, handling, fondling, and stroking express affectionate attention and care. From the earliest beginnings of life outside the uterus, it is believed that individuals learn to experience love and to express it to others through these sensory means. In infancy, this is thought to occur in relation to the development of an attachment between parents and infants. Early experiences in relation to the type of care given to an infant appear to play an influential role in determining later behavior and development.

All of this attention to the process of attachment helps to explain why the relationship established between an infant and its caregivers is very important. This has been studied extensively by a number of behavioral scientists, who have advanced what is known about the importance of attachment. For example, one of the classical methods for studying attachment in contemporary studies is the use of the "strange situation" test (Ainsworth, 1983). A mother and her infant enter a laboratory playroom that is equipped with interesting, appealing toys, as well as an adult stranger. Shortly after entering, the mother then leaves the baby with the toys and the stranger while observers record the baby's interactions with both. Later, the mother returns and the observers again record the infant's reactions. This is repeated eight times.

The reunion with the mother allows the observers to determine the three different types of attachment of the infant:

■ *Securely attached* infants are not overly animated when the mother returns and use her as a base for exploring the room and as a source of comfort upon reuniting.

■ *Insecure/avoidant* infants ignore or avoid the mother upon her return, do not appear to be distressed when the mother leaves them, and react to the stranger in a similar manner as to the mother.

■ *Insecure/resistant* infants are reluctant to explore the playroom, cling to the mother, and attempt to hide from the stranger. These infants initially seek contact with the mother upon her return, but then show signs of rejecting her. These children have been found to display more maladaptive behaviors and appear to be angrier children (Ainsworth, 1993).

Some researchers have wondered if the strange situation test is valid (Crittenden, Claussen, & Kozlowska, 2007). One of the main objections to this method of assessing attachment is that it may not be effective in other cultural settings. Researchers developed other ways to assess this, such as in-home observation by objective observers. This does not mean that the strange situation test cannot be used. Instead, researchers need to be mindful of the cultural context of families and the broad range of behaviors that indicate certain types of attachment in children.

In addition to behaving in accordance with the three main attachment patterns, some children respond in an atypical manner that has been described as *disorganized* attachment. Disorganized attachment may lack coherence, display contradictory patterns, and result in disorientation of the child. This kind of attachment may represent the child's response to being frightened of the caretaker or may be the child's reaction to an abusive situation.

Successful, secure attachment between the infant and the parents affects all participants and influences the baby's later behavior. There is some connection between attachment and a child's cognitive development. In addition, attachment continues to play an important role in a child's social relationships not only during childhood and adolescence, but particularly in adulthood, when it becomes manifested in a revised manner in intimate relationships.

Focus Point.   Attachment is a process in which both parents and infants participate. Secure attachment of an infant ensures its survival and impacts its development in other areas. For parents, attachment to their infant facilitates their nurturant caregiving behaviors, which, in turn, support the attachment process of the infant.

Developing Autonomy. While much parental attention and behavior is directed in ways that communicate nurture to infants and toddlers, a shift occurs when most children reach 18 months of age toward providing elementary measures of structure. This shift in parental behavior usually comes in response to a change in a toddler's behavior that indicates a drive toward establishing a sense of autonomy (from Erik Erikson's psychosocial theory). This drive is to establish one's independence from the parents as a separate entity and to dismantle the strong emotional ties promoted during attachment experiences with the parents. Essentially, from a family systems theory point of view, toddlers discover their ability to set personal boundaries between themselves and others as they discover that they are distinct individuals and not an extension of their parents. A toddler's attempts at self-differentiation are healthy, but may also produce conflicts and power struggles. Striving toward autonomy occurs when a toddler learns to be self-assertive in a variety of ways. Using the word "NO!" to show noncooperation with parental demands and requests, trying to dress without supervision, testing parental limits in play, and toilet training are examples of how personal autonomy is tested by toddlers.

Toilet learning or toilet training usually begins between 18 and 30 months of age and is typically completed by 36 months. Focusing on *toilet learning*

A sense of autonomy is established when toddlers accomplish self-differentiation in new ways.

acknowledges the neurological maturational process that occurs within the child and that allows the child to gain control over elimination (Wittmer, Petersen, & Puckett, 2013). *Toilet training*, in contrast, implies that the activity is adult directed. In reality, these two facets interact, as the parent responds to the cues provided by the child and provides the supportive environment to facilitate toilet learning.

Parenting FAQ 7–2

Do you have any suggestions on handling a toddler's temper tantrums? The outbursts that occur in public are especially troublesome.

Reacting to temper tantrums is an exercise in parental control. It is helpful to understand that these tantrums are not a personal attack on you, but the outcome of uncontrollable emotions. Adults can have temper tantrums, too, better known as *outbursts*. Children can learn to control these with a fair degree of success if taught by patient parents. With toddlers, you can begin the learning process by remembering to stay calm yourself. Try to analyze why the tantrum is occurring: Is it because the child is tired and needs to nap? If this is the case, just holding the child firmly and rocking gently will often help to calm things down. Going to a quiet place, if in public, may also contribute toward calming the child. Perhaps if you can reframe the temper tantrum as being similar to an electrical power outage, it can help you to stay calm. We don't plan an outage; it just happens, and often we just need to be patient and stay calm until the power returns. Recent research has also shown that a temper tantrum follows its own predictable cycle. When the child is intensely frustrated, interference by the parent only seems to aggravate matters. Wait until the child calms down a little and is more open to parental reassurance (Green, Whitney, & Potegal, 2011). A discussion about emotions and constructive ways of dealing with future situations can be introduced after the child has recovered and is calm.

An early step in the process of toilet learning is the awareness that elimination is occurring, and this progresses to anticipation of elimination and, later, the ability to void in appropriate contexts and places. Learning bladder and bowel control is usually easily accomplished if the child is developmentally ready. Guidelines can be found in most reputable child-care sources. The use of positive rewards and reinforcement is often the most successful route for encouraging toilet learning. Shaming a child for accidents or mistakes in toilet learning is likely to elicit a power struggle between the parent and the child and is not recommended. The resulting unhealthy attitude of shame and doubt can cause the child to question his or her ability to be autonomous (Erik Erikson). Being exposed in child-care programs to children who have mastered these skills can provide the appropriate behavioral and conformance cues.

• •

Parenting Reflection 7–3

Explain the long-term effects of the development of basic trust versus mistrust during infancy.

• •

Providing Appropriate Toys and Play Equipment. Infants need appropriate play equipment and materials to stimulate cognitive development and social skills. Simple toys are often all that is necessary. This is especially reassuring for parents who lack financial resources to provide what they see in stores and being used by other families. Infants can develop adequate cognitive skills by playing with toys and equipment that encourages visual and tactile exploration. These also promote the development of curiosity in the world, which will have long-range positive effects. During playtime, it is also helpful to introduce supervised *tummy time*, which promotes healthy development (www.healthychildcare.org/pdf/SIDStummytime.pdf).

Safety is an important factor in choosing toys. While most manufacturers meet safety standards, parents need to keep these points in mind when selecting toys for infants and older children: (1) no sharp edges, (2) no small parts that can be swallowed or inhaled, (3) no cords or strings, and (4) no loud noises (Consumer Product Safety Commission, n.d.). Parents can choose age-appropriate toys and play equipment by considering the chronological age of their child.

Promoting Cognitive Development.   Infancy encompasses the first stage of cognitive development according to Jean Piaget (1967). He termed this stage the *sensorimotor period*. This refers to the major developmental tasks that infants must accomplish whereby they coordinate motor skills with sensory data or perceptions of their environment. For example, they learn about the sources of sounds by walking toward them, touching them, and/or exploring them with their eyes. They become more adept at reaching for objects that they see and guiding their hands to grasp these and bring them to their mouths.

Focus On 7–4	**Age-Appropriate Play Equipment for Infants**		
	Birth to 1 Year	*1 to 2 Years*	*2 to 3 Years*
	Rattles	Bath toys	Tricycle
	Crib mobiles	Simple puzzles	Outdoor swings
	Teething rings	Musical instruments	Picture books
	Textured balls/boxes	Toy phone	Crayons
	Crib gyms	Simple picture books	Puzzles
	Stuffed toys	Interlocking blocks	Wooden blocks
	Push-pull toys	Wheeled toys (e.g., cars)	Sandpit
	Shape sorters	Musical toys	
	Squeaking toys	Ride-on toys (e.g., rocking horse, wagon)	
	Nesting/stacking toys		
	Cloth/hard cardboard books		

Another developmental task, according to Piaget, is an understanding of permanence in their physical and social environments. This is known as ***object permanence***. For about the first 6 months after birth, an infant becomes upset when the parent leaves its field of vision as it is thought that they believe that the parent has permanently disappeared; that is, what cannot be seen does not exist. As development takes place and interactions continue to take place, an infant will look for an object that's been covered up with a cloth by searching for it. The time-honored game of peek-a-boo is a classic exercise in helping infants to learn object permanence. In other words, with experience, an understanding develops that an object or person continues to exist even though it cannot be seen. Parents and caregivers play an important role in facilitating cognitive development through their interactions with infants and the experiences that they provide. This is the basis of what Vygotsky termed the *zone of proximal development*. Parents can support and guide infants in activities and interactions that they could not achieve on their own. Parents guide an infant to learn cues for appropriate behavior, to understand that it is appropriate to experience the world via their senses, and to be curious about exploring their environment. Essentially, when playing with their baby, parents begin to socialize the child into their family values system, their cultural system, and the importance of social interactions.

Research also points to the ability of parents to stimulate their baby's brain development through what are termed *enrichment activities*. These interactions include a variety of play equipment, sensory experiences, the use of language, and social interactions (Fowler, Ogston, Roberts, & Swenson, 2006). Rewarding or praising the baby when it is responsive to such activities is also important. In addition, when infants are securely attached to parents, their cognitive and brain development are enhanced as well.

Language acquisition. The role of *language* emerges during this period as the basis for learning and development during the later stages of cognitive development. Language acquisition is a crucial foundation in development and communication, and parents perform a significant role in helping infants to communicate. Behavioral scientists presume that there is a basic brain pattern and anatomy to support language development at birth (Chomsky, 1968; Chomsky, 1975), and this is shaped and influenced by parents when they talk to and interact with their baby, regardless of the particular language spoken in the home. Babies initially babble in universal sounds, but as they are exposed to role models, they imitate the sound ranges found within their mother tongue. The presence of mirror neurons in the brain is thought to contribute to language acquisition (Ferrari & Coudé, 2011; Pätzold, 2010).

It is important to talk to babies and infants in order to provide them with communication cues so that they learn the turn-taking behavior in the communication process and can model the language (see Figure 7–3). Under normal conditions, *receptive* language is acquired a little ahead of *expressive* language; in other words, a child will understand more than the child can verbalize. Receptive refers to the comprehension of a language, whereas expressive refers to producing speech and communicating meaning or intent. Later, with complete mastery of a language, these go hand-in-hand. When we learn another language as adults, we experience this same sequence; initially, we understand much more than we can speak until we become more fluent. By 18 months, children can usually use two-word combinations, and by age 3, the basics of a language system are in place—truly a developmental miracle! Linguistic ability forms one of the cornerstones of intelligence testing, and in normally developing children, verbal skills can be a good indicator of mental ability.

Although it is very tempting to use "baby talk" when speaking to a child, which is an emotional expression, it may be helpful to also use simple, correct language,

---

LANGUAGE DEVELOPMENT

- Expose infants to language by speaking to and with them.
- Give infants models of verbal expression.
- Allow infants to respond to language.
- Encourage speaking by listening; initiate verbal interaction.
- Encourage interactive activities and stories.
- Read stories; expose children to books.
- Expose children to another language in a consistent manner, if possible.

FIGURE 7–3. Fostering early language development.
Based on American Academy of Pediatrics (2012a). *Healthy Child Care America: Fostering Language Development of 3- to 5-Year-Olds*, Standard 2.1.3.6.

thereby modeling desirable language. Making up sounds and words in an emotionally expressive way, or calling the child by special names, is virtually universal. In all cultures, parents seem to find unique verbal ways of expressing their love for their child. But, ultimately, language connects us, and we have to agree on what words mean and how they are used to facilitate true communication.

We also know that bilingualism enhances brain development because the child will engage additional potential (Petitto, 2009; Westly, 2011). Children can become bilingual if exposed to the second language consistently and preferably before adolescence. There truly is a linguistic window of opportunity that should be used during childhood if the child is going to have the privilege of bilingualism, or even multilingualism. Languages should be separated by person or place. For instance, the parents could speak Spanish only, or if English is spoken at school, then Spanish could be spoken at home. Mixing languages within one sentence or providing a poor example of the language is not helpful.

Communication and Infant Crying.   An infant's first attempts at communication with the world come in the form of crying. Parents soon learn that they must decipher the meaning behind a particular cry in order to meet an infant's needs. For example, a fussy, tearful baby who cries relentlessly may be experiencing colic, a problem resulting from an immature digestive system. A baby may be expressing discomfort as a result of teething, sickness, a wet diaper, feeling lonely, being hungry, or needing comfort and human attention. Determining the cause of a baby's crying is best accomplished by spending time with the baby and learning to associate a particular cry with a particular need. Many infants use crying to indicate their desire to be held, nurtured, and comforted. Infants respond to being walked or rocked. Parents will need to rely on an infant's cries as a means of communicating until the simple elements of language have been acquired sometime between 18 and 24 months of age.

Even healthy babies cry, and parents need to learn what is normal and how to keep the baby safe. In essence, parents need to respond appropriately to the baby. They need to learn methods for soothing a baby, as well as *regulating their own emotions* (see Figure 7–4). They need to understand that developmentally, discipline is inappropriate for infants because, cognitively,

---

PREVENTING CAREGIVER DESPAIR

- Parents and/or caregivers who are sleep deprived or exhausted may act in irrational and desperate ways. They may become frustrated and angry, losing their ability to adapt and to be resilient.
- Recognize that caregiver despair is a real feeling that needs immediate intervention to prevent harm to the child.
- Establish a support system *before* despair sets in. Recognize and *anticipate* when caretaker's emotional resources are approaching depletion.
- Plan for some time off, utilizing support from family and friends or a caregiving facility to give the parent or caretaker a chance to recuperate. Make time for self-renewal and know that it is a valid need that has to be addressed.
- While the infant is young, try to sleep when the infant sleeps, even if this is during the day.
- If a caretaker feels that he or she is losing a grip on his or her emotions, it is necessary to call for help immediately. If that is not possible, the infant should be put in a safe place, such as a crib. The caretaker should then initiate an action which will interrupt the emotions of despair, such as counting to 50, breathing deeply, splashing one's face with cold water, phoning a friend and telling them of the despair, or calling a neighbor to come over. Hopefully, this short break is enough to regain control over one's emotions.
- Social isolation can contribute to the feelings of despair and depression that young parents may face. On becoming a parent, it is important to establish a peer network of fellow parents in an appropriate civic group and to solicit the support of family members, neighbors, and friends who will occasionally help with the caretaking tasks and who will respond in times of need.
- Recognize the despair, acknowledge that it is a valid emotion, and interrupt the overwhelming feeling so that no child is at risk at any time.
- As a parent and a caretaker, learn to anticipate and regulate your own emotions appropriately.

FIGURE 7–4.   Preventing parental/caregiver despair.

---

the infant cannot understand the intent. For toddlers, we introduce elements of structure. Parental education enhances appropriate parenting.

More information on infant crying can be obtained at Period of Purple Crying® (www.purplecrying.info).

This program is part of the National Center on Shaken Baby Syndrome (www.dontshake.org), whose mission is to reduce infant abuse, including shaken baby syndrome (see Figure 7–5). This evidence-based *infant abuse prevention program*, which educates parents and warns them about the dangers of shaking an infant, also explains the role of crying in infants.

Safety Precautions for Infants

Unintended injury is one of the leading causes of childhood mortality. It is important that parents and caregivers be familiar with precautionary safety measures and that they implement them consistently (see Table 7–1). Parents should consult their health-care provider. Safety precautions for infants, including suggested guidelines to decrease the risk of SIDS, are available. Generally, the following guidelines apply to infants under age 2.

Focus Point. Infancy is characterized by developmental tasks that are unique to this time of the life span. The infant achieves a variety of physical, social, and psychological abilities, such as walking, acquiring the healthy attitudes of basic trust and personal autonomy, learning basic sensorimotor and communication skills, and becoming emotionally attached to the parents. Parents are mindful of meeting the other needs of the infant, such as providing proper nutrition and health care, establishing sleeping patterns, and addressing safety issues.

Safety Concerns for Toddlers

When infants and toddlers become mobile, they experience a change in their perspective of their world. A toddler moves with increasing speed and can freely explore the physical world. Children at this age have a natural curiosity about their surroundings. As Piaget (1967) noted, children are the world's most natural scientists as they exercise their curiosity by discovering and experimenting with the things that surround them. Toddlers need the experiences of exploring their environment to recognize that they are distinct individuals, separate from other people and things, but also a part of their surroundings. Infants act on their environment and, in the process, discover how their environment acts upon them. Infants learn that balls make intriguing movements when they are kicked,

---

NONACCIDENTAL TRAUMA

- In the United States, *nonaccidental trauma* is the most common cause of mortality and morbidity associated with child abuse or maltreatment. The term refers to trauma or injury that is willfully inflicted. The phrase *nonaccidental injury* is also in use.
- Such abuse is often inflicted on infants during the first years of their lives.
- Ill-informed, frustrated, tired, and angry parents or caregivers sometimes act out irresponsibly and abusively when an infant continues to cry.
- The outcomes are nearly always tragic. A Canadian study showed that fewer than 7 percent of all survivors of shaken baby syndrome were reported as being "normal." Aside from death and coma, all other victims had lasting neurological deficits, visual impairment, and other permanent disabilities.
- It is important to train parents and caregivers to react responsibly to an infant's crying. If a caregiver feels despair, the baby should be put in a safe place, such as a crib, and the caregiver should step away, breathe deeply, and calm down. The caregiver should get help, such as calling a neighbor or friend, and do something constructive to prevent the cycle of despair and anger. Never ever act out at the expense of an infant; instead, learn to regulate emotions. Respond appropriately.
- Prior to leaving the hospital, every parent should be educated with regard to the following:
  - Adult emotional regulation
  - Methods for soothing an infant
  - Attitudes toward discipline
  - Basic knowledge of appropriate infant care.
- Perpetrators of abuse can be parents, grandparents, caregivers, boyfriends of the mother, or casual babysitters. A recent study showed that male perpetrators can inflict even greater harm. A combination of caregiver despair and a lack of child-care education can lead to a very dangerous situation. Substance abuse aggravates these circumstances.
- Abuse of children, as well as spouses or elders, is a criminal offense that is punishable by law.
- Educational material is available from the National Center on Shaken Baby Syndrome, whose mission it is to reduce infant abuse (see www.dontshake.org).

FIGURE 7–5. Nonaccidental trauma, including shaken baby syndrome.

Based on information from the National Center on Shaken Baby Syndrome (2012), www.dontshake.org and the American Association of Neurological Surgeons (2012), www.aans.org.

TABLE 7–1.   Safety Precautions for Infants

Knowledge is key	Take an infant and child CPR course, be prepared, and be safe. Read about infant care; consult reputable books written by experts such as pediatricians. Parents can attend courses recommended by their health-care team. Fathers can take courses on infant care, such as Boot Camp for Dads®. Consult informative and reputable websites such as www.healthychildren.org, which is written by pediatricians from the American Academy of Pediatrics.
Observe, supervise, and prevent a tragedy	Always be nearby. Never leave a child unattended. Be vigilant during diaper changes, when the child is on a high surface, and while bathing. Never leave an infant in bathwater. Leaving a child unattended in a car is against the law. Multitasking distracts the caretaker.
Remember "Back-to-Sleep" when putting a baby down in a crib	A baby needs to lie on its back. An increased risk of SIDS has been associated with putting babies on their stomachs (prone sleeping); they are not strong enough to roll over or lift their heads if they cannot breathe. The risk of suffocation is high.
Soft bedding can kill	The risk of suffocation increases dramatically if the bedding is soft. A baby can sleep in an approved sleep sack specifically designed for infants, where the top is a baby sleep/play suit that fits snuggly to keep it in place. Use a very firm mattress that is endorsed by the Consumer Product Safety Commission (CPSC). There should be no bedding or blankets in the crib. Do not swaddle infants older than 6 to 8 weeks of age as they can wriggle loose and risk suffocation.
Adult beds and bed sharing are dangerous	Never put a baby in an adult bed, and never let a baby share a bed with sleeping adults. Do not nurse in bed, as the risk of falling asleep with the infant is high. Adults could inadvertently squash the infant, or the infant could suffocate.
Crib safety	Safety standards for cribs changed in 2011. Only buy cribs that meet 2011 CPSC standards. There are to be no more drop-side cribs; in an older crib, such rails should be immobilized. Do not allow babies to share a crib.
Very young babies should sleep in their parents' bedroom	Very young babies should sleep in their parents' bedroom in their own bassinette or crib. This way, parents will hear if a baby is in distress and they can intervene immediately. Do not let a baby cry unsupervised. A baby is communicating something with its cries. Always check out the situation.
When feeding, "breast is best!"	The incidence of SIDS is lower in breast-fed babies. When bottle-feeding infants, hold the baby in one's arms in a slightly upright position. Burp well during and after each feeding. Never prop up bottles. An infant should not have a bottle in the crib because of the risk of choking. Check the bottle temperature carefully; it should be body temperature, which is lukewarm, not hot.
Pacifiers	Babies can use pacifiers if they are soothed by them. Never fasten a pacifier to a cord around a baby's neck or any other item as this could present a strangulation hazard.

(Continued)

TABLE 7–1. *(Continued)*

Choking and suffocation hazards	Many small objects can present a choking hazard. Supervise your child. Plastic bags can cause suffocation.
Car seats	• Never transport a baby without a car safety seat. It is illegal. • Buy a car seat that is age and weight appropriate, as well as CPSC endorsed. • Anchor the car seat according to the manufacturer's recommendations. Use the LATCH system in cars (Lower anchors and tethers for children). • Do not use secondhand car seats if the history or the safety status of the seat is unknown. • Learn how to buckle in the child correctly. • Follow the recommended guidelines for placing the car seat—use rear- or forward-facing position depending on the age and weight of the child. • Newer model cars automatically disable the air bag if a child car seat is anchored correctly. • A list of inspectors and installers is available on www. seatcheck.org
Baby/Infant carriers, slings, and papooses	Babies like the closeness of the parent. Check regularly that the baby can breathe; babies have been known to suffocate, especially if a young baby lies facing the parent's chest. Follow the manufacturer's instructions meticulously.
Strangulation hazards	Slightly older infants have been known to be strangulated by the cords on blinds, especially those found near cribs.
Temperature and direct sunlight	For baths, the water temperature should be lower than for adults, or lukewarm. Control room and car temperatures. Be aware of the baby's body temperature. Avoid direct sunlight during the first 6 months and cover exposed areas when going outside.
Supervise your child	Numerous situations and objects can be safety hazards. Be informed and make informed judgments. Supervise your child at all times.

Based on recommendations by pediatricians from the American Academy of Pediatrics (2012), www.healthychildren.org.

bounced, or thrown; pots and lids can clatter; and water is very attractive and makes interesting sounds and movements.

This ability to become involved with the environment creates its own challenges. Most parents can tolerate just so much noise and mess from children. A child's safety also becomes a preoccupation as parents learn that a toddler's movements can lead to dangerous situations, and they react to these behaviors by child-proofing the home to ensure that the child can explore and experience objects safely. Cleaning solutions are placed out of the child's reach, breakables are moved from tables, gates are placed across stairways, electrical outlets are capped, and so forth. Parents may provide a selection of toys that stimulate the toddler's curiosity and exploratory behavior, but household objects such as pots are just as fascinating to a child at this age (see Table 7–2).

The lifestyle of the family responds and is modified by a child's behavior and stage of development. This responsiveness demonstrates the ability of a family system to adapt to the changing developmental abilities of its members. In these ways, parents also provide structure for children's developmental progress.

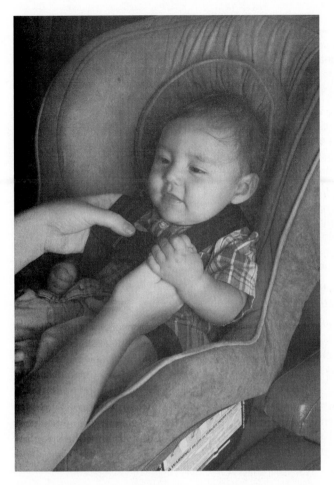

As toddlers become mobile, they should be monitored at all times to ensure safety. Unintentional injuries and accidents are leading causes of mortality in childhood.

Childhood accidents and unintentional injuries are leading causes of death in children (National Association of Children's Hospitals, 2012). Parents and caregivers need to be alert and take all of the necessary precautionary measures to ensure optimal safety.

EVOLVING PERSONAL CONCEPTS OF PARENTHOOD

Becoming a parent for the first time is a critical adjustment for the adults in a family. The first child has a major role in shaping the emergence of parenting skills for the new mother and father. While an infant is experiencing the psychosocial stages (Erik Erikson) of establishing basic trust and autonomy, parents are usually experiencing a new challenge in their own personal development by acquiring a sense of generativity. For many adults, the parenthood role adds a new, different, and perhaps more meaningful experience in acquiring generativity. With children, the adults turn their psychosocial focus more directly on the dimension of parenthood. They develop ideas about what it means to be a parent, the needs of children, what goals they have in child rearing, and what kind of parenting style they find appropriate.

People may not think much about parenting or how to behave in this role until the need arises. When children are born, adults discover opportunities to examine their existing beliefs, attitudes, and behavior as parents. This seems to be the time when adults consider and develop the self-regulating patterns for parenting behavior and parent–child interactions. These self-regulating patterns form the basis of how we act as parents, and the rules and roles we assume in regulating and evaluating our children's behavior.

TABLE 7–2. Safety Precautions for Toddlers

Useful website	Safe Kids USA (www.usa.safekids.org) provides important information regarding the prevention of injuries.
Supervision and childproofing	Older infants and toddlers are mobile, moving to get to things and moving the things themselves. Supervise and childproof the environment.
Traveling and outside the home	Use recommended restraints in vehicles. Never leave children unattended. Supervise, anticipate, and intervene to prevent injury.
Toddlers can pull things over	Children can pull over televisions. Furniture should be firmly anchored. Be careful with drawers that slide out completely. Furniture that is unstable can fall on toddlers. Doors can slam on little fingers.

(Continued)

TABLE 7–2. *(Continued)*

Toddlers can get into dangerous places	A mobile child can get to places and objects that present a danger. Use baby gates and lock windows. Remove low-level ornaments. Large chests, including freezers, should be locked or have the latches removed so that a child cannot be trapped inside.
Drowning hazards	Be cautious around water. Open toilets and standing water in a bathtub are drowning hazards. Never leave a child unattended in a bathtub or wading pool. Any activity involving water has to be constantly supervised. Washing machines and dryers are potentially dangerous places.
Burning and scalding	Protect children from hot surface or objects, including heating devices. When cooking, use the back burners and turn pot handles inward. Do not pour hot liquids while holding a child; do not multitask while scalding objects are being handled. Lower the thermostat of the hot water heater so that the water is not scalding. Bathwater should be lukewarm and checked before a child is immersed.
Sunburn	Take precautions with exposure to direct sunlight in order to avoid sunburn. Use an appropriate sunscreen on your child.
Choking hazards	Children explore with their mouths, so many objects will go into their mouths. Ban tiny objects that are choking hazards. Nuts, popcorn, and food on which children could choke should only be introduced to older children who understand the importance of chewing foods thoroughly.
For poison emergencies in the United States, call 911 or Poison Help at 1–800–222–1222	Lock up poisonous substances, cleaning materials, and medications. If your child takes a daily multivitamin that looks like candy, it should be locked up as well. Childproof lower cabinets in kitchens. Avoid poisonous plants in the home and the garden. Keep the number of Poison Help near your phone.

It is crucial that parents agree on their parenting strategies and think about how their parenting roles provide nurture for an infant with rapidly changing needs. Initially, the tasks that parents perform involve providing safety and care for the infant. Later, as the infant grows and changes, parents provide psychological and social stimulation. Later still, especially following the second birthday, parents use different parenting skills to support the child's socialization tasks related to gaining personal autonomy. New parents need to examine how they wish to respond to outbursts of emotion. Parents must find ways to allow the expression of independence without damaging the child's belief about his or her inner nature or self. During this stage of a family's development, parents learn an important lesson about working with children: One's behavior as a parent must change in tandem with the changing behavior and needs of children. Children have an important influence on one's conduct as a parent.

Parenting Reflection 7–4

Should new parents be given an emotional or virtual parenting kit to take home following delivery? What are some qualities and attributes that such a "kit" might contain that would be helpful, especially to the first-time parents of an infant?

Gender-Equal Parenting Roles

Many men and women who become parents see parenting differently according to how it played out in their family of origin. Increasingly, adults with young children in Westernized countries are moving toward a gender-equal approach toward parenthood in that parenting roles may be shared rather than being distinct or based on gender. Fathers are taking on greater responsibility in nurturing their children and may take paternity leave when a baby is born. Although both partners say they want to share parenting responsibilities equally, women continue to perform more of these tasks than men, and this can lead to *role strain*. Many men fully expect that they will be actively involved in providing care and support for their infants (Tikotzky, Sadeh, & Glickman-Gavrieli, 2011). Adults can experience some difficulties in sharing child-care responsibilities. The most difficult area reported is employers' rigidity regarding the time frame for performing work responsibilities.

Goodness of Fit. Another factor that can influence the nature and quality of parental care is **goodness of fit**. This refers to the congruence or match between the temperament of a baby and that of its parents and the family system (Chess & Thomas, 1987). Babies manifest individual temperaments or sensitivity, even before birth. Some highly sensitive infants display withdrawal, avoidance, and strong emotions. Others appear to need more than the ordinary levels of stimulation. These sensitivities may not match the temperament of the parents or the family. For example, some infants seek to be held and cuddled and appear to thrive on such treatment. Others find this uncomfortable. If a parent wants to hold the baby and cuddle it and the baby finds this undesirable, the quality of the relationship is adversely affected. The stage is set in infancy for the dance that occurs between the parent and the child. Parents of several children soon learn to accept each child as an individual with a one-of-a-kind style and personality. Each child demands an individual approach that takes into account their unique temperament and needs. When it comes to parenting, one size does not fit all.

• •

Focus Point. Few significant differences are found in the overall performance of men and women with regard to providing care for infants. Some differences are noted in interaction styles that relate more to the enactment of psychological scripts of appropriate parenting. Many middle-class men and women attempt to develop gender-equal parenting roles rather than those based on traditional gender-role stereotypes of fathers and mothers. Such parents share parenting roles.

The goodness of fit between the temperament of an infant and that of its parents influences how parenting may unfold. Although temperament may be inborn,

understanding the unique temperame[nt] enables the parent to develop an unde[r] ways that children express themselve[s] and children will benefit from a variety of life experiences as perceived and interpreted through the unique temperaments of their children. Children, in turn, get to know their parents, and preschoolers may already know how to pull a parent's heartstrings in remarkably sophisticated ways.

• •

SUPPORTS FOR PARENTS OF INFANTS AND TODDLERS

The topic of child care has received a great deal of attention. (The term "day care" is also frequently used in this context.) Consider the following statistics related to the use of nonparental child care by families of infants and young children in the United States (Federal Interagency Forum on Child and Family Statistics, 2010; U.S. Census Bureau, 2010b):

- The changing structure of American families has resulted in dramatic increases in the number of single-parent families in which the mother is the primary economic provider and in the numbers of dual-earner families in which both adults are gainfully employed.
- About 56 percent of all married women over 18 years of age were employed outside the home.
- About 75 percent of all children in the United States living with two parents had at least one parent who was gainfully employed year-round.
- About 60 percent of all children in the United States under the age of 5 had been in some type of child-care arrangement since they were born.
- Even if a mother is not employed outside the home, many families use child care and nonparental child care as enrichment experiences for children and to provide time for the mother's personal enrichment.

Given this information, questions arise about who is raising America's children and the quality of the care being given. Nonparental child care has not had a good reputation in the past, especially when infants are involved. Traditionally, the preferred mode of child care in our culture has been provided by the parents, typically the mother. Many families are finding this type of child-care arrangement impossible and perhaps even undesirable. An increasing number of families use nonparental child care provided by a relative (Federal Interagency Forum on Child and Family Statistics, 2007; Manlove, Vazquez, & Vernon-Feagans, 2008) Major cost savings result when this arrangement is used. In some young families, the fathers are the primary caregivers, staying home with young children to reduce the very high costs of child care. Concerns about the effects of child care or large-group care on children, and especially on infants, have been expressed (Lamb & Ahnert, 2006). Maternal deprivation was found to have serious deleterious effects on infant growth and development and was interpreted as strong evidence that infants should be cared for by their own mothers.

Popular opinion continued in this vein until the 1960s, when increasing numbers of women returned to the workforce. The use of nonparental child care increased accordingly. Researchers reversed the attitude that such care produced harmful effects on infants and children when it became apparent that attachment to the parents was not adversely affected. A national study found that about 46 percent of infant care programs were considered to be of high quality. Some studies suggest the following interpretations (Lamb & Ahnert, 2006; National Institute of Child Health and Human Development, 2006):

- Nonparental care of infants can offer an enriching experience that enhances and stimulates developmental progress.
- Quality care for infants had the greatest impact on infants from disadvantaged families.
- Some less desirable behavioral traits, such as boisterousness, heightened physical and verbal aggressiveness, and lack of cooperation with adults, could be observed at later ages in children who had been in infant group-care settings.

There is controversy among developmental researchers who have studied the effects of group care on infant and child development (Belsky, 1990; Belsky & Rovine, 1988). Infants who spend more than 20 hours a week in nonparental care are at risk of developing an insecure attachment, according to Bowlby's theory on attachment. Other researchers question this contention (National Institute of Child Health and Human Development, 2006). At issue are differences of opinion and interpretations regarding the research findings by the investigators. Most of the studies have found beneficial effects of nonparental infant care, but it always has to be seen in the context of the quality of the care provided.

One of the main sources of nonparental care of infants today is by a nonrelative in a private home, or by what is known as *family child care* (Federal Interagency Forum on Child and Family Statistics, 2010). The employment status of mothers contributes significantly toward choosing a child-care provider who is a relative. Forty-eight percent of employed mothers tend to have a relative rather than a nonrelative provide care for their babies.

The stability or consistent use of a nonparental care provider for infants is a major concern for both parents and researchers. Changes in the nonparental care provider occur less frequently for infants than for older children. In all, only about one fourth of the families change nonparental care providers within a year. Changes are more likely to occur when the provider is not a relative.

It may not be possible to foresee the long-term effects. What may be interpreted from the research findings is that quality infant care is apparently not harmful (National Institute of Child Health and Human Development, 2006; National Institute for Early Education Research, 2011), but the problem of how to provide adequate care for individuals at this vulnerable time in their lives remains.

Focus Point.   Due to the large number of women who are employed outside the home, an increasing number of families use nonparental care for their infants. Concerns have been raised about whether such experiences prevent adequate attachment of infants to parents. This is a controversial issue for which there are no clear answers. Some researchers report that nonparental care causes no harm to infants, while others suggest that it does. The *stability of the care* and the *quality of the experiences* may be crucial factors in determining the effects of nonparental care on infant and child development.

Parenting Reflection 7–5

What are some pros and cons of using nonparental child care for an infant when both parents must work outside the home?

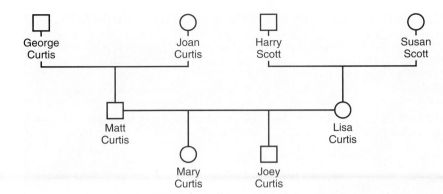

This simple family genogram depicts three generations. Men are depicted with squares and women with circles. Genograms can document a number of events that take place within family systems.

FAMILY SNAPSHOT

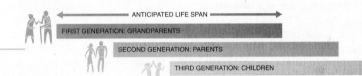

For this intergenerational family snapshot, we meet an imaginary family—the Curtis family. We briefly identify their coping skills and stressors, and observe how various family roles, patterns, and boundaries are established to maintain homeostasis (or balance) in the family.

The Curtis family is represented initially by a *genogram*, followed by a *family snapshot* (see Figure 7–6), outlining the stressors and developmental challenges that each generation can face. A **genogram** is a form of family notation, similar to a family tree. It has the added ability to indicate family relationships such as emotional qualities between the members. It is based on the work of McGoldrick & Gerson, 1985 and has been expanded by several contributors. It is frequently used in family therapy, and students who study families should be familiar with this form of family notation. We are keeping the genograms simple.

Parenting Reflection 7–6

Explain how this family snapshot reveals *interrelatedness* between the members of the family system at a particular point in developmental time. How does this family system cope with the effects of the various stressors?

POINTS TO CONSIDER

■ The basic developmental tasks of infancy focus on achieving significant physical milestones, mastery of basic motor competencies, and emerging social and mental competencies.

■ Parenting infants and toddlers focuses on meeting a variety of needs:
  ■ Facilitating the attachment between the parents and an infant.
  ■ Providing food and establishing self-feeding.
  ■ Attending to health and medical needs.
  ■ Observing an infant's sleep–wake cycle and good sleeping habits.
  ■ Providing nurture and structure.
  ■ Promoting brain development and cognitive development.
  ■ Providing stimulation through appropriate toys and equipment.
  ■ Initiating and supporting toilet learning.
  ■ Facilitating a sense of autonomy versus shame and doubt (Erik Erikson).

First Generation (Grandparents)

The older adults are the first generation in this particular family system. All have entered middle age in their adult development and are experiencing a typical progression through this developmental stage. The oldest of this generation, George Curtis, the paternal grandfather, is beginning to look forward to retirement. The Scotts, parents of Lisa Curtis and in-laws of Matt Curtis, are dealing with a particularly difficult situation as Susan was diagnosed with breast cancer 6 months ago and has been undergoing chemotherapy. She has found solace in her spiritual life, and for now this is what sustains her. The couple tends to be private about the situation, the feelings associated with their fears, or what the future could hold. The challenges for this generation are

- Adjusting to the aging process experienced in middle age.
- Adjusting to the midlife transitional experiences.
- Assisting adult children in completing their individuation process.
- Adjusting to the deaths of parents, relatives, and colleagues.
- Beginning the preparations for retirement, or having retired.
- Establishing grandparent and in-law roles.

Second Generation (Adult Parents)

Matt Curtis recently changed jobs after a long period of unemployment. Financially, things look better than they have in a long time. His wife, Lisa, carried a heavy burden in being the sole provider for her family while Matt was unemployed. They have to find child care for both of their children. Lisa wants to find someone to care for the children in their home. Both Matt and Lisa have managed to adjust to being parents for the first time and find that taking care of their second baby is more manageable than what they experienced after bringing Mary home. They feel fortunate to have Matt's parents nearby, and George and Joan have been generous in offering to take the children occasionally. Typically, families with very young children remain focused on this family task for 3 to 5 years. This phase in family life is preceded by a formal commitment or marriage. The challenges for this generation are

- Establishing work roles and objectives.
- Balancing work and family roles.
- Maintaining a household with infants and toddlers.
- Providing the finances for this household.
- Deciding on family size and adjusting to pregnancy, childbirth, and infants.
- Adjusting to changes in their committed relationship and additional family roles (e.g., parenthood, in-laws).
- Learning to parent infants and toddlers.

Third Generation (Children)

The children of this family are highly dependent on the adults for their care. Luckily, they have had good health and are growing as expected. At times, Lisa feels that she is neglecting the children because she can't be a full-time mother. She sees how well the children's needs are met and her job affords them food, medical care, and general necessities. Joey is having some problems with separating from his mother and father when taken to the sitter's home. Perhaps more than her husband, Lisa feels torn among the difficulties that her parents are having, her own situation, and the developmental changes that her children are undergoing. This is a stressful time for the first and second generations of this family system. The challenges for the children are

- Establishing an attachment with their parents.
- Establishing the attitudes of trust and autonomy.
- Mastering the cognitive tasks of infancy.
- Toilet learning.

FIGURE 7–6. Examples of stressors affecting each Curtis family generation.

- Becoming a parent, especially for the first time, is a significant event that requires critical adjustments for the adults in a family system. New parents evolve concepts of parenting from many sources, including social scripts developed in their families of origin, exposure to society's expectations of appropriate parenting behavior, and personal interpretations of parenting. New parents evolve ideas that serve as self-regulating patterns to fulfill roles within their family system. New parents anticipate the nature of their parenting experiences.

- First-time parents may be educated to parent infants effectively. Participation in these programs increase satisfaction and boost confidence.

- New parents often make a commitment to develop gender-equal roles as caregivers of their children. Gender does not factor into the assignment of role responsibilities.

- Many families with infants use nonparental child care, especially when both parents work outside the home. Nonparental care by a relative is the major source of supplemental child care. Controversy exists as to the effects of nonparental child care on infants.

- Unintended injury is one of the leading causes of childhood mortality. It is responsible to become familiar with safety and precautionary measures and to implement them consistently.

- A systemic family development snapshot reveals the stressors that may affect different generations of a family system and the ways that members cope with these stressors.

USEFUL WEBSITES

American Academy of Pediatrics
www.healthychildren.org
http://brightfutures.aap.org

American Academy of Pediatrics, Healthy Child Care America
www.healthychildcare.org

American Public Health Association, Publications: Caring for our children: standards and guidelines (3rd edition)
http://apha.org/publications/bookstore/

American SIDS Institute and National SUID/ SIDS Resource Center
www.sids.org and www.sidscenter.org

First Candle: Helping Babies Survive and Thrive
www.firstcandle.org

Mayo Clinic, Infant and Toddler Health
www.mayoclinic.com/health/infant-and-toddler-health/ MY00362

National Center on Shaken Baby Syndrome
www.dontshake.org

National Resource Center for Health and Safety in Child Care and Early Education
http://nrckids.org/CFOC3

Safe Kids, USA, Preventing Injuries: At Home, at Play, and on the Way
www.safekids.org

CHAPTER 8

Parenting Preschoolers

Learning Outcomes

■ ■ ■ ■ ■ ■ ■ ■ ■ ■ ■ ■ ■

After completing this chapter, readers should be able to

1. Explain why it is helpful to know the principal developmental landmarks of early childhood in order to facilitate effective parenting behavior.

2. Explain how the parent–preschooler relationship changes in comparison to the relationship during infancy.

3. Explain why positive methods of guidance work well with young children.

4. Describe some common behavioral problems observed in young children.

5. Describe the kind of community support required by families with preschoolers.

■ ■ ■ ■ ■ ■ ■ ■ ■ ■ ■ ■ ■

Early childhood is the period between ages 3 and 6 when children are also known as *preschoolers*. The interactions within a family system reflect the increasing involvement of young children as participating family members. A major challenge to parents is adjusting to a developing child whose behavior and personality traits are rapidly emerging. Preschoolers are adventurous, curious, and quickly learn many things. Parents enjoy their preschool-age child while also experiencing conflict as the child tests the limits and boundaries set by adults. During these years, the rate of developmental change is slower

than was observed during infancy and prenatal development, but it is still magical as each day seems to bring something new.

DEVELOPMENTAL LANDMARKS OF EARLY CHILDHOOD

A preschooler learns and accomplishes monumental tasks during the years before entering formal schooling. The power of language opens new worlds of interaction and communication. For the parent, language allows an evolving understanding of the child's universe. For the child, it becomes a tool for socialization and personal expression. Language and communication are the bridges that allow parents and their offspring to explore the shared world of parent–child relationships.

The basic skills of locomotion, communication, and interaction that were acquired during infancy are now being expanded. It is a time for learning the basic social skills that are necessary for effective interactions with others. Young children learn through modeling and observation of others and increasingly comprehend their parents' expectations and instructions. As young children acquire a number of physical and social skills, they become more oriented toward others rather than being largely self-oriented. This important change in perspective enables a developing child to capitalize on

a wide range of experiences as he or she learns to cope with and master the environment.

As with all other life stages, several unique developmental tasks and landmarks are associated with the early childhood stage. Expanding language skills, as well as increased social, emotional, cognitive, and physical abilities, contribute to increasing autonomy.

Focus Point. Early childhood is characterized by unique developmental tasks and specific landmarks. The period is notable as the time when young children actively acquire knowledge and basic skills that are both physical and social in nature.

PARENTING YOUNG CHILDREN

Meeting the Needs of Preschoolers

Parenting behavior undergoes modification as children grow from infancy into early childhood. These changes reflect the changing developmental needs and abilities of preschoolers. From the perspective of family systems theory, parenting adapts in response to what occurs that is new and different. Children present fresh challenges to parents as they attempt to master the developmental tasks of this age span.

The behavior of preschoolers is enhanced by parents who are *responsive* to changes in their children's needs. Parents find that their need to be needed by their children changes as well. Children, in effect, assist in shaping and modifying the parenting behavior of adults. Parents learn that their growing preschoolers also recognize the changes in their own maturity and resist being treated as if they were younger. Older preschoolers are particularly sensitive to adults who attempt to interact with them in a patronizing manner that fails to recognize their "big kid" status. From ages 3 to 6, the child increasingly expresses initiative, and parents, in turn, know that they can no longer take their child's behavior for granted. Throughout the years of early childhood, a child presents an attitude that says, "I can! Let me show you that I can!"

As children become verbally more skilled, parents react by shifting from physical methods of child rearing to those that are more verbal and psychological in nature. Parents who believe in permissive and authoritative methods of child rearing may begin to use increased reasoning and verbal direction in interacting with preschoolers. These reactions to children's changing nature guide the autonomous behavior that prepares children for their next stage of development.

Physical Aspects

Meeting Nutritional Needs. Preschool children typically have a small appetite, which results in the consumption of small amounts of food. Young children eat meals with their families and are taught table manners and to use utensils. Preschoolers are eating the same types of food as other family members and usually don't require a special diet. Because they require fewer calories, parents learn what they will eat at mealtime, often in smaller portions than other family members. Most parents understand that children require good nutrition to grow and need a balanced and nutritious diet that includes adequate amounts of protein. Preschoolers develop food preferences based on the foods to which they are exposed. For this reason, it is crucial that the early years are used to establish a foundation of good eating habits, which will set the child on the right nutritional path for life. Eating problems can develop as early as infancy and progress in early childhood. Childhood obesity is taking on alarming proportions. Parents contribute to obesity by requiring children to eat all of the food that they are served, by serving portion sizes that exceed the child's nutritional requirements, not cooking nutritious meals, routinely eating on the run,

It is crucial that the early years are used to establish a foundation of good eating habits, which will set the child on the right nutritional path for life.

Focus On 8–1

Major Developmental Tasks and Landmarks in Early Childhood

Physical

- ■ Slower rate of growth in weight and height
- ■ Small appetite; may be a picky eater
- ■ Uses a preferred hand
- ■ All primary teeth erupt
- ■ Major gross motor skills are mastered (e.g., running, climbing)
- ■ Fine motor skills emerge (e.g., creation of art)
- ■ High energy level

Psychosocial

- ■ Expanding awareness of self, others, and things
- ■ Gaining independence and some self-control
- ■ High curiosity level
- ■ Beginning socialization experiences (e.g., appropriate social and gender-role behaviors)
- ■ Learns by doing and from mistakes
- ■ Play is more social and creative

Cognitive

- ■ Preoperational, prelogical, and intuitive thought
- ■ Building a database of information about the world
- ■ Preoccupation with classification and the grouping of things
- ■ Expanding vocabulary
- ■ Improving memory
- ■ Flaws in thinking, such as egocentrism, animism, arriving at unwarranted conclusions, and self-centered thinking

using food as a reward, and not facilitating physical exercise (Nitzke, Riley, Ramminger, & Jacobs, 2010).

Parents sometimes miss the early signs of childhood obesity, partly because their own behavior is contributing to the situation. Additionally, social norms foster an atmosphere of politeness, avoiding topics that may offend. If health-care providers try to steer the family in the right direction, it is the responsibility of the adults to create the supportive environment for the children because the power to change the situation for the better lies within the control of the parents.

If parents model appropriate behavior, which strives toward healthy lifestyle choices, children almost always follow their good example, especially if they are supported in making healthful choices. Good parenting includes giving children the foundations for a healthy lifestyle, and the family system is a strong reinforcer of such behavior.

Focus Point. Parents should counteract childhood obesity by being good role models, cooking nutritious meals, and encouraging physical activity. In this way, they establish a foundation of good eating habits, which will set the child on the right nutritional path for life.

Health and Safety Issues. Young children do not yet have a fully mature immune system, nor have they developed enough antibodies to combat many illnesses. The wide availability of immunizations against a large number of formerly debilitating and fatal diseases has helped to extend life expectancy. It is important for preschoolers to have adequate health care, which includes immunizations.

Most deaths among young children are caused by injury in or near the home rather than illness (Federal

Interagency Forum on Child and Family Statistics, 2011b). Accidental injury is the leading cause of death during childhood and adolescence in the United States (U.S. Census Bureau, 2010a). During early childhood, this often occurs in relation to car accidents, either as a pedestrian, a passenger, or on a tricycle. The use of appropriately designed children's car seats is a legal requirement for all children. Other safety measures include the use of helmets while biking and skiing. Parents need to teach their children the rules of safety for inside and outside the home. Some children are more impulsive than others and can experience greater numbers of injuries and close calls. These children require an extra-strict parental eye and perhaps more intensive safety instruction than other children. Play equipment, both indoors and outdoors, should be safe and age appropriate. Children should never be left unsupervised, and leaving them alone in a parked vehicle for any amount of time is illegal. Although drowning deaths have declined over the past decade, any water activity requires extremely high vigilance, and pool areas need to be secured. Teaching preschoolers to swim can add to their safety.

Many accidental deaths involve a child's ingestion of poisonous or toxic substances, such as fertilizer, gasoline, cleaning products, and medication. While children in the United States are safer on playgrounds, at child-care centers, and in cars than in past decades, there are still too many deaths that could have been prevented. Even though we have become more safety conscious, suffocation and poisoning have increased (Centers for Disease Control and Prevention, 2012). Parents are urged to store medications and other dangerous substances out of the reach of children. It is wise to have the telephone number of a poison control center at hand and to insist on childproof caps for all medications.

Suffocation can be prevented with good child care and sleep practices, following the recommendations of the American Academy of Pediatrics. Suffocation in young children is sometimes linked to sharing a bed with an adult, sleeping in an adult bed, loose bedding in a crib, and the improper use of baby carriers or papooses. For preschoolers, loose cords on window blinds, necklaces, and strings can present a strangulation hazard. Also keep plastic bags away from young children.

Focus Point. Accidental injury is the leading cause of death of preschoolers, with the majority of deaths occurring within or near the home.

Parents should teach their children the rules of safety for indoor and outdoor play. Children should be supervised at all times, and safety precautions should be in place.

Cognitive, Behavioral, and Emotional Aspects

Providing Structure and Nurture for Young Children. During the early childhood period, child rearing increasingly includes greater attention to teaching children about structure as it is interpreted by the particular family system. Structure comes in several forms, such as the rules promoted by the family, the roles taught to children by precept and by example, and the ways that family members communicate with one another. In family systems theory, these are referred to as *family patterns.*

Nurture is provided when parents consistently attempt to meet the particular needs of young children and act in ways that are supportive of their psychosocial growth. There is a greater emphasis on providing assertive care rather than supportive care because preschoolers are not yet able to take greater control over their actions. Structure and nurture often go hand in hand because

TABLE 8–1. Structure and Nurture Are Two Cornerstones of Good Parenting

Behaviors that provide structure and nurture:

- Affirming developmental achievements appropriately.
- Providing a safe and loving environment.
- Encouraging appropriate and safe exploration of the environment.
- Modeling respectful and gender-equal behavior.
- Modeling good communication in the marital relationship.
- Encouraging the expression of feelings.
- Providing developmentally appropriate information.
- Providing appropriate feedback with regard to behaviors.
- Explaining the consequences of behaviors.
- Communicating clearly—no guilt trips!
- Being consistent.
- Being respectful of the child.
- Listening attentively.
- Having space in one's life for a child.

structural boundaries should be set by using a nurturing tone or attitude. Table 8–1 lists the behaviors that provide structure and nurture.

This time of a child's life is also crucial in setting the foundation for good self-esteem. Toxic parenting, which can crush the child emotionally, includes belittling, mocking, teasing, inconsistency, sarcasm, ridicule, and discounting the child. The parent–child relationship is not a competition that the parent should insist on winning. It is the parent's responsibility to do everything possible to create an environment that is conducive to the development of healthy emotions and positive self-esteem. The effects of this parental gift of good parenting will accompany the child for a lifetime.

Using Rules in Teaching Structure. Rules are used in family systems as a primary means for maintaining the group's efficient functioning. Rules are one means by which parents teach structure to children and help children to internalize controls that guide their behavior (J. I. Clarke & Dawson, 1998). When a family system evolves and formulates rules that promote healthy parent and child behaviors, some are negotiable and others are nonnegotiable. **Nonnegotiable rules** cannot be debated or changed, while **negotiable rules** are subject to discussion and alteration. In healthy families, a mixture of such rules guides the behavior of the family members. In these families, nonnegotiable rules generally relate to safeguarding the children's well-being in reasonable ways. These are not arbitrarily derived by the parents, nor are they abusive or rigid in nature. The purpose of such rules is to teach responsible behavior, good citizenship, and effective interpersonal skills. Nonnegotiable rules define limits and appropriate behaviors with which children are expected to comply for their own well-being. For example, the rule "Play in the backyard, not in the street" informs a preschooler that a parent cares about the child's well-being and is willing to define the places where the child can play safely. Other nonnegotiable rules might include "You must go to bed at eight o'clock," or "You must eat some breakfast every day."

Negotiable rules can be questioned by children and discussed with parents. Young children quickly learn which rules are negotiable and which are not. For example, an implicit rule in some families is that children are to eat whatever food is served to them, but children may learn that they can question what they are expected to

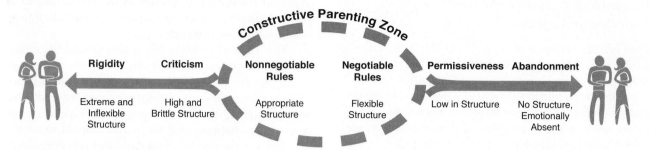

FIGURE 8–1. A balance between negotiable and nonnegotiable rules maintains appropriate family functioning.

eat. Perhaps children may resist eating certain foods. They may bargain with their parents regarding what they will eat and what they will not eat until some agreement is reached between them. In essence, negotiable rules help to teach children how to think and use discussion as a means of conflict resolution (see Figure 8–1).

Parenting Reflection 8–1

What are the implications if a family system has too few or too many rules that govern the behavior of family members? What effects would each of these situations have on young children, and what would be the implications for children's future development?

Enforcing rules and the consequences of rules can be a problem for parents, especially for first-time parents. It is often just as difficult for parents to remember to use positive reinforcement to help teach structure as it is to enforce the consequences of transgressions. Such structure is most effective when administered with nurturance and love by the parents.

Focus Point. Young children need to learn about structure from their parents. This is typically taught via rules, some of which are negotiable and some that are not. The consequences of these rules help preschoolers begin to learn self-control.

Parenting Reflection 8–2

How would you, as a parent of a preschooler, use rules to manage behavior and encourage a sense of initiative rather than a sense of guilt?

Beginning Socialization. *Socialization* refers to the processes by which children are taught to conform to social rules, to acquire personal values, and to develop attitudes and behaviors that are typical or representative of their cultural environment. The socialization process begins in earnest during early childhood, when parents and other caregivers begin to take an active role in teaching a young child these lessons. The lessons are not always given by formal instruction. Some are learned by observing the behavior of others, particularly adults.

Young children are expected to learn the patterns by which the family system functions and to adopt the rules, behavioral expectations, and limits or boundaries that the family system has established. Structure serves to internalize behavioral standards promoted by parents and other caregivers. A child who has incorporated structure has the information by which to judge any action as appropriate and acceptable or inappropriate and unacceptable. At the level of preschool children, such lessons are an introduction to family functioning. Implicit is the understanding that transgressions and mistakes are to be expected from young children as they learn.

BOOKS AND READING

- Have children's books in the home and make time to read with a child.
- Regularly accompany a child to the children's section of the library.
- Be a good role model: Convey your love of books.
- Books are an important part of development: They expand cognitive skills, language development, memorization, pre-reading skills, and much more.
- Stories can convey messages about prosocial behavior and lessons to be learned.
- Stories about a wide range of topics awaken interests in the child and foster the imagination.
- Help children find out at a young age how much joy can be found between the pages of a book!

FIGURE 8–2. Instilling the magic of books and reading.

Depending on the nature of a particular family system, certain standards may be promoted more than others. Despite the diversity of families today, almost all teach similar kinds of behaviors and values to children. Figure 8–2 illustrates the value of children's books in the home.

Prosocial Behaviors. Part of appropriate socialization is that children learn to show some degree of social interest in others. Prosocial behaviors promote helpfulness, empathy, and concern for others, as well as controlling impulsiveness, gaining self-control, and limiting aggression. These altruistic behaviors show an awareness of other people's feelings and appropriate ways of reacting to those feelings. This calls for knowledge in using the social skill *empathy*, which is the ability to accurately comprehend the thoughts, feelings, and actions of others. Empathy differs from sympathy, which is the ability to feel the same way that others do. Learning to be sympathetic, however, is the first step toward becoming empathic.

In early childhood, empathic responsiveness is observed when children share belongings and attempt to comfort or help others who are upset. These behaviors are not performed as spontaneously or as frequently as parents and others would prefer. It is unclear at this time how an adult model facilitates empathic behaviors in young children (van Kraayenoord, 2009). When children have opportunities to observe such behaviors, they tend to behave more empathically toward others.

Researchers note that these be throughout childhood, regardle parental influence or instruction

Aggression. Aggression is defi that causes fear and leads to forceful contact with anoth (Serbin, Temcheff, Cooperman, Stack, Ledingham, & Schwartzman, 2011). Aggressive actions directed at people or things can be verbal and/or physical.

Our culture values nonviolent social assertiveness. An example is a steady, determined, and controlled effort to reach a solution to a problem. In effect, this cultural concept of assertiveness is synonymous with, and is a logical extension of, the idea of initiative. Concern arises when aggression is expressed as hostile or violent behavior that harms others or excludes children from social interactions with others.

Some researchers believe that limited expressions of aggression in childhood follow a normal developmental progression (Pepler & Rubin, 1991). Aggressive expressions peak in early childhood and decline thereafter. Mild aggression in preschoolers is part of their normal growth and development. It may serve healthy functions such as helping them discover personal boundaries and communicate or enforce these boundaries with others.

Some researchers suggest a genetic tendency toward aggressive behavior. Others believe that the family environment promotes such behavior (Serbin et al., 2011). Children who are treated in harsh, aggressive ways by parents also act aggressively toward others. Children also adopt the model of aggressive behavior that they observe on television and in the movies. Young children clearly act aggressively at times for various reasons, and parents and other caregivers are challenged to teach young children how to control their aggressive impulses. Children are given a confusing message when they are spanked by adults for hitting others. Research points to the role of reinforcement as a powerful means for helping children learn to act in nonaggressive ways. When adults positively reinforce prosocial behaviors that are incompatible with aggressiveness, children learn that there are more beneficial ways to express themselves. One popular method is to isolate children from others briefly, as in time-out. Social learning theory suggests other alternatives, such as modeling for children appropriate ways of handling the feelings that motivate aggression.

Delaying Gratification.   Adults often ask preschoolers to delay getting what they want. This is a difficult task for a young child to master. Children are expected to defer having a smaller need satisfied immediately in exchange for receiving a greater benefit later. This is an important lesson in self-control. It helps to bring impulsiveness under willful restraint. Individuals can cope with difficult situations in later life more successfully if lessons about delaying immediate gratification are introduced in early childhood (Schwarzchild, 2000). Teaching young children to think "It is good if I wait" can also help them in controlling impulsiveness.

Self-Regulation.   As preschoolers progress developmentally, their ability to self-regulate improves. Self-regulation represents aspects such as expanding self-control; the ability to postpone or delay gratification; and waiting for an appropriate time or place, depending on the circumstances. These basic skills expand during each developmental stage until adulthood, when it supports longer range planning and aspects of socially acceptable behavior. It is an important skill which is acquired gradually in sync with cognitive development as the child develops the capacity to reason and understand why postponing the behavior may be beneficial.

Temper Tantrums.   Researchers have studied temper tantrums and found that children reveal a somewhat predictable rhythm that can be identified by the sound of the child's crying, as well as some other behavioral clues (J. Green, Whitney, & Potegal, 2011). There are two aspects to a tantrum, but they are not necessarily sequential. They can occur together. On the one hand, there is intense frustration, which can be linked to kicking, yelling, screaming, throwing objects, or pulling things over. The second cluster of emotions has more to do with seeking comfort and can be recognized by whimpering and sadness. The researchers (J. Green et al., 2011) concluded that the parental intervention should match where the child is emotionally during the tantrum. Trying to get beyond the angriest point is best done by not interrupting. Trying to console children while they are angry and frustrated seems to prolong the tantrum and escalate the behavior. Often the tantrum will suddenly "deflate" and be over with. Parents will learn to recognize the rhythm of a tantrum and to console their child when the child is consolable. Some children react with a tantrum when they are overstimulated or overtired.

It may be tough for a parent, especially if the tantrum occurs in a public place. If that happens, it may be best to leave the public venue with the child as quickly as possible, and to deal with the outburst in privacy. As children learn to self-regulate, they are better able to deal with minor frustrations. At the same time, parents become more competent at parenting appropriately, defusing inflammable situations, and anticipating their child's needs.

Encouraging Positive Gender-Role Development. An important aspect of an individual's self-concept is *gender identity*, the knowledge that humans are either male or female. An individual's biological sex immediately predicts a variety of reactions from others at birth. Children first learn gender or sex roles according to parents' interpretations of masculinity or femininity. In early childhood, parents and other caregivers use reinforcement to shape gender identity. These become modified and refined in middle childhood and adolescence. The result of such socialization experiences is that individuals make personal interpretations of masculinity and femininity at later ages. Gender-role development has both cognitive and behavioral aspects (Kendrick & Luce, 2000). Gender roles appear to vary from one culture to another in some respects. For example, the practice, in some cultures, that women and girls are allowed to eat only after the males in the family have eaten is obviously a cultural factor. On the other hand, the fact that males tend to exhibit more aggressive behaviors than females regardless of the culture would point to a biological factor.

Young children appear to acquire rigid stereotypes of what it means to be male or female (Dresner, 2000). It is to be expected that young children understand what they see as something that is factual. For example, preschoolers typically use visible physical cues, such as clothing and hairstyle, to recognize someone as either male or female. It is not unusual for young children to believe that long hair always indicates that a person is female, even when other features indicate that the person is a male.

A child's gender development begins at birth when parents are told, "It's a boy!" or "It's a girl!" This immediate classification is made more permanent and public by naming the child, usually with a name that conforms to the child's sex. From this point forward, children are channeled into one gender role or another by being dressed and given hairstyles that identify them as a male or female and cause others to treat them accordingly (Lester, 2003).

A preschool-age child's knowledge of gender-appropriate role behaviors comes from several sources (Eagley & Diekman, 2003). These behaviors are reinforced and modeled to children by adults and others in the family system. In addition, reinforcement from other same-sex children promotes gender-appropriate behaviors. A part of normal development can be that children explore aspects of different gender roles. Some children experience *gender dysphoria,* or feelings of dissatisfaction with their biological gender, which should be discussed with a physician.

Some gender-equal behaviors can be encouraged by involvement in activities and with toys that are traditionally associated with one gender only. For example, boys can be encouraged to take on roles such as playing house, and girls can be encouraged to play with building blocks. In addition, observing adult behavior in nontraditional roles can affect children's ideas about gender roles. Researchers have found that men who were raised in a family where the mother worked outside the home tend to be more gender equal in their attitudes. Girls who were exposed to mothers who worked outside the home were more likely to seek out any career option, regardless of the prevailing gender stereotypes. These subtle changes contribute to raising future generations that will strive for greater gender equality.

Children form a more balanced impression when they see both parents in a range of activities, regardless of whether these activities are traditionally gender stereotyped. Higher levels of social competence are found among adults who are comfortable adopting gender-neutral (androgynous) social and vocational roles.

Teaching Young Children About Sexuality.   It is commonly believed that children are not interested in or aware of their sexuality until puberty. This is a misconception that many parents soon discover when their children reach preschool age. Rather than relating just to physiological functioning and behavior, *sexuality* refers to the broad aspects of sexual interests, attitudes, and activities that are an expression of a person's total being. Sexuality plays a significant psychological role throughout an individual's life span, not just following puberty. Although it is difficult for behavioral scientists to study the sexual interests and activities of children, childhood sexuality has been investigated for many years.

Young children commonly ask many questions as a means of gaining information about their world, and questions relating to sexual issues and bodily functions are an expression of this interest. A typical question that can be expected from most 4-year-olds is "Where do babies come from?" It is also common for sexual themes to emerge in dramatic play activities, such as when young children play house or the proverbial scenario of playing doctor. Parents are the primary source of sexual socialization and information for young children (Kesterton & Coleman, 2010). Most parents are aware of their responsibilities in this regard, although some are anxious about answering a child's sexually oriented questions or feel incapable of providing accurate information due to their own ignorance or embarrassment about such matters. Although the accuracy of the information that parents provide in addressing young children's sexuality and sexual interests is important, perhaps of greater importance are the emotional tones and affect that parents communicate when discussing these issues. For example, although young children are unable to comprehend the mechanics involved in human reproduction due to their level of cognitive development, and an explanation at this level is not necessary, they easily absorb any feelings of embarrassment that accompany a parent's answers to sexual questions. This, in turn, may cause the child to develop feelings of embarrassment concerning sexual topics because this behavior is modeled by the parents. The child could also sense that this is a "secret" topic, or one that is best avoided.

Parents may read an abundance of excellent printed material about what kinds of sexually related questions to expect from young children. It may be helpful for parents to rehearse the answers they might provide to their preschoolers. Parents should understand that the messages they convey about sexuality, both verbal and nonverbal, will affect children's attitudes and values when they have reached maturity. Parents are encouraged to take an active role in shaping children's values and attitudes about sexuality in a developmentally appropriate way. Parents can guide their children toward appropriate choices as they mature by establishing a trusting relationship that allows open communication.

Teaching Young Children About Death and Dying.   Many parents find teaching children about the realities of death and dying to be especially difficult (Talwar, 2011). As unpleasant as this topic may be, parents should attempt to teach young children about mortality.

Parents need to remember that very young children cannot understand the finality of death. For example, when preschoolers play cops and robbers, they are able to resume normal functioning after playing dead. When they watch cartoon characters experience serious injury, they see them spontaneously recover. Another difficulty in this regard is the inability of preschool-age children to comprehend the full meaning of "forever" as relating to the finality of death. Many young children reach the conclusion that death happens only to those who are old, sick, or fatally injured. This belief leads to questions when a parent or sibling becomes ill about whether the person will die. When teaching young children about death and dying, one has to consider the cognitive abilities and developmental stage of the child and adjust the information accordingly.

Focus Point. A preschooler's first instructions about appropriate behaviors that are expected by the family and by society usually come from the parents. These instructions also guide children to understand gender roles, sexuality, and death and dying.

Attachment Revisited. The quality of the attachments that a child develops in infancy has long-term consequences, some of which begin to appear not only in late infancy, but also in the later stages of the life span. While this is not the only factor influencing other areas of a child's development, it contributes in significant ways.

Parenting FAQ 8–1

Our 4-year-old, who is just full of all kinds of questions, just asked me why the body of a woman who is obviously pregnant looked different. I had been expecting the usual "Where do babies come from?" question rather than this. I've delayed giving a complete answer. Can you give me some pointers?

"She is going to have a baby; I'll talk with you more about this later when I can explain it to you" would be a variation of an appropriate answer. Although it's always good to answer questions as completely as possible at the time they are asked, preschoolers sometimes have a knack for asking the toughest questions at inopportune times. Also, you cannot always hope that the question will quietly go away. Here are some suggestions:

■ Keep your explanations about the facts of life as simple as possible.
■ Don't make up stories; stick to the truth. For example, you might say, "The woman's tummy is larger because there's a special place inside where a baby is growing. It's called the uterus."
■ Don't immediately assume that your child is ready for the complete facts-of-life discussion. Remember that she or he is probably wondering after hearing your explanation just how a baby can be growing in there and how it eats. If you don't get additional questions after your explanation, you can either let the matter drop or perhaps ask your child other questions related to sex education.
■ Keep your child's level of cognitive development in mind. It is not necessary to go into significant detail about conception and pregnancy. Show that as a parent you are a resource of information on many topics of interest to children. You will want to encourage your child to develop the attitude that you can help her or him to interpret the world and can act as a reliable source of information. If you do not know something, admit it and include a statement about this being something that you both can learn about, and then research the topic.
■ Understand that children will ask many questions about sex and sexual matters. Don't count on a one-time explanation being sufficient for all time. Perhaps the best advice is to overcome any embarrassment you might feel and regard her or his curiosity as appropriate. Children will be asking the same question again, or in different forms, at later ages as they cognitively mature. Details can be added in an age-appropriate manner as they grow older.

Perhaps the most obvious way that the quality of attachments established in infancy becomes manifested in later life stages is seen in relationships that a child develops with others besides the parents (Ainsworth, 1989). For example, children who have established secure attachments in infancy appear to gain more satisfaction from relations with peers in early childhood and in the later years of development (Reuter-Kairys, 2011). In addition, researchers have also identified that the quality of the attachments affect preschool children's adjustment to nonparental child care (Howard, Martin, Berlin, & Brooks-Gunn, 2011).

In general, there are many benefits to acquiring secure attachments in infancy and early childhood, including higher levels of social competence and self-esteem, the ability to function independently, empathy, leadership skills, and problem-solving abilities in novel situations (James, 2006). Children coming from disadvantaged family systems are at a higher risk for developing insecure attachments and the likelihood of more serious problems in these areas. Parents of preschoolers also have their own attachment issues. Those parents who developed secure attachments during their own infancy have been found to be more responsive to their own children's signs of distress and to respond appropriately (Edelstein et al., 2004). In addition, other methods of intervention for at-risk parents who developed insecure attachments during childhood may be applied, such as home visitation from a social worker or child development specialist and participation in a community-based parent education intervention program (Gowen & Nebrig, 2002).

Reactive Attachment Disorder. Children who have been traumatized in early childhood through severe neglect or abuse or who spent the early months or even years of their lives in circumstances of severe neglect may present with *reactive attachment disorder*. This condition has been observed in some children who were adopted internationally and who may have spent the first months of life in orphanages, without opportunities for appropriate attachment (Belsky & de Haas, 2011; Nagel, 2012). These children may ultimately exhibit either inhibited or disinhibited attachments (www.mayoclinic.com/health/reactive-attachment-disorder/DS00988/METHOD=print). In the proposed fifth revision of the *Diagnostic and Statistical Manual of Mental Disorders* (*DSM-V*), a classification system developed under the leadership of the American Psychiatric Association, this condition is described as a *developmental trauma disorder*. It can result when children are exposed to prolonged multiple, complex traumas. The *DSM* has had several revisions, and the fifth major proposed revision (2013) reflects current approaches in the field of psychiatry.

Facilitating Cognitive Development. Children shift to a new type of thought process typically around age 3. Piaget (1967) calls this a change to the **preoperational** mode of thinking. Parents and other caregivers readily recognize that a preschooler thinks. Thinking becomes more noticeable as young children solve problems in their play and daily activities. They now have an active memory and information-processing skills. They also show the ability to use elementary logic (Flavell, Miller, & Miller, 2001).

During this period of mental changes, thought focuses on internalizing the environment. Children accomplish this by increasing their use of symbolic thought and mental imagery (Bruner, 1992). They rely on representational thought more frequently as they progress through early childhood. Parents may need to be informed that preschool-age children do not understand the world as an adult or even as an older child does. Piaget described the nature of preschool-age thought as intuitive in nature, meaning that these children often jump to conclusions, make decisions, and interpret the world based on insufficient facts. They are increasingly occupied with classifying things in their world according to their similarities. This stage reflects the beginnings of a more ordered, logical processing of information.

Preschoolers make judgments and reach conclusions based on their limited understanding of operations and rules. They use a minimal amount of cues and information in doing so because they cannot completely absorb and use extensive amounts of information to reach conclusions. This stage of cognitive development is a time when young children are acquiring knowledge about things, people, and their environment. Their later cognitive development allows them to make use of this information.

Mental changes are facilitated by new language skills and perceptual abilities, as well as changes in brain functioning. The preoperational label implies that a child's thought processes are prelogical in nature. These prelogical skills lay the foundation for many other, more complex mental changes that emerge in subsequent stages of the life span.

Preoperational thought among preschoolers is relatively inflexible in nature. Once young children adopt a particular point of view, they have difficulty understanding another competing viewpoint. Their thoughts are dynamically tied to their perceptions. Preschoolers, like infants, use sensory information extensively but in an entirely different manner. The maxim "What you see is what you get" is a good way to remember how preschoolers form their ideas of their world. An object's appearance is often the only means that preschoolers use for making judgments or evaluations about that object.

Piaget (1967) uses a number of concepts to describe the relative rigidity of preschoolers' thoughts: (a) equating appearance with reality, (b) egocentrism, (c) centering, (d) irreversibility, (e) inability to solve problems involving conservation, (f) preoccupation with classification, (g) animism, and (h) precausal thinking. These eight concepts are briefly outlined and the implications of parenting a preschooler to facilitate cognitive development follow:

1. *Appearance and reality.* Young children define reality almost exclusively as what they see, hear, and otherwise experience via their senses. They have almost no ability to generalize beyond the obvious or the information at hand. It is generally recognized that preschoolers' thought is bound by their perceptions. Judgments, decisions, and conclusions are based on what is seen in their world.

   The parents of a preschooler need to have realistic expectations about their child's inability to make reasonable judgments and conclusions. This is the basis for supportive care at this time in a child's life. Parents will need to make many decisions on behalf of their child to protect the child from harm. Keeping a watchful eye on the child is imperative because children at this age are not and cannot be made completely aware of the consequences of their actions.

2. *Egocentrism.* Piaget (1967) believed that the preoperational thought of young children is limited partly because of a cognitive trait known as **egocentrism**. Piaget did not use this word in our usual sense of meaning "selfish" or "conceited." Rather, he used it to describe how young children focus on their own viewpoint of the world and are unable to consider other alternatives. From their perspective, their own vantage point is all that is possible in understanding what they see in the world.

   Young children typically believe that they are the center of their universe and things happen solely for their benefit. Appearances fuel this conclusion. For example, a young child on a walk at night might be asked what the moon is doing. The child might explain that the moon follows her everywhere (after all, that is what it appears to be doing).

   Egocentrism is both a joy and a source of frustration for many parents of preschoolers. The joy comes from the opportunity to hear their child's charming perspective on the world. The parental frustration may be associated with misunderstanding a child's prelogical reasoning. Some parents become upset when they hear their preschooler tell a "tall tale" to explain his or her actions and punish the child for lying. For example, if a parent confronts a preschooler about a misbehavior, the child might create a story about how he or she was manipulated into doing so by a monster who has now escaped into the wild. Such logic is frustrating as many parents view this as unacceptable. It might help to stimulate creativity in the preschooler if the parent would continue with the story just to see where it will end. Parents need to understand that they would not be promoting a habit of lying because children outgrow this kind of thinking as they grow older.

3. *Centering.* Piaget called another aspect of preoperational thought centering (Piaget & Inhelder, 1969). Young children concentrate on only one aspect of an object they see or an activity they do. They have difficulty in perceiving other aspects or elements simultaneously. When young children are attracted to the color of something, they usually can't consider its size or shape at the same time. They can separate all of the yellow buttons from a large pile of assorted buttons, but the task of separating all of the yellow, wooden, round buttons is too difficult for them. The ability to make fine discriminations such as this occurs at later stages in the life span.

   When giving directions, it is important for parents to understand that preschoolers can follow only one concise, simple command at a time rather than a complicated series of actions. One approach used by the Montessori Method for educating children is to break down complex tasks into simple, easy-to-follow steps. The Montessori approach emphasizes the independence and autonomy of the child within a developmentally appropriate context. By taking this developmental context of the child into consideration, parents can avoid frustration. For example, when requesting that children pick up their toys and put them away following playtime, parents may find that the task is too complex for the preschooler, and must be broken down into simple steps.

4. *Irreversibility.* Young children typically cannot understand that some operations or processes can be reversed. To a young child, things operate in only one way and that way is irreversible (Piaget, 1967). For example, when asked if he has a sister, a preschool-aged boy can be expected to reply, "Yes, her name is Julie." However, when asked if his sister has a brother, the boy can be expected to reply, "No." Young children appear to be incapable of retracing the logic of their thinking.

   The trait of irreversibility implies that parents need to be mindful about their expectations of preschool-age children. We cannot expect them to have long memories and adequate information input and storage to retrieve information and trace events from beginning to end and then back again.

5. *Conservation problems.* Young children cannot understand that something retains the same properties when it is rearranged or reshaped. This mental skill comes in the next stage of cognitive development. Again, their comprehension of size, volume, and shape is influenced by what they see rather than understanding how these can be changed without disturbing the content or context of an object.

   Parents may be stymied when trying to explain complex notions such as the value of coins. In this case, young children often will believe that a nickel is worth more than a dime because it is larger in size. Understanding coins and what they will purchase comes with time, experience, and additional instructions from parents.

6. *Classification.* The mastery of **classification** skills is a challenge that is accomplished by age 6. Centering and egocentrism account for the inflexibility of thinking that prevents younger children from being able to group things according to shared properties.

   It is not easy for a young child to master this skill, but parents can help with a variety of learning experiences that foster classification skill development. Teaching a child about different animals is one example. At around 3 years of age or earlier, depending on individual cognitive development, children think that all animals are alike. Every animal that is seen is called a "dog," for example. Parents usually attempt to correct the child by pointing out that they are seeing a cat, perhaps. This is confusing to a preschooler because both animals have four legs, a tail, and fur. Parents usually discover that it is the vocalizations made by animals and their size that help the child understand that although they are alike in many respects, they can be identified correctly by their call.

   Parents may facilitate classification skill development by providing sorting tasks that take the preschooler's cognitive abilities into consideration. Classification skill development can also be facilitated when showing an older child an array of objects and asking him or her to identify the one that is not like the others. Parents can expect to repeat these kinds of activities many times with young children in order to help them master this skill.

7. *Animism.* Young children believe that all things, including inanimate objects, are alive (Saylor, Somanader, Levin, & Kawamura, 2010). **Animism** is a charming aspect of preschool-age thinking in which the child ascribes lifelike qualities to inanimate objects. It is often observed when young children are involved in solitary play and talk to their toys in "private speech," conversations intended for the toy as if the toy were alive and could take part in the discourse. In many respects, it is an extension of egocentrism and prelogical thinking, and it is an element of fantasy play Young children may use animistic thoughts to develop hypotheses about a complicated world.

   Appropriate parenting calls for accepting this type of thinking as part of the nature of a young child. To scorn the child and discount their beliefs about inanimate objects is inappropriate. This is a cognitive trait that will disappear as children gain experience and grow through the next stages of cognitive development.

8. *Precausal thinking.* Preschoolers often jump to conclusions. They base their decisions on a limited

amount of information or on how closely one event follows another. They simply do not have the ability to use deductive reasoning to reach conclusions.

Parenting calls for gently correcting children when they have come to erroneous conclusions with the expectation that children at this age will dispute their word.

One of the authors (Jerry Bigner) was an assistant working in a university preschool program as a graduate student. A memorable episode involving precausal thinking, egocentrism, and other cognitive idiosyncrasies took place one afternoon while he was supervising 4-year-olds playing dodge ball. The children tired of playing this game on level ground and moved the game onto a slight hill nearby. One ball thrower stood at the top of the incline and another at the bottom with the other children playing the game in between the two. The little boy at the bottom of the hill stopped the game after a few minutes. He said he had observed that the ball *always rolled back down the hill after stopping* and asked why this was so. Because this was a group of intellectually gifted children, Dr. Bigner had been instructed to explain such questions in detail using accurate information. In this regard, he had the opportunity to talk to the group about gravity, the shape of the ball, inertia, and so on. While they were fascinated by these ideas, the small questioner looked him squarely in the eye and said that he did not believe that to be correct. In reply, Dr. Bigner asked, "How so?" to which the child responded, "The ball always rolls down the hill because it knows I'm at the bottom." Dr. Bigner realized that the point could not be successfully argued with this 4-year-old.

Piaget (1967) also noted that a wide variety of experiences allow children to be exposed to the infinite elements of their world and stimulate cognitive and language development during these years. Parents play an important role in supervising preschoolers' experiences. Shopping at the supermarket, taking a walk, or just reading to their child are examples of ways that parents can stimulate their child's mind. Preschoolers will see their parents as a source of information about the world. This is particularly appealing to a 4-year-old who poses an endless stream of questions. While this constant bombardment may become irritating at times, these questions play a significant role in the child's life. Parents, in turn, act as interpreters and help give meaning to a child's understanding of the world. In this manner, parents begin to share their family values, beliefs, and worldview with their child.

Focus Point. Cognitive development during early childhood focuses on children acquiring a database of information about their world. Language skills facilitate this process. In addition, parents facilitate appropriate cognitive development by providing a variety of experiences and equipment for preschoolers.

The Role of Play. Toys and play equipment help preschool-age children to develop a number of different skills and abilities. Play is how young children begin to understand their world socially, physically, and mentally.

Preschool-age children explore various types of play as they gain social and mental skills. Three-year-olds may prefer solitary activities where they have no competition in exploring objects and things. Children at this age do not share possessions easily with others and often do well playing alone or in parallel play. Four-year-olds are becoming more creative and imaginative and are learning to share and interact with other children. A number of different kinds of toys and play equipment appeal to children at this age as they master gross motor skills and begin to explore fine motor skills. Five-year-olds can play fairly well with a small group of children and participate in more complex types of play and equipment, such as creating structures with building blocks, engaging in pretend play, doing artwork, and undertaking simple science projects. Many young children are somewhat familiar with computers because they have played games on their family's home computer.

Parents should always keep safety in mind when choosing toys and play equipment for preschoolers. Affordability may also be an issue. Some communities have toy lending libraries, which are especially helpful to budget-minded families or those who wish to expose their children to a wide variety of toys without spending a lot of money. Families may also trade toys with friends to increase the variety of play equipment.

Focus Point. Preschoolers need developmentally appropriate toys and play equipment to encourage appropriate physical, psychosocial, and mental skills.

Focus On 8–2

Examples of Preschool Toys and Play Equipment

Toys that encourage physical activity and promote gross motor skills

- Wagons
- Tricycles
- Scooters

Outdoor equipment

- Swings, gym sets, seesaws
- Playhouses
- Sandboxes
- Water-play equipment and games (supervision is needed)

Manipulative play equipment that encourages hand–eye coordination

- Blocks
- Connecting toys
- Simple puzzles
- Bead stringing
- Shape-sorting cubes, sorting/nesting toys
- Lotto matching games
- Sandbox toys
- Bath toys

Educational toys

- Picture and storybooks
- Simple computer games
- Simple board games

Equipment that encourages creativity

- Arts and crafts supplies (e.g., crayons, paint, modeling clay, markers, children's safety scissors, paper)
- Rhythm instruments
- Chalk

Dramatic play equipment

- Dress-up clothes and accessories
- Action figures, hand puppets
- Trucks and cars
- Play kitchen and accessories
- Role-play equipment
- Racially and culturally diverse dolls
- Small stage or low platform for performances

POSITIVE GUIDANCE METHODS WITH YOUNG CHILDREN

When a child enters the preschool years, parents can expect to alter or adapt their parenting style to include an increasing number of behaviors that are considered to be supportive care. These are blended with other behaviors that involve structure. To be effective at this stage, parenting must be customized to meet the needs of young children and also include the family values that a young child should learn. Additionally, ways to accomplish immediate goals, such as a child's compliance with

During early childhood, parents and caregivers foster healthy emotional development and promote positive self-esteem. This father nurtures by listening attentively and having together-time with his son.

parental wishes, feature strongly. In essence, parenting young children is geared toward what works best with a particular child at a particular level of development.

One of the biggest challenges facing parents of young children is communication as language becomes the vehicle for socializing experiences. Effective communication between parent and child is tested by the vocabulary and cognitive limitations of preschoolers. One of the time-tested approaches for helping parents work with children focuses on teaching preschoolers to learn to listen and, in turn, teaching parents how to gain a child's full attention when communicating (Ginott, Ginott, & Goddard, 2003). On the basis of the

work of Haim Ginott (1922–1973), an eminent parent educator, these methods were developed in progressive nursery schools during the 1940s and 1950s. Ginott's well-known parenting book *Between Parent and Child* (1965) became a trusted resource for an entire generation of parents. Among the book's key insights are the following:

1. *Communications with children are based on respect and skill.* Parents are advised not to attack a child's personality or character but to focus on the offensive behavior. Separate the misbehavior from the child who does it. For example, Ginott suggests that parents not say, "You're a rotten kid when you do that." Instead, he recommends parents say something like, "I'm very irritated by what you've done; I'm not angry at you." By making the distinction between the act and the child performing the act, parents help a child to avoid fusing the two, which can be damaging to a young child's healthy self-esteem and fuel feelings of guilt. Feelings of guilt are an unhealthy way for a child to learn to avoid poor behavioral choices because these tend to freeze higher thought processes and prevent critical thinking. When guilt is experienced, it overrules almost all other thinking. The opportunity to learn to think critically about how to act differently in the future in similar situations is thereby lost.

2. *Praise and positive reinforcement should not be overused by parents.* When these are used, they should be directed toward reinforcing a child's realistic attempts and accomplishments rather than to communicate how good he or she is in the parent's eyes.

3. *Constructively deal with conflicts or stress in interactions with children.* Ginott advises that parents accept the fact that a child's behavior is bound to cause tension at times. To gain a child's attention, he suggests using words that are likely to be new to the child, as this expands the child's vocabulary.

4. *A number of adult patterns are considered to be self-defeating.* Threats are invitations for misbehavior to occur because a child can view these as a dare to do something forbidden. Sarcastic comments serve only to make a child feel badly about him or herself, and a child will learn not to listen to parents who preach about faults and shortcomings.

5. *Communication is more effective when the physical differences between a parent and a child are minimized.* One way to achieve this is by getting down to eye level with a child. One can accomplish this by squatting down, sitting down with the child, or holding the child on the lap.

6. *A child needs to learn to take increasing responsibility for his or her behavior as he or she grows older.* A child can learn to do so when parents offer choices from among acceptable alternatives. Instead of asking yes–no questions or fill-in-the-blank questions such as "What do you want to wear this morning?" Ginott suggests that parents ask, "Do you want to wear your blue pants or the green ones?" This allows preschoolers a choice or even a sense of control. Lack of control is a major source of frustration and can lead to acting out in children at this age. Limited and age-appropriate choices gently guide a child toward greater autonomy.

7. *Discipline and responsibility are learned by a child through a parent's setting reasonable limits that can be understood.* Comments such as "Stop doing that!" identify unacceptable acts but fail to guide a child toward acceptable behaviors. Alternatives should be given: "If you need to hit something, Tommy, use the sofa cushion, not your sister" or "Tell your sister how angry you are; don't use your fists to communicate."

Haim Ginott's suggestions continue to be fully in line with the positive principles of child guidance. His recommendations are a consistent recognition of a humanistic approach to parent–child relations that recognize a child's contributions to interactions with the parents. These approaches promote effective communication, as well as mental health, in both parents and children.

Other methods of positive guidance that are found to be useful with preschool children include the following:

■ Try to discover the reason(s) underlying a child's misbehavior as a means for understanding the child's actions.

■ Don't expect a preschooler to behave like an older child.

■ Accept that mistakes are a part of human nature and view them as tools for learning how to act appropriately.

■ Use encouragement along with reinforcement, for example, "I can see how hard you've tried not to goof up; I hope you can try just as hard next time this happens. I'm proud of you for trying."

■ Clearly identify what is appropriate and what is not.

■ Use time-outs instead of spanking. Have the child sit in a corner or designated spot for a minute or two. Depending on the age of the child, the time-out period can become longer than the few minutes that were appropriate when the child was younger.

■ Talk out a problem rather than solving the problem for the child.

■ Take away a privilege.

■ Explain that there are alternative ways to act and help the child identify some of these.

■ Do not use shame or guilt to motivate a child toward exhibiting the appropriate behavior.

DEALING WITH THE BEHAVIOR PROBLEMS OF YOUNG CHILDREN

Many young children will experience varying degrees of behavioral problems as a normal part of their developmental progress. Although these problems are not necessarily detrimental to their progress, they are troublesome, especially from the parents' point of view.

Most of the behavioral problems are temporary. These behaviors present challenges for young children in their interactions with others, especially within the family system. Most problems are *stage specific*, that is, they are unique to the stage of the life span. Others problems are more common among older children.

Parents are often disturbed by the appearance and continued presence of certain kinds of behavioral problems among preschoolers. An immediate response is to attempt to eliminate the troublesome behavior from the child's repertoire, hoping that the behavior does not become permanent and habitual. Some parents turn to professionals, such as pediatricians, family physicians, child psychologists, and early childhood education specialists, for guidance in dealing with these problems. Others seek information from articles and books that address the specific problems of young children, such as toilet training, wetting the bed, or eating difficulties. The more problematic cases may require professional consultation and custom-designed treatment approaches. Those problems that occur more commonly among preschoolers are discussed briefly.

Bedtime and Sleeping Problems

The most common bedtime problems among young children include crying, resisting going to bed, repeatedly getting out of bed, and getting into bed with the parents (Spock & Needleman, 2011). Resistance to going to sleep is especially troublesome because a young child who gets too little sleep is irritable the next day. Several issues may account for resistance to sleeping. Infants normally whimper when they go to sleep. Parents who interpret this as cries of distress and rush to pick up the infant train him or her to expect such attention at bedtime. Eventually, a young child may prefer to go to sleep while being held and rocked by a parent or other caregiver.

Additionally, appropriate sleep routines are promoted if a young child is allowed time to wind down prior to bedtime. Parents can promote what experts call *sleep hygiene routines* beginning in early childhood. The period shortly before bedtime should be calming. Rough-and-tumble play should be saved for the mornings when children are alert.

Parents can help preschoolers develop good sleep hygiene habits that promote relaxation and preparation for sleep. Restful activities such as baths, reading stories, or quiet play serve as signals to preschoolers that bedtime is approaching. One of the more successful approaches is to use *planned ignorance* (Spock & Needleman, 2011), whereby parents give their full attention to a preschooler during the period prior to bedtime but do not reenter the child's bedroom after the child is in bed. This policy of "once in bed, you stay in bed" is established with the child's full knowledge and expected compliance. Usually, preschoolers will go to sleep within about 20 minutes after being put to bed.

Sleep routines vary with the developmental age of the child. The amount of sleep needed varies. Preschoolers should progress toward sleep that is not dependent on a parent's constant presence. A worst case scenario is parents who share a bed with a child in order to promote sleep. Bed sharing is an undesirable practice for preschoolers. Parents eventually become sleep deprived and fall into parental despair, promoting poor parent–child interactions. It also is detrimental to the marital relationship.

Ideally, good sleep routines should be established with *positive* routines so that children are not left to cry alone. Experts say that letting a child cry when attempting to establish good sleep patterns is not necessary, and that the same can be achieved with a non-crying approach. Being overly authoritarian, putting a very young child and even babies on an inflexible routine, and not responding to crying have been criticized as being undesirable practices that can lead to *failure to thrive* in children. Failure to thrive means that children do not develop optimally compared with other children of similar ages. By measuring, for instance, the weight and height of a child, the child's medical team can rank the results in terms of *percentiles*. In this manner, a child can be compared against the norm for children of the same age group. It is important to note that percentile rankings have to be professionally evaluated in the total context of a child's health and development.

The developmental readiness of a child is critical. Note, too, that there are temperamental differences in children. Some children fall asleep easily, others need more parent time and it will take longer to establish good sleep routines. Regardless, a child should never be abandoned in a crib or bed. Parents or caretakers should check on the child regularly to ensure that the child is well, and they should be within earshot.

Bad Dreams and Nightmares. Fears are common among young children and can take on additional dimensions in the fantasy world of dreams and nightmares. Although a nightmare may last only a few minutes, a young child may be able to recall it in intricate detail. Night terrors can last much longer, and a child is usually unable to recall specific details that were frightening. These are commonly observed among children who are experiencing extreme stress in their lives, such as when parents are divorcing (Spock & Needleman, 2011).

Talking with young children about their fears is often an appropriate approach for helping them to understand how fears can be manifested in frightening dreams. It may be helpful to hold the preschooler and rock him or her for a short time. Reassure the child that such a frightening experience is not real but is created by the imagination. Parents may examine the preschooler's bedtime and sleep hygiene routines and eliminate activities such as watching television shows that stimulate harmful fantasizing.

Problems with Elimination

Preschoolers can occasionally experience problems with the functions of bodily elimination. Typically, these have to do with regression during times of stress. Loss of control, such as bed-wetting (enuresis) and involuntary passage of feces (encopresis), is not considered problematic until a child reaches the school-age years.

Regression in toilet learning or toilet training might occur as a result of any of the following:

- The birth of a baby
- Sibling rivalry
- Extreme fatigue, excitement, anxiety, or illness
- Forgetting during periods of intense concentration and play activities

Commonsense measures help young children overcome these periods of regression. Reminding a child to use the bathroom may be all that is required to resolve the problem. In addition, protecting a child from situations that are overstimulating or frightening may be another easy way of supporting appropriate habits. Shaming or humiliating a child is inappropriate. Such negative interactions do not have a place among constructive parenting techniques. In some cases, a medical consultation is indicated.

• •

Parenting Reflection 8–3

How would you advise the parent of a young child that a behavior problem might be serious enough to warrant professional consultation, even though it is not indicative of abnormal developmental progress?

• •

Eating Problems

The foundation for lifelong nutritional habits is laid during childhood, and parents who guide their children toward healthy and nutritious choices give them a gift for life. Early exposure to healthy foods will mean that the child forms good associations with those choices and will usually maintain or return to that diet later in life. Food choices and taste preferences are reinforced culturally, and children need to be exposed to the same food several times before it becomes familiar and desirable. A child who receives fast food as a treat will return to that eating pattern when under stress.

Young children eat meals with other family members and share the family diet. Most parents understand that young children may eat the same foods as other family members, but in smaller portions. Culturally and socially, the shared meal is a powerful occasion for connecting with family members; families who eat together tend to have better communication. Parents lay the foundation for their children's nutritional habits by modeling desired behavior, by providing the appropriate foods in the home, and by not using food as a reward or a punishment. Childhood obesity is a serious problem that is increasing, and it can have lifelong consequences for the child, affecting not only health but also self-esteem.

Young children may acquire problems with eating such as

- Resistance to eating and dawdling over food served at meals.
- Overeating, obesity, and poor nutritional choices as a result of lack of parental responsibility and guidance in these areas.
- Developing peculiar desires for nonfood items, known as a *pica* (Spock & Needleman, 2011).

Many parents are knowledgeable about what constitutes a balanced and nutritious diet, and they become conscientious about the foods served to young children. Overzealousness can also cause young children to become resistant to eating. When children feel pressured to conform to parental desires and eating policies, they tend to resist eating certain foods. For example, if parents firmly believe that vegetables must be consumed when served at mealtime, some young children resent the pressure to comply with parents' expectations and stop eating vegetables altogether. Parents may react by becoming greatly concerned about the child's nutrition and fret about the short- and long-term effects on the child's health and well-being.

• •

Focus Point.   Many parents consider certain behavioral problems among preschool-age children to be a normal part of development. Many of these are related to conflicts between parents and children and with other family members. A variety of sources can help parents work with children in such situations.

• •

SUPPORTS FOR PARENTS OF PRESCHOOLERS

Community services that provide alternative forms of nonparental caregiving are more numerous and accessible to families with preschool-age children than to families with infants. In the United States, about 60 percent of all children younger than 5 years of age who were not in kindergarten were in some type of

Child care settings should have developmentally appropriate and planned activities. Staff should respect each child's individual needs and provide opportunities for children to play with peers.

nonparental child-care program, that is, they were not cared for by a stay-at-home biological parent. The type of supplemental care varies according to the age of the child and the type of care desired by the parents (Federal Interagency Forum on Child and Family Statistics, 2011b). While infants more typically receive home-based care by either a relative or a nonrelative, preschoolers who are not yet enrolled in a kindergarten program are more likely to be cared for by a relative or placed in a group program.

Relatives provide more than half of the child care for families with infants or very young children (Federal Interagency Forum on Child and Family Statistics,

2011b). Of the relatives who provide care, fathers, grandparents, and siblings provide the greatest amount of child care for preschool-age children when mothers are employed outside the home. Slightly more than half of all preschool-age children are cared for by child-care centers and by nonrelatives in their homes (see Figure 8–3).

Families use such services for a number of reasons. Many mothers of young children are employed outside the home, and this type of care is necessary to help the family provide for the children's needs. Some families with young children would like them to have enriching experiences that are not usually available in the home. Others wish for their children to experience educational opportunities in preparation for public school. Most programs today provide educational stimulation for young children in addition to custodial care.

Parenting Reflection 8–4

Give your opinion regarding the following statement and justify your response: Early childhood educational experiences should be required before a child enters first grade.

Child-Care Centers

There continues to be much discussion about the advantages and disadvantages of nonparental child care for preschoolers. In some contexts, child care is also referred to as *day care*. A variety of concerns have been raised about the short- and long-term effects of such care on children's developmental progress. There are several supervisory bodies who have published recommended guidelines for early childhood learning environments. Some issues of concern include the following:

- Stringent health and safety requirements for the facilities, supplies, equipment, and environmental health
- Licensure and state regulations
- Safe play area, playgrounds, and transportation
- Nutrition and food services
- Adequate staffing and qualified personnel
- Developmentally appropriate setting
- Curriculum and program activities

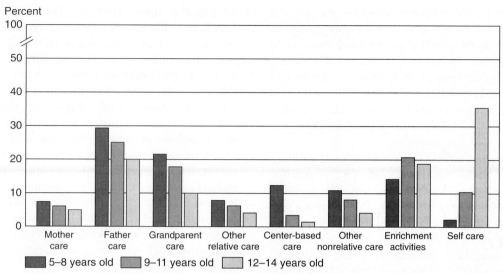

NOTE: The number of children in all arrangements may exceed the total number of children due to the use of multiple arrangements. Mother and father care refer to care while the mother worked.

FIGURE 8–3.   Children ages 5–14 child care arrangements.
Source: U.S. Census Bureau, Survey of Income and Program Participation.

- Quality and continuity of care
- Relationship with the caretaker and continuity of care
- Emotional climate
- Opportunities for comfortable play with other children
- Respect for children's individual needs.

Based on National Resource Center for Health and Safety in Child Care and Early Education, 2012a.

Researchers continue to investigate these complex issues (Belsky, 1990; National Institute of Child Health and Human Development, 2006). The context in which young children receive care may be associated with different child outcomes. It is important to take both the *quality* of child care and the *characteristics* of a family into consideration when examining long-term influences on children's development. For example, young children show the least competence in peer relationship skills when they acquire insecure attachments to parents, as well as to nonparental caregivers. This does not occur when they have a secure attachment to their child-care provider but not to their mother. Incompetent peer relationship skills can be counterbalanced by constructive modeling by nonparental caregivers, even if the parent–child relationship is suboptimal.

When nonparental care is sensitive and responsive to children's needs, young children are observed to be compliant, cooperative, and achievement oriented. The *relationship* that nonparental adults promote with children has a greater impact than the methods used in working with children. This parallel implies consequences based on the quality of nonparental care. The negative emotional attitudes of nonparental caregivers and their failure to respond to children's needs are thought to result in problem behavior. Generally speaking, the intellectual gains offered by preschool programs are greatest for low-income children rather than middle-class children because of the differences in the home environments (Children's Defense Fund, 2010).

When comparing in-home to out-of-home child care, we need to compare apples to apples. High-quality care that meets all health, safety, and developmental requirements can be optimal in any setting. A problem arises if we try to compare poor in-home parenting with good out-of-home child care, or we compare excellent in-home parenting with poor out-of-home child care. In such cases, we are not comparing the same dimensions of care, rather we are comparing apples to oranges. For the present, it may be safe to say that there appears to be little difference in the effects of parental and nonparental care on young children. There is one caveat: The quality of nonparental care must be high (National Institute of Child Health and Human Development, 2012). The most desirable choices are the ones that serve the *best interests of the child*. The features of each type of supplemental child-care program may vary.

Child-care centers typically offer care of children for a varying number of hours per day, depending on parental needs and work schedules. The kinds of programs most commonly used by families with pre-schoolers involve groups of children. They operate as a business venture. Some programs are nonprofit and are sponsored by companies, community agencies, churches, or educational institutions. A successful model is the co-op model for preschool, where at least a dozen pairs of parents pool their resources to run a children's preschool and they hire a teacher. Parents volunteer regularly and teach alongside the professional. Parent education and parental skill development is offered as part of this model.

Licensure and Accreditation of Child-Care Centers. During the past few decades, more staff members have been trained in early childhood education. Many universities with programs in child development and child education have child-care centers that fall under the auspices of the university and serve as training institutions while also serving the community. Typically, child-care centers are state licensed. They can also be subject to voluntary national accreditation.

A *licensed* center meets local and state requirements. The guidelines and rules differ from state to state. Guidelines include, for instance, standards and regulations set by a state department of human resources or a state department of health, as well as fire, safety, and other regulations. Licensure of child-care centers is mandatory, and the centers are monitored regularly to ensure compliance.

An *accredited* center meets stringent national standards and is monitored by an overseeing accrediting body. National accreditation is voluntary. An important resource in the Unites States is the National Association for the Education of Young Children (NAEYC), which is the national accreditation body that sets and monitors

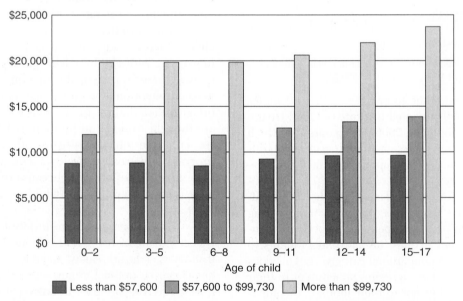

FIGURE 8–4. Family expenditures on a child, by income level and age of child,[1] 2010.

[1]U.S. average for the younger child in husband–wife families with two children.

professional standards of early childhood education and facilitates voluntary accreditation of child-care centers (www.naeyc.org/accreditation).

Parents should conscientiously check a center's licensure and accreditation status before sending their child there. Some guidelines can be found on state websites, as well as on the U.S government's website focusing on child care (www.childcare.gov).

Some unlicensed and unmonitored child-care settings in the United States have a questionable reputation and may provide nothing more than custodial care. At times, these settings have become notorious for practices that harm children.

. . . .

Parenting Reflection 8–5

Explain the implications for the family when an employer provides child care as an employee benefit.

. . . .

Preschool Programs

Preschool programs are more educational than custodial in nature. Most communities have several types of programs available for families with young children. Preschool programs are typically 2- to 3-hour sessions in the morning or afternoon, but the times can be synchronized to match parental work hours. The number of days that children attend can vary. The more common types of programs are discussed briefly.

Specialized Curriculum Programs.   Some preschool programs offer a particular curriculum, such as one based on Piaget's cognitive theory, the Montessori Method, or an open-classroom model. The theoretical philosophy of a particular program is emphasized over other factors. The materials used in a Montessori program foster sequential thinking skills. Young children are taught to proceed sequentially to reach goals or solutions to problems. A cognitive-based curriculum may provide an opportunity for young children to classify objects as one of the many activities available.

Programs for Exceptional Children.   Some families have a child with atypical needs. These children can benefit from preschool programs that are designed to meet their needs. Such programs typically involve children with special physical or mental challenges. Incorporating children with special needs into mainstream preschool programs allows all children to benefit and to gain greater empathy through these interactions. The Council for Exceptional Children is a good resource for matters pertaining to special education (www.cec.sped.org).

Compensatory Programs.   Compensatory preschool programs are specially designed to provide a variety of experiences for children from disadvantaged families. Head Start is an example of such a program. Activities promote a preschooler's acquisition of language and social and cognitive skills to enhance the child's self-concept and sense of initiative. Nutritional and health needs are also addressed. A unique aspect of such programs is parental and family involvement, which serves to strengthen family functioning.

Excellent long-range benefits result from participation in these programs (National Institute of Child Health and Human Development, 2012). Children who have attended Head Start programs score higher on achievement tests and have higher grades in elementary school. These children are also less likely to be placed in special education classes or to repeat a grade (U.S. Department of Health and Human Services, Administration for Children and Families, 2012).

. . . .

Focus Point.   Some parents arrange child care by using services from sources outside their family system. Agencies can provide screened au pairs and child-care professionals to take care of children in their parental homes. Generally, these are stimulating experiences for preschoolers if an educational component exists and the services are provided by qualified professionals. Parents should be concerned about the quality of these services and the effects on children's developmental progress. The care should meet quality standards. Caretakers should have background checks and clean records. References should always be checked. A variety of programs serve different needs and purposes in supplementing parental care for preschoolers. If well chosen, quality child care and preschool programming can be a very positive and enriching experience for children.

. . . .

FAMILY SNAPSHOT

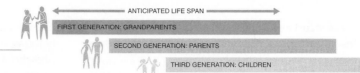

The intergenerational snapshot of the Curtis family is taken at the midpoint of the early childhood stage of the oldest child. Mary Curtis is now 4 years old. The second generation is experiencing increased stress due to the **role strain** that is affecting the young parents. Role strain refers to the pressures experienced when several competing roles must be managed simultaneously. When this occurs, role performance typically declines in at least one or two of the roles while another role is given priority. People also notice a decline in marital satisfaction, which can be confusing and upsetting (Talmadge & Talmadge, 2003). Women typically experience this role strain to a greater degree than men because they often bear greater responsibilities regarding parenting and household maintenance (Bianchi, Milkie, Sayer, & Robinson, 2000). Couples cope with this initial awareness of dissatisfaction in a variety of ways that can be healthy or unhealthy in nature. Figure 8–5 lists the different stressors that affect the Curtis family over the generations.

First Generation (Grandparents)

- Continuing adjustment to the aging process experienced in middle age.
- Continuing assistance to adult children in completing their individuation process.
- Continuing adjustment to the death of parents, relatives, and colleagues.
- Continuing preparations for retirement.

Second Generation (Young Adult Parents)

- Accumulating additional challenges in balancing work and family roles.
- Maintaining a household that meets the needs of preschoolers and toddlers.
- Providing finances for this household.
- Refining parenting behaviors and styles.
- Meeting personal adult needs while performing family and work responsibilities.
- Maintaining a healthy committed relationship while coping with marital dissatisfaction.
- Cultivating relationships with friends and other families.

Third Generation (Preschoolers and Toddlers)

- Completing the developmental tasks and milestones of infancy and early childhood.
- Developing language.
- Accomplishing toilet learning.
- Adapting to child-care settings.

FIGURE 8–5. Examples of stressors that affect each generation of the Curtis family: 2 years later.

Parenting Reflection 8–6

If changes in one generation affect the other generations to some degree, how do stressors that occur among the third generation affect the first generation? How does the role strain of the parents affect the children?

POINTS TO CONSIDER

■ The period of a child's life between ages 3 and 6 constitutes the stage of early childhood. During this time, a child's developmental tasks and milestones focus on continued physical changes, new psychosocial skills and abilities, and changes in mental development that allow for greater use of language skills and information processing. Preschoolers are characterized as

- Being highly curious in learning about their environments.
- Discovering emerging personal competencies and gaining in self-awareness.
- Beginning to learn family and cultural expectations for appropriate behavior.
- Discovering social roles and family interaction patterns.

■ Parenting behavior adjusts in response to the particular needs of preschoolers. Parents continue to provide nurture in the form of greater degrees of assertive, rather than supportive, care. Structure is introduced for the first time, often through the use and enforcement of rules to control children's behavior and to help them learn self-control. Parents begin to expose their preschooler to socialization practices. Young children begin to learn family, as well as cultural, expectations for appropriate *prosocial* behavior. Parents also teach preschoolers about gender roles as part of the socialization process. The socialization of children this age also includes some instruction about sexuality and about death and dying.

■ A general decline in the rate of physical growth during these years alters the provision of appropriate nutrition.

■ While the health of preschoolers is generally good, parents provide assertive care in protecting them from accidents and injuries, which largely occur within or near the home.

■ The quality of a child's attachment during infancy is manifested in various outcomes that continue to appear in early childhood.

■ Cognitive development during early childhood, known as *preoperational thought*, is characterized in unique ways. Various limitations exist that prevent the development of mature rational thought processes at this time.

■ Young children have limited cognitive and language skills, and parents must adjust their guidance methods. It is important to promote positive self-esteem.

■ Behavioral problems can be expected among many young children and are part of normal development. These are largely due to the problems that children experience in learning appropriate behavior, challenges in teaching children what is expected of them, and daily adjustment difficulties.

■ Nonparental child care includes child-care centers, home-based care by relatives and others, and substitute caregivers. Child-care programs vary according to philosophy and objectives. A variety of outcomes, mostly positive and beneficial, can be anticipated from a child's participation in such programs.

■ A systemic family development snapshot reveals examples of the stressors that may affect the different generations of a family system in healthy, as well as unhealthy, ways.

USEFUL WEBSITES

Center on the Developing Child, Harvard University
http://developingchild.harvard.edu

ChildCare.gov: Your Official Source for All U.S. Government Child Care Information
www.childcare.gov

Council for Exceptional Children
www.cec.sped.org

Head Start, an Office of the Administration for Children and Families Early Childhood Learning and Knowledge Center
http://eclkc.ohs.acf.hhs.gov/hslc

National Association for the Education of Young Children
www.naeyc.org

National Association of Children's Hospitals and Related Institutions, and its public policy affiliate
www.childrenshospitals.net

National Institute of Child Health and Human Development
www.nichd.nih.gov

National Resource Center for Health and Safety in Child Care and Early Education
http://nrckids.org

U.S. Department of Health and Human Services
www.healthfinder.gov

U.S. Department of Health and Human Services, Administration for Children and Families
www.acf.hhs.gov

CHAPTER 9

Parenting School-Age Children

Learning Outcomes

After completing this chapter, readers should be able to

1. Explain how the principal developmental landmarks of middle childhood support parents in applying parenting techniques that are developmentally appropriate.

2. Explain the subtle changes that occur in the transition from parenting preschoolers to parenting school-age children.

3. Explain how some common behavioral problems observed among school-age children differ from what was observed among younger children.

4. Describe the challenges that affect the ability of the parents of children with special needs to raise their children effectively and describe the kinds of assistance available to these families.

5. Explain how the effects of maternal employment exert a ripple effect on the entire family.

The period of the life span termed **middle childhood** begins when a child enters school at about 6 years of age and extends to about age 12. During this time, many children also enter puberty. Typically, puberty's onset can be from the age of 10 onwards, but for some children it is earlier. Girls tend to be slightly ahead of boys concerning the onset of puberty. The developmental events and changes that occur during this period lead to increased maturity and responsibilities. Middle childhood is characterized by more advanced levels of developmental abilities, accompanied by greater expectations by parents and others.

Parents and others hold higher expectations for school-age children than they did for preschoolers. They take a more serious approach to supervising and providing care for this age group, although preschool is a critical developmental window, underestimated by many. It is the foundation on which the school-age development is built.

Parents and children must work with the school system to ensure a successful academic experience and mastery of basic academic skills. Children begin to detach from their dependency on their parents as they separate from their families for longer periods during the day. There is an increasing orientation toward peers. School-age children also face the central psychosocial task (Erik Erikson) of developing a healthy sense of industry as opposed to a sense of inferiority. Although this focus constitutes the major concern of children at this time, many supplementary developmental tasks arise during this period as well. These tasks complement a child's emerging sense of self, and achieving these skills assist a child in developing healthy self-esteem that extends to many different, yet related, aspects of his or her life.

Parents continue to experience the challenges of interacting with a child whose emerging self-concept is sensitive to the psychological bruises inflicted by increasingly complex interactions with others outside of the family system. Parenting style and behaviors in caring for growing children are modified in response to their development. The methods and techniques of parenting or guiding children that were successful during a child's earlier years are no longer as efficient or effective. Essentially, parents must become psychological rather than physical helpers of a school-age child. The change in the nature of caregiving comes about subtly as a child progresses through elementary school.

THE DEVELOPMENTAL LANDMARKS OF MIDDLE CHILDHOOD

During the years of middle childhood, children are challenged by developmental events and changes that lead to increased maturity and responsibility. They are faced with the central task of acquiring a sense of industry as opposed to a sense of inferiority, according to Erik Erikson (1950, 1964). Although this challenge becomes the primary psychosocial focus of children in middle childhood, they are also expected to achieve additional developmental tasks during this period. These tasks complement a child's emerging sense of self, and achievement of these skills helps children acquire healthy self-esteem during their school-age years.

The events of early childhood lay the foundation for the developmental tasks and milestones addressed during middle childhood. Higher expectations are held for children during these years. Both parents and school systems expect children to acquire an attitude of duty and accomplishment (industry) as a result of the experiences that they have had in middle childhood. This attitude may be described in several ways:

- Acquiring a positive attitude toward work assignments and routine jobs leading to the development of a positive work ethic.
- Mastering the tools or mental and social skills that our culture expects children of this age to master over time (e.g., academic skills such as reading, writing, and calculation; learning group politics through group and individual activities with peers).
- Acquiring the ability to take responsibility for personal actions and behaviors.

The development of a healthy attitude toward work and duty in performing one's responsibilities means that school-age children are now expected to begin an assignment or task and complete it satisfactorily without having to be continually reminded to do so. The nature of the task may not be as important as the process of beginning the job and performing it to acceptable standard as outlined by those in authority. The overall feeling or reaction that should emerge during this life stage is pride in accomplishing a variety of skills and in demonstrating dependability in performing assigned tasks. Children acquire a work ethic as they are rewarded and reinforced if assignments are performed satisfactorily in the eyes of parents, teachers, and other authority figures.

Entry into the school environment signals changes and adjustments for the child, the parents, and the family system. An additional social group takes on increasing importance in children's lives. This group is composed of other children, approximately the same age and with similar abilities, who become the child's peers. As a child

Focus On 9–1

The Developmental Characteristics of School-Age Children

General

- Becomes increasingly independent
- Tends to be sensitive to criticism
- Enjoys privacy at times
- Becomes increasingly critical of adults
- Becomes more peer oriented

Physical/Motor

- Likes group activities and games
- Gender differences are observable in physical skills
- Well-established hand–eye coordination
- High energy level
- Appearance of permanent teeth
- Changing body configuration

Social/Mental

- Prefers activities with same-sex peers
- Enjoys light competition
- Curious about the world at large
- Develops a series of close friendships
- Improves with regard to group participation
- May construct self-concept based on social comparisons
- Develops reading and calculation skills
- Changes from intuitive to concrete thought processes

Interests

- Enjoys collections
- Enjoys silly jokes and humor
- Enjoys video and computer games and activities
- Likes adventure stories, movies, and biographies
- Likes creative activities and making things
- Acquires skills that display individual talents and abilities
- Enjoys sports, including organized and team sports

progresses through this stage and through adolescence, the peer group assumes an increasingly significant role in facilitating a child's socialization.

Throughout these years, the cultural expectations of parents and other authority figures concerning behavior and learning, combined with the maturation process, lead to new developmental objectives for school-age children. These objectives, which are largely social and mental, are communicated to children by parents and peers, as well as in the school and social contexts.

PARENTING SCHOOL-AGE CHILDREN

How Does Parenting Change?

As a child reaches school age, parenting changes in quality and style in response to the child's changing developmental needs. The developmental tasks and milestones of school-age children are entirely different from those experienced by preschoolers. During infancy and early childhood, the focus is on physical needs, whereas for school-age children, it shifts to increasingly social and psychological demands.

Physical skills acquired during this period play a significant role in shaping a child's self-concept.

Parenting children in middle childhood, as during the earlier stages, focuses on helping them accomplish their essential developmental tasks and milestones. Parents learn that they must respond and interact differently from when the child was younger. Parenting styles that worked well with preschoolers lose their effectiveness with school-age children. New accomplishments and abilities emerge during middle childhood. Parents learn that they need to become psychological rather than physical helpers for their school-age children.

During early childhood, parents begin training children with regard to increased self-control and self-regulation. The training from previous stages culminates in greater sharing of social power between the parents and the child. It also leads to **coregulation** as a predominant parenting style. Parents increasingly use psychological methods to help children achieve a higher level of self-control. Reassuring children, helping them recover from social blunders, and giving positive reinforcement for efforts to learn new skills are all helpful. The ratio of assertive versus supportive care shifts during this time because parents expect children to take more responsibility for their actions and decisions.

Parents of school-age children expect them to

■ Refine their social skills, exhibiting an increased ability to cooperate with adults and other children.

■ Increase the sophistication of their information-processing skills as reflected in their schoolwork.

■ Assume assignments without adult supervision, and complete them according to the standards set by adults.

Focus Point.   As a child reaches school age, parenting changes in quality and style in response to the child's changing developmental needs. Parents adopt different and more specific interaction styles based on the authoritarian, permissive, and authoritative models. During infancy and early childhood, the focus is on physical needs, whereas during the school-age years, it shifts to increasingly social and psychological demands.

Meeting the Needs of School-Age Children

Promoting Competent Eating.   Current research indicates that prenatal maternal nutrition, as well as childhood eating patterns, contribute to adult health outcomes (White House Task Force on Childhood Obesity, 2013). Ultimately, the goal is to establish *competent eating patterns* (L. E. Brown, 2011; Splett & Krinke, 2011). This paradigm for eating highlights aspects that characterize a competent eater, namely, being positive, comfortable, and flexible regarding food intake. A child needs to know that reliable sources for food are available and that there will be enjoyable and nourishing food at their disposal. Food intake should ideally be internally regulated in response to true hunger. The family's eating patterns should support structured and planned meals (Splett & Krinke, 2011), and this highlights the importance of the shared family meal. Ultimately, the goal is to maintain a normal, enjoyable eating experience that nourishes the body, yet does not lead to overeating or undereating. Attitudes toward eating should exhibit

Parenting FAQ 9–1

Every time my 8-year-old son wants something, such as a new computer game, he backs up his reason for wanting the item with "Everybody has one." Do you have any suggestions as to an appropriate, positive response?

When children at this age are told that they can't have something they want, this is the typical comment they will use because their peers are becoming increasingly important and they are beginning to explore conforming to peer pressure. Children learn subtle manipulative skills and they may even copy the techniques used by their own parents. Examine whether you use this pattern to manipulate your own child and whether the child is modeling your example. No one likes being denied something they desire, especially children. These situations are good opportunities to teach children about managing money. Give your child an allowance based on his contributions to household tasks and point out how the money can be used to fulfill some of these wishes. You can compromise by sharing the expense with him. You can teach your child (and yourself) to avoid power struggles and manipulation, and learn skills that will be useful in adulthood.

self-trust that the correct foods will be chosen. In short, a normalization of eating behavior is the desired outcome. Children are responsive to good role models and will incorporate the modeled healthy eating habits.

Of major concern is the increasingly high incidence of obesity and poor nutrition among school-age children. This paves the way toward health problems such as diabetes and hypertension. Several factors complicate this situation:

■ Parental role models and the nature and quality of family nutrition
■ Lack of knowledge regarding nutrition and a healthy lifestyle within the family home
■ Obese parents who condone obesity in their children
■ Exposure to fast foods, high-calorie drinks, and inadequately nutritious meals
■ Ready availability of high carbohydrate and high glycemic index foods
■ Lack of adequate physical activity, while increasing computer and television time
■ Skipping family meals because the family is not supporting healthy lifestyle choices
■ Chaotic home environments where children resort to "grazing" because there are no scheduled family meals
■ Pressures from food advertising in the media and during children's television programs
■ Exposure to vending machines and poor-quality cafeteria food in some schools

Childhood obesity becomes more apparent during this stage. Sadly, it is so prevalent that even parents do not notice, or choose not to notice, that their child is becoming overweight. As more children become overweight, children will have peers who look similar to them in terms of weight distribution. There has been a steady increase in the number of school-age children and adolescents who are overweight (Federal Interagency Forum on Child and Family Statistics, 2011b). About 17 percent of school-age children and adolescents are considered overweight. The incidence is rising, considering that since 1980 the prevalence has almost tripled (Centers for Disease Control and Prevention, 2012h). Boys and girls are similar in their rates of obesity. Ethnic heritage plays a role as Hispanic and African American children are at the greatest risk of being overweight. Socioeconomic class is an additional factor, with poverty increasing the chances of a lack of healthy nutrition and

knowledge of healthy lifestyle choices in the parental home.

Helping school-age children develop healthy eating habits and food preferences can be challenging for parents and other adults, especially if the older generation is facing weight and lifestyle struggles themselves. The parents are the most powerful influence during early childhood, and how family nutrition plays out in the parental home can set the stage for a lifetime of nutritional choices. One of the greatest gifts that parents can give their children is to instill appropriate nutritional and lifestyle choices from the start. If parents are struggling with food-related challenges, they can be perpetuating the poor habits learned from their own childhoods and inadvertently passing them on to the next generation. By educating the next generation and by raising awareness, perhaps the cycle can be broken. As a nation, Americans boast some success in decreasing cigarette smoking in adults. Similarly, with collaboration on many platforms, including positive influences in the schools, the incidence of overweight and obesity in children could be reduced, especially since there is so much room for improvement.

School breakfast and lunch programs can also promote good nutrition and eating habits among children at this age by offering healthful food choices through a la carte items and limiting the availability of junk foods in vending machines (White House Task Force on Childhood Obesity, 2013). Recess time offers many opportunities for physical activity, which contributes to good health. Physical education is required in most states at the elementary school level (Kann, Brener, & Wechsler, 2007).

Health and Safety Concerns.
Vaccinations.   In addition to promoting good health via healthy nutrition, physical activity, and lifestyle choices, parents have other health and safety concerns for school-age children. Children entering this stage should have received the basic series of vaccinations to prevent many infectious diseases. In the United States, immunizations are usually mandatory for child-care, preschool, and kindergarten enrollment. Some illnesses are common during this period. Because many children are in close contact with each other, it is likely that infectious diseases such as common colds and other conditions will spread easily (National Center for Health Statistics, 2011).

Dental and Orthodontic Care. Because permanent teeth appear at the beginning of this period, dental care is important. Many children are first introduced to a dentist in early childhood, and this becomes even more important in middle childhood. Dental professionals can assist parents in helping children learn the fundamentals of dental hygiene and how to prevent cavities. It is said that about half a century ago the bulk of a lifetime dental budget was spent in the second half of an adult's life. Nowadays, the bulk of the dental budget should be invested before age 20. Orthodontic care has become a virtual rite of passage for American teenagers.

Vision. Parents need to make sure that their children are not overexposed to computers and television because this keeps them inactive and indoors. Children should play outside and exercise in environments that require distance vision and outside light. Outside light can be tenfold that of indoor lighting conditions. Systematic reviews and meta-analyses of many research studies seem to support that reduced time in natural light and reduced time looking at distant objects, as well as genetic factors, can be contributing factors to myopia (American Academy of Ophthalmology, 2012; Khawaja & Sherwin, 2011). The prevalence of myopia has increased steadily in young adults. Good lifestyle practices, not spending too much time using near vision, and exposure to outdoor and daylight activities in which children exercise and use their distance vision all add up to healthier vision outcomes.

Accidents and Injuries. Every hour, a child dies in the United States as a result of an injury (Centers for Disease Control and Prevention, 2012c). Accidental injury involving vehicles and bicycles are the leading cause of death among children this age (Federal Interagency Forum on Child and Family Statistics, 2011b). Parents need to be assertive in preventing these kinds of accidents from occurring, if possible. Proper supervision during play, the use seatbelts, wearing helmets while biking and participating in snow sports, limiting where play may take place, and teaching personal safety on the street and in the home are just a few ways that child safety can be promoted. Flat-screen televisions may fall on children if they are not securely anchored.

Head Injuries and Concussions. Parents and coaches of children who take part in team sports need to be aware of the dangers of concussions and other head injuries. New guidelines have been established to prevent concussions from occurring while playing team sports. Repeated undetected and untreated concussions can lead to permanent brain damage. This is a serious matter as the effects may be lifelong and may not be reversible. About 40 percent of sports-related concussions involved children between the ages of 8 and 13, and it is a common injury that is likely to be underreported (Halstead & Walter, 2010).

Providing Structure and Nurture. Parents and other adults who work with school-age children recognize the value of children's experiences in earlier stages, which assist them in learning about structure. During middle childhood, adult caregivers are interested in helping children acquire even more refined abilities because children are expected to become more skilled at internalizing their own structure. An appreciation for rules is a basic part of experiences that help school-age children internalize and become more self-directed.

Parents should guard against the exclusive emphasis on rules in experiences that teach structure because it could come across as being very authoritarian. Ideally, structure should be combined with nurture. The nurturing of school-age children requires that parents and caregivers are sensitive to children's developmental needs and emerging abilities at this time (J. I. Clarke & Dawson, 1998). Adapting parenting styles is a major challenge for many parents; they must shift to more responsive methods than those established during a child's preschool years. This is a shift away from providing mostly physical care to providing psychological care that is supportive of school-age children. Psychological controls, such as reasoning, are more effective with 9-year-olds than with 3-year-olds. Taking privileges away is another method that some parents find to be useful.

Psychological guidance consists primarily of reassuring children, helping them rebound, and providing positive reinforcement for their efforts in acquiring new skills. The competitive nature of school-age children and how they expect immediate results and success in almost every endeavor requires secure and stable adult guidance. These adults appear, from the child's perspective, to weather every imaginable adversity or difficulty.

Parenting Reflection 9–1

Describe some family rules that promote structure for school-age children. Explain both the positive and the negative consequences of such rules.

Responding to a child's changing developmental demands in middle childhood means learning to lessen the more stringent controls imposed during early childhood (see Figure 9–1). It means allowing the child to gain freedom to practice making decisions within safe

The parenting style should be adjusted to meet the developmental needs of the child. Some behaviors that provide structure and nurture include

- Affirming developmental achievements appropriately.
- Providing a safe and loving environment.
- Encouraging appropriate and safe exploration of the child's environment.
- Modeling respectful, gender-equal behavior.
- Modeling good communication in the marital relationship.
- Communicating age appropriately and respectfully with the child.
- Encouraging the expression of feelings and responding respectfully.
- Providing developmentally appropriate information.
- Providing appropriate and respectful feedback regarding behaviors.
- Explaining the consequences of behaviors and setting appropriate boundaries.
- Being consistent and trustworthy.
- Providing a home environment that supports social and academic learning.
- Teaching the child appropriate decision making.
- Encouraging the child toward appropriate autonomous behavior.
- Supporting the child's interests and relationships with his or her peer group and friends.
- Teaching the child pro-civic behaviors and values.
- Facilitating engagement in prosocial groups in civic and/or religious contexts.

FIGURE 9–1. The behaviors of parents of school-age children.

limits. Parents learn that children desire and require increasing degrees of freedom during this time in their lives. The psychosocial focus of school-age children is facilitated when parents and other adults reinforce the greater desire for independence and provide opportunities for learning a sense of industry.

The increased involvement of children with peers, school activities, and activities outside of the family system means more frequent periods of absence from the home. Parents may find it difficult to keep a predictable schedule in the home. Keeping children's schedules from becoming chaotic and allowing periods of unstructured personal time can be challenging.

Letting go of school-age children means that parents accept the reality that they increasingly value peers and best friends as significant others in their lives. Letting go of children involves allowing them to sleep overnight at a friend's home and, during the later years of middle childhood, go on a camping trip with a youth group. Many children experience their first extended absence from their family during summer camp and visits with relatives.

Parenting Reflection 9–2

Parents can promote a sense of industry in school-age children by encouraging them to take part in arts and crafts projects. Describe how a parent could use both structured and unstructured projects to promote industry and creativity.

Promoting Peer Relations. Our culture is a composite of different subcultures, including various racial, ethnic, and age groups. Individuals have experiences with a number of subcultures throughout their life spans. During the middle years of childhood, children experience one of the first and most important subcultures—the **peer group**.

Peer groups may be formed spontaneously, as with neighborhood children who play together, or formally, as when children are grouped by age in elementary school. In the early part of middle childhood, peer group functioning is less structured and group adherence is loose in comparison with the latter part of this period. Children learn a number of social lessons from the group politics that take place within these groupings (Pellegrini, Kato,

Blatchford, & Baines, 2002). Like other social systems, peer groups have their own rules, communication styles, and boundaries; they also exhibit other functions:

- Developing companionship, especially for play activities.
- Creating a testing ground for behaviors, acceptable and otherwise.
- Transmitting information, accurate or inaccurate.
- Teaching rules and logical consequences.
- Promoting gender-role development.
- Influencing children's self-concept.

There are many sources that influence the development of a child's self-concept. These include past experiences, hypotheses that persons generate about themselves, and input from family members and teachers. The feedback provided by a peer group is seen by many school-age children as having a greater degree of truth in comparison to other sources. This feedback can be largely negative at times because of the all-or-nothing thinking style of school-age children, but it does not reflect the true inner character of a child. The characteristic thinking style of middle childhood (the next developmental stage) can confound an accurate perception of the self. As school-age children grow older, they shift away from using absolutes to determine levels of accomplishment and rely more on **social comparison** based on how they fare in relation to other children their age. Often, the children that serve as comparisons are considered to be less competent or successful, thereby protecting the self-image. This is a self-serving bias.

A healthy sense of self is promoted when children are helped to understand the extent of their personality traits, their collective strengths, and their weaknesses. A habit may be formed at this time in life when the feedback, especially the negative kind, may be overwhelming. By not knowing any different, it is only natural for school-age children to agree with the criticism and negative input about themselves that they hear from others their own age. Some children at this age can be very cruel in their comments and actions toward others who they wish to discount. For some children, crafting a positive personal self-concept occurs when others are discounted and ridiculed. When this is discovered by parents and teachers, it is possible for the adults to help these children construct a realistic sense of self. Parents and teachers are important as interpreters of reality for children. A parent or teacher who can provide accurate interpretations of others' behavior and unkind words can

counterbalance the negative impressions that children deduce from negative peer feedback. This healthy sense of self acknowledges both strengths and weaknesses. School-age children learn that everyone is a mixture of these elements and that other people have feelings and emotions just as they do. They can be helped to understand that the negatives and weaknesses attributed to them by peers do not cancel out the positive aspects and the strengths of their character.

Creating a Safe and Respectful School Environment.
Bullying and harassment.   Recent instances of school violence and killings in the United States have prompted parents, teachers, school systems, and communities to

Bullying is unacceptable behavior that can have tragic outcomes. Peer group empathy training and standing up for one's friends has been shown to reduce bullying and victimization.

examine the issues that have contributed to these tragedies. Several themes have emerged repeatedly:

■ The tendency of some children to become schoolyard bullies and cyberbullies
■ The role of the school and peers in preventing mistreatment
■ The long-term consequences of continued mistreatment or bullying

Almost all children experience some form of bullying or teasing by another child during the elementary and middle school years. While there are some personal characteristics of victims that may invite bullying, for example, being passive, a loner, or crying easily, children without such characteristics can also be mistreated by a bully.

Children who bully others tend to be abused by parents, watch more television featuring violence, and generally misbehave both at home and at school. They feel little remorse for their abusive actions and frequently lie to get around punishment. Many children who are labeled as a bully tend to be characterized as having a callous, unemotional nature that prevents them from comprehending the impact of their actions on their victims (Muñoz, Qualter, & Padgett, 2011).

Bullying and harassment are very real problems of everyday life for many school-age children, and they have long-term consequences. These problem behaviors will not go away on their own. Schools can be bully-proofed, whereby children who are victimized can be taught how to defend themselves, learn how to defuse situations that could lead to victimization, leave situations where bullying can occur, and increase their tolerance of taunts (Olweus, 1993; Ttofi, Farrington, Lösel & Loeber, 2011). Peers can be taught to rise up against bullying and to help defend other children against a bully. The role of peers can be a powerful counterfoil. In addition, schools can implement zero-tolerance policies that, in effect, outlaw bullying (www.stopbullying.gov).

Cyberbullying. Parents need to be aware of the risks of cyberbullying, in which children spread rumors and make derogatory remarks on social media. Again, if peers can be encouraged to support children who are being victimized rather than supporting the bully, then the actions of the bully will be deflated for lack of attention or reinforcement. Peer group empathy training has been shown to have a positive effect on reducing bullying and victimization (Sahin, 2012).

Parents and teachers are aware that some children will not fit easily or readily into peer groups and can sometimes be rejected by other children. When this occurs, adults often seek an explanation about why other children view the rejected child in negative terms. For example, children who are unpopular may be viewed as hostile and overly aggressive, immature, impulsive,

---

Focus On 9–2   **Preventing Bullying and Harassment**

Because bullying in schools has escalated over the past decade, schools are increasingly being held accountable to help curb the abuse of children by other children. Between 1999 and 2010, more than 120 bills were adopted by state legislatures to introduce or amend legislation that addresses bullying, harassment, or similar behavior in schools. Almost all states have laws in place that require schools to have clear policies pertaining to bullying (www.nasbe.org/healthy_schools/hs). The safe and supportive schools initiative provides guidance and has released a two-part training toolkit for use by teachers and educators. This training focuses on some of the following elements:

■ Developing a supportive classroom environment that includes good teacher-to-student and good student-to-student relationships.
■ Establishing a culture of respect for differences. Such a culture increases interstudent competence in interacting with individuals from diverse backgrounds.
■ Setting up a network of positive support throughout the school community. Such a network contributes to a bully-proof environment.

Material on training is available from Safe and Supportive Schools (www.safesupportiveschools.ed.gov).

different in appearance, or insensitive to others (Rodkin & Ahn, 2009). Adults should be concerned when children experience rejection because such experiences may contribute significantly to a negative self-image, conflict with other children, and impaired social development in later stages of the life span. Adults can arrange occasions for supervised play with other children so that these children can learn social skills that lead to more positive peer experiences.

● ●

Parenting Reflection 9–3

What are some steps you can take as a parent or a teacher to bully-proof a child who is being picked on constantly by another child? What would you do to help the child who is the bully?

● ●

Promoting Cognitive Skills. Psychologist Jean Piaget (1967) referred to cognitive development during middle childhood as a period of **concrete operations**. By the time that children reach their school-age years, they can understand and utilize certain principles or relationships between events and things. In using and comprehending these relationships, children interact with objects, symbols, and concepts. They are increasingly able to internalize the environment by using symbolic thought. They learn to add and subtract, classify and order, apply elementary rules of logic to reach conclusions, and apply rules in governing their behavioral choices. They begin to understand the functioning of systems in which they participate by learning that certain operations produce certain results. They are now able to use imagery to perform certain actions mentally that had to be performed physically in the past. Declining egocentrism helps to promote these changes in mental processing.

Certain characteristics are typical of concrete operational thought:

■ *Classification* improves as children become increasingly adept at employing a mental skill known as *decentering*. This means that school-age children can attend to several attributes or details of a task simultaneously. This may explain why children at this age are attracted to collecting objects such as dolls, model airplanes, buttons, and so forth.

■ Grasping the concept of *reversibility* allows a child to understand operations such as addition and subtraction. School-age children learn that subtraction is the reverse operation of addition. Science lessons also incorporate this concept as when sunlight is split into its color components using a prism, and by removing the prism, the sunlight is as before.

■ *Conservation* problems become better understood during this period. Piaget tested this concept with children by pouring a cup of water into differently shaped containers. Preschool-age children would think that a tall, thin container holds more water than a wide, flat one. School-aged children understood that the volume did not change and that it had been *conserved*. The solution to these problems is not confounded by the school-aged child's perceptions as is the case with preschool-age children. While they may be able to master conservation of volume problems, this ability does not easily transfer to the solution of other kinds of conservation problems, such as those involving weight or numbers. Additional experience with the use of mental imagery helps children to grow in this respect.

■ *Seriation* is an extension of classification problems where school-age children become able to scale objects according to the concepts of greater than (>) and less than (<). For example, Doll A is taller than (>) Doll B.

■ *Understanding time* is important in our culture and has a bearing on daily behavior. School-age children become capable of telling time by reading a clock, and they know the days of the week, the months, and the year. They become more knowledgeable regarding what constitutes the past and the future. An increased ability to understand cause-and-effect relationships helps children to predict what day will occur 3 days from now, for example.

Certain limitations are present in the logical processes. Just as thinking in early childhood is limited by egocentrism, thinking in middle childhood is limited by cognitive distortions in reasoning. One major limitation is known as all-or-nothing or black-and-white thinking, or **cognitive conceit** (Elkind, 1974). With regard to such problems in reasoning, a school-age child may reach a conclusion that there is only one right answer to a problem or situation. For example, school-age children eventually observe a teacher making a mistake. Because of cognitive conceit, they incorrectly conclude that the teacher cannot be trusted to provide correct information because of this one mistake. If a teacher is not always right, they reason, she must be frequently wrong. Similarly, a child might reason that because she can consistently give correct answers to several types of problems, she is, therefore, an authority on all matters. This is a type of cognitive distortion that may continue throughout someone's life span, or it may be resolved at a later stage in life (Burns, 2009).

School-age children increasingly use mental skills as part of their daily lives, many of them involving school activities. Parents and other adults play an important role in facilitating a school-age child's cognitive development. For example, children at this time make use of a large database of information that they have acquired earlier in the preschool years. They are attempting to expand this database and make greater sense of their world. Adults hold more challenging expectations of them than of preschoolers. As a result, it is often easy to expect things of school-age children that are beyond their capabilities at this time. By understanding that school-age children still are not able to think logically all of the time and that they are learning the basics of such thinking, parents can customize the ways that they provide structure and nurture at an appropriate developmental level. By understanding that school-age children see the world differently from adults, parents will not expect understanding beyond their child's ability.

Helping Children Adjust to School.   Entry into the school system is a significant event that influences a number of social and cognitive changes in middle childhood. In this setting, a school-age child is introduced to a larger group of peers. The child is also exposed to other adults who possess authority, such as teachers and group leaders, who assist in the child's growth process. Expectations with regard to children's behavior change yearly as children progress through the school system.

Although the education of children was once the responsibility of the family system, it is now partly institutionalized in other agencies. The school system has gained in significance as our culture has become more technologically oriented. Children in middle childhood are expected to become proficient in basic skills, such as reading, writing, and calculation. They are also expected to learn many facts about the world. Parents expect that children will succeed in their learning experiences if they are assigned to properly trained teachers. Teachers are

also expected to conduct effective educational programs that equip children with basic skills.

Some parents assume that once a child becomes part of a school environment, they need to relinquish more responsibility to teachers with regard to the child's academic success. On the other hand, many teachers feel that they cannot be expected to assume full responsibility for ensuring a child's success. Perhaps the best arrangement is that parents and teachers work as a team to help children succeed. When researchers studied how to motivate parents to become more involved in their children's homework, they found that parents are more involved when they are prompted by both their children and the school to provide assistance with assignments. The researchers point out that several positive outcomes could result from greater parental involvement in children's homework, such as being more aware of what was going on with their children at school.

Peer relationships become increasingly important for children in this age group. Some schools support peer group formation through *looping*, a practice that allows children to remain with the same cohort for several years, and the teacher may remain with the same group for more than a year. This provides the stability of ongoing attachments and contributes toward a positive outcome for students, teachers, and families (National Middle School Association, 2009).

Parental Involvement.   The research on parental involvement shows that the positive outcomes far outweigh any possible negative aspects. Parents can be involved in the lives of their children in a number of constructive ways without hampering the development of autonomy or negatively interfering with their peer relationships. Parents can assist a child's educational achievement by being involved with the school. Involvement can take several forms; six major areas are identified:

- *Parenting:* Parents acquire developmentally appropriate parenting skills.
- *Communicating:* Parents are informed and are interested in the school community.
- *Volunteering:*   Parents participate in volunteer activities to strengthen their relationships with the teachers and other parents.
- *Learning at home:* Parents facilitate the completion of homework through goal setting and providing some parental support.

- *Decision making:* Parents provide input and take some responsibility with regard to school policies.
- *Collaborating with the community:* Parents can become involved with those communities who have an interest in this age group (e.g., religious, social, and leadership groups; National Middle School Association, 2006).

Conducive Home Environment. Giving children their own space for quiet study and schoolwork is also important. This is part of creating a *conducive* home environment. It is important to provide structure for children, including an appropriate bedtime so that

Parental involvement with a child's education has many positive outcomes. Parents can volunteer at schools, facilitate learning at home, become involved in school policy decision making, and collaborate with community groups.

children are rested for school, limiting television or computer games, and having regular mealtimes. Many American children have a television in the bedroom. Television is distracting to children in the space where they also do homework, and it can disrupt bedtime. Children may also be exposed to endless influences via unsuitable programs of which the parents are not aware (Diehl & Toelle, 2012).

Talking with children about school and afterschool activities, what kind of play takes place with friends and what projects they are working on also provide support. Structured family mealtimes can provide excellent learning and social opportunities for children. These conversations around the dining table are one way that children learn the many *soft skills* of social interaction that can be an expression of *emotional intelligence*. Such interaction includes behaviors and attitudes that facilitate social engagement, including good manners, punctuality, a work ethic, and respect and appropriate concern for others.

Parents play an important role in encouraging their children's involvement in groups that foster civic engagement, as well as participating in the family's cultural and religious expressions. Children benefit from appropriate role models and mentors who will expand their opportunities for learning social skills that will serve them well in adulthood.

The type of parenting style employed with children this age also contributes to school success (Areepattamannil, 2010). Children who exhibit academic achievement are more likely to have parents who use an authoritative approach. These children tend to be independently motivated to learn and perform well in school. Children who underachieve and have difficulties at school are likely to have parents who use either an authoritarian or a permissive approach to child rearing. Children in authoritarian homes are likely to depend on extrinsic motivation provided by the parents to perform well academically, while parents in permissive homes do not appear to care how children fare in school.

· ·

Parenting Reflection 9–4

Beyond the basics, what are some topics that elementary schools should and should not teach children?

· ·

Focus Point. School-age children are challenged by a variety of developmental tasks that focus on complex social, mental, and physical skills that lead to increased maturity. Social development in middle childhood relates to adjusting to the school environment, establishing relations with peers, and experiencing refinement in the child's self-concept. New mental skills reflect refinement in cognition that allows a child to learn to read, write, and calculate. Parents play an important role in promoting children's academic performance and success.

Teaching About Sexuality. Children are initially educated about sexuality during middle childhood. Schools now play an important role in working with parents to help children grow up with healthy attitudes about sexual matters. Many school systems in the United States provide developmentally appropriate units on sex education, beginning in kindergarten and continuing throughout the elementary grades. These units are often presented in conjunction with input provided by parents who serve on school district advisory committees. Many parents apparently wish to have some assistance in helping children learn about sexuality and appreciate having teachers introduce the topic to their school-age children. On the other hand, there has been some protest from parents who feel that this type of education is best given by parents in the home.

School-age children occasionally ask questions about their bodies and sexual matters, and these questions deserve honest answers from parents. In such situations, parents may act as interpreters of family values for their children. Some parents fear that the school system would replace them in this role by providing children with formal educational experiences about sexuality. Most teachers prefer that parents take an even more active role in teaching children about such matters (P. Schwartz & Cappello, 2000).

Parents have an important responsibility in preparing older school-age children for the physical and psychological changes that they will experience in puberty. Beginning when children are about age 9, most parents can initiate discussions about this approaching developmental event. Opportunities for discussion are important because preteens are more likely to listen to parents' views on sexuality than are children who

have already entered adolescence. For example, it is important that girls be prepared for menstruation and that boys understand nocturnal emissions. Both boys and girls are also interested in their anatomy and desire more detailed information about the functioning of the reproductive system than do preschool-age children. Many excellent resources are available to assist parents in becoming more knowledgeable about preparing their children for puberty. In some communities, hospitals and other community centers provide age-appropriate lectures by experts.

Computers and the World Wide Web. Children need to become computer literate to prepare for their future. The use of computers and the Web augment children's learning in both the school and home environments. School-aged children should be able to use computers for writing reports, researching topics, and playing educational games. Some children may even desire to learn how to write software and develop the skills necessary for developing websites.

Most adults are aware that children need supervision when using computers and the Web. Parents need to learn about software filters that protect children from sites containing pornography and chat rooms that can attract people who want to exploit children. Parents should also monitor the use of social media as cyberbullying has been known to occur on these sites. Forbidding access to computers and the Web because of the inherent risks is not in the best interests of children because computer illiteracy places children at a distinct disadvantage. Parents need to guide and monitor their children so that this arena can be safely negotiated.

Parents should develop rules and regulations that outline how much time a child is allowed to use the computer and the Web. Additionally, children should be taught never to give out personal information to anyone or to post such information on a website. They should know how to deal with accidental viewing of unacceptable material and how to observe the rules of netiquette (appropriate etiquette while using social media and the Web). Parents should supervise the use of e-mail and instant messaging. If children do not observe the rules, parents may need to install programs that limit Internet use. Some children are determined to work around parental rules and limitations and may be exposed to the Web's more unsavory elements. In such cases, parents might wish to consult

---

Focus On 9–3   **Cyberbullying**

The occurrence of cyberbullying—the relentless harassing, intimidation, humiliation, and tormenting of an individual over the Internet via social media or by use of other digital technologies—is on the rise. Texting or instant messaging may be used to send hateful messages or threats to a child. The practice of writing anonymous and hateful attacks on a child's character, appearance, or behavior in notebooks called *slam books* has now moved to modern, digital platforms. Cyberbullying also occurs when a child uses computer software to alter a photo of another child in a demeaning manner.

Parents are not usually the first to learn that this type of misbehavior is being directed at their child, and they may not know how to handle the matter. The parent–child relationship should be sufficiently trusting so that a child feels comfortable discussing harassment and threats with his or her parents. Parents should also feel comfortable approaching professionals such as school officials and law enforcement in order to safeguard their children.

Parents also have a duty to make it clear to their own children that being a perpetrator who bullies is antisocial and destructive. By discussing these matters with children, parents can encourage empathic and prosocial behaviors. Parents, themselves, should be positive role models. Both girls and boys have been identified as being perpetrators and victims of cyberbullying; sadly, sometimes the parents of cyberbullies have been implicated as well.

When children are tormented and suffer in isolation, their despair has sometimes culminated in suicide. This is preventable, and schools are becoming increasingly proactive in curbing bullying and establishing zero-tolerance policies. Effective approaches include calling on peers to support their classmates who are being tormented and teaching children to be empathic. The Web contains many helpful resources for children who are experiencing this type of harassment and for their parents (www.stopbullying.gov).

---

websites for helpful assistance in fine-tuning methods to protect children. Google's Family Safety Center is just one site that offers guidelines that assist parents in regulating children's use of computers and the Web (see www.google.com/familysafety).

TYPICAL BEHAVIORAL PROBLEMS DURING MIDDLE CHILDHOOD

Part of effective and responsible parenting is imparting prosocial values while encouraging social responsibility and civic engagement in children. These lessons can start on a small scale and they need to be age appropriate to match the cognitive development of the child. Parents can teach social responsibility by encouraging children to contribute part of their allowance to charity, or by involving children in charitable events such as collecting toys for disadvantaged children. In this way, children are taught the joy of sharing. By discussing social and environmental stewardship and through modeling appropriate behaviors, parents teach children that trash cannot be dropped in public places, composting

is environmentally friendly, and we have a responsibility to recycle, to mention a few examples. Parents may choose to use religious instruction to support their values. These activities all contribute toward encouraging prosocial behavior throughout childhood. These values will be internalized by the child and will guide their behavior.

Despite parents' best intentions, children may still present with some behavioral problems. The types of behavioral problems observed in school-age children reflect the difficulties they experience in adjusting to the challenges of developmental tasks; therefore, these problems are considered to be age specific. Some, but not all, involve conflicts between parents and children regarding expectations concerning appropriate behavioral standards. Others may be negative, attention-getting behaviors. Some problems, such as learning disabilities, are diverse in their origins and can involve inherent developmental difficulties. Several types of commonly observed behavioral problems are discussed briefly. They include noncompliance, antisocial behaviors, and learning disabilities.

Noncompliance

One of the most common complaints of parents is that school-age children fail to comply with parental requests and they disobey the rules established by the family system. This issue, which begins to appear when children are preschool age, can escalate during middle childhood into a full-blown power struggle between adults and children.

Children at this age tend to test the limits of adults' patience, particularly if they are asked to do something they do not want to do. Standard replies to parental requests include, "In a minute, Mom," or "Just let me finish what I'm doing, Dad." Parents are elevating their expectations for children; instead of asking a child simply to get involved in an activity or chore, they insist that tasks be completed satisfactorily. Some adults may believe that a child should need only one prompt to perform a task before the consequences are enforced. But initially, most parents are patient, understanding that children must adjust as they learn what is expected of them.

There comes a time when parents know that their school-age child should be complying with the rules without exhibiting great resistance. Some of the most frequently prescribed methods for prompting children's compliance involve the use of behavior modification techniques. One technique teaches parents how to phrase their requests in a way that communicates exactly what is expected of children in keeping with family rules and policies. Essentially, parents are taught how to give clear, concise directions so that school-age children can understand parental expectations. Parents are told to give a child at least 5 seconds to comply, and to provide positive consequences or rewards for their appropriate, cooperative behavior.

Another method stresses the use of social reinforcement by using time-out, or separating a child from an activity to be alone for a specified period of time. Although rewards, such as hugging, tend to promote the appearance of compliant behavior, the use of time-out becomes associated in the child's mind with being noncompliant.

Antisocial Behaviors

Antisocial behaviors promote ill will, interfere with effective communication and interaction, constitute negative ways of getting attention, and serve as a means of expressing anger and hostility or coping with frustration and anxiety (Otten & Tuttle, 2010). Although some of these behaviors begin appearing in the latter part of early childhood, a number are typically observed during middle childhood. They reflect problems in adjusting to the demands of developmental tasks and can challenge effective, healthy functioning. Several behaviors are observed more commonly that cause particular concern among adult caregivers, including lying and stealing.

Lying. Lying refers to the deliberate falsification of information with the specific intent of deceiving the listener. Although young children are often unable to separate fantasy from reality, the ability to understand what is true and what is not follows a child's level of moral and cognitive development. Typically, most children come to understand the importance of truthfulness in their interactions by about age 6 or 7.

■ Parents can assist children with problem lying in several ways. It is helpful for a parent to evaluate his or her own behavior and actions so that children do not learn from the model that the parent presents. For example, parental honesty helps children learn how to be trusting and how to generate others' trust in their own integrity.

■ When parents observe a child knowingly giving false information, they should tell the child that lying is unacceptable behavior and will jeopardize their effective interactions with others. School-age children can be helped to understand how the consequences of such behavior are related to personal integrity. In such instances, reading "The Boy Who Cried Wolf," one of Aesop's fables, may be effective in instilling the importance of truthfulness.

■ Quizzing children about their misbehavior often promotes defensive lying. Parents can avoid this approach by informing a child that they are aware of his or her misbehavior. Discussions can proceed from this point in a straightforward manner to resolve the problem behavior.

■ Finally, parents should try to determine the causes that underlie a child's lying (Spock & Needleman, 2011).

Stealing. Stealing occurs more frequently among school-age children than most people imagine. Although many parents feel that stealing is an innocuous behavior in early childhood, it becomes a matter of concern among parents of school-age children and adolescents.

Children steal for a variety of reasons:

- They may lack training with regard to personal property rights.
- They may be trying to bribe friends, perhaps to avoid being teased, or to gain their approval.
- Stealing may be a means of coping with feelings of inferiority or of being in some way different from others.
- Children may steal simply because they cannot resist the temptation of obtaining something that they want very much.
- They may steal as revenge against parents or as a means of gaining their attention.

The problem of stealing is handled first by informing children that this behavior is unacceptable. Parents and other adults should deal fairly and honestly with instances of stealing. They may review their own behavior and reveal instances in which they have modeled dishonesty to children. Then parents can consciously work to avoid having their own actions contribute to the problem behavior of their child. Scrupulous attention to the details of property rights is important as well; parents should explain the difference between a child's property and that of others. It may be helpful to give children an allowance if they are not already receiving one. An allowance can help children learn the work ethics of the family system, including how one may obtain a desired object by saving money with which to purchase the object. Removing temptation, or at least reducing it, by putting money away may also be helpful.

Children with Disabilities

Special education is a highly specialized field, and children with disabilities require professional assessment and interventions. Typically, schools can guide parents toward accessing these services.

Specific learning disabilities that result in poor achievement in school are frequently observed in association with other types of behavioral problems in middle childhood. Children with behavioral problems also tend to demonstrate other types of maladaptive patterns.

Several conditions are classified as specific learning disabilities, including difficulties with reading, written expression, or mathematics. The proposed *DSM-V* uses the term *specific learning disorders* (American Psychiatric Association, 2012). Researchers generally understand that learning disabilities involve a complex variety of different, but related, conditions and factors that hamper the ability of a child to learn and progress in school. *Autism spectrum disorders* are increasingly diagnosed and require early intervention.

The following factors may play a role in learning and scholastic achievement:

- *Ability deficits* may account for many of the problems that school-age children experience with school performance.
- Many professionals attribute learning problems to children's *emotional disorders*, such as anxiety, depression, and unhealthy self-esteem.
- *Biological factors* can account for learning problems that stem from prenatal or postnatal exposure to harmful substances, such as maternal intake of alcohol or cocaine, oxygen deprivation, accidents that affect the central nervous system, infections, and inadequate protein in the diet.
- *Ecological factors* contribute to learning disorders when, for example, labeling a child as troublesome or as a slow learner negatively influences his or her behavior and learning skills.
- Children may lack *adequate knowledge* of how to learn, which may also contribute to such problems.

Attention deficit disorder (ADD) is commonly diagnosed in children. When accompanied by hyperactivity, it is called *attention deficit/hyperactivity disorder* (ADHD). These disorders are classified under neurodevelopmental disorders in the proposed *DSM-V* (American Psychiatric Association, 2012). They are believed to have strong neurobiological and genetic bases (Hallowell & Jensen, 2010; National Institute of Child Health and Human Development, 2010).

Families, especially the parents of children with ADD/ADHD, experience extreme frustrations while dealing with this condition, and it affects everyone involved. Children with ADHD can be in constant motion from the time they wake up in the morning until the time they finally go to sleep at night. Although the ramifications of this disorder are discouraging for children and parents, the condition is responsive to a variety of treatments (Rief, 2005), including medication and behavior modification techniques. Family therapy may be helpful in assisting a family system in dealing with the crises associated with a child whose behavior has a disruptive effect on family functioning.

Focus Point. Many behavioral problems in school-age children are linked to difficulties in achieving developmental tasks; other such problems relate more specifically to difficulties with interactions with parents and peers. Behavioral problems that are related to learning disorders are often discovered in the classroom. A variety of methods may be helpful in dealing with these problems.

PARENTING CHILDREN WITH SPECIAL NEEDS

Our society recognizes that some children have unique needs. These needs relate to disabilities that involve, for instance, visual, auditory, speech, and motor abilities, or providing self-care, together known as **activities of daily living** (Hildebrand et al., 2008). These needs create unusual demands on family systems and parents. In some situations, children have unique developmental difficulties and problems that label them as **exceptional**. In this regard, the term refers to individuals who are different in some manner from the majority of others their age. Community-based programs for assisting children with special needs and their families have been developed as a result of legislation at the state and federal levels.

The Characteristics of Children with Special Needs

The definition of *exceptional children*, or those with special needs, was formerly restricted to those with emotional, developmental, or intellectual disabilities that placed them at a disadvantage in their ability to function within the larger society. More recently, the meaning of exceptionality has been broadened to include those groups of individuals with learning disorders and other handicaps (L. G. Cohen & Spenciner, 2010). Some children have special needs because of chronic, potentially life-threatening conditions, such as diabetes or cancer, although they may have normal developmental capabilities. These children may miss school while undergoing treatment and may need some accommodations in the school environment.

Children with special needs represent about 13 percent of the student population of the United States. Generally, males with special needs outnumber females. This classification scheme is so broad that intellectually gifted children have also been termed exceptional because their needs are often misunderstood by others in their community. The process for including a child in any of these categories involves extensive, comprehensive evaluation by a variety of medical, psychological, and educational professionals.

Family Reactions

Unless there has been some indication prior to birth that a child is likely to have a developmental disorder, parents and other family members usually have little preparation for accommodating a child with special needs. Parents experience a variety of reactions. These reactions may vary according to the nature of the exceptionality, the degree of impairment, the socioeconomic status of the family system, the availability of professional assistance, the financial resources available, and the presence of unimpaired children in the family (Sileo & Prater, 2011). Parents can be expected to experience grief and mourning in reaction to the confirmation of a child's disability. The discovery that a child has special needs represents a loss for most parents, in particular, the loss of future normal developmental progress for the affected child.

In many respects, the diagnosis serves as a crisis or as a stressor event for a family system, and additional reactions follow. The family as a system must adjust to this newly recognized status of the affected child and begin to search for the numerous ways to meet the child's particular needs and those of the other family members. This process can take months, even years, as the family strives to accept and reconcile their unique situation. Ways must be found to include the child into the family's routines and patterns. Parents must learn ways to strengthen their committed relationship and find ways to meet the needs of the other children in the family. Those family systems that use the stresses of this situation to their advantage are likely to become stronger by developing healthy coping strategies that may also be applied in future family crises. On the other hand, those families that acquire unhealthy coping strategies experience even higher levels of stress and greater levels of family disorganization. Ultimately, some marriages will dissolve as the result of the chronic strain of these circumstances.

Many parents experience an adjustment process through which they gain an acceptance of the situation, although others experience ambivalence and even rejection of the child. For many, it is difficult to overcome the tendency to personalize this unfortunate circumstance. In some respects, mothers may react differently from fathers when it becomes known that their child is exceptionally different from others.

Parental attitudes about an exceptional child and the circumstances involved in having this child influence the nature and quality of caregiving. Mothers tend to become the family member who assumes the greatest amount of caretaking and nurturing of a child with special needs. Because fathers and other male family members are expected to be more actively involved in child care today, family stress diminishes and becomes more controlled when fathers lend active support.

The siblings of a child with special needs are also affected by the child's presence (Gopman, 2010). It is possible to observe the interrelatedness concept of family systems theory in this situation. Having a sibling with special needs brings some benefits to other children, such as learning empathy, gaining tolerance and compassion for those who are different, and developing a greater appreciation of personal health. On the other hand, siblings often report negative effects such as feelings of jealousy because of lack of parental attention, resenting the affected sibling's presence in the family, or shamefulness and guilt about the affected sibling. Parents should be mindful of the possibilities of these negative reactions. In addition, girls often complain that brothers aren't expected to assume surrogate parent or caregiver roles to a similar extent. By equalizing the responsibilities between male and female siblings, the psychological risks to girls, especially, are minimized.

The cultural backgrounds of families also influence their reactions to an exceptional child (Jacobs, Lawlor, & Mattingly, 2011). For example, in a Caucasian family, a child's disabilities are described and understood in medical and scientific terms; other cultures may attribute the situation to bad luck, an evil influence on the family, or punishment for ancestral sins.

Chronic stress is one of the most frequently observed family reactions (Alexander-Passe, 2008). Family members can learn healthy coping strategies, such as attending support groups, keeping a journal, participating in individual and family therapy, tapping into spiritual resources, sharing caretaking responsibilities

Having a sibling with special needs brings some benefits to other children, such as learning empathy, tolerance, and compassion. Children with special needs represent about 13% of the student population of the United States.

and time for self-renewal. Networking with other families who are experiencing similar circumstances is also helpful. Unhealthy coping may result in the child with exceptional needs being scapegoated, abused, or emotionally mistreated.

Support for Families with Exceptional Children

Families that have a child with special needs tend to be smaller in size than the average family and have lower incomes than the general population (U.S. Census Bureau, 2011c). Because of their unique circumstances, these families typically make use of more community services and resources in gaining assistance for their child. Several sources provide such support.

Federal Legislation. Federal legislation has helped to address the needs of exceptional children and their families. The Individuals with Disabilities Education Act (acronym IDEA: Public Law 94-142, first enacted in 1975) is based on two assumptions:

■ Children with special needs have a rightful and appropriate place in the public school system.
■ Parents play an important role in the education of their children with special needs.

Essentially, this law gives parents the right to monitor and judge the appropriateness of the educational experiences that their children with special needs receive. The law provides for appointing a guardian for children who are without parents and for funding special education programs.

The law requires that each child with special needs who is enrolled in a public school system be provided with an individualized educational program (IEP) developed by an education specialist working in conjunction with the child's parent(s). The IEP must include a statement regarding the present level of educational performance at the time of the initial implementation, a list of goals and objectives, and the specific educational services and support to be provided. It must also include plans for the child's participation in the classroom, the length of institutionalization (if applicable), and the manner in which the goals and objectives will be evaluated.

Amendments to the Individuals with Disabilities Education Act (Public Law 99-457) were enacted in 1986 and have influenced the assistance provided to families with exceptional children. It requires states to establish comprehensive multidisciplinary approaches to provide early intervention to infants and toddlers with special needs. It extends the ages of the children being served from birth through age 25, emphasizing a focus on services to be provided during the prekindergarten years. This law requires that individualized family service plans (IFSPs) be provided to children with special needs. An IFSP is written for each child between birth and age 3 by a multidisciplinary group of professionals and the parents. It includes the following:

■ An assessment of the child's present level of functioning and developmental status
■ A statement regarding the family's strengths and needs in facilitating the child's developmental progress
■ A list of goals and objectives for the child's progress

■ The means by which the child is expected to achieve these goals and objectives, or the experiences that will promote their accomplishment
■ The means by which the child will be transitioned from early intervention experiences into a preschool program
■ The time frame during which these services will be provided
■ The name of the child's case manager

Several additional laws strengthened the involvement of families in the process of educating children with special needs. Together, these laws comprise the Individuals with Disabilities Education Act of 2004. In complying with this legislation, the states have established an Interagency Coordinating Council that oversees the delivery of early intervention services to families and children with special needs. The Elementary and Secondary Education Act of 2001 (also known as the No Child Left Behind Act) contains provisions that address the needs of exceptional children by supplementing other legislation. This legislation allows school districts to provide programming that may increase parental involvement, reallocate financial resources to provide research-based curricula, and heighten the accountability of instructors. The act also permits children with certain disabilities to qualify for special education classrooms and programs that provide financial assistance.

The eligibility criteria for special education address the following 13 categories: Autism, deaf- and blindness, developmental delay, emotional disability, hearing impairment, intellectual disability, multiple disabilities, orthopedic impairment, other health impairments, a specific learning disability, speech or language impairment, traumatic brain injury, and visual impairment. The terminology used reflects the categories described in the eligibility criteria published by state educational departments.

Community Services. The kinds of services needed to assist exceptional children and their families often depend on the age and specific problems of the child. Some problems become evident long before a child enters the public school system. In some instances, these problems are noticed at birth or when expected developmental progress fails to occur within the months or years after birth. Problems can also be discovered through regular screening. When infants and young children are seen on a regular basis by a physician or health-care professional, the doctor or nurse may discover and evaluate the child's current or future developmental concerns. Early detection is crucial because treatment can alleviate some potential difficulties if it is implemented early. Available community services for parents of infants and young children with special needs include child-care centers, hospital programs, public school programs, Head Start programs, and programs offered through colleges and universities.

Respite care is a community service for families and individuals with disabilities. This supervisory service provides temporary relief for the caregivers of developmentally disabled individuals who live at home and also acts as an important element in preventing institutionalization. The service assists families in coping with emergency situations that require the absence of the primary caregivers and also provides relief from the daily stresses involved in caring for a disabled family member. It supports the caretaker in taking some time for self-renewal.

Educational Programs.   School-age exceptional children are included to the maximum extent possible in existing public school programs, a practice known as **inclusion**, formerly known as **mainstreaming**. These programs are supplemented by special education classes. Because not all children profit from this educational arrangement, some may be placed exclusively in special education classes. School districts offer a variety of programs and services for exceptional children, which vary in response to the needs of the children. These services may include the following:

- *Regular classrooms:*   Children receive special attention and an individualized program.
- *Resource rooms:*   Children are enrolled in regular classrooms, but they go to a specially equipped room to receive part of their daily instruction.
- *Consulting teachers:*   Special education teachers supplement the instruction provided by regular teachers.
- *Day schools:*   Special education programs are conducted in a separate room or building for children whose needs cannot be met in a regular classroom program.
- *Residential schools:*   These schools provide education and other treatment experiences that cannot be provided through any other means. Such schools are

usually reserved for those children with visual or hearing impairment, children with intellectual disabilities, and children with multiple severe disabilities.

- *Hospital or homebound programs:*   These programs serve the needs children who are confined to bed or who experience a lengthy convalescent period and children who are ill.

Other Services.   In addition to involving parents in the educational experiences of exceptional children, some support is offered to the adults and siblings in the family system. These families often need professional counseling, and several helpful strategies have been developed (Sileo & Prater, 2011):

- *Informational counseling* occurs when children are first diagnosed and parents are informed of the test results, prognosis, and treatment approaches.
- *Psychotherapeutic methods,* most prominently behavior modification and reflective counseling, are taught to parents and siblings. Pediatric psychotherapy is offered to the affected child in dealing with emotional and behavioral problems.
- *Group therapy* places a number of parents or siblings into a support network in which individuals share their feelings, reactions, and experiences to help each other cope with the stresses in their own family system.

• •

Focus Point.   Parents of children with special needs deal with issues in child rearing that are not usually confronted by other parents. Child rearing in these circumstances can be difficult, but can also have unique rewards. Members of such family systems experience numerous challenges that influence the quality and the nature of parent–child relations. These families need and receive community assistance that helps them deal with their particular challenges. Federal legislative efforts continue to provide much needed support.

• •

MATERNAL EMPLOYMENT AND CHILD REARING

Almost 71 percent of women with children are in the workforce (U.S. Bureau of Labor Statistics, 2010). Many women would like to reenter the workforce when their children reach school age because it is easier to coordinate work and school schedules. The entry or return of a woman to the workforce becomes a potential stressor for a family system. The change in a woman's employment status affects adaptations in boundaries, rules, and patterns that were formed earlier. Any significant change is disruptive to the efficient, smooth functioning of a family system. When one aspect of a system is altered, other aspects have to be adjusted to restore or maintain homeostasis. Family systems strive to maintain equilibrium. The change in a woman's role produces a ripple effect in the behavior and functioning of the other family members.

Adjusting to these changes effectively constitutes a crisis for many family systems. Job-related stress can have a negative impact on parent–child relationships (Haddock, 2002). On the other hand, the economic and self-actualization factors that accompany employment contain several positive elements that can affect the family system in rewarding ways.

Effects on Adults

Women in contemporary American society see their role as provider as part of their obligation within the family system. Currently, most women balance work outside the home with more traditional domestic responsibilities (U.S. Census Bureau, 2010a). In 1970, about 90 percent of married couples in the United States had conventional earning arrangements where the husband was the sole provider (S. B. Raley, Mattingly, & Bianchi, 2006), while only 9 percent of the wives contributed equally to the couples' earnings. By 2007, more than 60 percent of married couples were each bringing in an income. By 2008, about 26.6 percent of wives were earning more than their husbands, implying that the gender wage gap in the United States is narrowing (Catalyst, 2011).

Many sociological changes have supported these changes in the economics of marriage. Gender roles have become more equal. Women are fulfilling their aspirations for higher education, society is increasingly creating family-friendly workplaces, and a greater choice of child-care arrangements has become available (The Pew Research Center, 2007).

The entry of the oldest child into the school system initiates employment for a significant number of women. Many families need the additional income provided by

the woman's employment, but many women also find that full-time domestic roles have failed to provide sufficient personal fulfillment. Depression is high among stay-at-home mothers with preschool children. Many have college degrees and wish to utilize their educational training. Married women tend to increase their positive self-esteem, personal competence, and economic security while employed, leading to **role enhancement** (Chester & Elgar, 2007), but the entire family must make adjustments to accommodate this return to the workforce.

Researchers have examined the effects of women's employment outside the home on family systems, and they have noted that

- Family functioning requires adjustments in the roles of the other family members. These adaptations relate to household chores, leisure time, recreation, and interpersonal interactions.
- Evidence concerning the effects of women's employment on the couple's marital adjustment is conflicting. Much of this relates to gender roles within the marital dyad and child-care arrangements. Marital satisfaction is high within egalitarian relationships.

The greatest degree of adjustment in family systems to a woman's employment occurs in relation to role responsibilities. Changes usually occur in who does what and when. Many studies report that men become more involved in household chores, parenting responsibilities, and home life after the woman is employed (Bouchard & Lee, 2000). The degree of egalitarianism within the relationship will determine the extent of role sharing. The nature of the couple's jobs is also an important consideration. If one spouse has the night shift or travels extensively, the roles within the home are obviously adjusted to meet these challenges. In military families, one parent may act as a distant coparent while deployed. These families have to find role arrangements that suit the needs of their specific family challenges.

Research suggests that employed mothers experience **role overload** or **role strain** as they juggle the demands of work and the home. They continue to bear the principal household maintenance responsibilities in addition to holding a job outside the home (Chester & Elgar, 2007). Some factors that contribute to role strain in nonegalitarian relationships include the following:

- The division of family work is inequitable because male partners fail to contribute more time to housework or child care when women are employed.
- Traditional gender-role orientations and philosophies continue to determine what work is done by whom, even after women have been employed outside the home.
- Most women would like their partners to be more involved in household responsibilities and child care.
- Role overload has negative implications for women's health and well-being because they are constantly multitasking and juggling roles.
- Some men identify more with their work role than they do with a balanced work and family identity.
- A women's social power within a family system increases significantly after employment. As a woman's level of education increases, there is a greater likelihood of shared household responsibilities with a partner.

Adults in a dual-earner family system are challenged to balance work demands with family responsibilities. This can produce stress that is felt throughout the entire family system. Both men and women are able to achieve this balance successfully but with some differences (Milkie & Peltola, 1999). Men appear to be more challenged when they experience longer work hours, perceive unfairness in sharing housework, experience marital unhappiness, have a wife who works fewer hours than they do, and are unhappy with the trade-offs they make at work for their families, and vice versa. Women appear to be more challenged in achieving a balance when they are employed full-time and have young children.

The Effects on the Children

Many concerns are expressed about how dual parental employment affects children. Many interacting factors play contributory roles, such as the family structure, the ages of the children, the quality and continuity of alternative-care options, and socioeconomic constraints, to name a few (see Figure 9–2). Currently, there are more mothers who are working outside the home than there are those who are staying at home.

MATERNAL EMPLOYMENT

Many factors interact to determine the outcomes of maternal employment on children and adolescents, and there is no simple answer to this complex question. We do need to distinguish between dual-income couples where both parents work outside the home, and couples where the father fulfills the homemaker role.

- The father's support and involvement can influence the system positively.
- The stay-at-home father counteracts any potentially negative effects.
- Maternal employment effects vary by the children's developmental stage.
- Maternal employment effects vary by the mother's age and income.
- Maternal employment effects vary depending on the family structure.
- Maternal employment effects vary by the mother's educational status.
- Maternal marital, occupational, and socioeconomic status affect child rearing.
- Maternal employment affects shared family time.
- Racial and ethnic differences affect outcomes.
- Maternal income can add to the economic well-being of the family.
- Other family processes, such as support from the grandparents, play a role.
- Maternal employment can burden older children who then must take care of younger siblings.
- The effects vary depending on the quality and continuity of child care.
- The effects vary depending on the overall family support and economic resources.

FIGURE 9–2.   Maternal employment and child rearing.
Based on Crosnoe, R., & Cavanagh, S. E. (2010, June). Families with children and adolescents: A review, critique, and future agenda. *Journal of Marriage and Family, 72,* 594–611.

As with any other complex issue, researchers report a number of mixed findings on how this situation affects school-age children. Generally, they find no significant adverse effects on children (DeCaro & Worthman, 2007; Hangal & Aminabhavi, 2007). Children are thought to receive less supervision, less interaction time, and less discipline than do children where one parent stays at home. Some children have increased television time and an associated higher body mass index (Morrissey, Dunifon, & Kalil, 2011).

School-age boys and girls can benefit from their mother's employment, but girls may be especially influenced in positive ways. For example, the female children of employed mothers tend to have higher levels of emotional maturity and achievement, perhaps because of the roles that their mothers model. Both boys and girls tend to have fewer gender stereotypes and biases when their mothers are employed. Maternal employment can be a positive factor in role aspirations for girls, and boys tend to be more gender equal if they have grown up with mothers working outside the home.

Both boys and girls of employed mothers seem to be more self-sufficient than other children, and they tend to be given more responsibilities by their parents. Although they tend to be less compliant with regard to directions given by adults, these differences are generally minor. Other research indicates that employed mothers who feel the greatest levels of role strain are most likely to have children who display maladjustment and behavioral problems (Budig & England, 2001). It is reasonable to assume that those parents who have heavy work schedules or have more than one job are less likely to devote attention to their children and parenting roles and responsibilities. The *quality* of the parenting time can be influenced by the *quantity* of the time available, unless continuous, quality alternative care is in place.

Focus Point.   The entry or return of a mother to the workforce constitutes a crisis for a family system. Many adjustments occur in other aspects of the system to restore and maintain equilibrium, or homeostasis. Adults are affected by changes in their family roles and the use of their time. While many mothers experience role strain and overload, other mothers experience *role enhancement.* They feel that working outside the home widens their social network, keeps them intellectually stimulated, and enhances their autonomy.

Employment of mothers does not appear to cause detrimental problems for school-age children, depending on the quality and continuity of child care. Children benefit in various ways from their mothers' employment status, both economically and socially. Maternal employment can contribute to more gender-equal role perceptions in children of mothers who work outside the home.

The Sandwich Generation

Many employed mothers experience role overload and role strain as they continue to perform family roles in addition to work roles. A number of families have to look after aging parents. Here, the middle generation is *sandwiched* between the needs and demands of the previous, as well as the following, generation (Pierret, 2006).

FAMILY SNAPSHOT

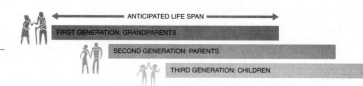

Our intergenerational snapshot of the Curtis family is taken at the midpoint of the middle childhood stage of the oldest child. Mary Curtis is now 9 years old. The first generation faces a critical adjustment following the death of Lisa's mother, Susan Scott, from complications related to breast cancer. The second generation in this family continues to experience great levels of stress because of role strain that affects

the young parents. They are a dual-income couple and have considerable responsibilities, including raising two school-aged children (see Figure 9–3). The third generation, the children, has to deal with adjustments as well, although children are often more resilient than adults in accepting the necessary changes. They lost a grandparent and have experienced a death in the family.

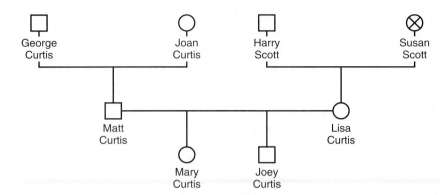

In this genogram, the death of the maternal grandmother is depicted with a cross across the circle bearing her name. The cross indicates that Susan Scott is deceased. Genograms can document a number of events that take place within family systems.

First Generation (Retiring Grandparents)

- Adjusting to the aging process that continues in the latter part of middle age.
- Adjusting to the increasing frequency of deaths among spouses, colleagues, and friends.
- The death of one spouse and widowhood for the surviving spouse.
- Making final preparations for retirement and retiring.
- Depending on the health status, continuing active involvement with the children.
- Mentoring the grandchildren.
- Passing on the heritage of the family through oral and written family history.
- Offering emotional and possibly financial support to their children and grandchildren.
- Having more free time to help adult children decompress.
- Greater reliance on children for support and care during health crises.

Second Generation (Young Adult Parents)

- Continuing adjustments in balancing work and family roles.
- Adding new roles to the existing array.
- Adjusting household and work routines to meet the needs of school-age children.
- Adapting parenting behaviors and styles to meet the needs of school-age children.
- Avoiding divorce and coping in healthy ways with the lowest level of marital satisfaction that will be experienced.
- Attempting to meet personal adult needs.
- Loss of a parent and thereby moving closer to becoming the oldest generation.
- Experiencing illness and death in the immediate family.
- Experiencing being in the sandwich generation, addressing demands from the generation above and the generation below.

Third Generation (School-Age Children)

- Mastering the developmental tasks and milestones of middle childhood.
- Experiencing greater autonomy related to the fact that both parents work outside the home.
- Increasing involvement with their peer group.
- Experiencing sibling relations.
- Enjoying their relationship with their grandparents, who pass on family history.
- Experiencing death in the family: the loss of a grandparent.
- Increasing involvement with team sports and organized social activities, such as youth groups.

FIGURE 9–3.   Examples of the stressors affecting each Curtis family generation.

POINTS TO CONSIDER

■ The time between ages 6 and 12 is called *middle childhood*. During this period, children master several developmental tasks and milestones, including
  ■ Achieving a sense of industry versus inferiority.
  ■ Developing a new sense of individuality.
  ■ Establishing relationships with peers.
  ■ Refining existing skills and acquiring new physical, social, and mental skills.

■ Parenting increasingly shifts to psychological assistance and guidance when children are school age. Parenting styles change and adapt in relation to the new developmental needs of children. Coregulation becomes a predominant approach by most parents of school-age children. Children take on greater responsibility for their own actions. Children are also allowed greater latitude in their activities and behavior because of their more advanced abilities. Parents increasingly provide more advanced levels of structure, best conveyed in terms of nurture. Many parents also incorporate new parenting styles to provide nurture and structure to children at this age.

■ Socialization experiences are part of parental efforts for school-age children, especially facilitation of moral development. Parents serve an important function in providing interpretation and acting as narrators. This role assists children in learning how to reason morally, consider options for their behavior, and gain knowledge about family values and a sense of right and wrong.

■ The school may assist parents in helping school-age children to appropriately learn more about sexuality. It is important for parents to prepare preteens for their approaching puberty. Parents also play an important role in helping their school-age children to become computer literate and in protecting them from unsavory, inappropriate Web content and online predators.

■ Certain behavioral problems can be expected in some school-age children that are specific to diffculties in adjusting to the developmental tasks of this life stage. They may involve
  ■ Problems in cooperating with adults' expectations of appropriate behavior.

  ■ Difficulties in attending school and in mastering the skills essential to successful functioning in an academic environment.
  ■ Problems in developing interpersonal skills and achieving the appropriate standards of behavior expected by those in authority.

■ Families of children with special needs face challenges that are not usually shared by other families and they experience a variety of reactions. A child with special needs influences the family system as a whole. The ability of families to cope with the stresses and demands of a child with special needs depends on the availability and nature of a variety of sources of assistance and support. Community programs and federal legislation address the needs of exceptional children and their parents.

■ Many married mothers become employed or reenter the workforce when their children are of school age. This change in a woman's employment status affects adaptations in family boundaries, rules, and patterns. Both adults and children are affected by this change, and the family system reacts by making major adjustments in roles, rules, and other patterns to regain and maintain homeostasis.

■ In a sandwich generation, the middle generation is sandwiched between the needs and demands of the previous, as well as the next, generation. The couple may be looking after elderly parents as well as raising their own children. This can lead to role strain.

■ A family snapshot reveals examples of the stressors that may affect the different generations of a family system with school-aged children.

USEFUL WEBSITES

Association for Middle Level Education
http://amle.org

Boy Scouts of America and Girls Scouts of America
www.scouting.org and *www.girlscouts.org*

Cyberbullying Research Center
www.cyberbullying.us

Learning Disabilities Association of America
www.ldaamerica.org

National Association of State Boards of Education: State School Healthy Policy Database
www.nasbe.org/healthy_schools/hs/

National Crime Prevention Council
www.ncpc.org

National Dissemination Center for Children with Disabilities
www.nichcy.org

National Resource Center on ADHD
www.help4adhd.or

National Safe Place
www.nationalsafeplace.org

Safe and Supportive Schools
www.safeandsupportiveschools.ed.gov

Stop Bullying
www.stopbullying.gov

Stop Cyberbullying
www.stopcyberbullying.org/index2.html

U.S. Department of Education
www.ed.gov

CHAPTER 10

Parenting Adolescents and Young Adults

Learning Outcomes

Parenting Adolescents

After completing this chapter, readers should be able to

1. Explain why it is important for parents to be familiar with the principal developmental milestones of adolescence.

2. Explain why parenting an adolescent is different from parenting a younger child.

3. Explain how parents adjust their parenting styles so that there is bidirectionality in meeting the particular needs of adolescent children, as well as the needs of the parents.

Parenting Young Adults

After completing this chapter, readers should be able to

1. Describe the unique challenges of parenting young adults while respecting their autonomy.

2. Describe why grandparenting is playing an increasingly important role in contemporary families.

3. Explain the factors contributing to this shift in family roles and some of the unique challenges of the grandparenting role.

Adolescence is the stage of the life span that represents a transitional period between childhood and adulthood. Chronologically, it begins at age 13 and extends through age 18. Development occurs gradually so that early and late adolescence can seem like two different stages. Early adolescence has some qualities of childhood, whereas late adolescence begins to model emerging adulthood (Arnett, 2000). The developmental event of puberty, which is usually in progress by early adolescence, signals the end of childhood. During this time, individuals become sexually mature and capable of reproduction. The term **puberty** refers to maturation in terms of physical sexual characteristics, whereas the term **adolescence** refers to the entire period between late childhood and early adulthood and includes social and emotional aspects as well as the physical dimension of puberty.

The stage of adolescence is technically divided into two periods:

1. *Early adolescence* typically encompasses puberty and involves a variety of physical changes associated with the achievement of sexual maturation. The onset of puberty varies. The average age at which breast development in girls begins is age 10, but can be as early as age 8. The average age of menarche (the first menstrual period) is about 12, but it can be earlier. The average age for male puberty is 12, but onset as young as age 9 is within the normal range. It typically ends at age 16.

2. *Late adolescence*, which begins at age 16 and continues until age 18, involves many psychosocial changes (Steinberg, 2010) as individuals seek increasing independence.

Parents and adolescents are part of the same dynamic family system, and they influence each other (Cui et al., 2007). Parents may anticipate the adolescent stage of their children's life span with mixed feelings. Traditionally, the period is described as stormy and stressful for teens, their parents, and the family system. Parents may fear for the safety of their increasingly independent children, whereas adolescents may feel as if they are disrespected or not trusted by their protective parents (B. K. Barber, Xia, Olsen, McNeely, & Bose, 2011).

A more contemporary view of adolescence describes this stage as one of expanding autonomy as children gain increasing degrees of personal responsibility at a time of significant transition (Steinberg, 2010). Parents may view these gains apprehensively, being aware of the many hazards that can threaten the health and well-being of adolescent children. As with other stages of the life span, adolescence presents both children and their parents with unique challenges for growth and adaptation.

Adolescence is a time of rapid change as individuals seek to establish a personal identity and embark on individuating from their family of origin.

THE DEVELOPMENTAL LANDMARKS OF ADOLESCENCE

Three features distinguish development during adolescence:

■ *Rapid physical and psychological change.* Adolescence is a period of metamorphosis in an individual's life that involves dramatic changes in body proportions and physical size, sexual maturation, and personality shifts.
■ *Individual emancipation.* Western culture emphasizes the teenage years as the appropriate time for establishing independence as a mature person and assuming full responsibility.
■ *Experimentation, idealism, and uncertainty.* These changing and developing ideals often bring teens into conflict with adults, especially their parents.

Adolescence is a transitional period between childhood and adulthood that has few guidelines for how to behave, what to expect, and how to remain secure about what the future holds. Adolescents are known for unrealistic expectations and aspirations. These attitudes are expressed in relationships with peers and family members. High hopes for the future lead teenagers to create dreams and idealistic notions about their own abilities and skills in coping with the world. Adolescents are known for self-exploration and self-expression, and the tendency to experiment is seen in their choice of clothing, musical tastes, friendships, and awakening sexuality. The specific developmental tasks and milestones that individuals encounter in adolescence focus on acquiring and refining more advanced skills, abilities, and attitudes that lead toward preparation for adulthood.

PARENTING ADOLESCENTS

When discussing parents' relationships with teens during adolescence, we need to look at both family status and family process. Family status is defined by aspects of family structure and positioning, such as marital union, single parenthood, socioeconomic resources, employment, and education. Family process concerns the relationships within the family. These relationships can occur *intergenerationally*, as when the grandparents are involved, and *intragenerationally*, as between siblings (Crosnoe & Cavanagh, 2010). Many parents anticipate conflict when a child reaches adolescence because this stage can be associated with rebellion, tension, and emotional turmoil. While some teenagers are rather extreme in their behaviors and attitudes, most adolescents do not act out, and the stereotypes do not normally apply.

Parenting styles and behaviors must adapt once again to meet the needs of a now maturing child. The adaptation is typically initiated by the adolescent, who may demand to be treated with more trust and respect, which is perceived as independence. The developmental need for autonomy and individuation from the family system presents unique, yet rewarding, challenges, and adolescents put a high value on being respected by their parents (B. K. Barber et al., 2011). Most parents

---

Focus On 10–1   **The Developmental Characteristics of Adolescence**

■ Establishing a sense of personal identity as opposed to role confusion.
■ Establishing new and more mature relationships with peers of both sexes.
■ Accepting the physical changes that accompany puberty.
■ Defining gender roles and accepting one's sexuality.
■ Initiating the process of individuation.
■ Initiating financial independence.
■ Preparations for higher education and/or an occupation.
■ Manifesting socially responsible behaviors.

The following steps begin in early childhood and continue to develop:

■ Acquiring and developing the skills needed to participate in healthy relationships.
■ Solidifying a set of values and an ethical system that will guide behavior.

understand that adolescents continue to need guidance, rules, and support during this process of growing toward maturity. The manner in which this guidance is offered needs to be respectful and acknowledge the emerging aspects of maturity, while being cognizant of the unique qualities that characterize adolescent thinking. The safety and shelter of parental guidance should allow appropriate self-exploration and autonomy.

Professionals who work with families stress that one of the more difficult challenges of parenting adolescents is the fine line that parents walk between being supportive of a teen's efforts to individuate and maintaining certain boundaries for appropriate behavior (Gnaulati & Heine, 2001). Adolescents need to learn how to make personal decisions, but sometimes their decisions can have drastic consequences. Family systems become unhealthy when there is a demand for complete conformity among all members, when everyone is expected to adhere to the same beliefs, values, and behaviors. Although parents and adolescents must agree on rules and other family patterns, this agreement ideally develops through negotiation and input from all concerned.

Revised Parenting Styles

Skilled parents adapt child-rearing strategies, methods, and interaction styles to meet the particular needs of the adolescent. Because of the expanding autonomy of adolescents, parents have to alter their parenting style as well. Parents become more authoritative, less authoritarian, and, eventually, more permissive.

Parents must discover ways to help teens learn to make decisions that minimize the potential harm to themselves and others. Communication between parents and teens requires patience and effort to achieve effective functioning in this microenvironment (Santrock, 2009). Parents must gradually relinquish control and place increasing amounts of personal responsibility onto teens so that they become self-regulating.

Some parenting styles are more common in subsets of society. Middle-class families tend to use methods based on persuasion and negotiation. Middle-class approaches include democratic, egalitarian, and authoritative styles. Under economic strain, stressful influences can contribute to parenting styles that emphasize control, especially by forceful, power-assertive methods (Areepattamannil, 2010). Financial independence may be valued if families are struggling, and they may expect that their adolescent children become financially independent at an earlier age. Parents with college educations tend to encourage their children to pursue further education, and the parents serve as role models.

Conflicts between parents and young adolescents occur more frequently than when children were younger (Steinberg, 2010). These clashes can happen because of the intense focus of young adolescents on identity formation. Predictably, many parents initially react to such efforts by using styles that are strict and controlling.

Research consistently shows that parent–adolescent relations are best when decisions are perceived by both parties as being consistent, fair, and collaborative and the needs of all family members are respected (Santrock, 2009). As in previous stages of parenting children, the authoritative parenting style continues to be associated with positive adolescent outcomes.

Historic Research.   The sociologist Glen Holl Elder (b. 1934) is best known for his historic work, *Children of the Great Depression* (1974, 1999). He studied human development against the backdrop of changing environments, and he showed how these changes in the environment could change lives. Elder examined how the chronosystem (time-related influences, according to Bronfenbrenner's family ecological theory) affected the outcomes of development over the life span. For instance, if all members of a cohort had to face a major life experience, such as the Great Depression, what influence would that have on their lives? He conducted a classic demographic study (1962) that described the styles commonly used by parenting adolescents. At a time when mainstream thinking undervalued the role of fathers as parents, and parent–child interaction was thought to be predominantly uni-directional, he studied the dimensions of parenting on a large scale. Elder's study included 7,400 adolescents from homes that had two parents, and it classified parenting styles on a continuum that differed in the degree of control exercised by the adults. According to the study, at least seven styles could be observed:

■ *Autocratic.*   Teens are allowed no freedom to express their opinions or to make any decision that affects how they conduct their lives.
■ *Authoritarian.*   Teens are allowed to express their opinions, but parents continue to make decisions that affect their lives.
■ *Democratic.*   Teens and parents share power, but parents have veto power over the decisions made by teens.

■ *Permissive.* Teens take an increasing degree of responsibility for their decisions and actions, but with the understanding that parents continue to have input into the decision-making process.

■ *Egalitarian.* Teens and parents have equal power and status, and they make decisions through joint effort.

■ *Laissez-faire.* Teens take complete control and responsibility for making decisions about their lives and conduct. Parents understand that they can contribute information and opinions, which teens can freely disregard.

■ *Ignoring.* Parents take no part or have no interest in an adolescent's behavior.

Most of the parents in this study used democratic or egalitarian styles. The stricter styles were more prevalent in larger family systems, among those with low incomes, and among those who had younger adolescents. Stricter parenting styles may be used more commonly in larger family systems because adults have greater time and resource management pressures. Contemporary family life is hectic when adolescents are present. Stricter methods among larger groups may facilitate family functioning to a certain degree, but this may occur at the expense of an adolescent's achievement of high-level individuation.

••

Focus Point. One of the challenges in relationships between parents and teens relates to how parents must adapt in providing structure and nurture. A significant task involves the ability of parents and teens to communicate effectively. Adults who use democratic styles in parenting adolescents usually have more positive interactions. Those using stricter styles experience more conflict, which frequently relates to adolescent attempts at individuation.

••

Meeting the Needs of Adolescents

Meeting Nutritional Needs. The focus on *competent eating* is important, and the nutritional foundation laid down by parents during earlier phases will now pay dividends. Family meals, family food choices, and positive parental role models remain important influential factors in spite of peer group pressures.

The appetites of both girls and boys increase dramatically during adolescence. With appropriate discussion

and modeling, modern adolescents are increasingly interested in healthy eating; although without this influence, they may gravitate toward easy-to-access and generally less nutritious food. Because adolescents are very peer oriented, it may be difficult to encourage or even insist on appropriate nutrition unless their peers care about healthy food choices. Most adolescents want to be like their friends, including the foods that they consume. Because adolescence is also associated with greater body awareness, which is linked to self-concept, there is a greater risk of eating disorders, especially in adolescent females. Obesity is increasing in both genders and can cause shame and erode adolescents' self-concept.

Health and Safety Issues   Health and safety issues occurring during this stage often have a significant impact on the present as well as the future. Some parents mistakenly skip the recommended medical checkups after children enter school because children have received most of the necessary vaccines. Continued health monitoring is a good practice that facilitates early recognition and treatment of any irregularities. Disorders such as poor growth can be missed if there are no health screenings.

Adolescents should continue annual visits with a health-care professional for routine medical checkups. These visits allow for confidential discussions of issues of a personal nature that a health-care professional can address. Health-care professionals can play an important role in supporting teens' acquisition of a healthy lifestyle, including safer sexual practices and limits with regard to alcohol.

Substance Abuse and Binge Drinking. Parents and other members of society are extremely concerned about adolescent drug use and binge drinking. The extent of drug use and illegal underage drinking of alcohol among teenagers is considerable (see Figure 10–1). There has been a moderate decline in illicit drug use among adolescents in recent years (National Institute on Drug Abuse, 2011). The misuse of prescription drugs and accidental fatal overdoses from these substances is on the rise and has become a new health hazard among this age group (Centers for Disease Control and Prevention, 2012d).

Despite the influences of the media and peers, adolescents who have been raised by parents who rely on an

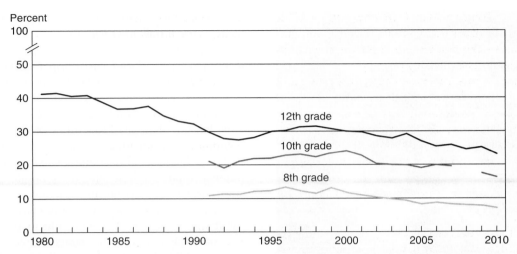

FIGURE 10–1.   Percentage of 8th-, 10th-, and 12th-grade students who reported having five or more alcoholic beverages in a row in the past 2 weeks by grade, 1980–2010.
Source: National Institute on Drug Abuse, Monitoring the Future Survey.

authoritative style appear to have stronger internalized standards that help to insulate them from peer pressure to abuse substances or to participate in underage drinking of alcohol (Luyckx et al., 2011). Teens do care what parents think about smoking and drinking and are less likely to drink alcohol, smoke cigarettes, or use other drugs if the parental role models are appropriate.

Adolescents are also at increased risk for injury and death from accidents involving alcohol and/or drug use and automobiles (U.S. Census Bureau, 2011d). Such accidents are still the leading cause of death among teenagers in the United States, resulting in much grief when friends, siblings, and children lose their lives in this manner. In addition to accidents and fatal injuries involving automobiles, teen text messaging while driving is taking its toll. Some states have enacted legislation that prohibits this practice.

Suicide.   Suicide is the third leading cause of death, following fatal accidents and homicides among individuals between 11 and 24 years of age (Miniño, 2011). Teenagers increasingly are completing suicide attempts successfully, and the rate has more than tripled within the past 30 years. No ethnic group is spared this phenomenon. Most adolescents who attempt suicide and fail are female, and males are more likely to succeed. The National Institute for Mental Health

states that, for every 25 suicides attempted, one is fatal (www.nimh.nih.gov). A teen suicide attempt should always be recognized as an expression of extreme distress that necessitates professional intervention (www.teensuicide.us).

Suicide may be related to a variety of factors, including clinical depression, which distorts the ability to reason logically. Life frequently seems hopeless to persons who are clinically depressed, and suicide may seem to be the only possible escape. Suicide among adolescents is also related to substance abuse, which is frequently accompanied by depression and increased impulsivity (National Alliance on Mental Illness, 2011).

Some teenagers who succeed in committing suicide are depressed regarding their sexual orientation (Teasdale & Bradley-Engen, 2010), and some are living with gender identity disorders where they identify more closely with the opposite gender. For instance, there are male teenagers who feel that they should be female (Spack, Edwards-Leeper, et al., 2011). Puberty can be an intensely distressing time for individuals who begin to develop external sexual characteristics that do not correspond to the gender with which they identify.

Young people who identify themselves as LGBT (lesbian, gay, bisexual, or transgendered) are more likely to attempt suicide than the average adolescent

Rates of suicide have more than tripled within the last 30 years. Suicide is often related to substance abuse and to depression. Crisis phone lines can offer additional support.

and increasingly schools are adopting a zero-tolerance stance against bullying behavior.

Teen Pregnancy and Sexually Transmitted Diseases (STDs).   There has been a recent decline in the number of teen pregnancies (Federal Interagency Forum on Child and Family Statistics, 2011b), but the decline has not eliminated this problem. Teen pregnancy continues to be a matter of concern for society, schools, and the adolescents and families who are affected. Teen parents, their children, and their families face many serious short- and long-term consequences.

The high frequency of unprotected sexual behavior and multiple sex partners results in an equally high rate of STDs among adolescents. Adolescents represent about 25 percent of all sexually active individuals. Almost one-half of all new STDs reported are contracted among those between 15 and 24 years of age (Centers for Disease Control and Prevention, 2010). The extremely high incidence of STDs is thought to be a combination of circumstances that include cognitive factors such as lack of information, ignorance, denial, and a misplaced sense of personal invincibility, as in "that won't happen to me." Social factors, such as coercion and peer pressure, are a reality. In addition, lack of planning and inappropriate shame associated with safer sexual practices play contributory roles. A growing number of high schools have school-based health clinics that provide sex education, STD screening and treatment, and, in some cases, condoms. A vaccine protecting against some types of human papilloma virus (HTP) is an option for both male and female adolescents. Abstinence or responsible sexual practices, including condom use as well as being informed concerning risks, contribute to safer outcomes.

Eating Disorders.   Some adolescents have a distorted body image (Le Grange & Lock, 2011). Many experience low self-esteem related to concerns about weight that may make them vulnerable to eating disorders. Eating disorders can be played out in the family system as a means of control. Eating disorders are increasingly recognized as a mental health disorder and should be treated seriously.

Anorexia nervosa and ***bulimia*** are serious eating disorders that affect the health, well-being, and lives of teenagers. Both conditions present predominantly in teenage girls. These conditions have serious consequences

population. These youths experience anguish and inner turmoil and choose to commit suicide rather than suffer rejection, disapproval, and shame, which are the reactions that they anticipate from family and friends. A more compassionate and informed society needs to reach out supportively and compassionately to these individuals. Crisis hotlines are available to take emergency calls 24/7.

Suicide can also occur as a result of *bullying*, where victims feel overwhelmed by the shaming and social abuse that they receive from their peers. Social awareness, respect for human and civil rights, and a growing acceptance of diversity make it very clear that this form of abusive behavior is unacceptable and cannot be tolerated. Increased awareness and empathy among peers has been shown to exert a protective influence, that can disturb normal adolescent behavior and development, and anorexia nervosa can result in death

Anorexic teenage girls appear to be obsessed with their body weight and have a distorted body image (Lock, 2011). The condition begins with dieting to achieve a particular weight, but continues to a point where it threatens their health and well-being. Controlling their weight and what they eat becomes the central life focus. Several factors interact:

■ Strong cultural pressures emphasize slim figures.
■ Within the family system, girls may react against strict, overprotective parents, the lack of adequate personal boundaries, or their inability to individuate and attain personal autonomy (Le Grange & Lock, 2011; Lock, 2011).

Anorexia is a psychological disorder that can have fatal consequences if left untreated. Therapy can involve hospitalization to treat malnutrition and individual psychotherapy to help a teenage girl become more autonomous in less self-destructive ways. Family therapy and cognitive behavioral therapy can be helpful in resolving enmeshed familial relationships, improving communication, and helping the family system acquire healthy ways of resolving conflict (Gowers & Green, 2009). Psychiatrists may be involved to treat comorbid depression and anxiety disorders.

Bulimia involves consuming huge amounts of food that are then purged from the body by vomiting or using excessive amounts of laxatives (Le Grange & Lock, 2011). Consumption occurs in periodic binges and during stressful situations as a means of coping. Unlike persons with anorexia, individuals with bulimia know that their behavior is not appropriate. They binge and purge in secret to avoid discovery and suffer from feelings of shame and guilt. The condition is similar to anorexia because it, too, revolves around the need to control one's eating and is motivated by a distorted body image.

Bulimia is a common method for weight control among adolescent girls, and bulimic-related death can occur as a result of suicide, a correlate of depression. Many adolescents with bulimia are clinically depressed and have a tendency toward perfectionism. They are described as having an obsessive desire to control and manage themselves, as well as others in their lives. They are considered to be heavily dependent on the approval of others as the basis of their self-worth. This condition, like anorexia, responds to treatment through group,

family, and individual psychotherapy and is also responsive to certain antidepressant medications.

Researchers have known for some time that cultural and family values influence the development of eating disorders, especially among female children (Davis, Shuster, Blackmore, & Fox, 2004). These factors can combine in a family ecology to produce a behavioral problem in adolescence. A critical family environment, coercive parental controls, and a dominating discourse about body weight within the household can work together to increase the likelihood of an adolescent developing an eating disorder. Research also points to biological influences that may cause a genetic predisposition. As with many conditions, several factors interact to precipitate the behavior (Steiner et al., 2003). With proper medical and psychotherapeutic treatment, both of these disorders can be brought under control and individuals can return to healthy, productive lives.

• •

Focus Point.   There are a variety of issues that affect the health and safety of adolescents. A significant number of adolescents behave in ways that have short- and long-term adverse effects on their development.

• •

Providing Structure and Nurture for Adolescents.   Family climate, rather than family structure, is related to the well-being of the members of the family, and is of greater importance in emotional satisfaction (T. Phillips, 2012). According to the U.S. Census Bureau (2011b), 27.2 percent of children under the age of 18 lived with only one parent. The cohesion of a family system is threatened when any change takes place that affects the system's functioning and equilibrium. Systems have a strong tendency to maintain the status quo because change in any aspect threatens the system's integrity. Family systems do face challenges that call for changes. When a child becomes an adolescent, the desire for individuation poses a serious threat to the family's functioning and the ability to maintain systemic cohesion.

Parents may seem particularly reluctant to release a teen from the controls, limits, and boundaries that were established in earlier developmental stages. Although many parents realize that this change must take place eventually, the equalization and transfer of power toward greater self-regulation occurs more slowly than most teens prefer.

Researchers have consistently validated the benefits of authoritative parenting styles in mediating positive developmental outcomes for children (Luyckx et al., 2011; Piaget, 1972). The benefits of this parenting style continue to remain in effect while parents make alterations in response to the individuation process of their teenagers. For example, the behavioral problems of adolescents appear to diminish while academic competence can be enhanced when parents maintain *detached involvement* or supervision. This variation on the authoritative parenting method relates to the perception that adolescents have regarding their parents' involvement in their lives, while allowing them enough slack from parental supervision in order to feel autonomous. Parents are still providing structure for adolescents, but the structure is perceived as being fairly administered, yet firm and warm in its tone (see Figure 10–2).

Parenting Reflection 10–1

Is there such a thing as a **generation gap,** or is this a media fabrication? How would this influence interactions, communication, and mutual understanding among the generations?

Parenting Reflection 10–2

How can parents guide their teenage children toward making constructive decisions and, at the same time, discourage them from making unwise choices?

Focus Point. One of the challenges found in the relationship between parents and teens relates to how parents must adapt in providing structure and nurture.

Peer Group Influences. The peer group plays a special role in the process of personal identity formation among adolescents. The interactions with peer groups in adolescence are similar in purpose to those

The parenting style should be adjusted to meet the developmental needs of the adolescent. Some behaviors that provide structure and nurture include

- All of the appropriate parenting behaviors up to this point of development.
- Supporting the emerging identity of the adolescent.
- Supporting positive self-image and the formation of positive body image.
- Introducing adolescents to appropriate adult roles and modeling appropriate behavior.
- Guiding adolescents toward educational and career goals.
- Modeling respectful and gender-equal behavior.
- Communicating age appropriately and respectfully.
- Explaining the consequences of behavior and setting appropriate boundaries.
- Providing a home environment that supports social and academic learning.
- Teaching adolescents appropriate decision making.
- Discussing the dangers of underage drinking and substance abuse.
- Discussing values, sexual decision making, and safer sex practices.
- Guiding adolescents toward sound financial decision making and modeling appropriate behavior.
- Encouraging adolescents to achieve appropriate autonomous behavior.
- Supporting interests and peer group relationships/friendships.
- Teaching adolescents pro-civic behaviors and values.
- Facilitating engagement in prosocial groups in civic and/or religious contexts.

FIGURE 10–2. The behaviors of parents of adolescents.

that occurred during middle childhood, but the peer group takes on additional functions for teens. Similar to school-age children, teenagers use their peers as a device for making self-evaluations. In adolescence, this group becomes a new source for redefining the teen's personal identity. Teens view their peers as an extension of their own self-image. There is an enmeshment of personal identity of the self with others.

The push for autonomy reaches its peak in adolescence. This change gives a teenager freedom to test limits, discover areas of ability and weakness, and make mistakes while learning many skills and problem-solving

During adolescence, peer pressure to conform to established or imagined standards is high. Most parents understand that adolescents continue to need guidance, rules, and support to enhance positive self-expression.

strategies. The boundaries between the self and the parents become more distinct, while the boundaries between the individual and the peer group begin to blur in early adolescence. Allegiance once felt toward the parents shifts to the peers. This change creates tension between an adolescent and the family system. Peer pressure to conform to established or imagined standards is high. Acceptance and validation from others bolster self-confidence, while rejection elicits strong feelings of alienation.

By late adolescence, changes in cognitive abilities occur. Peer opinions augment an adolescent's beliefs, attitudes, and perceptions of the self. These result in crystallization of personal identity as boundaries are drawn between the self and the social group. Experiences within the family, school, and social systems bring

Parenting FAQ 10–1

My 15-year-old has been hanging out with some kids I don't like. I think they are having a negative influence on him because he's dressing and talking in ways I don't approve of. What should I do?

This is tough for any parent. There are many factors that influence your child's social development. His peers are one of these and may seem to be the overriding influence socially, especially during adolescence. You and your family have a history with this child that is not discarded by your teen, despite his contact with his peers. Remember that this is a time of experimentation for your teen. First try to analyze what it is that troubles you about these kids. Is it really how they dress, or are you bothered by their being a part of your child's life while you take an increasingly lesser role as your teen grows older? Sometimes it's easy to blame a child's friends as being the catalyst for changes in your parenting relationship. If you forbid your teen to see his friends, you are inviting rebelliousness. Your child will find ways to deceive you in order to be with his friends. If you suspect that your child is becoming involved in dangerous activities with his friends, you can gain some control by not enabling the relationships that your teen has with those who you find troublesome. This can be accomplished by asking your teen to socialize with peers in situations and places where you can more closely observe, such as in your own home. Encourage him to invite his friends home.

adolescents into their own as individuals. 'Who am I' and 'where will I go with my life' are existential questions that seem to preoccupy teens.

The sense of identity that emerges from adolescent experiences is a foundational attitude that young adults retain throughout their life span. Young adults continue to acquire, develop, and refine other roles, as well as develop an understanding about the self, which becomes integrated into their basic personal identity during the years of adulthood.

Promoting the Individuation Process. The experiences of adolescence are a struggle toward the eventual emancipation of a teenager from the family of origin. The process leading to emancipation, or **individuation**, is part of the identity formation that is central to adolescent development. Although this process begins in adolescence, it may not be completed until later in adulthood. Some individuals never completely achieve the degree of emancipation or individuation they truly desire or that is expected of them by society. Becoming an individual who develops a personal belief system to guide decisions and behaviors, acquires financial independence, and assumes emotional self-care is a complex challenge.

Often a teen's advancement toward emancipation includes working at full- or part-time jobs. Making social decisions (such as choosing one's friends and dating) also helps teenagers take greater developmental steps toward maturity and personal autonomy.

Supporting Cognitive Changes. During adolescence, important changes take place in an individual's cognitive abilities. Thinking and comprehension during early and middle childhood are governed by perceptions. Children use their perceptions of the environment to develop hypotheses about their world and create a concrete understanding. In adolescence, an individual's understanding of people, events, and circumstances becomes more flexible, and abstract reasoning becomes possible.

Piaget (1967, 1972) labeled thought during adolescence as a period of *formal operations*. Thinking during this time of life can become increasingly abstract, characterized by scientific reasoning. This is the emergence of true deductive reasoning ability as a teen learns to generate hypotheses about something and logically work toward an acceptable conclusion. Experimentation helps adolescents rehearse this type of thinking.

Scientific reasoning gives rise to an increasing flexibility in thought. This requires divorcing oneself from reality and playfully considering various possibilities. For example, it is common for an adolescent to play the role of devil's advocate in discussions on moral issues. Teens who are developing formal operations cognitive skills apply these to a variety of different types of problems, including moral decisions, understanding the actions and words of others, and developing a basic belief or value system to guide their own behavior.

The weakening of egocentrism during middle childhood and adolescence allows the emergence of advanced, flexible thinking styles. As in middle childhood, cognitive egocentrism can distort or hinder mature thinking. In adolescence, egocentrism manifests itself in these ways:

- *Pseudostupidity.* This tendency to interpret something in more complex ways than is necessary or intended is "making a mountain out of a molehill" thinking that can persist as a habitual way of reacting to problems and the behavior of others. This tends to produce indecisiveness.
- *Imaginary audience.* Adolescents typically believe that they are the center of everyone's attention and that every move they make is under the scrutiny of an imaginary audience. This contributes to self-consciousness about appearance, what they say, and with whom they are seen.
- *Apparent hypocrisy.* Teenagers show a certain degree of apparent hypocrisy, meaning that there is incongruence between what they say they believe and how they act. This may be observed in arguments with adults, especially parents. Teens can be very critical of parental insensitivity to their needs, yet feel that they don't have to be sensitive to their parents' needs.
- *Personal invincibility.* Adolescents typically fall under the spell of a belief in their personal invincibility. They think that bad things happen only to other people and that they are protected or exempt from harm or injury when they take chances with risky behaviors. This cognitive flaw perhaps explains why some adolescents undertake risky experimentation with drugs, sexual activity, and reckless driving. Cognitive neuroscience indicates that the adolescent brain is not yet fully mature, which explains some of the irresponsible behavior and the sense of invincibility (Choudhury, McKinney, & Merten, 2012).

The Teenage Brain.   Some of the limitations and idiosyncrasies of the adolescent's cognitive functioning are thought to be the product of the unique neurological makeup of the teenage brain, which has not yet reached full maturity. It is thought that some teenagers are more irresponsible in their cognitive processes, do not think through consequences, and may feel invincible (Choudhury et al., 2012). There are many individual differences, and adolescents' cognitive abilities vary depending on their personal makeup and maturity. For that reason, it is best not to overgeneralize.

According to cognitive neuroscience, the adolescent brain continues its neurological development toward maturity, and changes in several cortical regions occur gradually (Choudhury et al., 2012). Teenage decision making is thought to differ from that of adults. It can be impulsive, focused on the immediate, lacking consideration of long-term detrimental outcomes, and lacking the anticipatory judgment required to think through consequences. Sadly, some decisions can have lifelong effects; for example, binge drinking, substance abuse, texting while driving, and reckless driving can all have dire consequences. Car insurance for young drivers, particularly young males, is expensive because they lack extensive driving experience and may not always exhibit the better judgment that is supposed to come with maturity. On the other hand, a number of adolescents are responsible and mature beyond their years, defying the stereotypes.

Puberty.   Puberty is perhaps the central developmental milestone of adolescence. Puberty refers to the physical maturation process occurring during adolescence. In this developmental event, a child becomes a sexually mature individual with the possibility of being able to reproduce sexually. Although puberty is a physical process (pertaining to the growth of the body), it is accompanied by psychological aspects. The psychological dimension influences the identity formation process. Because adolescents are not yet emotionally mature, the feelings that accompany the physical changes of puberty can be confusing and conflicting. Many parents are unsure about how to help their adolescent child handle the various aspects of puberty. It is important for a parent to maintain open lines of communication so that issues can be discussed openly and honestly.

Gender Roles and Sexual Orientation.   During adolescence, gender roles become more clearly established.

Sexual orientation serves as the foundation of sexual identity. A heterosexual orientation is the self-awareness that one is sexually attracted to people of the opposite sex. A homosexual orientation is directed toward the same sex.

The foundation for sexual orientation is influenced by interacting genetic, biological, and environmental factors beginning prior to birth. Adolescents who identify themselves as LGBT commonly experience great difficulty in accepting their sexual identity (Darby-Mullins & Murdock, 2007). Adolescents are sensitive to any behavior or social position in which they might be seen as being different from others. Young adolescents are especially fearful of rejection by peers because they interpret such reactions from others as an invalidation of self (D'Augelli, Grossman, Starks, & Sinclair, 2010; LeVay, 2011). Role confusion, rather than a fully integrated personal identity, occurs if adolescents fail to incorporate this aspect into their personal identity. Adolescents who are gay and lesbian are usually not afforded the equivalent types of dating experiences that are available to heterosexual teens.

Dating and Sexual Activity.   Adolescent romance is a topic that is increasingly studied by researchers. It is important as it represents part of the ongoing developmental tasks, and it can be influenced by factors in the family of origin (Cavanagh, Crissey, & Raley, 2008). Dating is the first interpersonal social experience that many teens have with sexuality. Teens are typically informal in the way they socialize. Much of this socialization is part of peer group activities rather than between individuals. The age at which adolescents begin to date is a significant predictor of the age at which sexual activity begins (Steinberg, 2010). Adolescent romances are also foundational in adult union formation (R. K. Raley, Crissey, & Muller, 2007). The age at which sexual activity begins also varies according to a teen's ethnic background. Predictors of early sexual involvement include opportunity (being in a steady relationship), sexually permissive attitudes, association with delinquent peers, and alcohol use.

While it is unlikely that completely accurate statistics can ever be obtained about the ages at which adolescents first become sexually active, it does appear that this occurs earlier among more adolescents than in previous decades (Centers for Disease Control and Prevention, 2010). The use of birth control methods is more prevalent than in the past, resulting in fewer teen pregnancies.

Sexual activity places teens at risk for exposure to sexually transmitted diseases, in addition to pregnancy. Sex education programs that promote abstinence from sexual activity apparently do not succeed in accomplishing this goal, because there is a high rate of STD infection among teen girls, especially those aged 15–19 (Centers for Disease Control and Prevention, 2012). The increased use of condoms may reflect the influence of more effective sex education programs that provide factual information, especially regarding the transmission of HIV.

Supporting Sex Education for Teens.   Exploration and experimentation are behavioral components that support identity formation during adolescence. Many adults are uncomfortable acknowledging that adolescents are curious about their sexuality. Because puberty has made them capable of reproduction, it is no longer an abstraction (Steinberg, 2010). Most adults favor sex education in schools and only a few prohibit their teenage children from participation (G. W. Woo, Soon, Thomas, & Kaneshiro, 2011).

Compounding the need for sex education is the fact that teens do not think logically about hypothetical issues in general (Flavell et al., 2001). Sexual decision making involves some of the skills that teens must acquire in this process of identity formation. They may obtain information in sex education courses, but it is unclear how teens use this information in making sexual decisions. Some adults fear that if teens are given information about sexual behavior or methods of birth control, they will become more curious, which may encourage sexual activity; but this response does not seem to be the case. Exposure to sexual information may delay the age at which adolescents begin to experiment sexually (Wagner, 2011).

One of the most important contributions that parents can make to their teen's exposure to sexual information is providing them with the skills to make healthy sexual decisions. For some parents, this means helping their teen to understand the reasons for sexual abstinence. For other parents, it means being sure that their adolescent understands the importance of safer sex practices. Each family system will need to determine how it will deal with this aspect of an adolescent child's identity development. Equally important is the balancing of information that is strictly factual with that which addresses the emotional aspects of sexuality. Teens need support as they explore their first romantic encounters. For many parents, this experience is a reminder of what they encountered as adolescents. Many parents of contemporary adolescents need to be updated on the sexual information they should discuss with their adolescent children. Adolescents from unstable home environments where parental role models might be absent or less than optimal may be influenced by their family of origin with regard to romantic relationships (Cavanagh et al., 2008).

Parenting Reflection 10–3

The transmission of HIV and other STDs has affected the long-running debate on what public schools should teach in sex education courses and what material is appropriate for which age group. Both parents and schools can play important roles in providing information pertaining to healthy lifestyle choices, including sexual matters. As a parent of a teenager, what sex education approach would you welcome?

FAMILY SNAPSHOT

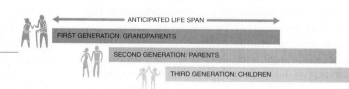

Our slice of developmental time is taken at the midpoint of the adolescence stage of the oldest child in the Curtis family. Mary Curtis is now 15 years old. Perhaps the greatest levels of stress are being experienced by both the third generation (the adolescent children) and the second generation (their parents). This is a time of challenges for the entire family system as homeostasis has been disrupted at all levels.

First Generation (Grandparents)

- Adjusting to the aging process that continues in the latter part of middle age and in the first years of late adulthood.
- Adjusting to the increasing frequency of deaths among spouses, coworkers, and friends.
- Adjusting to the decline in one's personal health and that of one's partner.
- Making the final preparations for retirement and adjusting to the life changes precipitated by retirement.
- Beginning life reviews.
- Adjusting to widowhood and to remarriage in late life.
- Preparing for one's death and the death of one's partner.

Second Generation (Adult Parents of Adolescents)

- Providing for the widely different needs of all family members.
- Experiencing the recovery of marital satisfaction.
- Bridging communication issues between the adults and the adolescent children.

- Supporting the individuation process of the adolescent children.
- Reworking and adapting family roles and rules.
- Adapting parenting styles to meet the needs of adolescents.
- Managing provider and family roles effectively.
- Facing the problems of the sandwich generation; being caught between the needs of their parents and those of their children.

Third Generation (Adolescent Children)

- Mastering the developmental tasks and milestones of adolescence.
- Increasing one's autonomy.
- Exploring gender roles, sexuality, and dating.
- Planning for higher education and a career.
- Establishing a philosophy of life and determining one's religious affiliation.
- Being increasingly able to think abstractly.

PARENTING YOUNG ADULTS

By the time a child has reached the years that we designate as early adulthood (ages 18 to 45), the general perception is that one's involvement as a parent ceases. The child is considered to be mature, responsible for his or her own welfare, and capable of making decisions and taking responsibility for the consequences of his or her own actions. In reality, the parenting relationship continues in an altered form. The transformation of the relationship between the parent and the child has been taking place all along in keeping with the developmental changes occurring over time. The child depended on the parent for protection, nurture, and training. With the child's adulthood, the relationship matures and takes on a new form.

When children arrive at adulthood, the overall goal of helping a child to become a fully functioning, mature person should have been accomplished, but this transformation is not simply accomplished with legal maturity at age 18. Dependencies continue in modified form, and there is some degree of similarity in all intimate relationships among adults in the family; the relationship transforms from one originally based on power and responsibility toward one in which the participants share

a more balanced interaction. The relationship between the parents and the adult children ideally acquires more adult characteristics.

Parenthood does not come to a complete halt when children reach their 18th birthday or even later; instead, the relationship between the parents and the young adults is modified in response to the new developmental needs of adult children. Most adult children experience these first years of adulthood as a transition period while they complete the final aspects of individuation from their family systems. Many are not yet completely financially independent while they complete their college education or for some time afterward. Others, although married, have not been employed long enough to build a sound financial base or establish themselves in occupations that ensure an optimistic financial future. Parents continue to provide support and often financial assistance to young adult children. In addition, they may provide support when young adult children temporarily return to live in the family home (boomerang children) and the structure is shifted to a renested family system.

Relations between the parents and the adult children during this stage can be strained and confusing.

Young adults individuate and form mature relationships. Parents adapt their roles by respecting the increasing autonomy of their adult children.

Parents are sometimes unsure about how to relate and communicate with adult children who are quickly becoming independent adults, but who are still partially dependent. They continue to feel responsible for giving advice to their adult children, but may feel unprepared and ill-equipped to do so in ways that are truly helpful. Adult children probably feel as many conflicting emotions as their parents. On the one hand, they may desire to confide in parents, but on the other hand, they may feel resentful about the intrusive and judgmental nature of parental advice.

Emerging Adulthood

We recognize a portion of early adulthood as *emerging adulthood*. This stage was first described by developmental psychologist Jeffrey Jensen Arnett (2000). In writing essentially about college-aged individuals, Arnett believes that a new developmental period in Western societies occurs between adolescence and adulthood, roughly the time between ages 18 and 25. During this advanced transition stage, individuals are characterized as experiencing five defining characteristics: (a) exploring one's identity, (b) feelings of instability, (c) focusing on one's self, (d) feeling emotionally in between adolescence and adulthood, and (e) experiencing a range of life's possibilities. Many of the traditional hallmarks that formerly defined one's entrance into adulthood have been altered. The age of first marriage increases, often following the completion of one's education or military service. More young adults focus for an extended period of time on exploring what life has to offer (Arnett, 2004; Arnett & Tanner, 2006).

Arnett (2010) questions the generally negative view often held by older adults regarding the character of young people and attributes these negative views to four factors:

- Later entrance into adult roles is misinterpreted by older adults as selfishness.
- Exploration of identity during emerging adulthood is misinterpreted as self-indulgence.
- Young adults who seek identity-based work are seen by older adults as being less motivated.
- Elders interpret the high hopes of young adults regarding their lives as grandiosity.

While Arnett believes that many young adults do hold high hopes for themselves, most adjust these dreams to fit with reality by the time they reach their 30s.

Emerging adulthood is an important transition phase that is characterized by the later age of finding a life partner and first marriage, widespread post-secondary education, and the search for satisfying work. (Arnett, 2000).

Prolonged Dependencies Between Parents and Young Adults

Unhealthy prolonged dependency can take place in a relationship between the parents and the children. Parents can maintain this state of dependency by providing financial and emotional support that exceeds normal expectations. Sometimes situations beyond the control of the family system maintain these ties. For example,

Parenting FAQ 10–2

About a year ago, I moved back into my parents' home because I am looking for a job. I'm having a hard time with my parents, who treat me like an errant teenager . . . which I'm not. I just haven't found the right job yet. They're trying to enforce rules as if I were a teen. I don't think that this is appropriate.

It's frequently difficult to raise parents, don't you think? You will need to work with your folks to help them realize that you are an adult. Persevere in being willing to work on this new relationship as everyone involved must learn to forge new roles, new rules, and new boundaries. Here are some additional thoughts to consider:

- Be willing to contribute to the work of the household in as many ways as possible, especially if you can't contribute financially.
- Talk rationally and keep a level head when you are discussing how you want to see this new relationship operate.
- Be willing to listen and contribute to the new relationship.
- Be willing to negotiate new rules and boundaries for your behavior that are acceptable to all involved.
- Suggest that new rules and boundaries be tested first, and then be willing to renegotiate any rule or boundary that doesn't seem to be working.

higher education is extremely costly, and young adults may seek assistance from their parents to meet financial obligations. Other situations can also prolong dependency, such as overparenting that promotes children's dependencies.

Some parents foster the extended dependency of adult children when they continue to be overinvolved in their children's lives. They may have given the child too many material possessions and not enough limits. They may not have fostered analytical and decision-making skills or used a parenting style that encouraged individuation during adolescence and early adulthood (S. Gordon, 2004). As a result, the adult child fails to individuate successfully from the family system. The usual, anticipated outcome of individuation is a redefined relationship between the parents and the adult child that is more adult in nature.

How Do Parents Promote the Prolonged Dependency of Their Adult Children?   Most parents want their children to grow up and achieve an independent existence. Essentially, most healthy parents want their child-rearing responsibilities to end at some point. Some parents continue to remain actively involved in a care-giving role.

Parents ideally shift away from authoritarian styles to those that are more democratic and egalitarian as children grow older. This shift occurs in response to the changing developmental nature of children as they mature. Egalitarian parenting styles support a child's individuation by shifting the source of social power to a more balanced position between the parent and the child. By reacting in ways that are authoritarian, overprotective, or disinterested, parents promote prolonged dependency in their adult children.

How Do Adult Children Promote Their Prolonged Dependency on Their Parents?   Prolonged dependency is not created and maintained by the parents alone. A child plays a part by maintaining a dependency role longer than is developmentally appropriate. Contributions stemming from the adult child that can promote abnormally prolonged dependence on the parents include (a) a fear of assuming responsibility for one's own life and decisions, (b) addictions and related disorders, (c) a fear of failure in the adult world, or (d) lack of motivation to leave the comforts of the parental home (Arnett & Tanner, 2006; van Poppel, Oris, & Lee, 2004).

Parenting Reflection 10-4

What happens when a family system does not accept or support the efforts of young adults to individuate completely from the family of origin? What are the short- and long-term effects of such prolonged dependence among family members?

Normalizing Parenting with Adult Children. Parents often realize that they are partially responsible for creating the dependency of adult children. Some understand what has happened when children do not master the appropriate developmental tasks for their age. Others become aware when adult children return home and do not move on with their lives. Therapists suggest a number of ways that parents can enhance their role configuration so that all family members can move forward developmentally. An obvious solution is to stop playing the role of a caretaker parent. Parents can let go of the ways in which they have usually responded to children's dependency needs. Boundaries can be adapted to reflect less involvement in the affairs of adult children. Another approach is to make a conscious and demonstrable change toward a more egalitarian stance. When prolonged dependency occurs as part of poor parenting skills, parents can change the relationship with their adult children by changing themselves (J. Adams, 2004). Another solution is to set a deadline for certain tasks to be accomplished, such as finding a job, moving into different quarters, and taking greater responsibility.

Parents sometimes wish to continue promoting their child's dependency, while the adult child wishes to individuate more fully. Often, changes are initiated in the parent–child relationship when children become aware that they are *adult children of dysfunctional families* (Ramey, 2004). In this case, the term "adult children" refers to adults who maintain certain aspects of the dependency of childhood, sometimes simply because circumstances dictate it. For instance, a child with Down syndrome, or a child with a serious disability, may require support throughout the life span. In some families, emotional factors stifle development, and children are never truly launched into adulthood.

This stifling can occur when children grow up in family systems where they are affected by physical, emotional, or sexual abuse; parental alcoholism or drug abuse; and/or ineffective and unhealthy parenting styles. Many people discover that they are such "adult children" when they try to recover from various addictions and related disorders manifested in early adulthood, including substance abuse, eating disorders, gambling, and sexual addiction.

When young adults struggle to achieve individuation from dysfunctional parents and family systems, they can find assistance in various forms of therapy and support groups. In this case, the adult child, not the parent, struggles to let go of dependencies and inappropriate patterns. This struggle can be immensely difficult for everyone involved.

Adult children make aggressive attempts to individuate from unhealthy parents as a means of resuming healthy developmental progress. The parents sometimes resist this significant change in the relationship. When one person in an unhealthy family system attempts to make changes, the system often reacts to the loss of equilibrium by becoming even more chaotic.

Parents who have a toxic relationship with their adult children can be expected to resist the children's attempts to individuate. Many individuals who are recovering from their experiences growing up in a dysfunctional family are parents themselves, and they do not wish to perpetuate unhealthy parenting patterns with their own children. By fully individuating from an unhealthy family system, these courageous individuals pursue a healthy developmental path toward their own full potential as human beings and that of their children (J. I. Clarke & Dawson, 1998).

Focus Point. The relationship between parents and young adult children can sometimes stagnate and fail to transform and mature. Both parents and adult children may bear some responsibility for this. Therapeutic intervention can normalize these relationships.

ATTACHMENT REVISITED

By establishing a basic identity in adolescence, an individual is prepared to move on to the next stage of psychosocial development. Erik Erikson (1950, 1964, 1982, 1986) believed that establishing a sense of intimacy is the primary developmental task of early adulthood. To achieve intimacy, people must learn how to lower the personal boundaries that they have constructed to protect their innermost, authentic selves from others. This requires trusting that one will not be harmed psychologically and emotionally by another in this intimate setting. Essentially, the lessons learned in infancy about trusting a parental caretaker laid the foundation for learning how to trust another in an intimate adult relationship. The attachment that was developed with parents serves as a template for this type of trust, which is an important component of an adult love relationship. When a young adult begins to pursue the development of an intimate relationship, it takes much practice and many opportunities to discover what is involved, what is required, what one wants, and with whom. There have been many attempts by behavioral scientists to identify and quantify how this takes place. One explanation about what adult love involves is the triangular theory of love (Sternberg, 1986, 1988). Sternberg believes that love is composed of three parts:

■ *Passion*, the physical and/or sexual attraction to someone
■ *Intimacy*, the emotional connection with another person that involves authentic self-disclosure leading to trust, closeness, and warmth
■ *Commitment*, the decision to love someone and remain with them over an extended period, "for better or worse"

When all three of these are experienced in an intimate relationship, then, according to Steinberg (1988), one is experiencing consummate love.

The nature of the love that is felt during infancy is thought to be self-directed. There is a significant need for an individual to learn, in the context of nurturing parenting, that he or she is the object of someone's intense love. It is believed that unless people learn self-love during infancy—that they are of importance and worth because of loving parental treatment—they are unable to love others later in life (Fromm, 1970). In the sequence of development, an infant who has been loved by nurturing parents learns such self-love. This self-love, or positive regard for oneself, is generated to the self, returned to the parents, and then given to other family members; later, it is shown toward possessions and other select people. As children grow older and make the accompanying shifts toward independence, they learn the need for interdependence. This characteristic assists them in developing healthy intimate relationships in adulthood in which they depend on another person,

as well as on themselves. A person progresses from infantile love ("I love you because I need you") to mature love ("I need you because I love you"; Fromm, 1970).

FUNCTIONING AS A RENESTED FAMILY SYSTEM

Families in which children have become adults are characterized by changes in the status and the roles of all family members. The emancipation of the children can cause conflict, adjustment problems, and even emotional crises for family systems. Launching children into the adult world may complete the parents' development of a sense of generativity. Because of various social and economic circumstances, some parents find that it takes many years to launch children successfully into an autonomous adulthood.

The transition of adult children into their own lifestyles does not happen as smoothly as one would hope (Secunda, 2004). Many young adult children, mostly males, return to the parental home to live there temporarily; these adult children are described as *boomerang children*. Usually, this is a limited arrangement that results because the adult child has become unemployed, seeks retraining or a change in career, or has experienced a divorce.

The kind of family structure experienced during childhood and adolescence may have a bearing on when adolescents and young adults launch themselves from their families of origin (Settersten & Ray, 2010). The family structure can also influence their return to the family of origin. Growing up in nontraditional family settings, such as stepfamilies, decreases the likelihood of an adolescent's enrollment into a program of higher education, and increases the likelihood of leaving the family of origin early to get married or to attain full individuation. Under such circumstances, there is also a lessened likelihood of returning to the family of origin after individuation.

In a family system where a child has returned to the parental home, everyone involved is likely to have mixed feelings about the situation. On the one hand, parents understand the need to be supportive of their adult children and wish to be as helpful as possible. On the other hand, parents may be understandably resentful of the demands on their resources, time, and energy imposed by the return of the adult child to their daily lives. The adult child may also harbor mixed feelings.

He or she may appreciate what the parents are providing in this time of need and, at the same time, resent the conflicts that can arise by the resumption of old patterns of interaction.

Both children and parents resent the dependency on the parents and view this period as developmentally off-time. Problems result from parents who continue to act intrusively in the lives of adult children who are used to independent functioning. Such families mention conflicts about the hours that adult children keep, the way they maintain their personal space, and lifestyle choices such as sexual behavior. During renesting, both the parents and the adult children may need to renegotiate the rules and patterns that govern their relationship.

Another trend is the continuing reliance of young adults on financial assistance provided by their parents, sometimes into the upper years of early adulthood, that is, age 39 and older. This is related to a downturn in the national economy where recessionary trends have influenced high rates of unemployment and job loss, significantly higher prices in commodities, and an unprecedented number of mortgage foreclosures. The necessity of continued financial reliance on the family of origin is likely to contribute to the challenges faced by a renested family.

Parenting Reflection 10–5

Generations from different periods can be identified by what defines them as a group. For instance, "baby boomers" were all born after World War II. Members of generation "X" were born after the baby boomers (1960–1970). A stereotype is formed concerning the commonalities of people born in the same decade. Thinking of your own generation, what sociological and other influences characterized your relationship with your own parents in your family of origin, and what influences do you expect will influence the relationships with your own children?

FAMILY SNAPSHOT

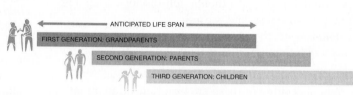

The intergenerational family snapshot shows the Curtis family dealing with adolescent and young adult children. Our slice of developmental time is taken at the beginning of the early adulthood stage of the oldest child in the Curtis family. Mary Curtis is now 25 years old. Perhaps the greatest levels of stress are being experienced by both the third generation (the young adult children) and the second generation (their parents). The first generation (the grandparents) continues to experience major life changes. This is a time of challenges for the entire family system.

Examples of Stressors Affecting an Intergenerational Family System

First Generation (Grandparents)

■ Adjusting to the aging process that continues in the latter part of middle age and in the first years of late adulthood.

■ Adjusting to the increasing frequency of deaths among peers.
■ Adjusting to declines in personal health and that of one's partner.
■ Continuing to adjust to the life changes precipitated by retirement.
■ Completing life reviews.
■ Preparing for one's death and that of one's partner.
■ Adjusting to widowhood.

Second Generation (Adult Parents of Adolescents)

■ Providing for the widely differing needs of all family members.
■ Experiencing the recovery of marital satisfaction.
■ Bridging communication issues between adults and young adult children.
■ Continuing to support the individuation process of emerging adult children.
■ Reworking and adapting family roles and rules.

- Adapting parenting styles to meet the needs of emerging adults.
- Preparing for and initiating retirement; adjusting to the changes brought by retirement.

Third Generation (Adolescent Children)

- Mastering the developmental tasks and milestones of emerging adulthood.

- Growing independence and individuation.
- Adjusting to the roles of early adulthood and career development.
- Developing relationships and addressing sexuality.
- Learning adult responsibilities.
- Attaining adulthood, legal age of majority.

GRANDPARENTING

At some point, it is likely that many parents will become grandparents. It is not unusual for someone in their early 40s to be a grandparent. Rather than taking a sedentary approach to life, today's grandparents might be physically active, still employed, and at times providing full-time care for grandchildren (Euler, 2011).

Considering the greater life expectancy, it is more likely that children will have the opportunity to know and have a relationship with both sets of grandparents. About 90 percent of Americans ages 65 years or older are grandparents. The most frequent activities that grandparents report sharing with grandchildren include having meals together, watching television, playing games and sports, reading together, and going shopping. A majority of those studied see a grandchild at least once a week, but many live long distances away, which prevents regular visits. Because grandparents usually have an empty nest, they can allocate more time to their grandchildren.

The high divorce rate in contemporary society has changed the nature of grandparents' relationships with their grandchildren. The legal status of grandparents is a nebulous issue, and few states have enacted statutes that outline grandparental rights with regard to visitation with grandchildren (Taft, 2010).

Many grandparents take an active role in raising and providing care for grandchildren (Federal Interagency Forum on Child and Family Statistics, 2011a). A substantial increase in the number of households headed by grandparents who provide primary care for their grandchildren has occurred, regardless of whether the children's parents are present or absent. Grandparents report that with regard to taking care of grandchildren, they are more relaxed, more involved, and wiser than when they parented their own children.

Although some grandparents are not especially involved with their grandchildren and their role is downplayed in family life, other grandparents make important contributions to family life and have a significant influence on the family system, such as

- Accepting the behaviors and traits of grandchildren that the parents are not able to tolerate.
- Providing nurture for grandchildren that parents may not be able to provide.
- Providing instruction to grandchildren on values, ethics, and morals.

Focus On 10–2	Developmental Characteristics of Emerging Adults

- Continuing to explore one's personal identity through interactions with others, work experiences, and experiences with one's environment.
- Dealing with feelings of personal instability in the areas of work, personal relationships, and life goals.
- Focusing on one's personal needs in establishing personal satisfaction.
- Difficulty fitting into a particular work role, career, or personal relationships.
- Experiencing a range of life possibilities.
- Establishing a sense of intimacy and learning about the complexity of close, personal relationships.

Grandparents often provide backup support to parents by raising grandchildren. By acting as family historians, grandparents strengthen family identity.

- Providing backup support for parents by raising or helping to raise grandchildren.
- Providing wisdom and advice if asked, and being the family historian.
- Acting as an equalizer to provide balance within a family system (Hurme, Westerback, & Quadrello, 2010).

The Role of Grandparents

The role of being a grandparent continues to lack clear definitions and boundaries. It is appropriate to view the role of grandparents as having diverse aspects based on the nature of the relationship with each particular grandchild (Hayslip, Glover, et al., 2009). When viewed from this perspective, a grandparent's role is composed of different aspects. Grandparents, like parents, may have a unique relationship with each grandchild and appreciate the differences that each child brings to the relationship.

For many, the transition to grandparenthood begins when they learn that the adult child is becoming a parent for the first time. The older adults fantasize about what they will experience as grandparents. Because this is the first time, the first grandchild often has a special place in the lives of the grandparents. This transition varies from person to person. Some find the experience to be difficult, especially if becoming a grandparent is perceived as being developmentally off-time rather than on-time (Kopera-Frye, Wiscott, & Begovic, 2003).

Childhood experiences with grandparents influence the future involvement of men and women with their own grandchildren (Hayslip, 2003). Individuals pattern their grandparenting role and behavior on the models they observed as children. Although there is general ambiguity about the role of the grandparent, several prominent components can be found:

- Grandparents may act as the family caretaker, providing support to adult children and grandchildren when needed, and ameliorating the negative effects of any problems that the adult child has, such as drug abuse, divorce, or chronic emotional or physical illness.
- Grandparents may provide nurture to all family members, especially unconditional love, which may not be available from other adults in the family.
- Grandparents serve as family historians, acting as a bridge between the past and the present that aids in developing a sense of family identity.
- Grandparents may provide companionship for grandchildren in shared social activities that promote close emotional attachment.

This evolution of grandparenting styles changes in tandem with grandchildren's development. Grandparenting styles may be mediated by a variety of factors (Hurme et al., 2010).

Gender may temper how someone approaches the grandparenting role. Women may be more actively involved with grandchildren than men because of their socialization and past experiences in parenting children. Grandfathers may emphasize interactions related to tasks outside the family, while grandmothers may emphasize issues related to interpersonal dynamics within the family. As gender-equality and shared-gender roles extend through the generations, these roles may blend over time.

Physical proximity is an important factor that mediates how the grandparent–grandchild relationship will unfold. The physical distance between the grandparents and the grandchildren will frequently determine how involved the older adults are and how interactions occur. Culture influences grandparenting style as well. A large majority of older Latinos report their desire to live in the same neighborhoods with adult children and grandchildren. Grandparents, who are heads of households where they raise grandchildren, are more likely to be members of ethnic minorities (Federal Interagency Forum on Child and Family Statistics, 2011a).

Grandparents have few legal rights to visit or be a part of their grandchildren's lives following the divorce of adult children. Because grandparents may play a very active role in the lives of their grandchildren, separation can be emotionally difficult for both parties. This can be relevant when the parents divorce. Unless a state has enacted legislation outlining such rights, grandparents may not be allowed to see their grandchildren if the custodial parent disapproves (Taft, 2010). If visitation rights are granted, the court allows such visitation because continuing to see the grandparents is perceived to be in the best interests of the child.

Step-Grandparenting

Divorce among adult children and the grandparents themselves can temper how the grandparent–grandchild relationship will play out. When the grandparents themselves divorce after years of marriage, some may reduce their involvement with grandchildren because of the circumstances surrounding the divorce. When adult children divorce, many grandparents are uncertain about their visitation rights. Mothers are typically awarded custody of children following a divorce; thus, the relationship of paternal grandparents and the grandchildren is often under greater duress than the relationship between the maternal grandparents and the grandchildren (Ahrons, 2007).

Divorce among the adult children can also strengthen the involvement of the grandparents and their relationship with the grandchildren. Grandparents may assume major caretaking responsibilities with regard to the grandchildren in the absence of one of the children's parents (Bryson & Casper, 1999). These circumstances present unique challenges. Grandparents may not be as capable of supporting grandchildren in school activities, and the age gap may present difficulties.

These arrangements typically occur when some type of serious family problem affects the adult child. Quality of life often becomes a prominent concern

Focus On 10–3	The Role of Grandparents in the Extended Family	
	Parental responsibilities	Coparenting, supporting their adult children in rearing the grandchildren
	Positive experiences	Because they are grandparenting part time, they can focus on enjoyable moments, leaving disciplinary matters to the parents
	Family historian	Knowing the family history and passing it on, ancestry
	Disengaged or distant	Emotionally disengaged and/or living far away
	Aging with health concerns, dependent	Health concerns can make grandparents dependent on their own children, needing help and support

because of financial constraints. Older adults may be on fixed incomes or dependent on public assistance, so their financial planning did not include providing for additional children.

• •

Parenting Reflection 10–6

How is the family system affected when three generations reside in the family home and the grandparents provide ongoing care for their grandchildren?

• •

Step-grandparenting has received relatively little attention from researchers. Because step-grandchildren are usually older when an adult-child remarries, there may be little opportunity for the step-grandparents to form a relationship with step-grandchildren. Because both parties have had experiences with this relationship prior to parental divorce, it is likely that both wish to take advantage of opportunities for the new relationship to develop.

CARING FOR AGING PARENTS

It is highly likely that, at some point, adult children will be called upon to provide care for an elderly parent. The American population is aging, and life expectancy is longer, with current averages in the mid-80s (U.S. Census Bureau, 2011e). Not all families can afford caregiving services for the elderly, and children have some responsibility to provide for aging parents (Gross, 2011).

Relationships between adult-child caregivers and elderly parents are characterized by some of the following (Zal, 2001):

■ Because more people are living longer than ever, family relationships are more numerous and complex. Younger members maintain ties with elderly parents, grandparents, great-grandparents, and older relatives.

■ A serious consequence of this increased life expectancy is that people may outlive their savings and experience more health problems.

■ Ethnic minorities tend to provide more care for their elderly parents.

■ Female adult children are more frequently the caregivers for the elderly.

■ Most adult-child caregivers are middle-aged, married, and parents themselves, and working full time.

Providing emotional support, services, and financial assistance to the elderly is referred to as *eldercare* (Abramson & Dunkin, 2011). Such care includes making phone calls on behalf of the parent, assisting the parent with personal hygiene, running errands, taking the parent to appointments, housekeeping, purchasing food and meal preparation, and paying bills. Adult-child caregivers can expect to perform informal caregiving for an estimated 18 hours a week or more, depending on the needs of the elderly parent. When this type of caregiving is not feasible, adult children hire caregivers to meet the needs of the parent, which adds financial stress. Many adult-child caregivers rely on siblings to help with these responsibilities. Some siblings are not reliable, making the burden of care especially heavy for the principal adult-child caregiver.

The relationship between the elderly parent and the adult-child caregiver follows a trajectory, beginning with concern about the welfare of an elderly parent and the expression of this concern to the siblings and others. This progresses to giving advice to the elderly parent on conducting their affairs. The adult-child caregiver assumes increasingly greater responsibilities and often consults with family members and professionals in making decisions.

It is at this point that conflicts between the elderly parent and the adult-child caregiver surface. The elderly parent may become resentful regarding his or her loss of power and control, and feel threatened by the loss of independence. The elderly parent may also disagree with the adult-child caregiver's decisions, causing increasing stress and tension in the relationship.

The Sandwich Generation.   Fueling the problems within the already strained parent–child relationship is the significant role reversal that takes place as the adult-child caregiver assumes greater responsibility, especially in light of chronic illness and disability. The adult-child caregiver progresses more swiftly toward *burnout*, resulting in poor-quality caregiving. When the adult-child caregiver works full time, tries to maintain a marital relationship, seeks to conduct their own parent–child relationships, and receives little assistance from siblings or a spouse, they are called the *sandwich generation* because of the demands from both the older and the younger generations (Pierret, 2006).

Elder Abuse.   Occasionally, excessive caregiver stress leads to emotional, physical, and/or verbal acting out, which can escalate to harmful *elder abuse* (Abramson & Dunkin, 2011). Several options may alleviate such situations and minimize caregiver burnout. These might include

- Encouraging men to become as involved as women in providing eldercare.
- Involving broader community support, such as eldercare and respite programs.
- Providing more governmental funding for programs that educate persons who will provide eldercare services.
- Making eldercare financially rewarding through tax credits and other incentives.

Focus Point.   Family systems enter a new stage when the oldest child enters early adulthood. Parenting focuses on assisting adult children to individuate fully and to maintain a home base while this process is taking place. Parents in healthy family systems shift to a more egalitarian style of interaction with adult children, which supports emancipation and entry into an adult lifestyle.

Grandparenting styles are modified by several factors, such as gender, ethnic identity, and geographic closeness. Divorce among the grandparents, as well as divorce of the adult children (i.e. the parents of the grandchildren), can significantly alter the nature of this relationship.

Many adult children can expect to provide care for an aging parent, especially if the parent has a chronic illness or a disability. The relationship between the parent and the adult child can become strained and contribute to caregiver burnout. The middle generation is called the *sandwich generation*, bookended on one side by an older generation, with a younger generation that requires support on the other side.

POINTS TO CONSIDER

Parenting Adolescents

- Parenting adolescents presents challenges that have not been encountered previously. One of the more difficult challenges of parenting adolescents is the fine line that parents walk between being supportive of a teen's efforts to individuate and maintaining certain limits and boundaries regarding appropriate behavior.
- Parenting styles and behaviors must adapt to meet the needs of a developing child. The adaptation is often not initiated by the parents but rather by the adolescent child who demands to be treated differently.
- The developmental tasks of adolescence require a rewriting of the rules and patterns that govern parent–child relationships. It is necessary to promote greater individuation and self-regulation in the adolescent, and to develop an equalization of power within this subsystem of the family system. If successful, such redefinition preserves the effective functioning of the family system. The challenge facing most parents of adolescents is learning to relinquish some level of control over the child so that appropriate development can take place.
- Parents, as well as peers, assist in a teen's development of a personal identity. This basic self-identity involves recognition that the self-concept is composed of many different, but related aspects that make up the total personality.
- Teenagers are concerned about individuating, or establishing independence from the influence of parents and other adults. Individuation is a healthy aspect of personal identity development at this period of the life span. Adolescents' emancipation is established in a variety of ways that can be both positive and negative. Positive demonstrations include working at part-time jobs, choosing their own friends, and displaying responsibility.
- Adjusting to the physical changes associated with puberty is a major developmental task of adolescence. Teens need assistance in understanding the physical, social, and psychological changes that are taking place. Parents usually recognize the importance of education about sexual issues. Teenagers need parental guidance in learning and implementing appropriate decision-making skills when it comes to health-promoting behavior, including that which pertains to sexuality.
- Several situations are related to health and safety during adolescence. Some are associated with negative acting-out behaviors, such as substance abuse and binge drinking, while others, such as eating

disorders, can reflect significant problems in the family system and may require professional intervention. Some teens are at risk of committing suicide, particularly if there is depression, undiagnosed mental illness, or sexual-orientation issues. Adolescents are increasingly abusing prescription medications, risking accidental overdose. Adolescents are also at a greater risk of being a victim of a violent crime and of contracting a sexually transmitted disease.

Parent–Young Adult Relations

■ The relationship between parents and adult children is evolving, becoming more mature and reflecting the new developmental status of the young adult. The individuation process is usually completed in early adulthood, and parents support this process in a number of ways. Difficulties sometimes occur when either the parents, the adult children, or both experience problems in releasing their mutual dependencies.

■ Changes take place in the family system; adult children leave the nest and occasionally return during times of personal crisis. These boomerang children may return as a result of difficulties related to finances or a change in marital status.

■ Many parents assume a more involved grandparenting role when their adult children become parents themselves. Grandparents evolve and bring their unique personalities and strengths to this role.

■ Adult children often provide care for elderly parents. Typically, more caregivers are from ethnic minorities and more are middle-aged women. The type of care provided is referred to as eldercare, which is largely informal in nature, but highly demanding of the caregiver's time and energies. While many providers rely on siblings or a spouse, such assistance may not always be available. The relationship between adult-child caregivers and parents usually becomes strained over time. As stressors increase, the likelihood of caregiver burnout increases, which may lead to elder abuse. Ways must be found to alleviate caregiver burnout.

USEFUL WEBSITES

Big Brothers Big Sisters of America
www.bbbs.org

Boys Town
www.boystown.org

Parent Involvement Matters
www.parentinvolvementmatters.org

YMCA of the USA
www.ymca.net

PART III

Challenges for Contemporary Parents and Children

The past half century has witnessed an evolution in family form and function. The roles and the division of labor of parents have become less clearly defined, stay-at-home fathers are more prevalent, and more mothers work outside the home than in previous decades. Families are blended, sandwiched, grandparents step in, children boomerang back into the home, same-sex parents raise families, and adoptions are frequently international. In short, fewer than 21 percent of all families in the United States fit the old cookie-cutter mold of one breadwinner father, one stay-at-home mother, and two picture-perfect children (U.S. Census Bureau, 2010b). Diversity in form and structure is the norm among contemporary American families.

Today, the pluralistic context in which people define their families unseats the concept of a typical family. Over the past 50 years, significant changes in many aspects of American society have influenced the kinds of families that have become more prevalent. These changes include the products of a high divorce rate, namely, binuclear families and an increasing number of remarriages. These, in turn, lead to parallel, blended families with unconventional configurations. Adolescent pregnancies and out-of-wedlock births continue, although teen pregnancies have been declining. Many adolescent girls and their families have chosen to retain custody of these children, creating unique parent–child relationships that involve three generations. Same-sex couples are becoming more visible throughout American society.

Families who face unique challenges and stressors, as well as fragile families, deserve special attention. Many families in the United States experience problems that affect their ability to function in healthy ways. Effective parenting may be difficult when a number of factors are counteracting this optimal goal. Some parents do not perform well and mistreat or neglect their children. Their parental rights may be temporarily or permanently suspended when their children are placed into foster care. In extreme and tragic situations, parents abuse their children physically, sexually, and/or emotionally. Effective parenting can also be seriously impaired by an adult parent's addictive disorders. These serious parental shortcomings harm all family members and lead to situations where the state may interfere with parental rights in order to prevent harm and to ensure the best interests of the child.

This text ends on a more positive note when best parenting practices are examined, with a special focus on how families display resilience in overcoming challenging situations. These themes draw on public and social policy and place the family into the larger societal context. Ultimately, many facets of the future of humankind lie within the sacred bonds of kinship. Can we learn from best practices in other developed countries? What have we done well in supporting the building blocks of society, namely, the family, and where do we need to venture in the future?

CHAPTER 11

Parenting in Single-Parent Family Systems

Learning Outcomes
■ ■ ■ ■ ■ ■ ■ ■ ■ ■ ■ ■ ■

After completing this chapter, readers should be able to

1. Explain the major factors responsible for creating single-parent family systems.

2. Explain how divorce affects parents as individuals and as caregivers.

3. Explain how children are affected by parental divorce.

4. Describe the important issues related to child custody decisions.

5. Describe the characteristics of a single-parent family headed by a woman and that headed by a man. Explain how parenting is conducted in each of these family systems.

6. Describe the major adjustments made by single-parent families. Describe the support systems available to these families.

■ ■ ■ ■ ■ ■ ■ ■ ■ ■ ■ ■

Traditional families that consist of two parents and their children with both parents in their first marriage have become less prevalent in the United States. These families constitute a distinct minority, accounting for only 21 percent of all families in the United States (U.S. Census Bureau, 2010b). The increasing rate of divorce over the years resulted in an increasing number of *binuclear* or single-parent families that are created when spouses go their separate ways (U.S. Census Bureau, 2010b). Many adults who divorce also remarry, which creates a new family system that resembles other families but

FIGURE 11–1. Distribution of people by poverty status, selected characteristics, 2004–2006.
Source: U.S. Census Bureau, Survey of Income and Program Participation, www.census.gov/sipp/source.html.

is unique in its functioning and structure. These families are called *blended families*, or stepfamilies. See Figure 11–1 for statistics on family types in the United States.

Divorce is the most common reason for single-parent families, although these families can also be created by persons who have never married or who choose a single lifestyle. Being a single parent is not necessarily devastating for adults or children. Divorce is a stressful experience that can be uncomfortable for the family system because old familiar patterns are dismantled by the separation of the adults. Family systems theory describes divorce as an event that produces disruption in a family system. In place of the chaos that emerges when a marriage is dissolved, a new family form evolves, known as a **single-parent family**, which is based on the former family system, but with significant modifications. The new family form reflects the children's membership in two separate and distinct households or families, hence *binuclear* family—one headed by the father and the other headed by the mother. Basically, these are separate one-parent households. Increasingly today, both parents hold joint custody of the children. One usually is designated as the physical custodian, meaning that the children reside the majority of time in this parent's household. For many individuals, these adjustments may be relatively temporary because the majority of divorced adults eventually remarry. Sometimes that means that they have divided responsibilities in two households.

Researchers continue to explore aspects related to the adjustment of individuals in the new single-parent family system following divorce (Mooney, Knox, &

Schacht, 2010). New patterns, rules, roles, and modifications to the parent–child subsystem restore equilibrium or homeostasis and allow the system to function. Several factors influence healthy adjustment as well as dysfunction. While divorce is the major factor in creating single-parent families, there is a significant trend in the increase of single, unmarried women who bear children (Federal Interagency Forum on Child and Family Statistics, 2011b).

DIVORCE, SINGLE-PARENT FAMILIES, AND PARENT–CHILD RELATIONS

Single-parent family systems are one of the more common types of families in the United States. These are composed of an adult male or female parent and one or more children less than 18 years of age. The parents of the children reside in separate households following divorce. This family type is increasing at the fastest rate of all family forms. In 1970, approximately 3.8 million families were headed by a single parent. By 2010, the number of family households headed by one adult, plus that adult's own children and without a spouse present, had increased to more than 11 million (U.S. Census Bureau, 2010b). About 22.4 percent of all Caucasian children in the United States lived with a custodial parent, while about 48.2 percent of all African American children lived with a custodial parent (Grall, 2009). About 25 percent of all Hispanic children lived with their custodial parent.

Parenting FAQ 11–1

Does a divorce have to be by mutual consent? How is child support determined? What happens if my partner doesn't comply with the terms of our divorce agreement?

Most states have no-fault divorce laws, and all it takes is for one person to declare legally that the marriage is irretrievably broken and the divorce proceedings may begin. You will need to consult a lawyer for legal advice. Many states have a formula by which child support is determined. Usually, a couple's gross annual income forms the basis to determine how much each adult will contribute to child support. In some states, this formula may include how health insurance, child-care, and/or educational expenses are shared by each adult. The divorce agreement will include stipulations about child support and visitation. You can return to court for legal redress of your complaints regarding any violations of the divorce agreement, and/or you can call upon the county sheriff's office for assistance in having the terms of your agreement enforced. Mediation may be helpful.

A single-parent family system can be created in several ways:

■ Divorce, desertion, or separation of the adults
■ Death of an adult
■ Birth of a child out of wedlock

Of these reasons, divorce is the most common. In 2010, about 66 percent of all children in the United States lived with both biological parents in comparison to the 23 percent who lived with either a single-parent mother or the 3 percent who lived with a single-parent father (Federal Interagency Forum on Child and Family Statistics, 2011b). The majority of single-parent families are those in which women have sole custody or are the physical custodian of children (about 83 percent), although there are significant increases in the numbers of such families where men are the head of the household. These families include an unmarried adult partner of the parent when adults cohabitate.

Much concern has been expressed over the effects of divorce and the experience of growing up in a single-parent family system. Differences are observed in a number of areas, such as interaction patterns, communication styles, parenting styles, and behavioral problems among children (Mooney et al., 2010). An insufficient number of people to adequately perform the roles needed in an efficient family system contributes to difficulties and can cause role strain.

Research suggests that while similarities exist in single-parent families headed by women and those headed by men, the gender of the parent is an important factor in determining the type of family life experience in each family system.

Each family system that loses one adult's presence has to adjust in distinct ways. Divorce, in particular, forces unique adaptation in the new single-parent family system. Divorce is one of the most difficult processes a family system can experience (Weimer, 2010). It has short- and long-term effects for both the original first-marriage family system and any subsequent relationships. In keeping with family systems theory, it is predicted that divorce will affect everyone in a family system.

In the case of the formation of two single-parent family systems following divorce, each family must construct new boundaries and patterns (i.e., rules, communication styles, and roles). All family members are affected in different ways by the many changes resulting from parental divorce. To adapt successfully, each family maintains homeostasis to avoid further confusion, disorganization, and chaos.

Parenting Reflection 11–1

Are there any advantages to single parenthood in comparison with a marriage?

Parental Adaptations

Family systems theory predicts that all members are affected when one key member experiences a major change. Divorce dissolves the effective functioning of the committed relationship between the adult partners. In turn, it disrupts the functioning of parent–child relationships, as well as the functioning of the entire family system. Divorce affects both adults and children. Adults experience a variety of reactions, especially when the divorce is seen as a solution to marital difficulties (Knox & Schacht, 2009). Emotional reactions such as depression, weight loss, sleep disturbances, and an increase in the likelihood of substance abuse may occur. Anger and hostility often color interactions between the divorcing adults and can take a long time to dissipate. Changes in lifestyle occur as a result of significant changes in the financial status of both adults. Single mothers may struggle financially and are often overrepresented among the impoverished.

Because divorce affects all family members, it is important for adults to be aware of what is happening to children so that they can understand the changes taking place (Knox & Schacht, 2009):

1. *Family metacognition.* The system acknowledges that divorce is imminent and that the adults no longer share similar feelings of love and attachment. It also acknowledges other feelings, such as sadness and even hate.

2. *Physical separation.* Separation of the adults has highly disruptive effects on the family system in that it dismantles the boundaries, rules, behavioral patterns, and roles that have made the system operate effectively. Removing the father's presence from the family system (which commonly occurs) can leave children with feelings of abandonment. In general, divorced fathers are emotionally more depressed than divorced mothers.

3. *Family system reorganization.* Divorced adults forge a new relationship with children, with different rules, roles, and interaction patterns. Their ability to resolve concerns in healthy ways allows appropriate reorganization. Failure to adjust constructively can lead to a dysfunctional family system. The new single-parent family adapts by evolving new rules, roles, interaction patterns, and living conditions.

4. *Family redefinition.* As the new single-parent family system assumes higher degrees of effective functioning, the members and the noncustodial parent see the system from different angles. The noncustodial parent also reorganizes interaction patterns, boundaries, and rules that govern how he or she relates to the single-parent family system and its members. Children often learn two sets of

patterns and rules because they are now members of two single-parent family systems. These binuclear systems are headed by the custodial parent and the noncustodial parent.

● ●

Parenting Reflection 11–2

Explain the factors that precipitate a breakdown of a marriage. Describe the effects on the family.

● ●

A major challenge for divorcing parents is to acknowledge that they continue to share parenting responsibilities and relationships with their children, even though their marriage has been dismantled (Knox & Schacht, 2009). Many people divorce with the expectation that their contact and involvement with the former spouse will cease completely. The relationship is transformed in several ways:

■ The visitation rights of the noncustodial parent forces some type of contact with the former spouse.
■ Children may perpetuate the remnants of the relationship by sharing information about one parent with the other and discussing life and events in their new family system.
■ With joint custody, spouses commit to sharing major decisions regarding the children.
■ While parents attend to their own adjustment to the divorce, they need to be mindful of their children's reactions as well.

● ●

Focus Point. Divorce elicits emotional and transitional adjustments as parents exchange their couple identity for single status. Even though adults adjust differently, they continue to share a connection by being their children's parents. A person is never completely divorced when children are involved.

● ●

Children's Adaptations

About one fifth (23 percent) of American children lived only with their mothers, 3 percent lived only with their fathers, and 4 percent lived with neither of their parents (Federal Interagency Forum on Child and Family

Statistics, 2011b). The number of single-parent families in the United States has increased considerably since 1960. This type of family system constitutes a sizable proportion of the population. The marital status of the parents influences where children will live and with whom, as well as the quality of life they will experience. In line with the increase in single-parent families, there has been a concomitant decrease in the number of children living with two parents. In 2010, for example, 75 percent of Caucasian, non-Hispanic children, 61 percent of Hispanic children, and 35 percent of African American children lived with two married parents (Federal Interagency Forum on Child and Family Statistics, 2011b).

Researchers have learned that children's reactions to parental divorce involve a process of adjusting to change rather than a single, simple reaction (Dush, Kotila, & Schoppe-Sullivan, 2011). This process is tempered by other factors, such as the child's age, gender, and past experiences. For many children, the parental divorce involves significant losses, and children can experience a variety of grief reactions. Children appear to undergo this process in three distinct stages:

1. The *initial stage* occurs after parents inform the child of their decision to separate. It is marked by high levels of stress, during which aggressive conflict and unhappiness increase markedly.
2. The *transition stage* commences about 1 year after the parents' separation and lasts for up to 3 years. Emotions normalize, and the restructuring process includes evolving new family patterns, changing the quality of life, and establishing visitation routines with the noncustodial parent.
3. The *restabilization stage* occurs about 5 years after the separation, when the new single-parent family system or blended family is more stable.

Divorce may be one of the few major family crisis events in which adults become more focused on their own needs than on those of their children (Dush et al., 2011). The functioning of the parent–child relationship is disrupted because of this changed focus. Children of divorcing parents can react uniquely in ways that express their own personalities (Knox & Schacht, 2009). Several factors appear to influence the course of children's adjustment to this family crisis:

■ Gender and age of the child when the parental divorce occurs

■ Adults' use of available social support networks to help the child adjust
■ Cultural attitudes toward divorce and single-parent families

The effects of parental divorce on children may be short- or long-term, positive or detrimental. Short-term effects include behavioral difficulties at home and at school that present in association with the initial reaction to parental separation.

Long-term effects may not appear until adolescence or adulthood, when individuals experience difficulties in establishing intimate relationships (Ahrons & Marquardt, 2010). Other long-term effects appear during later developmental stages. For example, the poor quality of the parents' marriage is reflected in troubled parent–child relationships as long as 8 to 12 years prior to divorce. The child's gender can also mediate such reactions. Boys have more adverse reactions to parental divorce than girls, but girls react more adversely to parental remarriage. Children who become part of blended families as a result of the death of one parent and the subsequent remarriage of the surviving parent also face unique emotional challenges.

The child's age at the time of the parental divorce seems to be one of the driving factors in how a child reacts and adjusts. Regressive behaviors, such as temporary loss of toilet training; increased aggression; fretting; and negative attention-getting behaviors, such as whining or destroying toys, may be observed among preschoolers whose parents are divorcing. School-age children may fear abandonment or rejection by their absent parent and experience a drop in school performance, adverse interactions with peers, or boundary shifts with their mother during or following parental divorce. Adolescents may manifest similar feelings, which can present as delinquency and negative acting-out behaviors, heightened conflicts with their parent, decline in school performance, and depression (Pedro-Carroll, 2010).

The first year after parental divorce may be the most difficult and stressful for both children and parents (Pedro-Carroll, 2010). Young children experience the disruptive effects beyond this first year. Boys generally experience more disruption than girls, especially if the parents continue to exhibit discord.

Divorce is more problematic for adolescents (Velez, Wolchik, Tein, & Sandler, 2011) and the context of the parent–child relationship is altered. Girls may

Divorce is the leading cause for single-parent families and is stressful and disruptive to the family system.

experience more serious difficulties than boys. Teenage girls target the custodial parent with the anger they feel for the noncustodial parent. Adolescent girls may resent this change in their relationship with their mothers and experience role reversal and boundary blurring. It is not unusual for some adolescents to have divided allegiances to both parents. This division is aggravated if conflict and hostility is high, and the parents do not collaborate. Teenagers can have divided loyalties for individual parents. Poor levels of adjustment are related to the disruptive changes precipitated by parental divorce.

Many adolescents make adequate adjustments in the years following a divorce and become competent adults. In a comprehensive, longitudinal investigation, half of the subjects entered adulthood as unhappy, angry, underachieving, self-deprecating, or fretful individuals. These unhealthy reactions were the scars from a parental divorce that had occurred many years ago.

A poorly managed, hostile divorce leaves children and adolescents emotionally scarred and handicaps them in future intimate relationships. On the other hand, the poor family climate that surrounds parents who are at war also has a high emotional price tag.

Parenting Reflection 11–3

Can growing up in a single-parent family be a healthy experience for children? What benefits might they gain from this experience?

The effects of divorce on children present as a negative and depressing scenario. Parents who are considering divorce should be aware that many complications await them:

■ Children experience the effects of parental divorce in ways that are more disruptive and stressful than those experienced by the parents.
■ Divorce is a process rather than an event, and the entire family system is affected, not just the divorcing couple.
■ Divorce has immediate and long-term effects on children. The effects vary depending on the age and gender of the child at the time of the divorce.
■ Children whose parents divorce during their developing years almost always see it as a milestone event that shaped the developmental aspects of adulthood.

The effects of parental divorce on children and adolescents are not clear-cut. Many conflicting and complex

Parenting FAQ 11–2

My friend is getting divorced, and he just told me that the court has appointed an attorney to be a Guardian ad Litem for the children. This seems unusual; please explain this.

It is not unusual for a court to appoint an attorney or another qualified professional to represent the best interests of the children of divorcing parents. This person is called a Guardian ad Litem (GAL), and serves as an agent of the court. This person acts as an advocate for the children in the divorce proceedings and will sometimes recommend actions that go against the parents' wishes. The appointment of a GAL usually happens when at least one parent requests it or because the court has reservations about the ability of either or both parents to act in the best interests of the children during the divorce proceedings.

findings are reported in the research literature. It is safe to state that not all children whose parents divorce react in the manner described. It is equally safe to conclude that no child of divorced parents completely escapes the disruption that divorce has on a family system (Amato & Sobolewski, 2004).

• •

Focus Point. Parental divorce affects children in a number of ways. Age at the time of the divorce is an important factor in determining their reactions. Many parents fear that their children will experience harmful outcomes as a result of the divorce. Researchers generally find that divorce is disruptive, but that most children adapt and adjust resiliently. Observers note that some residual effects may last for many years.

• •

Custody Arrangements

Parents must confront a major decision when they divorce: Who will have custody of the children, and how will the noncustodial parent and the children have access to each other for visitation? The Family Law Section of the American Bar Association lists several standards that court officials may apply in determining the custody arrangements of children following the divorce of their parents (American Bar Association, 2006). This includes the following:

1. Custody should be awarded to either or both parents according to the best interests of the child.
2. Custody may be awarded to persons other than the father or mother whenever such award serves the best interests of the child.

3. If a child is old enough and able to reason and form an intelligent preference, his or her wishes about custody should be considered by the court and given due weight.
4. Any custody award should be subject to modification or change whenever the best interests of the child require or justify such a change.
5. Reasonable visitation rights should be awarded to the noncustodial parent and to any person who is interested in the welfare of the child, at the discretion of the court, unless such rights of visitation are detrimental to the best interests of the child.

Before the 1920s, such issues were not considered in divorce proceedings because custody was automatically awarded to the father; the mother had no legal rights in this regard. In addition, women could neither vote nor sign contracts. In subsequent years, women have gained legal status in the United States, and the child-custody situation has changed. In almost 90 percent of such cases, child custody is awarded to the mother rather than the father.

• •

Parenting Reflection 11–4

What can divorced parents do to prevent their child from feeling like a ball that is tossed from one parent to the other in order to meet the requirements of joint custody or noncustodial visitation?

• •

Even though mothers stand a good chance of being awarded legal custody of a child, divorcing couples must still negotiate a decision about which parent should have full custody, or if both will share custody. They must reach visitation and support decisions, and consider other important details related to meeting the best interests of the child. Details regarding child support include how each parent will contribute to the child's medical, dental, educational, and other expenses, and what percentage of the costs each party will contribute. It can be challenging for couples to reach these decisions in an objective and amicable manner. They may arrive at this decision with the help of attorneys, mediation professionals, therapists, or even the intervention of the court.

When divorcing parents consider custody issues, five factors frequently favor one parent over the other (American Bar Association, 2006):

1. The preferences of the child
2. Whether or not a parent wants custody
3. The perceived need to place a child with the same-sex parent
4. The perceived need to keep a child with the mother because she may be the socially appropriate person for custody
5. A parent's ability to provide stable, continued support in the same residence or geographical area

Courts consider specific variables that are related to the quality of the child's life after parental divorce when custody decisions are made (American Bar Association, 2006). Sometimes a child is placed with a same-sex parent because he or she generally has better prospects for providing an environment that fosters healthy social adjustment.

A single parent's sole custody of a child can create problems that appear to outweigh the advantages. Single-parent families, especially those headed by women, can experience problem-ridden, stressful, and unpleasant custody negotiations. Many of the problems associated with sole custody reflect the noncustodial father's resentment, anger, and frustration in dealing with the perceived no-win situation. Many men feel they are systematically disenfranchised and have minimal input into making important decisions concerning their children and are prevented from having access to quality interaction with their children. As a result, postdivorce conflict with the ex-spouse continues or escalates, which affects the manner and context of children's interactions with their fathers. Noncustodial fathers typically disengage

from the parenting relationship because their ability to function adequately in this role is greatly diminished when they withdraw from the former family system (Nam, 2009).

The dismal record of defaulting on child-support payments by noncustodial fathers makes matters worse (Grall, 2009). Many fathers feel they are cut out of their children's lives and should not have to maintain financial support. They often use this claim when they live out of state.

Joint Custody.   A recent trend in custody decisions involves *joint custody*, or awarding the responsibility for child care and supervision to both parents. In many cases, joint custody, rather than single-parent custody, may be a viable solution that is in the best interests of the children (Knox & Schacht, 2009). This alternative has advantages, as well as disadvantages, in its implementation and execution. Many feel that the advantages outweigh the problems if the parents can work together in the best interests of their children. Advantages include

■ More contact between ex-spouses.
■ Fewer problems in securing the father's cooperation in meeting the financial-support agreement.
■ Fewer feelings of being overwhelmed by child-care responsibilities.
■ More access to beneficial interactions between children and fathers (typically not the case when mothers have sole custody).

Parenting Reflection 11–5

Should joint custody become the norm among divorced parents with children? Justify your answer.

Focus Point.   Fathers who share joint custody with the mother are more involved with parenting responsibilities, have more contact with their children, and use parenting resources more extensively than noncustodial fathers (Knox & Schacht, 2009). Fathers tend to be more satisfied with joint, rather than sole, custody arrangements, but mothers appear to prefer sole custody. When the father holds joint custody with the mother, the mother is more likely to receive support payments from the father, preventing a poverty-level existence (Grall, 2009).

Parenting Reflection 11–6

Is it right to force men to pay child support when they fall behind? Should a noncustodial mother pay child support to a custodial father even though she earns less than he does? Would noncustodial fathers be more willing to pay for child support if the federal government made this a line-item credit on annual tax returns?

Although joint custody seems to sidestep problems associated with sole custody of children, it does create other problems (Knox & Schacht, 2009):

■ It is more expensive to maintain because each parent must supply housing, equipment, toys, food, and often clothing for children.
■ It requires a degree of connection with ex-spouses that many people do not desire.
■ It will not work unless the adults are committed to maintaining civil discussions concerning child rearing.
■ Constraints on relocation to another state can impair decision making.
■ Children may feel confused and burdened because they have commitments to two family systems instead of one.
■ Children may have problems transitioning from one family system to another.
■ Disturbances in the relationships among siblings may occur due to split living arrangements.

Postdivorce Coparenting. Coparenting is performed jointly. Resources are shared, and parents collaborate. It is a legitimate form of parenting and often occurs in binuclear families (two households). It can have legal implications concerning parental rights and responsibilities.

At the heart of coparenting lies the ongoing commitment to a child's well-being. Coparents can be biological parents in binuclear families who take on the parenting roles based from two households because of divorce or separation. The adults could have a biological link to the children, but they need not have this connection. For instance, parents and stepparents in a postdivorce situation may coparent. Unmarried parents may coparent from two separate homes. Coparenting is undertaken by two or more adults who take on the care and upbringing of children for whom they share responsibility (McHale & Lindahl, 2011).

Managing Coparenting Arrangements. It is imperative that divorcing parents establish new rules and boundaries regarding their coparenting relationship. They must resist the temptation to involve children in the adult business of the divorce, making the children captive pawns. This is unhealthy for children, as well as parents. Many children feel obligated to take sides with one parent or another, which is detrimental to all concerned. The problems of the parents should not cross the hierarchical parental boundaries to contaminate the children, even though the children will feel many of the aftershocks of a divorce.

Parenting Reflection 11–7

Are two parents really better for children than a single parent? Justify your answer.

When parents are separating in preparation for divorce, it is important that they maintain open lines of communication to resolve their differences. Children are inevitably a part of the matters discussed. To avoid the feelings of anger, frustration, and guilt that can accompany these discussions, divorcing parents might limit the topics to the health needs and educational concerns of the children, and sharing time with the children (McHale & Lindahl, 2011). When these new rules and boundaries are followed, additional rules, patterns, and boundaries can be shaped to redefine the relationship between each individual parent and the children. This should allow for the development of new single-parent family systems.

Sometimes divorcing parents are tempted to express their hurtful feelings about their divorce and the divorcing partner by playing "pain games" that can interfere with effective parenting. Basically, three types of games may serve as unhealthy ways to express the unpleasant feelings associated with divorce:

1. *Discounting* of the other parent to a child, such as making negative comments or using derogatory labels. When children hear such statements, they feel that these also apply to them as well because they are half of each parent.
2. *Messenger or go-between.* One parent solicits a child to be a messenger or go-between with the other parent. Children can sometimes distort innocent, simple messages that they might be asked to give to the other parent. It is not healthy for children to play the go-between role in the altered relationship between divorcing parents.
3. *I Spy.* Divorcing parents may be tempted to use a child as a source of information about the other parent. This is a ploy to find out what the other parent is doing, whether they are dating, what purchases they are making, and so forth. Asking children to spy on the other parent violates parental trust.

Single-Parent Families Headed by Mothers

The majority of single-parent families in the United States are headed by women who have either never married or are divorced (Federal Interagency Forum on Child and Family Statistics, 2011b). Among these families, quality of life is a major concern. Divorced and single-parent women appear to face more economic and related employment difficulties than men. Family income is lowest among single-parent families headed by women (DeNavas-Walt, Proctor, & Smith, 2010). Because of the low level of income among these mothers, these family systems experience poverty-level existences that seriously affect the standard of living of children (see Figure 11–2). The majority of these families are found in Caucasian communities, although a substantial proportion of all children in the United States are born to African American and Hispanic unmarried mothers (Grall, 2009).

Financial Difficulties. Single-parent families headed by mothers can expect financial difficulties. A father's child support and maintenance payments are important sources of income and help provide an adequate standard of living. They do not adequately reflect the typical expenditures made by mothers who are physical custodians (Lino & Carlson, 2010). Because of this dependence on inadequate support payments and other factors, such as less education or fewer years in the labor force, most single-parent families headed by women have lower annual incomes than those headed by men. Child-support payments by the father can be absent or erratic (Grall, 2009). In 2007, about 76.3 percent of custodial parents received at least some payments. Of this amount, 46.8 percent received the full agreed-upon

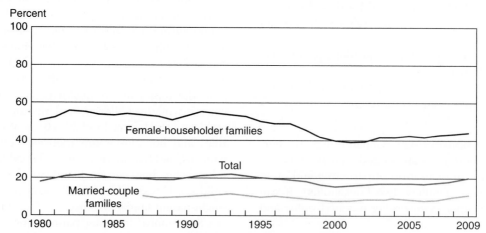

FIGURE 11–2.   Percentage of related children ages 0–17 living in poverty by family structure, 1980–2009.

Source: U.S. Census Bureau, Current Population Survey, Annual Social and Economic Supplements.

payment, and 29.5 percent received a portion of the payment.

••

Focus Point. Lack of education, poorly paying jobs, lack of work experience, and inadequate alimony all contribute to the likelihood that more custodial mothers have family incomes at or below the poverty level.

••

State laws differ in determining how much a parent must pay in child support. Many states have a requirement that 17 percent of a noncustodial parent's gross income should go toward child support. This figure increases with the number of children, and it can rise as high as 31 percent when four or more children require support. While these fathers most likely could afford to pay more in child support, many have established new families and must contribute to the support of additional biological children. The conflict between honoring the responsibilities owed to children from former marriages and those produced in new relationships creates a dilemma for the affected individuals.

Child support is determined at the time a divorce is finalized by court decree (Doskow, 2010). The divorcing individuals arrange a settlement that is finalized in a legally, binding contract. Either party may agree to something that has adverse financial consequences due to the emotional coerciveness of negotiations. It may be wise to request the assistance of a divorce mediator to help the couple reach objective decisions regarding child support and secure arrangements that help ensure adequate financial support.

The most common reason for failure to pay regular child support is attributed to the financial problems of the noncustodial parent. Some parents fail to honor their child support agreement for other reasons, including

■ Withholding payment as a means of expressing anger toward the custodial ex-spouse.
■ Feelings of discrimination about the amount awarded by the court.
■ Unemployment or underemployment.

In other instances, noncustodial parents provide support in a form other than money, such as gifts, paying for medical and dental expenses, or clothing (Grall, 2009).

A divorce means that most women with children will seek employment to provide support for their families. Typically, they earn wages and salaries at lower levels

Among single-parent families, quality of life is a major concern that often results in role strain. Family income can be compromised.

than men, often because of different levels of education, training, and work experience. Economic conditions are a primary source of stress among single-parent families headed by women (S. Reynolds & Bexton, 2009). One in three single-parent families headed by women exists below the poverty level, as compared with 1 in 10 two-parent families. This factor may contribute to a decrease in the quality of life and social functioning of the family, and affects the parent–child relationship as well (Grall, 2009).

The implications of economic conditions have both short- and long-term effects. Children who are not adequately supported experience the consequences more seriously than their mothers, although the quality of life affects everyone. Essentially, numerous ripple effects emanate from the dire financial conditions in single-parent families headed by mothers.

Role Strain. Single-parent mothers experience additional role strain within their new binuclear family system. Divorced women experience different degrees of role strain from that of divorced men. Because most women are granted full custody of children, they must now function as the sole full-time parent in their new family system. What was stressful in managing competing roles in a two-parent family system is even more stressful after divorce. The time demands in such systems are particularly exhausting (Federal Interagency Forum on Child and Family Statistics, 2011b). There is less time for most activities, and employment responsibilities receive the highest priority. Child care and personal needs receive the least time; although the quality of the attention paid to children does not appear to decline. As with role strain in intact families with children, performance in all of the competing roles falls as role strain and stress increases (Higgins, Duxbury, & Lyons, 2010).

Changes in the Parent–Child Relationship.   Many single-parent mothers experience changes in their relationship with their children. The parent–child subsystem changes as all participants redefine the parameters of the relationship. In many respects, two distinct parent–child subsystems emerge. There may be few differences in the relationship between mothers and daughters and mothers and sons in single-parent family systems when children are young. Children in family systems headed by single-parent mothers continue to experience adjustment difficulties 4 to 6 years following parental divorce in comparison with children whose mothers have remarried (Clarke-Stewart & Brentano, 2007).

One effect of role strain is the increased reliance on more authoritarian patterns of interacting with children (Clarke-Stewart & Brentano, 2007). The functioning of the parent–child subsystem is generally disrupted following divorce, and this is accentuated in the relationship between mothers and sons. It is less likely to affect mothers and their preadolescent daughters, who often forge a relationship that is emotionally more intimate. As the new family system evolves, new patterns establish a degree of stability, and single-parent mothers generally shift to more authoritative styles. This promotes healthier, well-adjusted children.

After divorce, it is not unusual for single-parent mothers to change the boundaries, patterns, and rules that define the usual adult and child roles (Everett & Everett, 2000). A mother may transform the definition of her role, particularly in relation to the oldest child, to that of a peer/partner. She may expect that child to be more mature than the developmental reality. As the mother transforms her relationship with this child, she significantly increases her shared personal feelings and opinions about a variety of topics. Accordingly, the child's role is transformed to that of the mother's *confidante*. The mother increasingly relies on this child for emotional support and assigns him or her much of the missing adult partner's responsibilities. As a result, the child may be forced into interaction patterns that call for developmental maturity beyond his or her years.

The pressures that children experience in these situations come from not having their emotional needs met by their mothers, who are usually unaware of this problem. When a mother transforms the child's role to one similar to the absent adult partner's, a conflict emerges that imitates the marital conflicts with the former spouse. The child discovers that it is a no-win situation. Some researchers also report a specific interaction between mothers and daughters. At times, they may experience competition, jealousy, and conflict that are not found between single-parent mothers and sons (Everett & Everett, 2000). Some children may not feel comfortable expressing their feelings of frustration and confusion. They respond with psychosomatic symptoms and acting-out behaviors that reflect their concerns and fears. Not surprisingly, when mothers disclose intimate details about personal problems, such as financial matters or negative feelings about ex-husbands, daughters report strong feelings of emotional distress.

Therapists and researchers who work with single-parent families note that parents may encounter certain pitfalls that can develop into clinical issues, including responding to children as a reminder of the former spouse, developing overdependence on children, seeing children as a burden, and focusing on survival rather than on parenting children and meeting the developmental needs of the children (Kaslow, 2000).

Focus Point.   Most single-parent families are headed by mothers who have been divorced. These families can expect financial problems. Researchers commonly observe role strain among these parents, who are holding several competing roles simultaneously. The relationship between mothers and children changes as the boundaries become blurred. Previously established adult and child roles transform. Many women find their status as single mothers stressful but manage to adjust in a variety of ways.

Single-Parent Families Headed by Fathers

Single-parent families headed by fathers constitute the minority of these family systems in the United States, although the percentage of families headed by men has increased steadily over the past 40 years. In comparison with single-parent mothers, fathers heading this type of family system earn considerably higher incomes, and this promotes a different standard of living, influencing the family's quality of life. They are reported as having fewer adjustment concerns compared to custodial single-parent mothers (Tyano & Keren, 2010).

Boys are more likely than girls to live with a custodial father. Some researchers attribute this tendency to the belief that boys in such situations benefit from being raised by fathers, while girls benefit from being raised by mothers (Baird & Hitchcock, 2011). Professionals within the legal system have become more flexible in awarding custody with the best interests of the child in mind. Nowadays, men are increasingly awarded custody following divorce. The quality of the parent–child relationship and the resources available to the custodial parent in providing a stable family life play a role in determining the best interests of the child.

Parenting Reflection 11–8

Divorced fathers are increasingly being granted sole custody of children. Why are women reluctant to relinquish full custody to the father?

Men assume the custodial parenting role for a variety of reasons. It continues to be customary in our culture for women to assume this role, although in the past, a man commonly accepted single parenthood after the death of his spouse. The idea that men can conduct their parenting activities as capably as women and that children are not harmed by single-parent fathering experiences is an emerging concept.

Unlike single-parent mothers, single-parent fathers gain custody of their children through two likely avenues:

1. Men may assert their right to gain custody of children because they feel capable and motivated to parent their children effectively, although the mother may contest their ability.
2. Men may assume custody when the mother shows no desire to continue parenting or is deemed unable to do so because of physical problems, mental illness, or addictive disorders.

Men adjust better to being cu___ when they have a strong desire to pe___ men wish to continue positive parentin___ may have been established when the childr___

Financial Stability. Single-parent fathers ___ earn higher incomes than single-parent mothers. Fathers achieve greater economic security, partly ascribed to higher levels of education and more years of employment. Those advantages may place them at higher income levels and a more favorable financial situation after they become single parents (Grall, 2009).

Discrepancies in income between single mothers and fathers account for many of the differences in the quality of life in these family systems. Single-parent families headed by men tend to have fewer people being supported by the father's income in comparison to families headed by women.

Role Strain. Single-parent fathers and single-parent mothers experience role strain differently. Like the single-parent mother, the single-parent father must adjust to the additional responsibilities of child rearing while providing for the family.

Many single-parent fathers were not involved in managing household tasks before the divorce, but they have little difficulty when they assume responsibility for home management (Everett & Everett, 2000). They report that shopping for food and preparing meals can be major problem areas because many of them lack these skills. Single-parent fathers tend to share household management tasks with children rather than secure help from outside resources. Single-parent mothers, in comparison, tend to perform these tasks themselves rather than expect children to help, which promotes greater levels of role strain. Single-parent fathers expect daughters to help more than sons and to assist with household management tasks, possibly due to differences in the socialization of children. When the families of single-parent fathers are compared with two-parent families, children in the single-parent systems do not perform as many household management tasks. This difference may be ascribed to several factors:

- Single-parent fathers may intentionally not involve their children in tasks in an effort to prove their own competence as household managers.
- These fathers may attempt to ease the transition and tensions that children experience when they shift to new family patterns after the divorce.

Children have difficulty becoming familiar with the routines and patterns of two different households.

Some single-parent fathers may have difficulty synchronizing child care, household duties, and wage-earning responsibilities into a manageable routine. Arranging child care may be a major problem, particularly for fathers with young children. Rather than hiring housekeepers or sitters, single fathers generally rely on the same child-care resources as other parents. These resources can include nonparental care, as well as support from their immediate and extended families. Frequently grandparents take on a significant caregiving role. Many custodial fathers are likely to work longer hours while holding a full-time job, which can contribute to role strain (Lin & Chen, 2006).

Structuring older children's activities is also a problem among single-parent fathers. Single fathers of older children typically rely on afterschool activities, such as dance instruction or athletics, to bridge the supervision gap.

Fathers and Gender-Neutral Parenting. Single-parent fathers can perform child-care responsibilities effectively (Baird & Hitchcock, 2011). One concern of authorities making custody evaluations and recommendations centers on a father's ability to perform effectively as a single parent. Researchers generally recognize that most men can take on caregiving responsibilities in a competent manner that is healthy and beneficial to the children. Fathers are particularly competent when they have been actively involved in providing care since a child's infancy and when they willingly accept child custody after divorce. Because individuals in our society have moved increasingly toward gender-equal parenting roles, many men have learned how to provide for children's needs and to express nurture in caregiving.

Single-parent fathers promote different expectations for their children than single-parent mothers (Knox & Schacht, 2009). For example, single-parent fathers demand more independence from children. As many gain experience in child-rearing activities, they shift away from authoritarian methods to an authoritative approach. They become less traditional, less discipline oriented, and more concerned about the quality of the care they provide and the experiences children have with nonparental caregivers. They are more interested in children's educational experiences and more

The number of single-parent families headed by fathers has grown significantly. When making the transition to this type of family, fathers must consider whether they are able to take on caregiving responsibilities in a competent manner that is healthy and beneficial to children.

protective about dangerous situations to which children might be exposed.

Many single-parent fathers also express concerns about raising a daughter in a family system that lacks the gender-role model provided by an adult woman. They wonder how they can provide socialization experiences for girls that will help them learn appropriate gender-role behaviors.

Single-parent fathers tend to seek advice and assistance from others outside of their family system when they need caregiving help. These sources include relatives, such as their own parents, professionals, religious leaders, physicians, and teachers. Many discover that these sources are helpful in providing information and guidance about child care that improves the father's ability to parent children effectively.

••

Focus Point.   Single-parent fathers experience situations that are similar to, as well as different from, those of single-parent mothers. Family systems headed by custodial fathers constitute a minority of single-parent families. Single-parent fathers are typically better educated than single-parent mothers and earn significantly higher incomes. They often have custody of sons rather than daughters. Men may gain custody of children after a divorce because they actively seek it or because the mother has defaulted on her parental rights by not being a responsible parent. Like single-parent mothers, single-parent fathers experience role strain as they add increased involvement with child rearing to their other responsibilities. These men usually perform adequately as caregivers, but researchers note certain differences in the interaction patterns with children when comparing these single families.

••

The Challenges of Nonresidential, Noncustodial Fathers

Fathers who do not share a home with their child face the risk of gradually fading from their child's life, other than for the obligatory child support. Research reveals a troubling picture. Being a nonresidential, noncustodial father seems to increase men's risk of injury, addiction, and premature death (Weitoff, Burström, & Rosén, 2004). These destructive lifestyles may be a reaction to the loss and grief experienced by nonresidential fathers, but it could also be a reflection of the type of irresponsible behavior that contributed to the divorce. Children's contact with their nonresidential father is important to both parties and has significant benefits (Stewart, 2010). The nonresidential fathers' payment of child support and emotional involvement are positively associated with the well-being of the children (Amato, Meyers, & Emery, 2009).

Two important aspects influence the role of nonresidential fathers in their children's well-being. The first is the degree to which the children feel close to their nonresidential father and the degree to which the father is able and willing to maintain contact with the child. The second hinges on the degree of marginalization that nonresidential, noncustodial fathers experience with regard to their involvement with their children (Hawthorne & Lennings, 2008).

Fathers may discover new dimensions in the relationship with their child. It is not uncommon for nonresidential fathers to transform the little time they have with their children into the most positive experiences possible. These fathers also tend to approach parenting from an adult-companion position. Positive outcomes are observed in the children's well-being when nonresidential fathers can maintain an age-appropriate balance between structure and nurture. This means that they act in authoritative ways, praise and discipline children, set and enforce limits, assist with schoolwork, and talk about problems (Amato & Sobolewski, 2004).

The Strengths of Single-Parent Families

The problems and challenges faced by single-parent families often overshadow the strengths (Yarber & Sharp, 2010). The challenges experienced provide opportunities for people to grow in ways they might not have done otherwise. Women generally state that their single-parenting experience helped build personal strengths and confidence. Strengths with regard to the family have also been identified (Weight, 2004):

- The ability to incorporate parenting skills traditionally found in two-parent families
- A positive attitude about changes in family life
- Effective communication among all family members
- Family management skills
- The ability to become financially independent

It is important to note that there are few differences between children raised by single-parent mothers and single-parent fathers (Everett & Everett, 2000; Kaslow, 2000). Modeling gender-equal roles to children offers many benefits that promote well-being far beyond the years of childhood and adolescence. Children are likely to learn resilience from their experiences in growing up in single-parent families, which is a life skill that will serve them well in adulthood (Greeff & Fillis, 2009).

In this genogram, the divorce between the parents is depicted with an interrupted line. Genograms can document a number of events that take place within family systems.

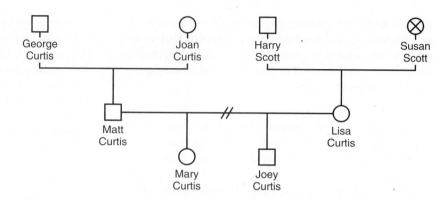

FAMILY SNAPSHOT

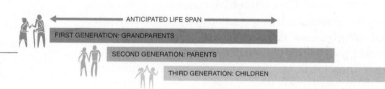

In this intergenerational snapshot of family life, the stressful and traumatic effects of divorce and single-parenting are observed rippling through three generations. One of the strengths of the systemic family development model is that it can be applied to all types of family forms and structures. It is possible to examine families who have experienced divorce and are facing numerous challenges. The example is of a single-parent family in which the divorced parents hold joint custody of two children (see Figure 11–3).

* *

Focus Point. For most divorcing parents, child custody is a central issue. Legal decisions are made with the best interests of children in mind. Sole custody is customarily awarded to the mother, although fathers are increasingly becoming sole custodians. Decisions about sole custody are sometimes difficult and can involve lengthy, expensive legal battles. Joint custody overcomes some of the disadvantages of sole custody, although it can present unique challenges.

POINTS TO CONSIDER

- There are a variety of family forms in the United States. Variations in family composition and structure result in differences in the parenting roles.
- The single-parent family is one of the most visible family systems in the United States. Most are headed by a woman who becomes the head of the household through divorce, separation, the death of her spouse, or the birth of a child while single.

- Divorce is the most common way that single-parent family systems are created.
- While many mothers continue to be granted custody of their children, the trend is toward joint custody. This arrangement has many advantages if parents can work cooperatively and communicate about parental role responsibilities. Joint custody can present problems as well. When a couple cannot reach an agreement about custody, they may need a mediator who can bring closure to their divorce and custody proceedings.
- Women have different experiences from men when they become single parents. Single-parent family systems headed by women are characterized by (a) financial difficulties, (b) additional role strain on the mother, and (c) changes in the parent–child relationship.
- An increasing number of men are gaining custody of their children. Single-parent family systems headed by men are characterized by (a) greater financial freedom in comparison to the families of single mothers, (b) additional role strain on the father, and

First Generation

Developmental Challenges Faced by Grandparents

- Adjusting to the divorce of their child
- Adjusting emotionally and socially, as divorce may have been less acceptable in the grandparents' generation
- Possible divided loyalties, maintaining contact with the former in-laws
- Increased responsibilities as the single-parent relies on the grandparents for support
- Greater involvement with the grandchildren, if they remain to live in close proximity
- Less involvement if the custodial parent moves away
- Effects on own life span development

Second Generation

Developmental Challenges Face

- Custody arrangements, possib
- Changed relationship with form
- Role strain and overload
- Children have to deal with parer
- Visitation by nonresident parent
- Child support
- Child care arrangements
- Circle of friends may be halved, d
- Social circles change, no longer in
- Grandparent relationships
- Finances and employment
- Becoming more competent in facing
- Considering dating and possible later
- Changes in the parent–child relations
- Effects on own life span development

Third Generation

Developmental Challenges Faced by Chil

- Custody arrangements affect the balance
- Changes in the parent–child relationship
- Possible divided loyalties
- New responsibilities in the household
- Children have to deal with parents living in t
- Visitation by nonresident parent
- Child support: effects when it is irregular or ab
- Child care and supervision; having different ca
- Grandparent relationships
- Becoming more competent in facing challenges
- Effects on own life span development

FIGURE 11–3. Systemic family development model.

(c) a less disruptive lifestyle than that experienced by single mothers.

■ Divorce has several effects on adults: (a) rediscovering feelings of self-worth, (b) experiencing a sense of failure about the former marital relationship, (c) developing a fear of intimate relationships, (d) experiencing depression and alienation, and (e) experiencing changes in lifestyle. The continuing relationship between the adults, despite the divorce, presents adjustment challenges.

■ Parental divorce has several effects on children. The timing of the divorce in a child's life results in different levels and types of adjustment. Generally, preschoolers exhibit regressive behaviors and some behavioral problems, particularly during the first year after the divorce. School-age children react to their parents' divorce by feeling angry with their parents, experiencing pervasive fears, feeling helpless about the situation, and feeling rejected by the absent parent. These children become more involved in household responsibilities and experience changes in interactions with both parents.

■ Adolescents often experience problems with personal identity; fears about being abandoned, rejected, and/or unloved; fears about the failure of their own future marriage; and delinquent behaviors. The effects of parental divorce on children are both short and long term. Researchers currently believe that some of these effects can be observed for years following the parents' divorce.

■ Single-parent families have strengths that derive from the experiences of adapting to the crisis of divorce and the resulting challenges by all members of the binuclear systems. These strengths provide opportunities for personal growth that might not have occurred in other types of family systems.

USEFUL WEBSITES

Educating Communities for Parenting
http://ecparenting.org

Center on the Developing Child, Harvard University
http://developingchild.harvard.edu

OnlyDads and OnlyMums (United Kingdom)
www.onlydads.org and *www.onlymums.org*

SingleFather.org
www.singlefather.org

Single Parents Alliance of America
www.spaoa.org

SingleParents.org
www.singleparents.org

CHAPTER 12

Parenting in Blended Family Systems

Learning Objectives

■ ■ ■ ■ ■ ■ ■ ■ ■ ■ ■ ■ ■

After completing this chapter, readers should be able to

1. Describe the distinguishing characteristics of blended families, and indicate how these families can be formed.

2. Distinguish between the stepmother and stepfather roles by referring to similarities, as well as differences.

3. Describe the developmental changes observed in blended family systems, and how these changes relate to the development of the individuals within that system.

4. Describe the strengths of blended families, as revealed when major adjustment challenges have to be resolved.

■ ■ ■ ■ ■ ■ ■ ■ ■ ■ ■ ■ ■

Families grow in various ways and different groups of people can form alliances to form **blended families**. There are several variations on the theme, where we depart from the formula of two biological parents with biological offspring. A new family system can be formed when a single parent remarries. A family can expand by fostering or adopting children. A *reconstituted* or *blended family system* typically brings together children who may have had different families of origin, and/or adults who have been married previously, or have children from previous relationships. They blend their resources to form a new family. Instead of focusing on how the children joined the blended family (remarriage, adoption, fostering), this chapter concentrates on the dynamics and challenges involved in blended family formation.

Typically, each one of the parents in a blended family can be the biological parent of some of the children while **stepparenting** the new spouse's children. Alternatively, neither parent has a biological link to the child, as in the case of adoption and fostering. Not all of the roles within the blended family are step relationships.

The remarriage of adults restores the adult family role that was vacant in a single-parent family. Because the vast majority of single-parent families in the United States are headed by women, the person usually filling the vacant adult role is a man who may or may not have been previously married. Occasionally, two single parents and their families are merged by the remarriage of the adults. Other variations of blended families are families who adopt and who foster children.

The problems and challenges facing blended families are different from those of other family systems. The adults face the usual tasks of establishing an intimate relationship as a newly married couple. This process is complicated by children who are not gradually introduced into the family structure, but who join the new family system with many memories of a former family system. The ability of the new blended family system to survive and cope with these challenges occupies much of the time, attention, and resources of the system, especially in the early years following remarriage.

THE CHARACTERISTICS OF BLENDED FAMILY SYSTEMS

Where there are marriages, there are also remarriages. In the past, many married adults became widowed and remarried after the death of a spouse. In recent decades, divorce has become the leading cause for single status after a first marriage (Berger, 2000).

Remarriage is more likely to occur if an adult has been divorced rather than if they were widowed. The probability of remarriage is highest among Caucasian divorced women and least likely among African American divorced women. Women who were under age 25 at the time of the divorce are more likely to remarry than women older than age 25. Remarriage is more likely if divorced women live in communities with lower rates of male unemployment, poverty, and welfare dependence. Interestingly, women living in nonurban areas are more likely to remarry than those living in cities. These patterns may be explained in part by the age of the individuals when they become single. People who are widowed are usually in late adulthood and are less likely to remarry because of their advanced age (Bramlett & Mosher, 2002; Clarke-Stewart & Brentano, 2007). Divorced individuals tend to be much younger. Remarriages are considered to be high-risk relationships as they have an even greater chance of ending in divorce (McCarthy & Ginsberg, 2007). Our knowledge of the factors that lead to second and even third divorces are limited (Ganong, Coleman, & Hans, 2006). The couples who have stable, functional remarriages report having higher satisfaction and greater pride in their new relationship than first-marriage couples.

Almost two thirds of the persons who divorce each year in the United States eventually remarry (Bramlett & Mosher, 2002). In the typical divorcing couple, the man is about 37 years old, the woman is about 33, and they have at least one child (Federal Interagency Forum on Child and Family Statistics, 2007). This suggests that many men and women remarry when they are about 10 years older than when they were first married. Generally, remarriage is more likely to occur among younger, rather than older, individuals (Bramlett & Mosher, 2002). The median interval between divorce and remarriage is about 3 years for women, with about half remarrying within 5 years of their divorce. Ethnic group identity also influences remarriage rates; more Caucasians tend to remarry than African Americans or Hispanics.

Cohabitation occurs more commonly post-divorce, and at greater rates than before first marriages (Fields, 2003). This may reflect the desire to test a relationship before making a marital commitment. Cohabitation prior to remarriage appears to have little effect on a couple's relationship (Stanley et al., 2006). Another distinction of courtship prior to remarriage is the influence of the children's presence. Not only do single parents, especially those who hold custody of children, have a more challenging time in locating prospective partners, they have other considerations as well. Single parents must be considerate of the developmental stages of their own children and the values they model when becoming involved in a serious relationship. Alternatively, how does one explain to children that the relationship has dissolved, especially if the children have developed an attachment to the potential partner?

Chapter 12 Parenting in Blended Family Systems ■ 269

Remarriages are characterized by the difference in developmental levels of the adults at the time of remarriage in comparison with those during their first marriage. Because of what they have experienced during their first marriage and because of developmental changes, divorced persons tend to have different expectations of remarriage and of themselves (Gerlach, 2003). Women with children who remarry may have stronger and more definite career goals than during their first marriage. Many know that they can survive a divorce and are more committed to making another marriage work successfully. Their ideas of what a marriage requires are clearer in comparison to during their first marriage. Remarriages do not differ significantly from first marriages in terms of marital happiness or in the degree of the partners' well-being (Ihinger-Tallman & Pasley, 1997).

The number of children involved in these diverse family arrangements is very high. There are an average of 2.5 stepchildren in American family systems. These children have dual roles in that they can be a stepchild to one parent and a biological child to the other parent. About 1.6 million adopted children have joined families in the United States (American Community Survey, 2008).

Parenting Reflection 12–1

Distinguish between a blended family and a first-marriage biological family.

Like other contemporary family structures, blended families are characterized by their diversity (Berger, 2000). Some blended families involve only one adult who has been previously married; in others, both adults may have been previously married once or more than once. Some involve a remarriage when children were infants and these children perceive the family as an ordinary family of origin.

Because remarriage most frequently involves individuals who have been previously divorced, it is likely that the children of one adult or both will be included as part of the new family system. Researchers describe seven characteristics of blended families that distinguish them from first-marriage families (Berger, 2000):

1. *When children are involved, a new family system is created instantaneously without the benefit of gradually adding new members.* In the developmental life span of first marriages, adults can gradually develop new patterns (rules, boundaries, and roles) for their family system that affect functioning. Blended families are challenged by the immediacy of developing patterns without gradually adding children to the system. In many cases, the patterns formed for one adult's single-parent family system after divorce is a template for those initially used in the new stepfamily system.

2. *The remarriage of adults may occur at a time when the necessities and tasks of the life span of the blended family are incompatible with the developmental needs and tasks of the adults.* In some situations, there is a conflict between what is required for healthy, individual adult development and what is required to establish a new marital relationship and new blended system patterns.

3. *Ex-spouses and ex-grandparents can continue to have input into and influence on the new blended family system.* Unlike the family systems based on first marriages, family functioning is complicated and seriously challenged by the influence of past relationships and former family systems. For example, the adults may continue to be influenced by their former spouses because they still share the biological parenthood of children who are part of the new blended family system.

4. *The desires and expectations of adult marriage partners may not be fulfilled by the new marriage relationship in the blended family system.* When adults remarry, they tend to anticipate that the new relationship will overcome or compensate for deficiencies in the previous marriage. This expectation places an unrealistic burden on the new marriage.

5. *Both children and adults may have mixed feelings of allegiance and guilt that interfere with effective blended family system formation.* Children in blended families can become confused concerning their loyalties because they are members of two separate and distinct family systems. It is not unusual for stepchildren to feel as if they are being pulled in several directions at once, which tests the strength of their personal boundaries. Adults also have mixed feelings about their past and its influence on their present functioning in the new family system. It is not uncommon for remarried men to feel torn between the need to provide for their

Remarriage of adults restores the adult family role that was vacant in a single-parent family.

biological children from their previous marriage and to meet the needs of the new family system to which they now belong. Whereas some men are relieved that their former relationship has ended, others continue to resent the continuing degree of involvement with that severed relationship through children and financial responsibilities.

6. *Children may not be willing participants in the new blended family system.* Although adults may consult children about a potential partner, they often do not seek a child's approval before deciding to remarry. Typically, children are not supportive or accepting of the new marriage, but they are often expected to cope with a situation they would rather avoid or ignore. Many children of divorced parents fantasize that their biological parents will somehow be reunited and that their family life will return to its former state. Others continue to resent the divorce, which makes life unpleasant in the new blended family system as children resist the efforts of the remarried adults to forge new family patterns.

7. *All blended family members experience role confusion.* A major task of the system is to establish new patterns that regulate the functioning and behavior

of all members. This task is common to all family systems, but it is especially difficult among blended families because of the past histories of the adults and the children. The role of a stepmother or stepfather is not clear, and the system must develop patterns to define this role, often by trial and error. New rules must be established that promote healthy family functioning. Boundaries are a special challenge to effective stepfamily functioning (Stewart, 2005). They may relate to personal property, psychological intimacy, and family routines or traditions. Clear communication, a commitment to the new family system, and a willingness to discuss issues and reach agreeable solutions are necessary to establish new patterns.

••

Focus Point. Blended families are created by the remarriage of at least one adult. Many persons who have been divorced remarry within 3 to 5 years. Children are frequently part of the new family system. Researchers note that these families can be distinguished from those based on first marriages in a variety of ways.

••

BLENDED FAMILY FORMATION

The problems that challenge blended family systems are unique, and these systems may experience a greater level of stress than usually encountered by first-marriage family systems. Problems are linked to the following (Hildebrand et al., 2008; Lee-Baggley, Preece, & DeLongis, 2005):

■ Merging different family cultures and identities as the new system establishes roles and patterns
■ Developing new modes of distributing time, energy, material goods, finances, and affection
■ Establishing new bonds of loyalty to the blended family system while learning to manage loyalty bonds to former family systems
■ Dealing with marital conflict and children's misbehavior

Blended family system formation involves different structures than in first-marriage systems (Papernow, 1993). First-marriage families have time to allow the adults to develop an intimate relationship and areas of shared interests and values, and habitual patterns that guide interactions and conflict resolution. The gradual addition of children to a biological family allows the adults to develop and adapt to parenting roles, learn to resolve differences, and create a shared value system.

When a first-marriage couple divorces, they create two single-parent family systems that most prominently affect the children, who become members of two distinct *binuclear* systems. A major consequence is the dismantling of the usual generational boundaries between adults and children. Adults often look toward children for the support and nurture formerly provided by the spouse.

At the beginning of a blended family's life, the stepparent at first seems to be an outsider to the existing alliance between the biological parent and his or her children. This alliance is based on the patterns established in the former single-parent family system and has its own history, rules, boundaries, patterns, and operational styles firmly in place. The greatest challenge to the survival and effective, healthy functioning of a blended family system may be overcoming the obstacles and resistance encountered in adapting previously established patterns and styles.

Patricia Papernow (1993) developed a model that describes blended family formation. She depicts three major stages that each involve substages. It takes a relatively long period for a blended family to find itself and its identity. Many difficulties can challenge effective family formation and functioning. The presence of adolescent children is a particular challenge to effective blended family formation (Leake, 2007). Because of their developmental focus on individuation from their families, struggles can be expected when the adults demand the teenager's participation in activities that are aimed to develop a family identity.

• •

Focus Point.   The structure of blended families is different from that of biological families. Single-parent families are created when adults divorce from their first marriage, changing the relationship between the biological parents and their children. When a biological parent's marriage to a new partner forms a blended family, other changes in the parent–child subsystem emerge, such as the alliance between the biological parent and the biological children. The development of a blended family progresses through distinct stages that may occur over a long period of time.

• •

Focus On 12–1   **Stages in Blended Family Formation**

Early Stages: Getting Started and Avoiding Pitfalls

Stage 1: Fantasy

Everyone involved commonly holds unrealistic expectations that they hope will be fulfilled in the new family system:

■ Children will be rescued from problems associated with the divorce of their biological parents.
■ Children will be able to get their biological parents to reunite by sabotaging the biological parent's new relationship.

(Continued)

Focus On 12–1

(Continued)

■ The biological family will be healed by introducing a new adult into the vacant role.
■ Stepparents will be adored by stepchildren and enthusiastically welcomed into the blended family.
■ The biological parent will finally have previously unmet needs satisfied by the new partner.
■ The biological parent will again be able to share parenting responsibilities with another adult.

Stage 2: Assimilating the New Adult

The biological parent attempts to merge the stepparent into the biological family but usually cannot accomplish this goal successfully at this time. The stepparent notices by now that he or she is an outsider and discovers feelings of jealousy, resentment, and inadequacy.

■ Both stepparent and stepchildren experience problems in establishing and working on a relationship.
■ Problems are perceived differently by everyone involved. The stepparent expresses frustration in dealing with what is seen as an impenetrable biological family solidarity. The biological parent doesn't understand the frustrations of the stepparent. The stepchildren may begin to experience loyalty conflicts regarding their absent biological parent and the stepparent.
■ The biological parent feels caught in the middle between wanting a good adult relationship and the problems experienced by the children in dealing with a new adult in their family.

Stage 3: Awareness

Many blended families stagnate in their development at this stage because of difficulties in communication among all of the parties. To avoid this, all family members need to

■ Apply labels to the feelings experienced.
■ Understand why the feelings are being experienced.
■ Articulate personal needs more clearly.
■ Listen to what the stepparent says regarding the rules and boundaries in the biological family, and note when the stepparent was not included.

Middle Stages: Remodeling the Family

Stage 4: Mobilization

The stepparent's role in initiating changes intensifies at this point. A showdown is inevitable, and if the changes and compromises cannot be made, there is considerable risk that the blended family will dissolve via the divorce of the adults.

■ Some changes may appear to be trivial, but these represent the need for further weakening of the biological family's alliances to accommodate the stepparent into a new family structure.
■ The biological parent may feel pulled in two directions: meeting the perceived needs of the children and giving more allegiance to the new relationship.
■ If the adaptations are successfully implemented (e.g., having more private time for the adult couple), the new blended family can be truly formed.

Stage 5: Action

In this stage, the changes and adaptations may be implemented on a larger scale to form the new blended family.

■ New family rituals and traditions are helpful for facilitating a sense of family.
■ Boundaries and rules are tested to define the adults' committed relationship and the stepparent–stepchild relationship more clearly (e.g., restricting discipline of the children solely to the biological parent, relieving the stepparent of this responsibility).

Focus On 12–1

(*Continued*)

■ The stepparent now plays an even greater role in the new family.
■ The adult couple works more closely as a team.

Later Stages: Putting It All Together

Stage 6: Contact

This stage serves to solidify the actions taken to forge a new blended family.

■ Children relinquish the role that was created in relation to the biological parent during the single-parent family experience and during the earlier stages of blended family formation.
■ A workable relationship has been negotiated for the stepparent and the stepchildren without the involvement of the biological parent.
■ Each member's family role has been validated and is authentic.

Stage 7: Resolution

The new blended family achieves a new identity.

■ The stepparent is accepted by the stepchildren as an "intimate outsider." A true friendship emerges between them.
■ The family gestalt differs completely from earlier; instead of uncertainty and stress, the feeling is one of confidence and comfort in relationships.
■ The family learns to let go of the dependencies that helped in forming the new family structure.

Sources: Based on Papernow, P. L. (1984). The stepfamily cycle: An experimental model of stepfamily development. *Family Relations, 33,* 355–363; Papernow, P. L. (1993). *Becoming a Stepfamily.* San Francisco: Jossey-Bass.

COPARENTING AND BLENDED FAMILY ROLES

Coparents agree to take on the parenting tasks together. In blended family systems, there may be two coparenting dyads at play. The first refers to the biological parents, who have to find ways to coparent successfully from binuclear households. The second dyad refers to the two persons fulfilling parental roles within the blended family, of whom one will be a biological parent and the other a stepparent. Coparenting has the best success rate if the best interests of the children are considered, and if parental systems can maintain the parental hierarchical boundaries. This means that the personal problems and challenges within the parental dyad should not spill over into the relationships with the children. Children should not be pulled into the intimacy problems of parents or be turned into go-betweens for warring parents. As responsible adults, the coparents have to set their personal agendas aside when it comes to parent–child relations and focus on the needs of the children, keeping their best interests in mind (Mangelsdorf, Laxman, & Jessee, 2011; Pruett & Donsky, 2011).

A stepparent's role is distinct from that of a biological parent. It differs in that it has a high degree of role ambiguity (Berger, 2000; Papernow, 1993). Our culture promotes many stereotypical images of stepparents that are largely negative in nature (Leon, 2005). These images can be found in stories and fairy tales told to children. Stepparents, particularly stepmothers, are depicted as evil, uncaring, self-centered individuals who mistreat stepchildren. To a certain degree, popular television shows and movies reflect the lack of clarity in the stepparent role.

Belief in these negative stereotypes varies according to someone's current family situation. Perceptions about stepparents, and particularly those about stepmothers, are generally negative when compared with perceptions

Parenting
FAQ 12–1

I'm seriously considering marriage to a wonderful woman I've been dating for almost 2 years. There are school-age children involved. I've never been married before. I have no clue what it's like to be a father, much less what is involved in being a stepfather. What can I expect?

You are in a unique position that may be to your advantage. Because you have never parented your own child, you may feel hesitant to take on the challenges of this new role. Some influences from your own family of origin, from your own experiences of having been parented, and from what you observe among your peers may contribute to your expectations concerning this role. This is an instant family situation. You are the newcomer in an already established and long-term relationship between the children and their mother. It might help to consider the relevant factors in the role of a stepfather. As an authority figure in a parental role, you should decide, together with the biological mother, what the most appropriate response in this family situation would be, especially concerning guidance, discipline, and rule enforcement. Show the amount of affection that is comfortable for all involved. When it comes to discipline, consider that the children may have divided loyalties, so make it a joint decision with your spouse. Gain clarity with your spouse concerning financial obligations and responsibilities. Roles will differ depending on the individual relationships and will transition toward greater informality and trust. A blended family is a work in progress.

about biological parents. Individuals currently living in single-parent family systems and blended families tend to hold less-negative opinions than those living in first-marriage families. Negative perceptions about stepparents seem to decrease as people become more sensitive, familiar, and appreciative of the problems and challenges that blended families face (Bloomfield, 2004).

Expectations about how someone should perform a social role influence actual behavior. Studies find that stepparents are expected to share equally in the parental status of the new family system, although expectations can contradict reality. Some stepparents are less involved than the biological parent (Berger, 2000). Special parenting problems may arise for a person who occupies the vacant role in a former single-parent family system. Both men and women who become stepparents may approach their new role with some trepidation. These individuals come into a family situation in which they are considered to be an outsider. The entire family's pattern of interaction must change to include the new person's cognitive style and personality. For example, a single-parent mother who marries or remarries has to relinquish her sole authority role in managing family affairs, and she must share decision-making responsibilities with her new partner. Although many women welcome this change, others state that they must work hard to realign their role with that of the new partner. As

we have seen in other situations, family systems tend to resist any change in the current homeostasis or functioning, whether this is healthy or unhealthy.

Although some remarriages are reported to be happier and more successful than first marriages, most of the problems associated with blended family functioning are related to parenting children from former marriages (Berger, 2000; Bloomfield, 2004). The difficulties encountered by a stepparent may be enhanced when stepchildren live with the remarried couple, particularly if they live with a stepmother.

● ●

Parenting Reflection 12–2

Why are clearly defined role functions and behaviors for stepparents lacking in our society?

● ●

Stepmothers

The uncertainty associated with stepparent role expectations causes many problems (Berger, 2000). The stepmother role is made more difficult by two myths: (a) a stepmother is bad, and (b) she requires instant love from the stepchildren. To counter the first myth, the stepmother may overcompensate by contributing too much to the relationship between herself and her stepchildren. The situation becomes impossible because the stepmother eventually realizes that she cannot possibly please everyone involved, including herself. Her biological children may complicate matters by feeling that they are being left out, ignored, or receiving less attention than their stepsiblings. Successful stepmothers experience the process of establishing an identity (Bradley, 2006). This process involves working through the stresses and ambiguities associated with the stepmother role, and developing new perspectives and an empathic understanding of what the role involves. Other stepmothers have deconstructed the myth of the evil stepmother by depicting the biological mother as the one who is bad, while portraying herself as the good mother (Christian, 2005).

●●●●●●●●●●●●●●●●●●●●●●●●●●●●●●●●●●●

Parenting Reflection 12–3

How do stereotypes about stepmothers typically depict these figures? Are there similar stereotypes of stepfathers? Do these truly influence the behavior of the individuals in these roles? Could these become self-fulfilling prophecies?

●●●●●●●●●●●●●●●●●●●●●●●●●●●●●●●●●●●

Families in which the mother role is filled by a stepmother have more problems than those with a stepfather. This may relate to the differences in the ways in which stepfamilies are formed. Fathers who gain custody of children after remarriage often do so because the mother has difficulties such as addiction disorders, which prove to be detrimental in the relationships with her biological children. Another challenging situation among families with stepmothers involves a woman who has never had children of her own but who quickly assumes a parenting role after her first marriage or remarriage.

Relationships with stepchildren may vary depending on the gender of the children. Stepmothers and stepdaughters are found to have the least favorable relationship of all steprelationships studied. Some of the girls in these relationships do not feel loved and report more feelings of hostility and lower self-esteem. Importantly, blended families have to find solutions that work for their unique challenges.

The age of stepchildren is a factor that influences the relationship with the stepmother, especially among those who have live-in stepmothers. Preschool-age children have the least problems interacting with stepmothers, while school-age and adolescent children have poorer relationships with their stepmothers. The stepmothers of these older children have more disagreements with their spouses, more conflicts over ways of disciplining children, and less satisfaction with their marriages than stepmothers of younger children.

There are successful stepmothers who adapt well to their new role and make significant contributions to their new family (Whiting, Smith, Barnett, & Grafsky, 2007). The methods most often used by these mothers include supports from outside, as well as inside, their family system; positive attitudes; the use of positive communication styles; and working toward the quality of the marital relationship.

Stepfathers

Stepfathers encounter similar problems in developing and performing their family role (Berger, 2000; Marsiglio, 2004). The stepfather–stepchild relationship may be at risk for as long as 2 years following the remarriage. Unlike the stepmother, the stepfather may not be as handicapped by myths and stereotypes regarding his new role and may be seen in a more positive manner, for instance as the provider (Claxton-Oldfield, O'Neill, Thomson, & Gallant, 2005). The fact that this role is less structured has both advantages and disadvantages. On the positive side, he can forge a new identity and impression when establishing a relationship with his spouse's children. Stepfathers are less likely to be authoritative in parenting style than biological fathers. Establishing disciplinary patterns and using controls related to stepchildren's behavior are often prime problem areas for stepfathers. Disagreements with the spouse may occur over how the stepfather disciplines the stepchildren.

Stepfathers also experience problems with financial affairs. Many make child support payments for their biological children from a former marriage. This money may be very much needed by the new blended family and can produce feelings of resentment about the former marriage. Guilt derives from the sense that the biological children have been abandoned after the new blended family system was formed. Some men feel that when another man becomes involved as a stepfather to their biological children, this man should help bear the financial costs of caring for these children. Research suggests that biological fathers reduce their social and economic investments in children if they no longer live with them and when they become involved in a blended family. One study reports that biological fathers in new blended families are likely to adjust child support payments to nonresidential children to accommodate the financial needs of supporting the new biological children produced in the subsequent marriage (Manning & Smock, 2000).

A man's satisfaction with being a stepfather is associated with several factors:

■ Being a biological father appears to work against a man's development of a positive relationship with his stepchildren. Men who do not have children of their own and who become stepfathers develop more positive relationships with their stepchildren.

■ Positive relationships between stepfathers and stepchildren are enhanced by the amount of communication between them.

■ When stepfathers feel that they have the biological mother's support to become involved in disciplining children, they report greater levels of satisfaction. Younger children can be more eager to accept a new father into their lives. Older children and adolescents are less willing to make adjustments and accept a new individual into their family life.

■ Finally, a critical event takes place in blended family formation when the stepfather accepts the stepchildren as his own and makes the transition from being an outsider to being a paternal figure (Marsiglio, 2004). This is all dependent on the contingencies of stepchildren making a similar transition in accepting the stepfather into the family circle.

Step-Grandparents

If we acknowledge that the family role of grandparents in contemporary times is ambiguous, consider the unique role of step-grandparents. The legal status of step-grandparents is not clear. Step-grandparents are more likely to view young step-grandchildren as a welcome addition to the family when an adult child remarries. When step-grandchildren live with the adult child, the likelihood of a relationship between step-grandparents and step-grandchildren increases (Christensen & Smith, 2002).

Research suggests that step-grandparents can improve their relationship with their step-grandchildren by increasing their active participation, including establishing a closer relationship with their adult child and increasing their visits with the step-grandchild at family gatherings and during the holidays (Haberstroh, Hayslip, Bert, & Wohl, 2001). The quality of the step-grandparent–step-grandchild relationship appears to be influenced to a greater extent by the adult child than by any factors that are exclusive to the step-grandparent–step-grandchild relationship. Step-grandchildren perceived the quality of the relationship with their biological grandparents to be stronger than their relationship with their step-grandparents.

Stepchildren and Stepsiblings

Usually, the quality of life for children is thought to be enhanced when their biological mother remarries. Single-parent families headed by a woman typically experience either a poverty-level existence or a borderline standard of living. When children live in these conditions, they fare less well than children living in more affluent families in terms of quality of life, medical care, nutrition, education, and economic security (Federal Interagency Forum on Child and Family Statistics, 2007).

Researchers report that children from stepfamilies fare neither better nor worse than children from single-parent families in terms of well-being (Berger, 2000). When compared with children from intact, first-marriage families, children from both blended families and single-parent families are rated as less well adjusted. It should be stressed that most children in these family forms do not have serious problems.

Children are expected to make a series of adjustments when biological parents divorce and later remarry. These adjustments typically focus on making a transition in family structure and functioning. These adjustments are stressful and affect school performance, behavior, and other socioemotional factors. Children living in intact, first-marriage families do not experience anything comparable that can affect their development.

Children, especially girls who grow up in blended families, tend to reject their stepfather and leave the blended family at an earlier age than those growing up in single-parent or two-parent households (Berger, 2000; Bray & Hetherington, 1993). They leave to establish their own homes and lifestyles or to get married.

These early departures may be the result of the tensions between them and their parents and stepparents. Exiting the blended family is seen as a more viable way to resolve these tensions. The friction that exists in blended families involving female children is attributed to the disruption of the mother–daughter relationship by the mother's male sexual partner who has an ambiguous relationship with the daughter.

The relationship among stepsiblings is complex when blended families are formed (Berger, 2000). Forging stepsibling relationships presents other challenges for blended families. The problems observed in biological sibling relationships, such as rivalry and jealousy, can become even more intense when stepsiblings are involved. It is not unusual for coalitions to form, creating a "my children are being mistreated by your children" scenario. Sexual tensions can exist when stepsiblings are pubertal or adolescent. On a more positive note, stepsiblings can also develop strong relationships where mutual support can be found and friendships flourish (E. R. Anderson, Greene, Hetherington, & Clingempeel, 1999).

Ex-Spouses and Ex-In-Laws

For persons in blended families, the relationships with ex-spouses and ex-in-laws are altered rather than severed. It is typical to feel displaced and alienated when divorce transforms the relationship (Berger, 2000). Although the rights and boundaries that define the altered relationship between ex-spouses begin with the divorce agreement, few legal rights or clear distinctions inform ex-in-laws about their altered relationship.

It is not uncommon for ex-spouses to experience feelings of jealousy, anger, and competition with their former partners (Berger, 2000). Likewise, ex-in-laws may harbor similar feelings of resentment. In other situations, ex-spouses and ex-in-laws collaborate to make the situation tolerable and even amicable.

• •

Focus Point.   Blended families involve challenging and complex relationships. The stepparent role differs from that of a biological parent. It is characterized differently for men and women. Many negative stereotypes are associated with the role. The expectations of a stepparent are ambiguous, and remarriages generally are happier than first betrothals. Most of the problems found in blended families relate to a stepparent's child-rearing function. The stepmother may encounter more

difficulties than the stepfather does, and her relationships can be influenced by the age and gender of the children. Stepfathers encounter similar problems, but their role is less restricted by structure and expectations, which allows for greater freedom in creating a unique role identity. Several factors affect a man's satisfaction with being a stepfather. Stepchildren and stepsiblings also experience challenging situations as new relationships are defined and developed. Ex-spouses and ex-in-laws, as well as step-grandparents, have to redefine their roles and relationships in the new family structure.

• •

Stepchildren and stepsiblings experience challenging situations as new relationships are defined and developed. All family members have to redefine their roles and relationships in the new blended family structure.

CHALLENGES AND ADJUSTMENTS IN BLENDED FAMILIES

The ability of blended families to adjust to their new status, roles, and patterns depends on three central themes (Hildebrand et al., 2008; Pasley & Ihinger-Tallman, 1987):

■ Giving up unrealistic expectations for the new family system.
■ Clarifying the feelings and needs of each family member.
■ Committing to new rules, roles, boundaries, and routines.

Blended family systems must accomplish several tasks to successfully transition from early disillusionment to total commitment to the new family system (Bloomfield, 2004; H. S. Glenn, Erwin, & Nelen, 2000). A variety of strategies are useful.

First, the biological parent and the stepparent need to determine the long-range goals for the organization of the new family system. This vision is determined by thinking about the needs of all family members. One helpful way to initiate the process is to have the remarried couple conduct a guided-fantasy exercise. This allows them to visualize how they want things to be at some future time in their family life. Discussion about the stepparent's role is especially important at this time. The couple can use input from the stepchildren, relatives, or a trained therapist in setting long-term goals.

Second, it is helpful if the remarried couple agrees that the biological parent is in charge of setting and enforcing limits for his or her biological children. It is recommended that when enforcing limits, the stepparent should learn to say, "Your parent says that you should . . ." When the biological parent is away and has left the stepparent in charge, it is helpful to instruct children to obey the stepparent in much the same way that they are expected to obey a sitter. The biological parent gives instructions to the children that they are expected to follow under the stepparent's supervision. When both adults have biological children, it is helpful for them to understand that it is acceptable to have various rules for the different children. There is a tendency for blended families to try to follow the former first-marriage family system's model of developing and imposing the same rules for all children. Instead, it is helpful to know that the new family system is not like the previous one.

Conflicts between the biological parent and the stepparent will probably occur, and couples may need assistance in learning how to negotiate compromises.

Third, stepparent–stepchild bonding may need assistance. This occurs in the same manner as between biological parents and their children during infancy. The process is characterized by nurturing without setting limits on children's behavior. When the stepparent insists that the biological parent should take over the limit-setting functions, bonding can occur between the stepparent and the stepchildren. This process may take a year or longer, depending on the age, personality, gender, and other factors relating to the children. The stepparent must also learn about individual differences that characterize each stepchild.

Fourth, adjustment to becoming a new family system is facilitated when the blended family develops its own rules, boundaries, and traditions. This may be as mundane or as important as determining who performs what household chores. Negotiation of the rules and traditions is helpful, and the stepparent and the stepchildren should engage in their own discussions. If the biological parent and the stepparent cannot reach an agreement, the stepparent should concede to the biological parent because the children are more likely to obey rules that are supported by their biological parent. Children play the biological parent off against the stepparent when they tell the stepparent, "You can't make me do that because you aren't my real parent."

Part of the negotiation strategy of the adults is to make compromises with the stepparent's point of view. It is supported by the biological parent's acknowledgment of the stepparent's positive contributions to the children's lives. If the biological parent refuses to negotiate, the stepparent has the option of withdrawing, although doing so does not send a message of a united parental dyad to the children. Sometimes professional help is needed to assist the remarried couple in reaching a settlement.

Fifth, both parents in a blended family system need to develop and maintain constructive patterns of interaction with ex-spouses. The blended family should differentiate itself from the former family by establishing its own boundaries. Encourage each family system to have its own rules and acknowledge that differences are acceptable. In therapeutic groups for couples, remarried spouses learn new ways of dealing with stressors and realize that the situation is not unique.

Parenting Reflection 12–4

What are some indicators that a blended family needs assistance to facilitate family cohesion?

Sources of support for blended families come from support groups, self-help publications, educational experiences, and therapeutic interventions (Carlson & Trapani, 2006; Michaels, 2006; Ziegahn, 2002). Educational strategies assist individuals in developing more realistic expectations of stepfamily life that facilitate the creation of long-term goals. Marriage and family enrichment programs are offered by churches and other organizations, and assist development (Hawkins, 2003). Family therapy can be helpful in restoring family balance and in guiding family members toward optimal functioning with one another (Berger, 2000).

Stepchildren are typically included in therapeutic programs. Children can call on teachers for help. Teachers can play an important role in helping children understand that the problems of blended family life can be resolved. Teachers may work with parents as well.

Because stepchildren complain about problems in their new family, it may appear as if the blended family home is a negative environment. Adjustment problems are more prevalent among children in blended families, and stressors can affect school performance. The children are not necessarily harmed by having a blended family experience.

Blended families can find online and community support through organizations that provide information concerning the following topics: judicial information, the importance of parenting time, legislation pertaining to blended families, and information on child support and custody.

Focus Point. The success of a blended family may depend on its ability to overcome obstacles that challenge the development of the new family system. The blended family may use several strategies, such as therapeutic and support groups.

FAMILY SNAPSHOT

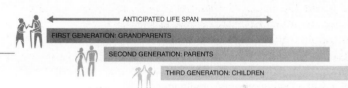

The intergenerational snapshot of a blended family system examines the family formed by the remarriage of Lisa Curtis, the mother of a single-parent family (see Figure 12–1). This snapshot is taken several years after Lisa's divorce was finalized. Her daughter, Mary, and her son, Joey, are teenagers. The children's maternal grandmother, Susan Scott, is deceased. Lisa's second husband is Tom Matthews, a divorced father of three children. These children live with their mother, Tom's ex-wife. Tom holds joint custody of his biological children with his ex-wife. Tom moved into Lisa's home, to which she gained the title following her divorce.

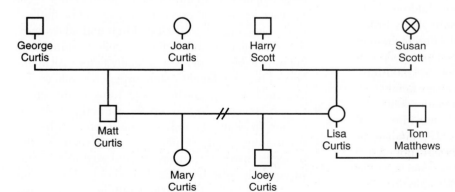

In this genogram, a line between Tom Matthews, to the right of Lisa Curtis, represents a second marriage for Lisa and a blended family system for the children. This genogram is increasingly complex, as it shows the death of the maternal grandmother, the divorce of the parents, and the formation of a blended family system. Genograms can document a number of events that take place within family systems.

First Generation

Grandparents and Step-Grandparents in a Blended Family

- Accepting the new family members.
- Supporting the remarriage of the adult child.
- Not being critical of the actions of the biological child who is remarrying.
- Maintaining good relationships with grandchildren.
- Offering support to the blended family.

Second Generation

Parents and Stepparents in a Blended Family

- Bonding with the new partner and establishing intimacy.
- Deciding on long-term goals for organizing the new family system.
- Initially, the biological parent is in charge of enforcing limits for his or her children.
- Facilitating the bonding process between the stepparent and the stepchildren.
- Developing rules, boundaries, and traditions for the new family system.
- Developing ways of interacting with the households of ex-spouses.
- Seeking assistance from educational strategies, counseling, and support groups.

Third Generation

Children and Stepchildren in a Blended Family

- Establishing new relationships with the stepparent and stepsiblings.
- Adjusting to the roles, boundaries, and rules of the blended family system.
- Maintaining a relationship with the biological parent who lives in a separate household.
- Visitation of biological parent in the separate household.
- Assimilating new extended stepfamily.
- Progressing through own developmental changes.
- Successfully meeting own developmental challenges.

FIGURE 12–1. Developmental challenges.

POINTS TO CONSIDER

■ Families grow in various ways and different groups of people can form **blended families**. There are several variations on the theme of two biological parents with biological offspring. A new family system can be formed when a single parent remarries. A family can expand by fostering or adopting children. A *reconstituted* or *blended family system* typically brings together children who may have had different families of origin, and/or adults who have been married previously, or have children from previous relationships. They blend their resources to form a new family.

■ Remarriage is likely to occur among individuals who have divorced or who were widowed. Individuals who remarry are generally young adults. The median interval between divorce and remarriage is about 3 to 5 years. Ethnic background influences remarriage; for example, Caucasians are more likely to remarry than African Americans.

■ Blended families differ from first marriages. When children are involved, a family system is instantly transformed and re-created without the benefit of the gradual addition of new members. The two remarried adults may be facing differing, and sometimes incompatible, developmental challenges. Ex-spouses and ex-grandparents can influence the new family system. Spouses' wishes and expectations may not be fulfilled in the new marriage. Both children and adults have mixed allegiances and feelings of guilt. Children may not want to be part of the new family system. All members of the new family system experience role confusion and have to negotiate new patterns of interaction.

■ Coparents agree to take on the parenting tasks together. In blended family systems, there may be two coparenting dyads at play. The first refers to the biological parents, who have to find ways to coparent successfully from binuclear households. The second dyad refers to the two persons fulfilling the parental roles within the blended family, of whom one will be a biological parent and the other a stepparent.

■ Coparenting has the best success rate if the best interests of the children are considered, and if the parental systems can maintain the parental hierarchical boundaries. That means that the personal problems and challenges within the parental dyad should not spill over into the relationship with the children. Children should not be pulled into the intimacy problems of parents or be turned into go-betweens for warring parents.

■ As responsible adults, the coparents have to set their personal agendas aside when it comes to parent–child relations and focus on the needs of the children, keeping their best interests in mind.

■ Blended families encounter a series of developmental tasks that are similar to those of single-parent family systems. They also experience seven stages:

■ Fantasy: All members hold unrealistic expectations for the new family system.

■ Assimilating the new adult: A new family member is assimilated into the existing family network.

■ Awareness: There is reorganization and identification of confused feelings.

■ Mobilization: The stepparent initiates changes in the family network to promote assimilation.

■ Action: There is renegotiation of boundaries, differences, and patterns of interaction.

■ Contact: Authentic interactions are developed.

■ Resolution: Relationship strengths are developed.

■ The stepparent has a high degree of role ambiguity. This is especially so for stepmothers. The role includes many interaction problems with other family members, especially children.

■ Families in which the mother role is filled by a stepmother may have more problems than those with a stepfather. This difference can be ascribed to the ways in which these new family systems originate. The quality of the relationship with a child depends on the child's age and gender.

■ Stepfathers have similar difficulties, but are less hampered by stereotypes about their role. They encounter problems in disciplining stepchildren and in dealing with the complex financial arrangements of the two separate family systems. The gender and age of the stepchildren are factors that influence the quality of the relationship with the stepfather.

■ Adjustments in stepfamilies hinge on resolving three challenges:

■ Discarding unrealistic fantasies and expectations regarding the new family system.

■ Clarifying the feelings and the needs of each family member.

■ Making a commitment to new rules, roles, boundaries, and routines.

■ A variety of strategies assist stepfamily members in adjusting to this new status.

■ Adults decide on long-term goals for organizing the new family system.

■ The biological parent is in charge of enforcing the limits for his or her children.

■ The biological parent facilitates the bonding process between the stepparent and the stepchildren.

■ Both parents in the blended family should develop rules, boundaries, and traditions for the new family system.

■ The parents in the blended family should develop ways of interacting with the households of ex-spouses.

■ They seek assistance from educational strategies, counseling, and support groups.

■ Stepfamilies have particular strengths, which include

■ Opportunities for stepchildren to learn problem solving, negotiation, and coping skills.

■ Becoming more flexible within a family system.

■ The presence of more adults for support.

■ Exposure to a wide variety of people and experiences.

■ Exposure to a good model of marital interaction.

■ The possibility of a better experience than that offered by the single-parent family.

USEFUL WEBSITES

Center for the Improvement of Child Caring
www.ciccparenting.org

Harvard Family Research Project
www.hfrp.org

HelpGuide.org, a nonprofit resource in collaboration with Harvard Health Publications and Harvard Medical School
www.helpguide.org

Search Institute: Discovering What Kids Need to Succeed and ParentFurther
www.search-institute.org and *www.parentfurther.com*

CHAPTER 13

Adolescent Parents

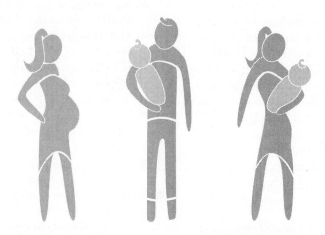

Learning Outcomes

After completing this chapter, readers should be able to

1. Describe the principal factors that contribute to adolescent parenthood.
2. Explain the implications for adolescents who become parents.
3. Distinguish between the short- and long-term consequences of a teen pregnancy.
4. Describe the role of community support for teenagers who become parents.
5. Explain initiatives that could contribute to lowering teen pregnancy rates.

Adolescence is a transitional period between childhood and adulthood that facilitates extended, tentative exploration of adult roles. If this exploration leads to adult responsibilities in the form of parenthood, the consequences may be overwhelming. An adolescent who is still searching for a niche in the world of employment, education, relationships, and other complex societal demands can be extremely challenged if the responsibility of an infant is added to this formula. Frequently, something gives way, and the loss may be in terms of further education and career preparation. A support network, including possible coparents, is crucial to helping the adolescent become the best parent

Rates per 1,000 women aged
15–19 in specified group

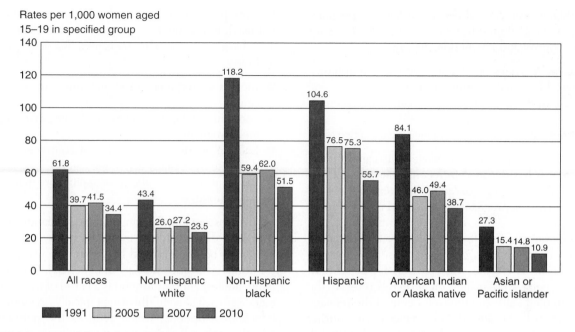

FIGURE 13–1.   Birthrates for women aged 15–19, by race and Hispanic origin: United States, 1991, 2005, 2007, and 2010.
Source: CDC/NCHS, National Vital Statistics System.

that he or she can be. Pregnancy among adolescents has been described as a problem with short- and long-term consequences for the adolescent parents, their child, and their families of origin.

The rate of adolescent pregnancy has been declining over the past 20 years and has reached a low point not seen since the 1950s (see Figure 13–1). This decline has been observed in every ethnic group surveyed in the

Educational programs about child development and parenting are helpful in making teens more competent in assuming parental roles.

United States. The general decline in teenage pregnancies might be attributed to several factors (Centers for Disease Control and Prevention, 2012i):

■ Increased participation in programs that emphasize responsible sexual decision making
■ A decrease in the number of sexually active teenage girls
■ Wider use of contraceptives among sexually active teens

While the number of teenage marriages in the United States has declined in recent years as well, the overwhelming majority of adolescents who become pregnant carry the pregnancy to term and retain custody of the child.

Two groups of females are considered at risk when pregnant: those *under* age 19 and those *over* age 35 (Martin et al., 2006; U.S. Census Bureau, 2011b). In relation to teenage pregnancy, the term *risk* refers to the dangers to the health and the well-being of the teenage girl and her baby because the pregnancy occurs during a period of her life that is not developmentally optimal. The teenage mother, the father of the baby, and the infant experience many ongoing negative consequences.

INCIDENCE, CAUSES, AND OUTCOMES OF TEENAGE PREGNANCY

Primary Factors

The teenage birthrate is continuing to decline in comparison to the previous decade. During 2010, about 368,000 infants were born to women ages 15–19 in the United States (Centers for Disease Control and Prevention, 2012i). Of those who become pregnant, about 10 percent experience a miscarriage or have a stillborn baby, about 29 percent have an induced abortion, and about 61 percent carry the pregnancy to term and give birth. Eleven percent of all births in the United States are to teen mothers. Fewer than half of these girls marry before giving birth; most are classified as unwed mothers. A large majority of the single girls who give birth choose to retain custody of their baby (Federal Interagency Forum on Child and Family Statistics, 2011a). The vast majority of adolescents who give birth are African American or Hispanic groups, rather than Caucasian.

Most adolescent girls do not choose to become pregnant (Wakschlag & Hans, 2000). The majority become pregnant because a birth-control method was not used. For some, the pregnancy is the result of rape. The basic reasons why teenagers become pregnant include

■ Increased frequency of sexual intercourse at earlier ages.
■ Social influences that decrease the negative stigma of teen pregnancy.
■ Lack of adequate knowledge of contraceptives and their use by sexually active teenagers.
■ Personal attitudes about sexuality, pregnancy, and parenthood.

Adolescent childbearing may be an adaptive strategy for some disadvantaged individuals; for example, the economic benefits reaped by young parents qualifying for public assistance may seem beneficial. On the other hand, adolescent parenthood is a cause of the disadvantaged status. Teen childbearing typically precludes their educational options, which reduces the potential for jobs that pay well and, in turn, maintains their receipt of public assistance (M. E. Collins, 2000). The overwhelming evidence suggests that parenthood is largely undesirable among adolescents, regardless of the outcomes for the young parents and their children (Breedlove, Schorfheide, & Wieczorek, 2000).

More Teens Are Sexually Active. Researchers believe that there has been a continued increase in the incidence of sexual engagement among teenagers (Alan Guttmacher Institute, 2012). Researchers estimate that about one fourth of all teenage girls have had intercourse by age 15 and that four out of five have had intercourse by age 19. This estimate contrasts with the figures for teenage boys. About 13 percent have had intercourse by age 15, and about 65 percent by age 19. Sexual activity becomes increasingly common with age during this period of life. Seven out of 10 teens are believed to have had sexual intercourse at least once by age 19. Many teenagers are sexually active at younger ages than most adults imagine (Alan Guttmacher Institute, 2012).

For the most part, sexual activity among teenagers is believed to occur frequently and with a variety of partners. Instead of being promiscuous, adolescents often become intensely involved with one person over a period of time and the relationship includes sexual intimacy. Sexual activity increases the risks of negative consequences, including exposure to sexually transmitted

Focus On 13–1

Contributing Causes of Teenage Pregnancy

- Serious emotional problems, such as lack of adequate social adjustment, extreme feelings of isolation, loneliness, or low self-esteem
- Embarrassment about sexual matters, which leads to reluctance to obtain information about conception and contraception
- Religious beliefs that may compound feelings of guilt, enhancing a reluctance to be informed about sexual matters
- Eagerness to participate in sexual activity without making the effort to ensure safer experiences, as well as impulsivity and peer pressure
- Feelings of resentment and anger toward a parent, which can facilitate a desire to punish the parent
- Feelings of guilt, a negative self-image, or low self-esteem, which can facilitate the need to be accepted socially, irrespective of the costs and outcomes
- A desire to prove one's masculinity or femininity
- A desire to be recognized as a person with adult social status
- An attempt to create a captive love or to trap a mate
- A desire to receive unconditional love from another person (perceiving a baby as a substitute for parental or marital love)
- Behavioral problems, including conduct disorders, involvement in criminal activity, acting-out behavior, or participation in delinquent behaviors such as substance abuse
- Certain family background markers, such as a single-parent versus a first-marriage family of origin, the level of the parents' educational achievement, a parent who was sexually active as a teenager, older siblings who are sexually active, experiencing a particular type of parental supervision in adolescence, parental involvement in elementary schooling, and racial or ethnic background

Sources: Breedlove, G. K., Schorfheide, A. M., & Wieczorek, R. R. (2000). *Adolescent Pregnancy*. White Plains, NY: March of Dimes Foundation; Kirby, D. (2001). *Emerging Answers: Research Findings on Programs to Reduce Teen Pregnancy*. Washington, DC: National Campaign to Prevent Teen Pregnancy; Mersky, J. P., & Reynolds, A. J. (2007). Predictors of early childbearing: Evidence from the Chicago longitudinal study. *Children and Youth Services Review, 29*(1), 35–52.

diseases, pregnancy, and a variety of deleterious psychosocial effects (Weinstock, Berman, & Cates, 2004). Researchers are particularly concerned about the spread of the AIDS-causing HIV virus among teenagers, who have a high level of sexual activity that is largely unprotected (Tinsley, Lees, & Sumartojo, 2004).

Another serious health concern regarding unprotected sexual contact is exposure to the human papilloma virus (HPV), which causes an estimated 70 percent of cervical cancer cases and can also play a role in rectal and throat cancers. A vaccine is now available to enhance immunity against many strains of this virus. Health professionals as well as the Centers for Disease Control and Prevention (2012g) are recommending that both adolescent girls and boys be vaccinated against HPV.

Several antecedent conditions contribute to the age at which teens become sexually active and the number of different partners (Alan Guttmacher Institute, 2012; Baumer & South, 2001; Franke-Clark, 2003; S. Phillips, 2003; Raffaelli & Crockett, 2003; Susman, Dorn, & Schiefelbein, 2003):

- The level of adolescent sex hormones may increase at earlier ages. These hormones establish the interest in and motivation for sexual activity.
- Adolescents' cognitive and emotional development usually lags behind physical development; therefore, teenagers may not be completely aware of the risks involved in early, unprotected sexual activity. For example, cognitive distortion may give them a sense of invulnerability.
- The family of origin is influential in shaping a teenager's attitudes about sexual activity, as it models behaviors that influence the adolescent's choices

Parents who maintain an open and trusting relationship with their adolescents can guide them toward responsible and safe decisions regarding sexual matters.

concerning sexual behavior. Some of these factors are (a) the sexual history of the mother during her adolescence, (b) older siblings who are sexually active, (c) living in a single-parent rather than a first-marriage family system, (d) unhealthy levels of family cohesion and adaptability, (e) highly involved mother–daughter and negative father–daughter relationships, and (f) the quality of the parent–child relationship. All of these factors affect the degree to which a child subscribes to family values regarding sexual behavior. The degree of adolescent girls' permissiveness about sexual activity may be related to friends and sisters who are sexually active, especially if an adolescent sister has become a mother herself.

■ Peer influences may affect a teen's sexual involvement. Many feel a great deal of social pressure to become sexually active, especially girls, who may be particularly susceptible to coercion by males to participate in sexual intercourse.

■ Sociocultural factors, such as religious participation, ethnic background, or the family of origin's socioeconomic status, may influence the probability of a teen's participation in sexual activity.

Changes in social attitudes about teenage sexual activity and those who become pregnant have occurred. In the past, pregnancy was a degrading, humiliating status that destroyed an adolescent girl's reputation and ability to fully participate in adolescent social development. Boys were taught that it was wrong to impregnate a girl outside of marriage. In the past, an adolescent girl who became pregnant had limited alternatives for dealing with her situation. She could try to arrange a dangerous, illegal abortion, or she could leave her community to bear her child in a facility for unwed mothers. These institutions were often run by charitable agencies or religious groups. Typically, she would give the child up for adoption.

Today, such attitudes no longer influence the course of teenage pregnancy. Fewer social stigmas are associated with teenage pregnancy, and families are more supportive of pregnant teenagers by providing emotional, financial, and physical assistance. A variety of community programs assist both expectant teenagers and those who have become parents. Some programs offer teens the opportunity to continue their education with as few disruptions as possible. Abortion is legal in the United States, although teenagers' access to such procedures is regulated. Most teenage girls who choose to continue their pregnancy retain custody of the baby. Many of these young mothers receive family assistance, especially from their own mother and grandparents, who care for the baby, fully integrating the child into the family.

Most pregnancies among teenagers occur because of a failure to use contraception. Few teenagers report a desire for pregnancy when they participate in sexual activity (Alan Guttmacher Institute, 2012). Adults are puzzled about why sexually active teenagers fail to use protective measures that will prevent pregnancy. The explanation is related to the meanings that adolescents attach to the use of contraception. For example, to use contraception is an obvious admission of sexual activity (Kosunen, Kaltiala-Heino, Rimpela, & Laippala, 2003). Teenagers' use of contraception reflects their understanding that consequences, such as pregnancy and disease, can result from sexual activity and that they are negative outcomes. Seeking and obtaining contraceptive devices have certain social, economic, and psychological costs that teenagers must weigh against the risks and costs of pregnancy. Many teens find it embarrassing and feel inept at discussing contraception and safer sex practices with a sexual partner.

• •

Parenting Reflection 13–1

What are the pros and cons if health clinics in junior and senior high schools dispense contraceptives and provide relevant informational material pertaining to safer sexual choices to any student who requests these services?

• •

The personal attitudes of adolescents play an important role in influencing their use or non-use of contraceptives (Strong, 2004). The total life situation of adolescents from low-income family systems promotes feelings of fatalism, depression, and apathy. These attitudes work against the effective use of contraception among those who are sexually active. Teenagers may be influenced in their sexual activity and use of contraception by a variety of cognitive distortions and beliefs about their ability to become pregnant. These distortions relate to a flaw in cognitive processing at this life stage called the *personal fable*. They may not use contraception because of the erroneous, irrational belief that other people become pregnant but that they are invulnerable.

What Influences Teenagers to Use Contraception?
American adolescents, in comparison with those of other countries studied, use contraception less consistently and effectively (Alan Guttmacher Institute, 2012; Hyde & DeLamater, 2000). As a result, we observe higher rates of adolescent pregnancy and parenthood than in other developed countries, such as Great Britain, Japan, and Scandinavia (Blum, 2001).

Certain antecedent conditions are associated with the use of contraception and safer sex practices among teenagers (Kershaw, Niccolai, Ethier, Lewis, & Ickovics, 2003; Longmore, Manning, Giordano, & Rudolph, 2003;

Stevens-Simon, Sheeder, & Harder, 2005; Topolak, Williams, & Wilson, 2001). Psychosocial factors, such as perceiving oneself as being sexually active, are crucial. Having the cognitive and psychological maturity to perceive oneself in this way without guilt influences a teen's use of birth control. If teens are able to delay becoming sexually active until late adolescence, the chances improve that they will use contraception because they have developed the skills that promote effective sexual decision making.

As teenagers become sexually experienced, they tend to use contraception more regularly and correctly and bypass feelings of embarrassment that prevent younger adolescents from obtaining and using contraception. If teenagers from disadvantaged backgrounds can be assisted in continuing their educational experiences, their chances of using contraception improve accordingly.

Families can influence the use of contraception by providing or failing to provide information concerning sexual choices. Parents who disapprove of and do not tolerate adolescent sexuality and sexual activity are more likely to have teens who become pregnant. Researchers generally find that, contrary to popular opinion, the parents' openness to communicate and their support of safer sexual decision making tends to increase adolescents' use of contraception.

When parents do not communicate with adolescents about sexual activity and pregnancy, peers provide information and are influential (Zabin & Cardona, 2002). When peers approve of the use of contraception, teenagers whose parents do not approve or do not discuss it appear to be influenced by their peers to also use contraception. On the other hand, if the peer group is not using contraception, the teenager will most likely follow suit.

When teenagers who are sexually active have access to family-planning services and information regarding sexual choices, either in their schools or their communities, there is a greater likelihood of preventing pregnancy and STDs (Topolak et al., 2001). School sex-education programs do not appear to have a significant effect on promoting teen sexual behavior or on increasing the likelihood of adolescent pregnancy in one way or another (Conner & Dewey, 2003).

Marriage as an Option.
Teenagers typically do not choose marriage as a consequence of becoming pregnant

Parenting FAQ 13–1

Our 16-year-old daughter recently revealed that she is pregnant. We worry that she will not continue her education and that she's ruined her life. We like the boy who's the father and believe the best solution is for them to marry and live with one set of parents until they finish high school. What do we need to know?

Research generally reports that teen marriages do not last and can be very stressful for everyone involved. The teens' parents and grandparents may have a difficult time being truly helpful. The new parents need a tremendous amount of support in order to deal with this difficult situation, and marriage may complicate things in the long run. It may be helpful to call in the support of an agency or health-care professional who deals specifically with these matters. A program such as Even Start by the U.S. Department of Education supports qualifying teen parents and their children, so that the teen mothers can complete their schooling while their children are cared for during the hours the mother is at school. In addition, the teen parents are required to participate in parenting education and interactive literacy activities involving parent and child (www2.ed.gov/programs/evenstartformula/index.html).

(U.S. Census Bureau, 2011b). Most frequently, the decision not to marry but to continue the pregnancy is influenced by a teenage girl's mother and the baby's father (Haveman, Wolfe, & Pence, 2001). Regardless of whether or not teens marry, they tend to encounter the poorest socioeconomic outcomes; marriage does not significantly improve their situation. Marriage under these circumstances is also considered to be high risk and prone to early divorce.

Another factor that contributes to the decision about whether or not to marry relates to welfare benefits (Boonstra, 2000). Teenagers who are unmarried are more likely to receive welfare benefits than teens who are married. Racial background is a contributing factor. African American adolescents who become pregnant are less likely to marry than Caucasian adolescents (Zabin & Cardona, 2002). This may be due partly to the unemployed status of these fathers. The tendency among African Americans to remain unmarried also reflects differences in values; the families may be more tolerant of unmarried parenthood in general. The decision not to marry and to carry a pregnancy to term implies that teenagers must rely on their families of origin for assistance. In reality, unmarried teens receive less assistance from their families than those who marry. Because of this situation, public assistance can be an essential resource.

Adoption as an Alternative. Adoption has been chosen less frequently as an option in adolescent pregnancy as more teenage girls choose to continue the pregnancy and retain custody of the baby (B. C. Miller & Coyl, 2000). In some cases, the fathers request custody. The adoption alternative enables the girl to continue her education, attend to otherwise normal adolescent developmental tasks, and avoid experiencing a disadvantaged existence. On the other hand, placing a baby for adoption produces feelings of guilt, grief, and loss that can have long-term effects. These feelings can harm a girl's psychological well-being and adversely affect her future sexual and intimate relationships. Placement of the baby for adoption may cause long-term consequences. Another alternative is that the teen father asks for custody of the baby if that would be in the best interests of the child.

The decision to place a baby for adoption is a difficult one for a teen mother. Many adolescent girls who give up their babies for adoption may rationalize this decision by noting that they feel unready or unable to be a parent and to provide an adequate environment for their child. On the other hand, parents who adopt a child mostly provide very good homes, the child is desired, and it may be a choice that is in the child's best interests. In **open adoptions**, the birth mother can remain in contact with the adoptive parents and follow the development of the child, even though she gives up almost all of her parental rights. The rights of the biological fathers are determined by their legal status in the child's life—for instance, whether they are married to the mother or not.

The majority of pregnant adolescents elect to keep their babies following birth.

Although most teenagers choose not to terminate their pregnancy or to place their baby for adoption, significant consequences result from the decision to retain custody of the child and to assume a parental role. As might be expected, teen mothers who choose to give up their child for adoption have more positive attitudes about adoption than those who choose to retain custody. There are complex consequences for the adolescent mother and father, as well as for their child, when they decide to retain custody.

....

Focus Point.   A variety of factors contribute to teenage pregnancy. The most obvious relate to the failure to use contraceptives among those who are sexually active. The majority of teens carry a pregnancy to term, although a substantial portion chooses abortion. Most of the girls who give birth choose to retain custody of their baby, and most do not marry during or following their pregnancy. Adoption as a means for resolving teen pregnancy has increasingly declined.

....

Adolescent Parents

There are short- and long-term considerations regarding parenthood for teenagers (Moore & Brooks-Gunn, 2002):

■ Educational implications
■ Marriage and family relations
■ Health considerations for the teen mothers

■ Workforce participation and economic consequences
■ Parent–child relations

Educational Implications.   Pregnancy appears to be the most common reason why an adolescent girl fails to complete her high school education (Alan Guttmacher Institute, 2012; Moore & Brooks-Gunn, 2002; Zachary, 2005). This is especially so if the girl is African American. The younger the girl at the time of conception, the less likely she is to return to school following the birth of her baby.

The most long-term effect of the disruption of a girl's education relates to economic consequences (Fergusson & Woodward, 2000). The lack of a high school diploma severely restricts the availability of jobs and the level of income. The teen mother can expect to have a less prestigious job, lower job satisfaction, and a decreased quality of life.

Some school systems are aware that these consequences affect adolescent girls for a lifetime. Special programs, such as Even Start by the U.S. Department of Education, promote the continuation of schooling by providing child care during school hours and teaching parenting and family life skills, as well as assisting in vocational development. School attendance can be enhanced when teen mothers reframe their anticipation of motherhood by prioritizing their educational goals to remain in school and to complete their education (SmithBattle, 2007). By remaining educationally motivated, they improve their grades, resolve to graduate, and show an interest in attending college. A number of competing demands, such as conflicting school policies, work demands, and parenting responsibilities, can complicate time management.

Marriage and Family Relations.   Adolescent pregnancy hastens early marriage, but this option is not necessarily an optimal solution. Teenage marriages are likely to be high risk, highly unstable, and prone to end in divorce (Moore & Brooks-Gunn, 2002). About 60 percent of adolescents who marry divorce within 5 years, in comparison with 20 percent for those who marry in early adulthood (Lichter & Graefe, 2001).

A classic study of adolescent marriage and parenthood (deLissovoy, 1973a, 1973b) points toward the unhappy nature of teenage marriages. Vladimir DeLissovoy studied the relationships of working-class, rural couples who were 17 years old and younger. The adolescent husbands were generally more dissatisfied than the adolescent wives. These young men felt that their wives did not participate enough in sexual activities, while the young women felt that husbands wanted too much sex. This dissatisfaction increased after 30 months of marriage. The young husbands were dissatisfied with the relative lack of sexual and social activity and opportunities to interact with mutual friends. They wished to continue their relationships with their male friends and to participate in sports after school. The young wives felt left out and lonely because many had been dropped by their former friends. Admittedly, this study occurred a generation or two ago, but it is still current in that it reflects the emotional immaturity of these young parents who take on a developmentally challenging role too early in their lives.

Most research findings suggest that early childbearing and marriage contribute to greater unhappiness than the pregnancy itself (N. Barber, 2001; Haveman et al., 2001). The correlates include disruption of education, restricted job opportunities, and limited earnings potential. When the teen father is involved in the pregnancy and is active in parenting following childbirth, then marriage is more likely to occur (Fagan, Schmitz, & Lloyd, 2007).

Health Considerations.   Early studies of adolescent pregnancy reported many adverse physical complications for the young mother, including elevated death rates, increased prevalence of maternal toxemia, precipitate or prolonged delivery, anemia, postpartum infections, and hemorrhaging. Most of these conditions are directly linked to lack of prenatal care, often because the mother is secretive about the pregnancy (Borja & Adair, 2003). Other factors contributing to the increased health risks are poverty and lack of access to health care (Haveman et al., 2001). Obtaining adequate prenatal care is unlikely unless the girl is open about her condition and has family support. Inadequate nutrition also presents significant problems because teenagers can make poor nutritional choices and may already have issues with obesity. Poor nutrition exacerbates problems associated with teen pregnancy by interfering with the normal growth patterns of the young mother. It also increases the likelihood that the baby will have a low birth weight, which jeopardizes survival and increases the chances of other birth complications (Stevens-Simon, Nelligan, & Kelly, 2001).

Mental health is also negatively affected by early childbearing (Turner, Sorensen, & Turner, 2000). Teen mothers have less social support and personal resources for coping with stress. The accumulation of major, potentially traumatic events could precipitate other mental health conditions. Substance abuse further jeopardizes the unborn child.

Workforce Participation and Economic Consequences.   When teenage girls drop out of school because of pregnancy, their future is jeopardized. Their ability to provide adequate incomes for themselves and their children becomes virtually impossible (Haveman et al., 2001). Most girls who fail to complete high school lack the entry-level skills to compete in the job market. The income of adolescent mothers is about one half that of mothers who have their first child in early adulthood (U.S. Census Bureau, 2011b).

Because of the combined effects of the loss of educational opportunities, the lack of sufficient support networks, the unavailability of adequate child care, extensive medical expenses, and other related factors, teenage parents face major economic consequences (Bissell, 2000). Their economic resources are severely limited, and their parents are frequently unable to provide the type of financial support that will ensure adequate prenatal care, equipment, and living conditions. Teen mothers often lack adequate resources to become effective parents, frequently fail to complete their educations, and fail to see parenthood as being personally or socially restrictive (Jaffee, 2002).

Economic instability in the months following a marriage between teen parents who have both dropped out of school typically leads to separation within 2 years. In the long run, teenage parents can expect to hold low-paying, low-level jobs in which little satisfaction or economic gain is evident. Another economic consequence is that children born to teenage parents ultimately are more costly to a parent than those born to women who have their child in their 20s (Alan Guttmacher Institute, 2012). This is related to the loss of potential income caused by dropping out of school, the average national annual income and hourly wage among women according to their level of educational attainment, and the direct costs of having additional children. The lack of adequate job skills and educational qualifications also causes adolescent mothers to seek financial assistance from public welfare programs (M. E. Collins, 2000).

Parent–Child Relations. Adolescents who become parents can expect to be single parents and to have large families, as compared with individuals who wait until early adulthood to have children (Wakschlag & Hans, 2000). Some investigations report that adolescent mothers are as competent as older mothers and that their interactions with infants and children are usually appropriate. Other studies report that teenage parents have troubled relationships with their children and may be abusive (Stevens-Simon et al., 2001).

Research points to problematic parent–child relationships among adolescents who are mothers, yet it does appear that there can be positive outcomes for children under certain circumstances (Luster, Bates, Fitzgerald, Vanderbelt, & Key, 2000). Children of adolescent mothers have been found to score high on certain measures that examine intellectual functioning when the mother has more years of education, is employed, has fewer children, lives in more desirable neighborhoods, and is living with a male partner.

Several studies point to the risks of poor teen parenting, which are highlighted by the following characteristics (Jaffee, 2002; Kimes, 2006; Moore & Brooks-Gunn, 2002; Stevens-Simon et al., 2001):

■ Lack of knowledge concerning children's developmental needs
■ Less of sensitivity to the behavioral cues of infants
■ Lack of interest in playing with children
■ Less time spent interacting with children, which is accentuated by ambivalent feelings about parenthood and a greater tendency to use physical punishment

The historical work by Vladimir deLissovoy (1973a, 1973b) is illuminating, as he studied adolescent parents in depth during the seventies. His work is better understood in the context of the time during which he completed his research. Since then, social attitudes have shifted, and access to information concerning child care has become easier. In deLissovoy's research, both adolescent mothers and fathers were questioned shortly after the birth of their baby regarding their knowledge of the developmental norms and growth of infants. This research found that teenagers were grossly ignorant about when to expect certain developmental events during infancy, a fact that had broad implications regarding the ability of these young parents to provide quality, nurturing caregiving for infants and children. For example, teenage parents indicated that toilet training should begin at 24 weeks (6 months) of age and that teaching infants about obedience to parental direction should begin at either 26 weeks or 36 weeks. The need for correct information and child-care training is important, including for the fathers. In contrast to the time when this research was done, current teen parents now have greater access to information on the World Wide Web, and most teenagers are computer literate. Nevertheless, teen parents may require guidance to access appropriate parenting material.

Adolescent parents typically demonstrate a range of nurturing, caregiving behaviors toward children, although immature and self-centered parenting styles also occur (Moore & Brooks-Gunn, 2002). Other works suggest that, rather than being at immediate risk of abuse and neglect because of parental ignorance, children of teenage parents may experience some developmental delays because they have not been engaged in ongoing constructive and teaching/learning oriented interactions with the caretaking parent (Jaffee, Caspi, Moffitt, Belsky, & Silva, 2001). Adolescent mothers tend to have more children, lower incomes, fewer sources of social support, interrupted educational experiences, and a lower quality of life, which cause stress and promote child abuse and neglect (Borkowski et al., 2002).

When adolescent mothers are compared with older mothers, the teen mothers are found to have competent parenting skills (Hess, Papas, & Black, 2002). Other factors, rather than age alone, may mediate the negative effects. Social class may produce differences in children's development manifested via maternal knowledge, attitudes, and behaviors that determine the quality of the parenting experience. These studies are unclear concerning the greater probability of abusiveness among teenage parents.

One researcher has described a culture of teen parenting that is competitive. The competitiveness can occur because teen mothers want to prove that they are competent. The consuming desire is to behave in ways that are not abusive, welfare-dependent, or incompetent. Despite their general ignorance about child development and caretaking, adolescent girls who are either pregnant or are parents were found to be more realistic than their nonpregnant cohorts in their expectations about child developmental milestones. This level of knowledge might be attributed to the participation of pregnant and parental adolescents in special education programs that prepare them for parenthood. When teen mothers have the support and involvement of grand-mothers in providing care for their infants, their parenting competence appears to improve considerably (Oberlander, Black, & Starr, 2007).

Adolescent mothers are reported to be more likely to feel depressed, nervous, tense, fretful, and ambivalent about their parenthood status (Schweingruber & Kalil, 2000). They are also less likely to feel positive about their child and about parenthood than older mothers (Stevens-Simon et al., 2001). The less positive outlook is reflected in adolescent mothers' perceptions of their infants as being more difficult, and this in turn can contribute to a negative self-concept in the child.

Like many teen fathers, this young man has a long-term and stable relationship with the mother of his child. He views teen parenthood as an opportunity to be an involved and responsible father.

•••

Focus Point. Adolescent mothers generally have difficulties acting in their role as a parent. A variety of short- and long-term consequences occur when adolescents assume the parental role. Generally, in contemporary American society, adolescent parenthood is developmentally off-time.

•••

Adolescent Fathers

Adolescent fathers have not received the same degree of attention from researchers as young mothers (Gielen & Roopnarine, 2004). Studies examine personality characteristics, a father's involvement during a girl's pregnancy and after the child's birth, his role in pregnancy resolution decisions, his problems, and social outcomes associated with becoming an adolescent father (Florsheim & Smith, 2005).

Because most adolescent girls who become mothers choose to retain custody of their baby and do not marry, an equal number of adolescent boys and young men are absent or nonresidential fathers. Some adolescent fathers may be uncaring, uninvolved, and immature, but it is not true for all adolescent fathers as some acknowledge their role in the pregnancy. Researchers describe these young fathers as frightened, withdrawn, confused, and feeling guilty about what has happened (Heaven, 2001). Many feel overwhelmed by the girl's pregnancy and may use denial as a defense mechanism to avoid the anxiety associated with their responsibility. The quality of a teen father's relationship with the teen mother of their child prior to their child's birth appears to positively influence their involvement with coparenting following the birth (Florsheim & Smith, 2005).

In many respects, adolescent fathers resemble teenagers who are not fathers, but a number of distinctive characteristics describe their particular situation (Madden-Derdich, Herzog, & Leonard 2002; Saunders, 2002; Xie, Cairns, & Cairns, 2001). For example, more teen fathers are members of minority groups. Teen fathers typically have lower high school grade point averages than teen boys who are not fathers. The relationship with the mother of the child is long term and stable. Most are nonresidential fathers but are involved with their child and the mother. They do not view teen parenthood as a negative life event because this is supported in their communities and families, and they feel that contraception is the responsibility of their female partner.

Adolescent fathers' lack of involvement in pregnancy resolution decisions may partly relate to the lack of clarity in their role as the father. This confusion tends to shape their behavior as parents (Madden-Derdich et al., 2002; Xie et al., 2001). For example, some adolescent mothers rely on the men in their extended family and social networks to act as fathers for their children. Different men may enact the role of the father at various times in a child's life, for example, the mother's current husband, the biological father, or the mother's biological father or stepfather. Once children are born, the majority of the young fathers have contact with their child and the mother. In addition, the extent, nature, and context of the teen father's involvement with his child may be highly dependent on the mother's support and expectations. Furthermore, a teen father's level of stress about parenting an infant appears to be positively mediated when both his parents and those of his child's mother are supportive (Fagan, Bernd, & Whiteman, 2007).

Many fathers of children born to adolescent girls are in their 20s, and the girls perceive them to be authority figures (Alan Guttmacher Institute, 2012). Investigators commonly report that adolescent fathers have been involved in an intimate relationship with their child's mother for a long time and frequently continue to maintain this relationship after the child's birth. Although many young men state that they love the mother, the relationship is often characterized by a lack of commitment and little promise for continuation into the future. One study notes that economic stressors affect almost all of these young fathers (Rozie-Battle, 2003). For these young men, who are usually out of work, joblessness accounts for a diminished role as a father, or becoming an absent father. The grandfather's support may increase the likelihood of a young teen father's involvement with his child (Madden-Derdich et al., 2002). On the positive side, the rate of teen fatherhood has declined in the past decade (Alan Guttmacher Institute, 2012).

The problems that these young men experience by virtue of their socioeconomic status and their educational and lifestyle experiences are poignant. They are essentially no different from the difficulties of many adolescent mothers (Bunting & McAuley, 2004). For example, both teen mothers and fathers typically have problems with the adolescent girl's parents, experience situations that are developmentally off-time, and find that they are ill prepared to be parents (Schweingruber & Kalil, 2000).

The fact that less attention has been paid to the adolescent father by researchers perhaps reflects both legal and social attitudes toward these young men. Although sophisticated laboratory tests are available using DNA, it is costly to prove the paternity of a child. The laws governing the custody and legal rights of out-of-wedlock children traditionally have recognized the rights of the biological mother over those of the father. These laws, which have origins in old English common law, were adapted in the formative years of the United States. They have not been questioned until recently, when fathers became interested in establishing their rights and access to out-of-wedlock children. Recently, cases brought before the U.S. Supreme Court have reversed the biological mothers' traditional rights, clearly outlining the legal rights of anyone who fathers a child out of wedlock. These rights range from custody and visitation to the child's right to an inheritance and support. They also guarantee a father's access to professional services when exercising his parental rights.

The following factors appear to predispose a teenager to becoming an adolescent father:

■ Having parents who assumed this role early in life.
■ Having parents with little formal education.
■ Being educationally disadvantaged.
■ Behaving in a delinquent or deviant manner (e.g., a history of arrest, gang involvement, having spent time in detention, living in a juvenile home, drug use, early sexual activity).
■ Experiencing adverse childhood conditions (e.g., household members who were substance abusers, mentally ill, or criminals).
■ Being of color (Alan Guttmacher Institute, 2012).

While not all teen males who experience these kinds of circumstances become fathers, the combined and interactive pressures put them at high risk.

Researchers have also identified factors which *do not* seem to contribute to the likelihood of teen fatherhood (Anda et al., 2002; Ornelas, 2007; Tan & Quinlivan, 2006):

■ Coming from a home without a biological father or a home that offers less supervision.
■ Having a parent who is experiencing depression.

■ Being exposed to family violence.
■ Having a commitment to school performance.

Some teen fathers make a better-than-expected adjustment to becoming a parent (Florsheim & Ngu, 2006). The young men in this study made a remarkable transformation to becoming committed coparents to their child. In addition, they developed an ability to empathize with their coparenting partner. A variety of social and educational programs have been developed to help teenage fathers address the changes in their lives when they become parents (Parra-Cardona, Wampler, & Sharp, 2006).

• •

Parenting Reflection 13–2

Can the parents of teenage expectant parents be held responsible for this situation?

• •

• •

Focus Point. Researchers have studied adolescent mothers more than adolescent fathers. The adolescent father's parental role is less well defined than that of the adolescent mother, although both parents share some of the same outcomes of pregnancy. Adolescent fathers have certain legal rights as a parent. Most continue to maintain a relationship with the child's mother after the birth of the baby.

• •

THE CONSEQUENCES FOR A CHILD OF AN ADOLESCENT PARENT

Although adolescent mothers may be competent in some aspects of parenting, the child born to an adolescent is at risk in numerous ways. These children are at greater biological, developmental, and psychological risk than those born to an older mother (Federal Interagency Forum on Child and Family Statistics, 2007). Prematurity and low birth weight is more common in adolescent pregnancy. Generally, there is a higher mortality rate among infants born to adolescent mothers than to women who have their first child in early adulthood.

Prematurity and low birth weight are associated with (a) lowered survival rates; (b) circulatory and respiratory difficulties; (c) higher incidence of brain damage, cerebral

palsy, hypoxia, membrane disease, epilepsy, and delayed developmental progress; and (d) prolonged hospitalization, which has severe physical, psychological, social, and economic implications (Levene, Tudehope, & Sinha, 2008). An infant is more likely to be born with physical, mental, and/or developmental challenges if the mother is age 15 or younger and the mother received no prenatal care. These disabilities include developmental delays and other health impairments. Girls age 15 and younger have the highest incidence of babies with low birth weight, resulting in an infant mortality rate that is twice that of babies born to women between ages 20 and 40 (Martin et al., 2006). Several factors account for the high rate of health problems for infants born to teenage mothers: the developmental immaturity of the mothers, their lack of adequate knowledge about the importance of prenatal care, their tendency to seek prenatal care later in the pregnancy, and their poor nutrition during pregnancy.

Researchers report other consequences for infants born to teenage mothers (Lefever, Nicholson, & Noria, 2007; Nicholson & Farris, 2007; Schatz & Lounds, 2007):

■ A tendency toward behavioral problems, especially among boys
■ The likelihood of becoming teen parents themselves, experiencing homelessness, incarceration, and/or juvenile delinquency
■ A tendency to repeat grades in school and to have some type of learning disability
■ A tendency to have developmental delays
■ The likelihood of experiencing disrupted marriages in adulthood
■ Early sexual activity and inconsistent use of contraceptives, increasing the chances of pregnancy
■ Greater likelihood of being abused, neglected, or abandoned

Researchers have also identified protective factors that can influence the adjustment of children born to teen parents, which include developing resiliency, having a father who is involved in their upbringing, having some type of religious affiliation, and having close ties to individuals in their communities (Howard, Carothers, Smith, & Akai, 2007).

• •

Focus Point. Children of adolescent parents also experience certain consequences, many of them negative in nature.

• •

SUPPORTS FOR ADOLESCENT PARENTS

A teenager who becomes a parent receives more support from his or her community today than in the past. Until about 20 years ago, the only type of assistance available was a residential program where an adolescent could live while awaiting the birth of her baby. Today, this type of service may continue to be helpful to some pregnant adolescents, especially those who have left their family or have dropped out of school. Services also target teens with substance abuse problems, those who are abused by their family or boyfriend, and those who have run away from home. In many places, community services have been expanded to include a number of other social and human services programs that address the needs of pregnant teens and those who become parents. Some of these programs also assist in preventing repeat teen pregnancy and parenthood (Akinbami, Cheng, & Kornfeld, 2002).

These programs may address educational needs, interpersonal skills, and/or parenting skill development. Regardless of the type of program, researchers identify those that are successful in achieving their goals as (a) providing individual attention to the participants, and (b) being multicomponent, multiagency, community-wide programs involving parents, schools, and religious groups to reach those teens most in need of services (Stevens-Simon, 2000). Programs that attempt to facilitate change in the lives of families with teenage mothers are also effective in minimizing the deleterious effects of adolescent pregnancy on the quality of life. Essentially, these programs offer long-term benefits to their adolescent participants (Honig & Morin, 2001).

The federal government has provided funding for three model programs that address adolescent sexual activity. These programs advocate abstinence or delayed sexual activity as a means of preventing pregnancy rather than focusing on the use of contraceptives. These include (a) Section 510 of the Social Security Act, (b) the Adolescent Family Life Act's teen pregnancy prevention component, and (c) Community-Based Abstinence Education (Alan Guttmacher Institute, 2012). Research reports that these programs are not as successful in preventing teen pregnancy as had been hoped (Centers for Disease Control and Prevention, 2012i).

Programs that provide counseling, peer education, or services to increase contraceptive use seem to be more effective in preventing adolescent pregnancy than abstinence approaches. Programs that inform teenagers that there is a high risk of contracting sexually transmitted diseases and that pregnancy can ruin their lives appear to be effective (Alan Guttmacher Institute, 2012). In addition, abstinence-only sex education programs appear to influence sexually active teens to delay or neglect the use of contraceptives, which increases their risk of contracting an STD and becoming pregnant (Bruckner & Bearman, 2005). In essence, sex-education programs that address both abstinence and contraceptive use comprehensively have been found to help teens delay becoming sexually active, reduce their numbers of sexual partners, and increase their use of contraceptives when they do become sexually active (Alan Guttmacher Institute, 2012).

Some programs specifically target teenage fathers or boys who potentially could become teen fathers (Brindis, Barenbaum, Sanchez-Flores, McCarter, & Chand, 2005; Kandakai & Smith, 2007; Saleh, Buzi, Weinman, & Smith, 2005). It is likely that programs targeting teenage girls would be more effective if combined with these programs aimed at the young males. Such programs are based on

- Changing males' sexual habits to include the use of condoms, not only to prevent the spread of STDs, but also to reduce pregnancy.
- Requiring males to assume financial responsibility for their children as motivation to avoid future unintended pregnancies.
- Increasing enforcement of statutory rape charges to reduce pregnancies and births.
- Strengthening the role of fathers in all families.
- Teaching teen fathers how to become more involved with their children.

One study suggests that lack of adequate material resources contributes significantly to negative life outcomes for both teen mothers and fathers (Mollborn, 2007). Programs that promote the availability and use of resources such as housing, child care, and financial support appear to facilitate teen parents' educational experiences, especially for teen fathers.

Educational Programming

Many different types of programs have been developed to mainstream pregnant adolescents into public schools or to maintain the public school educational programs of those who are already parents (Hoyt & Broom, 2002). Some programs support the continuation of a teenager's education while providing child development and parenting information that promotes competent caregiving skills (McDonell, Limber, & Conner-Godbey, 2007). The main function of these programs is to lower the high dropout rate observed among teenage girls who become pregnant. Disruption of schooling has long-range, largely negative effects on teen parents and their children. Other programs, such as Even Start, offer child-care services to promote school attendance while also providing students with opportunities to observe infant and child behavior as part of child development and parenting courses (Akinbami et al., 2002).

Many school districts in larger metropolitan areas have established support programs for pregnant teenagers or those who are already parents. These programs address the impending birth and provide instruction in parenting skills, maternal and child nutrition, and health and prenatal care. They also teach the required academic subjects.

Child-care services can provide practical experiences with infants and young children. One experimental program pairs adolescent mothers with older women who serve as mentors, role models, and friends (Waller, Brown, & Whittle, 1999). This apparently helps the young mothers learn parenting skills and acquire child development knowledge, motivates their participation in educational experiences, and results in fewer behavioral problems. Other programs feature peer education approaches and base programs on what teens believe are the best ways to prevent pregnancy, such as being given more access to information on contraceptives (Hacker, Amare, Strunk, & Horst, 2000).

When teenagers participate in such programs, they tend to return to, or stay in, school programs that lead to a high school diploma. Research reports that subsequent births among teen mothers are diminished when they remain in school, live at home with their parents, and are engaged in educational or work activities (Key, Barbosa, & Owens, 2001; Manlove, Mariner, & Papillo, 2000; Stevens-Simon, 2000).

Promoting Parenting Skills and Preventing Future Pregnancies

Participation in special programs can help teenagers who are pregnant or who already have children improve their parenting skills and prevent future unplanned,

unwanted pregnancies (Ammen, 2000; Key et al., 2001). When teenagers have information about sexuality, child development, contraception, and parenting, that knowledge may result in certain outcomes:

■ An increase in the number of teens using birth control
■ A reduction in the number of repeat pregnancies
■ A reduction in the number of child-abuse cases

These programs are as effective with teen fathers as they are with teen mothers. More programs are aimed at meeting the needs of adolescent mothers. These programs may be especially helpful to ethnic minority teens who are at high risk of pregnancy and parenthood (Gilliam, 2007).

One way to assess the effectiveness of teen parenting programs is to measure child outcomes following parental participation (Jaffee, Caspi, et al., 2001). If a program is truly successful, it will help teens parent competently, which will be reflected in a child's cognitive, emotional, intellectual, and physical development.

Many programs include information about child developmental norms and appropriate expectations regarding infant and child behavior. This information improves parenting skills and attempts to prevent abuse by teen parents by instilling appropriate expectations (Stevens-Simon, Nelligan, et al., 2001). Programs give teen parents and expectant teens opportunities to observe infants and young children. They offer lectures about child development and use special learning tools to promote appropriate parental attitudes and expectations.

Some programs are developed specifically to prevent adolescent pregnancy. For example, peer education involves students who train other students about the hazards and negative consequences of teen pregnancy (Akinbami et al., 2001). Small adolescent support groups discuss sexuality and sexual themes to promote responsible sexual decision making. Some programs work specifically with minority groups that are at high risk for adolescent pregnancy and other behavioral problems that interfere with attaining a good quality of life.

Some contend that the dilemma of adolescent parenthood can be most effectively addressed by implementing programs directed at the root of the issue: adequate sex education for teenagers that results in effective contraceptive practices. This is a controversial issue. It is commonly asserted that sex-education programs only stimulate teens' interest in having early sexual experiences that lead to pregnancy. Research has not been able to clearly support this assertion (Alan

Guttmacher Institute, 2012). Despite methodological problems, some evidence suggests that engaging adolescents in effectively using contraception is associated with their participation in sex-education programs. Youths who participate in sex-education programs have been found to delay sexual activity and are able to make more informed choices concerning sexual activity.

Parenting Reflection 13–3

Sex-education programs in junior and senior high schools include information on choices concerning sexual behavior and safer sexual practices. Why don't programs that stress abstinence or delayed sexual activity have a greater impact?

The federal government has been interested in developing programs that help prevent teen pregnancy. The Adolescent Family Life Act of 1981 was passed in an effort to achieve this goal, but with the stipulation that it would advocate abstinence as the most effective means of eliminating teen pregnancy and that certain topics, such as abortion and contraceptive practices, would not be included in the curriculum. The effectiveness of such programs in preventing pregnancy was disappointing (Centers for Disease Control and Prevention, 2012; Perrin & DeJoy, 2003).

A realistic strategy for helping teens avoid pregnancy makes use of a doll that looks, feels, and sounds like a real baby. It can register whether it was cared for adequately. This realistic educational tool is effective in helping adolescent girls and boys have experiences that are similar to those encountered by the parents of a newborn. This method is used in some teen pregnancy-prevention programs. It is likely that such simulation experiences may be more effective than other approaches in allowing teens to experience what it must be like to be a teen mother or father and the implications of early parenting on one's life plans (Barnett & Hurst, 2004; deAnda, 2006; Didion & Gatzke, 2004; Malinowski & Stamler, 2003; Mallery, 2002). One study questions the effectiveness of this approach (Barnett, 2006).

Focus Point. Programs that address the needs of adolescent parents are available in many communities in the United States. These programs offer a number of social and human services that assist adolescent parents and help to prevent future pregnancies. Public school systems provide programs that help teen parents pursue their educational goals. They also offer psychological support and training in parenting skills.

AN ADOLESCENT FATHER'S PERSPECTIVE ON PARENTING

Love is everything in a child's life. I know that being a parent has been the most blessed thing in my entire life. I live where every day is a new day, and my daughter is my life.

In the Parenting class, I became more confident as a parent. I learned the scholarly terminology for concepts and situations I had previously encountered as a parent, but for which I did not have the formal back-up of a theoretical model or of research findings. I learned techniques for parenting situations by relying on best practices as evolved by experts. I realized that there was a whole body of knowledge to help us face parenting challenges. Becoming more skilled as a parent helped me and improved my relationship with my daughter.

The information on parenting in single-parent systems really has driven me to try and overcome the stigmas in today's society. Even before reading the textbook chapters on adolescent and single parents, I was going through a joint custody battle. The stressors that are involved with custody agreements are like none other. Although the custody battle was not caused by divorce, an agreement was necessary to protect my rights as an involved and responsible father. I got a better understanding of what was going on when I added my personal experience to the words in the textbook.

The stigmas of being a single father do not really work in my favor. This has driven me far beyond what I thought I was capable of doing several years ago. Single fathers have assumed more responsibility, and it is a changing world. I did not like what I read in the research papers about single fathers; however, it is up to us as fathers to make that change. Being a single father is one thing, and reading textbook statistics is another. Without strong will and motivation, a single father becomes the self-fulfilling prophecy the research describes. But I will make it my mission to be the exception to the statistics. I want to be the best father I can be, and I am committed to that for life.

Perhaps the most important thing I learned from parenting class was from the article about a mother of a terminally ill son, Ronan. He has Tay-Sachs disease. She says: *"How do you parent without a net, without a future, knowing that you will lose your child, bit by torturous bit?"* (Rapp, 2011). It was very sad, and humbling. Ronan's mom refers to herself as a "dragon" mom because her love is so fierce, in the positive sense. Dragon parents are not embarrassing; they are an inspiration. Dragon parents only know one thing—absolute love. No one can really relate to these parents unless you are a dragon parent yourself. I can only imagine how it must feel to know that you could lose your child at any time and that every day is a blessing in itself. This is how life should be lived regardless of being a dragon parent or not.

"Parenting, I've come to understand, is about loving my child today. Now. In fact, for any parent, anywhere, that's all there is." —

Emily Rapp, mother of Ronan

Reference in Essay

Rapp, Emily (2011). Notes from a Dragon Mom. *New York Times*, October 15, 2011.

Used with permission of the author. P.W., the father who reflected on his experiences in this essay, had a child in late adolescence.

POINTS TO CONSIDER

■ Teenagers continue to become parents, although in recent years there has been a decline in the numbers who carry a pregnancy to term. Four basic factors influence teen pregnancy:
  ■ Increased incidence of sexual activity among adolescents
  ■ Lack of adequate contraceptive knowledge and use
  ■ Social and peer influences
  ■ Personal, family, and community attitudes about teen pregnancy

■ The majority of pregnant adolescents elect to keep their babies following birth. A minority place their infants for adoption. Some choose to get married; although married adolescents are at high risk for divorce within a relatively short period of time.

■ Teen pregnancy has consequences for adolescent mothers and fathers, their child, their families of origin, and society. Most of these consequences are long term in nature and scope. Adolescent mothers may expect interruption or disruption of their education; less than positive implications regarding the health of the mother and the child; the probability of lower economic status caused by low-paying, unsatisfying jobs; large families; and the likelihood of a troubled relationship with the child as a result of poor parenting skills.

■ Adolescent fathers have increasingly become the subject of studies. These young men usually play a less well-defined role in adolescent parenthood. A variety of characteristics distinguish these young men from those within their age range who are not fathers.

■ In many communities, a variety of support programs and services are available to assist adolescent parents. These are designed to help adolescent parents complete their education and learn adequate parenting skills. The programs also aim to prevent pregnancy among adolescents and repeat pregnancy among those who already are parents.

USEFUL WEBSITES

ABCD Parenting Young Adolescents (provides programs in several languages)
http://abcdparenting.org

Adolescent Counseling Services
www.acs-teens.org

Educating Communities for Parenting
http://ecparenting.org

Society for Adolescent Health and Medicine
www.adolescenthealth.org

CHAPTER 14

Family Formation and Parenting in Same-Sex Couples

Learning Outcomes

. . . .

After completing this chapter, readers should be able to

1. Explain how several complex factors interact in determining sexual orientation, and describe how both biology and the environment can play a role.

2. Explain the unique challenges, including legal challenges, that same-sex partners may face in forming families.

3. Discuss the research-based parenting concerns regarding children who are being raised by same-sex parents.

4. Describe some parental concerns if children identify themselves as lesbian, gay, bisexual, or transgender (LGBT).

. . . .

A family is traditionally considered to be the one place where people are nurtured emotionally, being accepted and loved unconditionally. It typically is the shelter within which we can develop our strengths, reveal our weaknesses, and trust those closest to us without wearing masks and pretending to be someone else. Family formation appears to be intertwined with our human condition; as humans, we seek the togetherness of a group of people who are closest and dearest to us. These persons of significance accept and nurture us for who we are, and love us as we are. They accept and respect the total person, which includes one's sexual orientation.

The *climate* of the family appears to be more important than the *structure* of the family in determining the well-being of family members, including the children (Phillips, 2012). Importantly, a summary of more than two decades of research did not reveal significant differences in the adjustment or development of children or adolescents reared by same-sex couples when these groups were compared to the offspring of heterosexual parents (Patterson, 2006). In essence, the outcomes of parent–child relationships are determined by the *quality* of the parenting and the family relationships, which have a stronger influence than the sexual orientation of the parents (Bos, Gartrell, Peyser, & van Balen, 2008; Cohn & Hastings, 2010; Tasker & Patterson, 2007). Patterson (2006, p. 241) sums it up in the following manner: "Results of the research suggest that qualities of family relationships are more tightly linked with child outcomes than is parental sexual orientation." What one would intuitively expect was supported by research (Patterson, 2006; Tasker & Patterson, 2007), namely that the children of parents who had good and close relationships with their children reported child social adjustment in more positive terms. In short, positive outcomes in parent–child relations are strongly influenced by the quality of the parenting.

Legal Matters

"As the legal landscape continues to evolve, some important trends are emerging" (Borelli & Littrell, 2011, p. F4). The trends these authors refer to are in the areas of relationship recognition, adoption, and parental rights. Internationally, 10 countries have legalized same-sex marriages over the past decade. A number of states have enacted legislation sanctioning same-sex marriages, or *marriage equality legislation*. Other states recognize domestic partnerships, which can be legalized with civil unions. In 2004, Massachusetts became the first state to officially sanction marriage equality legislation. (Rathus, Nevid, & Fichner-Rathus, 2011). Several states have ongoing same-sex marriage reforms (Lambda Legal, 2012). By 2011, 29 states had constitutional amendments, and an additional 11 states had statutes in place, barring such marriages (Borelli & Littrell, 2011). Marriage equality as a matter of civil rights has both supporters and opponents. It follows that legal and social policy contexts can vary vastly with the jurisdiction within which they occur (Patterson, 2007; Willetts, 2011). If a union is legally sanctioned as a marriage, it has a ripple effect that also involves aspects pertaining to family formation (Oswald & Kuvalanka, 2008).

Increasingly, persons who identify themselves as lesbian, gay, bisexual, and transgender (LGBT) are

Same-sex parents focus on providing a social support network based on love, intimacy, emotional warmth, interests, and a sense of community.

adopting children, or are finding a path toward parenthood through a number of other avenues (Telingator & Patterson, 2008), including reproductive technologies, ovum and sperm donation, and/or surrogate mothers. In most states, especially in the absence of marriage equality legislation, biological parents in a same-sex relationship usually have parental rights. The legal premise of "in the best interests of the child" is in operation as well. Nevertheless, a great number of states do not grant same-sex couples the opportunity to adopt jointly (Borelli & Littrell, 2011; Willetts, 2011). Difficulties also occur when parents move into a state where same-sex marriages are not legally supported, especially if same-sex couples face a situation that all married couples could potentially face, namely divorce. Following enactment of the Don't Ask, Don't Tell Repeal Act of 2010, with regard to armed services personnel, persons who identify themselves as gay or lesbian can be truthful about their sexual identity. Many religious groups have inclusive policies and welcome all persons into their places of worship.

In some areas, active discrimination has been legally disputed and overruled as unconstitutional (Borelli & Littrell, 2011). Historically, it is important to note that in 1973 the American Psychiatric Association declassified homosexuality as a mental disorder. By implication, no label based on a disease model or a normative value in terms of normality/abnormality could or should be attached to homosexuality. Increasingly, persons identifying themselves as LGBT request the same constitutional rights and privileges that others have as members of a diverse society. Same-sex couples express legal concerns in different ways: *before*, *with*, and *against* the law. These positions translate as challenging the law, using the law strategically, and intentionally resisting the law (Oswald & Kuvalanka, 2008). With same-sex couples, the challenges of family formation (for instance, adoption and coparenting situations) may necessitate some ingenuity. Parenthood in same-sex unions is changing traditionally held beliefs concerning family formation (Stacey, 2006).

Historically, homosexuality has always been recognized as an aspect of human nature and sexuality (Rathus et al., 2011). In cultures with a strong Judeo-Christian heritage, homosexuality was labeled most negatively; homophobia, an irrational fear, dislike, or disgust regarding homosexuality and homosexuals, and heterosexism, the belief that heterosexuality is superior

Photograph part of the "Living in Limbo" exhibition displayed at the Birmingham Civil Rights Institute in Alabama. Used with permission of the photographer, Carolyn Sherer (2012).

and preferable to homosexuality, had a strong presence (Herek, 1993). Ignorance, intolerance, and fearfulness can underlie negative feelings and behaviors (Bos et al., 2008). With increasing respect for diversity in its many expressions, including sexual orientation, cultural competence and understanding are displayed.

THE DETERMINANTS OF SEXUAL ORIENTATION

The majority of current research on sexual orientation seems to focus on several specific areas, including genetic influences; variations in brain structure; the role of prenatal hormones on the developing fetus during critical prenatal developmental stages; maternal variables; and individual variables, including life experiences. Despite ongoing investigations, there remains no simple answer to the etiology of sexual orientation. Several complex interacting genetic, hormonal, and other biological factors seem to underlie sexual orientation, and later environmental factors can add subtle layers to this complexity.

Biological Perspectives

Brain Structure and Genes. With the use of modern brain-imaging techniques, as well as through postmortem studies, the brains of persons who are homosexual have been examined to determine whether there are any significant identifiers in terms of structure. Carter (2010) addresses research findings concerning brain structure. She refers to the early studies by Simon LeVay (1991) that compare the structure of the nucleus in the hypothalamus of the brain. LeVay found that there are structural differences in the nucleus of men who are gay versus men who are heterosexual. Other researchers have found similar differences in the structure of the human brain in individuals who identify themselves as gay versus heterosexual. For example, lesbian women and heterosexual men have been observed to have slightly larger right brain hemispheres compared with gay men and heterosexual women. Some authors report that gay men and lesbians are more likely to be left-handed or ambidextrous than heterosexual men and women (Lalumiere, Blanchard, & Zucker, 2000).

Since handedness is inborn and dictated by an individual's dominant hemisphere, these findings led Simon LeVay to postulate the possibility of prenatal determination of sexual orientation (LeVay, 1991). A later study by Hamer in 1993 suggested that there could be a genetic link (Hamer, Hu, Magnuson, Hu, & Pattatucci, 1993). Hamer and his colleagues observed that male homosexuality within a family pedigree seemed to be more closely related to inheritance through the maternal line. Chromosomal linkage studies suggested that a particular gene on the X chromosome (Xq28) may be responsible for the inheritance of homosexuality. Mustanski et al. (2005) later performed a broader investigation into possible genes related to homosexuality and found new target genes, this time on autosomal chromosomes (those inherited equally from both parents as opposed to the sex chromosomes, which are inherited from either the mother or the father).

Epigenetics (the effects of the environment on gene expression) likely also contributes to the genetics of homosexuality. For example, exposure to estrogen in fetal and early postnatal life in certain critical windows turns on and off various genes that are important in sexual differentiation and the development of adult sexual behaviors in both males and females. The sensitivity of the estrogen receptor to estrogen plays a dominant role because all fetuses are exposed to maternal estrogens (Auger & Auger, 2011). Although the understanding of the role of genetics in determining sexual orientation is incomplete, some contribution, at least in some individuals, is highly likely.

Hormonal Influences and Genes. Research has thus far failed to conclusively prove the link between sexual orientation in either sex and exposure to sex hormones (testosterone and estrogen). The presence of these hormones in adulthood may be linked to the intensity of sexual desire, but they have not been found to be connected to sexual orientation (Rathus et al., 2011). Exposure to varying concentrations of sex hormones *prenatally*, particularly during certain critical windows, however, may contribute to gender identity and/or sexual orientation.

Human sexual development begins in the first trimester of pregnancy. The genetic sex (usually **XX** or **XY**) determines whether the bipotential gonads will become testes (in the presence of the SRY gene found on the Y chromosome) or ovaries (in the absence of the SRY gene). The differentiated gonads begin to produce hormones in utero at about 7 weeks of gestation. Until differentiation of the external genitalia occurs, the genitalia of all fetuses are identical and are referred to as *bipotential*, meaning that the same tissues have the ability to differentiate into either male or female genitalia. Additionally, the rudimentary structures that will become the internal organs for both males and females are present in all fetuses, with one set typically regressing after biologic sex (determined by the production of hormones) is established. The testes of male fetuses produce dihydrotestosterone and the undifferentiated *genital tubercle* enlarges and becomes a male phallus. In the absence of dihydrotestosterone, the same tissue that becomes a phallus in males becomes a clitoris in females (Migeon, 2003).

Current research is focused on understanding whether the human brain may have an analogous window of differentiation into male and female, leading to gender identity and ultimately perhaps to sexual orientation. One model used to understand the possible role of androgen exposure in the developing brain is that of an enzyme disorder that affects the production of sex hormones in utero, called congenital adrenal hyperplasia (CAH). In the most common form of CAH, 21 hydroxylase deficiency, the fetal adrenal gland overproduces androgen hormones, which are similar in action to, and include, testosterone. The 21 hydroxylase deficiency is one of the medical conditions that is labeled as a disorder of sex development (DSD) wherein genetic sex (XX female or XY male); the sex of rearing (a decision based on whether an individual would be most successful as a male or a female, using a combination of factors, including, but not limited, to the appearance of the external genitalia); and gender identity (whether an XX or XY individual identifies with being male or female) may not agree.

Female fetuses with 21 hydroxylase deficiency CAH are exposed to testosterone in utero, an exposure that would typically only occur for male fetuses. This causes not only virilization of their external genitalia (some appear as typical males and would be identified as boys at birth), but also creates early prenatal exposure for the developing female brain to testosterone. Postnatal exposure to testosterone continues until the condition is detected and treated. Most individuals with CAH are identified and treated as infants because CAH is screened for by the newborn screening program in almost all states.

Researchers have studied the effects of various forms of DSD on self-reported degrees of femininity and masculinity. Girls affected by 21 hydroxylase deficiency CAH reported more masculine behaviors with respect to toy preference, playmate preference, play activities, and styles compared to their sisters as young children and adolescents (Long, Wisniewski, & Migeon, 2004). By adulthood, the women in this group identified as being female, with similar masculinity scores to their sisters, although the women affected by the most severe form of 21 hydroxylase deficiency (and therefore exposed to the highest amount of androgen hormones in utero) remained slightly less feminine than their adult sisters. This finding suggests that although prenatal androgen exposure affects psychological masculinity in girls, there remains a societal influence that may play an important role in adult gender identity, at least in this group. Another group of individuals affected by XY DSD was similarly polled about perceived femininity and masculinity (Pappas, Wisniewski, and Migeon, 2008). XY DSD refers to a group of XY individuals who are genetically male, but for various reasons are exposed to less testosterone than would be typical. Some produce less testosterone, and some have androgen insensitivity, meaning that they produce, but cannot

respond normally to, testosterone. Some of the individuals in this study were raised as males and some as females. Those raised as males tended to report higher masculinity scores as adults compared to those raised as females, who reported higher femininity scores as adults. This adds support to the notion that socialization and learning contribute to gender role and gender identity. Despite the decreasing masculinity of girls with 21 hydroxylase deficiency over time, however, Zucker et al. (1996) still documented an increased likelihood of homosexuality in these girls. Conflicting reports about the masculinity and femininity of those affected by DSD, their sexual orientation, and their happiness in their assigned gender roles exist.

The following hypothetical question illustrates the complexity of the situation: If an XX genetically female individual with male external genitalia, who was raised as a male (but is only reproductively capable as a female), chooses a female sexual partner, is this person heterosexual or homosexual? Even for an expert, this is such a complex topic that there is no clear-cut answer.

Another model for understanding the role of prenatal exposure to hormones in the developing brain comes from the observation that males who are gay have a greater than average number of older brothers and can be expected to be of later birth order (Blanchard, Zuckey, Bradley, & Hume, 1995; Bogaert, 2003). Various theories have tried to explain this phenomenon. The most plausible explanation may be that mothers develop an immune reaction to the testosterone being produced by their male fetuses during pregnancy. This type of immune reaction is known to occur when mothers have babies of a differing blood type with respect to the Rh factor. Sensitization to the Rh factor can be so severe that it can lead to loss of the fetus in subsequent pregnancies. If a similar immune reaction to testosterone occurs, then the maternal immune response could serve to reduce the amount of circulating testosterone and therefore reduce testosterone exposure for the developing fetal brain. If the severity of this response increases with the number of male fetuses carried by a pregnant woman, then males later in the birth order would be exposed to progressively less testosterone during the critical fetal window, and this may lead to less masculine behaviors in adults and may also potentially alter sexual orientation.

An intriguing new area of research is in the area of the so-called endocrine disrupters, which are chemicals in the environment (such as the estrogenic compound bisphenol A found in hard plastic food containers) that may alter the usual course of pre- and postnatal hormone exposure. Bisphenol A so far has not been linked to changes in sexual orientation (Farabollini, Porrini, Seta, Bianchi, & Dessì-Fulgheri, 2002), but concern has been raised that exposure may affect the normal development of male genitalia and decrease sperm count, thus affecting fertility (Salian, Doshi, & Vanage, 2011). With increasing interest in this area as it relates not only to sexual development and fertility, but also to other aspects of human health, new information and understanding are expected to evolve rapidly. The National Institute of Environmental Health Sciences, under the auspices of the National Institutes of Health, has created a study section that is dedicated to this research (www.niehs.nih.gov/health/topics/agents/endocrine/index.cfm).

Many groups have tried to understand the delicate balance of the influence of genetics, sex hormones, and socialization on gender identity and sexual orientation. Without a complete understanding, the classic nature versus nurture debate continues, although both biology and the environment appear to play a role. It is important to note that most homosexuals and those who experience gender dysphoria (a feeling that they are living as the wrong gender) do not have any identifiable disorder, such as DSD. The etiology of gender identity and sexual orientation is clearly complex, with multifactorial influences that include some contribution from genetics, epigenetics, exposure to prenatal and postnatal sex hormones, other environmental factors, and individual variables, including life experiences. This is a cutting-edge research area; although we expect further findings to clarify aspects of sexual orientation, at this point, we have many leads but the picture is neither clear nor conclusive.

Psychological Perspectives

Historically, and from a more *psychological* angle, the *psychoanalytic* view, based on the work of Sigmund Freud, suggests that family influences, in particular, play a significant role. This approach proposed that male homosexual orientation occurred because an individual had an extremely dominant mother and a relatively submissive, emotionally distant, or absent father (Bieber, 1962). Other approaches proposed that sexual orientation

is *learned behavior* among males and females, which suggests that individuals can willfully choose, as well as change, their sexual orientation. Considerable, yet erroneous, popular support persists for the latter view that environmental factors are the sole cause of a homosexual orientation. There is no conclusive scientific support for such an opinion. Although learning is an important facet of adolescent and adult sexual behavior, learning theorists have not been able to conclusively point to a link between learned experiences and adult sexual orientation (Rathus et al., 2011).Evidence continues to grow in support of the position that people are born with a particular sexual orientation, which is manifested after reaching puberty (McKnight, 2000), and that numerous factors interact to present in this very complex scenario.

Queer Theory. The word *queer* has been used in previous decades in colloquial language to refer to homosexuals. It was especially used in British English, while its use in American speech is often viewed as derogatory, simple, or overly artsy. The word has regained attention because a very popular television show, which focused on home and personal makeovers, used this word in its title (Rathus et al., 2011), and the team doing the makeovers were proudly gay. The word has slipped back into mainstream use through reference to *Queer Theory*, and by referring to lesbian, gay, bisexual, transgender, and queer (LGBTQ), as well as to lesbian, gay, bisexual, and queer (LGBQ).

Queer theory, which started circulating in the early 1990s, tries to normalize the connotation of the concept of homosexuality by stating that it is not an opposite or another variant of heterosexuality. Queer theory is a critique, among other things, of *heteronormativity*. In other words, heterosexuality should not be the central point of reference (Berkowitz, 2009). This would be similar to ethnocentrism, where one's own culture (often the dominant culture) is used as the norm as well as the reference point. An ethnocentric view implies that one sees the world through a limited and very personal perspective; everything can be colored by this worldview. Putting this same type of thinking into the context of queer theory would mean that the world is generally viewed through heterosexual lenses, as it were, and heterosexuality then becomes the mainstream point of reference. Similarly, the historic marginalization of persons with disabilities resembles the marginalization of homosexuality (Sherry, 2004). It is proposed that the dichotomies of hetero- and homosexuality are deconstructed to allow more flexible and universal constructs that bypass restricting connotations (Berkowitz, 2009; Sherry, 2004).

Queer theory states that the approach whereby a categorization is made between hetero- and homosexuality should be challenged (Rathus et al., 2011) because they are social constructs. Queer theory acknowledges a continuum in sexual identification and expression, implying that sexuality is more varied than denoted by one label, and one can claim a Q *identity* (Russell & Licona, 2011).

INCIDENCE

A large number of family systems in the United States today include a child who identifies him or herself as LGBT. From historical sex research by Alfred Kinsey more than half a century ago, as well as from more recent research, it is estimated that individuals with exclusively homosexual orientation make up 7 to 12 percent of the male population and 5 to 7 percent of the female population (Kinsey, Pomeroy, & Martin, 1948; Kinsey, Pomeroy, Martin, & Gebhard, 1953; Strong, 2004). Assuming that these individuals come from average-size families of about four persons, the potential number of persons with a homosexual relative or close friend is nearly a third of the population of the United States. In addition, about 25 percent of the gay and lesbian population of the United States are biological parents of children from heterosexual relationships. There may be upwards of 10 million children in the United States who have a gay or lesbian parent.

There is no clear estimate of the number of families who know they have a member who identifies as LGBT because not all have disclosed their orientation to family members. This secrecy occurs for several reasons, including fear of rejection. Nonetheless, those who make their orientation known cause change in the identity of their family of origin as family members adapt and emotionally readjust to the greater sexual diversity within their own family. Those parents who are fully integrated and have strong support groups may be able to disclose their sexual orientation more easily and without fear of discrimination. This carries over into the relationships with their children where disclosure and openness may be adjusted to the level of acceptance and support within their communities (Telingator & Patterson, 2008).

FAMILY SYSTEMS WITH LGBT CHILDREN

It is common for parents to develop and acquire a variety of expectations about themselves and their children. These expectations shape parenting behavior and may serve as self-fulfilling prophesies for those involved in a family subsystem. Generally, these expectations are positive and reflect wishes, hopes, and dreams for parents, as well as for children. Most parents do not include an expectation that any of their children will reveal an LGBT identity or orientation upon reaching puberty. When it is revealed by a child that he or she does identify as LGBT, the revelation usually creates a crisis for the entire family system (M. M. Lee & Lee, 2006).

One of the most difficult, yet authentic, acts performed by a person who is gay or lesbian is disclosing this information and identity to others, especially family members. This process is known as *coming out*. For persons who identify as LGBT, the significance of the disclosure lies in presenting themselves to others as a whole, integrated person with a positive self-concept. They share this act of intimacy in the hope that the disclosure will result in honest acceptance and unconditional love.

It can add an added challenge for some youth who are LGBT to develop healthy, positive self-esteem growing up in a heterosexual family because they may be struggling to find their own sexual identity, while fearing rejection if they disclose their true sexual orientation (Connolly, 2005). If they keep their sexual orientation secret, they deny their basic identity. Clearly then, it would help to promote good self-esteem and other interpersonal strengths if acceptance can be found within the close and trusted family circle, as well as in the wider societal network.

Parenting Reflection 14–1

What would you do and say if your best friend shared the news with you that one of his or her siblings is gay or lesbian?

Family systems theory predicts that when one family member experiences change in some manner, all other members of the system are also affected to some degree. A child's disclosure of his or her sexual orientation is unlikely to be part of the vision that most parents hold for their child or for themselves as parents (Singer, 2001). Family disruption initially relates to members' difficulties in reconciling their negative attitudes, beliefs, and myths about homosexuality with what they know about the particular family member (D'Augelli, 2005; Rust, 2003). These beliefs and stereotypes may govern initial reactions of family members, but in a society more accustomed and accepting of diversity, the positive overrides. Family members and friends like to maintain the positive image they already have about the child as an individual and as a family member.

Disclosure as a Family Crisis

A child's disclosure of his or her sexual orientation acts as a stressor event for the family system, which most likely produces a crisis reaction. Family systems react in predictable ways to any significant change or crisis event that may be external to the system or internal among members (Savin-Williams, 2001; Savin-Williams & Dube, 1998). According to Hansen and Hill's (1964) ABCX model of family crisis management (see Figure 14–1), family systems demonstrate common ways of reacting when challenged by a significant stressor event. Families confront many stressor events and changes throughout the life span, such as an adult's job loss, moving, the chronic illness of one member, divorce, marriage, and even births. This model proposes that when A (a stressor event) interacts with B (the family's use of resources and their ability to cope with the stressor) and with C (the family's definition of the stressor event), then X (a family crisis) will occur. The family system's

reaction to the stressor event is a response or process based on these complex interactions (Smith, Hamon, Ingoldsby, & Miller, 2009).

Family coping strategies, B, differ in reaction to stressor events. These strategies include withdrawing from interactions with people outside of the system, discussing the situation only among the adults, denying that there is a problem, using anger and other negative emotions, and seeking assistance from others outside of the system. These coping strategies may or may not be immediately set into motion after a child's disclosure concerning sexual orientation. Factors that collectively represent the system's and its members' interpretations, C, may temporarily override the other means that the family eventually employs to resolve the crisis of disclosure.

According to the ABCX model, a family system's interpretation of the stressor event influences the system's reactions. The model predicts that when members perceive they are the cause of the problem, the family system as a whole suffers. The group is hampered in its ability to function in healthy, effective ways (S. R. Smith et al., 2009).

Some families interpret the revelation of a child's sexual orientation in serious terms. For example, some parents typically assume personal guilt for their child's homosexuality, believing they have done something wrong in their child rearing. They mistakenly believe that they have somehow performed poorly as parents and are failures. Parents also report feeling sad, fearful for their child, shocked, depressed, and hurt following their child's disclosure (LaSala, 2000a; Mosher, 2001). It is more typical of siblings to react with anger and confusion rather than guilt. They may experience feelings of alienation toward the homosexual sibling, who

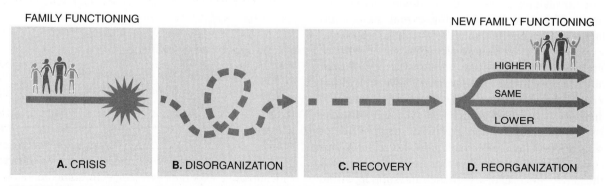

FAMILY FUNCTIONING　　　　　　　　　　　　　　　　　　　　　**NEW FAMILY FUNCTIONING**

HIGHER

SAME

LOWER

A. CRISIS　　　　　　**B.** DISORGANIZATION　　　　　　**C.** RECOVERY　　　　　　**D.** REORGANIZATION

FIGURE 14–1. **Phases in Family Functioning.** The exploding star can depict the crisis (X) in the ABCX model.

now seems to be a stranger rather than someone well known (Merighi & Grimes, 2000). Interestingly, a child identifying as LGBT often comes out to family members incrementally, reflecting the degree of emotional closeness that he or she feels toward specific family members. For example, the child may tell the mother first, then the siblings, and finally the father.

Observers also note other efforts as the system attempts to interpret the disclosure (Merighi & Grimes, 2000). Family members who are heterosexual frequently attempt to understand the child who is LGBT in relation to their family values concerning sexual orientation. It helps in the acceptance process to get to know persons who are open about their sexual orientation and to form good relationships with them, which reveals the diversity in sexual identity from a positive angle (Bigner & Wetchler, 2012).

In addition, sexual orientation is a private part of a person's identity, and an LGBT identity or acknowledgment is achieved late in the developmental sequence, usually in adolescence and early adulthood. Family members have had many opportunities to come to know the person without the benefit of this private knowledge about sexual orientation, which the person may choose to disclose or family members may discover accidentally. Even if parents have suspicions about a child's sexual orientation, the revelation of an LGBT sexual orientation constitutes a crisis for most parents and family systems. They may have previously assumed that the person is heterosexual like themselves. *Cognitive dissonance* may become evident as heterosexual family members try to reconcile negative family values about homosexuality with positive family values about the family member. They may have to go through phases of grief in order to reach a point where the child is accepted as the total person that he or she is.

Another aspect relates to the interpretation and definition a family system makes and ascribes to the homosexual child after disclosure. The members may negate the child's family role as brother, son, daughter, sister, or cousin. The *Gestalt*, or the bigger integrated picture, is revised. Essentially, the family recognizes that the homosexual identity and orientation is now public to the family. This recognition raises questions about intimacy and what else the family may not know about the child. It also challenges them to readjust the family system to keep the child within the safe and supportive realm of the family connections, and to offer their support during a time that must be a difficult transition for the disclosing child as well.

Several factors predict the nature and strength of a family's determination to constructively deal with a child's disclosure:

■ The more a family system subscribes to traditional, conservative teachings about homosexuality, the more negative the reactions to, and interpretations of, a child's disclosure.
■ If family members promote traditional, rigid conservative beliefs about gender roles, then these individuals generally react negatively to any person of LGBT orientation, whether or not the person is external or internal to the family system (Savin-Williams, 2001).
■ The rules that govern the functioning of a family system can influence the likelihood of negative reactions to disclosure (R. J. Green, 2002). For example, some family rules relate to maintaining an image or reputation in the community.
■ The age and gender of family members can influence reactions in positive or negative ways. Generally, the younger children and much older adults in a family system may be more accepting and react more favorably to the disclosure than others. Members of the same sex as the homosexual child can occasionally react more negatively than members of the opposite sex.

In keeping with the prediction made by the ABCX model, the degree to which a family system interprets a stressor as disruptive becomes a self-fulfilling prophecy. After taking stock of family values related to LGBT and combining them with interpretations and meanings given to the child's disclosure of their sexual orientation, the system often concludes that the family is experiencing a crisis caused by the revelation. If persons perceive a child's revelation as severe, their adjustments to new perceptions of the child are more difficult.

When a family system determines that the disclosure constitutes a family crisis, the system moves into a **phase of disorganization** in family functioning. Families typically resist the changes that accompany the stressor event that they interpret as a crisis because the ultimate goal of the system is to maintain the established **homeostasis**, or balance. A child's disclosure of sexual orientation temporarily disrupts the patterns of interaction and communication and the roles of all family members. They may try to keep the disclosure a secret from others outside the immediate or extended family.

Essentially, the reactions of family members can disrupt the stability of the family system, and disorder or chaos can result.

The disorganization phase begins to be resolved as a family system moves into a *recovery phase*. Members make an effort to reach solutions that are appropriate to their particular style of functioning. Depending on the particular family system, as members attempt to *reestablish homeostasis*, the resolutions reached in adjusting to an LGBT member may be healthy or unhealthy. A *healthy* family system moves toward *positive adaptation* in response to the child's disclosure. This tends to promote and enhance effective functioning of the family system. Such a family usually seeks assistance, which results in growth, change, innovation, and *adaptation* in structure and patterns (M. M. Lee & Lee, 2006; Planck, 2006). They recognize that family secrets are unhealthy and disruptive. Members may realize that an individual's sexual orientation is not a matter of personal choice. They may accept that a person's only choice is to be honest and to act authentically about his or her sexual orientation. Many family members, in seeking to understand a child who identifies as LGBT, acquire accurate information by educating themselves about homosexuality in appropriate ways and from reliable sources (R. J. Green, 2002; Savin-Williams, 2001). For example, they may seek out the services of a psychotherapist or counselor who has expertise in LGBT and read a variety of books on the topic. They may attend support groups devoted to helping families understand homosexual members, such as Parents, Family and Friends of Lesbians and Gays (PFLAG; see M. M. Lee & Lee, 2006). These efforts facilitate a family system's ability to create a climate of acceptance and tolerance for the LGBT child. The system's health is promoted by its understanding that *differences are appropriate* among members.

Some family systems fail to resolve the crisis in ways that are healthy and promote effective family functioning. Instead, a hostile, ambivalent family atmosphere, especially as it relates to the child who is gay or lesbian, becomes the normative family style to restore homeostasis to the system (LaSala, 2000b). Such attempts promote even greater disorganization in the system, which prevents effective functioning.

In some instances, a child who identifies as LGBT may feel forced to withdraw his or her participation in the family system due to the negative, unaccepting reactions of members. In more extreme situations, a family system's unhealthy resolution may contribute to the homosexual child's likelihood of developing serious depression. This depression can lead to suicide, which may account for the high suicide rate among adolescents who have difficulty accepting their homosexual orientation (M. Sullivan & Wodarski, 2002; van Wormer & McKinney, 2003). This distressing trend is counteracted by high-profile individuals publicly acknowledging their homosexual orientation and actively contributing to the understanding and acceptance of sexual diversity.

Those systems which resolve the crisis in healthy ways may reach levels in recovery that are similar to or greater than what existed before the crisis. These families turn the crisis into learning experiences that can result in personal growth and appreciation for all family members.

Parents, in their role as caregivers, must find constructive ways to express their need to give unconditional love, nurture, and visible support to a child who identifies as LGBT. Parents most likely need to express their grief about any losses that they may be experiencing, for example, no longer being potential grandparents, no longer having a child who is conventionally similar to other children in the family, no longer anticipating marriages and relationships that are sanctioned and recognized by the community, and no longer being like other parents of children who are heterosexual. Parents must allow the grieving and mourning processes to proceed in order to heal the feelings of loss. By doing so, they facilitate the healing of their family system and the reconstruction of a role definition for their child as an accepted, loved, and respected family member.

FAMILY FORMATION IN SAME-SEX COUPLES

Parenting forms the core of family life for most American adults. Regardless of sexual orientation, it can be a very rewarding aspect of adulthood (Patterson & Farr, 2011). Persons with a diverse sexual orientation (LGBT) participate in family forms that are very similar to those typically found in our society (Biblarz & Savci, 2010; Goldberg & Smith, 2009). As applied to family life, same-sex couples have reinvented the notion of what it means to be a family, how this family functions, and who participates in the family (Herek, 2006). These families are referred to as *families of choice* and represent a form of kinship formation (Riggle, Whitman, Olson, Rostosky, & Strong, 2008).

Membership, roles, and rules governing this type of family structure are custom designed according to mutually agreed-upon conditions. As such, families of choice are formed by a conscious decision about who constitutes the family, how it is defined, and what it means to each participant. Many persons who identify as LGBT do not feel the need to conform to family structure based on consanguinity or legally sanctioned marriage. They focus instead on providing a social support network based on compatibility, love, intimacy, emotional warmth, interest, and a sense of community. According to societal norms, these elements compose the *essence of family life*. When children are involved, it is difficult to distinguish families with same-sex parents from stepfamilies where the parents are heterosexual, except concerning the same-sex composition of the adults who act as parents (Biblarz & Savci, 2010; Herek, 2006; Patterson, 2006). Indeed, the parenting challenges and skills of same-sex couples are similar to those of heterosexual couples (Goldberg & Smith, 2009). In brief, "… regardless of gender, sexual orientation, and route to parenthood, new parents experience similar, positive changes in perceived [parenting] skills …" (Goldberg & Smith, 2009, p. 861).

The beginning of LGBT kinship formation takes place when an individual initiates what is known as the coming-out process. This multifaceted process occurs in stages and is perhaps never completed (Green, 2002). Persons who identify as LGBT develop a personal identity based on their sexual orientation, similar to that experienced by individuals who are heterosexual. Part of this identity is the desire to become emotionally close to another person, just as heterosexuals wish for closeness (Gottman et al., 2003). Same-sex couples participate in loving, committed relationships that often endure for long periods of time and resemble those found among heterosexuals. Some distinct differences are found in same-sex committed relationships. Primarily, their committed relationships strongly emphasize *egalitarian* functions because they are not forced to adopt and maintain the traditional gender-role models typically found among heterosexuals that emphasize differences in social power in the relationship (Gottman et al., 2003; Kurdek, 2003).

Like other families, those formed by persons who identify as LGBT bring strengths, as well as challenges, to family members (Biblarz & Savci, 2010; Goldberg & Smith, 2009; Lev, 2004). By expanding the very idea of

Photograph part of the "Living in Limbo" exhibition displayed at the Birmingham Civil Rights Institute in Alabama. Used with permission of the photographer, Carolyn Sherer (2012).

a family that transcends traditional limitations, same-sex couples demonstrate how to deal with societal challenges in healthy ways.

Parent–Child Relations in Same-Sex Couples

Not all parents are heterosexual; some are gay or lesbian. Their families are not significantly different from other family systems, although unique challenges are particular to their situations (Biblarz & Savci, 2010; Goldberg & Smith, 2009). The experiences of fathers who are gay are similar to those of mothers who are lesbian. Each type of family system faces unique challenges. Homosexuality per se does not prevent or hinder someone from being an effective parent. Research strongly confirms that it is the *quality* of the parent–child relationship that determines success (Bos et al., 2008; Farr, Forsell, & Patterson, 2010). Additionally, the *resilience* of the children is promoted with constructive parenting techniques, and the stability of the family provides a protective factor (Bos et al., 2008; Cohn & Hastings, 2010; Van Gelderen, Gartrell, Bos, & Hermanns, 2009). Regardless of sexual orientation, the difficulties in parent–child relations usually find their origins within the realms of psychological and/or psychiatric difficulties (Farr et al., 2010), the many societal and economic constraints that put families at *high risk*, and the various stressors that influence *fragile* families.

Because we are transitioning into greater acceptance and understanding of homosexuality, many people are reconciling their ideas concerning parenthood for adults who are gay or lesbian (V. Clarke, 2002; Tasker, 2002). The following discussion examines the issues related to parenthood in same-sex couples and how their sexual orientation affects their children.

Fathers. The father who is gay is a newly emergent figure in homosexual culture, and researchers have relatively little information about these men in comparison with fathers who are heterosexual. Males who are gay and are fathers have a unique and complex psychosocial environment. Their challenges of adjustment relate to identity issues, acceptance of self, acceptance by other men who are gay, and matters related specifically to parenting and child custody issues (Bigner, 1996). Other concerns focus on the development of a long-term, committed relationship with another man who is gay, who accepts and copes with children as a central issue of the relationship.

The man who is both a father and a homosexual is an enigma in our society. *Father* implies heterosexuality, while *gay* is associated with homosexuality. The problem lies in determining how both terms may be applied simultaneously to a person with a same-sex orientation who is also a parent. Researchers estimate that about 20 to 25 percent of self-identified men who are gay are also fathers (Bigner, 1999). This group clearly constitutes a minority within a minority in our culture. It is impossible to estimate accurately the number of men who are gay and who are also parents, because many are married to women or remain *closeted*, having not disclosed their sexual orientation for other reasons.

Some of the more historic research on the topic maintained that the process of *identity development* for a father who is gay required a reconciliation of perceptions. Because each identity, homosexual and heterosexual, is perceived with caution by the other group, the task of integrating both identities into a cognitive concept of the *father who is gay* can be challenging. This process is referred to as *integrative sanctioning* (Bozett,

1987; Bozett & Sussman, 1989). It involves the man's disclosure of his gay orientation and identity to non-gays and his father identity to gays, thus forming close liaisons with persons who tolerate or accept both identities simultaneously. It also involves distancing himself from those who are intolerant.

Fatherhood and Men Who Are Gay. The reasons why a man who is gay becomes a parent are not fully known (Bigner, 1996, 2006; Patterson, 2000). One might speculate that a man might not be able to accept his homosexual orientation; therefore, he marries a woman and fathers children as a means of denying his true sexual orientation. Later, he divorces his spouse to pursue his identity as a man who is gay. An estimated 20 percent of men who are gay marry women at some point, and approximately 2 million families are affected by the upheavals resulting from *mixed-orientation marriages* (Hernandez, Schwenke, & Wilson, 2011).

Alternatively, an increasing number of men who are gay are choosing parenthood because, like their heterosexual counterparts, they sincerely desire to have their own children for many reasons (Berkowitz, 2007). Men who are gay may not always be able to fulfill their desire to become a parent, and will then be *childless by circumstances* (Patterson & Riskind, 2010). A man who is openly gay may willfully choose to become a father as part of a liaison established between him and a woman who is lesbian because they both desire to become parents. Under these arrangements, a pregnancy is usually initiated via artificial insemination, although surrogacy is also an option (Green & Mitchell, 2007). Some men who are gay enter into marriage with a woman who is heterosexual, with both partners knowing the man's sexual orientation in advance. Other marriages involve *bisexual* men, and many of these marriages continue intact for years.

The large majority of fathers who are gay, until recently, were involved in heterosexual relationships in which children were produced (Bigner, 2006). Hernandez et al. (2011) state that mixed-orientation marriages face greater challenges than heterosexual marriages, and ultimately about half end up in divorce court. Some tried open relationships and others stayed together platonically for the sake of family commitments, but even then doubted that the relationships would last. Women stated that they did not feel they could seek support from family or friends because of the implied stigma, and this added to the stress (Hernandez et al., 2011).

Among men who identified themselves as gay in the 2002 National Survey of Family Growth, one in six men said that they had biological offspring (Gates, 2011). Having entered heterosexual relationships, often in denial about their actual sexual orientation or in trying to conform to societal pressures (Pearcey, 2005), many of these men eventually come to terms with their homosexual orientation and find it impossible to live a heterosexual lifestyle that is inauthentic, unfulfilling, and dishonest (L. M. Peterson, Butts, & Deville, 2000). These men frequently gain the courage to disclose their homosexual orientation to their wives, perhaps in conjunction with the midlife transition that ordinarily prompts much personal self-evaluation and reorientation of life goals (G. Sullivan & Reynolds, 2003). Their wives usually experience upsetting, disruptive reactions to the disclosure (Buxton, 2004, 2005, 2006; Grever & Bowman, 2008). Few of these marriages remain intact following the man's disclosure. The men usually want to pursue the development of their homosexual identity, and the women do not wish to continue an involvement with a man who is not heterosexual and who they feel has deceived them. Some marriages survive this crisis because one or both partners feel a strong commitment to children or because a divorce would lower the standard of living for the individual and/or the family.

The adjustment of men who divorce and pursue a homosexual lifestyle is difficult as the man acquires a new identity as a father who is gay (Benson, Silverstein, & Auerbach, 2005; Schacher, Auerbach, & Silverstein, 2005). These men enter the gay subculture at some disadvantage because they come out at later ages than other men who are gay. They usually seek to replicate the kind of relationships they experienced or desired in their heterosexual marriages. Because they are not like most other men who are gay, these fathers can experience discrimination and rejection from other gays who are not fathers. Many fathers who are gay are successful in forging a partnership with another man who is gay, based on long-term commitment, emotional and sexual exclusivity, and economic cooperation.

Little is known about the nature of these relationships or about the gay blended family system that may emerge from its formation (Lynch, 2000; Lynch & McMahon-Klosterman, 2006). It appears that the satisfaction of all persons involved in a gay blended family is improved when efforts are made to include the stepfather

who is gay (Current-Juretschko & Bigner, 2005). This is similar to what is found in heterosexual blended families as a means of improving the overall success of the family system.

Children of Fathers Who Are Gay.   It has been estimated that about 20 percent of gay men enter into a marriage with a heterosexual woman at some point in their adulthood, frequently leading to parenthood (Hernandez et al., 2011). There is no hard empirical evidence proving that the homosexual orientation of fathers or other caregivers is detrimental to children's welfare (Bigner, 1996, 1999; Herek, 2006; Lev, 2004; Patterson, 2006; Stacey & Biblarz, 2001; Tasker & Patterson, 2007). Furthermore, children of same-sex parents do not differ significantly from children of heterosexual parents on key psychosocial developmental outcomes (Goldberg & Smith, 2009; Tasker, 2005; Tasker & Patterson, 2007). In fact, fathers who are gay are as effective as fathers who are heterosexual in their ability to parent children and provide care.

Fathers who are gay are believed to be nurturing with children and less traditional in perceiving the provider role as a prime aspect of their parenting role. They have positive relationships with children and try hard to create stable home lives for them (Riggle et al., 2008).

These findings may be explained in the following ways:

■ Fathers who are gay may feel additional pressure to be proficient in their parenting roles because (a) they may feel guilty about the difficulties that divorce and disclosure create for their children, and (b) they are sensitive to the fact that their parenting behavior is being scrutinized by ex-wives and others, and they may fear that custody or visitation rights will be challenged because of their sexual orientation.

■ Fathers who are gay may be more gender equal than fathers who are heterosexual in their approach to parenting children. Their child-rearing styles may incorporate a greater degree of expressiveness and nurturing behaviors (Bigner, 1996; Riggle et al., 2008).

A common concern expressed in court proceedings, which determines the custody of children with a father who is gay, is that the children will also develop a homosexual orientation. The consensus of research is that although the causes of sexual orientation are complex, sexual orientation does not seem to be transmitted from parents with a particular orientation to the children they raise (Patterson, 2006; Strong, 2004; Tasker & Patterson, 2007). The parents of most homosexuals are heterosexual. The same patterns found in the general population concerning the incidence of homosexual orientation, appear to be replicated among sons of gay fathers (J. M. Bailey, Willerman, & Parks, 1991). More than 90 percent of adult sons of fathers who are gay reportedly have a heterosexual orientation. This data strongly suggests that the sons of fathers who are gay do not adopt the homosexual orientation by modeling their fathers, nor does living with a father who is gay appear to contribute in a substantial way to the sexual orientation developed by sons.

Gender-Equal Behavior

Perhaps one of the advantages that fathers who are gay offer to children of both sexes is the modeling of gender-equal behavior (Bigner, 1996, 1999, 2000; Riggle et al., 2008) and their acceptance of gender nonconformity (Kane, 2006). On the other hand, these couples may not function in a manner that is as genderless as is often believed (Biblarz & Savci, 2010).

Historically, the work of Bem (1975) identified *androgyny* as the ideal gender role. Androgynous individuals manifest characteristics associated with both genders regardless of their biological sex. Researchers have identified advantages to having such a gender role and identity. Gender-equal attitudes are perceived more positively (Hunter & Forden, 2002; Riggle et al., 2008). Adult males who are gender equal are described as having highly developed egos, showing greater flexibility in considering options to solving problems, and having a greater and deeper respect for individual differences in others. These individuals are also described as having an accepting attitude about sexual behavior, sexual

---

| Focus On 14–1 | Issues Related to Children of Fathers Who Are Gay |

The Father's Disclosure of Homosexual Orientation

■ Fathers who are gay have a more difficult time disclosing their homosexual orientation to children than do mothers who are lesbian. This difficulty may be especially pronounced among African American men.

■ Fathers who are gay describe their children's reactions to disclosure as "none" or "tolerant and accepting."

■ The age of the children at the time of disclosure may affect their reaction. Those who have not experienced puberty may be more accepting than those who have done so.

■ Children may have some difficulty relating to peers who are aware of the father's homosexual orientation, but the children apparently cope successfully with these problems, with little harm to their self-esteem.

Parenting Skills and Effectiveness

■ No empirical or descriptive evidence proves that having, being raised by, or living with a gay father is detrimental to the development of children.

■ Most fathers who are gay have positive relationships with their children. Fathers who are gay make serious attempts to create stable home lives and positive relationships with their children.

■ Fathers who are gay are similar to fathers who are heterosexual in their degree of involvement and intimacy with their children.

■ Fathers who are gay tend to be nontraditional, and more responsive to children's needs and provide more explanations for rules than fathers who are heterosexual.

■ Sexual orientation is not a factor in determining the quality of parenting behavior and relationships.

Sources: Based on Bigner, J. J. (2000). Gay and lesbian families. In W. C. Nichols, M. A. Pace-Nichols, D. S. Becvar, & Y. A. Napier (Eds.), *Handbook of Family Development and Intervention* (pp. 279–298). New York: Wiley; Committee on Psychosocial Aspects of Child and Family Health. (2002). Coparent or second-parent adoption by same-sex parents. *Pediatrics,*(109), 339–340; Patterson, C. J. (2000). Family relationships of lesbians and gay men. *Journal of Marriage and Family* (62), 1052–1069.

relationships, and interpersonal relationships with others in general.

Fathers who are gay can generally be expected to incorporate greater degrees of gender-equal behavior and identification than fathers who are heterosexual (Bigner, 1996, 1999, 2000; Riggle et al., 2008). Fathers who are gay can combine both *emotional expressiveness* and *goal instrumental behaviors* in their behavioral repertoire; children can learn to adopt these gender-equal behaviors as well and adopt gender-equal language. Research does indicate that clear and appropriate gender roles are expressed, while still incorporating gender equality as a value (Biblarz & Savci, 2010). The notion of genderless family situations should not be turned into a stereotype. The data strongly indicate that the sexual orientation of children, and that of sons in particular, is not transmitted by being parented by a father who is gay.

The benefits offered by fathers who are gay to their children relate to their ability to expand their interpretations of what it means to be a father beyond the limited traditional meanings of this family role (Bigner, 2000; Patterson & Farr, 2011; Tasker & Patterson, 2007). The benefits to children are likely to become even more apparent upon reaching adulthood, when their relationships with others can be expected to be based on equality rather than on who holds the most social and physical power (Riggle et al., 2008). Researchers have found that couples in which one person or both are gender equal (a) have higher levels of relationship satisfaction (Wharton, 2004), (b) divide decision making equally, (c) de-emphasize the use of power by either partner in the relationship, and (d) have greater long-term life satisfaction that extends far into the years of late adulthood than couples who have a traditional or undifferentiated gender-role orientation. This information provides even greater credibility to the consistent research findings that children experience no harmful influence on their developmental progress by being raised by, or living with, a father who is gay.

This is not to say that children of mothers and fathers who are homosexual do not have adjustment issues that relate to their parents' sexual orientation. Like children coming from other minority ethnic group families, these children face unique challenges. Adjustments are often facilitated by both parents (the father who is gay and the mother who is heterosexual) being committed to

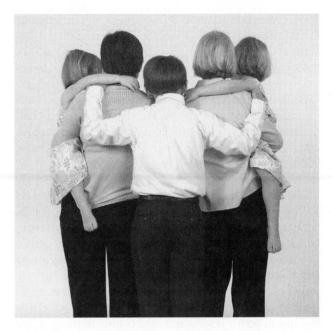

Photograph part of the "Living in Limbo" exhibition displayed at the Birmingham Civil Rights Institute in Alabama. Used with permission of the photographer, Carolyn Sherer (2012).

providing high-quality parent–child relations and supervision (Gottlieb, 2003; Snow, 2004). Children of parents who are gay or lesbian are assisted by the adults to learn to cope positively with bullying from peers (V. Clarke, Kitzinger, & Potter, 2004; Peplau & Beals, 2004). With greater tolerance of diversity and greater awareness of the dangers of bullying, this problem should decrease noticeably as adult role models encourage desirable attitudes and competencies.

Mothers Who Are Lesbian.   The parenting experiences of mothers who are lesbian are generally similar to those of fathers who are gay; but researchers observe some differences in family dynamics (R. Brown & Perlesz, 2007; V. Clarke, 2007; Mooney-Somers & Golombok, 2000; F. Nelson, 2007). Women who are lesbian differ from men who are gay in the ways in which they become involved as parents. For example, although many women acknowledge their homosexual orientation after being married to a man and having children, other lesbians use artificial insemination as a means of achieving parenthood (Green & Mitchell,

2007; Hermann-Green & Gehring, 2007; Stevens, Perry, Burston, Golombok, & Golding, 2003; Vanfraussen, Ponjaet-Kristoffersen, & Brewaeys, 2003). Adoption may also occur more frequently among women who are lesbian than among men who are gay (McClellan, 2001).

Couples who are lesbian face legal and social challenges when they use artificial insemination to conceive children within a committed relationship (Goldberg, 2006; McClellan, 2001). The laws of most states commonly recognize the biological mother's legal custody of the child, which leaves the nonbiological or social mother with no legal parental rights unless she legally adopts the child conceived by her partner (Patterson & Farr, 2011). Many states do not permit the names of two women to appear on a child's birth certificate or allow adoption by a nonbiological mother. The custody rights of fathers are relatively unclear in these situations as well, even if the identity of the father who was the sperm donor is known. Legal testing of these rights continues in various court cases that will set precedents for the future. Generally speaking, if the father is known to the lesbian-led family, it is possible to create legal documents that spell out the legal rights and responsibilities of the father, for example, regarding custody and visitation.

For many couples who are lesbian, parenthood via insemination is a well-planned, deliberate, and complex life decision. They address topics such as who the biological mother will be and how to choose a donor (known or anonymous; Chabot & Ames, 2004; Goldberg, 2006; Green & Mitchell, 2007). Children are greatly valued and desired; such motivation to attain parenthood may be a positive prerequisite for successful parenting outcomes.

Family Dynamics in Same-Sex Couples. Families formed by same-sex couples share common qualities with heterosexual blended families (Goldberg & Smith, 2009; Lynch, 2000; Lynch & McMahon-Klosterman, 2006). This is particularly the case with mothers who are lesbian, who more frequently have custody of children produced in a former heterosexual marriage (Hall & Kitson, 2000; Lorah, 2002). Among self-identified lesbians in the 2002 National Survey of Family Growth, one third of lesbians said they had biological children (Gates, 2011). The findings of the 2008 General Survey suggest

that 49 percent of lesbian, as well as bisexual women, say that they have biological offspring (Gates, 2011). Other similarities may involve relationship issues in the new blended family. The partner of the lesbian biological mother (the children's stepparent, coparent, or social parent) is rejected by the stepchildren, the stepchildren and stepparent compete for the attention and affection of the biological mother, and conflicts erupt over territoriality in the home.

Distinct differences within same-sex family systems headed by lesbians distinguish them from other family forms (Lev, 2004; Tasker, 2002; Tasker & Patterson, 2007). Four unique characteristics describe same-sex family systems headed by lesbians because their parental roles are more active than those of fathers who are gay (Bennett, 2003; Ciano-Boyce & Shelley-Sireci, 2002; Dundas & Kaufman, 2000; S. M. Johnson & O'Connor, 2001; J. M. Thompson, 2002):

- They experience a lack of legitimacy because they are not recognized as a family unit by their community. This presents unique problems, such as in dealings with school systems.
- These families must address their unique status, such as by more frequent confrontation with the stigmas associated with homosexuality. Fathers who are gay and who do not have full-time child custody do not usually experience these challenges. Parents often instruct children to keep the adults' sexual orientation a secret from others outside the family. Same-sex parents who are lesbian may isolate themselves and their children from other families. The pressure of maintaining family secrets is unhealthy to the effective functioning of the family. These mothers may fear losing custody of their children, which makes this possibility a continual threat to the well-being of the same-sex couple who is lesbian (Siegenthaler & Bigner, 2000). Children may not be allowed to invite friends home to play because the parents fear exposure.
- These families can experience strained relationships with ex-spouses and other relatives. The negative feelings of ex-spouses may be compounded during postdivorce interactions because of the mother's fear of losing custody of the children. But despite all of these problems, the children of mothers who are lesbian are well adjusted, and families typically find

creative and healthy ways for responding to the crises they experience.

■ The division of labor and parental roles take on unique assignments and situations. Each family must decide what each mother will be called, for example. Each family will need to determine if one mother or the other will be designated as the primary caregiver.

Same-sex couples base the structure of their committed relationship on the gender-equal principle of *equality of partners* (Gottman et al., 2003; Riggle et al., 2008). This differs considerably from the structure typically found among heterosexual couples that use gender to determine who does what tasks in the relationship. Families with children that are headed by lesbians report sharing household responsibilities, but the biological mother can be expected to be more involved in child care, while the nonbiological mother reports working longer hours at her job. Children are found to be better adjusted when both mothers divide the child-care responsibilities equally (Bennett, 2003; Ciano-Boyce & Shelley-Sireci, 2002).

Children of Mothers Who Are Lesbian.   The issues related to children of mothers who are lesbian do not differ significantly from those related to children of fathers who are gay (Tasker & Patterson, 2007). The main differences are that children of lesbians live in a different type of family system and have different kinds of parenting experiences (Lev, 2004). No differences in general adjustment, gender-role identity, or cognitive or behavioral functioning are consistently reported in studies comparing children of lesbian and nonlesbian mothers (Bos et al., 2007; Golombok et al., 2003; Patterson, 2006; Riggle et al., 2008; Tasker, 2002, 2005; Vanfraussen et al., 2003). Children, who display some behavioral issues add to the stress of their parents; this occurs regardless of the sexual orientation of the parents (Farr et al., 2010).

Four principal issues are relevant to children of mothers who are lesbians (Chrisp, 2001; S. M. Johnson & O'Connor, 2001; S. Kershaw, 2000; McClellan, 2001; Paechter, 2000; Stevens et al., 2003; Tasker & Patterson, 2007; Vanfraussen, Ponjaert-Kristoffersen, & Brewaeys, 2002, 2003): (a) dealing with the parent's disclosure of her sexual orientation, (b) dealing with the uniqueness of having lesbian parents and the effect on the parent–child relationship, (c) coping with custody concerns, and (d) dealing with the reactions of others.

Like the children of fathers who are gay, those growing up in same-sex family systems headed by women face the challenges of coping with parental divorce and the fact that their parents are different from other parents. Sons are more accepting than daughters when their mother establishes a lesbian partnership. Researchers generally find that the more accepting and relaxed the mother is about her sexuality, the more accepting the child will be. Another unique situation is the matter of whether and how to inform children who are conceived by artificial insemination by donor. Many children of mothers who are lesbian become aware of the uniqueness of their particular families in early childhood and begin to ask questions about the father. Most children react positively if this disclosure is appropriately managed.

The self-esteem of children whose mothers are divorced and lesbian appears to be no different from that of children of mothers who are divorced and heterosexual. Children from both groups experience problems that relate more directly to the effects of parental divorce than to the mother's sexual orientation.

Child custody is a central concern of mothers who come out. Many children of mothers who are lesbian wish to remain in their care and establish stable family relationships. This relates directly to custody and parental rights, which are matters that can threaten the continuation of a meaningful parent–child relationship in a family system that is headed by same-sex parents.

Because same-sex parental systems exist in a social environment that provides little support, many mothers who are lesbian turn to their children for implicit approval of their sexual orientation. At the same time, mothers do not want their children to feel different from other children (Bos et al., 2008). This is an especially troublesome problem for adolescents. When working through this concern in a therapeutic manner, children in families with same-sex parents learn that the child should not necessarily be expected to accept the parent's sexual orientation completely. It is important that the child respects the parents' lifestyle and the ways in which it is expressed. Some children need assistance in working through the love–hate feelings they have for their mother, precipitated by her sexual orientation, and the guilt that accompanies these feelings (Johnson & O'Connor, 2001).

Parenting Reflection 14–2

Suppose you are an attorney who is representing a parent who is gay or lesbian in a custody hearing. What evidence would you present to demonstrate the ability of this parent to raise a child in a developmentally appropriate manner?

Mixed-Orientation Marriage. Diversity in family forms is surfacing (Segal-Engelchin, Erera, & Cwikel, 2005). In a mixed-orientation marriage, sometimes referred to as a *heterogay* relationship, one of the spouses or partners identifies him or herself as heterosexual, while the other spouse or partner may be lesbian or gay (Hernandez et al., 2011). They conceive and raise children together and their sexualities may be expressed in ways that suit the individual needs of each partner. They may or may not share a common physical residence. If the couple is not legally married, this family type represents a variation of a *nonmarital family*. Part of the complexity of the situation revolves around how each partner wishes to express him or herself within the marriage and the qualities they seek from a marital union. Partners may seek a biological parent for their children who will also help them coparent. Because these families appear to be like heterosexual families to outsiders, they capture the characteristics of both traditional and nontraditional families. Researchers indicate that the children of these families appear to benefit from their family structure; they have a stable and predictable family environment with a father who is involved in their upbringing and shares in their financial support, and have generally positive psychosocial and developmental functioning (Hernandez et al., 2011).

Focus Points

- Some family systems include a member who is LGBT. A child's disclosure of his or her LGBT orientation frequently acts as a stressor event that disrupts family system functioning. Some parents and family members are influenced by the social stigma associated with homosexuality. The ABCX model facilitates an understanding of a family system's reaction to the disclosure of a child's homosexuality.
- Family members may negate the child's former family role as the system attempts to reconstruct a new role definition for the child that includes the child's sexual orientation. Healthy families resolve their conflicts about a child's LGBT orientation. They can educate themselves, participate in therapy and support groups. Family functioning can resume the levels of adaptation that they had prior to the disclosure. The family can also become more efficient. Unhealthy families fail to resolve these conflicts, which perpetuate the disruption in the family system.
- Not all parents are heterosexual; some are gay or lesbian. Their families are not significantly different from other family systems, although unique challenges can occur. The experiences of fathers who are gay are similar to those of mothers who are lesbian. Each type of family system faces unique challenges. Homosexuality per se does not prevent or hinder someone from being an effective parent. Research supports that these families can create a healthy environment that supports developmentally appropriate parent–child relations.

FAMILY SNAPSHOT

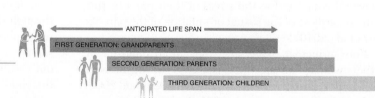

Our intergenerational family snapshot is taken from a family system that is about to experience a crisis resulting from the disclosure of a child's homosexual orientation. The grandparents are the first generation. The second generation includes the adult parents, Todd and Helen Jonas; the third generation includes their children: Donna, age 24; Ann, age 22; and Sam, age 18. This snapshot is taken at a time when the middle generation is focusing on two developmental stressors:

■ Dealing with their own midlife transition experiences.
■ Launching their children into adulthood.

The oldest daughter, Donna, has been grappling with sexual orientation issues since junior high school and has just disclosed to her parents that she is lesbian. Donna understands that coming out is a continual, life-long process that requires patience, empathy, and understanding on everyone's part. She is thankful to have a family where she knows she is loved and accepted. She looks confidently toward her future. We focus predominantly on the developmental challenges of the second generation (parents of Donna) and the third generation (Donna).

Developmental Challenges

First Generation (Grandparents)

■ Dealing with their granddaughter's coming out.
■ Accepting the sexual orientation of their grandchild.

Second Generation (Adult Parents)

■ Dealing with their own midlife transition experiences.
■ Dealing with their daughter's coming out.

■ Accepting the sexual orientation of their child.
■ Maintaining good relationships with the adult child and her partner.
■ Accepting their daughter's partner into their social support system.
■ Accepting the identity of the same-sex couple.
■ Dealing with changes in their own hopes for grandchildren.
■ Accepting the life path of the daughter and adjusting their expectations.
■ Dealing with their own sense of guilt concerning their role as parents.
■ Continuing their acceptance and love of their adult children.

Third Generation (Adult Child)

■ Coming out.
■ Dealing with the reactions of her family concerning the disclosure of her sexual identity.
■ Maintaining relationships with parents and siblings.
■ Forming a social support system.
■ Supporting her family and her partner in strengthening the relationships with each other.
■ Forming an identity as a same-sex couple.
■ Dealing with the possibility of family formation.

POINTS TO CONSIDER

■ Some family systems in the United States include a member who is LGBT. A child's disclosure of his or her sexual orientation or gender identity to parents and family members frequently serves as a stressor event for the family system. The ABCX model facilitates an understanding of family members' reactions to this crisis event. Many parents and family members are influenced by images of and beliefs about same-sex couples that color their initial reactions to a child's disclosure. The sources that a family uses to cope with the disclosure should support a positive transition toward acceptance of diversity in sexual orientation or gender identity.

■ Family systems may interpret the disclosure by reacting in ways that are healthy or unhealthy. Family values concerning diverse sexual orientation have to be merged with family members' positive knowledge of the child. Healthy families resolve their conflicts about having a child who identifies as LGBT by educating themselves about the topic. They may seek therapy for themselves, the child, and/or the family system to learn how to adjust constructively to the crisis. They may participate in support groups. In this way, families learn to extend unconditional love and acceptance as a new family role is created for the child with an LGBT orientation.

■ Same-sex couples become parents for several reasons. Research generally finds that these persons act effectively as parents and that children are positively supported by living with and being raised by same-sex parents. Many families headed by same-sex couples experience problems and circumstances that are similar to those encountered by single-parent family and stepfamily systems headed by a heterosexual person.

USEFUL WEBSITES

Family Equality Council
www.familyequality.org

Human Rights Campaign: Working for Lesbian, Gay, Bisexual, and Transgender Equal Rights
www.hrc.org

Lambda Legal
www.lambdalegal.org

National Center for Lesbian Rights
www.nclrights.org

National Gay and Lesbian Taskforce
www.thetaskforce.org

Parents, Families and Friends of Lesbians and Gays (PFLAG)
http://community.pflag.org

CHAPTER 15

Parent–Child Relations in High-Risk Families

Learning Outcomes

Abusive Parents and Their Children

After completing this chapter, readers should be able to

1. Name the major issues related to abusive parents and child neglect.

2. Describe the characteristics of abusive parents and their children, and explain the major consequences of abuse for children.

3. Describe intervention strategies that help parents control their abusive behavior and provide support for children.

Families Affected by Parents with Addictive Disorders

After completing this chapter, readers should be able to

1. Describe the effects observed in a family and its members when one or both adults are affected by substance use and addictive disorders.

2. Explain the factors that interact to place a family system at high risk. Reference the contexts that contribute to fragile families.

Families are frequently represented as happy groups of people committed to nurturing, sustaining, and supporting each other. This is the romanticized version that we prefer to hear about. The darker side reveals unpleasant and destructive realities.

An effective parenting outcome presumes a parental system that is healthy, resilient, and able to meet the requirements demanded by the parenthood role. Many families in the United States experience problems and situations that affect their ability to function in healthy ways. Effective parenting in these families is difficult to achieve because several factors counteract this optimal goal.

Fragile Families

In *fragile families*, the family system cannot withstand the numerous assaults on its well-being and may become dysfunctional or disintegrate. In this context, fragile means "liable to break." In extreme cases, the family becomes a dangerous place for children. Typically, several risk factors interact to escalate the detrimental effects on the family. One risk factor leads to another. Some of the factors that increase the fragility of families are

- Poverty and all of the factors linked to limited resources, economic or otherwise.
- Limited education, dropping out of school, and underserved schools.
- Unwed parenthood, lack of commitment to the family, and absent fathers.
- Lack of knowledge concerning child care and parenting.
- Lack of vocational skills, low-income jobs, and difficulty finding and retaining employment.
- Poor conditions in the family of origin and no role models for a healthy family life.
- Chronic illness, disability, depression, and children with behavioral problems.
- Mental illness, frequently untreated or noncompliant patients who stop treatment.
- Use of illicit substances and addictive disorders, alcoholism, and prescription drug abuse.
- Social isolation, lack of support systems, and dependence on welfare.
- Lack of integration into a social or civic community, for example, a social, religious, or other group that supports family values.

Based on The Research Forum at the National Center for Children in Poverty. (2012). *Fragile Families and Child Wellbeing Study*. Columbia University: Joseph L. Mailman School of Public Health.

Families can be considered as *high risk* or *fragile* because of economic, health, psychological, or social factors. These singly, or in combination, challenge effective functioning. Many families find they can cope by seeking help from professionals, social networks, relatives, and other sources. They learn to use healthy means for dealing with difficult circumstances. Other families fail to respond to such challenges in healthy ways, and their status becomes even more endangered. While every family can expect to experience crises, each family reacts in different ways to resolve critical situations.

These challenges are significant and have detrimental effects on parent–child relations. No family system is perfect, but many face problems that threaten the ability to function effectively and actually verge toward destruction and illegal behavior.

We will examine two groups of families. First, we will address families in which one or both parents abuse their children physically, sexually, and/or emotionally. Abusive parents present a clear risk to their children, and the effects of such treatment can have lasting, even life-threatening, effects on children. When abuse occurs, one or both parents create an unhealthy family environment that damages all of the members. Such behavior frequently leads to dissolution of the family via divorce, and parental rights may be terminated. Second, we discuss the effects of dependency and addictive disorders on an adult parent and how this affects the parent–child relationship. This condition has short- and long-range effects on the entire family system.

ABUSIVE PARENTS AND THEIR CHILDREN

Only within the intimacy of family systems do some people feel free to harm each other in physical, sexual, emotional, or other inappropriate ways. For some, the family system is a battleground where atrocities occur with all-too-frequent regularity (Brandt, 2002; Gelles, Loseke, & Cavanaugh, 2004).

Early explanations of family functioning recognized conflict as inevitable in human relations. This was thought to occur because individuals and social agencies tend to promote personal interests and needs over the welfare of the group. One of the primary tenets of the Freudian theory of personality development stresses the dual nature of human relations in which

Intergenerational transmission of abusive behavior is learned when children observe their own parents engaging in abusive behavior. This form of violence in their family of origin serves as a model for later aggressive behavior.

opposite emotions, such as love and hate, can be held simultaneously in relation to a love object. Recent research on family violence illustrates a renewal of interest in learning more about this unsavory aspect of family life (Wallace, 2007; Winkler, 2004).

Definitions and the Prevalence of Family Violence

Since the late 1960s, several cultural and social factors have promoted an interest in studying violence in families (Gelles et al., 2004). The women's movement has played a major role in focusing public attention on the issue of violence toward women and children, especially wife battering, marital rape, and incest. Researchers have demonstrated that valid research can be conducted on these sensitive issues, although they pose many methodological challenges (J. Miller & Knudsen, 2006; Miller-Perrin, Perrin, & Barnett, 2004).

Child Maltreatment or Abuse is defined as "behavior that causes significant harm to a child. It also includes when someone knowingly fails to prevent serious harm to a child" (Child-to-Child Trust, 2009). The World Health Organization (2011) states that child maltreatment or abuse constitutes "all forms of physical and/or emotional ill-treatment, sexual abuse, neglect, or negligent treatment or commercial or other exploitation, resulting in actual or potential harm to the child's health, survival, development or dignity in the context of a relationship of responsibility, trust or power." The World Health Organization considers **maltreatment** to be synonymous with **abuse**.

These definitions delineate four areas of cruelty to children:

■ *"Physical abuse:*   hurting, injuring, inflicting pain, smothering, drowning, poisoning
■ *Sexual abuse:*   direct or indirect sexual exploitation, coercion, or corruption by involving children in inappropriate sexual activities
■ *Emotional abuse:*   repeatedly rejecting, humiliating, and denying their worth and rights as human beings
■ *Neglect:*   the persistent lack of appropriate care of children, including love, stimulations, safety, nourishment, warmth, education and medical attention" (World Health Organization, 2012).

Note too that a child can be abused in more than one area simultaneously.

"Discrimination, harassment and **bullying** are also abusive and can harm a child, both physically and emotionally" (Child-to-Child Trust, 2009).

Neglect refers to acts of parental negligence, such as failing to supervise children or properly provide for their nutritional needs. While this is a basic premise of abuse, *maltreatment* of children and adolescents is the term increasingly used, which includes those acts that define abuse and neglect, as well as radical parental acts, such as excessive punishment, child abandonment, infanticide, murder of children, and abandonment of a child's corpse.

Violence is a rather broad concept that includes acts of force against family members, which often fall

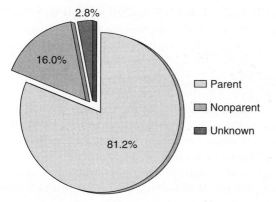

FIGURE 15–1. Perpetrators by relationship to victims, 2010.

under the guise of discipline and parental control of children. The term also relates to illegitimate acts of violence, occurring as part of a family conflict. Some dysfunctional families regard hitting as acceptable behavior and they consider spanking a child a necessary parental practice. Of particular concern is that the incidence of abuse is higher among children with disabilities (P. M. Sullivan & Knutson, 2000). The vulnerability of these children seems to bring out qualities of parental outrage, despair, and burnout.

A Canadian review of 37 studies on child abuse and neglect found that a child was likely to be removed from the home and placed into foster care if there was evidence of harm to the child, if the living quarters were unsafe, if there were older children involved, and if the parents were found to be negligent or incapable of parenting appropriately (Tonmyr, Quimet, & Ugnat, 2012).

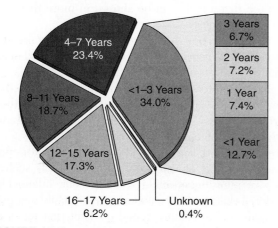

FIGURE 15–2. Victims by age, 2010.

Family or domestic violence represents any "abusive, violent, coercive, forceful, or threatening act or word inflicted by one member of a family or household on another" (National Center for Victims of Crime, 2008). Some definitions include *dating violence* as well. Examples of such acts include spanking, shoving, hitting, slapping, pinching, shooting, cutting, or pulling, as well as acts that cause psychological harm.

Violence in families can be directed at both children and adults, and perpetrators are typically parents or adolescent children. Child abuse and neglect have received a great deal of attention from both researchers and the media. Even though there is a wide range of abusive acts, a general categorization of physical and psychological abuse has emerged. This especially pertains to those acts that constitute child abuse and maltreatment.

Models of Family Violence

Seven basic theoretical models focus on reasons why parents and children act violently toward each other (Garbarino, Hammond, Mercy, & Yung, 2004; Gelles et al., 2004; Straus & Gelles, 2006; Wallace, 2007):

1. The **psychiatric model** assumes that abusive individuals in a family system are deviant or mentally and/or emotionally ill. This model isolates the personality characteristics of the offender as the primary cause of the abusive behavior. It attempts to link personality patterns or traits with the tendency to perform abusive acts and with other behavior patterns, such as borderline personality disorder, alcoholism, substance abuse, and mental illness.

2. The **ecological model** examines the child and the family from a systems theory perspective. It explores the child's development within the family system and the functioning of the family system within its community. For example, when the community supports parental use of physical force against children but does not provide support for families under stress, the likelihood of family violence increases. From this viewpoint, abuse is a family problem that affects everyone, and the entire family must receive treatment in order to promote healthier outcomes.

3. The **sociological model** stresses that social values and attitudes about violence shape violent behavior in family systems. From a cultural point of view, the

<table>
<tr><td>Focus On
15–1</td><td>Facts About Child Abuse and Neglect</td></tr>
</table>

Focus On 15–1

Facts About Child Abuse and Neglect

- More than 3 million reports of child maltreatment are received by state and local agencies in the United States each year. That is nearly six reports every minute, although not all are substantiated.
- An estimated 740,000 victims of child abuse or neglect are treated in hospital emergency rooms in the United States each year. Of course, not all victims receive medical care as needed.
- In 2008, 772,000 children were found to be victims of maltreatment by child protective services.
- Seventy-eight percent of child victims experienced neglect. Almost 17 percent were physically abused; fewer than 10 percent were sexually abused.
- Children from birth to age 1 had the highest rates of victimization at 20 per 1,000 children. Girls were slightly more likely to be victims than boys.
- About 1 in 50 infants in the United States are neglected or abused; nearly one third of these are newborns.
- Caucasian (44.8%), African American (21.9%), and Hispanic (21.4%) children had the highest rates of victimization.
- Child fatalities are the most tragic consequence of maltreatment. In 2008, an estimated 1,740 children died from abuse or neglect.
- Three quarters (79.4%) of children who were killed as a result of abuse were younger than 4 years old.
- Infant boys (birth to age 1) had the highest rate of fatalities.
- Of child fatalities, 32.6 percent were exclusively attributed to neglect. Physical abuse and sexual abuse were major contributors to fatalities.
- More than 40 percent of child fatalities were caused by multiple types of maltreatment.
- Of the perpetrators, 80 percent were the biological parents. Female perpetrators, mostly mothers, outnumbered men.
- Of all parents who were perpetrators, fewer than 8 percent inflicted sexual abuse.
- More than one half of all reports of child abuse and neglect were made by professionals such as medical personnel, teachers, police, attorneys, and social services staff. The remainder was reported by neighbors, friends, or relatives.

Based on Centers for Disease Control and Prevention. (2012f). Violence prevention (www.cdc.gov/ViolencePrevention/childmaltreatment/); Children's Bureau. (2012). *Child Maltreatment 2010*. Washington, DC: Author; U.S. Department of Health and Human Services, Administration for Children, Youth, and Families. (2008). *Child Maltreatment 2006*. Washington, DC: Author.

use of physical force, particularly against children, may be a sanctioned aspect of parenting behavior in certain subgroups or contexts. Violence is a means of settling disputes and conflicts with others. The model also emphasizes that adults' violent behavior toward children is a reaction to stress and frustration. The influences of these stimuli are closely related to the social status of the family system. Persons from lower social classes are thought to experience greater environmental stress and express their reactions through violent behavior that is often directed at children and other family members. Another tenet of this approach emphasizes that

family structure and organization lend their influence to violent behavior. Crowded living conditions, high levels of unemployment, strained financial resources, and social isolation from other families place additional stress on the parent–child microenvironment, which can trigger abusive behavior. Additionally, stressful living conditions, being an adolescent parent, or living in a stepfamily situation may increase the occurrence of this behavior.

4. The **social psychological model** covers a variety of approaches that explain violence among family members. Interaction patterns, the transmission of violent behavior from one generation to the next, and

Focus On 15–2

Classifications of Child Abuse and Neglect

- *Physical abuse:* Infliction of any type of injury on a child, such as burns, bites, cuts, and welts
- *Sexual abuse:* Forcing, tricking, or coercing sexual behavior between a young person and an older person, with an age difference of at least 5 years between the perpetrator and the victim, includes fondling body parts, penetration of the child's body by an object or the offender's sexual organ, and noncontact behaviors such as voyeurism or pornography
- *Physical neglect:* Failure to provide a child with an adequate and nurturing home environment, including the basic necessities of food, clothing, shelter, and supervision
- *Medical neglect:* Failure to provide a child with medical treatment when physical conditions necessitate such care and when withholding care could be life threatening to the child
- *Emotional abuse:* Speech, actions, and interactions that tend to destroy emotional well-being and a sense of self-worth, and hamper healthy personal and social development
- *Emotional neglect:* Failure to show concern for a child and his or her activities
- *Abandonment:* Failure to make provisions for the continual supervision of a child
- *Multiple maltreatments:* A combination of several types of abuse or neglectful acts

Based on Gelles, R. J., Loseke, D. R., & Cavanaugh, M. M. (2004). *Current Controversies on Family Violence.* Thousand Oaks, CA: Sage Publications; Straus, M. A., & Gelles, R. J. (2006). *Behind Closed Doors: Violence in the American Family.* Piscataway, NJ: Transaction Publishers; Wallace, W. (2007). *Family Violence: Legal, Medical, and Social Perspective* (5th ed.). Boston: Allyn & Bacon.

environmental stress are cited as prime motivators of violent behavior in families. According to this model, violence is learned by modeling and serves as a coping mechanism in response to stress. Child abuse is considered a product of inconsistent and excessive punishment. Violence may be learned within the sibling microenvironment as a means of solving problems.

5. The **patriarchy model** emphasizes that violence occurs in families as a result of the traditional social dominance of adult males, which places women in a subordinate position and condones the use of violence to support male dominance.

6. The **exchange/social control model** suggests that violence occurs in families when the costs of being violent do not outweigh the rewards. For example, the rewards of violent behavior might be getting one's own way, assuming superiority over others, gaining revenge, or expressing anger and frustration. The costs might include receiving violent behavior in retaliation, being arrested and jailed, or a divorce. These costs also act as social controls to prevent and limit the possibility of violent behavior. Factors that tend to limit the costs in controlling violence include (a) gender inequality; (b) the privacy of the family; and (c) subscription to cultural beliefs

in ultra-masculinity that is expressed in aggressive, hostile, and violent ways.

7. The **information-processing approach** proposes that neglectful parents fail to process information about children's need for care, which leads to physical neglect, a form of maltreatment. Reasons include the following:

- They do not perceive the behavioral cues given by children.
- They ignore such signals from children and do not respond with parental caregiving.
- They are aware that a parental response is required but fail to have one available.
- They choose a response that is either inappropriate or never implemented.

Factors Associated with Family Violence

A **cycle of violence** appears to be manifested in two basic ways:

1. Individuals who had violent and abusive childhoods tend to become abusers of their own children.
2. A three-phase sequence in the expression of violent behavior begins with increasing tension, a loss of

Socioeconomic status, stress, social isolation, substance abuse, and family form are all associated with expressions of violence. Incidence of violence is higher in families with limited social networks and support.

control that is manifested by violent behavior, and a reconciliation period that is characterized by the offender's regret and the victim's forgiveness.

Researchers describe several psychosocial variables that are related to the incidence and variety of violent behaviors expressed in families (Gallimore, 2002; Garbarino et al., 2004; Straus & Gelles, 2006):

■ The *socioeconomic status* of a family system is associated with expressions of violence, particularly in families from lower socioeconomic groups where the quality of life, environmental stressors, and cultural conditioning or standards may be felt more keenly than they are in other social groups.
■ *Stress* is closely related to domestic violence. Acts of violence or abuse form part of a person's coping mechanism for stress. Sources of stress may include poverty, unemployment or part-time employment, financial problems, pregnancy and childbirth, single parenthood, or a child with a disability.
■ *Social isolation* from other families increases the risk of abusive behavior directed toward children or a spouse. This may be a contributing factor to the likelihood of abuse occurring in single-parent families. The interactions provided by social networks and contact with other families tend to act as a control mechanism to reduce the risk of such behavior.

In addition to these variables, several other conditions can be linked to family violence. There is an association between **substance abuse** and addictive disorders in parents and the physical abuse and neglect of children. Substance abuse or chemical dependency may play a role in 50 percent to 90 percent of cases of physical abuse of children by parents. Intoxication and chemical dependency impair judgment, increase irritability, and enhance depressive reactions, increasing the likelihood that children will be mistreated.

Another factor associated with child abuse and neglect is *family form*. The majority of reported cases of child abuse occur in single-parent families. Rather than being a function primarily of single-parent household status, abuse of children may occur in these homes because of the effects of poverty on single-parent families. Stepfathers are more likely to abuse children than biological fathers.

There is strong evidence of intergenerational transmission of abusive behavior (Straus & Gelles, 2006). From this perspective, a child learns such behavior by being abused by his or her parents, and the maltreatment in the family of origin serves as a model for later aggressive behavior. This abusive behavior is replicated when the abused child becomes a parent. In this way, abuse is passed from one generation to the next.

Parenting Reflection 15–1

You are grocery shopping and have just witnessed a parent viciously slapping and shaking her preschool-age boy. The child is screaming and crying, and the parent is continuing to yell at the child, calling him names and shaming him for what he has done. What should you do?

Characteristics of Abusive Parents

Because it is unlike other family problems, the abuse of children by parents requires an understanding of the antecedents that lead up to the violent or abusive outbursts (Wallace, 2007). The parent is generally unaware that he or she is having an extremely difficult time dealing with a child's behavior. Statistics point to the mother rather than the father as being more likely to be the abusive parent (Children's Bureau, 2012).

Researchers observe several characteristics in adults who abuse their children. The child-rearing patterns typically reflect a rigid, harsh, authoritarian approach. For example, abusive mothers characteristically express inconsistency, hostility, and protectiveness (paradoxically) toward their children, often almost simultaneously. They seek to gain control over their children's behavior by eliciting anxiety and guilt in the child or through physical punishment (Timmer, Borrego, & Urquiza, 2002).

It is important to determine the characteristics of parents who maltreat children. The different types of abusive and neglectful parents are described below.

Neglect of Children.   Physical and emotional neglect of children constitutes the most frequently reported type of maltreatment. This accounts for more than 78 percent of all reported child abuse in the United States (Children's Bureau, 2012). Parents who neglect their children fail to physically provide for their basic needs, such as sufficient food to meet nutritional requirements, supervision, or medical care. Such inadequate care results in fatalities as frequently as physical abuse does. A child who is physically neglected is almost always also emotionally neglected because the inattentiveness and disinvested attitude of the parents affect the entire child. Good parenting requires ongoing *responsiveness* to the child, and this dimension is lacking or absent.

Parents, who are caught and reported for child neglect the first time may have recently experienced a family crisis such as an illness, divorce, or desertion. As might be expected, parents who are chronically neglectful of their children have poor parenting skills.

Such parents often live in poverty and experience high levels of stress that are accompanied by depression and anxiety. Aggravating circumstances include unemployment, inadequate nutrition, substance abuse, and low incomes. These are multiproblem families with a chaotic home environment and low personal functioning. The families are socially isolated and maintain closed boundaries that do not allow access to community support systems. The closed boundaries make them resistant to assistance and therapy. Parental neglect can be damaging to children. Our society must take this problem seriously. Although this type of child maltreatment may be overshadowed by the more dramatic aspects of physical and sexual abuse of children, it necessitates intervention (see Figure 15–3).

Physical Abuse of Children.   Many parents who physically abuse children are not aware that what they are doing is wrong and harmful (Flowers, 2000; Stark, 2000; Wallace, 2007). They see it as their parental responsibility to be in control of their children. This approach is founded on strong beliefs about using physical punishment to teach children how to behave and gaining control when children misbehave. These parents generally have a low tolerance for children's misbehavior. They are impatient, quick to anger, and have poor empathy and are insensitive to children's needs. Some are belligerent and suspicious and experience many negative interactions with other people. Physical abuse of children usually occurs when these parents are responsible for young children and they find themselves in situations that are highly stressful, without sufficient support, and without adequate coping skills (Stark, 2000). Several factors interact in abusive actions. These adults are vulnerable to stress and typically cope poorly. (Runyon, Deblinger, Ryan, & Thakkar-Kolar, 2004).

Being abused as a child is an important predictor of whether someone will abuse their own children. Substance and alcohol abuse is associated with physical abuse (Shultz, 2001). The abusive behavior occurs when parents are intoxicated or under the influence of drugs.

Focus On 15–3

Characteristics of an Abusive Parent

- Had an unhappy childhood.
- Was mistreated or abused as a child in the family of origin.
- Had parents who failed to provide an adequate model of good parenting.
- Is socially isolated from family, friends, or neighbors.
- Has few close friends or intimate outside contacts.
- Has low self-esteem; perceives self as inadequate, unlovable, incompetent, or worthless.
- Is emotionally immature.
- Has a dependent personality.
- Sees little joy or pleasure in life; may be clinically depressed.
- Holds distorted perceptions and unrealistic expectations of children.
- Is averse to the idea of spoiling his or her child.
- Strongly believes in physical punishment as a means of teaching children.
- Practices an authoritarian child-rearing style.
- Displays minimal nurturing behaviors toward the child; has frequent outbursts of temper.
- Has a very limited ability to empathize with others, particularly with his or her own children; displays a general insensitivity to the needs of others.

Based on Children's Bureau. (2012). *Child Maltreatment 2010: Summary of Key Findings.* Washington, DC: Author; Flowers, R. B. (2000). *Domestic Crimes, Family Violence, and Child Abuse: A Study of Contemporary American Society.* Jefferson, NC: McFarland & Company; Heyman, R. E., & Slep, A. M. S. (2002). Do child abuse and interparental violence lead to adulthood family violence? *Journal of Marriage and the Family, 64,* 864–870; Institute of Medicine Staff Board. (2002). *Confronting Chronic Neglect: The Education and Training of Health Professionals on Family Violence.* Washington, DC: National Academy Press; Malley-Morrison, K., & Hines, D. (2003). *Family Violence in a Cultural Perspective: Defining, Understanding, and Combating Abuse.* Thousand Oaks, CA: Sage Publications; Stark, E. (2000). *Everything You Need to Know About Family Violence.* New York: Rosen Publishing Group; White, J. W., Koss, M. P., & Kazdin, A. E. (2011). *Violence Against Women and Children: Mapping the Terrain.* Washington, DC: American Psychological Association.

When substance abuse is present, this same behavior was often modeled by a parent in the family of origin.

Emotional Abuse of Children.   Researchers have conducted fewer studies of emotionally abusive parents than other types of abuse (Wark, Kruczek, & Boley, 2003). It is difficult to prove that emotional abuse has occurred because the evidence is not as obvious. It may be possible that the emotional abuse of children is more widespread than previously thought, but it occurs within the confines of the family (Straus & Field, 2003; Straus & Gelles, 2006).

Parents who emotionally abuse children experience low levels of self-esteem (Miller-Perrin et al., 2004). They have poor coping skills and lack child management techniques. These deficiencies lead to situations in which parents express their anger and impatience with children in ways that damage children's self-esteem. The attainment of adulthood does not automatically confer emotional maturity upon an individual. Some parents experienced abuse in their family of origin that developmentally impaired them. Such life experiences result in a distorted emotional makeup (Ramey, 2004). Until adults who are disadvantaged by stagnated emotional development receive help to break the abuse cycle, it is likely that their children will experience emotional abuse as well.

When parents become emotionally abusive, they express their impatience, frustration, rage, personal hurt, and disappointment toward their children in ways that damage the children's trust and well-being. Discounting a child's feelings and actions through name-calling, put-downs, or sarcasm is considered emotional and verbal abuse. Telling children they will never amount to anything is abusive. Other examples include shaming children when they make mistakes; handing down punishments that are humiliating; not allowing children to express their feelings; ostracizing children by not

Discrimination, harassment, and bullying are abusive behaviors that can harm a child physically and emotionally.

speaking to them or ignoring their presence; and destroying their favorite toys. When children are abused in these ways, it increases the likelihood of depression (Driedger-Doyle, 2001). This difficult mental state is four times more prevalent in children who have been abused than among children from stable homes. Because depression is associated with suicidal ideation, these children are also at greater risk of suicide.

Sexual Abuse of Children.   For most people, it is abhorrent to even think that adults could abuse children in a sexual context and perform incestuous acts. There is a strong taboo against incest in almost all societies. *Incest* is sexual activity between members of the same family (bloodline) and is considered to be an aspect of sexual

abuse involving children. Children cannot give consent to such activity. In families where children are taught to obey their parents and other elders, children are incapable of declining and may not understand the intentions of the adult perpetrator (Witters-Green, 2003). Sexual abuse by parents is infrequent, occurring in an estimated 10 percent of abuse cases reported (Children's Bureau, 2007). The majority of adults who sexually molest children are other relatives and nonrelatives with whom the child is familiar.

Until half a century ago, researchers thought that sexual abuse or incestuous activity rarely occurred in American families. When child-abuse legislation was instituted at this time that required such cases to be reported, researchers discovered that sexual abuse of children was more widespread than they had anticipated. Victims have become more open in disclosing sexual abuse in childhood, even that which occurred many years earlier. Several high-profile court cases, some accusing persons from religious groups, as well as high-profile celebrities who have shared their stories, have thrown more light on these "silent" atrocities. The shocking aspect is that some persons not only abused children, but also used their positions of trust to perpetrate their crimes. Some persons who experienced such abuse as children are now seeking treatment and are helping others to acknowledge these experiences as part of their healing process. Although it may be impossible to gather exact figures concerning the extent of the sexual abuse of children, one national estimate is that, of the almost 6 million children who experience some form of abuse every year, an estimated 8.8 percent were sexually abused (Children's Bureau, 2012).

Sexual abuse involves inappropriate sexual touching and insinuations between parents and children. Children are abused sexually when parents engage in genital fondling, anal or vaginal intercourse, or oral–genital contact, for example. There are many risks involved with such activities for all concerned, but especially for the child. In cases where children have been diagnosed with STDs, health-care professionals have a duty to report the parents to the authorities, and the legal system will intervene.

Families in which the sexual abuse of children has occurred are characterized by poor boundary controls, especially between parents and children; the poor quality of the adult marriage relationship; less harmony and stability in the family system as a whole; and a father who

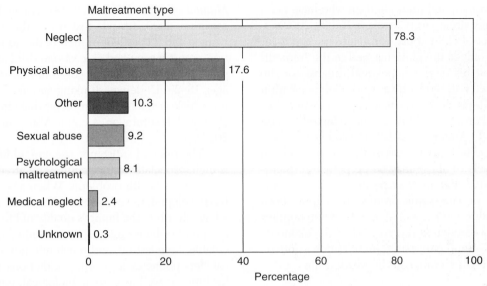

FIGURE 15–3.   Reported child maltreatment by type, 2010.

was probably physically abused as a child and acted violently within the family as an adult (Engel, 2000; Ferrara, 2001; Kinnear, 2007). Families in which the sexual abuse of children has occurred have significantly greater difficulty in regulating anger and greater degrees of chaos in managing roles (Howes, Cicchetti, Toth, & Rogosch, 2000). Some insights have emerged about the attitudes of men who have perpetrated sexual abuse. Compared to other men who have physically abused children, male incest offenders hold deviant attitudes that endorse male sexual entitlement and perceive children to be sexually attractive and sexually motivated. They minimize the harm caused to children by the sexual activity, especially among family members. In addition, interviews with perpetrators revealed that these individuals, regardless of their gender, see their incestuous actions as fair and loving, and a statement of their professed care for their child victims. These rationalizations serve to minimize and discount the harm that they inflict on children.

Treatment and Intervention for Abusive Parents

Many interventions are available to abusive parents (Feindler, Rathus, & Silver, 2003; Harway, 2000; Malley-Morrison & Hines, 2003; Miller & Knudsen, 2006; White, Koss, & Kazdin, 2011). Usually, this assistance

focuses on the adult, as well as the needs of the entire family. Services include medical care, counseling, psychotherapy, marriage and family therapy, mediation, support groups, a crisis hotline, child care, parenting education, and temporary foster care for the children. Some programs emphasize skill development that enhances prosocial parental attitudes and relationships. Other programs address family support for early intervention and prevention (Winkler, 2004). Where there is legal involvement, the courts may order participation in therapeutic programs (Wallace, 2004). In other instances, parents may seek these services voluntarily.

It is unclear if these programs are effective in preventing future child abuse and parental neglect (Garbarino et al., 2004). Some critics observe that most treatment programs are not particularly successful. Programs that emphasize parent education and early intervention may be more effective than others, especially in producing short-term effects. Programs may be most beneficial if abusive parents participate in support groups, such as Parents Anonymous or Parents in Distress, in addition to the parenting programs. These support groups are composed of self-referred individuals who are disturbed by their abusive behavior and fearful of the effects of the continued abuse on the family. Group members meet weekly and provide mutual support during and between meetings. Many communities also have safe houses that provide temporary shelter and initial assistance to women and their children who have been in abusive family situations (Correia & Rubin, 2002).

The impact of child abuse and maltreatment is far reaching. Not only is the child harmed in the immediate context, but his or her hopes and dreams for the future are pulled into the battle as well. Violence within families has effects on future marriage formation, cohabitation, and divorce and has also been linked to teen pregnancy (K. L. Anderson, 2010). It also has an effect on how these children will parent their own children because the cycle of abuse may be perpetuated (Sandberg et al., 2012). Family therapy that uses a systems approach may provide some promise of helping both parents and children (Gelles et al., 2004). When families are treated by a competent therapist, all of the elements of the abuse become part of the intervention strategy: the perpetrator, the victim, and the relationship.

....

Focus Point.   Violence in families is an unpleasant reality. Child abuse and neglect have received a great deal of attention in recent years. Seven theoretical approaches explain why maltreatment and neglect occur. Several psychosocial factors are associated with violent behaviors directed toward children and family members. Parents who abuse and neglect children have particular characteristics. The types of abuse range from physical neglect and maltreatment to the emotional and sexual abuse of children. Intervention and treatment programs have been developed, but the results are not promising.

....

FAMILIES AFFECTED BY SUBSTANCE USE AND ADDICTIVE DISORDERS

Various addictions have become a major concern of contemporary American society. Typically, alcohol, drugs, nicotine, and prescription medications come to mind when thinking of substance abuse. People become addicted to things, events, and experiences, as well as to substances. It is not possible to determine the exact number of adults in the United States who have a chemical dependency or some type of addictive disorder.

It is estimated that almost 7 percent of the U.S. population is, to some degree, dependent on alcohol, as reflected by 12-month prevalence estimates using the *DSM-IV-R* criteria from the *Diagnostic and Statistical*

Manual of Mental Disorders (American Psychiatric Association, 2000, 4th ed., text rev.). About 60 percent of women and 70 percent of men in the adult U.S. population report having had at least one drink during the past year. The highest alcohol consumption is found among ages 18–29. Underage drinking and alcohol-related motor vehicle accidents are problems that affect adolescents (National Institute on Alcohol Abuse and Alcoholism, 2012).

The price of substance use and addictive disorders is high, especially to the family. The affected individual experiences health problems. When a serious addiction has developed, the economic costs can be enormous and adversely affect the family's quality of life, sometimes to the point of bankruptcy. The emotional costs are incalculable, long lasting, and reach into adulthood. Chemical dependencies and other addictions may have behavioral, as well as genetic/biological, components and are frequently passed from one generation to the next. When a family member experiences such problems, the children are at risk for developing similar addictions because they are presented with the role models of their parents and other family members. The problem is compounded with each successive generation.

The abuse of substances and the development of an addiction lead to a crisis and problems that chronically affect all family members and put the children at risk. Among the most serious is the violence that almost always accompanies these problems. Children are especially vulnerable to emotional damage growing up in a family that is affected by parental addiction, and they may model the behavior. Although adolescents are vulnerable to developing dependencies and addictions, we will focus on families in which one or both parents have developed this problem and will examine the many effects on the family.

UNDERSTANDING THE EFFECTS OF SUBSTANCE USE AND ADDICTIVE DISORDERS

The Affected Adult Family Member

When an adult family member develops *substance use and addictive disorders* (American Psychiatric Association, 2012, *DSM–5*, 5th ed., draft), he or she believes that the solution to the problem can be addressed by using a substance. Some experts believe that an interaction between biological and environmental factors increases the likelihood that someone will develop substance abuse problems in adulthood.

It is thought that the adult affected by a chemical dependency or other addiction turns to the drug or substance for psychological, as well as physical, relief. The addictive substance functions to medicate the user in the short term, allowing him or her to cope with whatever difficulty is being experienced. The user may lose control over the ability to stop using the substance.

Definition.   A substance use disorder is defined as "[a] maladaptive pattern of substance use leading to clinically significant impairment or distress" (American Psychiatric Association, 2012, *DSM–5*, 5th ed., draft). It affects the functioning of the user in their work, school, and home roles, and in the context of the family it can lead to neglect of the children and the household. Social and interpersonal roles can be impaired as a result of the effects of the substance; for instance, anger can be aggravated, leading to physical fights and abuse, or neglect of the children or a spouse. A great deal of time and money is spent on obtaining the substance, leading to the depletion of financial resources and neglect of the family and the household. **Tolerance** of the substance may develop, meaning that there is a need for an increase in the amount ingested because the same dose fails to have the desired effect. **Withdrawal** may have severe physical and emotional side effects (American Psychiatric Association, 2012, *DSM–5*, 5th ed., draft).

Persons can develop dependencies and addictions to things other than illicit drugs, prescription medication, and other substances. The compulsive use of events, people, experiences, and nonchemical substances such as food can qualify as dependencies and addictions. Persons become addicted to relationships; the experience of falling in love; gambling; work; and a variety of other things, including tobacco, caffeine, and so forth. As long as the substance or the experience is capable of alleviating some kind of emotional pain, it serves as the basis for the problematic relationship that the person develops with the substance or the experience.

From a psychological point of view, it is not only the substance that causes the addiction but the relationship with the substance that becomes problematic as well. According to this line of thought, the process of dependency and addiction is a result of one's decreasing ability to choose not to have the relationship with the addictive substance. The person's relationship with the substance or the experience dominates his or her life—hence the neglect of the family and other obligations.

According to neuroscientific research, some mechanism in the pleasure centers of the brain seem to be triggered in addictive behaviors, even if these behaviors do not involve chemical substances such as drugs or medications (Esch & Stefano, 2010). It is also thought that various chemical substances made by the body can be released and can enhance a pleasurable effect and reduce pain. These substances are thought to bind to opiate receptors in the brain. When we talk about an "endorphin rush" in popular language, we are referring to the release of endorphins by the body that makes the person feel exhilarated. This may explain why the same agent causes some people no problem but becomes the focal point of addictions for others. Although there is a genetic basis for some portion of an addiction, it is the interaction with the environmental experiences that can ensure that the addiction is maintained.

Codependency was first used to explain why an alcoholic usually was married to a person who enabled their addiction by needing to be with someone who had serious personality and behavioral problems. Today, the concept has been greatly broadened to describe how people develop problems with dependency on others. It is thought that people who are codependent were not parented properly in infancy and childhood. This ineffective parenting refers to the inadequate caregiving by adults who failed to meet their children's dependency needs. This same aspect may partly explain why some abused spouses remain within the abusive relationship.

All children are dependent on adults to have their needs met in appropriate ways. This situation lasts for some time into adolescence when children gradually look less to others to meet their needs. The healthy developmental track is toward increasing independence, but in order for this to happen as intended, children need the assistance of healthy parents who assist them toward this goal. Persons who are codependent did not receive appropriate, adequate parenting experiences that allowed such developmental progress to occur. They experienced emotional and sometimes actual abandonment by their parents. Such abandonment takes many forms and, for all practical purposes, this kind of parental behavior is abusive. Parental abandonment reverses the order of the family structure. Instead of having parents who take care of them, children who are in such situations are forced to take care of parents, conform to their demands, and behave in ways that meet their needs.

It is thought that these behavioral problems occur because people experience some kind of deep emotional pain that responds to self-medication by using a particular substance or experience. When parents emotionally abandon children, the children come to the conclusion that something must be inherently wrong with them; why else would their parents neglect them in such ways? Parents who behave in this manner toward their children are emotionally damaged people who continue the abusive behavior that they experienced at the hands of their own parents in their family of origin. Unfortunately, the ability to parent children appropriately does not always develop. Some parents are not emotionally mature enough to provide adequate care because of their upbringing in families that were destructive. Other parents are emotionally or mentally ill and do not receive treatment. Some behave in this manner because of the stressful effects of poverty or the difficulties of being a single parent.

Ineffective parenting can occur on a continuum from overprotection to ignoring and neglecting children. When adults overprotect children, they continually take care of them, allowing little freedom for children to explore and discover themselves and their world. Nonnurturing parents are those who are overly strict and authoritarian in their approach to parenting. These parents overwhelm their children's ability to think critically, foster their dependence by having many nonnegotiable rules, and use physical punishment to enforce parental control over their children. At the opposite end of the continuum are those parents who ignore their children and neglect them.

Family systems theory predicts that when an adult is affected by some sort of dependency or addiction, everyone else in the family is also affected to some degree. Addicted adults and their codependent partners have developed a variety of self-defeating behaviors that are practiced in their relationship. These self-defeating behaviors emerged during their childhood and adolescent years as a means of coping with neglectful or abusive parents. The patterns also evolved as a means for gaining the approval, acceptance, and attention of parents who were failing to provide for their needs in appropriate ways. In adulthood, the patterns remain as a way of obtaining affection and love in an intimate relationship.

The relationship becomes even more dysfunctional because at least one partner's primary relationship is with an addictive substance or experience. The unhealthiness of this relationship affects the parenting behaviors within this family.

••

Focus Point. When children have been emotionally abused by parents, they acquire painful emotional beliefs that adversely affect their self-esteem. Growing up with such feelings about oneself harms the ability to form intimate relationships. These individuals discover substances and experiences later in life that at first alleviate this pain but later result in even greater shame and emotional pain because of the compulsive and self-destructive effects that the substance elicits in them. The intergenerational transmission of the tendency to develop dependencies and addictions is partially attributed to these interactions. Combined with a biological/genetic basis for substance dependency, the likelihood of maintaining the addictive cycle intergenerationally increases considerably.

••

Children Affected by Parents with Substance Use and Addictive Disorders

Children may not be aware that one or both of their parents have a substance use and addictive disorder because their parents deny it. These children are affected by living in a home where this problem exists, but the parents pretend that it does not exist. The effects can last a lifetime. Not only are the children likely to develop dependency problems that are similar to those of the parents at some time in their lives because they grew up seeing this behavior modeled, but they are likely to lack good parental role models as well. They may choose life partners who want to care for someone. Because they observed destructive patterns modeled by their parents, it is unlikely that they know what constitutes healthy family life. Invariably, they become involved in marriages and relationships with people who behaviorally resemble one or both parents in their family of origin.

The atmosphere in homes where one or both parents have an addictive disorder can be chaotic and abusive for children. Alcoholism is associated with an increased likelihood of physical and sexual abuse of children. Emotional damage is also inflicted on the children living in these families. Dependent and addicted family systems have very rigid rules that enable the system to function in unhealthy ways. The problem is a *family secret*, one that eats away at the integrity of the system as a whole and the individuals who are a part of it (Imber-Black, 1993). It also implies that children are not likely to seek help from school counselors or relatives because they are not allowed to breathe a word about what really happens at home. The patterns can be similar to spousal abuse. Three basic rules are strictly enforced in such families:

■ Do not talk about the parent's problem because it is a family secret.
■ Do not trust anyone outside the family to understand the problem.
■ Do not feel anything because this will destroy the integrity of the family.

Children typically become assigned to a special role in these dysfunctional families that helps to maintain the system's unhealthy homeostasis and protect the family secret from becoming public. While these roles can be observed in almost every kind of unhealthy family system, they are especially significant in dependent and addicted families because they help children cope with the chaotic climate of the family home.

These children often personalize the problems that their family experiences by feeling that they should be perfect children. When parents are intoxicated or high, children frequently presume that they are the cause of such behavior, and that somehow they ought to be able to correct the parent's problem and make their family healthy and whole again.

Having grown up in an unhealthy family system where the adults fail to function appropriately, children who have parents with an addiction disorder fail to develop in emotionally healthy ways, and they become victims of the dysfunctional system. Because these children have experienced chaotic, unpredictable parenting by adults who have abandoned them emotionally, they were left without the usual assistance that parents provide in nurturing children in healthy ways.

Children who grow up in such situations may exhibit compulsive behaviors and thinking, indecision, and difficulty in thinking clearly; experience hypervigilance; and have learning disabilities. These emotional and mental attributes are associated with having grown up in an unhealthy family system where

parental behavior created a chaotic, stressful environment (Fuller & Warner, 2000). Behavioral characteristics include crisis-oriented lifestyles, manipulative behavior with others, problems in intimate relationships, an inability to experience pleasure, fearfulness of being noticed by others, and a tendency toward substance use and addictive disorders.

Fortunately, help is available in most communities in the United States. The medical community provides rehabilitation programs, many of which are covered by major medical insurance. Many programs are available that serve community members who are living in poverty while experiencing these problems.

Among the most successful support programs, which have a long history of effectiveness in helping people overcome dependencies, are Alcoholics Anonymous and other related 12-step programs. Rational Recovery is another approach to dealing with addictions. These programs exist in communities throughout the United States. In addition, auxiliary programs are available for partners and children of addicted family members.

• •

Focus Point. Everyone in a family is affected when an adult develops an addictive disorder. Children growing up in families that are affected by an adult's addictive disorder also develop patterns that help them cope with their dysfunctional family. Children's emotional development typically is seriously affected if their normal childhood is sacrificed. Because these children have experienced chaotic, unpredictable parenting by adults who have abandoned them emotionally, they are left without the usual assistance that parents provide by nurturing children in healthy ways.

To report abuse or to get help in the United States, contact Childhelp: National Child Abuse Hotline at 1–800–4–A–CHILD (1–800–422–4453)

• •

POINTS TO CONSIDER

Abusive Parents

■ Violence in families occurs in a variety of ways and is frequently directed at children. Although it is difficult to obtain accurate information regarding the extent of such violence, child abuse appears to be the most prominent type of maltreatment among family members.

■ Seven basic models explain why violence takes place in families.

■ A number of psychosocial factors are associated with abuse, including a cycle of violence, a family's socio-economic status, the influence of stress, social isolation from other families, and the family form.

■ Parents who abuse their children share a variety of characteristics that often reflect a poor parenting experience in their own childhood family of origin. Children are not only neglected, but may be abused physically, sexually, and emotionally.

■ A variety of approaches are available to assist and treat abusive parents.

Families Affected by Adult Dependency or Addiction

■ It is possible for someone to become dependent or addicted to substances such as alcohol, illicit drugs, and prescription drugs, as well as to experiences (e.g., shopping, gambling), relationships (e.g., sexual), and so forth. Such problems affect an adult in a family, as well as the other family members.

■ It is believed that there are both physical and emotional aspects to substance use and addictive disorders. A family member may physically develop a tolerance to a substance and find withdrawal to be challenging. Psychologically, the substance may represent relief from emotional pain and a lifestyle for which they have no alternatives. A dependency or an addiction disorder represents a loss of control over the use of the agent.

■ Persons can develop codependent patterns that influence their functioning in adulthood. The basis for the patterns are laid in childhood and are likely to result from inadequate parenting that did not meet the child's dependency needs in an appropriate manner. In this way, the person was emotionally abused by his or her parents.

■ The children of dependent or addicted parents are likely to develop similar unhealthy dependency patterns. One of the significant outcomes is that they fail to experience normal emotional development and can be emotionally stunted. These patterns can cause difficulty in adult intimate relationships.

■ It is possible for persons in families affected by substance use and addictive disorders to undergo treatment for their problems and experience recovery. Typically, it requires intensive, professional intervention because relapse rates are high. In short, it is a very serious problem that requires complex interventions.

USEFUL WEBSITES

Centers for Disease Control and Prevention, Injury and Violence Prevention and Control
www.cdc.gov/injury

Child Welfare Information Gateway
www.childwelfare.gov

Childhelp: National Child Abuse Hotline, 1–800–4–A–CHILD (1–800–422–4453)
www.childhelp.org

Children's Bureau, Administration for Children and Families
www.acf.hhs.gov/

FRIENDS: National Resource Center for Community-based Child Abuse Prevention
www.friendsnrc.org

National Council on Alcoholism and Drug Dependence
www.ncadd.org

National Institute on Alcohol Abuse and Alcoholism
www.niaaa.nih.gov

CHAPTER 16

Best Practices in Parent–Child Relations

Learning Outcomes

After completing this chapter, readers should be able to

1. Describe the risk and resilience model in terms of good parenting outcomes.
2. Explain the ecological system of support promoting good parenting and resilient outcomes.
3. Describe the major protective factors in supporting good parent–child relations.

THE RISK AND RESILIENCE MODEL

"Positive early experiences lay a foundation for healthy development, but adverse experiences can weaken that foundation" (Center on the Developing Child, 2012). Societies are made up of the building blocks of families. Families, in turn, rely on societies to anchor them, allowing for a hopeful future. Responsible and informed parenthood is supported and embedded in all of the systems within a larger society. There is a constant mutual influence. Raising and maintaining a healthy family truly requires the entire village, it is not a task lightly undertaken. As a society, and as individual members within that society, we need to give all of the support we can to obtain the best outcomes. Optimal parenting cannot be the exclusive responsibility of an isolated family because it is bidirectionally embedded within the society where it occurs. We examine some of the factors that promote both risk and resilience, with an emphasis on resilience.

Ecological Perspective. Parenting is embedded within the family, which, in turn, is cushioned by societal institutions like educational facilities, places of civic engagement, centers for religious life, and many more. This collection is nested within the larger society, which exerts societal values and pressures, which with its social policies can be family friendly and exert support. It can create policies, allocate resources from national budgets,

and turn a listening ear to the risk factors, which, in some ways, concern all of us, and which have to be addressed to allow resilience to rise like the mythological Phoenix.

Both risks and protective factors exert an influence during childhood. Individual, interpersonal, and social factors, as well as environmental factors, interact (Jenson & Fraser, 2011). It is a similar approach to that of Urie Bronfenbrenner's ecological model where influential factors can operate in micro, meso, exo, and macro systems. These two approaches have been combined in Figure 16–1.

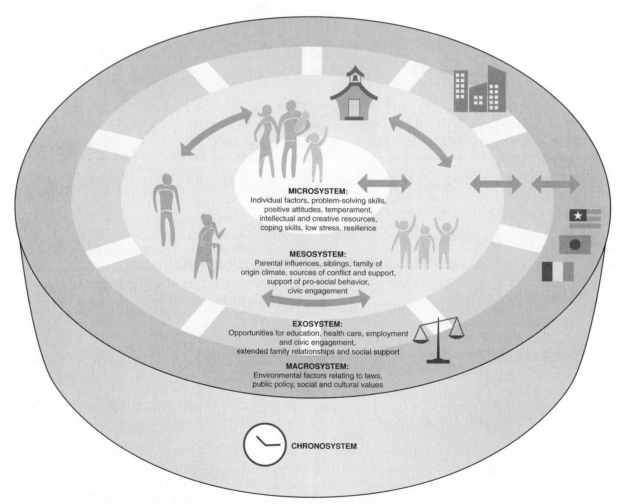

FIGURE 16–1. Protective factors for childhood and adolescence and Bronfenbrenner's ecological systems model.

Based on: Common Protective Factors for Childhood and Adolescent Problems by Level of Influence. *Source:* Jenson, J. M. & Fraser, M. W. (2011). *A Risk and resilience framework for child, youth, and family policy.* Chapter 1 in: Jenson, J. M. & Fraser, M. W. (eds.) *Social policy for children and families.* 2nd ed. Los Angeles: Sage.

Berk, L. (2012). Chapter 1: History, Theory and Research Strategies, Figure 1–4, page 26. Structure of the environment in ecological systems theory. In: *Infants, Children and Adolescents.* 7th ed. Upper Saddle River: Pearson.

As researchers in the field of parenting and family-related topics, we can study the ways in which individuals, families, and communities intersect and interface (Mancini & Roberto, 2009). Some relevant topics are intergenerational relationships, family stress, adaptation, and community resilience.

Bidirectional Interaction.   In an ecological and systemic model, the different levels interact in a *bidirectional* manner. It is an ongoing, interactive process of give and take between all parties involved. Our society influences us as individuals and as members of that society. But we, as individuals, shape the larger society as well. It is a constant and often almost imperceptible back and forth movement. Like the changing tides in the ocean, we see little if we watch the ocean from minute to minute; yet long term, the changes have remarkable effects.

Protective Factors

A glass of water is either half full or half empty, depending on how we look at it. Some youth seem to find it within them to use the half glass of water constructively and toward good outcomes, whereas others complain of thirst because they see the glass as half empty. The factors that contribute toward good outcomes despite adversity are *protective factors*. As members of the helping professions and groups that engage in matters of social concern, and as policy makers and members of this society, we will do well if we can strengthen those protective factors.

Risk and Resilience.   Research from the 1980s indicated that despite adversity, the presence of risk seemed to be lessened by the presence of the almost magical catalyst identified as resilience. Initially, it was thought that risk and resilience were opposite ends of the continuum. According to Jenson and Fraser (2011), social researchers asked whether these protective factors could be identified and measured. They also asked if risk and resilience go hand in hand or whether we could separate the constructs in our research and our policies. Rather than describing resilience as a personal asset such as a personality trait or characteristic, Coleman & Hagell (2007) felt that it was best described as a *process*. It is a process that engages personality traits, personal resources, and other aspects from the larger ecological system.

A key insight is that protective factors act as *buffers*; they stand between the youth or the family and adversity. They absorb the shock, like the crumple zone of a good car fender. In other words, protective factors are resources that the individual and the environment can access, which will then minimize or reduce the risk of impact (Fraser & Terzian, 2005). We can identify and name many of the buffering agents, and the intervention lies in implementing these protective buffers in high-risk situations. As with all complicated challenges, this may be easier said than done, but it is a beginning nonetheless, and a hopeful point of departure. Fraser and Terzian (2005) identify three steps, namely *Reduce, Interrupt*, and *Prevent*. We added illustrative metaphors for learning purposes:

■ *Reduce* whatever will cause the impact. If we are going to be hit by a truck, try to get the truck to slow down, or maybe it could be a smaller truck. Or reduce the amount of traffic and set speed limits. Reduction of the harmful agent will allow for a better outcome.

■ *Interrupt* the chain of risk. If we are going to get in harm's way, make sure there is a stop sign or a traffic light for the truck and the pedestrian. These will interrupt the chain of connected risks.

■ *Prevent* or block the factors that will cause the harm. No large vehicles are allowed in a pedestrian area; no unaccompanied children are allowed in traffic areas. Legislation makes this possible, and the system enforces it.

ENHANCING INDIVIDUAL RESILIENCE

Education.   "Education is one of the most powerful instruments for reducing poverty and inequality, and [it] lays a foundation for sustained economic growth" (World Bank, 2012). It is undisputed that learning is the key to improving socioeconomic outcomes. It is a powerful buffering agent. But in order to benefit fully from formal education, the opportunities for learning should also exist. These opportunities vary tremendously between developed and developing nations. Individuals can be held hostage by illiteracy because there are no facilities or opportunities to break the debilitating cycle. This educational disadvantage can be passed on from generation to generation unless the larger society implements those elements that will foster better educational outcomes.

The different ecological layers influence the outcomes as well. On the micro- and individual levels, family and personal factors interact to keep children in (or out of) school. For parents who missed out on their own education, helping their children reach their educational goals can be a major parental gift.

Parents need to be involved with the school and be attentive to their child's progress. The parent who prevents tardiness and absenteeism, and supports the child in simple things like catching the school bus on time and making sure the child has had adequate rest, meals, and clean clothes, is encouraging behavior patterns that send the message that the needs of the child and the role of schooling are important. Providing an environment that is conducive to learning, a time for age-appropriate play, and the support of pro-social values are important parental responsibilities. Children are quick to pick up these messages. It becomes difficult if the child has unsupported special needs or is exposed to parental examples where negative patterns may be reenacted.

The legislative building blocks for school attendance in the United States are in place, as mandatory and predominantly free schooling is available to all children until the minimum age of 16 or 17, depending on the state. The minimum age for employment is 15 (or 14 in some states). There typically is a 1-year gap. It is the state's intention that children are encouraged to attend schools at least until the minimum full-time employment age so that there is a seamless transition and no added temptation to leave school early for the lure of a paycheck. Worldwide, countries differ in enforcing mandatory school attendance. In many developing countries, the minimum age for employment is fairly low, encouraging children to enter the workforce to contribute to the family income. This, in itself, can perpetuate poverty through limited literacy.

For children and youngsters who reveal talent and motivation, many scholarships and educational support systems can be called upon. Legislation like the No Child Left Behind Act of 2001 in the United States, which sets goals and standards for best practices, seeks to improve outcomes for disadvantaged students and, in essence, supports literacy. The full title of this legislation is An Act to Close the Achievement Gap with Accountability, Flexibility, and Choice, So that No Child Is Left Behind (U.S. Department of Education, 2009).

In addition to the inner family circle, support from teachers and schools can the make the difference between success and failure. Underserved schools in poor neighborhoods present greater challenges in focusing on factors contributing to resilience because of fewer resources and often uninvolved parents. If a child is consistently mentored by someone who is truly interested in their well-being, even in the absence of a parent, this may be the catalyst for the child to obtain a better educational outcome (Ochse, 1990). Organizations such as Big Brothers Big Sisters of America (www.bbbs.org) provide mentoring that encourages positive self-image formation and better outcomes through role models and interpersonal encouragement. YMCA of the USA (www.ymca.net) operates afterschool programs and many other programs to contribute to "development, healthy living, and social responsibility," as reflected by their mission statement. Some of these programs provide a much needed and welcome support system to working parents.

Head Start (www.nhsa.org) and similar organizations step in to ensure that the foundation for early childhood education is solid. Head Start estimates that more than 27 million children in the United States have taken part in their programs since its inception in 1965, and that many of these children have progressed to positions of leadership and/or national eminence. Another organization that has positively affected the lives of thousands is Teach for America (www.teachforamerica.org). Students who have graduated in a variety of fields spend 2 transitional years teaching in low-income communities, contributing their skills and enthusiasm toward providing an education for children from underserved schools. This organization estimates that only 8 percent of children growing up in low-income communities in America will graduate from college by age 24, and that about 16 million American children "face the extra challenges of poverty" (Teach for America, 2012). Again, the bidirectional effect can be seen in operation. Virtually all of the participants who took on the teacher role state that they, too, were enriched by the experience, that it broadened their understanding and their compassion, and they felt rewarded by contributing to the greater good. It is very encouraging that a society such as illustrated here, can find it within in its own resource systems to make a palpable difference.

The W.K. Kellogg Foundation (www.wkkf.org) supports family stability through financial education, early learning, and child-care options. Through their investment and support, they encourage education and learning, and they use national organizations and their networks to achieve this goal. Part of their mission statement is "Whole child development, family literacy, and educational advocacy." Similarly, the Annie E. Casey Foundation (www.aecf.org) supports many social initiatives. They have produced a body of research that outlines some of the challenges and successes. They focus on children, but also on the communities that can bring about changes in children's lives. They have examined factors that pertain to juvenile justice, economic security, and education. They foster leadership and have set up networking sites where the poorest families can make connections and regain a sense of civic involvement. This is a key factor in feeling connected and wanting to make a difference at each level, even in the direst of circumstances. This organization estimates that 15.7 million children lived in poverty in the United States in 2010, representing 22 percent of all children (Annie E. Casey Foundation, 2012). In short, this foundation exemplifies that change has to occur on many levels to be truly effective because there is a reciprocal influence. These are a few select examples from countless organizations, initiatives, and foundations that are seeking to improve outcomes.

Worldwide, children face very diverse educational challenges. In developing countries, many children have no prospects of receiving an education; there simply are no schools or teachers to accommodate them. Others are forced into child labor or to enlist as soldiers in armed conflict. An estimated 73 million children worldwide are *not* attending school (UNESCO, 2010). These youngsters are referred to as "out-of-school children." Forty million of these children live in areas of civil conflict or war. Education is often compromised or unavailable. Children who are crippled by the effects of poverty, famine, and disease will not be able to reach their educational potential (UNESCO, 2012). In those societies where maternal educational level were increased, infant mortality was lowered and children had better nutrition and improved health outcomes. The Bill and Melinda Gates Foundation (www.gatesfoundation.org) applies substantial resources to improve outcomes for children on a global platform with numerous initiatives, including major vaccination programs. According to UNESCO,

> Education is a universal human right. However, enjoyment of that right is heavily conditioned by the lottery of birth and inherited circumstance. Opportunities for education are heavily influenced by where one is born and by other factors over which children have no control, including parental income, gender, and ethnicity. (UNESCO, 2009, p. 26)

Parents who are involved with their children's education and are attentive to their children's progress, model pro-social values and facilitate healthy socialization.

> **"Education is the most powerful weapon which you can use to change the world."**
> *Nelson Mandela*

Gender Equality in Educational Outcomes

The public consensus concerning the movement toward the changing role of women in society has been supportive, and nearly three quarters of American adults state that the trend of women entering the workforce is a welcome development. About 62 percent of adults in the United States believe that dual-income families have a more satisfying life and that both spouses should contribute to household and family-related chores (The Pew Charitable Trusts, 2012b).

The outcomes of gender equality in the workplace in the United States are cautiously optimistic. It is encouraging that women, in greater numbers than ever before in history, are seeking out tertiary or higher education and are graduating and entering the workforce in positions that match their expertise. They can be found in careers that had been male dominated in the past, such as in engineering, research, business, academia, and some of the medical specialties. Almost a quarter of small businesses list women as owners or co-owners (U.S. Census Bureau, 2012).

Less encouraging is that in key influential contexts, such as in boardrooms, in legislature, and in upper management, women's voices are in the minority. There are many contributing factors apart from education and work equality. The family life cycle tends to put much responsibility for family emotional wellness on the shoulders of women. Throughout the childbearing years, women's careers may be repeatedly interrupted, while social supports such as quality child care are limited and expensive. If women do have a career outside the home, they are frequently left managing their career and their family, and role overload ensues. With the fragility of families, single parenthood adds numerous difficulties to the challenges of fulfilling the parental role successfully, and single mothers and their children are more likely to live in poverty. There are always those who defy the norm, and children raised by single mothers have managed to reach their potential because they saw the parental sacrifices from close quarters and knew that the best way to thank their parent was to use the challenges of poverty or limited opportunity to strengthen them in their resolve to carve out different lives for their own families.

Around the world, the picture is bleak, especially for women in developing countries. Worldwide, women account for the majority of illiterate persons because of persistent gender disparities in accessing education. When these disadvantaged women become parents, their children perpetuate that same cycle of deprivation: infant mortality is higher, illnesses take their toll, and ultimately the chances of these children going to school are diminished (UNESCO, 2009, p. 28). Parents may hold universal dreams for their children, but some are shackled by the constraints of poverty.

Generational Differences

Research indicates that a cohort, or a generation of people, has a personality, in a similar manner to how individuals have personalities. There is a collective identity that defines these groups, and the group, in turn, is shaped by the many interactive layers of the community. Each group or cohort may reveal specific values, subtle cultural differences, attitudes, and visions of their own and of the larger world. One of the latest identified generations in the United States is the *Millennial Generation*, born from 1981 to 2000, the beginning of the new millennium, right at the cusp of the Internet paradigm shift (The Pew Charitable Trusts, 2012a). Characteristic of this group that grew up in the shadow of the World Wide Web is that they are hyperconnected, and this digital connectedness influences real face-to-face relationships.

The questions asked by the researchers of The Pew Charitable Trusts are about the current early adult generation: who they are, how they differ from their parents, how they are similar to their parents, how they are influencing the shaping of our society, how they are they being shaped in a bidirectional manner, and what their influence will be in the decades ahead (The Pew Research Center, 2012a). The characteristics that differentiate this generation are as follows:

■ Boomerang children are returning to the parental home after they receive their education.
■ Greater numbers are in college and are better educated.
■ Millennials face greater unemployment because of the economic downturn, hence the boomerang effect.

- Jobs are blocked by an aging workforce who is not retiring.
- Millennials are technologically more connected.
- This generation wants both a career and a family.
- Millennials want to be married (70%) and have children (74%).
- Significant numbers say they do not want to be married (25%) or have a family (19%).

Source: The Pew Charitable Trusts. (2011). "For Millennials, Parenthood Trumps Marriage."

ENHANCING FAMILY RESILIENCE

Changing Family Demographics

For both men and women of all age groups, being a good parent and having a successful marriage continue to rank high on their list of priorities, often more important than being successful or having a high-paying job or career. Women are placing more emphasis on their careers, but notably, this has not come at the expense of the marriage and the family (The Pew Charitable Trusts, 2012). The factor that best predicts marital success is level of education. College-educated spouses seem to have more resources at their disposal with which to create successful and rewarding marriages, while their education also protects them from poverty and related debilitating challenges (Karney, 2011).

Many men have stepped up to the challenge of family-related responsibilities by becoming involved with the nurturing and interactional aspects of child rearing. Frequently, these men are better educated and have been exposed to the role models of their own mothers who had been educated and have had careers outside the home. These men have expressed the pleasure that they experience in being involved in all facets of fatherhood.

Fathers are more visibly involved in their families, from the birthing room to the schoolroom. This means that they are present and involved during pregnancy, birth, and beyond. Men are better educated concerning child rearing, with programs such as Boot Camp for New Dads (www.bootcampfornewdads.org) contributing to the empowerment of fathers. When fathers are in the boardroom, they make it known that their families are important to them and their lives cannot be dictated by work demands. Public figures in high-visibility roles have been good role models for fathers. Increasingly, fathers are seeking a balance between work and their families. Some fathers have taken on the primary nurturing and caretaking role for their families by raising young children in the home while their partners become breadwinners, working outside the home. There is greater flexibility in matching personal preferences, economic opportunities, and the needs of the family.

Looking at the global picture, there is great variety in the educational and economic realms. In some countries, women are part of the top leadership, while, simultaneously, great economic and educational disparity between classes and genders persist. Some developed countries have made exceptional progress in these areas, and there are valuable lessons to be learned from their more successful approaches to providing family support and family-friendly work environments. In some countries, the effects of unrest place great burdens on families and children. Family life, parenting, and schooling are interrupted by war. Military families face separation and have to deal with distance coparenting and the risks of war to their survival and health.

Family Structure.   Family structure has changed dramatically over the last half century. Some key factors related to family stability are race, ethnicity, immigration status, men's and women's earnings, and family structure. Some of the characteristics of current families are

- Households are smaller and more fluid.
- Household composition and size change more frequently.
- Greater variation in the assignment of the parenting or primary caretaker role.
- Greater variation in family structure.
- Adults and children are more disconnected.
- Less family time, more television and media time.
- High rates of disruption in the parental union, including divorce.
- More children from nonmarital unions and many single mothers.
- Fathers' roles vary from being involved and responsible to being disengaged.
- Social connections and social support have atrophied.
- Little extended-family support.
- Families often live geographically far apart.
- Economic stressors, crises with the mortgage, and unemployment.

To maintain stability in the family unit, access to family support is an important strategy. That, in turn, is

h-promoting behaviors and general well-
......high school dropout rates, less education,
....d poorer job prospects facilitate economic disparities
(Waite, 2009). College-educated parents promote better educational and occupational aspirations in their
offspring and, generally, marital quality is better among
the educated (Karney, 2011).

Increasingly, institutional marriages that are supposed to last a lifetime are being replaced by nonmarital
relationships (Barlow & Probert, 2004). In practice, this
means that blended and reconstituted families are more
likely. The numbers of couples who choose to marry
are declining, with more marriages occurring at a later
age among the college educated. Americans still tend to
marry for love, and when that love fades, divorce rates
increase (Campbell & Wright, 2010).

Marriage and Family.   As marriage rates decline and
couples are tying the knot later in life, family formation
and the living arrangements of the children are affected.
In 2008, 53 percent of adults age 18 and older were
married, which was much lower than the 72 percent
recorded in 1960 (U.S. Census Bureau, 2010). There is
a widening of the "marriage gap," with college-educated
adults marrying later. They also tend to marry other
college-educated adults, often leading to dual-career
and dual-income couples. Many single mothers have

less education and are in the lower income groups (The
Pew Charitable Trusts, 2010).

Karney (2011) interprets some of the findings of the
U.S. Census Bureau (2010b) and research by The Pew
Charitable Trusts. He states that lower socioeconomic
status and concomitant poverty add to the probability of
divorce and to lack of satisfaction within the marriage.
Based on the Building Strong Families study, it was found
that marriage education curricula offered in order to decrease divorce rates had less of an effect than was hoped
for because many couples could not attend because of
lack of child care, holding down multiple poorly paying
jobs, transportation problems, and a generally lower motivation to attend (Karney, 2011). The unique problems
of low-income relationships were identified as follows:

- Marital problems that were more severe among low
  socioeconomic groups
- Problems related to money and the effects of poverty
- Addiction disorders (alcohol and drugs)
- Little investment in a monogamous, trusting relation-
  ship; infidelity
- Fewer friends, social isolation
- Lack of connectedness with civic organizations that
  provide social cohesion and support

All relationships, regardless of the educational
level or socioeconomic status, had difficulties or faced

Constructive family relationships
are important in maintaining
family stability.

challenges in the following areas: spending time to-gether, intimate marital relations, problems with parents or in-laws, problems with children and parent-ing children, communication, and the fair division of household chores (Karney, 2011; McNulty, O'Mara, & Karney, 2008). It appears that if there are problems in paying for food for the next meal, the luxury of relationship skills falls by the wayside. Low-income families face so many problems linked to survival that these problems take precedence, while independent relationship skills and attitudes are placed on the back burner (Karney, 2011; Karney & Frye, 2002). As stress and poverty add to the survival demands of families, husbands and wives, or committed partners, increas-ingly communicate in negative ways. It confirms what intuition would lead us to believe, namely that stress aggravates problems that might otherwise have been surmountable. Individuals from low-income com-munities report that negative life events and mental health incidents perpetuate the cycle of stress. We presume from the literature that couples in stressful environments communicate less and they do so less constructively, problem resolution is on a downward spiral, and stress then inhibits the adaptive process (M. D. Johnson et al., 2005). So at a time when it is most important to cope, the stress makes some couples less capable of coping. These are some of the factors that so clearly contribute to *caretaker despair*, where parents and caretakers feel overwhelmed by a tsunami of difficulties.

Marriage-friendly environments are created by taking care of the wolf howling at the door. Health care, quality child care, and a living wage for working people are the cornerstones that hold up the marital structure. Flaherty and Brown (2010) suggest that the actual community in which one lives has relatively little effect on the level of community attachment and commitment. We cannot pin all the blame on the socioeconomic aggregate of the neigh-borhood. What seems to be important is the level of en-gagement or attachment by members of the community. Are they investing in their community, or have they taken the approach of blaming the community, which ends up immobilizing the entire system? Other dimensions of the community experience seem to matter, especially civic en-gagement and emotional investment.

The separation of family status and family process can seem artificial. It follows along the same lines as the parenting argument concerning quality time. Researchers

ON FATHERHOOD

Being a father is a sacred responsibility, worthy of ven-eration and my highest level of attention. Maybe it's an art, but that too demands attention and devotion. Raised by what I like to call an in-home-child-support-paying father, one who paid the bills but little attention elsewhere, I'm sensitive to the need to spend time, daily, thinking about how I raise my two boys. That's what I mean by attention, serious time spent thinking about what it means to be a parent, not merely react-ing to my children as chaotic little creatures. They're mostly predictable, if you actually think about it. In Book II of his *Meditations*, Marcus Aurelius instructs us to "Say to yourself first thing in the morning: today I shall meet people who are meddling, ungrateful, treacherous, malicious, unsocial." He wishes to remind us that the world is intelligible, if we think about it and prepare ourselves for the day. This is a useful way to *think* about raising children; thinking that is. When they behave in ways I don't expect, I can say to myself, "See, you could have predicted that, if only you'd been mindful." For daily living, that means turning off the television or the radio, not shutting the car door in the middle of his sentence because I'm in a hurry, listening to his dreams every morning, asking questions, asking more questions.

As a poet I think a lot about what it means to be a maker, to be mindful of how my words form a made thing. My children are more important than my poems. Being a poet helps remind me seriously to look my children in the eyes (even the infant) and lis-ten to what they say. Sure, I respond with my share of thoughtless "uh huhs," "wows," and "awesome," for what parent doesn't find the chatter tiresome. But I still try to be mindful of my responses then listen more carefully. I came to fatherhood late in life and I wanted it dearly. My friends warned that it would steal my "inner life," that I would lose my sense of "Self." Romantic hogwash. My children, my wife, they are my inner life, as much as my poetry, the books I read, the students I teach, the friends and family I love. And that's what I mean to suggest, that if you see your children as something outside yourself, an append-age rather than an essential part of that elusive inner life, then parenting will be miserable and you'll raise miserable kids.

Bryan Johnson, Ph.D.
Director, Samford University Fellows, and
Associate Professor of English

Used with the permission of the author.

Respecting the differences of individual families and unique parent–child relationships in terms of qualitative differences, is key to being sensitive, aware, and in establishing multicultural competence.

have found that if there is not enough quantity, which is not enough time spent in parent–child relations, then it impacts the quality. Parents, who have to hold down daytime and nighttime jobs cannot spend time with children, and there is an effect in terms of parenting outcomes in this scenario, unless consistent and trusted caretakers step in. Sometimes this role is allocated to the grandparents.

We can maintain that the family climate overrides the family structure, but in some family structures, the cards are stacked against them, making it more difficult to maintain a good climate. For instance, for single parents, the role overload and the effects of poverty can be so overwhelming that this family form can face greater challenges than a family where two parents share parenting tasks, resources, and skills. Even if the parents part ways, it is always in the best interests of the child that the parents work out responsible ways of fulfilling the dual-household parenting roles. This means that the battles of the adults should never be fought with the children as go-betweens or pawns.

The Power of Family Support

Raising children successfully is a task that requires a thousand skills, among them responsibility, dedication, patience, foresight, and a sense of humor. If families are systems, and the members of each system are influenced by each other, then it follows that the support of the family can lighten the load and enable us to be more effective in our parent–child relations. Raising children successfully is a relay race. Even though the parents are the primary coaches, there is so much value in intergenerational parenting (Mancini & Roberto, 2009). Children can connect to the wisdom and grace of their own ancestors, while the grandparents are reminded that they have an important role to fulfill that extends to the third generation. They can be the link to ancestry and relay the family oral history, reminding us of our roots, which uniquely belong to each individual. As the American population is graying, it is more likely that grandparents can play a more active role in family relationships and also in sharing some of the child-care roles (Waite, 2009).

Siblings, too, can be a stabilizing factor for children. Children learn from brothers and sisters. There is a model for language, and they can interact in play. Later in life, the siblings become the reference group that uniquely understands how it was growing up in the family of origin. Siblings are cohorts who travel through time in a synchronized manner. They are the support when parents fall away. Even though much has been written about family position and children, each child may have different perspectives on the parents; the positives are that they represent the family of origin, and there normally is cohesiveness. Older siblings learn to share and empathize with the needs of younger siblings.

During normal, stable times, families oscillate in a range of connectedness, drawing closer or farther apart as the occasion demands. Typically, during key ritual and transitional moments in the family life span, the family will draw closely together, being almost enmeshed, as they go through the transition as a group. Transitional events can be happy ones, such as births, graduations, and marriages. There are also sad events, such as illness, loss, and death, when the family draws on each other for support, hope, and courage. These are times when the extended family is typically also involved. They know the family secrets, they know the code and the ritual; they subscribe to the same family culture. A young girl represents her family in a drawing in Figure 16–2.

Ideally, the nuclear and the extended families should fulfill some of the following roles:

- They provide nurture and structure.
- For growing children in these systems, there is the bond with primary caregivers.
- They should encourage and support a child's education.
- The family is the most intimate place, providing stability, shelter, and a sense of belonging.
- The family provides specific protective factors, such as celebrating and mourning together.
- Families communicate through the secret and overt codes of the family culture.

- Families are based on a business [...] financial obligations.
- Families provide a sense of contro[...] scaffolding upon which to acquire s[...]
- Families provide support that is anchored in a network of traditions.

The Power of Social and Civic Connectedness

Families and the children within families are more resilient if they can access and belong to organizations that emphasize social connectedness and promote civic engagement. These organizations can model appropriate behavior, provide a sense of belonging, and allow the children and the family to address developmental challenges while having a peer group for support as role models and as a reality check.

Schools are not only places of learning. They are social laboratories in which to learn how to connect interpersonally with peers and adults. Parents who become actively involved in their children's schools may find good connections with fellow parents that provide support and extend the child's social network. Any organization that promotes appropriate social engagement can act as a support system to the family and strengthen parent–child relations. A sense of belonging is an important component of the social nature of the family. Families will choose those settings that best meet their

FIGURE 16–2. Emily's drawing. The nurturing family environment provides stability, shelter, and a sense of belonging. Siblings form a unique support group.

needs and where they, too, can contribute to the fabric of society. Such settings include youth groups, social support groups, cultural organizations, volunteer opportunities, afterschool centers, and places of worship and communities with religious values.

Research in the field of psychology indicates that the sense of knowing there is concern and empathy from peers is an important part of getting support. A load shared is a load halved. Families who do not have extended family support nearby may form alliances with several other families who are facing similar challenges. They become each others' family and the children know that there are persons other than their parents who will look out for them.

In unfortunate situations where children and youth do not feel safe within their own homes, National Safe Place (based in the United States) has made it their mission to provide places of safety and shelter to support adolescents and to "create a safety net for youth" (www. nationalsafeplace.org). Typically, these shelters can be found at fire stations, police stations, schools, libraries, grocery stores, public transit, YMCAs, and other youth-friendly businesses. They are clearly identified by a yellow-and-black, diamond-shaped Safe Place sign. These sites are supported by qualified agencies that provide social services and trained volunteers.

Research Trends in the Family Sciences.   Five trends in family-related research are summarized (Crosnoe & Cavanagh, 2010). These do not necessarily reflect the challenges that families face in real life:

1. *Research into the meaning of parental behavior.*   Two parents may do similar things as part of their parenting behavior, but their motives may differ, and possibly the outcomes may differ. Self-disclosure is a product of positive parenting. Involvement and trust are foundations that develop and contribute to intimacy, which creates a sense of safety that allows disclosure and enhances emotional investment within the family.

2. *Relational components of the parent–child relationship.*   Shared family time is important. Shared time is positive for young people if it is actively and purposefully chosen and does not occur merely by default. Less family time signals problems if it is a symptom of disengagement. Even adolescents and young adults want some family time, although

their developmental needs may determine different types of shared activities. Family time is also reflected in the sharing of family meals and the celebration of rituals, events, and personally significant moments together. Parents do indeed learn from relationships and seem to parent better with subsequent children as reflected by chosen tine spent together.

3. *Importance of the father's role.*   Fathers are becoming increasingly visible, partaking in various roles, such as stepparenting, cohabiting, and adopting multiple father roles for different children in different contexts. The link between the father's involvement and parenting outcomes is of great importance. By the same token, absent fathers escalate problems in single-parent families.

4. *Unique strengths and qualities.*   The research is no longer simply dividing ethnicities or races by contrasting or comparing one group with another. Instead, there is an acknowledgment of specific strengths and unique qualities within the groups. Cultural expectations and strengths, as well as challenges stemming from the assimilation and blending of cultural heritage, address challenges that immigrant populations may face. With almost 20 percent of children having one foreign-born parent, this affects a much larger group than previously anticipated.

5. *Exploring diversity within general patterns of parent–child relationships.*   Increasingly, we respect the many ways that diverse groups parent. There may be differences in terms of timing, what is done when, and qualitative differences. Acknowledgment of the validity of different parental practices with differing outcomes add to the complexity of the unique parent–child relationship.

Some Global Initiatives for Young People.   With regard to research that pertains to global development and the empowerment of the next generation, some meaningful suggestions have been made (The World Bank, 2007, www.wdonline.worldbank.org):

■ *Civic engagement: Be a part of the solution, not a part of the problem.*   Expand opportunities for developing and engaging human capital. This is done by focusing on education and health care, and facilitating employment planning. The fresh element added to this mix is to involve youth in this planning, making their voices heard, because they need to be emotionally vested in these civic actions to ensure greater success rates. Young people need to feel that they are a *part of the solution*, and they need opportunities to participate in contexts where their input is valued. They need to feel that they are part of the initiative and the change. If we fail to do this, the younger generation will misread well-intended interventions as yet another form of authority, and the youth may rebel.

■ *Empowerment through constructive decision-making skills.*   Develop leadership skills in the younger generation, and guide them to choose well among the given choices. Their decision-making skills require strengthening so that when they do come to a fork in the road, they will choose the constructive option. They need to understand what is involved in decision making and the *consequences and outcomes*. They need to be well informed, have sufficient resources, and a sense of civic engagement. Hopefully, these principles come into play when young people face health- and lifestyle-related choices, such as the decision not to smoke or binge drink, and to adopt safe and responsible sexual practices. By empowering young people through the development of their decision-making skills, they will feel that they have control over their lives by making better decisions.

■ *Second chances and a purposeful life.*   Develop a system of *second chances* that works hand in hand with rehabilitation. If young people have made mistakes, there needs to be a way back into the system through programs that target young people who have made poor choices or have had bad luck. Given another opportunity, they may regain a sense of hope and purpose.

FINAL THOUGHTS

When best parenting practices are examined with a special focus on risk and resilience perspectives, it is apparent that in the United States, a number of major initiatives address the diverse challenges faced by parents and their children. Numerous public, educational, and social policies place the family into contexts that attempt to anchor and engage family life in civic networks that endeavor to cushion and sustain.

We have an outstanding network of information available in the public domain through websites maintained by major professional organizations and charitable foundations. Much of the research and the multitude of reports published on these websites and elsewhere point us in the right direction. Numerous gifted researchers have given these challenging questions their attention and have come up with tentative suggestions. We have learned from our past, both in terms of best practices and from outcome-based interventions.

Many systems interact to form a basis for good parenting. Parental love and structure may be a starting point, but it may not be strong enough to overcome the challenges of economic survival. Smaller families make it possible to give children the quality care and nurture they deserve for a better future, using the available resources.

Declaration of the Rights of the Child

On December 10, 1959, the General Assembly of the United Nations adopted the Universal Declaration of the Rights of the Child. The United Nations recommended that the declaration be publicized, especially in educational institutions, with the intent that ultimately it will be adopted universally. Here are some of the stated children's rights:

Children should be raised by their family or by those who will best care for them.

Children should have access to enough food and clean water.

Children should be raised under at least adequate circumstances.

Children have the right to health care and education.

Children with disabilities should have access to special care.

Children have the right to play.

Children have a right to safety and should not be hurt or neglected.

Children should not be abused as child labor or trained to fight.

Children have the right to express their own opinions.

Children should be allowed to speak their native language and practice their own religion and culture.

Children should be taught about peace and tolerance.

Source: Based on United Nations, Declaration of the Rights of the Child (Plain Language Version). In the Public Domain. Retrieved from http://www.un.org/cyberschoolbus/humanrights/resources/plainchild.asp

Numerous policies attempt to anchor and engage family life in sustaining networks.

Families are culturally anchored and in some ways they differ widely. But in other ways they face the same challenges of providing support and nurture to offspring. These goals are universal for all parents, regardless of their resources.

Ultimately, many facets of the future of humankind lie within the sacred bonds of kinship and civic responsibility. Can we learn from best practices in other contexts, are there ways in which we can empower and support the building blocks of society, namely the family? As we are educating the next generation of parent educators, we hope that they, too, will venture toward securing improved outcomes for children and their parents. After all, public wisdom tells us that there is no better investment than allocating appropriate resources to our children, who, in turn, hold the promise of becoming the next generation of parents.

USEFUL WEBSITES

The Annie E. Casey Foundation
www.aecf.org

Big Brothers Big Sisters of America
www.bbbs.org

The Bill and Melinda Gates Foundation
www.gatesfoundation.org

Child Welfare Information Gateway, Administration for Children and Families, U.S. Department of Health and Human Services
www.childwelfare.gov

Healthy Marriage Initiative, Administration for Children and Families, U.S. Department of Health and Human Services
www.acf.hhs.gov/healthymarriage

National Fatherhood Initiative
www.fatherhood.org

National Head Start Association
www.nhsa.org

National Responsible Fatherhood Clearinghouse
www.fatherhood.gov

National Safe Place
www.nationalsafeplace.org

Teach for America
www.teachforamerica.org

W.K. Kellogg Foundation
www.wkkf.org

YMCA of the USA
www.ymca.net

References

AARP. (2010). GrandFacts: State fact sheets for grandparents and other relatives raising children. Retrieved November 7, 2012, from www.aarp.org/relationships/friends-family/grandfacts-sheets

Abdul-Adil, J. K., & Farmer, A. D., Jr. (2006). Inner-city African American parental involvement in elementary schools: Getting beyond the urban legends of apathy. *School Psychology Quarterly, 21*(1), 1–12.

Abramson, A., & Dunkin, M. A. (2011). *The caregiver's survival handbook: How to care for your aging parent without losing yourself.* New York: Berkley Publishing Group.

Acs, G., & Nelson, S. (2002). The kids are alright? Children's well-being and the rise in cohabitation. Retrieved July 10, 2007, from www.urban.org/url.cfm?ID=310544

Adams, B. N. (2004). Families and family study in international perspective. *Journal of Marriage and the Family, 66,* 1076–1088.

Adams, J. (2004). *When our grown kids disappoint us: Letting go of their problems, loving them anyway, and getting on with our lives.* New York: Simon & Schuster.

Ahrons, C. R. (2007). Family ties after divorce: Long-term implications for children. *Family Process, 46*(1), 53–65.

Ahrons, C., & Marquardt, E. (2010). Does divorce have positive long-term effects for the children involved? In B. Slife (Ed.), *Clashing views on psychological issues* (16th ed., pp. 134–154). New York: McGraw-Hill.

Ainsworth, M. D. S. (1973). The development of infant–mother attachment. In B. Caldwell & H. Riciuti (Eds.), *Review of child development research* (Vol. 3). Chicago: University of Chicago Press.

Ainsworth, M. D. S. (1977). Attachment theory and its utility in cross-cultural research. In P. Leiderman, S. Tulkin, & A. Rosenfield (Eds.), *Culture and infancy: Variations in the human experience.* New York: Academic Press.

Ainsworth, M. D. S. (1989). Attachment beyond infancy. *American Psychologist, 44,* 709–716.

Ainsworth, M. D. S. (1983). Patterns of infant–mother attachment as related to maternal care: Their early history and their contribution to continuity. In D. Magnusson & V. L. Allen (Eds.), *Human development: An interactional perspective* (pp. 35–55). New York: Academic Press.

Ainsworth, M. D. S. (1993). Attachment as related to mother–infant interaction. *Advances in Infancy Research, 81.*

Akinbami, L. J., Cheng, T. L., & Kornfeld, D. (2002). A review of teen–tot programs: Comprehensive clinical care for young parents and their children. *Adolescence, 36,* 381–393.

Alan Guttmacher Institute. (2012). Facts on American teens' sexual and reproductive health. Retrieved November 7, 2012, from www.guttmacher.org/pubs/FB-ATSRH.html

Aldous, J. (1978). *Family careers: Developmental change in families.* New York: Wiley.

Alexander-Passe, N. (2006). How dyslexic teenagers cope: An investigation of self-esteem, coping and depression. *Dyslexia, 12*(4), 256–275.

Alexander-Passe, N. (2008). The sources and manifestations of stress amongst school-aged dyslexics, compared with sibling controls. *Dyslexia, 14*(4), 291–313.

Amato, P. R., Meyers, C. E., & Emery, R. E. (2009). Changes in nonresident father–child contact from 1976 to 2002. *Family Relations, 58*(1), 41–53.

Amato, P. R., & Sobolewski, J. M. (2004). The effects of divorce on fathers and children: Nonresidential fathers and stepfathers. In M. E. Lamb (Ed.), *The role of the father in child development* (4th ed., pp. 341–367). Hoboken, NJ: Wiley.

Ambert, A. M. (2001). *Families in the new millennium.* Boston: Allyn & Bacon.

American Academy of Ophthalmology. (2012). Daylight hours at birth and high myopia. Retrieved November 7, 2012, from www.aaojournal.org/article/s0161-6420(08)01024-5/abstract

American Academy of Pediatrics. (2012). Breastfeeding and the use of human milk: Section on breastfeeding. *Pediatrics, 129*(3), 827–841.

American Academy of Pediatrics. (2012a). *Healthy Child Care America: Fostering Language Development of 3- to 5-Year-Olds,* Standard 2.1.3.6.

American Academy of Pediatrics. (2012b). Retrieved November 7, 2012, from www.healthychildren.org

American Academy of Pediatrics, Committee on Substance Abuse. (2001). *Substance abuse: A guide for professionals* (2nd ed.). Washington, DC: Author.

American Association of Neurological Surgeons. (2012). Shaken baby syndrome. Retrieved November 7, 2012, from www.aans.org/Patient%20Information/Conditions%20and%20Treatments/Shaken%20Baby%20Syndrome.aspx

American Bar Association. (2006). *The ABA guide to family law.* Retrieved November 7, 2012, from www.americanbar.org/groups/public_education/resources/law_issues_for_consumers/books_family_home.html

American Civil Liberties Union. (2012). Violence against women. Retrieved November 7, 2012, from www.aclu.org/womens-rights/violence-against-women

American College of Obstetricians and Gynecologists. (2010). *Your pregnancy and childbirth; month to month* (5th ed.). Washington, DC: Author.

American Community Survey. (2008). 2008 data release. Retrieved November 7, 2012, from www.census.gov/acs/www/data_documentation/2008_release

American Medical Association. (2012). AMA resources for patients. Retrieved November 7, 2012, from www.ama-assn.org/ama/pub/patients/patients.page

American Pregnancy Association. (2012a). What is a pre-conception visit? Retrieved November 7, 2012, from www.americanpregnancy.org/gettingpregnant/PEpreconceptionvisit.html

American Pregnancy Association. (2012b). Miscarriage. Retrieved November 7, 2012, from www.americanpregnancy.org/pregnancycomplications/miscarriage.html

American Psychiatric Association. (2000). *Diagnostic and statistical manual of mental disorders* (4th ed., Text revision). Washington, DC: Author.

American Psychiatric Association. (2012). *Diagnostic and statistical manual of mental disorders* (5th ed., draft). Washington, DC: Author.

Ammen, S. A. (2000). A play-based parenting program to facilitate parent–child attachment. In H. G. Kaduson & C. E. Schaefer (Eds.), *Short-term play therapy for children* (pp. 345–369). New York: Guilford Press.

Anda, R. F., Chapman, D. P., Felitti, V. J., Edwards, V., Williamson, D. F., Croft, J. B., et al. (2002). Adverse childhood experiences and risk of paternity in teen pregnancy. *Obstetrics and Gynecology, 100,* 37–45.

Anderson, C. (2003). The diversity, strength, and challenges of single-parent households. In F. Walsh (Ed.), *Normal family processes: Growing diversity and complexity* (3rd ed., pp. 121–152). New York: Guilford Press.

Anderson, E. R., Greene, S, M. Hetherington, E. M., & Clingempeel, W. G. (1999). The dynamics of parental remarriage: Adolescent, parent, and sibling influences. In E. M. Hetherington (Ed.), *Coping with divorce, single parenting, and remarriage: A risk and resiliency perspective* (pp. 295–319). Mahwah, NJ: Lawrence Erlbaum.

Anderson, K. L. (2010). Conflict, power, and violence in families. *Journal of Marriage and Family, 72*(3), 726–742.

Angelou, M. (1997). *I shall not be moved.* New York: Random House.

Annie E. Casey Foundation. (2012). Major initiatives. Retrieved November 7, 2012, from www.aecf.org/MajorInitiatives.aspx

Areepattamannil, S. (2010). Parenting practices, parenting style, and children's school achievement. *Psychological Studies, 55*(4), 283–289.

Arnett, J. (2004). Adolescence in the twenty-first century: A worldwide survey. In U. P. Gielen & J. Roopnarine (Eds.), *Childhood and adolescence:*

Cross-cultural perspectives and applications (pp. 277–294). Westport, CT: Praeger Publishers/ Greenwood Publishing Group.

Arnett, J. (2010). Oh, grow up! Generational grumbling and the new life stage of emerging adulthood—Commentary on Trzesniewski & Donnellan (2010). *Perspectives on Psychological Science, 5*(1), 89–92.

Arnett, J. J. (2000). Emerging adulthood: A theory of development from the late teens through the twenties. *American Psychologist, 55,* 469–480.

Arnett, J., & Tanner, J. (2006). *Emerging adults in America: Coming of age in the 21st Century.* Washington, DC: American Psychological Association.

Aroian, K. J. (2006). Children of foreign-born parents. *Journal of Psychosocial Nursing & Mental Health Services, 44*(10), 1518.

Astington, J. W. (1993). *The child's discovery of the mind.* Cambridge, MA: Harvard University Press.

Ateah, C. A., & Durrant, J. E. (2005). Maternal use of physical punishment in response to child misbehavior: Implications for child abuse prevention. *Child Abuse & Neglect, 29*(2), 169–185.

Aucoin, K. J., Frick, P. J., & Bodin, S. (2006). Corporal punishment and child adjustment. *Journal of Applied Developmental Psychology, 27*(6), 527–541.

Auger, A. P., & Auger, C. J. (2011). Epigenetic turn-ons and turn-offs: Chromatin reorganization and brain differentiation. *Endocrinology, 152*(2), 349–353.

Azar, B. (2005). How mimicry begat culture: Researchers from varied disciplines look to mirror neurons to explain many aspects of human evolution. *Monitor on Psychology, 36*(9), 54.

Bacallao, M. L., & Smokowski, P. R. (2007). The costs of getting ahead: Mexican family system changes after immigration. *Family Relations, 56*(1), 52–66.

Bailey, A. B, McCook, J. G., Hodge, A., & McGrady, L. (2011). Infant birth outcomes among substance using women: Why quitting smoking during pregnancy is just as important as quitting illicit drug use. *Maternal & Child Health Journal.* Retrieved November 7, 2012, from www.etsu.edu/tips/documents/Smoking_and_Illicit_Drugs.pdf

Bailey, J., Willerman, L., & Parks, C. (1991). A test of the maternal stress theory of human male homosexuality. *Archives of Sexual Behavior, 20*(3), 277–293.

Bailey, M. (2003). The corporal punishment debate in Canada. *Family Court Review, 41*(4), 508–516.

Baird, C., & Hitchcock, T. (2011). *A complete guide for single dads: Everything you need to know about raising healthy, happy children on your own.* Ocala, FL: Atlantic Publishing Group.

Baldwin, D. A., & Moses, I. J. (1996). The ontogeny of social information gathering. *Child Development, 67,* 1915–1939.

Balkcom, C. T. (2002). African American parental involvement in education: A phenomenological

study of the role of self-efficacy. *Dissertation Abstracts International, 63,* 495.

Bandura, A. (1977). *Social learning theory.* Englewood Cliffs, NJ: Prentice Hall.

Barber, B. K., Xia, M., Olsen, J. A., McNeely, C. A., & Bose, K. (2011). Feeling disrespected by parents: Refining the measurement and understanding of psychological control. *Journal of Adolescence, 35*(2), 273–287.

Barber, N. (2001). On the relationship between marital opportunity and teen pregnancy: The sex ratio question. *Journal of Cross-Cultural Psychology, 32,* 259–267.

Barker, D. P. (2004). The developmental origins of chronic adult disease. *Acta Paediatrica. Supplement, 93*(s446), 26–33.

Barker, D., Eriksson, J., Forsén, T., & Osmond, C. (2002). Fetal origins of adult disease: Strength of effects and biological basis. *International Journal of Epidemiology, 31*(6), 1235–1239.

Barlow, A., & Probert, R. (2004). Regulating marriage and cohabitation: Changing family values and policies in Europe and North America—An introductory critique. *Law & Policy, 26*(1), 1–11.

Barnett, J. E. (2006). Evaluating Baby Think It Over® infant simulators: A comparison group study. *Adolescence, 41*(161), 103–110.

Barnett, J. E., & Hurst, C. S. (2004). Do adolescents take Baby Think It Over® seriously? *Adolescence, 39*(153), 65–75.

Barry, J. (2007). *Environment and social theory.* New York: Routledge.

Barth, R. P., Webster, D., II, & Lee, S. (2002). Adoption of American Indian children: Implications for implementing the Indian Child Welfare and Adoption and Safe Families Acts. *Children and Youth Services Review, 24,* 139–158.

Bateson, P., Barker, D., Clutton-Brock, T., Deb, D., D'Udine, B., Foley, R. A., et al. (2004). Developmental plasticity and human health. *Nature, 430*(6998), 419–421.

Baumer, E. P., & South, S. J. (2001). Community effects on youth sexual activity. *Journal of Marriage & the Family, 63,* 540–554.

Baumrind, D. (1966). Effects of authoritative parental control on child behavior. *Child Development, 37,* 887–907.

Baumrind, D. (1991). The influence of parenting style on adolescent competence and substance abuse. *Journal of Early Adolescence, 11,* 56–95.

Baumrind, D. (1994). The social context of child maltreatment. *Family Relations, 43,* 360–368.

Baumrind, D. (1996). The discipline controversy revisited. *Family Relations, 45,* 405–414.

Baumrind, D., Larzelere, R. E., & Cowan, P. A. (2002). Ordinary physical punishment: Is it harmful? Comment on Gershoff (2002). *Psychological Bulletin, 128*(4), 580–589.

Bausch, R. S. (2006). Predicting willingness to adopt a child: A consideration of demographic and attitudinal factors. *Sociological Perspectives, 49*(1), 7–65.

Bean, R., Barber, B., & Crane, D. (2006). Parental support, behavioral control, and psychological control

among African American youth: The relationship to academic grades, delinquency, and depression. *Journal of Family Issues, 27*(10), 1335–1355.

Becerra, R. M. (1998). The Mexican-American family. In C. H. Mindel, R. W. Haberstein, & R. Wright, Jr. (Eds.), *Ethnic families in America: Patterns and variations* (pp. 153–171). Upper Saddle River, NJ: Prentice Hall.

Bech, B. H., Obel, C., Henriksen, T. B., & Olsen, J. (2007). Effect of reducing caffeine intake on birth weight and length of gestation: Randomised controlled trial. *British Medical Journal, 334*(7590), 409–412.

Becvar, D. S., & Becvar, R. J. (1998). *Systems theory and family therapy: A primer* (2nd ed.). New York: University Press of America.

Becvar, D. S., & Becvar, R. J. (2008). *Family therapist: A systematic integration* (7th ed.). Boston: Allyn & Bacon.

Belsky, J. (1990). Child care and children's socioemotional development. *Journal of Marriage and the Family, 52,* 885–903.

Belsky, J., & de Haan, M. (2011). Annual research review: Parenting and children's brain development: The end of the beginning. *Journal of Child Psychology & Psychiatry, 52*(4), 409–428.

Belsky, J., & Rovine, M. J. (1988). Nonmaternal care in the first year of life and the security of infant–parent attachment. *Child Development, 59,* 157–168.

Bem, S. (1975). Sex-role adaptability: One consequence of psychological androgeny. *Journal of Personality and Social Psychology, 31,* 634–643.

Bengston, V. L., Acock, A. C., Allen, K. R., Dilworth-Anderson, P., & Klein, D. M. (2005). *Sourcebook of family theory and research.* Thousand Oaks, CA: Sage.

Bennett, S. (2003). Is there a primary mom? Parental perceptions of attachment bond hierarchies within lesbian adoptive families. *Child & Adolescent Social Work Journal, 20,* 159–173.

Bensley, L., Ruggles, D., Simmons, K. W., Harris, C., Williams, K., Putvin, T., et al. (2004). General population norms about child abuse and neglect and associations with childhood experiences. *Child Abuse & Neglect, 28*(12), 1321–1337.

Benson, A. L., Silverstein, L. B., & Auerbach, C. F. (2005). From the margins to the center: Gay fathers reconstruct the fathering role. *Journal of GLBT Family Studies, 1*(3), 1–30.

Berger, R. (2000). Remarried families of 2000: Definitions, description, and interventions. In W. C. Nichols, M. A. Pace-Nichols, D. S. Becvar, & A. Y. Napier (Eds.), *Handbook of family development* (pp. 371–390). New York: Wiley.

Bergman, K., Rubio, R. J., Green, R., & Padron, E. (2010). Gay men who become fathers via surrogacy: The transition to parenthood. *Journal of GLBT Family Studies, 6*(2), 111.

Berkowitz, D. (2007). A sociohistorical analysis of gay men's procreative consciousness. *Journal of GLBT Family Studies, 3*(2/3), 157–190.

Berkowitz, D. (2009). Theorizing lesbian and gay parenting: Past, present, and future scholarship. *Journal of Family Theory & Review, 1*(3), 117–132.

Berkowitz, D. (2011). "It was the Cadillac of adoption agencies": Intersections of social class, race, and sexuality in gay men's adoption narratives. *Journal of GLBT Family Studies, 7*(1/2), 109.

Bialystok, E., Luk, G., Peets, K. F., & Yang, S. (2010). Receptive vocabulary differences in monolingual and bilingual children. *Bilingualism: Language and Cognition, 13*(4), 525–531.

Bianchi, S. M., Milkie, M., Sayer, L., & Robinson, J. (2000). Is anyone doing the housework? *Social Forces, 79,* 191–228.

Biblarz, T. J., & Savci, E. (2010). Lesbian, gay, bisexual, and transgender families. *Journal of Marriage and Family, 72*(3), 480–497.

Bieber, I. (1962). *Homosexuality.* New York: Basic Books.

Bigner, J. J. (1996). Working with gay fathers: Developmental, post-divorce, and therapeutic issues. In R.-J. Green & J. S. Laird (Eds.), *Lesbian and gay couple and family relationships: Therapeutic perspectives* (pp. 370–403). San Francisco: Jossey-Bass.

Bigner, J. J. (1999). Raising our sons: Gay men as fathers. *Journal of Gay and Lesbian Social Services, 10,* 61–77.

Bigner, J. J. (2000). Gay and lesbian families. In W. C. Nichols, M. A. Pace-Nichols, D. S. Becvar, & A. Y. Napier (Eds.), *Handbook of family development and intervention* (pp. 279–298). New York: Wiley.

Bigner, J. J. (2006). Disclosing gay or lesbian orientation within marriage: A systems perspective. In C. A. Everett & R. E. Lee (Eds.), *When marriages fail: Systemic family therapy intervention and issues.* Binghampton, NY: Haworth Press.

Bigner, J. J., & Wetchler, J. L. (2012). *Handbook of LGBT-affirmative couple and family therapy.* New York: Routledge.

Bigner, J. J., & Yang, R. K. (1996). Parent education in popular literature: 1972–1990. *Family and Consumer Sciences Research Journal, 25,* 3–27.

Billingsley, A. (1993). *Climbing Jacob's ladder.* Upper Saddle River, NJ: Prentice Hall.

Bissell, M. (2000). Socio-economic outcomes of teen pregnancy and parenthood: A review of the literature. *Canadian Journal of Human Sexuality, 9,* 191–204.

Bitler, M., & Zavodny, M. (2002). Did abortion legalization reduce the number of unwanted children? Evidence from adoptions. *Perspectives on Sexual and Reproductive Health, 34,* 25–33.

Blanchard, R., Zuckey, K. J., Bradley, S. J., & Hume, C. S. (1995). Birth order and sibling sex ratio in homosexual male adolescents and probably prehomosexual feminine boys. *Developmental Psychology, 31,* 22–30.

Bloch, J. S. (2003). The ultimate discipline guide. *Child, 18,* 88–89.

Bloomfield, H. H. (2004). *Making peace in your stepfamily: Surviving and thriving as parents and stepparents.* San Diego, CA: Peace Publishing.

Bluestone, C., & Tamis-LeMonda, C. S. (1999). Correlates of parenting styles in predominantly working- and middle-class African American mothers. *Journal of Marriage and the Family, 61,* 881–893.

Blum, R. W. (2001). Trends in adolescent health: Perspectives from the United States. *International Journal of Adolescent Medicine & Health, 13,* 287–295.

Bogaert, A. F. (2003). The interaction of fraternal birth order and body size in male sexual orientation. *Behavioral Neuroscience, 117,* 381–384.

Bold, M. (2001). *Boomerang kids.* Denton, TX: University of Northern Texas, Center for Parent Education.

Boonstra, H. (2000). Welfare law and the drive to reduce "illegitimacy." *The Guttmacher Report on Public Policy, 3,* 7–10.

Borelli, T., & Littrell, B. (2011). Legal trends in protecting lesbian and gay parents' relationships with their children. *National Council on Family Relations Report, 56*(4), F4–F6.

Borja, J. B., & Adair, L. S. (2003). Assessing the net effect of young maternal age on birth weight. *American Journal of Human Biology, 15,* 733–740.

Borkowski, J. G., Bisconti, T., Weed, K., Willard, C., Keogh, D. A., & Whitman, T. L. (2002). The adolescent as parent: Influences on children's intellectual, academic, and socioemotional development. In J. G. Borkowski & S. L. Ramey (Eds.), *Parenting and the child's world: Influences on academic, intellectual, and socioemotional development* (pp. 161–184). Mahwah, NJ: Lawrence Erlbaum.

Bornstein, R. F., & Masling, J. M. (Eds.). (2002). *The psychodynamics of gender and gender role.* Washington, DC: American Psychological Association.

Bornstein, M. H., & Toole, M. (2010). Assessment of parenting. In S. Tyano, M. Keren, H. Herrman, & J. Cox (Eds.), *Parenthood and mental health: A bridge between infant and adult psychiatry* (pp. 349–355). Hoboken, NJ: Wiley-Blackwell.

Bos, H. M. W., Gartrell, N. K., Peyser, H., & van Balen, F. (2008). The USA National Longitudinal Lesbian Family Study (NLLFS): Homophobia, psychological adjustment, and protective factors. *Journal of Lesbian Studies, 12*(4), 455–471.

Bos, H., & van Balen, F. (2010). Children of the new reproductive technologies: Social and genetic parenthood. *Patient Education & Counseling, 81*(3), 429–435.

Bos, H. M. W., van Balen, F., & van den Boom, D. C. (2007). Child adjustment and parenting in planned lesbian-parent families. *American Journal of Orthopsychiatry, 77*(1), 38–48.

Boss, P. (1988). *Family stress management.* Beverly Hills, CA: Sage.

Bouchard, G., Boudreau, J., & Hébert, R. (2006). Transition to parenthood and conjugal life: Comparisons between planned and unplanned pregnancies. *Journal of Family Issues, 27*(11), 1512–1531.

Bouchard, G., & Lee, C. M. (2000). The marital context for father involvement with their preschool children: The role of partner support. *Journal of Prevention & Intervention in the Community, 20*(1–2), 37–53.

Bowen, M. (1978). *Family therapy in clinical practice.* New York: Aronson.

Bowie, F. (2004). *Cross-cultural approaches to adoption.* New York: Routledge.

Bowlby, J. (1952). *Maternal care and mental health: A report prepared on behalf of the World Health Organization as a contribution to the United Nations programme for the welfare of homeless children.* Geneva, Switzerland: World Health Organization.

Bowlby, J. (1982). *Attachment and loss.* New York: Basic Books.

Bozett, F. W. (1987). Gay fathers. In F. W. Bozett (Ed.), *Gay and lesbian parents* (pp. 3–22). New York: Praeger Publishers.

Bozett, F. W., & Sussman, M. B. (1989). Homosexuality and family relations: Views and research issues. *Marriage & Family Review, 14*(3–4), 1–8.

Bradbury, T. N., Fincham, F. D., & Beach, S. R. H. (2000). Research on the nature and determinants of marital satisfaction: A decade review. *Journal of Marriage and the Family, 62,* 964–980.

Bradley, J. M. (2006). Finding their way: An exploration of stepmother role identity and discovery. *Dissertation Abstracts International, Section B: The Sciences and Engineering, 66*(9-B), 5120.

Bramlett, M. D., & Mosher, W. D. (2002). Cohabitation, marriage, divorce, and remarriage in the United States. *Vital Health Statistics, 23*(22). Hyattsville, MD: National Center for Health Statistics.

Brandt, D. (2002). *Homes of fear: The curse of family violence.* Monrovia, CA: World Vision International.

Bray, J. H., & Hetherington, E. M. (1993). *Families in transition: Introduction and overview. Journal of Family Psychology, 7*(1), 3–8.

Breedlove, G. K., Schorfheide, A. M., & Wieczorek, R. R. (2000). *Adolescent pregnancy.* White Plains, NY: March of Dimes Birth Defects Foundation.

Brindis, C. D., Barenbaum, M., Sanchez-Flores, H., McCarter, V., & Chand, R. (2005). Let's hear it for the guys: California's male involvement program. *International Journal of Men's Health, 4*(1), 29–53.

Broderick, C. B. (1993). *Understanding family process: The basics of family systems theory.* Thousand Oaks, CA: Sage.

Bronfenbrenner, U. (1979). *The ecology of human development.* Cambridge, MA: Harvard University Press.

Bronfenbrenner, U. (1985). The parent–child relationship and our changing society. In L. E. Arnold (Ed.), *Parents, children, and change.* Lexington, MA: Lexington Books.

Bronfenbrenner, U. (1986). Ecology of the family as a context for human development: Research perspectives. *Developmental Psychology, 22,* 723–742.

Bronfenbrenner, U. (1993). Ecological systems theory. In R. H. Wozniak (Ed.), *Development in context* (pp. 44–78). Hillsdale, NJ: Lawrence Erlbaum.

Brott, A. A., & Ash, J. (2010). *The expectant father: Facts, tips, and advice for dads-to-be.* New York: Abbeville Press.

Brown, J. E., (Ed.). (2011). *Nutrition through the life cycle* (4th ed.). Stamford, CT: Cengage Learning.

Brown, R., & Perlesz, A. (2007). Not the "other" mother: How language constructs lesbian co-parenting relationships. *Journal of GLBT Family Studies, 3*(4), 267–308.

Brown, S. L. (2000). Union transitions among cohabitors: The significance of relationship assessments and expectations. *Journal of Marriage and the Family, 63,* 833–846.

Bruckner, H., & Bearman, P. S. (2005). After the promise: The STI consequences of adolescent virginity pledges. *Journal of Adolescent Health, 36*(4), 271–278.

Bruner, J. (1992). Another look at New Look 1. *American Psychologist, 47*(6), 780–783.

Bruner, J. S. (1966). *Studies in cognitive growth: A collaboration at the Center for Cognitive Studies.* Oxford, England: John Wiley & Sons.

Bryson, K., & Casper, L. M. (1999). Coresident grandparents and grandchildren. *Current Population Reports,* P23-198. Washington, DC: U.S. Government Printing Office.

Bubolz, M. M., & Sontag, S. (1993). Human ecology theory. In P. Boss, W. J. Doherty, R. LaRossa, W. R. Schumm, & S. K. Steinmetz (Eds.), *Sourcebook of family theories and methods: A contextual approach* (pp. 419–448). New York: Plenum Press.

Bunting, L. (2004). Parenting programmes: The best available evidence. *Child Care in Practice, 10*(4), 327–343.

Bunting, L., & McAuley, C. (2004). Research review: Teenage pregnancy and parenthood: The role of fathers. *Child & Family Social Work, 9*(3), 295–303.

Burgess, E. (1926). The family as a unity of interacting personalities. *Family, 7,* 3–9.

Burns, D. (2009). *Feeling good together: The secret to making troubled relationships work.* London: Vermilion.

Buxton, A. P. (2004). Paths and pitfalls: How heterosexual spouses cope when their husbands or wives come out. *Journal of Couple and Relationship Therapy, 3*(2/3), 95–110.

Buxton, A. P. (2005). A family matter: When a spouse comes out as gay, lesbian, or bisexual. *Journal of GLBT Family Studies, 1*(2), 49–70.

Buxton, A. P. (2006). Healing an invisible minority: How the Straight Spouse Network has become the prime source of support for those in mixed-orientation marriages. *Journal of GLBT Family Studies, 2*(3/4), 49–70.

Byrd, M. M., & Garwick, A. W. (2006). Family identity: Black–White interracial family health experience. *Journal of Family Nursing, 12*(1), 22–37.

C., Kim. (2010). 100+ reasons to have children. Retrieved November 7, 2012, from http://inashoe.com/2010/07/reasons-children

Callaway, E. (2012). Fathers bequeath more mutations as they age: Genome study may explain links between parental age and conditions such as autism. Retrieved November 7, 2012, from www.nature.com/news/fathers-bequeath-more-mutations-as-they-age-1.11247

Campbell, D. A., Lake, M. F., Falk, M., & Backstrand, J. R. (2006). A randomized control trial of continuous support in labor by a lay doula. *Journal of Obstetric, Gynecologic, & Neonatal Nursing, 35*(4), 456–464.

Campbell, K., & Wright, D. W. (2010). Marriage today: Exploring the incongruence between Americans' beliefs and practices. *Journal of Comparative Family Studies, 41*(3), 329–345.

Caplan, N. J., Whitmore, J. K., & Choy, M. H. (Eds.). (1989). Culture values, family life, and opportunity. In N. Caplan, M. Trautmann, & J. K. Whitmore. *The boat people and achievement in America: A study of economic and educational success* (pp. 94–127). Ann Arbor, MI: University of Michigan Press.

Carl, J. D. (2012). *A short introduction to the U.S. Census.* Upper Saddle River, NJ: Pearson Education.

Carlson, C., & Trapani, J. N. (2006). Single parenting and stepparenting. In G. G. Bear & K. M. Minke (Eds.), *Children's needs III: Development, prevention, and intervention* (pp. 783–797). Washington, DC: National Association of School Psychologists.

Carlson, M. J., Pilkauskas, N. V., McLanahan, S. S., & Brooks-Gunn, J (2011). Couples as partners and parents over children's early years. *Journal of Marriage and Family, 73*(2), 317–334.

Carter, R. (2010). *Mapping the mind* (2nd ed.). London: Phoenix.

Casper, L. M., & Bryson, K. R. (1998). U.S. Census Bureau, March 1998 Working Paper #26. In L. Casper & J. Bryson (Eds.), *Co-resident grandparents and their grandchildren: Grandparent maintained families.* Washington, D.C.: U.S. Census Bureau.

Catalyst.org. (2011). Women's earnings and income. Retrieved November 7, 2012, from http://catalyst.org/publication/217/womens-earnings-and-income

Cavanagh, S. E., Crissey, S. R., & Raley, R. K. (2008). Family structure history and adolescent romance. *Journal of Marriage and the Family, 70*(3), 698–714.

Center on the Developing Child: Harvard University. (2012). *Science of early childhood.* Retrieved November 7, 2012, from http://developingchild.harvard.edu/topics/science_of_early_childhood/

Centers for Disease Control and Prevention. (2004). Blood mercury levels in young children and childbearing aged women—United States: 1999–2002. *Morbidity and Mortality Weekly Report, 53*(43), 1018–1020.

Centers for Disease Control and Prevention. (2010). 2010 sexually transmitted diseases surveillance. Retrieved November 7, 2012, from www.cdc.gov/std/stats10/default.htm

Centers for Disease Control and Prevention. (2011). Births—Method of delivery. Retrieved November 7, 2012, from www.cdc.gov/nchs/fastats/delivery.htm

Centers for Disease Control and Prevention. (2012a). Breastfeeding. Retrieved November 7, 2012, from www.cdc.gov/breastfeeding

Centers for Disease Control and Prevention. (2012b). 2012 CDC Breastfeeding report card—United States, 2011. Retrieved November 7, 2012, from www.cdc.gov/breastfeeding

Centers for Disease Control and Prevention. (2012c). CDC childhood injury report. Retrieved November 7, 2012, from www.cdc.gov/safechild/Child_Injury_Data.html

Centers for Disease Control and Prevention. (2012d). Poisoning in the United States: Fact sheet. Retrieved November 7, 2012, from www.cdc.gov/HomeandRecreationalSafety/Poisoning/poisoning-factsheet.htm

Centers for Disease Control and Prevention. (2012e). Saving lives and protecting people from injuries & violence. Retrieved November 7, 2012, from www.cdc.gov/injury

Centers for Disease Control and Prevention. (2012f). Child maltreatment prevention. Retrieved November 7, 2012, from www.cdc.gov/ViolencePrevention/childmaltreatment

Centers for Disease Control and Prevention. (2012g). HPV vaccines—Questions & Answers. Retrieved November 7, 2012, from www.cdc.gov/vaccines/vpd-vac/hpv/vac-faqs.htm

Centers for Disease Control and Prevention. (2012h). Overweight and obesity. Retrieved November 7, 2012, from www.cdc.gov/obesity

Centers for Disease Control and Prevention. (2012i). Teen pregnancy: The importance of prevention. Retrieved November 7, 2012, from www.cdc.gov/teenpregnancy

Chabot, J. M., & Ames, B. D. (2004). "It wasn't 'let's get pregnant and go do it'": Decision making in lesbian couples planning motherhood via donor insemination. *Family Relations, 53,* 348–356.

Chakraborty, R. (2002). Better late than never. *Femina, 43,* 94–96.

Chamberlain, P., & Patterson, G. R. (1995). Discipline and child compliance in parenting. In M. H. Bornstein (Ed.), *Handbook of parenting, Vol. 4: Applied and practical parenting* (pp. 205–225). Hillsdale, NJ: Lawrence Erlbaum.

Chasmoff, L. P., Schwartz, L. D., Pratt, C. L., & Neuberger, G. J. (2006). *Risk and promise: A handbook for parents adopting a child from overseas.* Chicago: NTI Publications.

Chawla, N., & Solinas-Saunders, M. (2011). Supporting military parent and child adjustment to deployments and separations with filial therapy. *American Journal of Family Therapy, 39*(3), 179–192.

Cheal, D. (2007). *Families in today's world*. New York: Routledge.

Cherlin, A. (2004). The deinstitutionalization of marriage. *Journal of Marriage and the Family, 66,* 848–861.

Cherlin, A. (2005). American marriage in the early twenty-first century. *Future of Children, 15(2),* 33–55.

Cherlin, A. J. (2010). Demographic trends in the United States: A review of research in the 2000s. *Journal of Marriage & Family, 72(3),* 403–419.

Chess, S., & Thomas, A. (1987). *Know your child: An authoritative guide for today's parents.* New York: Basic Books.

Chester, A., & Elgar, K. (2007). The mental health implications of maternal employment: Working versus at-home mothering identities. *Australian E-Journal for the Advancement of Mental Health, 6(1),* 1–9.

Child-to-Child. (2009). Child-to-child trust: Child protection policy. Retrieved November 7, 2012, from www.child-to-child.org/about/childprotection.htm

Child Welfare Information Gateway. (2011). Adopción de "necesidades especiales": ¿Qué significa? ["Special needs" adoption: What does it mean?] Washington, DC: U.S. Dept. of Health and Human Services, Administration for Children and Families, Children's Bureau.

Children's Bureau. (2012). *Child abuse and neglect prevention and intervention.* Washington, DC: Author. Retrieved November 7, 2012, from http://www.acf.hhs.gov/programs/cb/areas/child-abuse-neglect-prevention-intervention

Children's Defense Fund. (1996). *The state of America's children yearbook, 1996.* Washington, DC: Author.

Children's Defense Fund. (2003). *The state of children in America's union, 2002.* Washington, DC: Author.

Children's Defense Fund. (2004). *The state of America's children, 2004.* Washington, DC: Author.

Children's Defense Fund. (2010). Number of children in foster care decline: Fewer children entered care and they didn't stay as long. Retrieved November 7, 2012, from www.childrensdefense.org/child-research-data-publications/number-of-children-in-foster-care-decline.pdf

Chomsky, N. (1968). *Language and mind.* New York: Harcourt, Brace & World.

Chomsky, N. (1975). *Reflections on language.* New York: Pantheon Books.

Choudhury, S., McKinney, K. A., & Merten, M. (2012). Rebelling against the brain: Public engagement with the "neurological adolescent." *Social Science & Medicine, 74(4),* 565–573.

Chrisp, J. (2001). That four letter word—sons: Lesbian mothers and adolescent sons. *Journal of Lesbian Studies, 5,* 195–209.

Christensen, F. B., & Smith, T. A. (2002). What is happening to satisfaction and quality of relationships between step/grandparents and step/grandchildren? *Journal of Divorce & Remarriage, 37,* 117–133.

Christian, A. (2005). Contesting the myth of the wicked stepmother: Narrative analysis of an online stepfamily support group. *Western Journal of Communication, 69(1),* 27–47.

Christoffersen, M., & Lausten, M. (2009). Early and late motherhood: Economic, family background and social conditions. *Finnish Yearbook of Population Research, XLIV,* 79–95.

Chuang, S. S. (2009). Transformation and change: Parenting in Chinese societies. In J. Mancini & K. Roberto (Eds.), *Pathways of human development* (pp. 191–206). Plymouth, United Kingdom: Lexington Books.

Ciano-Boyce, C., & Shelley-Sireci, L. (2002). Who is mommy tonight? Lesbian parenting issues. *Journal of Homosexuality, 43,* 1–13.

Clark, R. A., Richard-Davis, G., Hayes, J., Murphy, M., & Theall, K. (2009). *Planning parenthood: Strategies for success in fertility assistance, adoption, and surrogacy.* Baltimore, MD: Johns Hopkins University Press.

Clarke, J. I., & Dawson, C. (1998). *Growing up again: Parenting ourselves, parenting our children* (2nd ed.). Center City, MN: Hazelden Information and Educational Services.

Clarke, V. (2002). Resistance and normalization in the construction of lesbian and gay families: A discursive analysis. In A. Coyle & C. Kitzinger (Eds.), *Lesbian and gay psychology: New perspectives* (pp. 98–116). Malden, MA: Blackwell Publishers.

Clarke, V. (2007). Men not included? A critical psychology analysis of lesbian families and male influence in child rearing. *Journal of GLBT Family Studies, 3(4),* 309–350.

Clarke, V., Kitzinger, C., & Potter, J. (2004). "Kids are just cruel anyway": Lesbian and gay parents' talk about homophobic bullying. *British Journal of Social Psychology, 43(4),* 531–550.

Clarke-Stewart, A., & Brentano, C. (2007). *Divorce: Causes and consequences.* New Haven, CT: Yale University Press.

Claxton-Oldfield, S., O'Neill, S., Thomson, C., & Gallant, B. (2005). Multiple stereotypes of stepfathers. *Journal of Divorce & Remarriage, 44(1–2),* 165–176.

Coggins, T. E., Timler, G. R., & Olswang, L. B. (2007). A state of double jeopardy: Impact of prenatal alcohol exposure and adverse environments on the social communicative abilities of school-age children with fetal alcohol spectrum disorder. *Language, Speech, and Hearing Services in Schools, 38(2),* 117–127.

Cohen, L. G., & Spenciner, L. J. (2010). *Assessment of children and youth with special needs* (4th ed.). Upper Saddle River, NJ: Prentice Hall.

Cohn, T. J., & Hastings, S. L. (2010). Resilience among rural lesbian youth. *Journal of Lesbian Studies, 14(1),* 71–79.

Cohn, D., Passel, J., Wang, W., & Livingston, G. (2011). Barely half of U.S. adults are married—a record low. Retrieved November 7, 2012, from www.pewsocialtrends.org/2011/12/14/barely-half-of-u-s-adults-are-married-a-record-low/2

Coleman, J., & Hagell, A. (2007). *Adolescence, risk and resilience: Against the odds.* Hoboken, NJ: Wiley & Sons.

Collins, M. E. (2000). Impact of welfare reform on teenage parent recipients: An analysis of two cohorts. *American Journal of Orthopsychiatry, 70,* 135–140.

Collins, W. A., Maccoby, E. E., Steinberg, L., Hetherington, E. M., & Bornstein, M. H. (2000). Contemporary research in parenting: The case for nature and nurture. *American Psychologist, 55,* 218–232.

Committee on Psychosocial Aspects of Child and Family Health. (2002). Coparent or second-parent adoption by same-sex parents. *Pediatrics, 109(3),* 339–340.

Connolly, C. M. (2005). A process of change: The intersection of the GLBT individual and their family of origin. *Journal of GLBT Family Studies, 1(1),* 5–20.

Connor, J. M., & Dewey, J. E. (2003). Reproductive health. In M. H. Bornstein & L. Davidson (Eds.), *Well-being: Positive development across the life course* (Crosscurrents in contemporary psychology, pp. 99–107). Mahwah, NJ: Lawrence Erlbaum.

Consumer Product Safety Commission. Think toy safety. Retrieved November 7, 2012, from

Coontz, S. (2006). *Marriage, a history: How love conquered marriage.* New York: Penguin Group (USA).

Correia, A., & Rubin, J. (2002). *Housing and battered women.* Washington, DC: U.S. Department of Justice, Office of Violence Against Women.

Cosmi, E., Fanelli, T., Visentin, S., Trevisanuto, D., & Zanardo, V. (2011). Review article: Consequences in infants that were intrauterine growth restricted. *Journal of Pregnancy, 2011.* Article ID 364381. Retrieved November 7, 2012, http://www.hindawi.com/journals/jp/2011/364381/ref/

Cowan, C. P., Cowan, P. A., & Pruett, M. K. (2007). An approach to preventing coparenting conflict and divorce in low-income families: Strengthening couple relationships and fostering fathers' involvement. *Family Process, 46(1),* 109–121.

Crittenden, P., Claussen, A., & Kozlowska, K. (2007). Choosing a valid assessment of attachment for clinical use: A comparative study. *Australian & New Zealand Journal of Family Therapy, 28(2),* 78–87.

Crosnoe, R., & Cavanagh, S. E. (2010, June). Families with children and adolescents: A review, critique, and future agenda. *Journal of Marriage & Family, 72(3),* 594–611.

Cui, M., Donnellan, M., & Conger, R. D. (2007). Reciprocal influences between parents' marital problems and adolescent internalizing and externalizing behavior. *Developmental Psychology, 43(6),* 1544–1552.

Cunningham, H. (2005). *Children and childhood in western society since 1500.* New York: Pearson Longman.

Current-Juretschko, L., & Bigner, J. J. (2005). An exploratory investigation of gay stepfathers' perceptions of their role. *Journal of GLBT Family Studies, 1*(4), 1–20.

Darby-Mullins, P. B., & Murdock, T. B. (2007). The influence of family environment factors on self-acceptance and emotional adjustment among gay, lesbian, and bisexual adolescents. *Journal of GLBT Family Studies, 3*(1), 75.

D'Augelli, A. R. (2005). Stress and adaptation among families of lesbian, gay, and bisexual youth: Research challenges. *Journal of GLBT Family Studies, 1*(2), 115–136.

D'Augelli, A. R., Grossman, A. H., Starks, M. T., & Sinclair, K. O. (2010). Factors associated with parents' knowledge of gay, lesbian, and bisexual youths' sexual orientation. *Journal of GLBT Family Studies, 6*(2), 178.

Davidson, J. K., & Moore, N. B. (1992). *Marriage and family.* Dubuque, IA: W. C. Brown.

Davis, C., Shuster, B., Blackmore, E., & Fox, J. (2004). Looking good—family focus on appearance and the risk for eating disorders. *International Journal of Eating Disorders, 35*(2), 136–144.

deAnda, D. (2006). Baby Think It Over: Evaluation of an infant simulation intervention for adolescent pregnancy prevention. *Health & Social Work, 31*(1), 26–35.

DeBlander, T., & DeBlander, D. (2004). *Parents by choice: An insightful guide exploring adoption to build your family.* Lincoln, NE: iUniverse.

DeCaro, J. A., & Worthman, C. M. (2007). Cultural models, parenting behavior, and young child experience in working American families. *Parenting: Science and Practice, 7*(2), 177–203.

Diehl, D. C., & Toelle, S. C. (2012). Making good decisions: Television, learning, and the cognitive development of young children. *University of Florida IFAS Extension.* Retrieved November 7, 2012, from http://edis.ifas.ufl.edu/fy1074

deLissovoy, V. (1973a). Child care by adolescent parents. *Children Today, 2,* 22–25.

deLissovoy, V. (1973b). High school marriages: A longitudinal study. *Journal of Marriage and the Family, 35,* 245–255.

Del Vecchio, T., & O'Leary, S. (2008). Predicting maternal discipline responses to early child aggression: The role of cognitions and affect. *Parenting: Science & Practice, 8*(3), 240–256.

Dembo, M. H., Switzer, M., & Lauritzen, P. (1985). An evaluation of group parent education: Behavioral, PET, and Adlerian programs. *Review of Educational Research, 55,* 155–200.

De Mol, J., & Buysse, A. (2008). Understandings of children's influence in parent–child relationships: A Q-methodological study. *Journal of Social and Personal Relationships, 25*(2), 259–380.

DeNavas-Walt, C., Proctor, B. D., & Smith, J. C. (2010). Income, poverty, and health insurance coverage in the United States: 2009. Retrieved November 7, 2012, from www.census.gov/prod/2010pubs/p60-238.pdf

Derbort, J. J. (2006). A cultural look at parenting. In K. H. Rubin & O. B. Chung (Eds.), *Parenting beliefs, behaviors, and parent–child relations:*

A cross-cultural perspective (pp. 25–40). New York: Psychology Press.

Dere, J., Ryder, A. G., & Kirmayer, L. J. (2010). Bidimensional measurement of acculturation in a multiethnic community sample of first-generation immigrants. *Canadian Journal of Behavioural Science/Revue Canadienne Des Sciences Du Comportement, 42*(2), 134–138.

Detzner, D. F., & Xiong, B. (1999, June). Southeast Asian families straddle two worlds. *NCFR Report,* 14–15.

Dickerson, J., Allen, M., & Pollack, D. (2011). *How to screen adoptive and foster parents.* Washington, DC: NASW Press.

Didion, J., & Gatzke, H. (2004). The Baby Think It Over-Supertm experience to prevent teen pregnancy: A post-intervention evaluation. *Public Health Nursing, 21*(4), 331–337.

Dinkmeyer, D. (1979). A comprehensive and systematic approach to parent education. *Journal of Family Therapy, 7,* 46–50.

Dinkmeyer, D., & Dreikurs, R. (2000). *Encouraging children to learn.* New York: Brunner/Mazel.

Dinkmeyer, D., & McKay, G. D. (1981). *Parents' handbook: Systematic training for effective parenting.* Circle Pines, MN: American Guidance Service.

Dobbs, D. (2006). A revealing reflection. *Scientific American Mind, 17*(2), 22.

Dodge, K. A., McLoyd, V. C., & Lansford, J. E. (2005). The cultural context of physically disciplining children. In V. C. McLoyd, N. E. Hill, & K. A. Dodge (Eds.), *African American family life: Ecological and cultural diversity* (pp. 245–263). New York: Guilford Press.

Doherty, W. J., Erickson, M., & LaRossa, R. (2006). An intervention to increase father involvement and skills with infants during the transition to parenthood. *Journal of Family Psychology, 20*(3), 438–447.

Dolbin-MacNab, M. L. (2009). Becoming a parent again: An exploration of transformation among grandparents raising grandchildren. In J. Mancini & K. Roberto (Eds.), *Pathways of human development: Explorations of change* (pp. 207–226). Plymouth, United Kingdom: Lexington Books.

Doskow, E. (2010). *Nolo's essential guide to divorce* (3rd ed.). Berkeley, CA: Nolo.

Douglas, E. M., & Straus, M. A. (2006). Assault and injury of dating partners by university students in 19 countries and its relation to corporal punishment experienced as a child. *European Journal of Criminology, 3*(3), 293–318.

Downs, B. (2003). Fertility of American women: June 2002. *Current population reports,* P20-548. Washington, DC: U.S. Census Bureau.

Dreikurs, R. (1950). *The challenge of parenthood* (Rev. ed.). New York: Duell, Sloan, & Pearce.

Dresner, B. (2000). *Sex-role stereotyping: Changes in attitude of 3-, 4-, and 5-year-old children.* Knoxville: University of Tennessee.

Driedger-Doyle, S. (2001). Overcoming depression. *Maclean's, 114*(46), 34–38.

Drum Major Institute for Public Policy. (2006). *Saving our middle class.* New York: Author.

Dundas, S., & Kaufman, M. (2000). The Toronto lesbian family study. *Journal of Homosexuality, 40,* 65–79.

Dush, C., Kotila, L., & Schoppe-Sullivan, S. (2011). Predictors of supportive coparenting after relationship dissolution among at-risk parents. *Journal of Family Psychology, 25*(3), 356–365.

Dussich, J. J., & Maekoya, C. (2007). Physical child harm and bullying-related behaviors: A comparative study in Japan, South Africa, and the United States. *International Journal of Offender Therapy & Comparative Criminology, 51*(5), 495–509.

Duvall, E. M. (1988). Family development's first forty years. *Family Relations, 37,* 127–134.

Duvall, E. M., & Miller, B. C. (1985). *Marriage and family development* (6th ed.). New York: Harper & Row.

Eagly, A. H., & Diekman, A. B. (2003). The malleability of sex differences in response to changing social roles. In L. G. Aspinwall, & U. M. Staudinger (Eds.), *A psychology of human strengths* (pp. 103–115). Washington, DC: American Psychological Association.

Edelstein, R. S., Alexander, K. W., Shaver, P. R., Schaaf, J. M., Quas, J. A., Lovas, G. S., et al. (2004). Adult attachment style and parental responsiveness during a stressful event. *Attachment and Human Development, 6,* 31–52.

Edmisten, K. (2007). 40 reasons to have kids. Retrieved November 7, 2012, from http://karenedmisten.blogspot.com/2007/10/40-reasons-to-have-kids.html

Edwards, O. W., & Daire, A. P. (2006). School-aged children raised by grandparents: Problems and solutions. *Journal of Instructional Psychology, 33*(2), 113–119.

Elder, G. H. (1962). *Adolescent achievement and mobility aspirations.* Chapel Hill, NC: University of North Carolina.

Elder, G. H. (1999). *Children of the great depression: Social change in life experience.* Boulder, CO: Westview Press.

Elkind, D. (1974). *Child development and education.* New York: Oxford University Press.

Engel, B. (2000). *Families in recovery: Healing the damage of childhood sexual abuse.* New York: McGraw-Hill.

Erikson, E. (1950). *Childhood and society.* New York: Norton.

Erikson, E. (1959) Identity and the life cycle: Selected papers. *Psychological Issues, 1*(1), 1–171.

Erikson, E. (1964). *Insight and responsibility.* New York: Norton.

Erikson, E. (1982). *The life cycle completed.* New York: Norton.

Erikson, E., Erikson, J., & Kivnick, H. (1986). *Vital involvement in old age.* New York: Norton.

Eriksson, J., Forsén, T., Tuomilehto, J., Osmond, C., & Barker, D. (2003). Early adiposity rebound in childhood and risk of type 2 diabetes in adult life. *Diabetologia, 46*(2), 190–194.

Esch, T., & Stefano, G. (2010). Endogenous reward mechanisms and their importance in stress reduction, exercise and the brain. *Archives of Medical Science, 6*(3), 447–455.

Euler, H. A. (2011). Grandparents and extended kin. In C. Salmon, & T. K. Shackleford (Eds.), *The Oxford handbook of evolutionary family psychology* (pp. 181–207). New York: Oxford University Press.

Evans, J. M., & Aaronson, R. (2005). *The whole pregnancy handbook.* New York: Penguin Group.

Everett, C. A., & Everett, S. V. (2000). Single-parent families: Dynamics and treatment issues. In W. C. Nichols, M. A. Pace-Nichols, D. S. Becvar, & A. Y. Napier (Eds.), *Handbook of family development and intervention* (pp. 323–340). New York: Wiley.

Faber, A. (1995). *How to talk so kids can learn—at home and in school.* New York: Rawson Associates.

Fagan, J., Bernd, L., & Whiteman, V. (2007). Adolescent fathers' parenting stress, social support, and involvement with infants. *Journal of Research on Adolescence, 17*(1), 1–22.

Fagan, J., & Palkovitz, R. (2011). Coparenting and relationship quality effects on father engagement: Variations by residence, romance. *Journal of Marriage and Family, 73*(3), 637–653.

Fagan, J., Schmitz, M. F., & Lloyd, J. J. (2007). The relationship between adolescent and young fathers' capital and marital plans of couples expecting a baby. *Family Relations, 56*(3), 231–243.

Farabollini, F., Porrini, S., Seta, D. D., Bianchi, F., & Dessì-Fulgheri, F. (2002). Effects of perinatal exposure to bisphenol A on sociosexual behavior of female and male rats. *Environmental Health Perspectives, 110*(3), 409–414.

Farr, R. H., Forssell, S. L., & Patterson, C. J. (2010). Parenting and child development in adoptive families: Does parental sexual orientation matter? *Applied Developmental Science, 14*(3), 164–178.

Faul, M., Xu, L., Wald, M. M. & Coronado, V. G. (2010). Traumatic brain injury in the United States: Emergency department visits, hospitalizations, and deaths. Retrieved November 7, 2012, from www.cdc.gov/TraumaticBrainInjury/index.html

Federal Interagency Forum on Child and Family Statistics. (2007). *America's children: Key national indicators of well-being: 2007.* Washington, DC: U.S. Government Printing Office.

Federal Interagency Forum on Child and Family Statistics. (2010). *America's children: Key national indicators of well-being: 2010.* Washington, DC: U.S. Government Printing Office.

Federal Interagency Forum on Child and Family Statistics (2011a). Federal report shows drop in adolescent birth rate. Retrieved November 7, 2012, from www.nichd.nih.gov/news/releases/070711-annual-federal-statistics.cfm

Federal Interagency Forum on Child and Family Statistics. (2011b). *America's children: Key national indicators of well-being: 2011.* Washington, DC: U.S. Government Printing Office.

Federal Interagency Forum on Child and Family Statistics. (2012). *America's children: Key national indicators of well-being: 2012.* Washington, DC: U.S. Government Printing Office.

Feindler, E. L., Rathus, J. H., & Silver, L. B. (2003). *Assessment of family violence: A handbook for researchers and practitioners.* Washington, DC: American Psychological Association.

Fergusson, D. M., & Woodward, L. J. (2000). Teenage pregnancy and female educational underachievement: A prospective study of a New Zealand birth cohort. *Journal of Marriage and the Family, 62,* 147–161.

Ferrara, F. F. (2001). *Childhood sexual abuse: Developmental effects across the lifespan.* Belmont, CA: Wadsworth.

Ferrari, P., & Coudé, G. (2011). Mirror neurons and imitation from a developmental and evolutionary perspective. In A. Vilain, J. Schwartz, C. Abry, & J. Vauclair (Eds.), *Primate communication and human language: Vocalisation, gestures, imitation and deixis in humans and non-humans* (pp. 121–138). Amsterdam, Netherlands: Benjamins.

Fields, J. (2003). Children's living arrangements and characteristics: March 2002. *Current Population Reports,* P20-547. Washington, DC: U.S. Census Bureau.

Fix, M., Zimmerman, W., & Passel, J. S. (2001). *The integration of immigrant families in the United States.* Washington, DC: The Urban Institute.

Flaherty, J., & Brown, R. B. (2010). Attachment: Assessing the relative importance of the community and individual levels. *American Journal of Sociology, 116*(2), 503–542.

Flavell, J. H., Miller, P. H., & Miller, S. A. (2001). *Cognitive development.* Upper Saddle River, NJ: Prentice Hall.

Fletcher R., Vimpani G., Russell, G., & Sibbritt, D. (2008). Psychosocial assessment of expectant fathers. *Archives of Women's Mental Health, 11*(1), 27–32.

Flora, S. R. (2004). *The power of reinforcement.* New York: State University of New York Press.

Florsheim, P., & Ngu, L. Q. (2006). Fatherhood as a transformative process: Unexpected successes among high-risk fathers. In L. Kowaleski-Jones & N. H. Wolfinger (Eds.), *Fragile families and the marriage agenda* (pp. 211–232). New York: Springer Science+Business Media.

Florsheim, P., & Smith, A. (2005). Expectant adolescent couples' relations and subsequent parenting behavior. *Infant Mental Health Journal, 26*(6), 533–548.

Flowers, R. B. (2000). *Domestic crimes, family violence, and child abuse: A study of contemporary American society.* Jefferson, NC: McFarland.

Fowler, W., Ogston, K., Roberts, G., & Swenson, A. (2006). The effects of early language enrichment. *Early Child Development & Care, 176*(8), 777–815.

Framo, J. L., Weber, T. T., & Levine, F. B. (2003). *Coming home again: A family-of-origin consultation.* Philadelphia: Brunner-Routledge.

Francis-Connolly, E. (2003). Constructing parenthood: Portrayals of motherhood and fatherhood in popular American magazines. *Journal of the Association for Research on Mothering, 5,* 179–185.

Franke-Clark, M. J. (2003). The father–daughter relationship and its effect on early sexual activity. *Dissertation Abstracts International, Section B, The Sciences and Engineering, 63*(8-B), 3957. Ann Arbor, MI: University Microfilms International.

Fraser, M. W., & Terzian, M. A. (2005). Risk and resilience in child development: Principles and strategies of practice. In G. P. Mallon & P. M. Hess (Eds.), *Child welfare for the 21st century: A handbook of practices, policies, and programs* (pp. 55–71). New York: Columbia University Press.

Fromm, E. (1970). *The art of loving.* New York: Bantam.

Fronczek, P. (2005). *Income, earnings, and poverty from the 2004 American Community Survey.* Washington, DC: U.S. Census Bureau.

Frost, G. S. (2009). *Victorian childhoods.* Westport, CT: Praeger.

Fuller, J. A., & Warner, R. M. (2000). Family stressors as predictors of codependency. *Genetic, Social, & General Psychology Monographs, 126,* 5–22.

Gabbe, S. G., Niebyl, J. R., & Simpson, J. L. (2003). *Obstetrics: Normal and problem pregnancies* (4th ed.). Philadelphia: Elsevier.

Galinsky, E. (1987). The six stages of parenthood. In R. L. Newman (Ed.), *Building relationships with parents and families in school age programs* (pp. 56–69). Reading, MA: Perseus Books.

Galinsky, E. (2002). *Navigating work and family: Hands-on advice for working parents.* New York: Families and Work Institute.

Gallimore, T. (2002). Unresolved trauma: Fuel of the cycle of violence and terrorism. In C. E. Stout (Ed.), *The psychology of terrorism: Clinical aspects and responses* (Vol. II, pp. 143–164). Westport, CT: Praeger/Greenwood.

Gameiro, S., Moura-Ramos, M., Canavarro, M., Almeida Santos, T., & Dattilio, F. M. (2011). Congruence of the marital relationship during transition to parenthood: A study with couples who conceived spontaneously or through assisted reproductive technologies. *Contemporary Family Therapy: An International Journal, 33*(2), 91–106.

Gameiro, S. S., Moura-Ramos, M. M., Canavarro, M. C., & Soares, I. I. (2011). Network support and parenting in mothers and fathers who conceived spontaneously or through assisted reproduction. *Journal of Reproductive and Infant Psychology, 29*(2), 170–182.

Gámez-Guadix, M., Straus, M. A., Carrobles, J., Muñoz-Rivas, M. J., & Almendros, C. (2010). Corporal punishment and long-term behavior problems: The moderating role of positive parenting and psychological aggression. *Psicothema, 22*(4), 529–536.

Ganong, L., Coleman, M., & Hans, J. (2006). Divorce as prelude to stepfamily living and the consequences of redivorce. In M. A. Fine & J. H. Harvey (Eds.), *Handbook of divorce and relationship dissolution* (pp. 409–434). Mahwah, NJ: Lawrence Erlbaum.

Garbarino, J., Hammond, W. R., Mercy, J., & Yung, B. R. (2004). Community violence and children: Preventing exposure and reducing harm. In K. I. Maton & C. J. Schellenbach (Eds.), *Investing in children, youth, families, and communities: Strengths-based research and policy* (pp. 303–320). Washington, DC: American Psychological Association.

Gates, G. J. (2011). Family formation and raising children among same-sex couples. *NCFR Report, 56*(4). Retrieved November 7, 2012, from www.ncfr.org/ncfr-report/focus/lgbt-families/family-formation-and-raising-children-among-same-sex-couples

Gelderen, L. V., Gartrell, N., Bos, H., & Hermanns, J. (2009). Stigmatization and resilience in adolescent children of lesbian mothers. *Journal of GLBT Family Studies, 5,* 286–279.

Gelles, R. J., Loseke, D. R., & Cavanaugh, M. M. (2004). *Current controversies on family violence.* Thousand Oaks, CA: Sage.

Genosini, L., & Tallandini, M. A. (2009). Men's psychological transition to fatherhood: An analysis of the literature, 1989–2008. *Birth, 36*(4), 305–318.

Gerhardt, S. (2004). *Why love matters: How affection shapes a child's brain.* New York: Brunner-Routledge.

Gerhardt, C., & Gerhardt, C. M. (2009). Creativity and group dynamics in problem-based learning context. In O. Tan (Ed.), *Problem-based learning and creativity* (pp. 109–126). Singapore: Cengage Learning.

Gerlach, P. (2003). *Build a co-parenting team: After divorce or remarriage.* Philadelphia: Xlibris Corporation.

Gibbs, J. T. (2003). Biracial and bicultural children and adolescents. In J. T. Gibbs & L. N. Huang (Eds.), *Children of color: Psychological interventions with culturally diverse youth* (pp. 145–182). San Francisco: Jossey-Bass.

Gielen, U. P., & Roopnarine, J. L. (2004). *Childhood and adolescence.* Westport, CT: Praeger.

Gilliam, M. L. (2007). The role of parents and partners in the pregnancy behaviors of young Latinas. *Hispanic Journal of Behavioral Sciences, 29*(1), 50–67.

Ginott, H. (1965). *Between parent and child.* New York: Macmillan.

Ginott, H. G., Ginott, A., & Goddard, H. W. (2003). *Between parent and child.* New York: Three Rivers Press.

Glenn, H. S., Erwin, C., & Nelen, J. (2000). *Positive discipline for your stepfamily: Nurturing harmony, respect, unity, and joy in your new family.* New York: Crown.

Glick, J. E. (2010). Connecting complex processes: A decade of research on immigrant families. *Journal of Marriage & Family, 72*(3), 498–515.

Glover, G. (2001). Parenting in Native American families. In N. B. Webb (Ed.), *Culturally diverse parent–child and family relationships: A guide for social workers and other practitioners* (pp. 205–231). New York: Columbia University Press.

Gnaulati, E., & Heine, B. J. (2001). Separation–individuation in late adolescence: An investigation of gender and ethnic differences. *Journal of Psychology, 135,* 59–70.

Goldberg, A. E. (2006). The transition to parenthood for lesbian couples. *Journal of GLBT Family Studies, 2*(1), 13–42.

Goldberg, A. E., Kinkler, L. A., & Hines, D. A. (2011). Perception and internalization of adoption stigma among gay, lesbian, and heterosexual adoptive parents. *Journal of GLBT Family Studies, 7*(1/2), 132.

Goldberg, A. E., & Smith, J. Z. (2009). Perceived parenting skill across the transition to adoptive parenthood among lesbian, gay, and heterosexual couples. *Journal of Family Psychology, 23*(6), 861–870.

Golden, M. (1993). *Children and childhood in classical Athens.* Baltimore: The John Hopkins University Press.

Goldfarb, W. (1945). Psychological privation in infancy and subsequent adjustment. *American Journal of Orthopsychiatry, 15,* 247–255.

Golombok, S., Murray, C., Brinsden, P., & Abdalla, H. (2003). Social versus biological parenting: Family functioning and the socioemotional development of children conceived by egg or sperm donation. In M. E. Hertzig & E. A. Farber (Eds.), *Annual progress in child psychiatry and child development: 2000–2001* (pp. 155–175). New York: Brunner-Routledge.

Golombok, S., Perry, B., Burston, A., Murray, C., Mooney-Somers, J., Stevens, M., et al. (2003). Children with lesbian parents: A community study. *Developmental Psychology, 39,* 20–33.

Goodrich, S. M. (1990). *Boundaries: Development of self within a family system. Dissertation Abstracts International, Section A, 50,* 4218.

Gopman, B. (2010). Tolerance: Our voice—an elementary school package in support of siblings of children with special needs. *Dissertation Abstracts International, Section A, 70*(12), 4581.

Gordon, S. (2004). *When living hurts: For teenagers, young adults, their parents, leaders, and counselors.* New York: UAHC Press.

Gordon, T. (1975/2000). *Parent effectiveness training: The tested way to raise responsible children.* New York: Wyden.

Gorman, J. C. (1988). Parenting attitudes and practices of immigrant Chinese mothers of adolescents. *Family Relations, 47,* 73–80.

Gottlieb, A. R. (2003). *Sons talk about their gay fathers: Life curves.* New York: Harrington Park Press.

Gottman, J. M., Levenson, R. W., Gross, J., Frederickson, B. L., McCoy, K., Rosenthal, L., et al. (2003). Correlates of gay and lesbian couples' relationship satisfaction and relationship dissolution. *Journal of Homosexuality, 45,* 23–43.

Gowen, G. W., & Nebrig, J. B. (2002). *Enhancing early emotional development: Guiding parents of young children.* Baltimore: Brookes.

Gowers, S. G., & Green, L. (2009). *Eating disorders: Cognitive behaviour therapy with children and young people.* New York: Taylor & Francis Routledge.

Grall, T. (2009). Custodial mothers and fathers and their child support: 2007. *Current Population Reports.* Retrieved November 7, 2012, from www.census.gov/prod/2009pubs/p60-237.pdf

Gray, M. R., & Steinberg, L. (1999). Unpacking authoritative parenting: Reassessing a multidimensional construct. *Journal of Marriage and the Family, 61,* 574–587.

Greeff, A. P., & Fillis, A. (2009). Resiliency in poor single-parent families. *Families in Society, 90*(3), 279–285.

Green, J., Whitney, P., & Potegal, M. (2011). Screaming, yelling, whining, and crying: Categorical and intensity differences in vocal expressions of anger and sadness in children's tantrums. *Emotion, 11*(5), 1124–1133.

Green, M., & Piel, J. A. (2009). *Theories of human development: A comparative approach* (2nd ed.). Richmond, Surrey, United Kingdom: Allyn & Bacon.

Green, R. J. (2002). Coming out to family … in context. In E. Davis-Russell (Ed.), *The California School of Professional Psychology handbook of multicultural education, research, intervention, and training* (pp. 277–284). San Francisco: Jossey-Bass.

Green, R. J., & Mitchell, V. (2007). Different storks for different folks: Gay and lesbian parents' experiences with alternative insemination and surrogacy. *Journal of GLBT Family Studies, 3*(2/3), 81–104.

Greenfield, P. M., & Suzuki, L. K. (2001). Culture and parenthood. In J. C. Westman (Ed.) *Parenthood in America: Undervalued, underpaid, under siege* (pp. 20–33). Madison: University of Wisconsin Press.

Greenfield, P. M., Trumbull, E., Keller, H., Rothstein-Fisch, C., Suzuki, L. K., & Quiroz, B. (2006). Cultural conceptions of learning and development. In P. A. Alexander & P. H. Winne (Eds.), *Handbook of educational psychology* (pp. 675–692). Mahwah, NJ: Lawrence Erlbaum.

Grever, C., & Bowman, D. (2008). *When your spouse comes out: A straight mate's recovery manual.* New York: Haworth Press-Taylor & Francis Group.

Griffin, G., McEwen, E., Samuels, B. H., Suggs, H., Redd, J. L., & McClelland, G. M. (2011). Infusing protective factors for children in foster care. *Psychiatric Clinics of North America, 34*(1), 185–203.

Grogan-Kaylor, A., & Otis, M. D. (2007). The predictors of parental use of corporal punishment. *Family Relations, 56*(1), 80–91.

Grolnick, W. S., & Pomerantz, E. M. (2009). Issues and challenges in studying parental control: Toward a new conceptualization. *Child Development Perspectives, 3*(3), 165–170.

Gross, J. (2011). *A bittersweet season: Caring for our aging parents and ourselves.* New York: Vintage Books.

Gunnar, M. R., & van Dulmen, M. H. M. (2007). Behavior problems in postinstitutionalized internationally adopted children. *Development and Psychopathology, 19*(1), 129–148.

Haberstroh, C., Hayslip, B., Jr., & Wohl, E. (2001). Perceptions of grandparents and stepgrandparents by young adults. *The Gerontologist, 41*, 35.

Hacker, K. A., Amare, Y., Strunk, N., & Horst, L. (2000). Listening to youth: Teen perspectives on pregnancy prevention. *Journal of Adolescent Health, 26*, 279–288.

Haddock, S. A. (2002). A content analysis of articles pertaining to therapeutic considerations for dual-income couples (1979–1999). *American Journal of Family Therapy, 30*(2), 141–156.

Hall, C. M. (2005). Physical discipline and child externalizing problems in Caucasian and Korean immigrant families. *Dissertation Abstracts International, Section B: The Sciences and Engineering, 65*(8-B), 4320.

Hall, K. J., & Kitson, G. C. (2000). Lesbian stepfamilies: An even more "incomplete institution." *Journal of Lesbian Studies, 4*, 31–47.

Hallowell, E. M., & Jensen, P. S. (2010). *Superparenting for ADD: An innovative approach to raising your distracted child.* New York: Ballantine Books.

Halstead, M. E., & Walter, K. D. (2010). Clinical report—sport-related concussion in children and adolescents. *Pediatrics, 126*(3), 597–615.

Hamer, D. H., Hu, S., Magnuson, V. L., Hu, N., & Pattatucci, A. M. (1993). A linkage between DNA markers on the X chromosome and male sexual orientation. *Science, 261*(5119), 321–327.

Hamilton, B. E., Martin, J. A., & Ventura, S. J. (2010). Births: Preliminary data for 2009. *National Vital Statistics Reports, 59*(3), 1. Retrieved November 7, 2012, from http://www.cdc.gov/nchs/data/nvsr/nvsr59/nvsr59_03.pdf

Hangal, S., & Aminabhavi, V. A. (2007). Self-concept, emotional maturity, and achievement motivation of the adolescent children of employed mothers and homemakers. *Journal of the Indian Academy of Applied Psychology, 33*(1), 103–110.

Hansen, D. A., & Hill, R. (1964). Families under stress. In H. Christensen (Ed.), *Handbook of marriage and the family* (pp. 355–375). Chicago: Rand-McNally.

Harlow, H. F. (1958). The nature of love. *American Psychologist, 13*(12), 673–685.

Harlow, H. F., Harlow, M. K., & Hansen, E. W. (1963). *The maternal affectional system of rhesus monkeys.* New York: Wiley.

Harlow, M., & Laurence, R. (Eds.). (2010). *A cultural history of childhood and the family in antiquity* (Vol. 1). Oxford, United Kingdom: Berg Publishers.

Harms, R. W., Johnson, R. V., & Murry, M. M. (2004). *Mayo Clinic guide to a healthy pregnancy.* New York: HarperCollins.

Harway, M. (2000). Families experiencing violence. In W. C. Nichols, M. A. Pace-Nichols, D. S. Becvar, & A. Y. Napier (Eds.), *Handbook of family development and intervention* (pp. 391–414). New York: Wiley.

Harwood, K., McLean, N., & Durkin, K. (2007). First-time mothers' expectations of parenthood: What happens when optimistic expectations are not matched by later experiences? *Developmental Psychology, 43*(1), 1–12.

Haveman, R., Wolfe, B., & Pence, K. (2001). Intergenerational effects of nonmarital and early childbearing. In L. L. Wu & B. Wolfe (Eds.), *Out of wedlock: Causes and consequences of nonmarital fertility* (pp. 287–316). New York: Russell Sage Foundation.

Hawkins, A., Danielson, C., de Arellano, M. A., Hanson, R. F., Ruggiero, K. J., Smith, D. W., et al. (2010). Ethnic/racial differences in the prevalence of injurious spanking and other child physical abuse in a national survey of adolescents. *Child Maltreatment, 15*(3), 242–249.

Hawkins, D. B. (2003). *When you're living in a stepfamily.* Colorado Springs, CO: Cook Communications Ministries.

Hawthorne, B. J., & Lennings, C. J. (2008). The marginalization of nonresident fathers: Their postdivorce roles. *Journal of Divorce & Remarriage, 49*(3/4), 191.

Hayslip, B., Jr. (2003). The impact of a psychosocial intervention on parental efficacy, grandchild relationship quality, and well-being among grandparents raising grandchildren. In B. Hayslip, Jr., & J. H. Patrick (Eds.), *Working with custodial grandparents* (pp. 163–176). New York: Springer.

Hayslip, B., Glover, R., Harris, B., Miltenberger, P., Baird, A., & Kaminski, P. (2009). Perceptions of custodial grandparents among young adults. *Journal of Intergenerational Relationships, 7*(2–3), 209–224.

Heaven, P. C. L. (2001). *The social psychology of adolescence.* Basingstoke, United Kingdom: Palgrave.

Herek, G. M. (1993). The context of antigay violence: Notes on cultural and psychological heterosexism. In L. D. Garnets & D. C. Kimmel (Eds.), *Psychological perspectives on lesbian and gay male experiences* (pp. 89–107). New York: Columbia University Press.

Herek, G. M. (2006). Legal recognition of same-sex relationships in the United States: A social science perspective. *American Psychologist, 61*(6), 607–621.

Hernandez, B. C., Schwenke, N. J., & Wilson, C. M. (2011). Spouses in mixed-orientation marriage: A 20-year review of empirical studies. *Journal of Marriage and Family Therapy, 37*(3), 307–318.

Herrmann-Green, L. K., & Gehring, T. M. (2007). The German lesbian family study: Planning for parenthood via donor insemination. *Journal of GLBT Family Studies, 3*(4), 351–396.

Hess, C. R., Papas, M. A., & Black, M. M. (2002). Resilience among African American adolescent mothers: Predictors of positive parenting in early infancy. *Journal of Pediatric Psychology, 27*, 619–629.

Heuveline, P., & Timberlake, J. M. (2004). The role of co-habitation in family formation: The United States in comparative perspective. *Journal of Marriage and the Family, 66*, 1214–1230.

Heyman, R. E. & Slep, A. M. S. (2002). Do child abuse and interparental violence lead to adulthood family violence? *Journal of Marriage and Family, 64*, 864–870.

Higgins, C. A., Duxbury, L. E., & Lyons, S. T. (2010). Coping with overload and stress: Men and women in dual-earner families. *Journal of Marriage and Family, 72*(4), 847–859.

Hildebrand, V., Phenice, L., Gray, M., & Hines, R. (2008). *Knowing and serving diverse families* (3rd ed.). Upper Saddle River, NJ: Prentice Hall.

Hobbs, F., & Stoops, N. (2002). Demographic trends in the 20th century. *Census 2000 Special Reports,* Series CENTER-4. Washington, DC: U.S. Government Printing Office.

Hochschild, A., & Machung, A. (2003). *The second shift.* New York: Penguin Books.

Hofferth, S. L., & Goldscheider, F. (2010). Family structure and the transition to early parenthood. *Demography, 47*(2), 415–437.

Hoffman, L. (1973). Deviation-amplifying process in natural groups. In J. Haley (Ed.), *Changing families* (pp. 135–168). New York: Grune & Stratton.

Honig, A. S., & Morin, C. (2001). When should programs for teen parents and babies begin? Longitudinal evaluation of a teen parents and babies program. *Journal of Primary Prevention, 21*, 447–454.

Howard, K. S., Carothers, S. S., Smith, L. E., & Akai, C. E. (2007). Overcoming the odds: Protective factors in the lives of children. In J. G. Borkowski, J. R. Farris, T. L. Whitman, S. S. Carothers, & K. Weed (Eds.), *Risk and resilience: Adolescent mothers and their children grow up* (pp. 205–232). Mahwah, NJ: Lawrence Erlbaum.

Howard, K., Martin, A., Berlin, L. J., & Brooks-Gunn, J. (2011). Early mother–child separation, parenting, and child well-being in Early Head Start families. *Attachment & Human Development, 13*(1), 5–26.

Howes, P. W., Cicchetti, D., Toth, S. L., & Rogosch, F. A. (2000). Affective, organizations, and relational characteristics of maltreating families: A system's perspective. *Journal of Family Psychology, 14*, 95–110.

Hoyt, H. H., & Broom, B. L. (2002). School-based teen pregnancy prevention programs: A review of the literature. *Journal of School Nursing, 18*, 11–17.

Huebner, A. J. (2009). Exploring processes of family stress and adaptation: An expanded model. In J. Mancini & K. Roberto (Eds.), *Pathways of human development: Explorations of change* (pp. 227–242). Plymouth, United Kingdom: Lexington Books.

Huebner, A. J., Mancini, J. A., Bowen, G. L., & Orthner, D. K. (2009). Shadowed by war: Building community capacity to support military families. *Family Relations, 58*(2), 216–228.

Huebner, A. J., Mancini, J. A., Wilcox, R. M., Grass, S. R., & Grass, G. A. (2007). Parental deployment and youth in military families: Exploring uncertainty and ambiguous loss. *Family Relations, 56*(2), 112–122.

Hughes, D. (2003). Correlates of African American and Latino parents' messages to children about ethnicity and race: A comparative study of racial socialization. *American Journal of Community Psychology, 31*, 15–33.

Humes, K. R., Jones, N. A., & Ramirez, R. R. (2011, March). *Overview of race and Hispanic origin: 2010.* Washington, DC: U.S. Census Bureau. Retrieved November 7, 2012, from www.census.gov/prod/cen2010/briefs/c2010br-02.pdf

Humphries, N. A., & Parks, C. A. (2006). Seeking a child through international adoption: Lucy's and Robin's story. In L. Messinger & D. F. Morrow (Eds.), *Case studies on sexual orientation & gender expression in social work practice* (pp. 57–59). New York: Columbia University Press.

Hunter, A. E., & Forden, C. (Eds.). (2002). *Readings in the psychology of gender: Exploring our differences and commonalities.* Needham Heights, MA: Allyn & Bacon.

Hurme, H., Westerback, S., & Quadrello, T. (2010). Traditional and new forms of contact between grandparents and grandchildren. *Journal of Intergenerational Relationships, 8*, 264–280.

Hyde, J. S., & DeLamater, J. D. (2000). *Understanding human sexuality* (7th ed.). New York: McGraw-Hill.

Ihinger-Tallman, M., & Pasley, K. (1997). Stepfamilies in 1984 and today—a scholarly perspective. In I. Levin & M. B. Sussman (Eds.), *Stepfamilies: History, research, and policy* (pp. 19–40). New York: Haworth Press.

Imber-Black, E. (1993, May–June). Ghosts in the therapy room. *Family Therapy Networker,* 18–29.

Ishizawa, H., Kenney, C. T., Kubo, K., & Stevens, G. (2006). Constructing interracial families through intercountry adoption. *Social Science Quarterly, 87*, 1207–1224.

Jacobs, L., Lawlor, M., & Mattingly, C. (2011). I/We narratives among African American families raising children with special needs. *Culture, Medicine & Psychiatry, 35*(1), 3–25.

Jaffee, S. (2002). Pathways to adversity in young adulthood among early childbearers. *Journal of Family Psychology, 16*, 38–49.

Jaffee, S., Caspi, A., Moffitt, T. E., Belsky, J., & Silva, P. (2001). Why are children born to teen mothers at risk for adverse outcomes in young adulthood? Results from a 20-year longitudinal study. *Development & Psychopathology, 13*, 377–397.

James, M. (2006). Implementing attachment theory in Head Start to enhance social competence: A program development. *Dissertation Abstracts International, Section B: The Sciences and Engineering, 67*(4-B), 2259.

Jarrett, R. L. (1995). Growing up poor: The family experiences of socially mobile youth in low-income African American neighborhoods. *Journal of Adolescent Research, 10*, 111–135.

Jenson, J. M., & Fraser, M. W. (Eds.). (2011). *Social policy for children and families: A risk and resilience perspective* (2nd ed.). Thousand Oaks, CA: Sage.

Joe, J. R., & Malach, R. S. (1992). Families with Native American roots. In E. W. Lynch & M. J. Hanson (Eds.), *Developing cross-cultural competence: A guide for working with young children and their families* (pp. 89–119). Baltimore: Paul H. Brooks.

Johnson, J. O. (2005). Who's minding the kids? Child care arrangements: 2002. *Current Population Reports,* P70-101. Washington, DC: U.S. Census Bureau.

Johnson, M. D., Cohan, C. L., Davila, J., Lawrence, E., Rogge, R. D., Karney, B. R., et al. (2005). Problem-solving skills and affective expressions as predictors of change in marital satisfaction. *Journal of Consulting and Clinical Psychology, 73*(1), 15–27.

Johnson, S. M., & O'Connor, E. (2001). *For lesbian parents: Your guide to helping your family grow up happy, healthy, and proud.* New York: Guilford Publications.

Jones, D. J., Forehand, R., Brody, G. H., & Armistead, L. (2002). Positive parenting and child psychosocial adjustment in inner-city single-parent African American families: The role of maternal optimism. *Behavior Modification, 26*, 464–481.

Joselevich, E. (1988). Family transitions, cumulative stress, and crises. In C. J. Falicov (Ed.), *Family transitions: Continuity and change over the life cycle.* New York: Bruner/Mazel.

Julian, T. W., McHenry, P. C., & McKelvey, M. W. (1994). Cultural variations in parenting: Perceptions of Caucasian, African-American, Latino, and Asian-American parents. *Family Relations, 43*, 30–37.

Jungmarker, E. B., Lindgren, H., & Hildingsson, I. (2010). Playing second fiddle is okay—Swedish fathers' experiences of prenatal care. *Journal of Midwifery & Women's Health, 55*(5), 421–429.

Kagan, J. (1976). The psychological requirements for human development. In N. Talbott (Ed.), *Raising children in modern America.* Boston: Little, Brown.

Kandakai, T. L., & Smith, L. C. R. (2007). Denormalizing an historical problem: Teen pregnancy, policy, and public health action. *American Journal of Health Behavior, 31*(2), 170–180.

Kane, E. W. (2006). "No way my boys are going to be like that!": Parents' responses to children's gender nonconformity. *Gender & Society, 20*(2), 149–176.

Kann, L., Brener, N., & Wechsler, H. (2007). Overview and summary: School health policies and programs study 2006. *Journal of School Health, 77*(8), 385–397.

Karney, B. (2011). "What's (not) wrong with low-income couples: Maintaining intimacy in more and less affluent marriages." National Conference on Family Relations, Families and the Shifting Economy, Closing Plenary Session. Orlando, FL.

Karney, B. R. & Crown, J. A. (2007). *Families under stress: An assessment of data, theory, and research on marriage and divorce in the military.* Santa Monica, CA: RAND Corporation.

Karney, B. R., & Crown, J. S. (2011). Does development keep military marriages together or break them apart? Evidence from Afghanistan and Iraq. In S. Wadsworth, & D. Riggs (Eds.), *Risk and resilience in U.S. military families* (pp. 23–45). New York: Springer.

Karney, B. R., & Frye, N. E. (2002). "But we've been getting better lately": Comparing prospective and retrospective views of relationship development. *Journal of Personality and Social Psychology, 82*(2), 222–238.

Kaslow, F. W. (2000). Families experiencing divorce. In W. C. Nichols, M. A. Pace-Nichols, D. S. Becvar, & Y. A. Napier (Eds.), *Handbook of family development and intervention* (pp. 341–368). New York: Wiley.

Kazdin, A. E., & Benjet, C. (2003). Spanking children: Evidence and issues. *Current Directions in Psychological Science, 12*(3), 99–103.

Kelley, M., Schwerin, M., Farrar, K., & Lane, M. (2007). A participant evaluation of the U.S. Navy parent support program. *Journal of Family Violence, 22*(3), 131–139.

Kelly, P. (2011). Corporal punishment and child maltreatment in New Zealand. *Acta Paediatrica, 100*(1), 14–20.

Kendall-Tackett, K. A. (2001). *The hidden feelings of motherhood: Coping with stress, depression, and burnout.* Oakland, CA: New Harbinger.

Kendrick, D. T., & Luce, C. L. (2000). An evolutionary life-history model of gender difference and similarities. In T. Eckes & H. M. Trautner (Eds.), *The developmental social psychology of gender.* Mahwah, NJ: Lawrence Erlbaum.

Kennedy, R. (2004). *Interracial intimacies: Sex, marriage, identity, and adoption.* New York: Knopf.

Kershaw, S. (2000). Living in a lesbian household: The effects on children. *Child & Family Social Work, 5*, 365–371.

Kershaw, T. S., Niccolai, L. M., Ethier, K. A., Lewis, J. B., & Ickovics, J. R. (2003). Perceived susceptibility to pregnancy and sexually transmitted disease among pregnant and nonpregnant adolescents. *Journal of Community Psychology, 31*, 419–434.

Kesterton, D., & Coleman, L. (2010). Speakeasy: A UK-wide initiative raising parents' confidence and ability to talk about sex and relationships with their children. *Sex Education, 10*(4), 437–448.

Key, J., Barbosa, G. A., & Owens, V. J. (2001). The Second Chance Club: Repeat adolescent pregnancy prevention with a school-based intervention. *Journal of Adolescent Health, 28*, 167–169.

Khawaja, A., & Sherwin, J. (2011). More time out-doors may reduce kids' risk for nearsightedness, research suggests. *ScienceDaily*. Retrieved November 7, 2012, from www.sciencedaily.com/releases/2011/10/111024084639.htm

Kim, P., & Swain, J. E. (2006). Why love matters: How affection shapes a baby's brain. *Journal of the American Academy of Child & Adolescent Psychiatry, 45*(1), 122–123.

Kimes, L. M. (2006). Adolescent parents' under-standing of the social and emotional develop-ment of their very young children. *Dissertation Abstracts International, Section B: The Sciences and Engineering, 67*(6-B), 3483.

Kinnear, K. L. (2007). *Childhood sexual abuse* (2nd ed., rev.). Santa Barbara, CA: ABC-CLIO.

Kinsey, A. C., Pomeroy, W. B., & Martin, C. E. (1948). *Sexual behavior in the human male*. Phil-adelphia: Saunders.

Kinsey, A. C., Pomeroy, W. B., Martin, C. E., & Geb-hard, P. H. (1953). *Sexual behavior in the human female*. Philadelphia: Saunders.

Kirby, D. (2001). *Emerging answers: Research find-ings on programs to reduce teen pregnancy*. Washington, DC: National Campaign to Prevent Teen Pregnancy.

Knowles, C. (1997). *Family boundaries: The inven-tion of normality and dangerousness*. Peterbor-ough, ON, Canada: Broadview Press.

Knox, D., & Schacht, C. (2009). *Choices in relation-ships: Introduction to marriage and the family* (10th ed.). Belmont, CA: Cengage Learning.

Koonce, D. A., & Harper, W., Jr. (2005). Engag-ing African American parents in the schools: A community-based consultation model. *Journal of Educational & Psychological Consultation, 16*(1/2), 55–74.

Kopera-Frye, K., Wiscott, R. C., & Begovic, A. (2003). Lessons learned from custodial grandparents involved in a community support group. In B. Hayslip, Jr., & J. H. Patrick (Eds.), *Working with custodial grandparents* (pp. 243–256). New York: Springer.

Kosunen, E., Kaltiala-Heino, R., Rimpela, M., & Laip-pala, P. (2003). Risk-taking sexual behavior and self-reported depression in middle adolescence—a school-based survey. *Child: Care, Health & Devel-opment, 29*, 337–344.

Krebs, L. (1986). Current research on theoretically based parenting programs. *Individual Psychol-ogy: The Journal of Adlerian Theory, Research & Practice, 42*(3), 375.

Kreider, R. M. (2003). *Adopted children and step-children: 2000*. Washington, DC: U.S. Census Bureau.

Kreider, R. M. (2005). *Number, timing, and dura-tion of marriages and divorces: 2001. Current Population Reports*, P70-97. Washington, DC: U.S. Census Bureau.

Kuczynski, L. (2003). Beyond bidirectionality: Bi-lateral conceptual frameworks for understand-ing dynamics in parent–youth relations. In L. Kuczynski (Ed.), *Handbook of dynamics in par-ent–youth relations* (pp. 3–24). Thousand Oaks, CA: Sage.

Kuczynski, L., & Kochanska, G. (1995). Function and content of maternal demands: Developmen-tal significance of early demands for competent action. *Child Development, 66*, 616–628.

Kurdek, L. A. (2003). Differences between gay and lesbian cohabitating couples. *Journal of Social and Personal Relationships, 20*, 411–436.

Kyriacou, C. (2002). A humanistic view of discipline. In B. Rogers (Ed.), *Teacher leadership and be-havior management* (pp. 40–52). London: Paul Chapman.

LaFollette, H. (2004). Licensing parents. In P. Tittle (Ed.), *Should parents be licensed?: Debating the issue* (pp. 51–63). Amherst, NY: Prometheus Books.

Lalumiere, M. L., Blanchard, R., & Zucker, K. J. (2000) Sexual orientation and handedness in men and women: A meta-analysis. *Psychological Bul-letin, 126*(4), 575–592.

Lamanna, M. A., & Reidman, A. (2006). *Marriages and families: Making choices in a diverse society* (9th ed.). Belmont, CA: Wadsworth/Thomson Learning.

Lamb, M. E., & Ahnert, L. (2006). Nonparental child care: Context, concepts, correlates, and conse-quences. In *Handbook of child psychology* (6th ed., pp. 950–1016). Hoboken, NJ: John Wiley & Sons.

Lambda Legal. (2012). Legal work: Marriage, re-lationships and family protections. Retrieved November 7, 2012, from www.lambdalegal.org/issues/marriage-relationships-and-family-protec-tions

LaSala, M. C. (2000a). Gay male couples: The impor-tance of coming out and being out to parents. *Jour-nal of Homosexuality, 39*, 47–71.

LaSala, M. C. (2000b). Lesbians, gay men, and their parents: Family therapy for the coming-out crisis. *Family Process, 39*, 67–81.

Laszloffy, T. A. (2002). Rethinking family develop-ment theory: Teaching with the systemic family development (SFD) model. *Family Relations, 51*, 206–214.

Lawrence, E., Nylen, K., & Cobb, R. J. (2007). Pre-natal expectations and marital satisfaction over the transition to parenthood. *Journal of Family Psychology, 21*(2), 155–164.

Lawrence, F. R., & Blair, C. (2003). Factorial invari-ance in preventive intervention: Modeling the development of intelligence in low birth weight, preterm infants. *Prevention Science, 4*, 249–261.

Layne, S. L. (2004). *Over land and sea: The story of international adoption*. Gretna, LA: Pelican.

Leake, V. S. (2007). Personal, familial, and systemic factors associated with family belonging for step-family adolescents. *Journal of Divorce & Remar-riage, 47*(1/2), 135–155.

Lee, M. M., & Lee, R. E. (2006). The voices of ac-cepting and supportive parents of gay sons: To-wards an ecosystemic strengths model. *Journal of GLBT Family Studies, 2*(2), 1–28.

Lee-Baggley, D., Preece, M., & DeLongis, A. (2005). Coping with interpersonal stress: Role of big five traits. *Journal of Personality, 73*(5), 1141–1180.

Lefever, J. B., Nicholson, J. S., & Noria, C. W. (2007). Children's uncertain futures: Problems in school. In J. G. Borkowski, J. R. Farris, T. L. Whitman, S. S. Carothers, & K. Weed (Eds.), *Risk and resilience: Adolescent mothers and their children grow up* (pp. 69–99). Mahwah, NJ: Lawrence Erlbaum.

Le Grange, D., & Lock, J. (2011). *Eating disorders in children and adolescents: A clinical handbook*. New York: Guilford Press.

Leon, K. (2005). Portrayals of stepfamilies in film: Using media images in remarriage education. *Family Relations, 54*(1), 3–23.

Lester, T. P. (Ed.). (2003). *Gender nonconformity, race, and sexuality: Charting the connections*. Madison: University of Wisconsin Press.

Lev, A. I. (2004). *The complete lesbian & gay parent-ing guide*. New York: The Berkley Publishing Group.

LeVay, S. (1991). A difference in hypothalamic struc-ture between heterosexual and homosexual men. *Science, 253*(5023), 1034–1037.

LeVay, S. (2011). *Gay, straight, and the reason why: The science of sexual orientation*. New York: Ox-ford University Press.

Levene, M., Tudehope, D. I., & Sinha, S. (2008). *Essential neonatal medicine* (4th ed.). Ames, IA: Blackwell.

Lichter, D. T., & Graefe, D. R. (2001). Finding a mate? The marital and cohabitation histories of unwed mothers. In L. L. Wu & B. Wolfe (Eds.), *Out of wedlock: Causes and consequences of non-marital fertility* (pp. 317–343). New York: Russell Sage Foundation.

Lin, F.-T., & Chen, J. (2006). Custodial fathers—Do they work more or fewer hours? *Journal of Fam-ily and Economic Issues, 27*(3), 513–522.

Lincoln, A., Swift, E., & Shorteno-Fraser, M. (2008). Psychological adjustment and treatment of children and families with parents deployed in military combat. *Journal of Clinical Psychology, 64*(8), 984–992.

Lino, M. (2011) *Expenditures on children by fami-lies, 2010*. Washington, DC: U.S. Department of Agriculture.

Lino, M., & Carlson, A. (2010). Estimating housing expenses on children: A comparison of methodol-ogies. *Journal of Legal Economics, 16*(2), 61–79.

Littler, W. (1997). *A Victorian childhood: Recollec-tions and reflections*. Belbroughton, Worcester-shire, United Kingdom: Marion Seymour.

Lock, J. (2011). Evaluation of family treatment mod-els for eating disorders. *Current Opinion in Psy-chiatry, 24*(4) 274–279.

Locke, J. (1697). *Some thoughts concerning educa-tion* (4th ed., enlarged). London: H. Clark for A. and J. Churchill.

Long, D. N., Wisniewski, A. B., & Migeon, C. J. (2004). Gender role across development in adult women with congenital adrenal hyperpla-sia due to 21-hydroxylase deficiency. *Journal* of Pediatric Endocrinology and Metabolism, 17(10), 1367–1373.

Longmore, M. A., Manning, W. D., Giordano, P. C., & Rudolph, J. L. (2003). Contraceptive self-efficacy: Does it influence adolescents' contraceptive use? Journal of Health & Social Behavior, 44, 45–60.

Lorah, M. A. (2002). Lesbian stepmothers: A grounded theory study of women who cohabit with biological, custodial mothers of children from previous heterosexual relationships. Dissertation Abstracts International, 62, 4074.

Lumeng, J. C., Cabral, H. J., & Gannon, K. (2007). Pre-natal exposures to cocaine and alcohol and physical growth patterns to age 8 years. Neurotoxicology and Teratology, 29(4), 446–457.

Luster, T., Bates, L., Fitzgerald, H., Vanderbelt, M., & Key, J. P. (2000). Factors related to successful outcomes among preschool children born to low-income adolescent mothers. Journal of Marriage and the Family, 62, 113–146.

Luyckx, K., Tildesley, E. A., Soenens, B., Andrews, J. A., Hampson, S. E., Peterson, M., & Duriez, B. (2011). Parenting and trajectories of children's maladaptive behaviors: A 12-year prospective community study. Journal of Clinical Child and Adolescent Psychology, 40(3), 468–478.

Lynch, J. M. (2000). Considerations of family structure and gender composition: The lesbian and gay stepfamily. Journal of Homosexuality, 40, 81–95.

Lynch, J. M., & McMahon-Klosterman, K. (2006). Guiding the acquisition of therapist ally identity: Research on the GLBT stepfamily as resource. Journal of GLBT Family Studies, 2(3/4), 123–150.

Maccoby, E. E., & Lewis, C. C. (2003). Less day care or different day care? Child Development, 74(4), 1069–1075.

Maccoby, E., & Martin, J. A. (1983). Socialization in the context of the family: Parent–child interaction. In P. H. Mussen (Ed.), Handbook of child psychology, Vol. 4: Socialization, personality, and social development (4th ed., pp. 1–101). New York: Wiley.

MacDermid-Wadsworth, S. (Ed.), Stress in U.S. military families (pp. 131–147). New York: Springer.

Madden-Derdich, D. A., Herzog, M. J., & Leonard, S. A. (2002). The coparental involvement of teen-aged fathers: The mediating role of mothers' desire to have fathers involved. Paper presented at the 64th Annual Conference of the National Council on Family Relations, Houston, Texas.

Magnuson, K. A., & Waldfogel, J. (2005). Preschool child care and parents' use of physical discipline. Infant and Child Development, 14(2), 177–198.

Malinowski, A., & Stamler, L. L. (2003). Adolescent girls' personal experience with Baby Think It Over infant simulator. American Journal of Maternal/Child Nursing, 28(3), 205–211.

Mallery, J. G. (2002). Practicing parenting? Effects of computerized infant simulators on teenage attitudes toward early parenthood. The Journal of Early Education and Family Review, 9, 18–28.

Malley-Morrison, K., & Hines, D. (2003). Family violence in a cultural perspective: Defining, understanding, and combating abuse. Thousand Oaks, CA: Sage.

Malpass, R. S. (1993, August). A discussion of the ICAI. Symposium presented at the Annual Convention of the American Psychological Association, Toronto, Ontario, Canada.

Mancini, J. A., & Bowen, G. L. (2009). Community resilience: A social organization theory of action and change. In J. Mancini & K. Roberto (Eds.), Pathways of human development: Explorations of change (pp. 245–265). Plymouth, United Kingdom: Lexington Books.

Mancini, J. A., & Roberto, K. A. (Eds.). (2009). Pathways of human development: Explorations of change. Lanham, MD: Lexington Books.

Mangelsdorf, S. C., Laxman, D. J., & Jessee, A. (2011). Coparenting in two-parent nuclear families. In J. P. McHale, & K. M. Lindahl (Eds.), Coparenting: A conceptual and clinical examination of family systems (pp. 39–59). Washington, DC: American Psychological Association.

Manlove, J., Mariner, C., & Papillo, A. R. (2000). Subsequent fertility among teen mothers: Longitudinal analyses of recent national data. Journal of Marriage and the Family, 62, 430–448.

Manlove, E., Vazquez, A., & Vernon-Feagans, L. (2008). The quality of caregiving in child care: Relations to teacher complexity of thinking and perceived supportiveness of the work environment. Infant & Child Development, 17(3), 203–222.

Mann, M., & Peabody, E. (1863). Moral culture of infancy, and kindergarten guide … by Mrs. Horace Mann and Elizabeth P. Peabody. Boston: Burnham.

Manning, W. D., & Smock, P. J. (2000). "Swapping" families: Serial parenting and economic support for children. Journal of Marriage and the Family, 62, 111–122.

March of Dimes Foundation. (2011). Cytomegalovirus. Retrieved November 7, 2012, from www.marchofdimes.com/pregnancy/complications_cytomegalovirus.html

Marlow, N., Wolke, D., Bracewell, M. A., & Samara, M. (2005). Neurologic and developmental disability at six years of age after extremely preterm birth. New England Journal of Medicine, 352, 9–19.

Marshall, J. (2011). Infant neurosensory development: Considerations for infant child care. Early Childhood Education Journal, 39, 175–181.

Marsiglio, W. (2004). Stepdads: Stories of love, hope, and repair. Lanham, MD: Rowman & Littlefield.

Marsiglio, W., Hutchinson, S., & Cohan, M. (2000). Envisioning fatherhood: A social psychological perspective on young men with kids. Family Relations, 49, 133–142.

Martin, C., & Fleming, V. (2011). The birth satisfaction scale. International Journal of Health Care Quality Assurance, 24(2), 124–135.

Martin, J. A., Hamilton, B. E., Ventura, S. J., Sutton, P. D., Ventura, S. J., Menaker, F., et al. (2006).

Births: Final data for 2004. National Vital Statistics Reports, 55(1). Hyattsville, MD: National Center for Health Statistics.

Matsumoto, D., & Juang, L. (2008). Culture and psychology (4th ed., pp. 7, 27). Belmont, CA: Wadsworth Cengage Learning.

Matsumoto, D., & Juang, L. (2012). Culture and psychology. (5th ed.). Belmont, CA: Wadsworth Cengage Learning.

Mattessich, P., & Hill, R. (1987). Life cycle and family development. In M. Sussman & S. Steinmetz (Eds.), Handbook of marriage and the family. New York: Plenum Press.

Mayo Clinic. (2011a). Mayo clinic: Guide to a healthy pregnancy. Intercourse, PA: Good Books.

Mayo Clinic. (2011b). Pregnancy and exercise: Baby, let's move! Retrieved November 7, 2012, from www.mayoclinic.com/health/pregnancy-and-exercise/PR00096

Mays, L. C., & Lechman, J. F. (2007). Parental representations and subclinical changes in postpartum mood. Infant Mental Health Journal, 28(3), 281–295.

McCarthy, B. W., & Ginsberg, R. L. (2007). Second marriages: Challenges and risks. The Family Journal, 15(2), 119–123.

McClellan, D. L. (2001). The "other mother" and second parent adoption. Journal of Gay & Lesbian Social Services, 13(3), 1–21.

McCoyd, J. M. (2010). A bio-psycho-social assessment of maternal attachment in pregnancy and fetal loss. Social Work Review/Revista de Asisten?? Social?, (2), 131.

McDonell, J. R., Limber, S. P., & Connor-Godbey, J. (2007). Pathways teen mother support project: Longitudinal findings. Children and Youth Services Review, 29(7), 840–855.

McGoldrick, M., & Gerson, R. (1985). Genograms in family assessment. New York: Norton.

McGuinness, T., & Pallansch, L. (2000). Competence of children adopted from the former Soviet Union. Family Relations, 49, 457–464.

McHale, J. P., & Lindahl, K. M. (Eds.). (2011). Coparenting: A conceptual and clinical examination of family systems. Washington, DC: American Psychological Association.

McHale, J. P., & Rotman, T. (2007). Is seeing believing? Expectant parents' outlooks on coparenting and later coparenting solidarity. Infant Behavior & Development, 30(1), 63–81.

McKnight, J. (2000). Editorial: The origins of male homosexuality. Psychology, Evolution & Gender, 2, 223–228.

McLoyd, V. C., Cauce, A. M., Takeuchi, D., & Wilson, L. (2000). Marital processes and parental socialization in families of color: A decade review of research. Journal of Marriage and the Family, 62, 1070–1093.

McLoyd, V. C., Kaplan, R., Hardaway, C. R., & Wood, D. (2007). Journal of Family Psychology, 21(1), 165–175.

McNulty, J. K., O'Mara, E. M., & Karney, B. R. (2008). Benevolent cognitions as a strategy of relationship maintenance: "Don't sweat the small stuff"… But it is not all small stuff. *Journal of Personality and Social Psychology, 94*(4), 631–646.

Merighi, J. R., & Grimes, M. D. (2000). Coming out to families in a multicultural context. *Families in Society, 81,* 32–41.

Mersky, J. P., & Reynolds, A. J. (2007). Predictors of early childbearing: Evidence from the Chicago longitudinal study. *Children and Youth Services Review, 29*(1), 35–52.

Michaels, M. L. (2006). Stepfamily enrichment program: A preventive intervention for remarried couples. *Journal for Specialists in Group Work, 31*(2), 135–152.

Migeon, C. J. (2003). Gender assignement in newborns: Gender identity/role differentiation in genetic males affected by abnormal sex differentiation. *Minerva Pediatrica, 5536*–5540.

Milgrom, J., Holt, C. J., Gemmill, A. W., Ericksen, J., Leigh, B., Buist, A., & Schembri, C. (2011). Treating postnatal depressive symptoms in primary care: A randomised controlled trial of GP management, with and without adjunctive counselling. *BMC Psychiatry, 11,* 1–10.

Milgrom, J., Schrembri, C., Ericksen, J., Ross, J., & Gemmill, A. W. (2011). Towards parenthood: An antenatal intervention to reduce depression, anxiety, and parenting difficulties. *Journal of Affective Disorders, 130*(3), 385–394.

Military Child Education Coalition. (2011). Coordinated treatment and support enhance access to care for veterans with post-traumatic stress disorder and traumatic brain injury and their families. Retrieved November 7, 2012, from www.innovations.ahrq.gov/content.aspx?id=3335

Milkie, M. A., & Peltola, P. (1999). Playing all the roles: Gender and the work–family balancing act. *Journal of Marriage and the Family, 61,* 476–490.

Miller, A. (1990). *For your own good: Hidden cruelty in childrearing and the roots of violence.* New York: Noonday Press.

Miller, A. (2002). *The truth will set you free: Overcoming emotional blindness and finding your true adult self.* New York: Basic Books.

Miller, A. (2006). *The body never lies: The lingering effects of hurtful parenting.* New York: Norton.

Miller, B. C., & Coyl, D. D. (2000). Adolescent pregnancy and childbearing in relation to infant adoption in the United States. *Adoption Quarterly, 4,* 3–25.

Miller, J., & Knudsen, D. D. (2006). *Family abuse and violence: A social problems perspective.* Lanham, MD: Alta Mira Press.

Miller-Perrin, C. L., Perrin, R. D., & Barnett, O. W. (2004). *Family violence across the lifespan: An introduction* (2nd ed.). Thousand Oaks, CA: Sage.

Miniño, A. (2011). Death in the United States, 2009. *NCHS Data Brief,* (64), 1–8.

Mintz, S. (2006). *Huck's raft: A history of American childhood.* Boston: Harvard University Press.

Minuchin, S. (1974). *Families and family therapy,* Miscellaneous Publication No. 1528-2010. Cambridge, MA: Harvard University Press.

Mitchell, B. A. (1998). Too close for comfort? Parental assessments of "boomerang kid" living arrangements. *Canadian Journal of Sociology, 23,* 21–46.

Mitchell, B. A. (2006). *The boomerang age: Transitions to adulthood in families.* New Brunswick, NJ: Aldine.

Mitchell, B. A., & Gee, E. M. (1996). "Boomerang kids" and midlife parental marital satisfaction. *Family Relations, 45,* 442–448.

Mitchell, V., & Green, R.-J. (2008). Different storks for different folks: Gay and lesbian parents' experiences with alternative insemination and surrogacy. *Journal of GLBT Family Studies, 3*(2/3), 81–104.

Mollborn, S. (2007). Making the best of a bad situation: Material resources and teenage parenthood. *Journal of Marriage and Family, 69*(1), 92–104.

Molter, N. C. (2003). Creating a healing environment for critical care. *Critical Care Nursing Clinics of North America, 15,* 295–304.

Monk, C., Fifer, W. P., Meyers, M. M., Sloan, R. P., Trien, L., & Hurtado, A. (2000). Maternal stress responses and anxiety during pregnancy: Effects on fetal heart rate. *Developmental Psychology, 36,* 67–77.

Mooney, L. A., Knox, D., & Schacht, C. (2010). *Understanding social problems* (7th ed.). Belmont, CA: Wadsworth.

Mooney-Somers, J., & Golombok, S. (2000). Children of lesbian mothers: From the 1970s to the new millennium. *Sexual & Relationship Therapy, 15,* 121–126.

Moore, M. R., & Brooks-Gunn, J. (2002). Adolescent parenthood. In M. H. Bornstein (Ed.), *Handbook of parenting, Vol. 3: Being and becoming a parent* (2nd ed., pp. 173–214). Mahwah, NJ: Lawrence Erlbaum.

Morris, B. J., & Masnick, A. M. (2008). Making numbers out of magnitudes. *Behavioral & Brain Sciences, 31*(6), 662–663.

Morris, D. (1986). *The illustrated naked ape: A zoologist's study of the human animal.* New York: Crown.

Morris, D. (1996). *The human zoo: A zoologist's classic study of the urban animal.* New York: Kodansha International.

Morrissey, T. W., Dunifon, R. E., & Kalil, A. (2011). Maternal employment, work schedules, and children's body mass index. *Child Development, 82*(1), 66–81.

Mosher, C. M. (2001). The social implications of sexual identity formation and the coming-out process: A review of the theoretical and empirical literature. *Family Journal: Counseling & Therapy for Couples & Families, 9,* 164–173.

Muñoz, L., Qualter, P., & Padgett, G. (2011). Empathy and bullying: Exploring the influence of callous-unemotional traits. *Child Psychiatry & Human Development, 42*(2), 183–196.

Munson, M. L., & Sutton, P. D. (2006). Births, marriage, divorces, and deaths: Provisional data for 2005. *National Vital Statistics Reports, 54*(20).

Hyattsville, MD: National Center for Health Statistics.

Murdock, K. W. (2012, February 6). An examination of parental self-efficacy among mothers and fathers. *Psychology of Men & Masculinity.*

Murphy, A. (2003). Daddy boot camp: How an increasingly popular program prepares rookie fathers to hit the ground crawling. *Child, 18,* 85–86, 88, 90.

Murphy, M.-K., & Knoll, J. (2003). *International adoption: Sensitive advice for prospective parents.* Chicago, IL: Chicago Review Press.

Mustanski, B. S., Dupree, M. G., Nievergelt, C. M., Bocklandt, S., Schork, N. J., & Hamer, D. H. (2005). A genomewide scan of male sexual orientation. *Human Genetics, 116*(4), 272–278.

Nagel, M. C. (2012). *In the beginning: The brain, early development and learning.* Camberwell, Victoria, Australia: ACER Press.

Nam, K. (2009). Program participants' understanding about program rules and its effect on program outcomes: Non-custodial parents' knowledge about child support rules and its impact on child support payments. *Dissertation Abstracts International, Section A, 69.*

Nanda, S., & Warms, R. L. (2007). *Cultural anthropology* (10th ed.). Belmont, CA: Wadsworth.

Nation, M. (2007). Empowering the victim: Interventions for children victimized by bullies. In J. E. Zins, M. J. Elias, & C. A. Maher (Eds.), *Bullying, victimization, and peer harassment: A handbook of prevention and intervention* (pp. 239–255). New York: Haworth Press.

National Alliance on Mental Illness. (2011). Suicide in youth. Retrieved November 7, 2012, from www.nami.org/Template.cfm?Section=By_Illness&Template=/TaggedPage/TaggedPageDisplay.cfm&TPLID=54&ContentID=23041

National Association of Children's Hospitals. (2012). Children's hospitals combat #1 killer of kids: 2011 survey of injury prevention services at children's hospitals. Retrieved November 7, 2012, from www.childrenshospitals.net/AM/Template.cfm?Section=Injury_Prevention1&TEMPLATE=/CM/ContentDisplay.cfm&CONTENTID=62186&cmpid=hp_injury_surveyresults2012

National Center for Chronic Disease Prevention and Health Promotion & American Society for Reproductive Medicine. (2009). *Assisted reproductive technology success rates: National summary and fertility clinic reports.* Atlanta, GA: U.S. Department of Health and Human Services.

National Center for Health Statistics. (2011). Vaccines and immunizations. Retrieved November 7, 2012, from www.cdc.gov/vaccines/default.htm

National Center on Shaken Baby Syndrome. (2012). Physical consequences of shaking. Retrieved November 7, 2012, from www.dontshake.org/sbs.php?topNavID=3&subNavID=23

National Center for Victims of Crime. (2008). Domestic violence. Retrieved November 7, 2012, from http://www.victimsofcrime.org/our-programs/public-policy

National Coalition for the Homeless. (2006). *Encyclopedia of world poverty*. Thousand Oaks, CA: Sage.

National Foster Parent Association. (2011). Foster parent training requirements. Retrieved November 7, 2012, from http://www.nfpaonline.org/Default.aspx?pageId=1105687

National Institute for Early Education Research. (2011). State pre-k evaluations. Retrieved November 7, 2012, from http://nieer.org/research/state-pre-k-evaluations

National Institute of Child Health and Human Development. (2006). *The NICHD study of early child care and youth development: Findings for children up to 4½ years*. Washington, DC: Author. Retrieved November 7, 2012, from http://www.nichd.nih.gov/publications/pubs_details.cfm?from=&pubs_id=5047

National Institute of Child Health and Human Development. (2010). Child Development & Behavior (CDB) Branch. Retrieved November 7, 2012, from www.nichd.nih.gov/about/org/crmc/cdb

National Institute on Alcohol Abuse and Alcoholism. (2012). Underage drinking. Retrieved November 7, 2012, from www.niaaa.nih.gov/alcohol-health/special-populations-co-occurring-disorders/underage-drinking

National Institute on Drug Abuse. (2011). Adolescents and young adults. Retrieved November 7, 2012, from www.drugabuse.gov/publications/research-reports/prescription-drugs/trends-in-prescription-drug-abuse/adolescents-young-adults

National Middle School Association. (2006). Parent involvement. Retrieved November 7, 2012, from www.amle.org/Research/ResearchSummaries/ParentInvolvement/tabid/274/Default.aspx

National Middle School Association. (2009). The power of looping and long-term relationships. *Middle Ground, 12*(3). Retrieved November 7, 2012, from www.nmsa.org/Research/ResearchSummaries/Looping/tabid/2090/Default.aspx

National Resource Center for Health and Safety in Child Care and Early Education. (2012). Safe sleep practices and SIDS/suffocation risk reduction. Retrieved November 7, 2012, from http://nrckids.org/SPINOFF/SAFESLEEP/SafeSleep.pdf

National Resource Center for Health and Safety in Child Care and Early Education. (2012a). Caring for our children. Retrieved November 7, 2012, from http://nrckids.org/CFOC3/CFOC3-grayscale-small.pdf

Nelson, F. (2007). Mother tongues: The discursive journeys of lesbian and heterosexual women into motherhood. *Journal of GLBT Family Studies, 3*(4), 223–266.

Newburn-Cook, C. V., White, D., Svenson, L. W., Emianczuk, N. N., Bott, N., & Edwards, J. (2002). Where and to what extent is prevention of low birth weight possible? *Western Journal of Nursing Research, 24*, 887–904.

Nicholson, J. S., & Farris, J. R. (2007). Children's uncertain futures: Socioemotional delays and psychopathologies. In J. G. Borkowski, J. R. Farris, T. L. Whitman, S. S. Carothers, & K. Weed (Eds.), *Risk and resilience: Adolescent mothers and their children grow up* (pp. 101–123). Mahwah, NJ: Lawrence Erlbaum.

Nitzke, S., Riley, D. Ramminger, A., & Jacobs, G. (2010). *Rethinking nutrition: Connecting science and practice in early childhood settings*. St. Paul, MN: Redleaf Press.

Oberlander, S. E., Black, M. M., & Starr, R. H., Jr. (2007). African American adolescent mothers and grandmothers: A multigenerational approach to parenting. *American Journal of Community Psychology, 39*(1–2), 37–46.

Ochse, R. R. (1990). *Before the gates of excellence: The determinants of creative genius*. Cambridge, NY: Cambridge University Press.

Office of Immigration Statistics. (2007). Immigrant orphans adopted by U.S. citizens by gender, age, and region and country of birth: Fiscal year 2007 [data file]. Retrieved November 7, 2012, from www.dhs.gov/files/statistics/publications/LPR07.shtm

Olmos, J. E., Ybarra, L., & Monterrey, M. (1999). *Americanos: Latino life in the United States*. New York: Little, Brown.

Olson, S. (2007). Extending tours, stressing troops. *In These Times*. Retrieved November 7, 2012, from www.inthesetimes.com/article/3295/extending_tours_stressing_troops/

Olweus, D. (1993). *Bullies on the playground: The role of victimization*. New York: SUNY Press.

Olweus, D. (1995). Bullying or peer abuse at school: Facts and intervention. *Current Directions in Psychological Science, 4*, 196–200.

Ornelas, E. P. (2007). Hispanic and white non-Hispanic adolescent fathers: An exploratory study using socio-cultural variables. *Dissertation Abstracts International, Section B: The Sciences and Engineering, 67*(8-B), 4761.

O'Rand, A. M., & Krecker, M. L. (1990). Concepts of the life cycle: Their history, meanings, and use in the social sciences. *Annual Review of Sociology, 16*, 241–262.

Orthner, D. K., Bowen, G. L., & Beare, V. G. (1990). The organization family: A question of work and family boundaries. *Marriage and Family Review, 15*, 15–36.

Ostrea, C. (2003). *Family bound: One couple's journey through infertility and adoption*. Lincoln, NE: iUniverse, Inc.

Oswald, R. F., & Kuvalanka, K. A. (2008). Same-sex couples: Legal complexities. *Journal of Family Issues, 29*(8), 1051–1066.

Otten, K., & Tuttle, J. (2010). *How to reach and teach children with challenging behavior (K–8): Practical, ready-to-use interventions that work*. San Francisco: Jossey-Bass.

Paechter, C. (2000). Growing up with a lesbian mother: A theoretically-based analysis of personal experience. *Sexualities, 3*, 395–408.

Papernow, P. L. (1984). The stepfamily cycle: An experimental model of stepfamily development. *Family Relations, 33*, 355–363.

Papernow, P. L. (1993). *Becoming a stepfamily*. San Francisco: Josey-Bass.

Pappas, K. B., Wisniewski, A. B., & Migeon, C. J. (2008). Gender role across development in adults with 46,XY disorders of sex development including perineoscrotal hypospadias and small phallus raised male or female. *Journal of Pediatric Endocrinology and Metabolism, 21*(7), 625–630.

Parke, R. D., & Buriel, R. (2006). Socialization in the family: Ethnic and ecological perspectives. In N. Eisenberg, W. Damon, & R. M. Lerner (Eds.), *Handbook of child psychology, Vol. 3: Social, emotional, and personality development* (6th ed., pp. 429–504). Hoboken, NJ: John Wiley & Sons.

Parra-Cardona, J. R., Wampler, R. S., & Sharp, E. A. (2006). "Wanting to be a good father": Experiences of adolescent fathers of Mexican descent in a teen fathers program. *Journal of Marital & Family Therapy, 32*(2), 215–231.

Pasley, K., & Ihinger-Tallman, M. (1987). *Remarriage*. Beverly Hills, CA: Sage.

Patterson, C. J. (2000). Family relationships of lesbians and gay men. *Journal of Marriage & the Family, 62*, 1052–1069.

Patterson, C. J. (2006). Children of lesbian and gay parents. *Current Directions in Psychological Science, 15*(5), 241–244.

Patterson, C. J. (2007). Lesbian and gay family issues in the context of changing legal and social policy environments. In K. J. Bieschke, R. M. Perez, & K. A. DeBord (Eds.), *Handbook of counseling and psychotherapy with lesbian, gay, bisexual, and transgender clients* (2nd ed., pp. 359–377). Washington, DC: American Psychological Association.

Patterson, C. J., & Farr, R. H. (2011). Coparenting among lesbian and gay couples. In J. P. McHale and K. M. Lindahl (Eds.), *Coparenting: A conceptual and clinical examination of family systems*. Washington, DC: American Psychological Association.

Patterson, C. J., & Riskind, R. G. (2010). To be a parent: Issues in family formation among gay and lesbian adults. *Journal of GLBT Family Studies, 6*, 326–340.

Pätzold, H. (2010). Review essay: Mirror neurons in the discourse of social sciences. *Forum: Qualitative Social Research, 11*(3). Retrieved November 7, 2012, from www.qualitative-research.net/index.php/fqs/article/view/1536/3037

Paulson, J., & Bazemore, S. (2010). Prenatal and postpartum depression in fathers and its association with maternal depression: A meta-analysis. *Journal of the American Medical Association, 303*(19), 1961–1969.

Pavao, J. M. (2004). *The family of adoption*. Boston: Beacon Press.

Pearcey, M. (2005). Gay and bisexual married men's attitudes and experiences: Homophobia, reasons for marriage, and self-identity. *Journal of GLBT Family Studies, 1*(4), 21–42.

Pedro-Carroll, J. (2010). *Putting children first: Proven parenting strategies for helping children thrive through divorce*. New York: Avery/Penguin Group.

Pellegrini, A. D., Kato, K., Blatchford, P., & Baines, E. (2002). A short-term longitudinal study of children's playground games across the first year of school: Implications for social competence and adjustment to school. *American Educational Research Journal, 39*(4), 991–1015.

Peplau, L. A., & Beals, K. P. (2004). The family lives of lesbians and gay men. In A. L. Vangelisti (Ed.), *Handbook of family communication* (pp. 233–248). Mahwah, NJ: Lawrence Erlbaum.

Pepler, D. J., & Rubin, K. H. (1991). *The development and treatment of childhood*. Hillsdale, NJ: Lawrence Erlbaum.

Perez, A., O'Neil, K., & Gesiriech, S. (2004). *Demographics of children in foster care*. Washington, DC: The Pew Commission on Children in Foster Care.

Perrin, K. K., & DeJoy, S. B. (2003). Abstinence-only education: How we got here and where we're going. *Journal of Public Health Policy, 24*, 445–459.

Peterson, G. W., Steinmetz, S. K., & Wilson, S. M. (2005). Cultural and cross-cultural perspectives on parent–youth relations. In G. W. Peterson, S. K. Steinmetz, & S. M. Wilson (Eds.), *Parent–youth relations: Cultural and cross-cultural perspectives*. Binghamton, NY: Haworth Press.

Peterson, L. M., Butts, J., & Deville, D. M. (2000). Parenting experiences of three self-identified gay fathers. *Smith College Studies in Social Work, 70*, 513–521.

Petitto, L. (2009). New discoveries from the bilingual brain and mind across the life span: Implications for education. *Mind, Brain, and Education, 3*(4), 185–197.

The Pew Charitable Trusts. (2010). Family structure and the economic mobility of children. Retrieved November 7, 2012, from www.pewstates.org/research/reports/family-structure-and-the-economic-mobility-of-children-85899376379

The Pew Charitable Trusts. (2011). For millennials, parenthood trumps marriage. Retrieved November 7, 2012, from www.pewtrusts.org/our_work_report_detail.aspx?id=328700

The Pew Charitable Trusts, the Pew Research Center. (2012). Report on women, work, and motherhood. Washington, DC: The Pew Research Center.

The Pew Hispanic Center. (2012). *Net migration from Mexico falls to zero—and perhaps less*. Retrieved November 7, 2012, from www.pewhispanic.org/2012/04/23/net-migration-from-mexico-falls-to-zero-and-perhaps-less

The Pew Research Center. (2007). Motherhood today: Tougher challenges, less success. Retrieved November 7, 2012, from http://pewresearch.org/pubs/468/motherhood

Phillips, S. (2003). Adolescent health. In A. M. Nezu & C. M. Nezu (Eds.), *Handbook of psychology: Health psychology* (Vol. 9, pp. 465–485). New York: Wiley.

Phillips, T. (2012). The influence of family structure vs. family climate on adolescent well-being.

Child & Adolescent Social Work Journal, 29(2), 103–110.

Piaget, J. (1967). *Six psychological studies*. New York: Random House.

Piaget, J. (1972). Intellectual evolution from adolescence to adulthood. *Human Development, 15*, 1–12.

Piaget, J., & Inhelder, B. (1969). *The psychology of the child*. New York: Basic Books.

Pierret, C. R. (2006). The "sandwich generation": Women caring for parents and children. *Monthly Labor Review, 129*(9), 3–9.

Pinsof, W. M. (2002). The death of "till death us do part": The transformation of pair-bonding in the 20th century. *Family Process, 41*(2), 135–157.

Piper, B., & Balswick, J. C. (1997). *Then they leave home: Parenting after the kids grow up*. Downers Grove, IL: InterVarsity Press.

Pittman, F. S. (1987). *Turning points: Treating families in transition and crisis*. New York: W. W. Norton.

Planck, C. (2006). Connection and community: How the Family Pride Coalition supports parents and children of GLBT families. *Journal of GLBT Family Studies, 2*(3/4), 39–48.

Pollak, S. D. (2008). Mechanisms linking early experience and the emergence of emotions: Illustrations from the study of maltreated children. *Current Directions in Psychological Science, 17*(6), 370–375.

Pollak, S. D., Nelson, C. A., Schlaak, M. F., Roeber, B. J., Wewerka, S. S., Wiik, K. L., et al. (2010). Neurodevelopment effects of early deprivation in postinstitutionalized children. *Child Development, 81*(1), 224–236.

Posada, G., Longoria, N., Cocker, C., & Lu, T. (2011). Child–caregiver attachment ties in military families: Mothers' view on interactions with their preschooler, stress, and social competence. In S. MacDermid-Wadsworth (Ed.), *Stress in U.S. military families* (pp. 131–147). New York: Springer.

Postpartum Support International. (2012). Perinatal mood & anxiety disorders overview. Retrieved November 7, 2012, from www.postpartum.net/Get-the-Facts.aspx

Proverbs 22:6. (1986). *The Ryrie study bible* (New international version). Chicago: Moody Press.

Pruett, M., & Donsky, T. (2011). Coparenting after divorce: Paving pathways for parental cooperation, conflict resolution, and redefined family roles. In J. P. McHale, & K. M. Lindahl (Eds.), *Coparenting: A conceptual and clinical examination of family systems* (pp. 231–250). Washington, DC: American Psychological Association.

Radtke, K. M., Ruf, M. M., Gunter, H. M., Dohrmann, K. K., Schauer, M. M., Meyer, A. A., et al. (2011). Transgenerational impact of intimate partner violence on methylation in the promoter of the glucocorticoid receptor. *Translational Psychiatry, 1*(7), 21.

Raffaelli, M., & Crockett, L. J. (2003). Sexual risk taking in adolescence: The role of self-regulation and attraction to risk. *Developmental Psychology, 39*, 1036–1046.

Raley, R. K., Crissey, S., & Muller, C. (2007). Of sex and romance: Late adolescent relationships and young adult union formation. *Journal of Marriage and Family, 69*(5), 1210–1226.

Raley, S. B., Mattingly, M. J., & Bianchi, S. M. (2006). How dual are dual-income couples? Documenting change from 1970 to 2001. *Journal of Marriage and Family, 68*(1), 11–28.

Ramey, M. (2004). *Adult children, adult choices: Outgrowing codependency*. Chicago: Sheed & Ward.

Rapp, E. (2011, October 15). Notes from a dragon mom. *New York Times*, Retrieved November 7, 2012, from www.nytimes.com/2011/10/16/opinion/sunday/notes-from-a-dragon-mom.html

Ratcliffe, S. D. (2007). *Family medicine obstetrics* (3rd ed.). St. Louis, MO: Elsevier.

Rathus, S. A., Nevid, J. S., & Fichner-Rathus, L. (2011). *Human sexuality in a world of diversity* (8th ed.). Boston: Prentice Hall/Allyn & Bacon.

The Research Forum at the National Center for Children in Poverty. (2012). *Fragile families and child wellbeing study*. New York: Columbia University, Joseph L. Mailman School of Public Health.

Reuter-Kairys, M. (2011). Effects of early attachment on adult attachment and adult self-soothing. *Dissertation Abstracts International*: Section B: The Sciences and Engineering, 71(9-B): 5802.

Reynolds, S., & Bexton, R. (2009). *250 personal finance questions for single mothers: Make and keep a budget, get out of debt, establish savings, plan for college, secure insurance*. Avon, MA: F+W Media.

Ribble, M. A. (1943). *The rights of infants, early psychological needs and their satisfaction*. New York: Columbia University Press.

Richardson, R. W. (1999). *Family ties that bind: A self-help guide to change through family of origin therapy*. Vancouver, British Colombia, Canada: Self-Counsel Press.

Rief, S. F. (2005). *How to reach and teach children with ADD/ADHD: Practical techniques, strategies, and interventions*. San Francisco: Jossey-Bass.

Riggle, E. D. B., Whitman, J. S., Olson, A., Rostosky, S. S., & Strong, S. (2008). The positive aspects of being a lesbian or gay man. *Professional Psychology: Research and Practice, 39*(2), 210–217.

Ring, S. (2001). Use of role playing in parent training: A methodological component analysis of systematic training for effective parenting. *Dissertation Abstracts International, Section B: The Sciences and Engineering, 61*(11-B), 6121.

Robi, J. L., & Shaw, S. A. (2006). The African orphan crisis and international adoption. *Social Work, 51*(3), 199–210.

Robinson, M. M., & Wilkes, S. E. (2006). "Older but not wiser": What custodial grandparents want to tell social workers about raising grandchildren. *Social Work & Christianity, 33*(2), 164–177.

Robinson, P. W., Robinson, M. P. W., & Dunn, T. W. (2003). STEP parenting: A review of the research. *Canadian Journal of Counselling, 37*(4), 270–278.

Rodkin, P. C., & Ahn, H. (2009). Social networks derived from affiliations and friendships, multi-informant and self-reports: Stability, concordance, placement of aggressive and unpopular children, and centrality. *Social Development, 18*(3), 556–576.

Rogoff, B. (1990). *Apprenticeship in thinking: Cognitive development in social context.* New York: Oxford University Press.

Rogoff, B. (2003). *The cultural nature of human development.* Oxford, United Kingdom: Oxford University Press.

Rosenthal, D. A., & Feldman, S. S. (1992). The relationship between parenting behavior and ethnic identity in Chinese-American and Chinese-Australian adolescents. *International Journal of Psychology, 27,* 19–31.

Ross, M. E., & Aday, L. A. (2006). Stress and coping in African American grandparents who are raising their grandchildren. *Journal of Family Issues, 27*(7), 912–932.

Rothstein-Fisch, C., Greenfield, P., Trumbull, E., Keller, H., & Quiroz, B. (2010). Uncovering the role of culture in learning, development, and education. In D. Preiss & R. Sternberg (Eds.) *Innovations in educational psychology: Perspectives on learning, teaching, and human development* (pp. 269–294). New York: Springer.

Rozie-Battle, J. (2003). Economic support and the dilemma of teen fathers. *Journal of Health & Social Policy, 17,* 73–86.

Runyon, M. K., Deblinger, E., Ryan, E. E., & Thakkar-Kolar, R. (2004). An overview of child physical abuse: Developing an integrated parent–child cognitive-behavioral treatment approach. *Trauma, Violence & Abuse, 5,* 65–85.

Russell, S., & Licona, A. (2011). LGBTQ families—the changing discourse. *NCFR Report, 56*(4):F11-F12.

Rust, P. C. (2003). Finding a sexual identity and community: Therapeutic implications and cultural assumptions in scientific models of coming out. In L. D. Garnets, & D. C. Kimmel (Eds.), *Psychological perspectives on lesbian, gay, and bisexual experiences* (2nd ed., pp. 227–269). New York: Columbia University Press.

Ryder, A. G., Alden, L. E., & Paulhus, D. L. (2000). Is acculturation unidimensional or bidimensional? A head-to-head comparison in the prediction of personality, self-identity, and adjustment. *Journal of Personality and Social Psychology, 79,* 49–65.

Ryder, A. G., & Dere, J. (2010). Canadian diversity and clinical psychology: Defining and transcending cultural competence. *The CAP monitor, 32,* pp. 1, 6–13. Retrieved November 7, 2012, from www.cap.ab.ca/pdfs/capmonitor35.pdf

Saadeh, W., Rizzo, C. P., & Roberts, D. G. (2002). Spanking. *Clinical Pediatrics, 41*(2), 87–88.

Sahin, M. (2012). An investigation into the efficiency of empathy training program on preventing bullying in primary schools. *Children and Youth Services Review, 34*(7), 1325–1330.

Saleh, M. F., Buzi, R. S., Weinman, M. L., & Smith, P. B. (2005). The nature of connections: Young fathers and their children. *Adolescence, 40*(159), 513–523.

Salian, S., Doshi, T., & Vanage, G. (2011). Perinatal exposure of rats to bisphenol A affects fertility of male offspring—an overview. *Reproductive Toxicology, 31*(3), 359–362.

Salonen, A. H., Kaunonen, M., Åstedt-Kurki, P., Järvenpää, A. L., Isoaho, H., & Tarkka, M. T. (2009). Parenting self-efficacy after childbirth. *Journal of Advanced Nursing, 65*(11), 2324–2336.

Sandberg, J. G., Feldhousen, E. B., & Busby, D. M. (2012). The impact of childhood abuse on women's and men's perceived parenting: Implications for practitioners. *The American Journal of Family Therapy, 40*(1), 74–91.

Sanders, M. R., Markie-Dadds, C. K., & Turner, M. T. (2003). Theoretical, scientific, and clinical foundations of the triple-P Positive Parenting Program: A population approach to the promotion of parenting competence. *Parenting Research and Practice Monograph, 1,* 1–21.

Santrock, J. (2009). *Adolescence* (14th ed.). Boston: McGraw-Hill.

Sassler, S., Miller, A., & Favinger, S. (2009). Planned parenthood? Fertility intentions and experiences among cohabiting couples. *Journal of Family Issues, 30*(2), 206–232.

Satir, V. (1972a). Family systems and approaches to family therapy. In G. D. Erikson & T. P. Hogan (Eds.), *Family therapy: An introduction to theory and technique.* Monterey, CA: Brooks/Cole.

Satir, V. (1972b). *Peoplemaking.* Palo Alto, CA: Science and Behavior Books.

Saunders, J. A. (2002). African American teen parents and their non-parenting peers: Differences in high school and young adulthood. PhD dissertation, Washington University of St Louis, *Dissertation Abstracts International-A, 62,* 4335.

Savic, I., & Lindström, P. (2008). PET and MRI show differences in cerebral asymmetry and functional connectivity between homo- and heterosexual subjects. *Proceedings of the National Academy of Sciences of the United States of America, 105*(27), 9403–9408.

Savin-Williams, R. C. (2001). *Mom, Dad. I'm gay. How families negotiate coming out.* Washington, DC: American Psychological Association.

Savin-Williams, R. C., & Dubé, E. M. (1998). Parental reactions to their child's disclosure of a gay/lesbian identity. *Family Relations: An Interdisciplinary Journal of Applied Family Studies, 47*(1), 7–13.

Savin-Williams, R. C., & Ream, G. L. (2003). Suicide attempts among sexual-minority male youth. *Journal of Clinical Child & Adolescent Psychology, 32,* 509–522.

Schacher, S. J., Auerbach, C. F., & Silverstein, L. B. (2005). Gay fathers expanding the possibilities for us all. *Journal of GLBT Family Studies, 1*(3), 31–52.

Schatz, J. N., & Lounds, J. J. (2007). Child maltreatment: Precursors of developmental delays. In J.

G. Borkowski, J. R. Farris, T. L. Whitman, S. S. Carothers, & K. Weed (Eds.), *Risk and resilience: Adolescent mothers and their children grow up* (pp. 125–150). Mahwah, NJ: Lawrence Erlbaum.

Schulz, M. S., Cowan, C. P., & Cowan, P. A. (2006). Promoting healthy beginnings: A randomized controlled trial of a preventive intervention to preserve marital quality during the transition to parenthood. *Journal of Consulting and Clinical Psychology, 74*(1), 20–31.

Schwartz, L. L. (2000). Families by choice: Adoptive and foster families. In W. C. Nichols, M. A. Pace-Nichols, D. S. Becvar, & A. Y. Napier (Eds.), *Handbook of family development* (pp. 255–278). New York: Wiley.

Schwartz, P., & Cappello, D. (2000). *Ten talks parents must have with their children about sex and character.* New York: Hyperion.

Schwarzchild, M. (2000). *Helping your difficult child behave: A guide to improving children's self-control—without losing your own.* Lincoln, NE: iUniverse.

Schweingruber, H. A., & Kalil, A. (2000). Decision making and depressive symptoms in black and white multigenerational teen-parent families. *Journal of Family Psychology, 14,* 556–569.

Scommegna, P. (2002, September). Increased cohabitation changing children's family settings. *Research on Today's Issues, 13.* Bethesda, MD: Demographic and Behavioral Sciences Branch, Center for Population Research, National Institute of Child Health and Human Development.

Sears, W. & Sears, M. (2001). *The attachment parenting book: A commonsense guide to understanding and nurturing your baby.* New York: Little, Brown.

Secunda, V. (2004). *Losing your parents, finding yourself: The defining turning point of adult life.* Collingdale, PA: Diane.

Segal-Engelchin, D., Erera, P. I., & Cwikel, J. (2005). The hetero-gay family: An emergent family configuration. *Journal of GLBT Family Studies, 1*(3), 85–104.

Serbin, L. A., Temcheff, C. E., Cooperman, J. M., Stack, D. M., Ledingham, J., & Schwartzman, A. E. (2011). Predicting family poverty and other disadvantaged conditions for child rearing from childhood aggression and social withdrawal: A 30-year longitudinal study. *International Journal of Behavioral Development, 35*(2), 97–106.

Settersten, R. A., & Ray, B. (2010). *Not quite adults: Why 20-somethings are choosing a slower path to adulthood, and why it's good for everyone.* New York: Bantam Books.

Shelov, S. (2010). *Your baby's first year* (3rd ed.). New York: Bantam Books.

Sherry, M. (2004). Overlaps and contradictions between queer theory and disability studies. *Disability & Society, 19*(7), 769–783.

Sherwin, J. C., Reacher, M. H., Keogh, R. H., Khawaja, A. P., Mackey, D. A., & Foster, P. J. (2012). The association between time spent outdoors and myopia in children and adolescents: A systematic review and meta-analysis. *Ophthalmology, 119*(10): 2141–2151.

Shiraev, E. B., & Levy, D. A. (2010). *Cross-cultural psychology: Critical thinking and contemporary applications* (4th ed.). Boston: Pearson/Allyn & Bacon.

Shreffler, K. M., Greil, A. L., & McQuillan, J. (2011). Pregnancy loss and distress among U.S. women. *Family Relations, 60*(3), 342–355.

Shultz, S. K. (2001). Child physical abuse: Relationship of parental substance use to severity of abuse and risk for future abuse. *Dissertation Abstracts International, Section B: The Sciences and Engineering, 62*(1-B), 605.

Siegenthaler, A., & Bigner, J. J. (2000). The value of children to lesbian and nonlesbian mothers. *Journal of Homosexuality, 39*, 73–92.

Sileo, N. M., & Prater, M. A. (2011). *Working with families of children with special needs: Families and professional partnerships and roles.* Boston: Prentice Hall.

Sinclair, J. C. (2003). Weighing risks and benefits in treating the individual patient. *Clinics in Perinatology, 30*, 251–268.

Singer, A. (2001). Coming out of the shadows: Supporting the development of our gay, lesbian, and bisexual adolescents. In M. McConville & G. Wheeler (Eds.), *The heart of development* (Vol. 11, pp. 172–192). Cambridge, MA: Gestalt Press.

Skinner, B. F. (1938). *The behavior of organisms.* New York: Appleton-Century-Crofts.

Skinner, J. H. (2001). Acculturation: Measures of ethnic accommodation to the dominant American culture. *Journal of Mental Health and Aging, 7*, 41–52.

Smith, C., Perou, R., & Lesesne, C. (2002). Parent education. In M. H. Bornstein (Ed.), *Handbook of parenting* (Vol. 4, 2nd ed., pp. 389–410). Mahwah, NJ: Lawrence Erlbaum.

Smith, S. R., Hamon, R. R., Ingoldsby, B. B., & Miller, J. E. (2009). *Exploring family theories* (2nd ed.). Oxford, United Kingdom: Oxford University Press.

SmithBattle, L. (2007). "I wanna have a good future": Teen mothers' rise in educational aspirations, competing demands, and limited school support. *Youth & Society, 38*(3), 348–371.

Smithgall, C., & Mason, S. (2004). Identified problems and service utilization patterns among kinship families accessing mental health services. *Journal of Human Behavior in the Social Environment, 9*(3), 41–55.

Snow, J. E. (2004). *How it feels to have a gay or lesbian parent: A book by kids for kids of all ages.* New York: Harrington Park Press.

Sobol, M. P., Daly, K. J., & Kelloway, E. K. (2000). Paths to the facilitation of open adoption. *Family Relations, 49*, 419–424.

Sokol, R. J., Jr., Delaney-Black, V., & Nordstrom, B. (2003). Fetal alcohol spectrum disorder. *Journal of the American Medical Association, 290*, 2996–2999.

Spack, N. P., Edwards-Leeper, L., Feldman, H. A., Leibowitz, S., Mandel, F., Diamond, D. A., et al. (2012). Children and adolescents with gender

identity disorder referred to a pediatric medical center. *Pediatrics, 129*(3), 418–425.

Spillman, J. A., Deschamps, H. S., & Crews, J. A. (2004). Perspectives on nonresidential paternal involvement and grief: A literature review. *The Family Journal, 12*(3), 263–270.

Spitz, R. (1945). *Hospitalism: An inquiry into the genesis of psychiatric conditions in early childhood.* New Haven, CT: Yale University Press.

Splett, P. L., & Krinke, U. B. (2011). Adult nutrition. In J. E. Brown (Ed.), *Nutrition through the life cycle* (4th ed., pp. 405–427). Stamford, CT: Cengage Learning.

Spock, B., & Needleman, R. (2011). *Dr. Spock's baby and child care.* (9th ed.). New York: Gallery Books.

Stacey, J. (1998a). *Brave new families: Stories of domestic upheaval in late-twentieth-century America.* Berkeley: University of California Press.

Stacey, J. (1998b). Dada-ism in the 1990s: Getting past baby talk about fatherlessness. In C. Daniels (Ed.), *Lost fathers: The politics of fatherlessness in America* (pp. 51–84). New York: Palgrave Macmillan.

Stacey, J. (2006). Gay parenthood and the decline of paternity as we knew it. *Sexualities, 9*(1), 27–55.

Stacey, J., & Biblarz, T. J. (2001). (How) does the sexual orientation of parents matter? *American Sociological Review, 66*, 159–183.

Stafford, J. J. (2004). Remembered parental corporal punishment and its relation to attitudes and abuse: A cross national study. *Dissertation Abstracts International, Section B: The Sciences and Engineering, 64*(11-B), 5769.

Stanley, S. M., Rhoades, G. K., & Markman, H. J. (2006). Sliding versus deciding: Inertia and the premarital cohabitation effect. *Family Relations, 55*(4), 499–509.

Staples, R., & Mirande, A. (1980). Racial and cultural variations among American families: A decennial review of the literature on minority families. *Journal of Marriage and the Family, 42*, 887–903.

Stark, E. (2000). *Everything you need to know about family violence.* New York: Rosen Publishing Group.

Stein, M. T., Kennell, J. H., & Fulcher, A. (2004). Benefits of a doula present at the birth of a child. *Journal of Developmental & Behavioral Pediatrics, 25*(5S), S89–S92.

Steinberg, L. (2010). *Adolescence* (9th ed.). Boston: McGraw-Hill.

Steinberg, L., Elmen, J. D., & Mounts, N. S. (1989). Authoritative parenting, psychosocial maturity, and academic success among adolescents. *Child Development, 60*, 1424–1436.

Steiner, H., Kwan, W., Shaffer, T. G., Walker, S., Miller, S., Sager, A., et al. (2003). Risk and protective factors for juvenile eating disorders. *European Child and Adolescent Psychiatry, 12*(Suppl 1), I38–I46.

Steinmetz, S., Clavan, S., & Stein, K. F. (1990). *Marriage and family realities: Historical and contemporary perspectives.* New York: Harper & Row.

Sternberg, R. J. (1986). A triangular theory of love. *Psychological Review, 93*(2), 119–135.

Sternberg, R. J. (1988). *The triangle of love: Intimacy, passion, and commitment.* New York: Basic Books.

Stevens, M., Perry, B., Burston, A., Golombok, S., & Golding, J. (2003). Openness in lesbian-mother families regarding mother's sexual orientation and child's conception by donor insemination. *Journal of Reproductive & Infant Psychology, 21*, 347–362.

Stevens-Simon, C. (2000). Participation in a program that helps families with one teen pregnancy prevent others. *Journal of Pediatric and Adolescent Gynecology, 13*, 167–169.

Stevens-Simon, C., Nelligan, D., & Kelly, L. (2001). Adolescents at risk for mistreating their children. Part I: Prenatal identification. *Child Abuse & Neglect, 25*, 737–751.

Stevens-Simon, C., Sheeder, J., & Harder, S. (2005). Teen contraceptive decisions: Childbearing intentions are the tip of the iceberg. *Women & Health, 42*(1), 55–73.

Stewart, S. D. (2005). Boundary ambiguity in stepfamilies. *Journal of Family Issues, 26*(7), 1002–1029.

Stewart, S. D. (2010). Children with nonresident parents: Living arrangements, visitation, and child support. *Journal of Marriage and Family, 72*(5), 1078–1091.

Stiles, J. (2008). *Fundamentals of brain development: Integrating nature and nurture.* Boston: Harvard University Press.

Straus, M. A., & Field, C. J. (2003). Psychological aggression by American parents: National data on prevalence, chronicity, and severity. *Journal of Marriage and the Family, 65*, 795–808.

Straus, M. A., & Gelles, R. J. (2006). *Behind closed doors: Violence in the American family.* Piscataway, NJ: Transaction Publishers.

Strong, B. (2004). *Human sexuality: Diversity in contemporary America.* New York: McGraw-Hill.

Stuebe, A., & Schwarz, E. (2010). The risks and benefits of infant feeding practices for women and their children. *Journal of Perinatology, 30*(3), 155–162.

Sullivan, G., & Reynolds, R. (2003). Homosexuality in midlife: Narrative and identity. *Journal of Gay & Lesbian Social Services, 15*, 153–170.

Sullivan, M., & Wodarski, J. S. (2002). Social alienation in gay youth. *Journal of Human Behavior in the Social Environment, 5*, 1–17.

Sullivan, P. M., & Knutson, J. F. (2000). Maltreatment and disabilities: A population-based epidemiological study. *Child Abuse & Neglect, 24*(10), 1257–1273.

Sun, J., Helgason, A., Masson, G., Ebenesersdóttir, S., Li, H., Mallick, S., et al. (2012). A direct characterization of human mutation based on microsatellites. *Nature Genetics, 44*(10), 1161–1165.

Sunley, R. (1955). Early nineteenth century American literature on child rearing. In M. Mead & M. Wolfenstein (Eds.), *Childhood in contemporary cultures.* Chicago: University of Chicago Press.

Susman, E. J., Dorn, L. D., & Schiefelbein, V. L. (2003). Puberty, sexuality, and health. In R. M. Lerner & M. A. Easterbrooks (Eds.), *Handbook of psychology: Developmental psychology* (Vol. 6., pp. 295–324). New York: Wiley.

Swinford, S. P., DeMaris, A., Cernkovich, S. A., & Giordano, P. C. (2000). Harsh physical discipline in childhood and violence in later romantic involvements: The mediating role of problem behaviors. *Journal of Marriage and the Family, 62*, 508–519.

Swize, J. (2002). Transracial adoption and the unblinkable difference: Racial dissimilarity serving the interests of adopted children. *Virginia Law Review, 88*, 1079–1118.

Taft, C. N. (2010). Are laws granting grandparents rights a good or bad thing? Retrieved November 7, 2012, from http://ezinearticles.com/?Are-Laws-Granting-Grandparents-Rights-A-Good-Or-Bad-Thing?&id=3871566

Talmadge, L. D., & Talmadge, W. C. (2003). Dealing with the unhappy marriage. In S. B. Levine & C. B. Risen (Eds.), *Handbook of clinical sexuality for mental health professionals* (pp. 75–92). New York: Brunner-Routledge.

Talwar, V. (2011). Talking to children about death in educational settings. In V. Talwar, P. L. Harris, & M. Schleifer (Eds.), *Children's understanding of death: From biological to religious conceptions* (pp. 98–115). New York: Cambridge University Press.

Tan, L. H., & Quinlivan, J. A. (2006). Domestic violence, single parenthood, and fathers in the setting of teenage pregnancy. *Journal of Adolescent Health, 38*(3), 201–207.

Tasker, F. (2002). Lesbian and gay parenting. In A. Coyle & C. Kitzinger (Eds.), *Lesbian and gay psychology: New perspectives* (pp. 81–97). Malden, MA: Blackwell Publishers.

Tasker, F. (2005). Lesbian mothers, gay fathers, and their children: A review. *Journal of Developmental & Behavioral Pediatrics, 26*(3), 224–240.

Tasker, F., & Patterson, C. (2007). Research on gay and lesbian parenting: Retrospect and prospect. *Journal of GLBT Family Studies, 3*(2/3), 9–34.

Taylor, C., Hamvas, L., Rice, J., Newman, D., & Dejong, W. (2011). Perceived social norms, expectations, and attitudes toward corporal punishment among an urban community sample of parents. *Journal of Urban Health, 88*(2), 254–269.

Teach for America. (2012). A solvable problem: Change is possible. Retrieved November 7, 2012, from www.teachforamerica.org/our-mission/a-solvable-problem

Teasdale, B., & Bradley-Engen, M. S. (2010). Adolescent same-sex attraction and mental health: The role of stress and support. *Journal of Homosexuality, 57*(2), 287–309.

Telingator, C. J., & Patterson, C. J. (2008). Children and adolescents of lesbian and gay parents. *Journal of the American Academy of Child and Adolescent Psychiatry, 47*(12), 1364–1368.

Therrien, M., & Ramirez, R. R. (2000). The Hispanic population in the United States: March 2000. *Current Population Reports*, P20-535. Washington, DC: U.S. Census Bureau.

Thompson, G. L. (2003). *What African American parents want educators to know*. New York: Praeger.

Thompson, J. M. (2002). *Mommy queerest: Contemporary rhetorics of lesbian maternal identity*. Amherst: University of Massachusetts Press.

Thompson, R., & Lee, C. (2011). Fertile imaginations: Young men's reproductive attitudes and preferences. *Journal of Reproductive & Infant Psychology, 29*(1), 43–55.

Tikotzky, L., Sadeh, A., & Glickman-Gavrieli, T. (2011). Infant sleep and paternal involvement in infant caregiving during the first 6 months of life. *Journal of Pediatric Psychology, 36*(1), 36–46.

Timmer, S. G., Borrego, J., Jr., & Urquiza, A. J. (2002). Antecedents of coercive interactions in physically abusive mother–child dyads. *Journal of Interpersonal Violence, 17*, 836–853.

Tinsley, B. J., Lees, N. B., & Sumartojo, E. (2004). Child and adolescent HIV risk: Familial and cultural perspectives. *Journal of Family Psychology, 18*, 208–224.

Tittle, P. (Ed.). (2004). *Should parents be licensed?: Debating the issues*. Amherst, NY: Prometheus Books.

Tonmyr, L., Quimet, C., & Ugnat, A. M. (2012). A review of findings from the Canadian incidence study of reported child abuse and neglect (CIS). *Canadian Journal of Public Health, 103*(2), 103–112.

Topolak, R., Williams, V., & Wilson, J. (2001). Preventing teenage pregnancy: A multifaceted review. *Journal of Psychological Practice, 7*, 33–46.

Trosper, T. B. (2002). Parenting strategies in the middle class African-American family. *Dissertation Abstracts International, Section A: Humanities and Social Sciences, 63*, 864.

Trumbull, E., Rothstein-Fisch, C., & Greenfield, P. M. (2000). Bridging cultures in our schools: New approaches that work. Retrieved August 3, 2007, from www.wested.org/cs/we/view/rs/81

Ttofi, M. M., Farrington, D. P., Lösel, F., & Loeber, R. (2011). The predictive efficiency of school bullying versus later offending: A systematic/metaanalytic review of longitudinal studies. *Criminal Behaviour & Mental Health, 21*(2), 80–89.

Tudge, J. H., Mokrova, I., Hatfield, B. E., & Karnik, R. B. (2009). Uses and misuses of Bronfenbrenner's bioecological theory of human development. *Journal of Family Theory and Review, 1*(4), 198.

Turner, R. J., Sorenson, A. M., & Turner, J. B. (2000). Social contingencies in mental health: A seven-year follow-up study of teenage mothers. *Journal of Marriage and the Family, 62*, 777–791.

Tyano, S., & Keren, M. (2010). Single parenthood: Its impact on parenting the infant. In S. Tyano, M. Keren, H. Herrman, & J. Cox (Eds.), *Parenthood and mental health: A bridge between infant and adult psychiatry* (pp. 31–38). Hoboken, NJ: Wiley-Blackwell.

UNICEF. (1959). Convention on the rights of the child. Retrieved November 7, 2012, from http://unicef.org/crc

United Nations Educational, Scientific and Cultural Organization. (2009). *Education for all global monitoring report*. Retrieved November 7, 2012, from www.unesco.org/new/en/unesco/partners-donors/the_actions/education/education-for-all-global-monitoring-report/

United Nations Educational, Scientific and Cultural Organization. (2010). *Education for all global monitoring report: Reaching the marginalized*. Oxford, United Kingdom: Oxford University Press.

United Nations Educational, Scientific and Cultural Organization. (2011). *Education for all global monitoring report: The hidden crisis: Armed conflict and education*. Paris, France: United Nations Educational, Scientific and Cultural Organization

United Nations Educational, Scientific and Cultural Organization. (2012). *Education for all global monitoring report: Youth and skills: Putting education to work*. Retrieved November 7, 2012, from www.unesco.org/new/en/education/themes/leading-the-international-agenda/efare-port/reports/2012-skills

U.S. Bureau of Labor Statistics. (2008). Women in the labor force: A databook. Retrieved November 7, 2012, from www.bls.gov/cps/wlf-databook2008.htm

U.S. Bureau of Labor Statistics. (2010). Women in the labor force: A databook. Retrieved November 7, 2012, from www.bls.gov/cps/wlf-databook-2010.pdf

U.S. Census Bureau. (2007a). *Statistical abstract of the United States: 2006*. Washington, DC: Author.

U.S. Census Bureau. (2007b). Population profile of the United States: Dynamic version (Internet Release). Retrieved July 12, 2007, from http://www.census.gov/econ/census07/

U.S. Census Bureau. (2010a). Statistical abstract of the United States. Retrieved November 7, 2012, from www.census.gov/prod/www/abs/statab2006_2010.html

U.S. Census Bureau. (2010b). Households and families: 2010. Retrieved November 7, 2012, from www.census.gov/prod/cen2010/briefs/c2010br-14.pdf

U.S. Census Bureau. (2010c). Overview of race and Hispanic origin: 2010. Retrieved November 7, 2012, from www.census.gov/prod/cen2010/briefs/c2010br-02.pdf

U.S. Census Bureau. (2010d). The Asian population: 2010. Retrieved November 7, 2012, from www.census.gov/prod/cen2010/briefs/ c2010br-11.pdf

U.S. Census Bureau. (2010e). The American Indian and Alaska Native population: 2010. Retrieved November 7, 2012, from www.census.gov/prod/cen2010/briefs/c2010br-10.pdf

U.S. Census Bureau. (2010f). U.S. POPclock projection. Retrieved November 7, 2012, from www.census.gov/population/www/popclockus.html

U.S. Census Bureau. (2011a). Maternity leave and employment patterns of first-time mothers: 1961–2008. Retrieved November 7, 2012, from www.census.gov/prod/2011pubs/p70-128.pdf

U.S. Census Bureau. (2011b). One-parent unmarried family groups with own children under 18, by marital status of the reference person: 2011 [Data file]. Retrieved November 7, 2012, from http://www.census.gov/population/www/soc-demo/hh-fam/cps2011.html

U.S. Census Bureau. (2011c). Disability. Retrieved November 7, 2012, from www.census.gov/hhes/www/disability/disability.html

U.S. Census Bureau. (2011d). Section 23: Transportation. Retrieved November 7, 2012, from www.census.gov/prod/2011pubs/11statab/trans.pdf

U.S. Census Bureau. (2011e). Section 2: Births, deaths, marriages, and divorces. Retrieved November 7, 2012, from www.census.gov/prod/2011pubs/11statab/vitstat.pdf

U.S. Census Bureau. (2011f). Economic data by survey title. Retrieved November 7, 2012, from www.census.gov/econ/survey.html

U.S. Census Bureau. (2012). Business enterprise: Women and minority-owned businesses. Retrieved November 7, 2012, from www.census.gov/compendia/statab/cats/business_enterprise/women_and_minority-owned_businesses.html

U.S. Department of Education. (2009). *No Child Left Behind: Elementary and Secondary Education Act.* H. Rep. No. 107-63, H. Rep. No. 107-334, and S. Rep. No. 107-7. Retrieved November 7, 2012, from www2.ed.gov/nclb/landing.jhtml

U.S. Department of Health and Human Services. (2004). *How many children were adopted in 2000 and 2001?* Washington, DC: Child Welfare Information Gateway.

U.S. Department of Health & Human Services. (2008). Administration on Children, Youth and Families (ACYF). Retrieved November 7, 2012, from www.hhs.gov/open/contacts/admin_youth_families.html

U.S. Department of Health & Human Services. (2011). Income, poverty, and health insurance coverage in the United States: 2010. Retrieved November 7, 2012, www.census.gov/prod/2011pubs/p60-239.pdf

U.S. Department of Health and Human Services. (2012). Administration on Children, Youth and Families: Children's Bureau. Retrieved November 7, 2012, from www.acf.hhs.gov/programs/cb/

U.S. Department of Health and Human Services. (2012). National Institutes of Health: National Institute on Alcohol Abuse and Alcoholism. Retrieved November 7, 2012, from www.niaaa.nih.gov/research/major-initiatives

U.S. Department of Health and Human Services, Administration on Children, Youth and Families. (2008). *Child maltreatment 2006.* Washington, DC: Author.

U.S. Department of Health and Human Services, Administration on Children and Families. (2012).

Head Start. Retrieved November 7, 2012, from http://eclkc.ohs.acf.hhs.gov/hslc

Vanderwert, R. E., Marshall, P. J., Nelson, III, C. A., Zeanah, C. H., & Fox, N. A. (2010). Timing of intervention affects brain electrical activity in children exposed to severe psychosocial neglect. *PLOS ONE, 5*(7), 1–5.

Vanfraussen, K., Ponjaert-Kristoffersen, I., & Brewaeys, A. (2002). What does it mean for youngsters to grow up in a lesbian family created by means of donor insemination? *Journal of Reproductive & Infant Psychology, 20,* 237–252.

Vanfraussen, K., Ponjaert-Kristoffersen, I., & Brewaeys, A. (2003). Family functioning in lesbian families created by donor insemination. *American Journal of Orthopsychiatry, 73,* 78–90.

Van Gelderen, L., Gartrell, N., Bos, H., & Hermanns, J. (2009). Stigmatization and resilience in adolescent children of lesbian mothers. *Journal of GLBT Family Studies, 5*(3), 268–279.

Van Houten, R., & Hall, R. V. (2001). *The measurement of behavior: Behavior modification* (3rd ed.). Austin, TX: Pro-Ed.

van Kraayenoord, C. (2009). In others' shoes: Research and the development of empathy. *International Journal of Disability, Development & Education, 56*(3), 201–204.

van Poppel, F. W. A., Oris, M., & Lee, J. Z. (2004) *The road to independence: Leaving home in western and eastern societies, 16th to 20th centuries.* New York: Peter Lang.

van Wormer, K., & McKinney, R. (2003). What schools can do to help gay/lesbian/bisexual youth: A harm reduction approach. *Adolescence, 38,* 409–420.

Varon, L. (2003). *Adopting on your own: The complete guide to adoption for single parents.* Collingdale, PA: Diane.

Velez, C. E., Wolchik, S. A., Tein, J., & Sandler, I. (2011). Protecting children from the consequences of divorce: A longitudinal study of the effects of parenting on children's coping processes. *Child Development, 82*(1), 244–257.

Volk, A. (2011). The evolution of childhood. *Journal of the History of Childhood & Youth, 4*(3), 470–494.

von Bertalanffy, L. (1968). General systems theory and psychiatry. In S. Arieti (Ed.), *American handbook of psychiatry* (Vol. 1, pp. 247–300). New York: Basic Books.

von Bertalanffy, L. (1974). *General systems theory.* New York: Braziller.

Vontver, L. A. (2003). *Appleton and Lange's review of obstetrics and gynecology.* New York: McGraw-Hill.

Vygotsky, L. S. (1962). *Thought and language.* Cambridge, MA: MIT Press.

Vygotsky, L. S. (1987). Thinking and speech. In R. W. Reiber & A. S. Carton (Eds.), *The collected works of L. S. Vygotsky: Problems of general psychology* (Vol. 1, pp. 37–285). New York: Plenum.

Wagner, P. A. (2011). Socio-sexual education: A practical study in formal thinking and teachable moments. *Sex Education, 11*(2), 193–211.

Waite, L. J. (2009). The changing family and aging populations. *Population and Development Review, 35*(2), 341–346.

Wakschlag, L. S., & Hans, S. L. (2000). Early parenthood in context: Implications for development and intervention. In C. H. Zeanah, Jr. (Ed.), *Handbook of infant mental health* (2nd ed., pp. 129–144). New York: Guilford Press.

Wallace, W. (2007). *Family violence: Legal, medical and social perspective* (5th ed.). Boston: Allyn & Bacon.

Waller, M. A., Brown, B., & Whittle, B. (1999). Mentoring as a bridge to positive outcomes for teen mothers and their children. *Child and Adolescent Social Work Journal, 16,* 467–480.

Wallerstein, J. S., Lewis, J. M., & Blakeslee, S. (2001). *The unexpected legacy of divorce: A twenty-five year landmark study.* New York: Hyperion Press.

Walsh, W. (2002). Spankers and nonspankers: Where they get their information on spanking. *Family Relations, 51,* 81–88.

Wark, M. J., Kruczek, T., & Boley, A. (2003). Emotional neglect and family structure: Impact on student functioning. *Child Abuse & Neglect, 27,* 1033–1043.

Warren, E., & Tyagi, A. W. (2004). *The two-income trap: Why middle-class mothers and fathers are going broke.* New York: Basic Books.

Watson, J. B. (1928). *Psychological care of infant and child.* New York: W. W. Norton.

Weight, C. E. (2004). *Divorce in America: A reference handbook.* Santa Barbara, CA: ABC-CLIO.

Weimer, T. E. (2010). *Thriving after divorce: Transforming your life when a relationship ends.* New York: Atria Books/Beyond Words.

Weinstock, H., Berman, S., & Cates, W., Jr. (2004). Sexually transmitted diseases among American youth: Incidence and prevalence estimates, 2000. *Perspectives on Sexual and Reproductive Health, 36,* 6–10.

Weitoff, G. R., Burström, B., & Rosén, M. (2004). Premature mortality among lone fathers and childless men. *Social Science & Medicine, 59*(7), 1449–1459.

Wells, G. (2011). Making room for daddies: Male couples creating families through adoption. *Journal of GLBT Family Studies, 7*(1/2), 155–181.

Westheimer, R. K., & Lopater, S. (2004). *Human sexuality: A psychosocial perspective.* New York: Lippincott, Williams, & Wilkins.

Westly, E. (2011). The bilingual advantage: Learning a second language can give kids' brains a boost. *Scientific American Mind, 22*(3), 38–41.

Wharton, A. S. (2004). *The sociology of gender: An introduction to theory and research.* Malden, MA: Blackwell.

White, J. W., Koss, M. P., & Kazdin, A. E. (2011). *Violence against women and children: Mapping the terrain.* Washington, DC: American Psychological Association.

The White House Task Force on Childhood Obesity. (2012). Childhood obesity task force unveils action plan: Solving the problem of childhood obesity within a generation. Retrieved November 7, 2012, from www.whitehouse.gov/the-press-office/childhood-obesity-task-force-unveils-action-plan-solving-problem-childhood-obesity-

Whiting, J. B., Smith, D. R., Barnett, T., & Grafsky, E. L. (2007). Overcoming the Cinderella myth: A mixed methods study of successful stepmothers. *Journal of Divorce & Remarriage, 47*(1/2), 95–109.

Wiley, A. R., Warren, H. B., & Montenelli, D. S. (2002). Shelter in a time of storm: Parenting in poor, rural African-American communities. *Family Relations, 51*, 265–273.

Willerton, E., Wadsworth, S. M., & Riggs, D. (2011). Introduction: Military families under stress: What we know and what we need to know. In S. Wadsworth & D. Riggs (Eds.), *Risk and resilience in U.S. military families* (pp. 1–20). New York: Springer.

Willetts, M. C. (2011). Registered domestic partnerships, same-sex marriage, and the pursuit of equality in California. *Family Relations, 60*(2), 135–149.

Williams, S. S., Norris, A. E., & Bedor, M. M. (2003). Sexual relationships, condom use, and concerns about pregnancy, HIV/AIDS, and other sexually transmitted diseases. *Clinical Nurse Specialist, 17*, 89–94.

Winkler, R. (2004). *The family—where violence begins, recognizing and stopping it.* Lincoln, NE: iUniverse.

Witters-Green, R. (2003). Parental expression of physical intimacy with young children: Influences on subjective norms about what is appropriate. *Dissertation Abstracts International,*

Section B: The Sciences and *Engineering, 64*(3-B), 1556. Ann Arbor, MI: University Microfilms International.

Wittner, D. S., Peterson, S. H., & Puckett, M. B. (2013). *The young child: Development from prebirth through age eight* (6th ed.). Boston: Pearson.

Woo, G. W., Soon, R. R., Thomas, J. M., & Kaneshiro, B. B. (2011). Factors affecting sex education in the school system. *Journal of Pediatric & Adolescent Gynecology, 24*(3), 142–146.

Woo, H., & Raley, R. K. (2005). A small extension to "Costs and rewards of children: The effects of becoming a parent on adults' lives." *Journal of Marriage and Family, 67*(1), 216–221.

Wood, B., & Talmon, M. (1983). Family boundaries in transition: A search for alternatives. *Family Process, 22,* 347–357.

Wood, C., & Davidson, J. (2003). Helping families cope: A fresh look at Parent Effectiveness Training. *Family Matters, 65,* 28–33.

The World Bank. (2007). World development report. Retrieved November 7, 2012, from http://web.worldbank.org/WBSITE/EXTERNAL/EXTDEC/EXTRESEARCH/EXTWDRS/0,,contentMDK:23062361~pagePK:478093~piPK:477627~theSitePK:477624,00.html

The World Bank. (2011). World development report 2012: Gender equality and development. Retrieved November 7, 2012, from http://econ.worldbank.org/WBSITE/EXTERNAL/EXTDEC/EXTRESEARCH/EXTWDRS/EXTWDR2012/0,,contentMDK:22999750~menuPK:8154981~pagePK:64167689~piPK:64167673~theSitePK:7778063,00.html

World Health Organization. (2011). Youth violence. Retrieved November 7, 2012, from www.who.int/violence_injury_prevention/violence/youth/en/

World Health Organization. (2012). Child maltreatment. Retrieved November 7, 2012, from www.who.int/topics/child_abuse/en

Xie, H., Cairns, B. D., & Cairns, R. B. (2001). Predicting teen motherhood and teen fatherhood: Individual characteristics and peer affiliations. *Social Development, 10,* 488–509.

Yarber, A. D., & Sharp, P. M. (2010). *Focus on single-parent families: Past, present, and future.* Santa Barbara, CA: Praeger.

Zabin, L. S., & Cardona, K. M. (2002). Adolescent pregnancy. In G. M. Wingood & R. J. DiClemente (Eds.), *Handbook of women's sexual and reproductive health* (pp. 231–253). New York: Kluwer Academic/Plenum.

Zachary, E. M. (2005). Getting my education: Teen mothers' experiences in school before and after motherhood. *Teachers College Record, 107*(12), 2566–2598.

Zal, H. M. (2001). *The sandwich generation: Caught between growing children and aging parents.* New York: Da Capo Press.

Ziegahn, S. J. (2002). *The stepparent's survival guide: A workbook for creating a happy blended family.* Oakland, CA: New Harbinger.

Zucker, K. J., Bradley, S. J., Oliver, G., Blake, J., Fleming, S., & Hood, J. (1996). Psychosexual development of women with congenital adrenal hyperplasia. *Hormones and Behavior, 30*(4), 300–318.

Index